THE INNOCENCE OF PONTIUS PILATE

DAVID LLOYD DUSENBURY

The Innocence of
Pontius Pilate

*How the Roman Trial of
Jesus Shaped History*

OXFORD
UNIVERSITY PRESS

OXFORD
UNIVERSITY PRESS

Oxford University Press is a department of the
University of Oxford. It furthers the University's objective
of excellence in research, scholarship, and education
by publishing worldwide.

Oxford   New York

Auckland   Cape Town   Dar es Salaam   Hong Kong   Karachi
Kuala Lumpur   Madrid   Melbourne   Mexico City   Nairobi
New Delhi   Shanghai   Taipei   Toronto

With offices in

Argentina   Austria   Brazil   Chile   Czech Republic   France   Greece
Guatemala   Hungary   Italy   Japan   Poland   Portugal   Singapore
South Korea   Switzerland   Thailand   Turkey   Ukraine   Vietnam

Oxford is a registered trade mark of Oxford University Press
in the UK and certain other countries.

Published in the United States of America by
Oxford University Press
198 Madison Avenue, New York, NY 10016

Library of Congress Cataloging-in-Publication Data is available
David Lloyd Dusenbury.
The Innocence of Pontius Pilate: How the Roman Trial of Jesus Shaped History.
ISBN: 9780197764923

Printed in the United Kingdom on acid-free paper

"Great coherences stand out through our secular blur"

W. H. Auden

For my father, J. D. Dusenbury II

amicus Jesu

CONTENTS

AUTHOR'S NOTE

This book originates in a thoughtless decision to review Giorgio Agamben's little book *Pilate and Jesus* in 2015. I never wrote the review, but Agamben is still the "illegitimate father"—in Ernst Kantorowicz's tangy phrase—of *The Innocence of Pontius Pilate*.[1]

I warmly thank Rupert Shortt of the Von Hügel Institute at St Edmund's College, University of Cambridge, for commissioning more than one *TLS* essay on the Roman trial of Jesus, and for introducing me to Hurst. He is a *sine qua non* of this book.

In my early days researching the Roman phase of Jesus' trial, I gave lectures at the law faculties of the University of Edinburgh and University of Leuven, and a seminar at Tilburg University. I wish to thank Paul du Plessis, Stephan Dusil, and Randall Lesaffer for those invitations.

Chapters were drafted at the De Wulf–Mansion Centre in Leuven; the Hardt Foundation in Geneva; Loyola University Maryland in Baltimore (especial thanks to Lisa Flaherty, secretary to the Department of Philosophy); Dumbarton Oaks Research Library in Washington, D.C.; the Abbaye d'Orval in Villers-devant-Orval; and the Center for the Study of Christianity in Jerusalem.

In Jerusalem, where I write this—within sight of the gold cupolas of Gethsemane, the white-walled Church of the Condemnation, and the grey-domed Church of the Holy Sepulchre—my debts are most pronounced to Brouria Bitton-Ashkelony, Francesco Celia, Paula Fredriksen, Oded Irshai, Isidoros Katsos, Yonatan Moss, and Guy Stroumsa. It is an honour to conduct research with them.

AUTHOR'S NOTE

Immensely learned comments on a draft of the book were made by Dante Fedele, Samuel Noble, Guy Stroumsa, and Joseph Verheyden. I regret that I could not incorporate more of their questions, subtilizations, and original insights.

Chapters received state-of-the-art comments from Miriam Goldstein, Arnold Hunt, Ian Hunter, Johan Olsthoorn, Samuel Pomeroy, Gabriel Said Reynolds, Andrea Robiglio, and Okihito Utamura. They nuanced many passages, sharpened many statements.

Other hints and references are due to Paul Richard Blum, Helen Bond (in conversation, and in the pages of her *Pontius Pilate in History and Interpretation*), Annabel Brett, Gianluca Briguglia, Wim Decock, Hugo Drochon, Amir Engel, Colum Hourihane (in correspondence, and in his monograph *Pontius Pilate, Anti-Semitism, and the Passion in Medieval Art*), Serena Masolini, Talila Michaeli, Jürgen Miethke, Alessandro Mulieri, Hindy Najman, Tilke Nelis, Carlos Steel, and the late Laurent Waelkens (deceased June 2020).

My editor at Hurst, Lara Weisweiller-Wu, is nonpareil. A thousand thanks to her.

Many thanks, too, go to Alasdair Craig, Jonathan de Peyer, and Michael Dwyer at Hurst—for commissioning, commenting on, and publishing *The Innocence of Pontius Pilate*.

The scholarly readers consulted by Hurst were sympathetic and astute, and I owe signal debts to them both.

Finally, it is a pleasure to thank Samuel Noble for afterhours conversations on arcane topics, and Timothy Dusenbury for finessing my prose. They're the best at what they do.

But as Pilate says in *John* (it is not a tautology): "What I have written I have written." Any errors here are mine.

My debts to the dedicatee, Julian Delano Dusenbury, and to the rest of my family, lie somewhere beyond the limits of my language.

"You have to simplify sometimes", as one of Michel Houellebecq's louche narrators says, "or you end up with nothing."[2] Throughout this book, I am simplifying. But however bold the strokes and glaring the lacunas, I promise the reader this: You will not end up with nothing.

Jerusalem, 2020
D.L.D.

LIST OF FIGURES

LIST OF FIGURES

NOTE ON CITATIONS

Wherever a citation takes the form ABB. *Taf.* 1:1 or VIDA *Christ.* I 1, it refers to a work written before 1600. Consult the list of premodern titles at the back of the volume.

I have relied on the editions and translations listed in the bibliography. Translations of Greek and Latin texts are rarely my own, but they have throughout been compared with the originals, and often modified.

Unless otherwise noted, translations of biblical texts are from the New Revised Standard Version in *The Book of Common Prayer ... According to the Use of the Episcopal Church* (New York, 2007), or from the Revised Standard Version in the Nestle-Aland *Greek–English New Testament* (Stuttgart, 1994). They, too, have been compared with the originals and often modified.

PROLOGUE

THE DRAMA OF PILATE AND JESUS

At the heart of every European city lies a mystery: the figure of the cross.[1] From the hulk of Saint Paul's in the sleek, financialized core of London to the dome of Saint Peter's in the Vatican statelet within Rome; from the spare façade of Saint Dominic's on the island of Corsica to the pale-wood-panelled apse of the Svalbard Church in Longyearbyen, Norway: the architectural lines of European settlements converge on a cruciform structure, a church, at the heart of which is set, in a state of semi-darkness and silence, the figure of the cross.

This is not just true of Europe, but of what Fernand Braudel called the "European civilizations".[2] I first drafted this page in Baltimore, Maryland, a new-world port city studded with imposing Neo-Gothic churches (though this is not why Jacques Lacan, an intense Catholic, said that Baltimore at first light is "the best image" of the unconscious).[3] The only interest of this, here, is that these structures elevate a symbol in which late modern culture is fundamentally uninterested, and that many feel to be bleak and inert: the cross. This book is a historical reflection on that mystical and juridical figure.

What is the cross? It is the image of a stake and crossbeam on which a Galilean prophet, whose birth marks the beginning of our era, died.[4] And who is the Galilean? As Porcius Festus, a Roman procurator, put it circa 60 CE,[5] the "dead man" in question is "someone called Jesus". This is a man the first Christ-believers conceded to have died, says Festus, yet "alleged to be alive".[6] And to this day, Christians allege that Jesus, who breathed his last normal breath circa 30 CE, is, in some sublime and mysterious way, supremely alive.[7]

One of the most astonishing sequences in political history is that the faith of those whom Roman judges, like Festus, were the first to call 'Christians' ultimately converted the Roman emperors.[8] It is because of this conversion, or revolution of empire, that a cross—originally the sign of Rome's murder of an innocent man—came to signify the Roman legacy in Europe and its former colonies.[9] (See fig. 1.) But who is this innocent convict, Jesus?

In this twenty-first century after his trial and death, Jesus is revered by more than half of humankind—Christians and Muslims—as Christ (Greek *Christos* and Arabic *Masih*, both from the Hebrew *Mashiah*).[10] Roughly a third of humankind—Christians—venerate Jesus as the Son of God (one of the legal charges brought in the gospels is that Jesus "made himself out to be the Son of God")[11] and as *God* (the Creed of Constantinople, promulgated in 381 CE, chants that Jesus is "Light of Light, true God of true God"). His divinity is not thought, by Christians, to vitiate Jesus' own confession of the unity of God ("The Lord is one"), or the stress in *John* on the invisibility of God ("No one has ever seen God").[12] But this sketch of the Christ-idea is only necessary because its features are rapidly dimming in our cultural memory.

This is not a book of theology.

This is a book, in the first instance, about the *brute fact* that Jesus died a convict's death in Jerusalem, after a formal interrogation by the Roman prefect of Judaea, Pontius Pilate (flourished 26–37 CE).[13] "During the rule of Tiberius", says historian Tacitus circa 115 CE, Jesus was crucified "by the sentence of ... Pontius Pilatus".[14] This harmonizes perfectly with what we read in early Christian texts. For instance, Ignatius of Antioch avers circa 107 CE that Jesus died "in the time [of] ... Pontius Pilate".[15] When a line from the early second century's hardest-headed annalist, Tacitus—who loathed Christians—supports the earliest Christian testimonies, it constitutes a datum.

This is a book, in the second instance, about a centuries-long reception of Jesus' trial and death as a *legal fact*. What could this mean? Of course, Jesus' death is the bitter exaction of a Roman sentence. His presence on a Roman cross is *itself* a legal fact. And in purely juridical terms, the cross belongs to Pilate, not Jesus. But what is more intriguing, though harder to define, is that Jesus' trial and death function in later centuries as a legal fact in a more sublime sense. The passion is analysed by many of the master thinkers of European legal history— from Paul of Tarsus in the first century to Hans Kelsen in the twenti- eth—as "the decisive event of history", which takes, significantly, in Giorgio Agamben's phrase, "the form of a trial".[16]

This is the first book to retrace the *brute fact* of Jesus' trial and death as a *legal fact* of epoch-defining significance. My claim is that the drama of Pilate and Jesus has decisively shaped, and still subtly shapes, the legal and political cultures of Europe and the Americas. If Jesus had not been tried by Pilate, and if the Pilate trial had not been lavishly nar- rated in the four canonical gospels, then the political history of Europe and the Americas would be unrecognizable. But why?

I have come to believe that, without Pilate's judicial hand in the death of Jesus, it would not have been possible for medieval and early modern legal thinkers to effect the bright and lasting line demarcating secular power (*potestas*) and sacred authority (*auctoritas*). The demarca- tion of coercive secularity (*saecularitas*) and non-coercive religion (*reli- gio*) underlies, and unsettles, all recognizably 'modern' configurations of legal and political culture. The drama of Pilate and Jesus is thus not only a religious memory. Pilate's crucifixion of an innocent man, held by Christians to be the God-Man, is a secular tragedy without which no convincing record can be written of what Michel Foucault calls "the form of Western history".[17]

And what is that drama?

In *Matthew*, it is a dream by Pilate's wife that reveals Jesus' innocence. According to the Danish philosopher-memoirist Søren Kierkegaard, in a jotting from 1849: "Pilate's wife, who dreamed by day, was more awake than Pilate, who did not dream by day."[18] But beyond this dream of Procla (her name in Christian tradition), it seems to me that the gospels' narratives take on an oneiric quality after Judas Iscariot—one of Jesus' cohort, the Twelve—betrays his rabbi with a kiss.[19] The gos- pel-writers register, in proto-realistic lines, early Christian memories of a charcoal fire, an open gate, a melancholy glance, a relentless girl, a naked boy, a blindfold, and a bird's call on the night before Jesus' death.[20] Yet the scenes in which these images flare up are montage-like, and the dramatic sequence of the passion narratives is, like a dream, both inexorable and mystifying.

In the first half of the twentieth century, Rudolf Bultmann deemed whole blocs of the gospels' passion narratives to be mythical. A glance at Bultmann's field-altering book, *The History of the Synoptic Tradition* (1921), suggests that many of the elements just cited are "manifestly legendary", "strongly disfigured by legend", and so on.[21] I am not convinced, and I am not alone.[22] But this is not the place to assess the conclusions reached by Bultmann and his school. Our concern here is only with the *canonical data* that biblical commentators, legal theorists, and dramaturgs have been recollecting, now, for 2,000 years. And our data, roughly, come to this.

On the chaotic night before his death in the restive province of Judaea, Jesus is led with hands bound to the house of the Judaean high priest Caiaphas (in *Matthew*, *Mark*, and *Luke*)—or first, to the house of a former high priest, Annas (in *John*).[23] He is interrogated by Jerusalem's Temple elites in the dead of night. Some sort of Judaean "pre-judgement", or Latin *praejudicium*, is made on the night of his arrest (in *Matthew* and *Mark*),[24] or at dawn the next day (in *Luke*).[25] The Italian classicist Emilio Gabba concludes that in the hours after Jesus' arrest, a high-priestly judge or Judaean council found him to have committed "a crime that carried the death penalty".[26]

On the morning of his death, Jesus is led from Caiaphas' house to a palace in Jerusalem occupied by the Roman prefect, Pontius Pilate, who then remands Jesus (only in *Luke*) to a palace occupied by the Galilean tetrarch, Herod Antipas (reigned 4 BCE–39 CE). According to Fergus Millar, there is "no inherent improbability" in this Herodian trial.[27] But regardless of historicity, we read in the passion narrative in *Luke* that after a brutal but inconclusive interrogation, Herod returns Jesus to Pilate *without a conviction*. Unconvinced that Jesus is guilty of treason—in Latin *laesae majestatis*, or in modern legal parlance *lèse-majesté*—Pilate nevertheless sentences him to death.

Myth 1: Pilate's innocence

The Christian myth of Pilate's innocence is tied to Pilate's reluctance, in all the canonical passion narratives, to crucify Jesus. Pilate's reluctance is, without doubt, a canonical datum. This is not the place to elaborate, but I have come to believe this reluctance, and his unctuous handwashing in *Matthew*, have been grossly misinterpreted by whole traditions of Christian, and post-Christian, commentary. A glance at *Luke* will have to suffice.

In *Luke* 23, Pilate says of Jesus—not once, but three times—"I have not found this man guilty."[28] Like certain early Christian commentators, many modern critical exegetes have seen in this recurring declaration a half-concealed tendency of the writer of *Luke–Acts* to 'redeem' the Roman prefect. That is a poor interpretation. For *Luke*'s Pilate is not the only non-priestly ruler to declare Jesus innocent; *Luke*'s Herod declares Jesus innocent, too. After Pilate's second objection to Jesus' accusers, "I have not found this man guilty", he says this: "Neither has Herod."[29] Yet there is no tendency in *Luke* to 'redeem' Herod.[30] On the contrary, *Luke* portrays the Herodian tetrarch as a thoroughly depraved ruler. It is only *Luke* who tells us, for instance, that Herod wanted to see Jesus—but *Luke* makes it clear that this is hardly a pious desire. For, Jesus is rumoured to be like John the Baptist. And what is John's fate? Herod mutters to himself, in the only sentence *Luke* puts in his mouth: "John, I beheaded."[31] It is only in *Luke* that Jesus dictates a message for Herod, in which he calls the tetrarch a "jackal".[32] And it is only *Luke* that tells us that Herod and Pilate become "friends" on the day of Jesus' death, adding, "before this they had been enemies".[33] It is certainly damning, for the writer of *Luke–Acts*, that this new friendship is a bond created by torturing (Herod) and killing (Pilate) an innocent man.[34]

That *Luke*'s Herod is unconvinced by the Temple elites' charges against Jesus is not remotely, for the writer of *Luke–Acts*, a sign of *Herod's innocence*. It is only a sign of *Jesus' innocence*. The gospel-writer concludes Herod's interrogation of Jesus in a way that is clearly meant to incriminate the tetrarch of Galilee: "Herod with his soldiers treated Jesus with contempt and mocked him."[35] Similarly, I believe that the writer of *Luke–Acts*—like the other gospel-writers—is totally uninterested in 'redeeming' the Roman prefect. *That Pilate declares Jesus innocent deepens his guilt*—since in *Luke*, Pilate decides to "chastise" the innocent prisoner, and then sentences him to death.[36]

Myth 2: Pilate's non-judgement

It is common for premodern Christian writers—and indeed, for modern critical commentators—to deny that Pilate condemns Jesus in the gospels. One of the darkest denials may come from a German jurist and Nazi Reichsjustizministerium officer, Wilhelm von Ammon, who insists that there is no "talk" in the gospels of a Roman "death sentence".[37] Von Ammon likely had a sinister investment in the gentile's non-judgement—yet in his mid-century study *The Trial of Jesus*, Josef Blinzler treats von Ammon's line as doctrinaire.

Introducing the question of Pilate's judgement, Blinzler writes: "The evangelists do not explicitly say that Pilate pronounced a formal death sentence. Many researchers have concluded from this that his decision was not a verdict in the technical sense (*kein Urteilsspruch im technischen Sinn*)."[38] One researcher to have concluded this is the estimable Millar, who believes that in all four canonical passion narratives, Pilate's decision to have Jesus killed "is *not* represented as a verdict concluding a trial".[39]

That is false. Pilate's judgement of Jesus is cited as a "sentence" more than once in *Luke* 23–4.[40] The idea that Pilate utters no sentence in the canonical gospels is a myth. But this is not to deny that it is necessary to "decipher allusions to juridical facts which the sacred authors assumed their readers knew", as classicist Elias Bickerman stressed in the 1930s.[41] One such juridical fact—crucial for us—is Pilate's judgement.

In *Mark* and *Matthew*, the prefect's judgement is implicit. When we read in *Matthew* that "having scourged Jesus", Pilate "delivered him to be crucified", we must infer that his order was that Jesus be led out and put to death. A Latin formula for this is *duci iussit*.[42] The Roman judgement is unmissable in *Luke*, but many commentators have somehow missed it. In *Luke* 23, we read: "Pilate gave sentence."[43] The writer of *Luke–Acts* not only depicts Pilate uttering his sentence but then cites it as a "sentence"—once in his crucifixion scene, once after the resurrection.[44]

The dramaturgy of Pilate's judgement is most elaborate in *John*. On *John*'s telling, the prefect "sat down on the judgement seat at a place called The Pavement" before he handed Jesus over "to be crucified".[45] The judgement seat symbolizes the judgement. Yet it is crucial to note, here, *who crucified Jesus* after the Roman prefect sentenced him to that cruel Roman punishment.

Myth 3: a Judaean crucifixion

There is a tenacious myth in Christian circles that Judaean zealots crucified Jesus (more on this in chapters 6 and 12), but the canonical passions nullify this. "The soldiers", reads a line in *John*, "crucified Jesus."[46] And *Matthew* calls the men who crucify Jesus "soldiers of the governor".[47] The canonical data are clear. Contrary to various Christian traditions, *it is Pilate's gentile troops who crucify Jesus*, and who pin Pilate's judicial notice to the stake on which Jesus expires.[48] (See the letters *I. N. R. I.*, a Latin code for Pilate's death-script, in fig. 2.)

This is why we read in *Acts of the Apostles* 2 that Jesus was "killed *by the hands* of those outside the law"—a definite reference to his crucifixion by gentiles.[49]

Who, then, is Pilate in the gospels? He is the Roman judge whose caustic sentence is placed on Jesus' cross (one of the foci of chapter 3). And Jesus is not the only Galilean whom Pilate kills in the gospels. We read in *Luke* 13 of a cohort of "Galileans whose blood Pilate ... mingled with their sacrifices", seemingly in the Jerusalem Temple.[50] And it is not only in the gospels that Pilate is Jesus' judge. For we read in *Acts of the Apostles* 4 that God's "holy servant Jesus" was tortured and killed by "both Herod *and Pontius Pilate*, with the gentiles and the peoples of Israel".[51] There is a proto-creedal moment, too, in the letter of *I Timothy* where Jesus testifies "before Pontius Pilate" (the topic of chapter 2).[52]

From the first pages of the Christian archive, then, Pilate is a Roman judge who formally interrogates Jesus (*pro tribunali*), and who sentences him to death at the conclusion of a Roman trial for non-citizens (*cognitio extra ordinem*).[53]

Having introduced the myth of Pilate's innocence, we can return to Kierkegaard for a moment. In his *Philosophical Fragments*, Kierkegaard cites a letter by the eighteenth-century "meta-critic" Johann Georg Hamann in which Hamann calls Pilate "the wisest author and most obscure prophet, the executor of the New Testament".[54] Roughly a century after Hamann's letter is written, Friedrich Nietzsche is irritated that, in his words, "Christians today like to set up Pilate ... as an advocate of Christ."[55] How could the Pilate of Hamann (a Christian) be a "prophet", and the Pilate objected to by Nietzsche (a post-Christian) be an "advocate of Christ"? As we will see in the coming chapters, Christians' exculpation of Pilate is nothing like a modern phenomenon, as it seems to originate in the early second century CE (if not before).

This book is a *premier coup* outline, in thick 'cubist' strokes, of the history of Pilate's innocence and guilt, and the strange and deep ways in which depictions of Pilate both reflect and influence the history of empire. For Pilate's 'innocence' is not only a neglected theological question; it is a recurring theme in the history of European political thought, and a neglected *topos* in the history of philosophy. Philosophical reflections on Jesus' death arc from the fragmentary texts of 'pagans' such as Celsus and Porphyry in the second and third centuries CE, to books such as *Atheism in Christianity* by the heterodox Marxist Ernst Bloch in the late twentieth century.[56]

Nietzsche himself, years after he rejects the Christian myth of Pilate's innocence, becomes a post-Christian mythicist of Pilate's innocence.[57] He writes this in *The Anti-Christ*:

> Do I still need to say that in the whole of the New Testament there is only *one* honourable figure? Pilate, the Roman governor. To take Jewish affairs seriously—he could not convince himself to do this ... The noble scorn of a Roman when faced with an unashamed mangling of the word 'truth' [by Jesus] gave the New Testament its only statement *of any value*—its critique, even its *annihilation*: "What is truth!"[58]

The question of Nietzsche and 'the Jews' is vexed.[59] What matters here is that he cites Pilate's saying, "What is truth?", as the annihilation of Christian faith.[60] But if Pilate is the first 'anti-Christ', on Nietzsche's reading, is the writer of *The Anti-Christ* the last? Could we perhaps suspect that Nietzsche sees himself as a sort of new Pilate?

It is certainly not meaningless that Nietzsche's literary autobiography-manifesto, *Ecce Homo*, takes its name from one of Pilate's lines in *John*: "Behold the man" (in Latin, *ecce homo*).[61] In choosing that title for his most autobiographical book, Nietzsche seems to identify himself with Pilate—who says 'ecce homo', *and who crucifies Jesus*. One text that indicates that Pilate is a critical figure for *Ecce Homo*, and for Nietzsche's efforts to 'crucify' the whole Platonic-Christian legacy, is his 20 November 1888 letter to a Danish atheist and literary critic, Georg Brandes (died 1927). Nietzsche writes to Brandes: "The book is called

Ecce Homo and is an assassination without the slightest regard for the Crucified."[62] In the gospels, Pilate hesitates to kill Jesus; Nietzsche means to do him one better. This time, Jesus will be crucified—and with him, Christian Europe—"without the slightest regard".

But how could we forget that Nietzsche signs a couple of his last letters—to the Vatican's Secretary of State Cardinal Rampolla, and King Umberto I in Rome—"The Crucified"?[63] The meaning of this cryptic, half-crazed signature lies, I think, in lines of Nietzsche's Zarathustra-poem that he cites in *Ecce Homo*. "The good", Nietzsche sings in his counter-gospel, "crucify those who write *new* values on new tablets."[64]

Nietzsche's *Ecce Homo* could thus be read as an "assassination without the slightest regard for the Crucified" (in the November 1888 letter), *and* Nietzsche could be regarded as "the Crucified" (in January 1889 letters). Nietzsche is, in his own mind, a new Pilate who degrades and kills the Platonic-Christian legacy; *and* he is the writer-of-new-values who is 'crucified' by a nineteenth-century Europe that, in his own epochal words, killed God.

Returning, however, from Nietzsche: I have come to believe that, without the drama of Pilate and Jesus, the history of empire—and the history of European philosophy—would have been radically different.

The thesis of this book is that what we now call the 'secular' is not a Roman (pre-Christian) inheritance, or a late modern (post-Christian) innovation. On the contrary, the 'secular' is constituted by Christian philosopher-bishops, legal theorists, and polemicists—in a thousand bright and murky ways—from the sayings of Jesus and the letters of Paul. More concretely, I am inclined to think that the term-concept of the 'secular' owes incalculably much (1) to a single utterance in the Roman trial of Jesus as it is narrated in the fourth gospel: "My kingdom is not of this world" (*John* 18:36); and (2) to a singular interpretation of this utterance in the early fifth century by a formidable African bishop, Augustine of Hippo, in his *Homilies on the Gospel of John* (from which we will read in chapter 13).

One way to think of this is territorial. Wherever Augustine's commentary on *John*'s Pilate trial is not read—as in much of the Byzantine and Islamicate zones—the 'secular' never crystallizes.[65] This of course means that the secular is at its inception a Christian concept—and, more concretely, a *Latin* Christian concept. This indicates, further, that the secular is an *African* concept that is only elaborated in *Europe* by medieval and early modern philosophers and jurists. It is not a self-conception of the late antique church *in Rome*, but of the late antique church *in Roman Africa* that is revived and valorized by the earliest theorists of the secular *in Europe*. At the heart of European modernity, and of *late* modernity, lies a constellation of legal concepts and political impulses that emerge from a uniquely African interpretation of the moment in Jesus' Roman trial in *John* when—as Thomas Hobbes writes in *Leviathan*—the "Saviour himself expressly saith, 'My Kingdom is not of this world.'"[66]

What we call 'the secular' is first exegetically formulated in the port city of Hippo Regius in late antique Roman Africa, and it is first theoretically formulated in late medieval Europe by readers of Augustine. Early modern advocates of the secular are conscious of the roots of this term-concept in Augustine's reading of the Roman trial in *John*, and of late medieval theorizations of papal authority and imperial power in light of the African bishop's reading of the Roman trial in *John*.

Beginning in the eighteenth century, there is a tendency to forget, or repress, the Latin Christian logic of the secular. This book resists that forgetting.

PART 1

A WORLD-HISTORICAL TRIAL

1

"IN THE NAME OF OUR LORD"

THE MOST SUBLIME IRONY IN THE HISTORY OF EMPIRE

There is no undivided point of origin for European law. On the contrary, it is characteristic of European legal history that every possible point of origin we might posit is doubled or mirror-imaged. The most glaring case of this may be the double-tradition of civil law and common law—with one predominating on the Continent (and many of its former colonies), the other rooted in England (and many of its former colonies). Because of this double-tradition, there is no clear answer to such a basic question as: Is European law written or unwritten? Common law is (in a certain sense) unwritten and verdict-based; civil law is written and code-based. And both are, incontestably, European traditions.

But there is no undivided point of origin for either of those legal traditions. For code-based Roman law was a systemic influence on common law in the medieval period.[1] And it must be said in the most neutral tones that European code law is, and will continue to be, a strong influence on English common law. Similarly, canon law—the law code of the Church of Rome—exerted a continent-forming influence on the civil law traditions well into the modern period (and in some jurisdictions, to the present).[2] This is the reason why Europe's most revered legal theorists and practitioners—some of whom will figure in the coming chapters—were styled masters of "both laws" (*utrumque ius*). Double-mastery of the law was a mark of competence precisely because the law in Europe was for many centuries (and to some extent, is still today) a *double-structure*, with one law code regulating 'sacred' jurisdictions, and another law code regulating the 'secular' jurisdictions of Europe.

This division of laws and institutions into 'sacred' and 'secular', which is so characteristic of Europe (and many of its former colonies), and of what most of us would call the politics of modernity, is one of my main interests in this book. But we have not yet finished tracing out the origins of European law—which we left at a division into canon ('sacred') law on the one hand, and civil ('secular') law on the other. What, we could now ask, are the origins of "both laws" (*utrumque ius*)? And a thoroughly inoffensive reply would be that both European laws, canon and civil law, have a double origin.

This is impossible to miss in the case of canon law, since the Christians' sacred book is itself a two-part collection, a diptych. It is composed, first, of an *Old Testament*, a collection of texts written in Hebrew (and Aramaic) before the life and death—and, in Christian belief, the resurrection—of Jesus; and second, of a *New Testament*, a collection of texts written in Greek (and conceivably Aramaic) after Jesus' life and death and "resurrection-event" (as it is called in the modern critical literature). The terms *Old* and *New Testament* are so familiar that we tend to forget—as early Christians, and many generations of European legal theorists, did not—that the word 'testament' is, in both Greek (*diathēkē*) and Latin (*testamentum*), a legal term.[3]

That being the case, the editorial division of the sacred book into 'testaments' suggests a *legal division* of sacred history—and sacred institutions—into 'old' and 'new'. History that is divided into 'testaments' is necessarily a *legal* history; and this legal history, which lies at the root of canon law—of European 'sacred' law—is dramatically divided into *old* and *new laws*. This is what Paul of Tarsus, a legal critic who is still unsurpassed for passion and influence, evokes when he writes of both a "new covenant" (in *I Corinthians*) and an "old covenant" (in *II Corinthians*) in the middle of the first century CE.[4] And this is what the African courtier Firmianus Lactantius means when he writes in the early fourth century that the risen Christ had "regulated all things concerning the institutions of the new testament (*testamenti novi*)".[5] Lactantius is not referring to a collection of texts, but to the constitution of a new form of life—or to what he later calls "the law and religion of God".[6]

This division of human history into epochs of old and new laws is one that has never ceased to thrill, and mystify, Christian theologians and jurists. In the first centuries of our era, pagan philosophers often criticized the conflict of laws they noticed in the Christians' Old and New Testaments.[7] "Who is wrong?" one philosopher asks: "Moses or Jesus?"[8] And by the middle of the second century CE, Christians of a gnostic bent were condemning the "enormous body of legislation" in the Five Books of Moses as unworthy of a high, perfect deity.[9] There is much more in this for modern historians of politics and law than they tend to recognize.

It is certainly not meaningless that the first surviving occurrence of the words "ancient and modern laws" (*antiquis et modernis legibus*) is in a Latin text by a sixth-century bishop of Pavia, Magnus Felix Ennodius.[10] And it is suggestive that the strange, late antique Christian neologism— 'modern' (*modernus*)—occurs more than once in the writings of one of Ennodius' contemporaries, Pope Gelasius I (reigned 492–6), on whom there will be more in a later chapter.[11] Not unlike Ennodius, Gelasius differentiates the newest decrees of the church (*admonitiones modernas*) from its older rules and binding decisions (*antiques regulis*).[12]

Legal innovation—the changing of laws, and the legitimacy of 'modern laws'—is thematized in European history, *in part*, because it is so visible in Christian holy writ.[13] This is true even when legal innovation is thought of as repristination: as the return to a more pristine law. We see this in a third-century Syrian text, *The Doctrine of the Apostles*, where Christians are taught to observe God's original "Law" (the Mosaic Decalogue, which is ratified by Jesus),[14] but not to observe the "Second Law" (the more elaborate legal-sacrificial order in the Five Books of Moses).[15] Here, the 'old' and the 'new' seem to be convoluted, yet the division of human history into a dispensation of 'old' and 'new' laws is still decisive.[16] And this is one of the crucial double-structures at the origin of European 'sacred' law.[17]

But what of a double-structure at the origin of European 'secular' law? No one doubts that the origins of European 'secular' law lie, in the first instance, with the Romans.[18] But some of Rome's most

5

iconic legists were not natives of the imperial city or of the Italian peninsula. How is this possible? In 212 CE, a half-African, half-Syrian emperor, Caracalla, granted citizenship "to virtually the entire free population of the empire".[19] It was through Caracalla's edict that the Roman Empire was reborn, or reconceived, in the early third century.[20] And two of Roman law's most formidable authorities, Ulpian and Papinian, were natives of Syria. They were, for that reason, close to the Syrian dynasty to which Caracalla belonged—the Severans.[21] And it is not unimportant that this pair of Roman legal master-thinkers were a new kind of 'Roman'. Their Syrian provenance seems to have informed their theories of legal universality—in other words, of late antique cosmopolitanism—which are still a defining influence in European law and politics.

Similarly, Roman law was reborn in its most conclusive form not in the city of Rome but in Constantinople, known for many centuries as the "New Rome" (note the mirroring).[22] In European intellectual history, Roman law was born in the 530s CE, when the Christian emperor Justinian I promulgated several huge legal collections, in a series of editions, which are known as the *Body of Roman Law* (*Corpus juris civilis*). There will be more on this collection—or rather, on the first words of the introductory text of this collection, Justinian's *Institutes*—in a moment. Here, we can only note that Roman legal theorists—including those who compiled Justinian's *Body of Roman Law*—believed that their legal culture originated in a myth-clouded law code, now lost, called the Twelve Tables (circa 450 BCE). And by the first century CE, many Romans—Pliny the Elder, to name one—believed that the Twelve Tables were modelled on a Greek law code, or were even written by a Hellene from the city of Ephesus named Hermodorus.[23] According to Roman tradition, this Hermodorus was a friend of Heraclitus—a citizen of Ephesus, and a philosopher who says in one fragment that "all human laws are nourished by a divine one".[24]

Our question here is not whether Hermodorus ever went to Rome—or whether, for that matter, the Twelve Tables were ever inscribed on twelve bronze tablets.[25] Regardless of whether Hermodorus is a Roman myth or a dim memory, his presence in the tradition reveals that some of the most celebrated Roman legists *wanted* the point of origin of civil law to be double—that is, not only Roman but Greek. *QED*. The thought of

Greece—by which I mean, too, the myth of Greek thought—constitutes one deep double-structure at the origin of European 'secular' law in Rome and in the New Rome, Constantinople.

Where has this breakneck history of European law brought us? It is common and civil—sacred and secular—old and new—Greek and Roman. In all these ways, there is no undivided point of origin for European law. As a tradition, it is constitutively double. But if there *were* such a point of origin, I suspect that it might be a handbook of Roman law that I have already mentioned—the *Institutes* of Justinian.

The first words of the Body of Roman Law

The sixth-century emperor Justinian was under no illusions that his *Institutes*—which he promulgated but did not write—were original. On the contrary, he (and his legal secretaries) pointed out that his *Institutes* mark only a new, epochal contribution to a Roman legal genre. Justinian himself tells us that his *Institutes* have been "compiled from all the books of *Institutes* written by the classical lawyers, and especially from the works of our Gaius, both his *Institutes* and his *Quotidian Law*".[26]

We are fortunate to still have substantial fragments of Gaius' *Institutes*, which Justinian cites here. Yet Gaius' second-century text vanished for many centuries. A half-obscured copy was only recovered in 1816 by a diplomat-historian, Barthold Niebuhr, in the holdings of Verona's cathedral library.[27] And it is Justinian's *Institutes* that initiated countless generations of lawyers—and still initiates some—to the shape of Roman law.

Justinian's *Institutes* is the foyer to the vast *Body of Roman Law* that inspired many of the 'secular' law codes that still regulate European governance, commerce, and domestic life. If there is a point of origin for the European legal tradition, then, it is Justinian's *Institutes*. And the foyer to this foyer-text is Justinian's preface to the *Institutes*, which is known by its first words, "Imperial Majesty" (*Imperatoriam maiestatem*). According to most legal histories, it is these words that serve as the opening (or incipit) of Justinian's colossal edifice of law. But these are not, in fact, the words that open his text—and with it, the century-spanning history of Roman law in Europe (and many of its colonies).

I therefore want to set the narrative arc of this book by reflecting, in the briefest possible way, on the first words of Justinian's prologue to his *Institutes*. I will give them first in Latin, since it is worth remembering that Latin is the European language par excellence.[28] In the early modern period, when modern 'secularization' begins to be theorized (and this book will end), Latin is not "a parochial dead language"—as Anthony Grafton writes—"but a universal living one".[29] Latin was not only a living tongue in churches and law courts but in university lecture halls. For, beginning with the chartering of the first university in the late eleventh century, all 'readings' of Europe's canonical texts—all *lectiones*—were conducted in Latin. This continent-wide Latin culture lasted much longer than many of us think.

One sharp blow to this culture only comes in the autumn of 1687, when a liberal Protestant jurist, Christian Thomasius, decided to give his law lectures at the University of Leipzig in German.[30] (We will later read Thomasius' Latin text *On the Unjust Judgement of Pontius Pilate*.) It was utterly outré, in the 1680s, to lecture in a vernacular on Justinian and his early modern commentators—or anything else—and the displacement of Latin was slow. When a young Johann Gottfried Herder made his lecture notes at Königsberg in the 1760s, his lecturer— Immanuel Kant—still held the floor in Latin.[31]

It is no coincidence that the decline of Latin culture in the long nineteenth century is mirrored by the rise of nationalism in Europe.[32] And it is revealing that the modern European term for a borderless language—*lingua franca*—is not cast in seventeenth-century Italian, nineteenth-century French, or twenty-first-century English.[33] The original 'lingua franca' may have been "a corrupt Italian contact language" of the late medieval Mediterranean, stemming from the Venetian dialect.[34] But the concept itself, *lingua franca*, is cast in Latin. And to this day, Latin is not only a learned language that structures medicine and law, theology and philosophy. It lives on in our technological lexicons, giving us the words 'digital', 'computer', 'information', and, of course, 'data' (from the Latin *digitalis*, *computator*, *informatio*, and *data*).

This, then, is the 'data' from Justinian that we want to begin with:

In nomine domini nostri Jhesu Christi
Imperator Caesar Flavius Iustinianus

"IN THE NAME OF OUR LORD"

Alamannicus Gothicus Francicus Germanicus Anticus Alanicus Vandalicus Africanus
Pius Felix Inclitus Victor ac Triumphator Semper Augustus

Now, what does this mean?

In the name of our Lord Jesus Christ
The Emperor Caesar Flavius Justinian
Conqueror of the Alemanni Goths, Franks, Germans, Antes, Alani, Vandals,
and Africans
Devout, Fortunate, Renowned, Victorious and Triumphant, Forever
Augustus.[35]

A vainglorious beginning. Why, then, have we chosen this—a text that even legal historians pass by in disinterest—as *our* point of origin?

There are three things I want us to notice in Justinian's formal opening, since this book is—among other things—an attempt to set these three things in a new light, and to draw them into a new relation. There is, in this opening, a curious presence; an epochal absence; and a superlative irony.

A curious presence

First, and most simply, the presence. It would not be glib to point out the presence in Justinian's opening lines of both the French and Germans—or rather, of their remote ancestors—since even now, European policy and commerce tend to hinge on France and Germany. And it is not uninteresting that Justinian claims both nations—together with a Slavic nation, the Antes—for his Roman, which is to say proto-European, legal culture.[36] (A joke could perhaps be made, too, about the absence of Britons.)[37] But these are not the presences that interest me, here.

What I am struck by is the presence of Africa—or, more precisely, of Africans—in Justinian's incipit. Of course, Justinian's Africans are evoked—like the Franks, Germans, and Antes—as a subject nation (or collection of nations). This is not the place to sketch Justinian's hard-fought reclamation of the Romanized northern coastline of Africa (and parts of the inner countryside) in the early sixth century, or to reflect on the subtleties of imperial and post-imperial law and culture in the African provinces that later fell, in the seventh century, to the Islamic conquest.[38] Without entering into that history and the many questions

9

it raises, there is reason simply to note *the presence of Africans in the first lines of the defining corpus of European law.*

Their presence reminds us that when we read, in the first sentences of Justinian's *Institutes*, that "by the law of nature, all humans were initially born free *(omnes homines liberi nascebantur)*",[39] the peoples of Africa are envisioned, no less than the peoples of Gallia or Germania. Now, that all humans are born free is a thought that most of us mistakenly credit to the first sentence of Jean-Jacques Rousseau's *Social Contract*. But when Rousseau says there that humans are "born free" and are "everywhere in chains", he knows that it is the second half of his line—not the first—that is revolutionary.[40] It is not often remarked—and it should be—that the first pages of Rousseau's *Social Contract* are in conversation with the first pages of Justinian's *Institutes*.[41]

Still, it is the mere presence of *Africans* in Justinian's opening that introduces one of the themes of this book—namely that the history of European law and politics cannot be written without reference to Africa. From the beginning, and in surprising ways, I believe that European legal history is rooted in Romanized north Africa—and retracing the interpretation of Jesus' Roman trial will help us to see that.

An epochal absence

Second, and more subtly, the absence. Justinian calls himself "Devout, Fortunate, Renowned, Victorious and Triumphant, Forever Augustus"—but there his imperial title ends. What is missing? Two words of immense importance: Supreme Pontiff. For that is how the traditional imperial titular ends,[42] with the emperor being designated "Forever Augustus" *(semper Augustus)*—or some such—and then, "Supreme Pontiff" *(pontifex maximus)*.

For instance, when we glance at one of the edicts marking the end of the most vicious period of anti-Christian persecution before Constantine I begins to Christianize the empire in the fourth century CE, we see that both of the *Augusti* who promulgate the edict are introduced as "Unconquered Augustus, Supreme Pontiff" *(invictus Augustus, pontifex maximus)*.[43] In the pre-Christian Roman Empire, as this indicates, the legal systems of Roman punishment and sacrifice, criminal law and ritual law, culminated in a single person, the emperor—or, in the late third and early fourth centuries, in a 'college' of emperors.

The Roman emperors were not remotely 'secular' figures but "sac-rificers in chief on behalf of the state"[44]—the Roman ecumene's high priests—when they were not, like Tiberius, a "son of the divine"; like Nero, a "lord of the whole world"; or like Domitian, a "lord and god".[45] Even towards the end of the fourth century, the Christian Emperor Valentinian could style himself "Devout, Fortunate ... Victorious and Triumphant, Forever Augustus, *Supreme Pontiff*".[46] Yet after Valentinian's reign, Christian emperors ceased to call themselves "supreme pon-tiff".[47] The bishops of Rome then begin to be called Rome's "highest pontiff" (*summus pontifex*), though it is not until the Renaissance that popes, seizing on the old imperial formula, begin to style themselves "supreme pontiff" (*pontifex maximus*).[48]

This is world-historical. For by the 490s, Pope Gelasius, who was "African by birth", could claim that the title of *pontifex maximus* marked one of the sharpest signs of the difference between Christian Rome and pre-Christian Rome.[49] The Christian era, argues Gelasius, is marked by an irreversible split in the highest offices that bear the authority of Caesar (empire) and of God (church). After the coming of Christ, this African pope reasons, it is impossible for one man to legitimately be both Caesar and Supreme Pontiff. And it is certain that Justinian and his legal secretaries, writing after Gelasius' papacy, mean for Justinian *not* to be styled the "Supreme Pontiff", since they *do* call him "Renowned" (*Inclitus*). As Alan Cameron has shown, *inclitus* (or *inclytus*) is a term that systematically replaces *maximus* in the imperial titulature after the Christian Emperor Gratian (reigned 367–83).[50]

The mere absence of *pontifex maximus* from Justinian's title, then, introduces a second of this book's themes, namely that the division of 'sacred' and 'secular', which is so characteristic of European legal cul-ture, is in process from the first centuries of our era. This division is a *question* for European law in a way that it is not for many other legal cultures (notably, for pre-Christian Roman law),[51] even when the signs of it are no more eye-catching than the conclusion of Justinian's titula-ture in the first lines of his *Institutes*. Few of Justinian's contemporaries, and far fewer of ours, would feel that conclusion to be abrupt—yet it is, in a world-historical way. And what might be an epochal cause—not a *sole* cause, but a *necessary* cause—of Justinian's decision to merely call himself "Renowned" (*Inclitus*)?

11

A superlative irony

This brings us back to the first words of Justinian's preface—in which we can hear, I think, the supreme irony in the history of empire: *In nomine domini nostri Jhesu Christi*. What is the irony of Justinian's invocation of "the name of our Lord Jesus Christ"?

This emperor calls himself "Devout" (*Pius*), and there is no reason to doubt the fanatical intensity of his Christian conviction.[52] The irony of Justinian's words is not subjective, then. It does not lie in his mind, nor—that I have seen—in the minds of any of his interpreters. It is an *objective* irony that I sense here—by which I mean an irony that is not intended (or perceived), and an irony that is *intensified* by it not having been intended (or perceived). This irony could not be simpler; and it could not, to my mind, be more sublime. It is this: Justinian inscribes, at the head of his foyer-text to his monumental code of Roman law (and with it, of much European code law), as a sanctifying and legitimating figure, *the name of a man who was crucified by a Roman judge as a Roman convict*.[53]

No end of studies could be written about the influence of this historically, institutionally, and mystically dense fact.[54] It is the name of a Roman convict—an innocent man, so Justinian believes, who was tortured and killed at the close of a valid Roman process (*cognitio extra ordinem*)[55]—that sanctifies and legitimates Justinian's immense system of Roman law, and in later centuries, other European law codes. (See figs. 3 and 4.)

The presence of Africans in Justinian's incipit, and the absence of the pagans' *pontifex maximus* title, both help to introduce the themes and structure of this book. Throughout, however, what the book represents is a new attempt to interrogate the fact that European politics and law, like European philosophy—I am thinking of the twinned deaths of Socrates and Jesus[56]—begin, in a meaningful sense, *with the court-ordered execution of an innocent man who claims to be a witness to the truth*.

Conclusions

There is no undivided point of origin for European law, but if there *were* such a point of origin, it might be one that modern Europeans tend to forget. European law might begin with the conviction of an innocent man who is now revered by roughly a third of humankind, twenty-one centuries on, as divine. European law might begin, in some caliginous sense, with the *court-ordered death of God*. "God has been murdered", as a second-century Christian poet—whom we will later meet—intones.[57] This is an ear-splitting fore-echo of Nietzsche's line about God's death in the late nineteenth century.

But if that is the case—or if that is even vaguely or conjecturally the case—then Jesus' judge, Pontius Pilate, might be a pivotal and recurring figure in the history of European legal and political theory. And that, ultimately, is the wager of this book.

2

"YOU SAY I AM A KING"

THE MOMENT WHEN JESUS CONFESSES TO PILATE

In modern parlance, it is only the guilty who confess. One confesses to a priest, a judge, or a lover because one has sinned in some way, or broken a law, or strayed from one's commitments. Yet we read in one of the New Testament letters, *I Timothy*—likely written towards the end of the first century CE—that Jesus "witnessed under Pilate of Pontius a *good confession*" (as a fourteenth-century English translation puts it), or that Jesus "testified to the *good confession* in the time of Pontius Pilate" (as a twentieth-century classicist renders it).[1] And the ancient languages are unequivocal. In the Greek of *I Timothy*, we read that Jesus made a *kalē homologia* before his Roman judge. This clearly means that Jesus made a "good confession", which is why the phrase becomes *bona confessio* in the quasi-canonical Latin version of scripture finalized by Jerome (the so-called Vulgate).[2] Whether in Greek, Latin, or English, *I Timothy* claims that Jesus made some sort of confession during his Roman trial.[3]

What is an innocent man, or in Christian belief the *most* innocent man in human history—early Christians called Jesus, simply, "the Just One"[4]—doing making a confession to a contemptuous, brutal, emperor-worshipping man like Pontius Pilate (which is how our first-century Judaean sources portray him)?[5] In one of his last lecture courses at the Collège de France, Foucault clarifies this for us—in a different context, however, and without reference to Jesus' trial.

"We should not forget", Foucault tells his auditors in 1980, "that the notion of confession ... in the Latin Church" is a double one. In the medieval period, it comes to mean pre-eminently the confession of sin (*confessio peccatorum*), which Foucault prefers to call a "confession of self'". But this is not the oldest meaning of Christian confession. "In the Latin of the Church Fathers, practically up to the seventh and eighth century", Foucault reminds us, "the word '*confessor*' refers to someone who is prepared to make the profession of faith right to the end, that is to say to the point of risking death."The word 'risking' here is critical. In early Christian texts, those who die for the faith are called martyrs; and those who risk death, without defecting, are called confessors.[6] But however the lines are drawn in different periods, Foucault concludes his thought by stating that Christianity really is "the *religion of confession*".[7]

What we now think of as 'confession' is not the only, or the most essential, historical meaning of that term. When Jesus 'confesses' to Pilate, he is not conceding guilt or confessing sins. On the contrary, he is testifying, or giving witness to a truth. This is why Pilate sneers at him, "What is truth?"[8] And this is why, as perhaps we failed to notice, *I Timothy* says that Jesus "*witnessed* under Pilate" (in the late medieval version I quoted), or that he "*testified to* the good confession" (in the modern version).[9] The words I have just italicized render the Greek verb *marturein*, from which we take the English word 'martyr'. In Greek, a martyr is anyone who testifies in court. But in early Christian thought,[10] a martyr is one who is killed for testifying in court to a perilous truth—namely "I am a Christian" (*Christianus sum*, or, for women such as the African martyr Vestia in her reply to a Roman prefect at Carthage in the year 180: *Christiana sum*).[11] Multitudes died in the first centuries of our era after making that confession—and many still die, in this century, after making that confession.[12]

The very word 'martyr' suggests that the archetypal drama of Christian suffering is, beginning with Jesus himself, a *courtroom drama*. Jesus' trials in the gospels lead inexorably to the later trials, in *Acts of the Apostles*, of those who were the first to preach Christ-belief (Peter, John, James, Paul, and others), and the first to formally confess it (Stephen and unnamed other Christ-believers who are prosecuted in

Acts).[13] Much of the New Testament canon is structured by trials, and by 'martyrdoms'.

And Jesus himself is a martyr—so *I Timothy* indicates. He is one who voiced a prophetic truth before a Roman tribunal, and who went to his death—the cross—because of it. Jesus did not confess that he was a 'Christian' (despite Nietzsche's claim that "there was really only one Christian, and he died on the cross").[14] Without straying onto theological terrain, the term 'Christian' postdates Jesus' crucifixion by a couple of decades and originates in non-Christian circles.[15] But if Jesus is the Christians' first and incomparable martyr, and if he certainly did not confess that he was a 'Christian', then what is the 'good confession' he made before Pilate?[16]

"The mystery of religion is great"

The substance of Jesus' confession to Pilate is never stated in *I Timothy*.[17] But the context indicates that it may have had something to do with the reign of God, whom *I Timothy* calls "the blessed and single ruler … the King of Kings and Lord of Lords". This divine reign is barely visible in "the present age" (*nun aiōni* Greek, *huius saeculi* Latin), but it will be revealed in a world-culminating future, at the end of this world-age, with "the appearance of our Lord Jesus Christ".[18] The writer of *I Timothy* insists that what he calls "power everlasting" (*kratos aiōnion* Greek) or "empire without end" (*imperium sempiternum* Latin) belongs to God, and to no one but God.[19]

Written, as it is, in the late-first- or early-second-century empire, that would seem to be a seditious claim. But is it? The reign of God is absolute in *I Timothy*, but—weirdly—it seems not to be a *political* reign. This is indicated by one of the first paragraphs in the letter, where we read:

> I ask you first of all to make your prayers, entreaties, intercessions, thanksgivings, for all people, for kings and all who are of high degree, so that we may live a quiet and peaceful life in all piety and dignity. This is good and acceptable in the sight of God our saviour, who wishes all people to be saved, and to come to the recognition of the truth.[20]

The impression this gives is of an early Christian liturgy in which "empire without end" is ascribed to the Christians' God,[21] and yet intercessions are made for all people—this means Judaeans and Hellenes, Christians and "barbarians"[22]—and for emperors and other rulers, not least because they, too, are human.[23] Tertullian of Carthage notes in his *Apology* (197 CE) that African Christians prayed for emperors in their liturgies.[24]

According to *I Timothy*, the reign of God is not revealed in this world-age by violent conflict and political machinations, but by Christians living a "peaceful life" (*hēsuchion bion* Greek, *tranquillam vitam* Latin). How could this be?[25] How could the divine imperium *not* conflict with the Roman imperium—or, in later centuries, with the Persian imperium?[26]

One reply to these questions seems to be given in *I Timothy* itself, where we read that "the mystery of religion is, confessedly, great".[27] The reign of God is not a seditious tenet at the end of the first century, because—as Eusebius of Caesarea will write a couple of centuries later—early Christians held that the divine reign was "mystical" (*mustikōs*), not "material" (*sōmatikōs*).[28] Devotion to Jesus is the source of a mystery-religion in *I Timothy* precisely because Christians confess *a mystical reign of God*. In *I Timothy*, the church seems to be a ritually and liturgically constituted body that calls "*all people* ... to come to the recognition of the truth"[29] but that *coerces no one* to recognize that truth.

From Hugo Grotius' Annotations on the New Testament

Whether or not this is a convincing reading of *I Timothy*, it is of immense historical interest that one of the premier legal theorists of early modern Europe, Hugo Grotius (died 1645), read *I Timothy* in this way.[30] Grotius' influence on modern law—and particularly on modern international law—is vast. His 1609 essay *The Free Sea* influenced the laws of navigation in the *longue durée*. Colonial and neoliberal trade-regimes owe much to his thought.[31] What is more, Grotius' 1625 treatise *The Rights of War and Peace* is a canonical modern treatment of the laws of war, and a decisive influence on several of the philosophers who will concern us later in the book—Hobbes, Samuel Pufendorf, Thomasius, and Rousseau.[32] More recently and more concretely, as legal historian Martti Koskenniemi reminds us, some of the architects of the post-Soviet world order hailed the 1990s as "a 'Grotian moment'".[33] In a word, Grotius is a colossus.

Yet Grotius' stature is misjudged by most intellectual and legal historians,[34] since they tend to forget that his bulkiest text is not a legal summa but a fabulously learned twelve-volume biblical commentary, *Annotations on the Old and New Testament*.[35] (His forerunners in the *Annotations* genre are Lorenzo Valla—on whom, more in chapter 15—and Erasmus of Rotterdam.)[36] Late modern theologians ignore Grotius because he is a jurist; legal historians disregard his commentaries because they are biblical. But Grotius, and most of the figures in this book, would have found such distinctions unconvincing.

In any event, Grotius believes he can identify the moment in Jesus' Roman trial when he makes his 'good confession' before Pilate. It occurs at an unexpected point in the trial narrative in *John* when Pilate urges the accused to face the gravamen of his trial—namely that Jesus claims to be a 'king'. "Pilate said to him", we read in *John* 18, "You are a king? Jesus answered: *You say* I am a king."[37] And in his brief comment on this exchange, Grotius writes: "This is that *kalē homologia* (*bona confessio*), *I Timothy* 6:13"—which is to say, this is the 'good confession' that Jesus made per *I Timothy*.[38]

Is Grotius serious? How could Jesus' half-convinced and half-convincing statement to Pilate, "*You say* I am a king", be the 'good confession' that inspires the writer of *I Timothy*, and the letter's first hearers? One contemporary legal historian reads it as Jesus' refusal to testify.[39] How could one of early modern Europe's foremost legists see in Jesus' retort anything but a sullen evasion?

To begin with, Grotius notes that the form of Jesus' reply is a Hebraism—meaning a form of speech that reflects Jesus' Semitic mother tongue, Aramaic.[40] Grotius read Hebrew and knew many rabbinic texts. (Citing Paul, he expressed a hope that Christians would "unite into one church with the Hebrews"—through, merely, "the abolition of their law"!)[41] When Jesus says to Pilate, "You say" (*su legeis* in the gospel-writer's Greek), what he means to convey is: "You are right" (*recte dicis* in Grotius' Latin). Jesus is not evading Pilate's question, but affirming his kingship.

Nevertheless, there is a subtlety here—a nuanced resistance to the rubric of 'king'—that Grotius is quick to observe. There is a legalistic subtlety hidden in this scene in *John*—or, in Grotius' interpretation of *John*—that I believe to be of world-historical significance. For Grotius reads Jesus as saying to Pilate, here: "I am a king *in a certain sense.*" It is this shading of the meaning of his 'kingship'—which is to say, of the reign of God—that Grotius believes is the 'good confession' of Jesus. He is a king, *and* he is not a king—that is what Grotius hears Jesus saying when he confesses to Pilate that he is "a king in a certain sense *(certo sensu)*".[42] But what is that 'certain sense'? Grotius clarifies.

Jesus is not a king "in the vulgar sense" *(sensu vulgari)*, says Grotius. He is not a rebel or an insurgent. His kingship is not hostile, per se, to the Roman *imperium.* To bolster his interpretation, Grotius cites an intriguing scene that we will return to (in chapter 5), when Jesus' cousins tell the first-century emperor Domitian that Rome's jurisdiction is "worldly or terrestrial", but that Jesus' jurisdiction is not.[43] On the contrary, they say, Jesus' kingdom is "heavenly and angelic" *(celeste et angelicum,* in Grotius' Latin).[44]

And what is an 'angelic' kingdom? The concept is, to be sure, a nebulous one. But Grotius is capable of giving it a hard-edged, institutionally legible meaning that is on hand for him—as we will see in parts 4 and 5—because he is heir to a long line of interpretation of the Roman trial of Jesus. The 'angelic' kingdom that Jesus limns in *John* 18, writes Grotius, "is not coercive *(coactivum)*, but persuasive *(persuasivum)*". That, for Grotius, is the 'good confession' that Jesus made before Pilate. He is a king, but he is a king *in a certain sense.* This is to say that his is an *angelic kingdom*, by which Grotius means *a kingdom of persuasion.* Those who obey the laws of Jesus' kingdom, Grotius goes on, obey of their own volition *(sua sponte)*, and never under duress *(nulla coacti)*.[45] All this, according to Grotius, can be heard in the 'good confession' that Jesus made before Pilate.

From Hugo Grotius' poetic drama, Christ Suffering

But where does Jesus' confession of his 'angelic' kingdom leave Pilate? How can a Roman prefect judge a man who insists that he is a king *in a certain sense*? We will have occasion to mention Grotius' *Annotations on the New Testament* later in the book. They are often cited by Thomasius, for instance, in his 1675 text *On the Unjust Judgement of Pontius Pilate*.[46] Here, we can glance at a Senecan tragedy that Grotius penned on Jesus' trial and death. This dramatic poem, *Christ Suffering* (1608),[47] appeared a year before his epoch-shaping legal brief *The Free*

Sea (1609).[48] It is in his passion play, far more vividly than in his commentary, that Grotius shows how Pilate behaves when he is faced with a man "that Rome", perhaps, "should fear".[49] And we should note, in passing, that Grotius' lines in the coming pages are taken from George Sandys, who "Englished" parts of Ovid during his stay at a Virginia colony in the 1620s—one of the first classical translations to be made in the Americas.[50]

Returning, though, to Grotius. In the lines of *Christ Suffering*, Jesus confesses that he is a king. But this confession is a confusing one. For, as Pilate reflects to himself in Grotius' drama:

he avers his Kingdom is unknown,
Nor of this World, and bows to Caesar's Throne.
Proved by the event: for when the Vulgar bound
His yielding hands, they no resistance found.[51]

What sort of king would offer "no resistance" to being bound, tortured, and killed by legionnaires of a foreign power? (See figs. 5 and 6.) And how is a Roman prefect to judge a king whose "Kingdom is unknown, Nor of this World"? These are some of our core questions in this book.

Grotius' Pilate chances on the expedient that is only narrated by *Matthew* out of the four canonical gospels. He decides to wash his hands in the presence of Jesus and his accusers.[52] Pilate turns to his functionaries in *Christ Suffering*. "You my Attendants", he says, "hither quickly bring spot-purging Water from the living Spring." Pilate continues, addressing the water itself, his "innocent hands", and his conscience:

Thou liquid Chrystal, from pollution clear;
And you my innocent hands like record bear,
On whom these cleansing streams so purely run;
I voluntarily have nothing done.
Nor am I guilty, though he guiltless die.

It is not by chance that the image of an innocent Pilate—courtesy of Grotius—first comes into view, for us, as he is laving the blood of a 'guiltless' convict off his hands. Nor is it by chance that it is at this moment of Jesus' trial that Grotius has Pilate speak harshly to the Judaeans (in Sandys' rendering, "the Jewes").[53] "*Yours* is the Crime", Pilate jabs at Jesus' accusers, "his Blood upon *you* lie." And this is the Judaeans' reply:

Rest thou secure. If his destruction shall
Draw down celestial Vengeance, let it fall
Thick on our heads, in punishment renew:
And ever our dispersed Race pursue!

This is Grotius' terse articulation of a blood-drenched, Christian myth of undying Judaean blood-guilt—more on that in chapter 12— which is dramatically tied to the Christian myth of Pilate's innocence. Both myths coalesce in the first centuries of our era—as we will see in chapter 6. But both Christian myths stem, to my mind, from misreadings of the canonical gospels—and Augustine of Hippo deconstructs the latter in the early fifth century, as we will see in chapter 13.

Returning to Grotius, it is shocking how uncritically he reads the scene of Pilate's handwashing, not only in *Christ Suffering* but in his *Annotations* on the trial narrative in *Matthew*.[54] Far more cynical—and for that reason, far more exegetically astute—are William Shakespeare's lines, composed roughly a decade before Grotius', where Richard II says to his enemies:

Though some of you with Pilate wash your hands,
Showing an outward pity, yet you Pilates
Have here delivered me to my sour cross
And water cannot wash away your sin.[55]

Less hard-headed than the English poet, the Dutch jurist dully echoes a long tradition of Christian epic poetry in which—as we will see in chapter 10—Pilate is not a corrupt judge of Jesus, but, *like* Jesus, a victim of this Roman trial.

What is *less* common, and no less critical to the book's narrative arc, is that Grotius shows his victim-judge, his 'innocent' Pilate—in *Christ Suffering*, as in his *Annotations on the New Testament*—in the act of sentencing Jesus to death.[56] This is Pilate, preparing to utter the sentence of death:

Then I, from this Tribunal, mounted on
Embellished Marble, Judgement's awful Throne,
Thus censure: Lead him to the Cross; and by
A servile death let Judah's King there die.[57]

The last line ("servile death") could call to mind George Herbert's description of Jesus' cross, in a seventeenth-century poem, as "a servile death in servile company". (The "company" that Herbert alludes to being the two convicts nailed up at Jesus' sides.)[58] But what is crucial for us, here, is simply to observe how Grotius—in his *Annotations on the New Testament*, and in his tragic poem, *Christ Suffering*—introduces us to the question of Pilate's innocence (and Judaean blood-guilt). Grotius tries to somehow maintain this 'innocence' though his Pilate sentences Jesus; though his Jesus is guiltless; and though Jesus' kingdom is, for Grotius, *unknown*—which is to say, echoing the Roman trial in *John* 18, that it is "not of this world".

Conclusions

With Grotius—though it is not original to him, as we will see in part 5—Jesus' innocence is formulated in terms of coercion and persuasion. The reign of God, as Jesus states during his interrogation by Pilate, is a reign of *persuasion*. By contrast, the reigns of Tiberius in Rome and Pilate in Judaea are marked by grotesque forms of coercion—as Jesus' trial reveals. And Grotius' Jesus is innocent because, though he is a non-citizen of Rome (*peregrinus*) and a 'king', he has renounced the use of force. He offers 'no resistance' to Rome's functionaries and punishers, as Grotius' Pilate says to himself.

Grotius' elaboration of Jesus' innocence is distinctly Christian—as is his representation of Pilate's innocence. For Grotius' Pilate sentences Jesus only after he has disavowed his sentence of Jesus, and so on. But there is an ancient, far more direct account of Pilate's innocence. And this is a pagan claim—revived and re-elaborated in the eighteenth century by H. S. Reimarus (more on him in chapter 19)—that Jesus was *not* innocent, since he did *not* renounce the use of force.[59] According to a certain number of surviving pagan texts, Jesus'—failed—kingdom *was* 'of this world'; and Pilate was a guiltless judge for the simple reason that the man he crucified was *guilty*. To begin to see how that counter-narrative runs in history, we can turn to a fascinating character of the twentieth century.

3

"THESE THINGS WERE REPORTED TO TIBERIUS"

THE MYSTERY OF WHAT PILATE WROTE

One day in the spring of 1927, Walter Benjamin and Gerhard Scholem sat in an echoey flat on the Rue de Lille in Paris listening to Robert Eisler—a visiting lecturer at the Sorbonne—introduce his riveting new theory about the trial and death of Jesus. "It was an eerie scene", Scholem writes in one of his memoirs, recalling that Benjamin, "who had a special feeling for situations of that kind, was spellbound". Later in the day, Scholem and Benjamin—both of whom had known Eisler in Munich in the early 1920s—went to hear one of his lectures.[1] The conjectures that Eisler made in conversation that day and during his Sorbonne lecture course came out several years later in a colossal book that went to press in Heidelberg as *Jesus, the King Who Did Not Reign*,[2] and in London and New York as *The Messiah Jesus and John the Baptist*.[3]

Here, it is only necessary to know that Eisler became convinced, on the strength of one of the Oxyrhynchus fragments and a dossier of Slavonic (Old Russian) manuscripts—on which, more below—that Jesus went to the holy city, in the last days of his life, with a cohort of "secretly armed" disciples.[4] Once in Jerusalem, Eisler conjectures, Jesus must have called for an "occupation of the Temple". Jesus and his cohort of fighters must have been "reinforced by partisans from the city", Eisler goes on, before they gained control of "the strongly forti-

25

fied Temple".[5] (Gore Vidal seems to recollect this theory in a trashy 1990s novel, *Live from Golgotha*.)[6] But Jesus "could be under no delusion", Eisler then writes. The Galilean prophet must have "expected himself to be taken prisoner and executed"—not by the Romans, however, and not on a cross. This is Eisler: "Jesus was not prepared for the *servile supplicium* [servile death] of crucifixion, but for the horrible sanguinary fate of kings—to be hewn in pieces before the Lord; of Roman legislation on the punishment of an *auctor seditionis* [head of a rebellion], he had scarcely thought."[7]

Eisler's source for this vivid depiction of Jesus? Not much more than a boldly phrased claim that "many Gospels must have perished at an early date".[8] It is from 'gospels' we do not have, rather than the gospels we do, that Eisler takes his Jesus—and his Pilate. And where the canonical Pilate is unconvinced of Jesus' guilt but nevertheless, in a dilatory way, condemns him to death, Eisler is sure that "the passing of sentence upon the *auctor seditionis* taken *in flagranti* and in the midst of armed followers"—meaning, Jesus—"certainly detained the court not an instant longer than was necessary".[9] Eisler's Pilate is resolute—and innocent—because his Jesus is the head of a rebellion. Yet when Eisler writes that Jesus' Roman trial "*certainly* detained the court not an instant longer than was necessary", there is no certainty to be had. He is brazenly contradicting all our first-century narratives of Jesus' Roman trial.[10]

The strange life of Robert Eisler

Eisler is a figure whose theories are bold when they are not incredible, and much in his life verges on the incredible, too. For instance, Eisler headed up a Paris bureau of the League of Nations. Yet the Austrian government bitterly objected to him being chosen for the position—though he was Austrian, and though his call to Paris was by then a *fait accompli*. This accounts for the "eerie scene" that met Benjamin and Scholem when they stepped into Eisler's rooms on the Rue de Lille. He had rented a mansion flat before it became clear that all the "official people" in Paris would have nothing to do with him. As a result, Eisler's flat was never properly furnished—his suite of rooms felt deserted, Scholem recalls—and he served for several years as a *non grata* official in Paris.[11]

Eisler's circle of friends included some of Europe's most imposing minds, such as the German cultural theorist and "image historian" (*Bildhistoriker*) Aby Warburg. Long after Warburg's death in 1929, Eisler's contributions can be found in the pages of the *Journal of the Warburg and Courtauld Institutes*. (I have in mind a five-page *tour de force* on the frontispiece of a Renaissance astrological text.)[12] And the bulk of Eisler's papers are now housed at The Warburg Institute in London, with one stray box at The Griffith Institute in Oxford. This is a mark of his seriousness.

Roughly a decade after his visiting lecturership at the Sorbonne, Eisler held a visiting lecturership at the University of Oxford.[13] But he never held a professorship. Perversely, Eisler's only chair was at the fictitious University of Muri. This 'university' only existed as a joke between Scholem and Benjamin, who had lived in Muri—a village near Zurich known for its eleventh-century, Habsburg-founded monastery—in 1918 and 1919. In later years, these 'rectors' of the University of Muri installed Eisler—unknown to him—in a chair that obligated him to lecture on a set of frothy twentieth-century topics "in light of the history of religion".[14] Eisler presumably held this dubious chair until his death in Oxford in 1949.

Yet Eisler's professorship at the University of Muri is nothing like the strangest item on his vita. In the long decade that fell between his lecturerships in Paris and Oxford, he was invited to speak at one of Carl Jung's *Eranos* conferences, in 1935.[15] A couple of years later, he was interned in the Nazi camps at Dachau and Buchenwald (as prisoner number 16547)—he was then released and permitted to emigrate to England in 1938.[16] Eisler's imprisonment was, of course, due to his Jewish descent (he had formally converted to Catholicism long before the *Nazizeit*). It is not many who made it from the cells of Buchenwald to the corridors of Oxford.

And Eisler's literary biography is harder yet to believe. A couple of years after the second volume of his *Jesus* book appeared, he published a 300-page book of monetary theory that is still being cited by impeccably credentialed economists.[17] What Willem Buiter—formerly of the Bank of England's Monetary Policy Committee—calls "the Eisler economy" is notable for the function it assigns to virtual currencies. It is striking to see Buiter conclude in a 2007 paper that

Eisler's 1932 text theorizes an "important and much-neglected issue in monetary economics".[18]

If Eisler's lasting contribution to monetary theory feels vaguely credible after we glance at a page of his 1902 text *Studies on Value-Theory*,[19] it begins to feel much less predictable after we run our eyes down the contents of his 1921 monograph *Orpheus—The Fisher*,[20] and then move on to his 1938 historical-critical study *The Enigma of the Fourth Gospel*.[21] When we finally come to Eisler's extravagantly anno-tated lecture *Man into Wolf: An Anthropological Interpretation of Sadism, Masochism, and Lycanthropy*—a lecture he read before the Royal Society of Medicine, and that appeared posthumously in 1951—the hair on the backs of our necks begins to prick up. Can this be real? And do the professors of economics know they are citing a man whose theory of *homo economicus* is linked to the 1949 trial and hang-ing of a Kensington serial killer, John George Haigh, whom Eisler is drawn to as "a clear case of vampirism"?[22]

Eisler's contributions are real. His wilder conjectures are fascinat-ing, even when they are not convincing. Scholem describes his friend as "inconceivably erudite", and Eisler's contributions bear this out. He represents a rebellious sort of erudition that could only live on the fringes of the early-twentieth-century university (except the University of Muri). Yet Scholem warns that Eisler, whose ingenuity and learning are undeniable, is nevertheless a man with a flair for devising "bril-liantly false solutions" to historico-religious problems.[23] And it is one such 'false solution' that leads us into the question of Pilate's innocence in the fourth century CE.[24]

What Pilate wrote

In this chapter, our main interest is with what Eisler conjectures about Pilate and his writings. For it is one of the novelties of Eisler's book on Jesus—which one of his critics, Ernst Bammel, calls a "departure of the greatest importance"[25]—that he poses the ques-tions: What did Pilate write about Jesus and his trial? And do we possess any of those writings?

It is rarely phrased in this way, but we do seem to have a legal text on record that Pilate himself composed. It is not much—a slight fragment—but the canonical gospels all claim that the Roman prefect had a judicial notice (*titulus*) mounted on Jesus' cross, in keeping with the Roman custom. This brief text stated the legal cause for Jesus' death. According to the Roman consul Dio Cassius (died 235), such scripts consisted of "words setting out the crime for which a man was dying".[26]

The canonical gospels give slightly different versions of this notice, but there is no reason to doubt that Jesus' claim to kingship was pinned, as the cause of his punishment (*causa poenae*), to the stake on which the Romans hanged him. In Paul Winter's words, there are "cogent reasons which forbid the reader" to treat Jesus' *titulus* as a Christian fabrication.[27] Without entering further into this: the Romans' use of such notices is attested by Dio Cassius and Suetonius,[28] and the possibility "seems remote" that first-century Christians would compose a *titulus* that blares the charge of sedition.[29] Citing Cyril of Alexandria, Winter notes that "the words of Pilate's *titulus* were even offensive to the Christian appreciation of Jesus' person".[30] With that said, the canonical versions of Jesus' *titulus* are

1. "The King of the Judaeans" (*Mark* 15:26),
2. "This is Jesus, the King of the Judaeans" (*Matthew* 27:37),
3. "This is the King of the Judaeans" (*Luke* 23:38),
4. "Jesus of Nazareth, the King of the Judaeans" (*John* 19:19).

It is the Latin acronym of the *titulus* in *John*, reading *Iesus Nazarenus Rex Iudaeorum*, that is emblazoned on European altars and chasubles, using the initials *I. N. R. I*. And it is on seeing this acronym that Leopold Bloom, an early-twentieth-century European Jew who finds himself in church in James Joyce's *Ulysses*, half remembers and half conjectures that it means: "Iron nails ran in."[31]

Though a *titulus* is recollected in all four gospels, it is only the gospel of *John* that tells us that "Pilate *wrote* an inscription"—"'Jesus of Nazareth, the King of the Judaeans'"—in Latin (the language of Roman bureaucracy and law), Greek (the empire's *lingua franca*), and Aramaic (the convict's mother tongue).[32] And it is only *John* that tells us that Jesus' accusers urged the Roman prefect to change the wording of this notice. "Do not write: 'The King of the Judaeans'", they ask Pilate, "but write *that he said*: 'I am King of the Judaeans.'" Pilate refuses to emend his *titulus*, saying: "What I have written, I have written."[33] (See figs. 7 and 8.)

Eisler deems that to be a "thoroughly credible statement, for the invention of which no apparent reason can be imagined".[34]

Like Jesus' accusers in *John*, both non-Christians and Christians have been unhappy, from the first century on, that Pilate did not write more about himself and the Galilean he put to death. But what Pilate has *not* written, he has not written—and others have obliged. We will glance in chapter 6 at a skein of forged Christian texts that is often called "the Pilate cycle".[35] They are all written by a 'Pilate', or concoct new speeches for a 'Pilate', and most of them contain naive protestations of the prefect's innocence and bitter imprecations of "the wicked Hebrews".[36] These forgeries are historically important, since they exerted a long and diffuse influence on Christian thought (and lamentably, on Christian politics). But they are certainly forgeries. No modern historian or theologian believes that Pilate wrote them, or that a historical Pilate figures in them.

Eisler's theory of what Pilate wrote

One of Eisler's boldest claims in his *Jesus* book is that Pilate's writings about Jesus—the Roman prefect's notes and impressions of Jesus' physiognomy, trial, and conviction—were exhumed in the 1860s by Alexander Popov from a collection of Old Russian manuscripts made in the early modern period,[37] and then published in the 1920s by Konrad Grass in a (posthumous) German edition by the Estonian philologist Alexander Berendts.[38] Eisler's claim is so momentous that I will be forgiven for restating it: Pilate's forensic notes on the trial and death of Jesus—his *hupomnēmata* in Greek, *commentarii* in Latin—were rediscovered in a set of Old Russian manuscripts in the mid-nineteenth century and published in a critical edition in the early twentieth century. It is now possible to read *Pilate's own memoranda of the trial and death of Jesus*, and even *how Pilate perceived the bone-structure of Jesus' face*. For instance, Jesus is a "crooked", "horse-faced" man with eyebrows that meet over his nose—or so we read in one medieval fragment that Eisler is ready to attribute to Pilate himself.[39]

This is not the place to reconstruct the long chain of texts, and versions of texts, and highly original conjectures—and conjectures within conjectures[40]—that lead Eisler to claim in the early 1930s that we now possess extracts made from "the official commentaries of Tiberius" (the emperor when Jesus died). Eisler means by this that, in his words, we now possess "nothing more and nothing less than extracts from the official reports of Pilate".[41] This conjecture can be called 'wild' because there is precisely *no* hard evidence backing it. There is *no* indication, however subtle, in the Old Russian 'Josephus'—the text on which Eisler's *Jesus* book hangs—that whoever composed the material about Jesus consulted "the official commentaries of Tiberius" or "the official reports of Pilate".[42] The idea that Pilate's own writings about Jesus are extant in Old Russian copies of Josephus is nothing more, and nothing less, than an idea that occurred to Eisler—a philologist of immense learning—in the late 1920s in Paris.

According to Per Bilde, Eisler's is a "notorious hypothesis" that can now "be said to have been invalidated".[43] The scholarly consensus—with which I concur—is that Pilate's writings about Jesus, whatever they may have been, are lost without a trace.[44] Outside of Jesus' *titulus* in the gospel, that is to say, we seem to have no access to any scrap of writing—much less to a forensic commentary—that Pilate may have written about Jesus.

The question of Pilate's writings in the first centuries CE

Eisler's wild conjecture about Pilate's writings is now inert, and scholars have forgotten it because they legitimately can. The late-twentieth-century authority on the Slavonic Josephus, Nikita Meščerskij, is right to stress how "unreliable Eisler's philological arguments can prove".[45] It is nevertheless, to my mind, unfortunate that Eisler's *Jesus* book—which James Carleton Paget calls his "magnificent, if flawed, work"[46]—is no longer read. Benjamin and Scholem recognized that Eisler's "theories on the origin of Christianity" were "uncommonly ingenious" (though erroneous).[47] And they *are* uncommonly ingenious (though erroneous). One mark of their ingenuity is the salience that Eisler gives, in his history of Christian origins, to *the question of Pilate's writings*.

Let me restate this. Eisler is wrong to claim that we still have Pilate's writings in Old Russian copies of Josephus. That conjecture is without merit and can be forgotten. Yet Eisler is right to argue that *the question of Pilate's writings* is a critical one in the early history of Christianity, and during the Christianization of Rome. It is this question of Eisler's that should not be forgotten—and that chapter 4 will centre upon. Here, we can only ask—in a cursory way—what are the facts about Pilate's writings of which Eisler reminds us in his *Jesus* book, and of which he presumably told Benjamin and Scholem that day in 1927?

In the first place, it is not improbable that Pilate would have written something (making use of his secretaries, naturally) about the trial and death of Jesus. This is Eisler:

> We know ... from the Egyptian papyri ... the habits and usages of the Roman bureaucracy, which kept a running index of even the smallest incidents of their official life as they came up. Such notices were collected so as to form the official diary (*commentarii*) of the governor, copies of which were kept in provincial and central archives, whilst extracts were regularly sent to the Emperor in Rome.[48]

It is wild of Eisler to conjecture that we still have, in a cache of early modern manuscripts, the forensic notes composed by Pilate and submitted to the imperial archives in Rome. But there is nothing wild in Eisler's claim that such notes are likely to have been extant, if only in archival copies, for a time—perhaps centuries—after Jesus' death.

In the second place, as Eisler notes, early Christian intellectuals show some cognizance of Pilate's notes on the trial of Jesus—or rather, of Christian texts that passed as such, and that seem to have circulated in the first centuries of our era. For instance, Justin the Philosopher (and Martyr) cites a text he calls circa 150, the *Acts of Pontius Pilate*. "After Jesus was crucified", Justin writes, "they cast lots for his clothing, and his crucifiers divided it among themselves. You can ascertain that these things really happened from the *Acts of Pontius Pilate*."[49] And again, this is Justin:

> Concerning the prophecy that our Christ should cure all diseases and raise the dead to life, hear ... the exact words of the prophecy: "At his coming the lame shall leap like a stag, and the tongue of the dumb shall be clear; the blind shall see, and the lepers shall be cleansed ..." That Christ did perform such deeds you can learn from the *Acts of Pontius Pilate*.[50]

What we cannot learn from Justin is the form in which his second-century *Acts of Pontius Pilate* circulated, or what this text's provenance could have been. The biblical tenor of the second passage naturally suggests that it is not a forensic report written by Pilate, but a forgery by some early Christian.

Similarly, in his third-century defence of Christian faith, Tertullian of Carthage—*nota bene*, an African writer—invokes the figure of Jesus' Roman judge:

> This religion of ours depends upon very ancient Judaean records—although most people know it only as something of a novelty which came to birth during the reign of Tiberius (a fact that we ourselves acknowledge) ... As for Jesus' teaching ... the teachers and elders of the Judaeans ... finally brought Jesus before Pontius Pilate, who at that time was governing Syria in the interests of Rome, and by the violence of their demands they forced Pilate to hand him over to the Judaeans to be crucified.[51]

Tertullian is wrong to tie Pilate to Syria. Pilate is not a Roman legate of Syria (*legatus Syriae*), but a prefect of Judaea (*praefectus Judaeae*).[52] And it is erroneous of Tertullian to say that Pilate handed Jesus "to the Judaeans to be crucified". That is a tenacious Christian error that comes from a crude reading of the canonical passion narratives (on which, more in chapter 12).

Our interest here, though, is precisely in the fact that Tertullian is *not* citing the canonical passion narratives. Instead, he writes:

> All these things about Christ were reported to Tiberius, the reigning Caesar, by Pilate who was by now a Christian, as far as his conscience was concerned. And the Caesars, too, would have believed about Christ, had Caesars not been necessary for the world-age (*saeculo*), or if Christians could have been Caesars.[53]

It is by no means certain that Tertullian is referring to the *Acts of Pilate* cited by Justin, but both seem to believe that documents written by Pilate could be consulted in the second and third centuries of our era. That the 'Pilate' texts cited by both Justin and Tertullian attest the divine power and resurrection of Jesus suggests they were early Christian forgeries, and not Pilate's forensic notes on the trial of Jesus.

But note what Tertullian says about the Caesars. They would have converted to the Christian faith, he opines, if they had "not been necessary for the world-age (*saeculo*)". The presence of the Latin word *saeculum* in this text on Pilate is of immense interest. This is a very early contrast, in the Christian archives, between a Roman governmental *saeculum* and the church. In this text, Caesar represents the "world-age", and Christians represent Christ. And this early contrast between the 'secular' and 'sacred' is linked to Jesus' trial before Pilate.

That Tertullian—as just noted—is an African theologian will take on a clearer significance later in the book (particularly in chapters 13 and 14). For the arc of 'secularity' in European history, I will argue in the coming chapters, is set by a distinctive interpretation of the Roman trial of Jesus that is rooted in Roman Africa. It is not true of European secularity, as Foucault joked in a 1977 interview on the history of European sexuality, that the "originator of it all was Tertullian".[54] But it is certainly suggestive, apropos of the history of European secularity, that Tertullian is still being cited in seventeenth-century legal texts on Jesus' Roman trial (as we will see in chapter 19). And it is striking that Tertullian takes it to be inarguably the case, in the early third century, that Christians *cannot* be Caesars.[55] A multitude of histories turn on the fact that, a century later—in the early fourth century—one of the Caesars, Constantine I, declares himself a Christian.[56]

Conclusions

The striking title of Eisler's opus, *Jesus, the King Who Did Not Reign*, is lifted from a passage in the Slavonic Josephus where we read of "Jesus, [a] king who had not reigned, *crucified by [the] Jews*, because he foretold the destruction of the city and the devastation of the Temple."[57] The words I have italicized, "crucified by the Jews", signal the lateness of Eisler's text. This could not have come from Pilate's hand. For the Judaean crucifixion of Jesus is not only a myth but—from what I can tell—a uniquely Christian one (though it reverberates in Judaic and Islamic traditions).

Now, when I refer—here and hereafter—to the 'myth of a Judaean crucifixion', I am not suggesting that *Jesus' crucifixion* is a myth (on the contrary, it is a historical datum), or that *Jesus' Judaean trial* is a myth (to my mind, it is not).[58] The 'uniquely Christian myth' that I refer to is the idea that *Judaeans, rather than Romans, nailed Jesus to the cross*. This is a myth. And the oldest Christian text that attests this myth seems to be the *Apology* of Aristides.[59] Though this second-century *Apology* only says

that Jesus was "pierced by the Judaeans",[60] we can read in a hugely influential fourth-century text that "Judaeans fastened Christ to the cross."[61]
There will be more on this myth in chapter 6. Here, it suffices to say
that the 'myth of a Judaean crucifixion' is not rooted in the canonical
gospels—but seems to be ineradicable in Christian tradition.

Whatever the errors of *Jesus, the King Who Did Not Reign*, Eisler is
unique in his stress on the question of Pilate's writings in early
Christian history. He is unique, too, in his recognition that the
Christianization of the Roman Empire in the fourth century is signalled
by, and reflected in, a contest between pagan texts and Christian texts
that are attributed to Pontius Pilate.

PART 2

THE HIGH POLITICS OF PILATE AND JESUS

4

"CHRIST HIMSELF COMMITTED ROBBERIES"

THE *MEMOIRS OF PILATE* AND THE LAST PAGAN EMPEROR

It is not common knowledge that the English philosopher Thomas Hobbes wrote a 2,000-line anti-clerical poem in Latin iambic pentameter by the name of *Ecclesiastical History*.[1] Hobbes's epoch-shaping political treatise, *Leviathan*, will concern us in chapter 17, and our interest in this chapter is with a huge *Ecclesiastical History* written in prose by the fourth-century Christian historian Eusebius of Caesarea (died 339/40). Hobbes's poem is a sort of counter-blast to Eusebius' chronicle.[2] But as the hostile echo in Hobbes's title suggests, late antique church history is a looming presence in the early modern political imaginary. And it is with Hobbes's antagonistic poem in mind that we can glance now at the last book of Eusebius' *Ecclesiastical History*.

Here, Eusebius recalls the solemn Christian rites that marked the end of the Great Persecution, as it is called, in the years 303 to 311 CE.[3] Influenced by a reactionary strain of Platonic philosophy,[4] and sanctioned by the god Apollo (on whom more in chapter 7),[5] the Great Persecution seems to have started with the gutting of a basilica and the burning of Christian scriptures near the imperial court at Nicomedia on *Terminalia*, the feast-day of the god Terminus, in February 303.[6] The date may have been chosen to symbolize the persecutors' intent "to terminate ... the Christian religion".[7] Needless to say, they failed. And

39

in April 311, an edict of toleration was posted in Nicomedia, near Byzantium—soon to become Constantinople, the Christian world-city of Constantine I, and the "New Rome" (*Nova Roma*).[8]

"Ineffable symbols of the Saviour's Passion"

Much has been written about the "terrible and gloomy spectacles" of that critical decade in which Christians,[9] in many parts of the empire, were judicially tortured, mutilated, burned alive, fed to beasts, or worked to death in the mines. Those scenes pose immense problems of reconstruction and interpretation that we cannot hope to clarify.[10] Our interest is much narrower—and we will begin by noting a single phrase in Eusebius' massive history. During the Christians' celebration of the end of persecution after the suicide (or natural death) of the last pagan emperor,[11] Eusebius writes that "the ineffable symbols of the Saviour's Passion were present".[12]

Eusebius is doubtless referring to the eucharistic bread and wine that were consecrated in what he calls the "divine and mystical services" of the church, and which—he adds—were tasted by "all together, of every age, male and female".[13] But Eusebius is also surely referring to the sign of the cross made by believers over the forehead, and to the image of the cross sewn into vestments and blazoned in the churches.[14] What is the relevance, here? A distinctive style of cross (or Christogram) known as the *labarum* had begun to represent the government of the western empire and the armies of Constantine "the Greatest" (*Maximus*), as the Roman Senate styled him,[15] in October 312.[16] It was during Constantine's reign that the "heavenly sign" of Jesus' cross came to symbolize the military prowess of Rome.[17] And with the death of the last persecuting emperor in the summer of 313,[18] the cross now rose as a symbol of Rome in the eastern provinces, such as Syria and Palestine.[19]

When Eusebius observes that "the ineffable symbols of the Saviour's Passion were present" in the newly restored basilicas of Syria and Palestine in the year 313, then, it helps to mark a world-historical threshold.[20] This is the moment at which the symbol of the cross begins to be elevated over both zones of the late antique Roman Empire—zones that will become, in later centuries, a 'Byzantine'

Empire (centred on Constantinople), and a 'Holy Roman' Empire (symbolically centred on Rome)—shaping the legal and political history of the globe. And this threshold is constituted, on Eusebius' telling, by the death of the last pagan emperor, by a repellent sickness or by his own hand, in Tarsus (the native city of the apostle Paul),[21] in the late summer of 313.[22]

"A man from Dacia"

The last pagan emperor? It is a vague and contentious description, and it is one that Eusebius does not use. But Eusebius wrote book X of his *Ecclesiastical History* soon after the death of Maximin Daia (or Daza),[23] a pagan who held the highest imperial offices in the Diocese of the East (*Diocesis Orientis*) between 305 and 313 CE.[24] The name 'Daia' simply marks him off as "a man from Dacia", or Dacia Ripensis, one of the empire's outermost provinces covering the bulk of modern Romania.[25]

It is critical for us to note that Maximin Daia ruled within an imperial 'college' that modern historians call the Tetrarchy.[26] In 293, Emperor Diocletian had introduced a system that split the governance of Roman territories between two older rulers styled *Augusti*, both of whom were shadowed by younger rulers called *Caesares*. And it was within a rapidly and violently disintegrating Tetrarchy that Daia came to be the supreme ruler of the east—or, as Eusebius prefers to call him, "the tyrant of the east".[27] Daia's diocese covered the Roman territories in the Near East—from Bithynia (in modern Turkey) and Syria in the north, to Palestine and Egypt in the south. During much of his reign, Daia brutally persecuted Christians.[28] Because of this, referring to 313—the year in which Daia died—Eusebius calls him "the only one of the enemies of piety".[29] Eusebius means by this that Daia was the last of the Tetrarchy's persecuting emperors to be vanquished—and to die.

But does this make Daia the 'last pagan emperor'? It could of course be suggested that there *is* no 'last pagan emperor' (until, say, Napoleon Bonaparte). The lines between pagan and Christian are blurred and contested in late antiquity (and in many later centuries).[30] Or, less radically, it could be argued that Daia is not the 'last pagan emperor'. After all, Emperor Licinius—who put an end to Daia's reign in 313 and then ruled in the east for more than a decade—was not a Christian.

On rare occasions, it seems that Licinius himself persecuted Christians.[31] Isn't Licinius, then, the 'last pagan emperor'?

Through Eusebius himself, we learn that this is how Constantine, who deposed Licinius in 324 and likely had him killed in 325, chose to portray him.[32] But Licinius' victory over Daia in 313 is remembered by early-fourth-century Christians as a 'Christian' victory over the last fanatical pagan emperor.[33] It is unlikely that Licinius ever converted (though Christian texts claim he did in his final moments). Yet he is still, in some sense, a 'Constantinian' emperor—and not simply a 'pagan' one. Licinius is portrayed in one fourth-century Latin text, for instance, as exhorting Christians to restore the basilicas that Daia had seized or destroyed.[34]

What is more, in the wake of Daia *and* Licinius there will come a brilliant pagan reactionary, Julianus Augustus, alias Julian the Apostate, whom Hans Teitler has denominated *The Last Pagan Emperor*.[35] Julian reigned for nineteen months in the years 361 to 363,[36] decades after Eusebius wrote the *Ecclesiastical History*. As Julian's epithet—'Apostate'—blares, he was reared as a Christian. For Julian was a nephew of Constantine, as he often bitterly reminded the Romans.[37] Julian may have died by a Christian hand, too. If one early rumour can be trusted, the Apostate was slain in Persia by an Arab Christian serving in the Roman ranks.[38]

All that matters here is that, though Julian may have come to be one of the "enemies of piety" (in Eusebius' phrase), he was not *simply* a pagan.[39] Not like the roughneck Daia, and not like Rome's other pagan emperors. Not in a pre-Constantinian sense.[40] This is why inscriptions from Julian's reign call him a "restorer of the temples", a "restorer of the sacred rites".[41] Julian's reign is a *pagan restoration* led, not by a 'pagan', but by a *post-Christian*.

For our purposes here, then, it is possible to say that Licinius is a *conflicted* non-Christian, Julian is an *apostate* Christian—and Daia is the last pagan emperor of Rome. As Marta Sordi suggests, Daia's demise marks the end of the Roman imperium's smouldering hostility to, and recurring persecution of, the early church.[42] That being the case, it should be of interest that "the ineffable symbols of the Saviour's Passion" come to new prominence in the months and years following Daia's death.[43] And crucial to the arc of this book is one of Daia's tactics for thwarting this elevation of the cross.

"Memoirs about Our Saviour"

Daia seems to have sensed the supreme irony (evoked in chapter 1) of a Roman convict's death-pole being taken by one of his rivals, Constantine, as a symbol of Rome's sacred laws and empire. Daia seems to have believed that Jesus was not a guiltless mystic (as sketched in chapter 2), but an insurgent 'king'. And Daia seems to have claimed (like Eisler in chapter 3) that the forensic notes made by Pilate could still be read. Unsurprisingly, this text of Daia's proved Jesus' guilt—and Pilate's innocence.

It is strange that historians of early Christianity and late antiquity have not made more of this, but in the years before his death Daia tried to demystify the cross by promulgating a text called the *Memoirs of Pilate*.[44] What this means is that one of the last tactical moves of Rome's last pagan emperor centred on the figure of Pilate. What is more, Daia's *Memoirs of Pilate* seem to have dramatized Pilate's innocence.[45] In a very broad sense, we could perhaps even say that the last political 'doctrine' promulgated by Rome's last pagan emperor was the innocence of Pontius Pilate. For it is Pilate's name that seems to preside, in Daia's eastern territories, during pre-Christian Rome's last concerted persecution of the church. But what do we know about Daia's *Memoirs of Pilate*?

Daia's *Memoirs of Pilate* are first mentioned in book I of *Ecclesiastical History*, when Eusebius is chronicling the life and death of Jesus. He dates Jesus' prophetic life back to his baptism by John the Baptist. And this baptism occurred, according to Eusebius—who is drawing here on the gospel of *Luke*—when "Tiberius Caesar was in the fifteenth year of his reign and Pontius Pilate the fourth of his governorship."[46] Having settled on this chronology, Eusebius notes that *Luke*'s dating of Pilate's prefectship conflicts with the dating of Jesus' death in Daia's *Memoirs of Pilate*.[47] For Eusebius, this is "clear proof of the forgery of those who recently ... issued a series of *Memoirs* about our Saviour".

But Eusebius' chronology is not only based on *Luke*. He also cites the first-century Judaeo-Roman historian Flavius Josephus—"*if* Josephus", the Christian chronicler shows some hesitation, "may be used as a witness".[48] And *if* Josephus can be trusted by late antique Christians, then the crucifixion in Daia's *Memoirs* will have occurred in a year in which "Pilate was not yet in charge of Judaea." Because Eusebius is convinced that "the crime of the Saviour's death" is misdated in Daia's text, he believes that he can "convict the forgers" of the fourth-century *Memoirs of Pilate* of their "untruth".[49]

When Eusebius later returns to the topic of Jesus' death, he cites the fantastically contentious Testimony of Josephus (*Testimonium Flavianum*), which states—in Eusebius' version—that "Pilate condemned Jesus to the cross."[50] Given the discrepancies between Josephus' text and Daia's *Memoirs*, Eusebius asks rhetorically: "What alternative is there but to convict of shamelessness those who have concocted the *Memoirs*?" Again, Eusebius is clearly referring to, and denying the authenticity of, Daia's *Memoirs of Pilate* (though he adverts to false reports about John the Baptist that seem to have been circulating at the time).[51]

On the question of Jesus' death and resurrection, Eusebius further cites Tertullian (whom we met in chapter 3), adding that the Carthaginian "had an accurate knowledge of Roman laws".[52] Many early Christian writers, for that matter, had legal formations, or philosophical formations, or both. Supplementing his knowledge of Tertullian, Eusebius seems to be familiar with at least some of the forged Christian texts that modern historians call "the Pilate cycle" (to which we will return in chapter 6),[53] and he affirms—with Tertullian—that Rome's imperial archives once held a copy of the original *Memoirs of Pilate*. This is Eusebius:

> In keeping with an ancient custom that those who ruled over the nations should report to him who held the imperial office any new movement among them, in order that no event might escape his notice, Pilate communicated to the Emperor Tiberius the story of the resurrection from the dead of our Saviour Jesus as already rumoured among all throughout all Palestine, together with the information he had gained of Jesus' other wonders and how he was already believed by many to be God (*theos einai*), in that after death he had risen from the dead.[54]

Whatever else we could say about this passage, it demonstrates that both Christians and pagans on the cusp of the Constantinian revolution believed that Pilate had composed *Memoirs* about Jesus' trial and death—a set of formal governmental memoranda (*hupomnēmata* in Greek) for Tiberius' court and the imperial archives. The Christians claimed, moreover, that the rumours and hopes in Palestine concerning Jesus' resurrection were described in Pilate's *Memoirs*.

Both pagans and Christians seem to have sensed, in the last years and decades of the pre-Christian Roman Empire, that Pilate was a critical figure. This inference from Eusebius' *Ecclesiastical History* is confirmed by numerous passages on the Pilate trial in an early-fourth-century apology by Macarius of Magnesia, composed in reply to an unnamed pagan philosopher (Plotinus' disciple Porphyry? Julian the Apostate?).[55] And this is not unreasonable. For who better than Pilate to tell the Romans who Jesus—the man crucified in Palestine and "believed by many to be God"—might have been, or must have been?[56]

"Forged to insult us"

The ferociously anti-Christian Daia clearly thought that Pilate—which is to say, the *figure* of Pilate—was crucial in his fight to save the pagan *imperium*. For this is what we read in *Ecclesiastical History* IX of Daia's last, devastating wave of persecutions of the Christians in Syria, Palestine, and other eastern territories:

> Having forged—to be sure—memoirs (*hupomnēmata*) of Pilate and our Saviour, full of every kind of blasphemy against Christ, [the new pagan 'high priests' of Daia's Diocese of the East] sent them,[57] with the approval of [Daia], into every part of his dominions, with edicts that they should be exhibited openly for everyone to see in every place, in the country and the cities, and that the grammar-teachers should give them to the children, instead of lessons, to be studied and committed to memory.[58]

Eusebius seems, here, to recollect a propagandistic text titled *Memoirs of Pilate*—or even, conceivably, *Memoirs of Pilate and Jesus*[59]—that was put into circulation when Daia's sanguinary new policies went into effect.[60] But what is most striking is that the *Memoirs of Pilate* that were penned—on Eusebius' telling—in the world-historical moment that Constantine began to Christianize the imperial machinery in Rome were promulgated in the eastern provinces *by edict*. Daia permitted this text to move through the formal, imperial channels in the east. The pagan *Memoirs of Pilate* were issued as a sort of legal text, a highly visible counter-narrative to the passion narratives in the canonical gospels and in forged Christian texts by 'Pilate'.

Eusebius seems to be certain that Daia's pagan version of the Roman trial of Jesus was not only posted throughout the Roman

Empire's eastern provinces but chanted in the schools. For he returns to this image of the late pagan empire's children chanting about the Roman trial of Jesus:

> So intensely, indeed, did that hater-of-the-good, Maximin Daia, come against us, that this persecution which he had stirred up seemed to us much more severe than the former one. In fact, in the midst of the cities—a thing that had never happened before—petitions presented against us by cities, and rescripts containing imperial ordinances in reply, were set up, engraved on bronze tablets, while the children in the schools had on their lips every day the names of Jesus and Pilate and the *Memoirs* forged to insult us.[61]

It is arresting to think of the sing-song recitation of the *Memoirs of Pilate* in the grammarians' schools of Arabia and Palestine, Syria and Anatolia, circa 312 CE—the year in which Constantine vanquished Rome under his cruciform sign (the *labarum*). "The children", in the last days of pre-Christian Rome, "had on their lips every day the names of Jesus and Pilate."[62] This image is a structuring motif in Eusebius' history of the last pagan emperor, and it represents a failed attempt by Daia—a pagan—to shape history by means of the Roman trial of Jesus. As we will see, certain later attempts by Christians did not fail.

But Eusebius says that the "memoirs of Pilate and our Saviour" were "full of every kind of blasphemy against Christ".[63] Is it possible for us to conjecture what these 'blasphemies' might have been, that the children of Daia's Rome were taught to chant? And is it possible, in that way, to see more clearly what the importance of Pilate, for Daia, might have been? In other words, what might have led Daia's pagan high priests to compose and promulgate the *Memoirs of Pilate* as an "insult" to the Christians?[64]

"A force of 900 men"

Eusebius gives no real indication of the contents of Daia's *Memoirs of Pilate*, but I suggest that we can obtain a probable indication.[65] This indication emanates from Daia's milieu; it is not unrelated to Eusebius' oeuvre;[66] and it is reported by one of Eusebius' contemporaries, Lactantius (whom we will meet in chapter 6).[67] It is unnecessary to give much context or an elaborate interpretation. It should suffice to say that in Lactantius' book *Divine Institutes*, he tells us that one of the Christians' enemies during the Tetrarchy "asserted that 'Christ himself, put to flight by the Judaeans, had carried on robberies by collecting a force of 900 men.'"[68]

Lactantius never names his source, here—and he is hardly impressed by his pagan antagonist. "Who would dare to refute such great authority?" he laughs.[69] (Note that Lactantius, apparently, was a pagan by birth.) But the implication of this pagan claim, circa 300 CE, is clear: Jesus was a criminal. And, what is more, Jesus was an enemy of the human race (*hostis humani generis*)—in modern parlance, a 'terrorist'.[70] For that is how a gangster-king at the head of a 900-man force would be defined by Roman law.[71] Legally, there is no question that a judge who nailed up such a 'king' would be *innocent*. And legally, if Jesus *had* headed a cohort of marauders, he would have deserved to be crucified.

It is worth noting that this claim about Jesus and his 900 gangsters seems to derive from Sossianus Hierocles, a Platonic philosopher and high Roman official who wrote a polemic against the Christians titled *Lover of Truth*.[72] (Christians loved to mock this title and its "truth-loving" author.)[73] Lactantius only tells us that the claim about Jesus and his 900 fighters originates in a text by someone who was "one of the first instigators" of the Great Persecution; and that this person, "not content with that crime", terrorized in the courts Christians "he had afflicted with his writings".[74]

Given that Hierocles belonged to the highest imperial circles during the Great Persecution, and was notorious for his hostility to Christians (though he may have been a Christian by birth),[75] it is plausible that Hierocles' claim about Jesus' 900 fighters may have been one of the 'blasphemies' contained in Daia's *Memoirs of Pilate*.[76] We can already see in *Acts of the Apostles* how Roman officials confused the apostle Paul, in 58 CE (or so), with the partisan of an Egyptian gangster-king who headed a force of 4,000 "knife men" (*sicarii*) in the desert.[77]

Conclusions

Since neither Hierocles' *Lover of Truth* nor Daia's *Memoirs of Pilate* is extant, we can only speculate that the pagan philosopher's text may have influenced the last pagan emperor's propaganda. But regardless of whether (what we may take to be) Hierocles' line about Jesus' violence illuminates Daia's *Memoirs of Pilate*, it is a line of thought that is forcefully opposed by Eusebius—and by two of Jesus' cousins—in the pages of *Ecclesiastical History*.

5

"DOMITIAN DID NOT CONDEMN THEM"

ECHOES OF JESUS IN THE TRIAL OF HIS COUSINS

Eusebius is a bold theorist of Constantine's Christianization of the Roman Empire, a volte-face in Roman policy and identity that implicates Christianity in a centuries-long history of violence.[1] Yet Eusebius denies that Jesus or his cohort of disciples ever resorted to violence. This is important to remember. For in the same passage where Eusebius exults in "the royal and sovereign authority of the only true Christ, the Word of God who reigns over all", he stresses that Jesus was not elevated "to a kingdom by the armed force of men".[2] Constantine and the later Christian emperors had their legions and elite palace guards—but Jesus, according to Eusebius, was an unguarded king. How could this be?

The first answer is, of course: Jesus was crucified. The disarmed king died violently—which is to say, predictably. But a second answer is more revealing, since it shows us what sort of kingdom Jesus inaugurated—a kingdom that survived his death, and that perhaps survives twenty-one centuries later. We can take this second answer from the Roman trial of Jesus in *John* 18—as it is echoed, somehow, by a couple of Jesus' cousins. For there is a remarkable scene in Eusebius, which Eisler misconstrues on the last page of his book *The Messiah Jesus and John the Baptist* (treated in chapter 3),[3] and which illuminates the place—real or imagined—of Jesus' Roman trial in late-first-century Roman politics.

The Lord's People

It is bizarre that scholars have not made more of "the human relatives of the Saviour" in first-century Palestine.[4] They were called the Lord's People (*hoi desposunoi* in Greek).[5] Some of them seem to be referred to in one of Paul's undisputed letters as "the Lord's brothers",[6] and Hegesippus (flourished after 150 CE)—on whom, more below— defines them as "those who were, in a human sense, the Lord's relatives".[7] Eusebius tells us in an extract from Julius the African, a third-century Christian chronographer who created the library at the Pantheon in Rome,[8] that the Lord's People kept genealogical "records for themselves" that legitimated "the memory of their good birth", by which he means their descent from the legendary house of David.[9]

Apparently, the Lord's People lived in the Galilean settlements of Nazareth and Cochaba (now Kaukab, Israel),[10] and there is "an ancient story" (*palaios ... logos*) about them that Eusebius gives us in *Ecclesiastical History* III.[11] He is copying from a lost book by Hegesippus, a native of Palestine or Syria, who reports in the second century that towards the end of the first century CE, two of the Lord's People were summoned by the pagan emperor Domitian, during whose reign, it seems, the mightily anti-Roman *Book of Revelation* was composed.[12]

"Christ and his kingdom"

"The ancient story goes", says Eusebius, that Domitian himself interrogated two of the male descendants of Jesus' brother Jude, because they claimed Davidic descent.[13] Whether this Roman trial of Jesus' cousins is historically credible is irrelevant for us.[14] Some of history's most revealing scenes have never occurred;[15] and something like this scene *may* have occurred.

Richard Bauckham reminds us that "the tradition of Jesus' Davidic descent is an early one". It is mentioned by Paul in the letter he wrote to Christ-believers in Rome a couple of decades after Jesus' death.[16] And the source of Eusebius' trial scene, Hegesippus, seems to have been a native of Palestine or Syria, and is rumoured (by Eusebius) to have been a convert "from among the Hebrews", who ultimately settled in Rome. As such, Hegesippus would have had knowledge of Judaean-Christian traditions that are irrecoverably lost to us.[17] If nothing else, the scene is consistent with a tradition of Roman hostility to those in Palestine who claimed, like Jesus and the Lord's People, to be descendants of the Hebrew monarch David.[18]

The late Italian classicist Marta Sordi suggested that the core of this trial scene is credible.[19] What Sordi meant is that "descendants of the house of David" were likely to have been harassed by the Flavians in Palestine. She found it believable that Jesus' cousins might have been interrogated, not by a provincial governor (for reasons we cannot enter into), and not by Domitian (who cannot be placed in Palestine), but by one of the other Flavians—namely Vespasian (Domitian's father), or Titus (Domitian's brother).[20] A Roman 'trial' of Jesus' cousins may well have taken place in Palestine, and it could be a memory of that 'trial' that Hegesippus recorded and Eusebius transmitted. The mistake may lie, Sordi concluded, not in the scene's Palestinian setting, and not in the memory of a Flavian's interrogation of Jesus' cousins—but only "in the name given the emperor".[21]

Whatever we make of this trial scene's fictionality or historicity, we read in Eusebius that Domitian asked Jesus' cousins "if they were of the house of David"—much as Pilate asked Jesus in the gospels if he was the King of the Judaeans. Note in passing that Pilate's question to Jesus—"Are you the King of the Judaeans?"—is the only element of Jesus' trial narratives that is recollected in *identical Greek wording* by all four gospel-writers.[22] Returning to Eusebius, we then read that Jesus' cousins "confessed it"[23]—much as Jesus is said, in *I Timothy*, to have made a "good confession" before Pilate.[24]

The Roman 'trial' of Jesus' cousins is worth reading in full. This is Eusebius, copying a tradition written down by Hegesippus:

> [Domitian Caesar then] asked them how much property they had, or how much money they controlled, and they said that all they possessed was 9,000 *denarii* between them, the half belonging to each. And they stated that they did not possess this in monetary form, but that it was the valuation of only 39 *plethora* of ground [some 29 acres] on which they paid taxes, and lived by their own work.[25] They then showed

Domitian their hands, adducing as testimony of their labour the hard-ness of their bodies, and the tough skin which had been embossed on their hands from their incessant work.

They were asked concerning Christ and his kingdom, its nature, origin, and time of appearance, and explained that it was neither of the world nor earthly, but heavenly and angelic, and it would be at the consum-mation of the age, when he would come in glory to judge the living and the dead and give back to each in keeping with what they have done.

At this, Domitian did not condemn them at all, but despised them as simple folk, released them, and decreed an end to the persecution against the church. But when they were released, they were leaders of the churches, both for their testimony (*marturas*) and for their relation to the Lord. And they remained alive in the peace which ensued until [the reign of] Trajan.[26]

Domitian's behaviour in this scene is reminiscent of Pilate's in the canonical passion narratives. He despises Jesus' cousins, but he is inclined to release them. This is not because Eusebius (or his source, Hegesippus) is blind to Domitian's hostility to the church: Domitian is called "a Nero in cruelty" on the same page of *Ecclesiastical History* III.[27] Rather, it is because the strange conception of a 'kingdom' that Jesus' cousins confess is not seen as a threat to Domitian's imperium. In the context of this scene, Jesus' kingdom is pathetic, not menacing. And this is likely Pilate's impression—at least in certain moments of Jesus' Roman trial, as narrated in the gospels.[28]

But most decisive, for us, is that the reply of the Lord's People in this scene is reminiscent of Jesus' in *John* 18 when Pilate asks him, "What have you done?" The prisoner's reply echoes down the centu-ries: "My kingdom is not of this world. If my kingdom were of this world, my followers would fight."[29] The critical moment of the 'trial' of Jesus' cousins is signalled by the cousins' *seeming* echo of the Roman trial of Jesus in *John* (the last canonical gospel to be written).[30] When the descendants of one of Jesus' brothers are asked by Domitian, in the last years of the first century, about "Christ and his kingdom", they confess to the emperor that it is "neither of the world nor earthly".[31] What is more, Jesus' cousins seem (in Hegesippus' text) to gloss this by saying that Jesus' kingdom is not of this 'world-age', since it will only be revealed "at the consummation of the age".[32]

Conclusions

The Platonic philosopher Hierocles claimed—and some modern exegetes have claimed—that Jesus and his followers *did* fight (touched on in chapter 4). That non-Christian tradition is contradicted, not only by the gospels but by a piece of tradition from Palestine in which Jesus' cousins, facing a Roman emperor—in an early Christian fiction or a minimally confused history—echo the words of Jesus before Pilate.

If this piece of early Christian tradition can be trusted, then the Roman trial of Jesus—when it is recollected by the Lord's People—may have changed the Roman policy towards Christians in the latter part of the first century CE.[33] But the historicity of the trial of Jesus' cousins is immaterial. The main argument of this book is that the *saying* attributed to Jesus by *John*, and the *idea* attributed to Jesus' cousins by Hegesippus (via Eusebius), has altered the history that we still inhabit. That idea, which will be recollected by Grotius in the seventeenth century, is that the kingdom that Jesus bore witness to is "neither of the world nor earthly, but heavenly and angelic".

6

"PILATE DID NOT UTTER A SENTENCE"

THE FORGERIES OF 'PILATE' AND THE COURT
OF CONSTANTINE

It is not only the high priests of Maximin Daia who forged writings by Jesus' Roman judge. Christians did the same. "The earliest Christians—I mean those of the second and third centuries—liked these pious frauds", says an ultra-erudite bishop, Pierre-Daniel Huet, in a letter dated January 1662. "And those centuries have bequeathed to us", he goes on, "an infinite number of books that have fooled many people."[1]

One of the most consequential Christian forgeries is the *Acts of Pilate*, which may have been concocted as a refutation of Maximin Daia's *Memoirs of Pilate*.[2] We will come to the *Acts of Pilate* in a moment. First we must notice that, though there is nothing strange in the fact that Daia's pagan *Memoirs of Pilate*, chanted in the school-halls of Palestine and Syria, whitewashed Pilate, it is strange that an array of Christian texts, one of which emanates from the core of a rapidly Christianizing Rome—namely from Constantine's court—sought to 'redeem' Jesus' Roman judge.

This is a striking thing. Pagans and Christians, on the cusp of the Constantinian revolution, are alike intrigued by the Roman trial of Jesus. But what is more, pagans and many Christians seem to agree that the judge in that trial—Pilate—is *innocent*. And like Daia's forgers, Christians who hold to Pilate's innocence seem keen to let the Roman prefect state that innocence. Jesus' judge is far more loquacious in apocryphal texts, as in the canonical gospels, than is the taciturn prophet from the Galilee (as he is called in *Matthew*).[3]

The imagined letters and deaths of 'Pilate'

The oldest Christian text by 'Pilate' may be a letter he writes to Emperor Claudius.[4] Now, the chronology itself is erroneous. It is Tiberius, not Claudius, who sent Pilate to Judaea—though this did not prevent Irenaeus of Lyon from bizarrely insisting, circa 200 CE, that Jesus died during Claudius' reign.[5] In any event, this early 'Pilate' opens his letter to Claudius in a muted tone: "There happened recently something which I myself brought to light." Of course, 'Pilate' is referring to the death of Jesus. And he is keen to absolve himself of that death.

This 'Pilate' tells Claudius that it is not he or his legionnaires but the Judaeans who crucified Jesus: "*They* crucified him", 'Pilate' avers. This is a tenacious Christian myth that reverberates, too, in Judaic and Islamic traditions (as we will see in part 3). And this 'Pilate' closes his letter by saying: "I have reported this lest anyone should lie about it and lest you should think that the lies of the Judaeans should be believed."[6] It is curious that he is concerned—or feigns concern—that the Judaeans will try to blame him for the crucifixion. For that is a concern that seems to be recollected in one of the canonical books, *Acts of the Apostles*, but rarely outside it.

In *Acts* 5, the Temple elites object to Jesus' (newly reconstituted) circle of Twelve: "You are determined to bring this man's blood on us!" They are referring, of course, to Jesus' blood.[7] We can only assume from this scene in *Acts* 5 that the Temple elites wanted (or were thought by the writer of *Luke–Acts* to have wanted) the death of Jesus to be imputed to Pilate, and not to them. I will indicate in chapter 8 that this is not how the Judaic authorities of later centuries thought of Jesus' death, or of Pilate's hand in it. But regardless, if this apocryphal letter from 'Pilate' to Claudius can be dated to roughly 200 CE, then it is one early witness to the Christian myth of Pilate's innocence.

This myth is stated even more naively in a Christian forgery called *The Tradition of Pilate*, in which we get to see 'Pilate' on trial for his life in Rome. Here, 'Pilate' is made to testify before Caesar and the Senate regarding the death of Jesus. "I am innocent of these things", he wails.

"It is the multitude of the Judaeans", he assures his Roman judges, "who are reckless and guilty!"[8] The anti-Judaic bent of this forgery is artless and dark. Yet it is interesting that such protestations of innocence do not save his life, and vaguely satisfying to read that Caesar "commanded an officer called Albius to behead Pilate".

In *The Tradition of Pilate*, Jesus' Roman judge protests his innocence to the end. And when he is nearing the deathsman, 'Pilate' prays to Jesus—that is, to the 'Lord' he had condemned to death: "'Lord, do not destroy me with the wicked Hebrews, for ... you know that I acted in ignorance!'" Sighing out an anti-Judaic prayer, the head of 'Pilate' is lopped off—"and look! an angel of the Lord received it".[9] Jesus himself thunders out of the clouds in the death scene of his former judge: "All generations ... shall call you blessed, because in your governorship everything was fulfilled which the prophets foretold about me!"[10]

A version of the 'Pilate' letter that is hard to date—it is first attested in Renaissance copies—is not sent to Claudius, but to Tiberius.[11] If nothing else, the chronology of this forged letter has been corrected, since it is certainly Tiberius who made Pilate the prefect of Judaea, and then recalled him to Rome. (Tiberius died weeks before Pilate's return to the imperial city in 37 CE.)[12] In this letter, 'Pilate' laments the "cruel punishment" inflicted on Jesus "by the will of the people"—he means, of course, the people of Judaea. He then informs Tiberius that, throughout the Roman trial of Jesus, "I was unwilling and apprehensive." The victimization of Pilate is a Christian literary trope that survives into the early modern period, as we will see in chapter 10.

Yet the reconstruction of Jesus' trial in this forgery is still closest to the canonical passions. For this is what 'Pilate' tells Tiberius, in what may be a late medieval or a Renaissance version of a much older forgery: "Had I not greatly feared an uprising of the people, who were on the point of rebelling, that man would perhaps still be alive."[13] The role of a Jerusalemite crowd in Jesus' Roman trial is strongly attested in all the canonical passion narratives. So, too, is Pilate's inclination to release Jesus—an inclination that might reflect nothing more than his contempt for the Galilean (as we saw in chapter 5 with 'Caesar Domitian' and Jesus' cousins), and his irritation with the Temple elites (who insist on Jesus' death in the gospels—but not only in the gospels).

It is eye-catching that the 'Pilate' of this letter concedes to Tiberius: "I did not strive to the utmost of my power to prevent the loss and suffering of righteous blood."[14] This 'Pilate' is defensive, but *he is not innocent*. And as this slightly more realistic forgery indicates, the Christian 'Pilate' traditions are not uniformly lenient to Jesus' Roman judge.

A vivid, convoluted tradition

The sources of a vivid, convoluted Pilate tradition reach from the Christian cities of ancient Ethiopia—Adulis on the coast, and Aksum farther inland—to the statelets of medieval Europe.[15] This Christian tradition can be convincingly divided into demonizing and canonizing strains.

According to the demonizing legend, Pilate is a vicious pagan who is pursued by "malignant and filthy spirits" that spectacularly defile his corpse after he is killed, or commits suicide, in Rome—or perhaps farther north.[16] Medieval Europe seems keen to claim the mortal remains, and immortal name, of Jesus' Roman judge. He is said to haunt one of the peaks circling Lucerne, Switzerland—the eponymous Mount Pilatus.[17] Other rumours that come down to us in *The Death of Pilate* (*Mors Pilati*) inter him in the icy waters of the Rhone at the Gallic colony of Vienne (near modern Lyon, France). Why Vienne? Because it is "called, as it were, *Via Gehennae*, the Way of Hell".[18] This etymology is fabulous, but the early Christian tradition that Pilate died in exile, in Gaul, *may not* be pure fiction. For there is reason to believe that one of Jesus' other judges (according to *Luke–Acts*), Herod Antipas, may have died in exile in Gaul.[19]

Since the 'Pilate' forgeries are full of "curious imaginings", they make for good reading;[20] but they are not 'innocent' texts. They are fictions, but not *l'art pour l'art*. The basic intuition of the canonizing Pilate legend is that the Roman prefect is "already a Christian in his own conscience"—the phrase is Tertullian's—at the time of Jesus' trial.[21] This canonizing 'Pilate' legend feeds, and is fed by, some of the darkest undercurrents of Christian political and intellectual history. But even the demonization of 'Pilate' can take sinister, anti-Judaic forms.

The transmutation of Pontius Pilate

In a brilliant study of Pilate's portrayal in European sarcophagi, altar-pieces, and manuscript illuminations up to the sixteenth century,

Colum Hourihane retraces the diverging Pilate legends.[22] In the canon-izing arc, Pilate's handwashing becomes linked to the Christian rite of baptism. Pilate becomes united to the mystical body of Christ, and accepts his share in the mystical sufferings of Christ, in the very act of consigning the physical body of Christ to the cross.

In the demonizing arc, however, Pilate is exculpated *as a Roman judge* by a surreal trend that becomes unmistakable towards the end of the tenth century—that of depicting Pilate *as a Jewish judge*. In this uniquely European tradition, Pilate's features and garments—his headpiece, beard, and so on—are transmuted into those of Caiaphas and his func-tionaries in medieval art.[23] (See fig. 9.)

Of course, the stylized deformation of 'the Jews' in late medieval passion imagery is no secret. And in the fifteenth century, as Hourihane writes, Christian artists further 'degrade' the image of Pilate. He begins in the early modern period to "change physically into a devil".[24] In this circuitous way, then, it is not only the myth of Pilate's innocence that incites—or hardens—premodern Christians against European Jews.[25] Even the recognition of Pilate's *guilt* can be bent to that end.

It would of course be incorrect to fuse the demonization of Pilate in premodern literature, or his 'Judaization' in premodern art, with the narrative of Pilate's innocence. His demonization and his 'Judaization' are both techniques of enhancing the Roman's guilt, and of 'rational-izing'—within the late antique and medieval Christian imaginaries—the "unspeakable judgement of blind Pilate", in the words of a poem long misattributed to Lactantius.[26] Those techniques are deeply tied to other, recurring crimes in European history.

But it is remarkable that in the most elaborate text of the 'Pilate cycle', the *Acts of Pilate*, Jesus' Roman judge is portrayed as clearly *Roman* and as Jesus' *judge*. At the heart of the Christian 'Pilate' tradition in Europe, in other words, we encounter a 'Pilate' who is not innocent.

"According to the law of the pious emperors"

The most momentous text in the 'Pilate cycle' is a fourth-century composition called the *Acts of Pilate*, which may have been circulated to neutralize Daia's *Memoirs of Pilate*.[27] For us, the interest in this forgery lies in it contradicting the Constantinian interpretation of the Pilate trial by a fourth-century courtier, Lactantius—on whom, more presently. In the *Acts of Pilate*, which circulated for twelve centuries in six languages (Greek, Latin, Coptic, Syriac, Armenian, and Georgian),[28] 'Pilate' clearly judges Jesus.

This judgement of Jesus by 'Pilate' can already be observed in the apocryphal reconstruction, in the *Acts of Pilate*, of the moment in *John* 18 that is with us throughout this book. We can begin to read this half-apocryphal scene when Pilate peremptorily asks Jesus, "What have you done?" According to the *Acts of Pilate*,

> Jesus answered, "My kingdom is not of this world; for if my kingdom were of this world, my servants would fight, that I might not be handed over to the Judaeans. But now my kingdom is not from here." Pilate said to him, "So you are a king?"

> Jesus answered him, "You say that I am a king. For this cause I was born and have come, that everyone who is of the truth should hear my voice." Pilate said to him, "What is truth?"

> Jesus answered him, "Truth is from heaven." Pilate said, "Is there not truth upon earth?"

> Jesus said to Pilate, "You see how those who speak the truth are judged by those who have authority on earth."[29]

There is much material here from *John*, but Jesus' final reply to 'Pilate'—his diamond-hard line about "those who speak the truth"—is apocryphal. Our interest here with this non-canonical line is that Jesus utters, in it, a Greek term for 'judgement'. In this line, Jesus signals that 'Pilate' is not only interrogating him in the *Acts of Pilate* but *judging him.* "You see", Jesus says, "how those who speak the truth *are judged* (*krinontai*)."[30] (Of course, we still see how those who speak the truth are judged by those who have authority on earth.) 'Pilate' is rarely a judge in Christian forgeries. Yet Jesus states in this line, with epic sang-froid, that he is being judged—or rather, misjudged—by *this* 'Pilate'.

What is more, the very judgement of 'Pilate' is handed down several chapters later in the *Acts of Pilate*, where the Roman says to Jesus:

> Your nation has convicted you of being a king. Therefore I have decreed that you should first be scourged according to the law of the pious emperors, and then hanged on the cross in the garden where you were seized. And let Dysmas and Gestas, the two malefactors, be crucified with you.[31]

This Roman judgement by no means contains only canonical material. The names for the malefactors crucified with Jesus are non-canonical (though the Greek term for 'malefactor', *kakourgos*, is taken over from *Luke*).[32] The specificity of a crucifixion in the garden of Gethsemane is non-canonical, too.[33] But this apocryphal judgement by 'Pilate' is introduced by a gloss on the line in *John* 18 where Pilate tells Jesus, "Your own nation and chief priests have delivered you up to me."[34] And the idea of a Roman judgement, or punitive decree, harmonizes with the gospels' trial narratives and could have been inspired by a crucial verse in *Luke* 23: "Pilate gave sentence."[35]

Decisive for us is the concocted line where 'Pilate' informs Jesus that he will be flogged and crucified "according to the law of the pious emperors".[36] The *Acts of Pilate* is a rich and strange text. But the crucifixion of Jesus, in it, is decreed by a Roman judge and carried out by Roman hands *in the name of Roman law*. What we see, in this judgement scene in the *Acts of Pilate*, is 'how those who speak the truth are judged' *by the Romans*.[37] But that is not what we see when we turn to other Christian texts of the first centuries CE.

"Pierced by the Judaeans"

The two most pernicious Christian myths about the crucifixion are that Pilate refused to sentence Jesus, and that Judaeans—not Romans—crucified him. The myths are interlocking, and the narrative is clear. Rather than condemning him, Pilate lets Jesus' accusers—the Judaean Temple elites, and a mob of zealots—drive him off to the place of death, where the grisly work of nailing him up is done, not by Pilate's legionnaires, but by Judaean fanatics.

Modern historians are right to conclude, first, that "Jesus could never have been put to death by the manner of crucifixion"—in Winter's words—"unless a verdict … had been given by a Roman magistrate";[38] and second, that gentile conscripts would have exacted the Roman penalty by nailing Jesus to a cross.[39] Both myths are contradicted, too, by the presence of Pilate's name in an early Christian formula that is still recited in all the churches (the Latin *Credo*),[40] and by close readings of the canonical gospels. Nullifying the Christian myth of Pilate's non-judgement is this line in *Luke* 23: "Pilate gave sentence."[41] And cancelling the myth of a Judaean crucifixion is this line in

John 19: "The soldiers ... crucified Jesus."[42] Yet these Christian myths are not only pernicious; they are unbelievably tenacious.

Both myths seem to date back to a second-century *Apology*,[43] though the lines in question may have been inserted later. The titles of this *Apology* vary, but one holds the eye: *To the Emperor Hadrian Caesar from the Athenian Philosopher Aristides*. A believing philosopher, Aristides is rumoured to have composed this *Apology*—a legal defence of Christianity, bearing the same title as Plato's *Apology*—to mark Hadrian's imperial visit to Athens in 125 CE.[44] From roughly that date on—to the present—Aristides' (or his redactors') misrepresentations of the crucifixion have not ceased to circulate in Christian circles. The reception of Aristides' *Apology* is diffuse, and its wide influence is due in part to the fact that it came to be folded into a tremendously popular medieval novel, *The Lives of Barlaam and Ioasaph*,[45] thanks to which medieval Europeans came to revere the figure of Buddha, mistaking him for a Christian saint.[46] But that is a different story.[47]

Aristides seems to have formulated both of the undying Christian myths about the crucifixion—though there are indications that his text may have been altered by later, bitterer hands. First, in its Greek form, Aristides' *Apology* claims that though the Judaeans "delivered Jesus to Pilate, the governor of the Romans", it is the Judaeans themselves—not Pilate—who "condemned him to the cross".[48] This is a very early statement of the Christian myth of Pilate's non-judgement. And second, in its Syriac form, this *Apology* says that Jesus was "pierced by the Judaeans".[49] This seems to be a maliciously garbled reference to the *coup de lance*, a moment in *John* 19 (it only occurs in *John*) when a Roman conscript stabs Jesus' chest with a spear, rather than to the crucifixion itself.[50] However that may be, Aristides' lines—or the scene they evoke—seem to morph into a Christian myth of Judaean crucifixion, which may, even, be recollected in *Qur'an* 4 and elements of the Islamic tradition.[51] And both of Aristides' myths are put into Latin by Lactantius in his *Divine Institutes*—a text that was offered, like Aristides' *Apology*, to a Roman emperor.

"Crucified by the Judaeans"

There may be an echo of Lactantius' *Divine Institutes* in the *Institutes of Divine Jurisprudence* by Thomasius, an innovative eighteenth-century jurist we will meet in chapter 19. But Lactantius was a late-third-century pagan convert whose patron in the early fourth century was, significantly, the epoch-making Constantine I.[52] Before he came to Constantine's court, Lactantius was a rhetor in the province of Bithynia, where he seems to have moved in the circles of a pagan governor and Platonic philosopher we met in chapter 4—Hierocles,[53] who wrote *Lover of Truth*.[54]

The fourth book of Lactantius' *Divine Institutes* is a critical text in the history of Christian passion exegesis, and of Pilate's innocence. Reflecting his later position at Europe's first Christian court, Lactantius refers by name to Constantine in the first line of (his re-edited text of) *Divine Institutes* IV.[55] This means that it is to Constantine himself that Lactantius says, later in *Divine Institutes* IV, that "in Tiberius' fifteenth year, in the consulship of the two Gemini … the Judaeans fastened Christ to the cross (*Iudaei Christum cruci adfixerunt*)".[56] We read the same in Lactantius' book *On the Deaths of the Persecutors*. There, he writes that "in the latter days of the Emperor Tiberius, in the consulship of the two Gemini … Jesus Christ was crucified by the Judaeans (*Iesus Christus a Iudaeis cruciatus est*)".[57]

It calls for no elaborate comment that in this uniquely 'Constantinian' version of the passion, the Roman prefect is exculpated. Lactantius is writing "once the Pilates and Neros" have themselves "turned Christian", in Bloch's acid phrase.[58] What is more, he is writing at the court of the first emperor to have 'turned Christian'. In this setting, as in Aristides' oration before Hadrian, Pilate's innocence would be a highly politic supposition to make.[59] But whatever his complex of motives, Lactantius imputes the crucifixion to the Judaeans. According to Lactantius, the death of Jesus is not chargeable to Rome.

Throughout *Divine Institutes* IV, the Judaeans' guilt is a recurring note. This culminates in Lactantius' graphic claim, for which there is no backing in the canonical gospels, that "the Judaeans hoisted Jesus up between two criminals".[60] Pilate only figures briefly in Lactantius' passion as a Roman functionary who questioned Jesus before "the Judaeans … killed him".[61] What, on Lactantius' telling, is Pilate's role in Jesus' death? It is emphatically not judicial. There is no Roman judgement of Jesus in the *Divine Institutes*. Pilate may have indulged a Jerusalem lynch mob, but he "did not himself utter a sentence". That remains a crucial line in passion exegesis—to the present day. But if Pilate never judges him, how is it that Jesus comes to be crucified? Lactantius writes only that Pilate "handed Jesus over to the Judaeans".[62]

Remarkably, Lactantius' interpretation of the Pilate trial is not dead. A legal and cultural philosopher of some celebrity, Giorgio Agamben, has reflected on Jesus' trial in his book *Pilate and Jesus*.[63] Agamben's twenty-first-century reprise of the juridical drama—or rather, of the *lack* of juridical drama—in *Divine Institutes* IV could hardly be more precise. For Agamben now writes that Pilate "did not pronounce his sentence", but "simply 'handed over' the accused to the Sanhedrin".[64] That is a passable translation of Lactantius' fourth-century Latin, *nec tamen ipse sententiam protulit, sed tradidit eum Iudaeis*—which means, again, that Pilate "did not himself utter a sentence, but handed Jesus over to the Judaeans".[65] Lactantius is never mentioned, however, in Agamben's *Pilate and Jesus*.

Conclusions

Iconic European jurists like Grotius and Thomasius are still citing Lactantius' reading of the Roman trial of Jesus, in *Divine Institutes* IV, in the seventeenth century. The myth of Pilate's non-judgement, and the myth of a Judaean crucifixion—both of which Lactantius canonizes,[66] and Agamben seems to still detect in the gospels[67]—seem to be datable to texts written by Christians within a century of the crucifixion. The Christian myth of Pilate's innocence—which is vascularly tied to the Christian myth of a Judaean crucifixion—is nearly as old as the Christian confession of Jesus' death. I believe that both myths could be retraced in unbroken traditions, in the Byzantine zone (and the modern Orthodox zones) and in Europe, from the second century to the twenty-first. What is perhaps most remarkable, though, is that aspects of both myths are shared—as we will see in part 3—by Christian and non-Christian traditions.

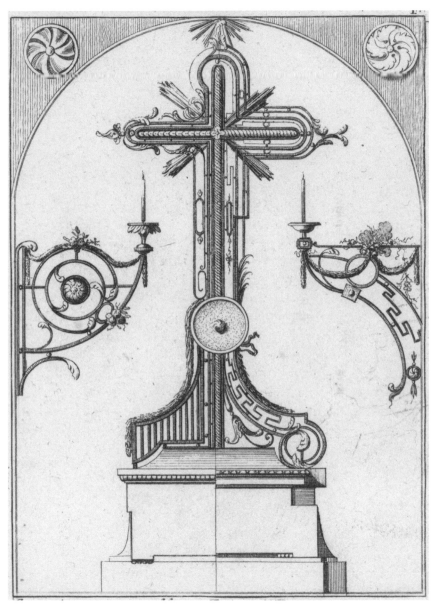

Fig. 1: *Cross with architectural ornaments*, by Johann Thomas Hauer, 1781.

Fig. 2: *Christ on the cross*, by Hieronymus Wierix (after an image by Marten de Vos), before 1619.

Fig. 3: First page of Justinian's *Institutes* in a medieval manuscript. Justinian's text occupies the centre. It is encased by commentary and peppered with marginalia.

Fig. 4: Detail of Justinian's *Institutes*. Beneath the enthroned figure of a Roman emperor, likely Justinian, we read in a compressed cursive script: "In the name of our Lord Jesus Christ" (*In nomine domini nostri Jhesu Christi*).

Fig. 5: *Christ collapsing under the weight of the cross*, by Agostino Veneziano (after Raphael), 1517.

Fig. 6: Detail of Veneziano's *Christ collapsing under the weight of the cross*. The ensign that bears the letters SPQR, fluttering over Jesus' cross, signals that he will be crucified by Romans—not Judaeans.

Fig. 7: *Crucifixion of Christ*, by Pieter Soutman (after Pieter Paul Rubens), before 1657.

Fig. 8: Detail of Soutman's *Crucifixion of Christ*. Here we see Pilate's inscription on Jesus' cross, as recollected in the gospel of *John*. It reads in Hebrew, Greek, and Latin: "Jesus of Nazareth, the King of the Judaeans."

Fig. 9: Detail of *Christ before Pilate*, by Israhel van Meckenem, before 1503. This early modern depiction of Pilate is in a tradition that Colum Hourihane has retraced in his monograph *Pontius Pilate, Anti-Semitism, and the Passion in Medieval Art*. In this uniquely European tradition, which becomes unmistakable towards the end of the tenth century, Pilate is portrayed *as a Jewish judge*. The Roman's features and garments—his headpiece, beard, and so on—are transformed into those of Jesus' high-priestly judge, Caiaphas, in the medieval Christian imagination.

Fig. 10: *Christ on the cold stone*, by Jacob Binck, before 1569. In this early modern *Ecce homo*, Jesus is an object of mockery and a subject of melancholy. This reflects the duplicity of the passion scenes in Augustine's *Homilies on the Gospel of John*—though I am not suggesting that Binck is inspired by Augustine. I do suggest that there are postural and structural resemblances to Albrecht Dürer's celebrated engraving, *Melancholia I* (1514), which invite reflection.

PART 3

TWENTY CENTURIES OF INNOCENCE

7

"THE MAN WHO WAS CRUCIFIED IN PALESTINE"

PILATE'S INNOCENCE IN PAGAN TRADITION

Writing in the year 180 or so, the Syrian satirist Lucian of Samosata calls Jesus "the man who was crucified"—literally, impaled—"in Palestine because he introduced *new mysteries* into the world".[1] It is the novelty of Christianity that pagans most objected to in the first centuries of our era, since what Christians (and post-Christians) call 'paganism' is a worship of archaic gods by means of immemorial rites.[2]

This is why a first-century Stoic master, Epictetus, defines "piety" as a universal human obligation "to make libations, sacrifice, and offer first fruits in the ancestral way (*kata ta patria*)".[3] This is why a shadowy second-century philosopher, Celsus, takes the archaic poet Pindar's line—"Law is the king of all"—to be a sublime contradiction of Christian faith. He has in mind the myth-sanctioned cultic laws of Greco-Roman cities.[4] And this is why a fourth-century edict by one of the last pagan emperors, Galerius, defines what we call 'paganism' as "the observance of the ancient institutions".[5]

To the 'pagan' mentality—or, better, to the *forma mentis* inculcated by pre-Christian cities—a new cult is a menacing one, and a new mystery is a deceptive one. This connection is made by a second-century Roman historian, Suetonius, who writes that Christians were in the grip of "a new and malignant superstition".[6] The newness of the

Christian faith was, for Suetonius, one sign of its malignancy. When Celsus sniffs that Christians worship "this man who appeared recently", Jesus' modernity is taken to annul his claims to divinity.[7] And Dio Cassius urges in his *Roman History* that the menace of new mysteries is political. "People who introduce new gods", Dio warns, "are a danger to the monarchy." What is more, Dio calls them "atheists".[8]

It is for political reasons—or rather, for theologico-political reasons—that the first generations of Christians were perceived as 'atheists'.[9] Those who reject the deities of a pre-Christian city reject the city, since the pre-Christian city is a temple-state. (This is equally true of Rome and Jerusalem in Jesus' lifetime.)[10] It is no mistake that Cicero, in the first century BCE, dates the origin of Roman religion to the founding of the city. The religion of Rome belongs to the city, the city to its religion.[11] Because of this, 'atheism' is not a crime of conscience in a Greco-Roman milieu; it is a threat of revolution. This is what Celsus means when he calls Christians "rebellious".[12] The church, for him, is a cabal that subverts the Roman temple-state.

It is hard for late moderns to see early Christians—or even Jesus and the apostles—as 'atheists'. But in a first- and second-century 'pagan' milieu, if we respect our sources, it is hard for them *not* to be seen that way.[13] For Christians refuse to honour the archaic nature-cults, family-cults, city-cults, and empire-cults of pre-Christian Rome. And to repeat myself, this is not only an insult to the Roman 'temple-state', but a threat. For the "rulers and emperors among humans", Celsus stresses, must not be thought to "hold their position without the might of the daemons (*daimonias*)".[14] It is shocking to us, but this urbane philosopher even argues that Christians should not be permitted "to live to marriageable age", since they "refuse to worship in the proper way the lords in charge" of weddings, meaning, "the beings who have been entrusted with these things"—the Greco-Roman gods and daemons.[15]

Without entering into the fascinating history of early Christians' historicizing critique of the gods (or Euhemerism), we can note that the apostle Paul writes contemptuously in his first letter to Christ-believers at Corinth of the empire's "so-called gods" (*legomenoi theoi*).[16] It is in a similar tone that the writer of *I Peter* alludes to the "foolish ancestral form of life" in the ecumene's non-Judaean cities.[17] Early Christian 'atheism' is real.

Hundreds of big, intricate books have been written on these themes. Much more could be said, but the recognition of new and foreign cults is a difficulty that 'paganism' had consciously faced—and tactically negotiated—many centuries before Jesus. It is only necessary to remember the cultic drama in Euripides' *Bacchae* (and that some of the cultic excesses charged to early Christians resemble those of the *Bacchae*).[18] But we must remember, too, that Euripides' friend Socrates was put to death for "introducing *new* divinities" in Athens,[19] and that many pagans of the first centuries CE faulted Christianity for its 'novelty'.[20]

Tertullian of Carthage's retort in his book *On the Soul* could be said of many Christian claims and ideas. "Truth does not cling to antiquity", he tells 'pagans', "nor does falsehood shun novelty (*novellitas*)."[21] Truths, like errors, can be new. We could recall that the word 'modern' (*modernus*) is a late antique Christian neologism,[22] and Guy Stroumsa elucidates the 'modernity' of Christianity in one of his recent books. Summarizing "the huge and diverse Patristic literature", which he calls "a veritable cathedral of glosses on both the Old and New Testaments"—a beautiful phrase—Stroumsa writes that "in early Christianity one finds the emergence of a *complete novelty* in the context of ancient societies: a clear delineation between the sacred and the secular".[23] The Christian logic of that delineation is, of course, one of this book's themes.

The motif of novelty is present, too, in Stroumsa's study *The Making of the Abrahamic Religions in Late Antiquity*. There, he concludes that "the church fathers were quite aware ... of the originality of their thought". He continues: "Christian authors usually insisted with pride upon the novelty of their religion." It was "this novelty", he stresses, that "the traditionalists feared most".[24] And from the middle of the first century CE, the traditionalists' reaction to Christian novelty was often bloody.

The savagery of 64 CE

The pagan confrontation with 'Christians' predates them, since it was a pagan prefect—Pontius Pilate—who sentenced their eponymous 'Christ', as our earliest Roman sources call Jesus. Writing circa 115, historian Tacitus notes that Christ suffered the extreme punishment "by the sentence of the procurator Pontius Pilate".[25] The tone is impassive, but it becomes clear, once we read this line in context, that Tacitus is not only convinced of Pilate's innocence (as judge) and Christ's guilt (as convict) but of the collective guilt of the first generation of Christians in Rome.

The setting for Tacitus' only reference to Christ and Christians is a city-levelling fire in Rome during the reign of Emperor Nero. Pagan cults, far more than early Christianity, were observed as a means of warding off such disasters.[26] (This is one reason why pagans liked to take a jab at early Christians with the question: "Why, if you are the servants of the almighty God ... does he allow you to suffer so much persecution?")[27] After Tacitus tells us that the Romans sought to propitiate the goddess Juno "at the nearest point of the seashore, where water was drawn for sprinkling the temple and image of the goddess", he recalls that Christians in Rome were convicted en masse by Nero of "hatred of the human race" (*odium humani generis*) and then "covered with wild beasts' skins and torn to death by dogs", or "fastened to crosses, and when the daylight failed ... burned to serve as lamps by night".[28]

Predictably, some late modern historians hold that this "never happened". It has been argued in the twenty-first century that these Bosch-like torture scenes are nothing but a first-century textual "mirage".[29] But that argument has been shown, conclusively, to be a mirage.[30] And however much contemporary historians may prefer to believe such things never happened, this is what Tacitus—our most hard-headed Roman annalist, and our only source on the savagery of 64 CE—tells us:

> Nero substituted as culprits and punished with the utmost refinements of cruelty those whom the crowd call *Christians*, who are hated for their crimes.[31] *Christ*, the founder of the name, had suffered the death penalty in the reign of Tiberius, by the sentence of the procurator Pontius Pilatus, and the pernicious superstition was halted for a moment—only to break out once more, not only in Judaea, the source of this disease, but in Rome itself.[32]

For Tacitus, Christ is a criminal—sentenced and killed by Pilate—and the Christians are a contagion from the restive province of Judaea. Pilate is justified for having crucified Jesus in Jerusalem, and Nero is justified for having crucified Christians in Rome. They disturb the

Roman 'temple-state' and must be eliminated. The matter is that simple—which is to say, that brutal.

We could recall here that the philosopher Celsus says, darkly, to all second-century Christians, that it is because "you blasphemously assert that the other gods ... are phantoms" that "you are crucified".[33] The Christians, for him, are like sirens—they lure the ignorant to their destruction.[34] And it is right, he says, that "the death penalty ... hangs over them".[35] It is in the same tone that the philosopher Porphyry asks at the close of the third century: "What punishments are too severe to inflict on those"—he means Christians—"who desert the laws of their fathers?"[36] In the fourth century, a Christian historian traces Nero's ferocity to a first-century fear that many were forsaking Rome's "old ways" and converting to a "new religion" (religionem novam).[37] Note the recurring motif of Christianity's novelty. The violence inflicted on Christians in the first centuries of our era was, in a strict sense, reactionary. "It was as deviant pagans", in Paula Fredriksen's words, that "gentile Christians were coerced"—and, beginning in Nero's reign, killed.[38]

The martyred slave girls of 112 CE

Ignatius of Antioch writes circa 107 CE that Jesus died "in the time ... of Pontius Pilate".[39] More graphically, he says in one of his letters that Jesus was "nailed to a tree in the flesh ... under Pontius Pilate".[40] Similarly, Justin the Philosopher writes circa 150 that Jesus was executed "under Pontius Pilate ... in the times of Tiberius".[41] It is important to remember that both Ignatius and Justin—a Syrian and a Palestinian Christian—were martyred at Rome for their confession.[42] And to the end, both confessed that Jesus had been martyred by Rome.

Jesus' crucifixion is not a banal or inconsequential fact in the first centuries CE. On the contrary, in this period the trial and death of Jesus represent a fact—a historical and liturgical memory—for which many Christians are willing to die. Jesus' crucifixion is also a fact for which many pagan magistrates are willing to kill. (The violence—as Ramsay MacMullen comments—was "always anti-Christian" in the period before Constantine.)[43] The first surviving non-Christian text that gives us a glimpse of this sort of ordeal is a much-cited letter sent by Pliny the Younger to Emperor Trajan (reigned 98–117). Among Pliny's numerous surviving letters, we find several charming ones that he wrote to his friend Tacitus, whom we just met. The letter I have in mind, though, is short on charm.

Here, Pliny is consulting Rome's master (*dominus*) on what he takes to be an ephemeral question of penal law. Pliny is unsure how he is meant to handle Roman subjects who are being denounced to him as Christians in the remote coastal province of Bithynia–Pontus, on the Black Sea, that he is tasked with governing in the early second century, circa 110–12.[44] There is a mention of Christians in Bithynia and Pontus in the canonical letter of *I Peter*, and a couple of Latin manuscripts indicate that the Johannine letters were addressed to Pontic Christians.[45] That being noted, Pliny writes this in his letter to Trajan: "I have interrogated [the accused], asking if they are Christians (*Christiani*). If they confess it, I put the same question to them until they have replied a third time, warning them of the punishment. And if they persist, I order them to be led away (*duci iussi*)."[46]

What is the punishment (*supplicium*) of which Pliny, here, repeatedly warns the accused? And what fate should we assign to these convicted Christians once they have been led out of his tribunal? James Corke-Webster writes that the Christians who flit through Pliny's letter "were almost certainly executed, since *duci iussi*"—the Latin formula that concludes our extract—"refers to capital punishment in parallel judicial contexts".[47]

Pliny's letter suggests that he executes those in his province who persist in identifying as Christians—unless, he stresses, they are "Roman citizens" (*cives Romani*). Most provincials, in Pliny's day—as in Jesus' and Paul's day—were not citizens. Christian *non-citizens* of Bithynia–Pontus are interrogated, warned, and put to death by Pliny; but Roman *citizens* who are charged with being Christians, and who confess this to Pliny, are held with other suspects in the province who must be "sent to Rome for trial".[48] This conveyance of Christians from the provinces to Rome is a judicial drama that structures the New Testament's *Acts of the Apostles*. For, a couple of decades after Jesus' death, Paul is arrested in Jerusalem. Since Paul—unlike Jesus—is a Roman citizen, he is sent after a number of hearings in provincial courts to Rome, to be heard "in Caesar's tribunal".[49] This is why Paul dies as a Roman convict *in Rome*, and not in Corinth, or Lystra, or Caesarea Maritima, or—like his Lord Jesus—in Jerusalem.[50]

Judicial torture is commonplace in Pliny's court—as in most Roman courts of the first centuries CE. Pliny mentions airily a couple of slave girls (*ancillae*) who, he says, were called "deaconesses" (*ministrae*). He questioned these girls—or women, *ancillae* is vague—under torture, he tells Trajan, before having them killed.[51]

Trajan's brisk reply to Pliny's query is collected in Pliny's *Letters* and fits into the Roman legal genre of imperial rescript (*rescriptum*). The rescript is a letter composed by the emperor (or his legal office) in reply to a written query, originating somewhere in the imperial bureaucracy, on an obscure point of Roman law or policy. The decision communicated in a rescript has the force of law. (It is intriguing to note that the papal 'decretal', a genre that seems to be born in the late fourth century, is an offshoot of the imperial rescript.)[52] "You have chosen the right course of procedure", comes Trajan's reply, "in your handling of these cases."[53]

Trajan sanctions the killing of slave girls who insist, in Pliny's words, that "their offence or error consisted of no more than this: they had often come together before dawn on a fixed day"—the first day of the week, we can infer—"to chant songs ... in honour of Christ, as if to a god (*quasi deo*)".[54] This is vile, but politically comprehensible.[55] Pliny's cool air after the killing of two Christian girls calls to mind Pilate's demeanour in the gospels, after the death of Christ. There is no animus.[56] Like Pilate with Christ in Jerusalem, Pliny is *willing* to kill Christians in Bithynia—yet he is *reluctant* to.

In this, Pliny not only resembles the canonical Pilate (as Albert Kalthoff noticed in the early twentieth century)[57] but also the Roman magistrates Gallio and Felix in *Acts of the Apostles*, who are in no rush to condemn Paul—though he will ultimately be martyred in Rome.[58] There is no avidity to kill Christ in Pilate, or Christians in Pliny—but kill they did.

A pagan oracle on the death of Jesus

When reading Tacitus' and Pliny's pages on the Christians, we must not forget that their Rome is a deity (*dea Roma*). By the late first century

CE, the imperial city is itself a divinized entity with temples, priests, and a sacrificial cult.[59] It seems that divinized Rome never spoke, in the character of a city-god, about the rise of Christianity—but, remarkably, one of the archaic Greco-Roman gods may have done.

In Augustine of Hippo's vast counter-history, *The City of God against the Pagans*, shining Apollo, son of Zeus and Leto (and deuteragonist of Nietzsche's rhapsodic essay *The Birth of Tragedy*), speaks to the trial and death of Jesus. Or so the Platonic philosopher Porphyry appears to have claimed in his lost book, *Philosophy from Oracles*. (As the coming chapters show: Porphyry is nothing like the first or the last philosopher to deal with Jesus' trial and death. It is a philosophical *topos*.) What follows is a prophet of Apollo—via Porphyry, via Augustine[60]—replying in poetic form to a suppliant who asked the god "what god he should appease in order to recall his wife from Christianity".[61] The pagan god says:

> You will, perhaps, be more able to write enduring letters on water, or to open light wings and fly through the air like a bird, than to bring your defiled and impious wife back to her senses. Let her continue as she likes, persevering in her vain delusions, singing lamentations for a god who died deluded himself—a god who was condemned by just judges and sentenced to die cruelly by the worst of deaths.[62]

The 'hysterical female' is a common trope in pagan critiques of Christian origins.[63] It is impossible not to think, here, of Celsus' critique of the gospels' resurrection narratives, in which it is Mary Magdalene and other women who find that Jesus' tomb is empty.[64] "Who saw this?" Celsus prods the Christians. "A hysterical female", is his derisive reply. He suggests that Mary Magdalene must have "dreamed" the resurrection "in a certain state of mind"—or "more likely", Celsus goes on, she merely "wanted to impress the others by telling this fantastic tale".[65]

It is good that the god Apollo, unlike the man Nero, has no desire for *this* 'hysterical female'—his suppliant's wife—to be torn to death by dogs or fastened to a cross. She is a hopeless case, says Apollo, but she is to be left to do "as she likes" (*quo modo vult*)—by which, Apollo means, she must be permitted to mourn her dead god (*mortuum deum*). Our only question here is *why* this woman's god—Christ—is 'dead' in *Philosophy from Oracles*.[66] And Apollo tells us: Jesus was "condemned by just judges" (*iudicibus recta*). Pilate is here declared, by the oracle of a pagan deity, innocent. Jesus is a criminal and, it seems, a maniac—since he "died deluded himself". But Pilate's verdict is just, and Pilate is a "just judge".

However, we have failed to notice something in Apollo's lines: Pilate, who may be remembered but is not named by Porphyry, *is not alone.* For what is it that the god says? Jesus "was condemned by just *judges*" (*iudicibus*). The plural here implies a council, or a succession of trials and judgements (as in the gospels, where Jesus is interrogated first by the Temple elites, and then by Pilate—or, in *Luke*, by Herod Antipas and Pilate). Both the god (Apollo) and the philosopher (Porphyry) must have known that what they call "the worst of deaths"—the stake and crossbeam—is a Roman punishment. But who are the other "just judges" to whom Porphyry and his deity allude? And are they Romans, or non-Romans?

A pagan philosopher on the Judaean trial of Jesus

Augustine copies out a comment by the Platonic philosopher on Apollo's oracle concerning Jesus. "Apollo made clear", Porphyry says, "that the Judaeans are more ready to defend God (*suscipiunt deum*) than the Christians are". And Augustine then adds a comment of his own on Porphyry's reasoning:

> See how Porphyry denigrates Christ … confessing that the Judaeans defend God? For he interprets the verses of Apollo, where Apollo says that Christ was condemned to death by just judges, as if these verses meant that the judges were just in their punishment and that Christ deserved his punishment … Porphyry says that the Judaeans, as defenders of God (*dei susceptores*), rightly gave judgement against Christ in pronouncing him worthy to be tormented (*excruciandum*) by the worst kind of death.[67]

Whatever the provenance of Apollo's oracle (Augustine is sceptical that it is a real 'oracle'); and whatever its inner meaning (Augustine is not convinced that, if it is a real mantic utterance, Porphyry has read it correctly), there can be no doubt that Porphyry, a consummate pagan, held that "the Judaeans … gave judgement against Christ" (*iudicasse de Christo*). This is important, precisely because Porphyry *commends the*

Judaeans for this judgement, saying that they "*rightly (recte)* gave judgement against Christ".[68]

Beginning in the mid-twentieth century, much of the New Testament critical literature reflects a modern notion that the gospels' report of a decisive Judaean moment in Jesus' legal ordeal—a Sanhedrin trial (in *Matthew*, *Mark*, and *Luke*), or a high-priestly interrogation (in *John*)—must be a 'Judaeophobic' fiction concocted by the earliest Christians.[69] But Porphyry's claim of Jesus' condemnation by Judaean judges is not remotely 'Judaeophobic', and neither Porphyry nor any other non-Christian writer in antiquity treats that claim as fictitious.

Conclusions

It is not a modern theoretical nuance but a relic of Christian Latin to speak of "paganisms" (*paganiae*),[70] and Porphyry's condemnation of Jesus is not the only 'pagan' reaction to his death. Neither is Lucian's bitterness, or Tacitus' revulsion. We have what seems to be a letter by a Syrian philosopher of the late first century, Mara bar Serapion, who believes that Jesus—like Socrates—was unjustly condemned.[71] And it is said that the last Severan emperor, Severus Alexander, not only revered cult-icons of the "deified emperors" but of "certain holy souls" such as Abraham (a prophet), Orpheus (a mystagogue), Apollonius (a philosopher)—and Christ (a saviour).[72]

There were not only "synagogue-going pagans" but Christ-revering pagans in pre-Constantinian Rome.[73] Augustine tells us in his *Harmony of the Gospels* that Jesus was lauded by many pagans for his "unsurpassed wisdom" (*excellentissima sapientia*).[74] And what is more, there were Christ-revering *gods* in the first centuries CE. For, in his *Demonstration of the Gospel*, Eusebius highlights pagan oracles about Jesus that attest to "his holiness, his wisdom, and his ascension into heaven", and that were collected by Porphyry in his *Philosophy from Oracles*.

"What I am about to say may seem surprising to some", writes Porphyry (per Eusebius). "It is that the gods have pronounced Christ to have been most holy and immortal, and they speak of him reverently."[75] Though Celsus ridicules "apparitions of Hecate",[76] a century or so later Porphyry transmits an oracle (via Augustine) in which this night-goddess, Hecate, calls Christ "a supremely righteous man". It is suggestive that Hecate, a deity of the dead in late antiquity, becomes evasive when her devotees ask why Christ was "condemned to death" (*damnatus*).[77] In this case, Hecate is uninterested in death.

But in conclusion, what seems to have been a common—perhaps the most common—conviction in pagan circles in the first centuries CE is intoned by Apollo's oracle in Porphyry's lost text: Jesus was justly "sentenced to die ... the worst of deaths". For Porphyry, the crucifixion of Jesus is neither a mystery nor a tragedy. It is a proof of Judaean piety, and of Roman legal efficacy.[78] As we have seen (in chapter 4), it is only in the fourth century CE, during the reign of Maximin Daia, that Pilate's innocence becomes something like a state doctrine of the eastern empire. But the pagan commitment to Pilate's innocence is older than that. Before it is promulgated by a pagan emperor (Daia), the idea of Pilate's innocence has the sanction of a pagan god (Apollo).

The crux is this. For all the pagan intellectuals and deities mentioned in this chapter, the figure of Pilate is—if he is remembered—an innocent man and a just judge. And it is no different when we turn, as we now will, to the death of Jesus in the Judaic tradition.

8

"JESUS IS GOING TO BE STONED"

PILATE'S INNOCENCE IN JUDAIC TRADITION

It is a twentieth-century critical cliché that Jesus' condemnation by a Judaean court, prior to his condemnation by Pilate, is a Christian fabrication. In line with a nineteenth-century tradition of "tendency criticism" (*Tendenzkritik*), Jesus' Judaean 'trial' is seen by many commentators as a mark of the gospel-writers' anti-Judaic bias. But I am not convinced.[1] One reason for this is that the Judaean hand in Jesus' death is less salient in the gospels than in certain pagan texts of the first centuries CE. Far more damaging to this modern conviction is the fact that the Judaean condemnation of Jesus is less salient in the gospels than in certain *Judaic texts*.[2] This suggests, to me, that mid-twentieth-century anti-Semitic crimes of demonic proportions may have distorted late-twentieth-century readings of pre-Nazi texts, beginning with the gospels.[3]

The death of Jesus is without doubt, in Bat-Sheva Albert's phrase, the "most resentment-laden" theme in Christian history.[4] Yet it is not per se a sign of resentment that the gospels recollect a Judaean moment in Jesus' judicial murder in the temple-state of Jerusalem—culminating in a Roman verdict, and a Roman punishment—circa 30 CE.[5] For it is Josephus—not one of the gospel-writers—who says that the Temple-governing elites of Jerusalem, in Jesus' day, were "more heart-

79

less than any of the other Judaeans" when they sat in judgement.[6] And Josephus himself comes from this "heartless" elite. As he tells us in *The Life of Josephus*, he was born of a line of Jerusalem priests.[7] From birth, he bore a Judaean name, Yosef ben Mattityahu, not his post-revolutionary Roman *nomina*, Flavius Josephus;[8] and his father likely offered sacrifices in the Temple with Caiaphas, the high priest who interrogates Jesus in the gospels.[9]

It is 'Josephus'—not one of the gospel-writers—who wrote that Pilate crucified Jesus "because of an accusation made by the leading men among us".[10] Now, the provenance of this text—the notorious *Testimonium Flavianum*—has been doubted since the sixteenth century.[11] I am not competent to judge, though my sense is that this text has an authentically Josephan core with an originally non-Christian meaning, and that Christian corruptions were identified in the late nineteenth century.[12] (Eisler, for one, thought the *Testimonium Flavianum* had been reduced by Christians—not embroidered.) But nothing in this chapter, or book, rests on the *Testimonium Flavianum*—which belongs, however suspect, to a text-history we call 'Josephus'. For there is no extant manuscript of the *Judaic Antiquities* that does not contain the lines of Josephus (or pseudo-Josephus) about the death of Jesus, under Pilate's sentence, at the urging of Jerusalem's Temple elites.[13]

And it is Josephus—not one of the gospel-writers—who reports that the Judaean high priest Ananus, a successor of Caiaphas, "convened the judges of the Sanhedrin and brought before them a man named James, the brother of Jesus who is called 'Christ'". Josephus then tells us that Jesus' brother was convicted by a first-century Jerusalem court, and stoned to death. Now, the stoning of James in 62 CE led to charges of a mistrial. Ananus, who condemned Jesus' brother, was deposed— and replaced, as it happens, by a man named Jesus.[14] But the point is this. It is impossible to write a history of first-century Jerusalem—or of any great city in any century—without referring to mistrials and the 'heartlessness' of governing elites.[15]

The anti-Semitic crimes of Nazis (and others) are monstrous, unpardonable, and—tragically, as of this writing—unended.[16] It cannot be denied that malicious Christian interpretations of the gospels and Christian hostility towards Jews are both rooted, in terribly complex ways, in the first centuries of the Christian era.[17] But I nevertheless think that we misjudge premodern Christian texts if the criterion by which we judge them 'anti-Judaic' also renders premodern *Judaic* texts—and anti-*Christian* pagan texts—'anti-Judaic'.

In this chapter, the figure of Pilate—in his presence and absence, his guilt and innocence—will help us to set a vast network of premodern texts, from the ancient canonical gospels to Renaissance anti-gospels, in a new light.

"We condemned him"

It is not a Judaean text, but it may reflect an early Judaean tradition[18] when the pagan philosopher Celsus has a Judaean figure in one of his books say of Jesus: "*We* convicted him and condemned him and decided that he should be punished."[19] Pilate seems to be not so much forgotten, here, as he is dramatically cut out of Jesus' execution narrative.[20] "As an offender", Celsus holds, "he was punished by the Judaeans (*para Ioudaiois dikēn*)."[21] And the text in which this hard assertion is made is not anti-Judaic, but anti-*Christian*.

We will recall how philosopher Porphyry said that "the Judaeans, as defenders of God, *rightly gave judgement against Christ* in pronouncing him worthy to be tormented by the worst kind of death".[22] Like Porphyry in the third century, Celsus in the second century is not scandalized by the Judaeans' claim that they tried and killed Jesus. On the contrary, Celsus is offended by *Christians* who elevate a dead convict—the crucified Jesus—to the status of a god. Celsus is not troubled by the fact that the Judaeans (on his telling) claim that they killed Jesus; he is incensed by the fact that Christians worship a man who was "arrested and punished".[23] For this pagan, the implications of Jesus' condemnation are fatal—not for Jesus, but for Christian faith. Celsus, or his Judaean source, is ruthless:

> "We regard him as Son of God because he was punished" ... What then? Have not many others also been punished and that no less disgracefully? ... Why may we not think that everyone else as well who has been condemned and come to an unfortunate end is an angel greater and more divine than Jesus? ... Anyone with similar shamelessness could say even of a robber and murderer who had been punished that he ... was not a robber but a god.[24]

What Celsus' text demonstrates is that a Judaean condemnation of Jesus can be celebrated by a pagan who perceives Jesus as a criminal. Because there is no doubt of Jesus' guilt in Celsus' mind, he charges the Judaeans with Jesus' death without incriminating them. For Celsus, the idea that they killed Jesus is a strike against *Christians*, and not—as in many centuries of European history—against Judaeans. It is a similar logic that seems to underlie the trial and death of Jesus in the Babylonian Talmud.

The question of 'Jesus in the Talmud'

Before we proceed, it is crucial to note that the Talmudic text I have in mind, and will quote in a moment, is only finalized in late antiquity. No one questions this. But there is much uncertainty about the traditions inscribed in this text (by how many centuries do they antedate their Talmudic form?),[25] and the question of whether they refer to Jesus of Nazareth (and not to some other 'Jesus').[26]

A minimalist tone predominates in much of the modern literature, leading many to assume that Talmudic texts that mention a 'Jesus' are very late traditions (or post-Talmudic interpolations), or that they cannot refer to Jesus of Nazareth. Emblematic of this tendency is Johann Maier's book *Jesus of Nazareth in the Talmudic Tradition*, which nullifies its title by trying to prove that Jesus is an illusory figure in Talmudic tradition.[27] However, there is a maximalist or "deliberately naïve" tendency that is represented by Peter Schäfer's study, *Jesus in the Talmud*.[28] Since I am not a Hebraist, I am not competent to judge between Maier and Schäfer. But I am drawn to Schäfer's 'naïve' reading of the Talmud—and I am not alone.

Citing Schäfer, Peter Frankopan writes that the Babylonian Talmud's "sophisticated counter-narratives" of Jesus' life and death "show how threatening Christian advances had become" in fifth- and sixth-century Persia. The "scathing position on Christianity" taken in the Babylonian Talmud, but not in the Palestinian Talmud, signals for him a well-attested shift in imperial history.[29] In her path-breaking study *Early Christian Monastic Literature and the Babylonian Talmud*, Michal Bar-Asher Siegal claims that the Babylonian Talmud has even more "Jesus material taken from the gospels" than Schäfer catalogues.[30] And Thierry Murcia's comprehensive monograph, *Jesus in the Talmud and Ancient Rabbinic Literature*, is very much in line with Schäfer's tendency, though Murcia criticizes some of Schäfer's formulations.[31]

In the present context, I find Schäfer's 'naïve' reading of the Talmud convincing for the simple reason that aspects of the Talmudic material on 'Jesus'—some of which will be quoted in the coming pages—can be correlated to pre-Talmudic *and* post-Talmudic traditions that certainly refer to Jesus of Nazareth. William Horbury noticed this fifty years ago,[32] and Samuel Krauss has concurred.[33] Murcia now writes that there is "no doubt" that we can trace real continuities in ancient and medieval Judaic texts on Jesus.[34] There may even be a presence of Jesus' mother, Mary, in Talmudic tradition.[35] And crucially for us, there even seems to be one cryptic reference to Pilate in the Babylonian Talmud.[36]

To my mind, the most creditable research indicates that there are a number of claims and motifs that link the 'Judaic' traditions concerning Jesus' death in ancient pagan and Christian texts, to late antique Talmudic texts, and to the medieval and Renaissance *Toledot Yeshu* genre.[37] That being the case, it seems odd to isolate the Talmudic texts on Jesus' death from pre-Talmudic and post-Talmudic traditions that— shockingly, to us—tie the death of Jesus *only* to a Judaean court and a Judaean judgement.[38]

The death of Jesus in the Babylonian Talmud

Without entering further into the question of 'Jesus in the Talmud' (the title, already, of a 1699 German book, *Jesus in Talmude*): What is the text in question?[39] It is this, from the tractate *Sanhedrin* of the Babylonian Talmud:

> On the eve of the Passover Jesus the Nazarene was hanged.[40] And a herald went before him forty days, heralding: "Jesus the Nazarene is going forth to be stoned because he practiced sorcery and seduced Israel to idolatry. Whoever knows anything in his defence may come and state it." But since nothing was brought forward in his defence, they hanged him on the eve of Passover!
>
> Ulla retorted: Do you suppose that Jesus the Nazarene was one for whom a defence could be made? Was he a not an enticer to idolatry,

concerning whom the Merciful says: "Show him no compassion and do not shield him" (*Deuteronomy* 13:8–9)?

With Jesus the Nazarene, however, it was different, for he was close to the government (*malkhut*).[41]

No word of this rabbinic tradition (Hebrew *baraita*) is uncontroversial, and the Talmud is a literary form that is both inspired and structured by controversy.[42] But there seems to be a clear recollection, here, of the chronology of Jesus' crucifixion in *John* 19 on "the eve of the Passover".[43] This seems, then, to be a *baraita* about the death of the Christians' Jesus. He is "hanged" on the day before Passover in a locale that is not named, but we can take to be Jerusalem.[44]

"The Babylonian Talmud has its own version of the execution of Jesus", is Murcia's comment.[45] Murcia believes that the text just quoted is confusing, referring first to a 'hanging' and then to a 'stoning', because it marks a confluence of differing traditions—one in which a sorcerer named Ben Stada is stoned, the other in which Jesus is crucified. (Murcia rejects the traditional notion that 'Ben Stada' is Jesus.) It is a mark of this confluence of traditions that, in Murcia's words, "Jesus is condemned to be stoned" in this *baraita*, but "ends up 'hanged'".[46]

What is crucial for us is that, in this Talmudic version of the passion, Jesus is charged, sentenced, stoned, and 'hanged' *by Judaeans*. The Talmudic death of Jesus is a thoroughly Judaean affair. In juridical terms, the Babylonian Talmud's narrative is identical to the line that Celsus puts in the mouth of a second-century 'Judaean': "*We* convicted him and condemned him and decided that he should be punished."[47] And in juridical terms, the Talmudic passion anticipates a claim that *Qur'an* 4 will attribute to seventh-century 'Judaeans': "It is *we* who killed … Jesus son of Mary."[48] We will return to the *Qur'an* in chapter 9.

Here, though, it is imperative to note that the Talmudic 'passion' differs from the Christian myth of a *Judaean crucifixion*. This is because the hanging of Jesus, in this *baraita*, refers to a rabbinic form of post-mortem suspension in which a dead convict's hands were bound together "after the fashion of butchers" (in the Talmud's blunt phrase),[49] not stretched out and nailed as in the crucifixion of a living man.[50] The Talmudic hanging of Jesus is not a crucifixion—which means, of course, that it is not a Roman punishment. This may be why Pilate is absent from the tractate *Sanhedrin*. Or is he?

We may have noticed that Jesus is rumoured, in this *baraita*, to have been "close to the government". Some modern commentators have taken that to mean, 'close to *the Romans*'.[51] Reading 'Romans' for 'government' in this *baraita* would conflict, of course, with the zealot-Jesus tradition—in its pagan (mythic) and modern (critical) forms. This alone is highly interesting. But Schafer holds that the "claim of Jesus's closeness to the Roman government reflects some knowledge", by the rabbis of Babylonia, "of the New Testament narrative". Schäfer then comments, with some consternation, that this *baraita* "exonerates the Roman government from the blame of Jesus's condemnation".[52] I would only add that a person or government that is exonerated—Schäfer's word—is declared innocent.

This could suggest a new question: Is Pilate concealed in the line, "Jesus the Nazarene ... was close to the government"?[53] In which case, is Jesus 'close to' Pilate in the Talmud? Before turning to this question, we should glance at another text in the Babylonian tractate *Sanhedrin*.

Pilate and Jesus in the Babylonian Talmud?

Joseph Perles, a learned Hungarian rabbi of the nineteenth century who "stood in constant communication on matters of learning with a number of eminent Catholic theologians" (as his Munich obituary reads),[54] was the first to suggest that there might be a reference in the Babylonian Talmud to Pilate's hand in Jesus' death.[55] For there are lines in the tractate *Sanhedrin* where one of the rabbis says: "I personally have seen Balaam's chronicle in which it is stated: 'Balaam the lame was thirty-three or thirty-four years old when Phinehas the Robber killed him.'"[56] What could this mean?

It is easiest to pose the questions that Perles and others have posed, and then to offer a uniform reply. Is 'Balaam's chronicle' a coded reference to the gospels? Perhaps. Is 'Balaam' a cipher of Jesus in the Talmud? Perhaps. And is 'Phinehas' a cryptic reference to Pilate? Perhaps. This 'Balaam' text in *Sanhedrin* is, by design, intensely murky. Unlike the Targum, where, in one place, Jesus (*Yosos*) and Pilate (*Apolitos*) are named,[57] this Talmudic passage is heavily encrypted.[58] We can only glance, here, at the figures through which the Babylonian Talmud *may* evoke Jesus and his Roman judge.

To begin with, Balaam is a gentile prophet in the biblical book of *Numbers*. For us, this prophet's memory is tied to his beast of burden: Balaam's "ass saw the angel" (as in the title of Nick Cave's glowering novel).[59] But for the rabbis of Babylonia, Balaam is a figure of deviance and false prophecy.[60] It is because of this that 'Balaam' may be a recurring Talmudic cipher for Jesus.[61] And it is not unlikely that 'Balaam' symbolizes Jesus in this *baraita*—and thus, that 'Balaam's chronicle' refers to a gospel (or to the collection of four gospels). The age at which 'Balaam' is killed may echo *Luke* 3, where we read—and where, conceivably, the rabbis had read: "Jesus was about thirty years old when he began his work."[62]

But if 'Balaam' *is* a cryptonym of Jesus, the figure of 'Phinehas'— who kills him—is much harder to determine. 'Phinehas' could be a code name for Judas Iscariot (who is prominent, too, in certain Islamic Jesus-traditions).[63] Or 'Phinehas' could be no more than an esoteric *jeu de mots* on the Hebrew title of 'Balaam's chronicle'.[64] But if 'Phinehas' *is* a cipher for Pilate, he may be called 'the Robber' to differentiate him from Phinehas 'the Zealot' (who, like Balaam, is a character in the book of *Numbers*).[65]

If 'Phinehas' is Pilate, then there is a single Talmudic reference to Pilate's hand in Jesus' death at the age of "thirty-three or thirty-four".[66] And this returns us to our earlier question: Is Jesus 'close to' Pilate in the Babylonian Talmud? We *may* have now read in the same tractate that Jesus was close to the Roman government, and that Pilate killed Jesus. Isn't that a conflicting narrative? Of course. But that does not preclude us seeing Jesus and Pilate in both *Sanhedrin* texts. For the Talmud is a palimpsest.[67]

Whatever we make of Pilate and Jesus in the Babylonian Talmud, there is no doubt that Pilate is 'innocent' of Jesus' death in the main currents of medieval and early modern Judaic tradition. We can see this by glancing at a post-Talmudic Judaic genre, *Toledot Yeshu* (*The Life of Jesus*), which seems to have been inspired by the Talmud.[68]

"Our rabbis, blessed be their memory, said to Pilate"

Toledot Yeshu is not a text, but a genre of counter-texts. *The Life of Jesus* is a Judaic text-tradition that is viscerally and structurally linked, word by word and line by line, to a complex body of Christian (and perhaps Islamic) texts and images.[69] By satirizing non-Judaic 'lives of Jesus'—in the first instance, the four gospels—*The Life of Jesus* seeks to nullify the lure of Christianity (and perhaps, too, of Islam).[70]

The first witness we have to this parodic 'gospel' genre comes from a Christian bishop, Agobard of Lyon (died 840), who wrote the book *On the Superstitions of Jews* in the hopes of nullifying the lure of Jewish learning at the Carolingian court of the 820s.[71] Agobard's influence on medieval legal culture is negative when it comes to the rights of Carolingian Jews (though not their slaves),[72] but he helped to weaken the non-Roman culture of "judicial ordeal".[73] Agobard opposed the pre-Christian European customs of trial by water, by hot iron, and so on. And his critique of trial by combat cannot be bettered: *non est lex, sed nex*. Which means: "It is not law, but slaughter."[74]

In his book *On the Superstitions of Jews*, Agobard—who cites a number of other interesting texts from Babylonian Jewish circles, and indeed, several Hebrew verses from the *Psalms*[75]—informs his readers that ninth-century European Jews could read in their traditions that Jesus was "suspended on a 'fork' like an execrable sorcerer, and there he was hit in the head with a stone and killed in this way *(hoc modo occisum)*".[76] Note what modern commentators have called the "sequence of hanging and stoning" in Agobard's text. This is common in early Aramaic instances of the *Toledot Yeshu* and seems to resemble the Babylonian Talmud *baraita* in which Jesus is both stoned and 'hanged'.[77]

This is not the place to say more about Agobard or the intricate, long, and occasionally murderous Christian reception of the *Toledot Yeshu*.[78] What matters here is that the text Agobard reads in Lyon in the early ninth century seems to emanate from the Byzantine and Islamicate east (in what is now Syria or Iraq), and may date back to the fifth century (though it reflects second- and third-century traditions).[79]

In one of the 'early oriental' versions of the *Toledot Yeshu*, a medieval Aramaic manuscript from Babylonia,[80] we read that the rabbis of Israel—in concert with "the king Tiberius Caesar" and "Pilate the governor"[81]—had a gallows (or cross) constructed on which they wished for Jesus to be hanged.[82] After some high jinks—Jesus flies to Mount Carmel, where he sulks for a while—one rabbi seizes him by his cloak, before a second rabbi sentences him to death. Tiberius and Pilate are not in the picture when we read that "they lifted him up and executed him". More concretely, we are told that "they hanged him on the gallows alive and stoned him with stones and he died on the gallows".[83] Though Pilate and Tiberius are both named in this 'early oriental' text, the arrest, sentencing, and killing of Jesus are unmistakably done by rabbis and enforcers of "the Law" (meaning, the Law of Israel).[84] The sequence of hanging and stoning in this Judaic narrative of Jesus' death is recognizable from the Babylonian Talmud, and indeed, from Agobard's Latin precis of the *Toledot Yeshu*.

It is much the same in a 'Byzantine' copy of *The Life of Jesus*—this time, in an early modern Hebrew manuscript.[85] The first line of this manuscript couples Pilate and Jesus in a way that might vaguely remind us of Daia's *Memoirs of Pilate and Jesus*.[86] "This is a book of the governor and Jesus the Nazarene", it begins.[87] This copy of the Judaic *Life of Jesus* could perhaps be called *The Story of Pilate and Jesus*—for "the governor" is definitely Pilate. "In the fourth year of Tiberius Caesar the king", we read later on, "there was a man ... Pilate the governor."[88] This Pilate even imprisons Jesus, who is brought to him by Judas (*Yehudah*), for a stint of nine months.[89] But it is Tiberius—not Pilate—who instructs the rabbis that Jesus is to die under "the sentence given by your Scripture".[90]

This 'Byzantine' text then informs us that rabbis and the partisans of Scripture (meaning the Scripture of Israel) "hanged Jesus", once he had been "captured by the hand of Israel". It is the "hand of Israel" in this Judaic *Life of Jesus*—as in Melito of Sardis' *anti*-Judaic second-century homily *On the Pascha*—that "hanged Jesus on the tree and stoned him", so that he "died on the tree".[91] Pilate is a prominent character in this Judaic satire, but he is not one of Jesus' judges. And though Jesus is virtually 'crucified' in this text, it is done by the "hand of Israel"—not the hand of Rome. The sequence of hanging and stoning should, by now, require no comment.

The last of the genre we will glance at is a sophisticated 'European' copy of *The Life of Jesus* made in Amsterdam in 1699.[92] Here, the New Testament borrowings are constant and bold. This is what makes it so interesting that, once "the sages of Israel and the violent ones" have led Jesus to Pilate—"the judge from the city of Rome"—Pilate asks Jesus: "Are you the Messiah?" Jesus replies: "You and not me."[93] (This is a parody of the moment that Grotius interprets, decades before this

Amsterdam manuscript was made, as the "good confession" of Jesus.)[94] Unlike the gospels' Pilate, though, this seventeenth-century Judaic Pilate concludes Jesus' Roman trial without a judgement. "He is in your hands", Pilate says to the sages of Israel. "Judge him in your court, and according to your religion and law you shall sentence him."[95] Now, we can read that much in *John*—but this early modern *Life of Jesus* then diverges from the Johannine narrative of Jesus' Roman trial. For in *John*, after Pilate tries to deny his jurisdiction—and the Judaean elites renounce theirs—he takes his seat on the dais and concludes Jesus' legal ordeal.[96]

In this European *Life of Jesus*, we read that after Pilate denied his jurisdiction, the sages of Israel "took Jesus and brought him before the rabbinic court and the Sanhedrin".[97] The gospels' chronology—in which a Judaean trial *precedes* a Roman trial—is consciously inverted here. "What did the sages of Israel do?" asks the compositor of this early modern Judaic text. He then tells us:

> They immediately pushed Jesus and dragged him to the stoning house and stoned him at the time. It was the sixth hour of Passover eve and Sabbath eve. After they stoned him, they took him from the stoning house and hanged him on a tree, according to the law of the stoned ones ... and they left him there till sunset. Afterwards, they buried him in the graves of the stoned ones.[98]

From a Christian precis in ninth-century Lyon to a Judaic copy in seventeenth-century Amsterdam, the *Toledot Yeshu* is a Judaic text-tradition in which Jesus is killed by Judaeans, not Romans. As in the Babylonian Talmud, Jesus is 'hanged' in the *Toledot Yeshu*, yet he is first killed by stoning. Pilate is a recurring figure in this text-tradition, but he is always 'innocent'. For what is it that "our rabbis, blessed be their memory", say to Pilate in one of the 'early oriental' manuscripts of the *Toledot Yeshu*? "Give us permission to kill!"[99] It is never Pilate, in this Judaic counter-genre, who condemns and crucifies Jesus. The condemnation and 'hanging' of Jesus are invariably done by the rabbis and their enforcers.

That the Jewish compositor of our 1699 Amsterdam manuscript, one Zaddiq Belinfante,[100] cuts Pilate from the trial narrative his text is parodying is of course not a sign that he is 'more anti-Judaic' than the writer (or redactor) of *John*. But if a twentieth-century exegetical cliché is useless in reading a late-seventeenth-century European text on the death of Jesus, we can be sure that it is useless in reading a first-century Mediterranean text like *John*. The presence of a Judaean trial of Jesus in the gospels is simply not, per se, a mark of anti-Judaic hostility or bias.

Conclusions

Schäfer concludes his reconstruction of Jesus' death in the Babylonian Talmud in the following way:

> What we then have here in the [Babylonian Talmud] is a powerful con-firmation of the New Testament Passion narrative, a creative rereading, however, that ... proudly proclaims Jewish responsibility for Jesus' execution. ... [We] do accept, it argues, responsibility for this heretic's death, but there is no reason to be ashamed of it and feel guilty for it. We are not the murderers of the Messiah and Son of God, nor of the king of the Jews, as Pilate wanted to have it. Rather, we are the rightful executioners of a blasphemer and idolater.[101]

For Schäfer, the Babylonian Talmud offers a defiant Judaic counter-narrative to the passion narratives in the gospels. For Murcia, however, the Babylonian Talmud offers a sui generis narrative of Jesus' death—not a counter-narrative.[102] What is most arresting for us is just that the rabbis of Babylonia seem to have had some cognizance of Jesus' death in the gospels. They may have had some cognizance, too, of the figure of Pilate. And if so, they seem to have eliminated him from their only sustained 'passion' narrative in the tractate *Sanhedrin*. When we read in the Talmud that "they hanged Jesus on the eve of Passover", this 'hang-ing' is not a crucifixion, and it is not inflicted by Romans. Jesus' con-demnation and punishment are both claimed for their ancestors by the rabbis of Babylonia.[103]

The truth seems to be that a Judaic 'passion' in which Jesus dies, and Pilate is innocent, is much older—and much newer—than the Babylonian Talmud. It is recollected in the 'Judaean' parts of Celsus, in the late second century—and it is still circulating in the *Toledot Yeshu* when Voltaire, a virulent anti-Semite, seeks to weaponize the genre in the late eighteenth century.[104]

This narrative of Jesus' death is present in many of the most lustrous Judaic texts.[105] The towering philosopher-exegete Maimonides (died

1204) writes in his *Repetition of the Torah*, which is no mere repetition of the Torah,[106] that "Jesus the Nazarene ... posed as Messiah and was put to death by the court." In context, "the court" seems to refer to a Judaean court, a Sanhedrin.[107] To be sure, it must not be forgotten that Christian courts in Europe incinerated Maimonides' texts, and copies of the Talmud, beginning in the thirteenth century.[108] Yet it is worth remembering that Maimonides, like the Talmud, seems to negate Pilate's hand in Jesus' death and to attribute that death—by stoning, not crucifixion—to a Judaean court.

"I am aware that these truths are scarcely welcome", as the late Harold Bloom says in a related context, "but what truth is?"[109]

One desperately unwelcome truth is that this Judaic counter-*passion* is shadowed (and overshadowed) by a mercilessly counter-*Judaic* passion that originates in Christian circles, and that seems to thrive with a special intensity in late antique Syria and Arabia—resurfacing in the Islamic tradition. It is hard, perhaps impossible, to determine which of these narratives—Judaic or anti-Judaic—informs the one Quranic text on the crucifixion of Jesus.

9

"CHRIST WAS NOT THE ONE CRUCIFIED"

PILATE'S INNOCENCE IN ISLAMIC TRADITION

Suras seem to have had no titles in the earliest written copies of the *Qur'an*,[1] but sura 4 of the *Qur'an*—which is sura 2 in early Quranic lists—bears the conspicuous title "Women".[2] Early Islamic chronologies place the first utterance of sura 4 in Muhammad's time in Yathrib (renamed Medina after his death).[3] Modern text-critics concur, dating it to roughly 625 CE, within the first five years of the Islamic era.[4]

In the lines of sura 4 that concern us in this chapter, since they touch on the death of Jesus, the *Qur'an* voices bitterness towards the Judaeans of Yathrib. Gabriel Said Reynolds may be right to conclude that the main intent of the crucifixion-text in sura 4 is to "condemn the enmity" that keeps seventh-century Judaeans from venerating Jesus, whom the *Qur'an* holds to be a prophet and the Christ (Arabic *Masih*).[5] Yet later in the sura, the Christians of Arabia are censured for flawed doctrines,[6] and Philip Alexander may be right to suggest that Muhammad is "deliberately cutting out", in this text, the Christian hope in Jesus' redemptive death.[7]

However we contextualize the brief crucifixion-text in *Qur'an* 4, its contents are these. First, a "painful torment" awaits unbelievers among the Judaeans.[8] This is because—second—they have committed blasphemy by "killing prophets unjustly",[9] by uttering "words of slander

93

against Mary",[10] and by saying: "It is we who killed the Christ Jesus son of Mary, the messenger of God." Third, that final claim is flatly denied in *Qur'an* 4: "They killed him not."

But more than Jesus' death is denied, here. For a critical line of sura 4 reads, fourth: "They killed him not, *nor* did they crucify him." Couldn't this doubling of the Quranic negation reflect a consciousness of, and a rejection of, two related traditions?[11] The claim, "It is *we* who killed the Christ Jesus son of Mary", is a Judaean one. But the notion that Judaeans "killed *the Christ* Jesus" is a Christian one. It seems to me that the *Qur'an* could be negating, here, both a seventh-century Judaean claim to have *killed* Jesus,[12] and a seventh-century Christian claim that Judaeans *crucified* Jesus.[13]

Regardless, Jesus' death and crucifixion at the hands of Judaeans are both denied. "They killed him not, nor did they crucify him", reads the *Qur'an*.[14] That much is clear.

The Quranic verses then become obscure. For the text concedes—fifth—that, though the Judaeans did not crucify Jesus son of Mary, "so it was made to appear to them". The ones who make a false claim in sura 4—namely that they killed and crucified Jesus—seem to have been misled by their own senses. It appeared to them, in a tenebrous past, that they both crucified and killed Jesus. The Judaeans seem to have suffered a delusion that they were torturing and killing "the Christ Jesus". How could that happen? As we will see in the coming pages, there are various theories.

But whatever meaning we give to that decisive yet obscure line, "so it was made to appear to them", the *Qur'an*'s only crucifixion-text closes—sixth—with a solemn attestation of Jesus' ascent to God. "Assuredly they killed him not", we read, "but God raised him up to him."[15]

Who killed? Who died?

Pilate is not named in the *Qur'an*, or in the bulk of Islamic tradition.[16] The question of the culpability for Jesus' death is much simpler in the *Qur'an* than in the gospels.[17] For in the gospels, Jesus is interrogated by Caiaphas and Annas (Judaean priests), by Herod Antipas (a part-Judaean hereditary ruler), and by Pilate (a non-Judaean office-holder). In sura 4 of the *Qur'an*, Jesus is faced only with the hostility of Judaeans—as in the Babylonian Talmud (but there is no 'Phinehas' in the *Qur'an*, no coded reference to Pilate).[18] In the Talmud and Judaic tradition, Judaeans kill Jesus; in the *Qur'an* and Islamic tradition, they do not.

Yet there is still a crucifixion in the *Qur'an*. And we can say, in the most rigorous sense, that there *appears to be* a crucifixion *of Jesus* in sura 4. The question then becomes: If Jesus is not crucified and does not die in sura 4, who *is* crucified and who *does* die? The dominant Islamic interpretation of the cryptic words in sura 4, "so it was made to appear to them", is that a man *other than Jesus* died in his place on the cross.[19]

What the London solicitor and *Qur'an* commentator George Sale wrote in the 1730s is still basically correct.[20] It is the "constant doctrine" of Muslim exegetes, Sale says, that "it was not JESUS himself who underwent that ignominious death, but somebody else in his shape and resemblance".[21] In other words, Jesus had a body double.

Now, the body-double theory of the crucifixion is not preferred by late modern Quranic commentators.[22] Some critical exegetes seem reticent to go into it.[23] But the theory's roots are deep, and its presence in Islamic tradition is—to lift Sale's term—constant. Since our concern here is with Pilate and Jesus in that tradition, the body-double theory is decisive.

The crucifixion of a shadow

The first hint of a body-double theory in Islamic thought comes from a Christian, not a Muslim. I am thinking of Cyrene bar Mansur,[24] a high-born Christian official of the Umayyad caliphate who left Damascus during the harsh reign of 'Umar II—the first Umayyad caliph to try to induce Christians to convert.[25] Cyrene became a monk, taking the name 'John' and dying circa 750 in the Palestinian monastery of Saint Sabbas (which is still a thriving desert monastery).[26] In much of the later tradition, Cyrene is therefore 'John of Damascus'.[27]

John could read Arabic and had been "surrounded", at the Umayyad court, "by Qur'anic phraseology".[28] This fact seems to have complicated his reception in the Byzantine Empire. For in a condemnation of John (under the name of 'Mansur') by the Iconoclastic Synod of 754, he is attacked as having been "Saracen-minded" (*Sarrakēnophroni* in

Greek),[29] though it is not clear what exactly that means. How much of the *Qur'an* John had read is unclear, too, since the early history of the *Qur'an* is unclear. He cites Islamic "scripture" and a "book" (*graphē* and *biblos*, in his Greek), but Peter Schadler cautions that John could not have read the *Qur'an* "in its present form".[30]

John makes a significant early comment on sura 4, which he calls "the scripture on 'Woman'".[31] John's comment on this scripture is made in chapter 100 of his book *Against the Heresies*, suggesting that Islam—which he calls "Hagarism"—is, to his mind, the hundredth heresy.[32] And whatever he may have heard in Damascus, or whatever text he had before him, John—a scrupulous copyist—relates that he had read in "Woman" that "the Judaeans, having broken the law, wanted to crucify Jesus, but having arrested him they crucified his shadow. But Christ, it is said, was not crucified, nor did he die, for God took him up because of his love for him."[33]

A number of John's lines in this chapter of *Against Heresies* seem thrillingly close to the text of *Qur'an* 4.[34] I am not an Arabist, but when John writes in Greek that Christ "was not crucified, nor did he die",[35] he seems to me to dutifully convey the meaning (though inverting the structure) of the Quranic line: "They killed him not, nor did they crucify him."[36] And it is intriguing that he says that the Judaeans were thought by early Muslims to have crucified the "shadow" of Jesus (Greek *skia*), and not a body double.

The crucifixion of "their man"

A body-double theory of the crucifixion is attested in Quranic commentaries within a couple of centuries after Muhammad's death.[37] One notable gloss is made in the commentary of al-Tabari (died 923), highly revered for his learning.[38] Tabari registers a consensus in Islamic thought that the Judaeans nailed up "that which was made to appear similar" to Jesus.[39] But what is that?

A legend transmitted by al-Tha'labi (died 1035), who is known simply as "the Commentator" in later centuries,[40] sharpens the concept. It is Jesus' betrayer, Judas, who perished on the cross. And how could that be? Tha'labi opines that "the shape of Jesus was cast upon Judas ... and they crucified him instead, thinking he was Jesus". In this tradition, the betrayer of the Islamic Christ is made "similar to Jesus" and hoisted to die in his place.[41]

The logic is similar in the *Tafsīr Ibn 'Abbas*, a commanding *Qur'an* commentary of uncertain date that is erroneously named for one of Muhammad's companions, 'Abdullah Ibn 'Abbas (died 687). We read in this *tafsīr* that "because of their saying, 'It is we who killed the Christ Jesus son of Mary' ... God destroyed their man Tatianos." Who is Tatianos? This is all that matters: Tatianos is "their man". The Judaeans who try to destroy Jesus destroy one of their own. But how is Tatianos made to resemble Jesus? The *tafsīr* says only that "God made Tatianos look like Jesus." And why is God called "All-Wise" in this text? Because, the *tafsīr* reasons, "he saved his prophet and destroyed their man".[42]

Many other post-Quranic variations could be catalogued.[43] But the origins of the body-double theory lie in a pre-Quranic past. The crucifixion-text in *Qur'an* 4 seems to have been informed, not only by Talmudic or Syriac Christian traditions of the seventh century, but by gnostic Christian traditions of the first centuries CE.[44] We should glance, now, at them.

"Another was the one"

The body-double theory of the crucifixion seems to surface for the first time in connection to a second-century Egyptian heresiarch, Basilides, whose passionate "hatred of the God and the religion of Israel" may have inspired his heterodox theory of the 'passion'.[45] He is rumoured to have written a lost *Gospel according to Basilides*,[46] and it is perhaps because this 'gospel' is lost that Basilides is a recurring figure in the rumour-filled oeuvre of Jorge Luis Borges.[47]

Borges delights in being distrusted. But if Irenaeus of Lyon's treatise *Against the Heresies* can be trusted, Basilides claimed that

> Jesus did not himself suffer death but Simon, a man of Cyrene, being compelled, bore his cross for him. And this Simon was transformed by him so that he might be thought to be Jesus. Simon was crucified through ignorance and error, while Jesus himself received the form of Simon. And standing by, Jesus laughed at them.[48]

This Basilidean scene of Jesus grinning at Simon as he writhes on a stake is still horrifying, nineteen centuries on. "One does not have to be a Christian", as Stroumsa stresses, to recoil from this image of "Christ laughing as the poor Simon of Cyrene ... suffers in his place".[49] But this gnostic image of the 'passion' is baseless.

A twentieth-century form-critic, Martin Dibelius, pointed out that Simon of Cyrene's sons are named in *Mark* 15. Here, in the oldest crucifixion scene in our possession, we read that Pilate's troops "compelled a passer-by, Simon of Cyrene, who was coming in from the country, *the father of Alexander and Rufus*, to carry Jesus' cross".[50] The naming of Simon's sons, Alexander and Rufus, is certainly not gratuitous. It suggests to Dibelius that they must have known the gospel-writer (or some of those in his circle) and watched the crucifixion—of Jesus, not of Simon.[51] Eisler agrees with Dibelius' reasoning here, and he is not alone.[52] With Dibelius, Eisler, and other critical exegetes, I regard the crucifixion of Simon—and the laughter of Jesus—as hideous ancient fictions.

Yet Stroumsa has shown in a dazzling study of "Christ's laughter" that Jesus' hilarity at the agony of Simon (or some other unfortunate) is a recurring scene—a recurring nightmare?—in gnostic texts of the first centuries CE.[53] For instance, in one of the Nag Hammadi codices that Stroumsa cites, a Coptic manuscript that is probably influenced by Basilides,[54] 'Christ' says this:

> My death which they think happened, [happened] to them in their error and blindness. They nailed *their man* up to their death. For their minds did not see me, for they were deaf and blind. But in doing these things, they render judgement against themselves. As for me, on the one hand they saw me; they punished me ... *[But] it was not I* ... Another was the one who lifted up the cross on his shoulder, who was Simon. Another was the one on whom they put the crown of thorns. But I was rejoicing in the height ... and I was laughing at their ignorance.[55]

Note the crucifixion of "their man" in this gnostic text. No analysis of the Coptic and Arabic has been made, and I cannot make it. But at first glance, this ancient Egyptian apocryphon seems to eerily resemble a medieval Persian commentary on the *Qur'an*. Remember what we have just read in the *Tafsīr Ibn 'Abbas*: "He saved his prophet and destroyed their man."[56]

There is no laughter in the one Quranic crucifixion-text, or from what I can tell, in the Quranic commentary tradition. Yet the haunting claim in this gnostic text—"Another was the one who lifted up the cross ... Another was the one on whom they put the crown of thorns"—seems to be reformulated, if not recollected, in the Quranic denial of Jesus' crucifixion and the great Islamic commentaries on it.

Echoes of Basilides' lost gospel—real or imagined—have been heard in Qur'an 4 since the Renaissance. In a text that a Christian philosopher, George of Trebizond (died 1472), composed after the fall of Constantinople in 1453 in hopes of converting the Ottoman sultan, Mehmed II—the new "Caesar of Rome" (Turkish *kayser-i Rum*)[57]—he notes that "Christians and those who maintain the doctrines of Muhammad agree on virtually everything." Why, then, are they fighting? Christians and Muslims are only in schism, Trebizond reasons, because the *Qur'an* rejects "the cross and death of Christ".[58]

On Trebizond's telling, Basilides is the source of this schism. "Nearly seven hundred years after Basilides", Trebizond writes to the Turkish conqueror, Muhammad "revived" Basilides' tenet. Basilides and Muhammad both hold "that Christ was neither put on the cross nor died".[59] And Trebizond then cautions that they are "the only two who hold that opinion".[60] But Mehmed II never saw, or heard of, Trebizond's text. And he certainly never converted.

A startling Renaissance reading of sura 4

In the same text by George of Trebizond—which he obsequiously calls *On the Eternal Glory of the Autocrat*—he writes that if "the cross and the death of Christ" never occurred, the resurrection never occurred. And "if the latter never was", he reasons, "then neither is salvation".[61] Trebizond's sense that sura 4 cuts at the root of Christian faith is common to many exegetes, Christian and Muslim, in many centuries. Yet there are subtle variations in the way premodern Christians read that sura—or *azoara*, as 'sura' charmingly reads in Renaissance Latin.[62]

The most startling variation may occur in the writings of one of Trebizond's literary patrons, a Renaissance cardinal and thousand-sided intellect, Nicholas of Cusa (died 1464). Cusa commented more than once on sura 4 in books he wrote after the Turkish capture of Constantinople: *On the Peace of Faith* (1453) and *Sifting the Qur'an* (1461).[63] The first book is a collection of symbolic conversations. We

99

can only note here that in one conversation between a Turk and a Christian, the Turk observes that Christians say that "Christ was crucified by the Jews, while others"—read Muslims—"deny it."

In his reply, in *On the Peace of Faith*, the Christian argues that those who "deny that Christ was crucified"—read Muslims—are "ignorant of the mystery of his death". The 'mystery' of that death, for Cusa, is this: It is not shameful for Christ to die "a most shameful death". On the contrary, Christ "gave the life that he had in *this* world"—Cusa reasons—so he could "free the world from the ignorance by which it prefers *this* life to the future one". The glory of the cross lies in the hope of our redemption from the *saeculum*.

Notice, though, that in his book *On the Peace of Faith*, Cusa stresses that "Christ was crucified by the Jews."[64] (George of Trebizond similarly asserts, in his text for Mehmed II, that "the race of the Hebrews ... crucified Christ" after Pilate "declared himself to be guiltless".)[65] Cusa is certain that "Christ died in this manner"—namely by being *crucified*, and by being crucified *by the Jews*. This means that the Turk, as just quoted, is right. Christians *do* say that "Christ was crucified by the Jews." And for Cusa in 1453, a Jewish crucifixion is a historical datum that Muslims must come to confess.[66]

Yet by the time Cusa writes *Sifting the Qur'an*—less than a decade later—he himself no longer confesses that "Christ was crucified by the Jews."[67] "Muhammad denies", he notes in *Sifting the Qur'an*, "that *the Jews* killed Christ."[68] This Quranic denial is undeniable. But Cusa's close reading of sura 4 in *Sifting the Qur'an* seems to mark a new moment in the history of Quranic interpretation.

To begin with, Cusa concedes to Muslim exegetes that "Christ, as regards his *soul*, was not killed by the Jews." The cardinal then advances, contrary to most Islamic tradition,[69] the idea that "in the whole of the *Qur'an* there is no denial that Christ was crucified". It is only denied in sura 4 "that *the Jews* hung up Christ". If Cusa can be trusted—and more recent critical exegetes seem inclined to trust him—the oracular lines of sura 4 hint at the possibility that "*Pilate*, not the Jews, could have carried out this crucifixion in the way stated by the gospel."[70]

Unlike Trebizond, Cusa never mentions Basilides. And unlike Trebizond, Cusa hopes to overcome the 'Basilidean' reading of *Qur'an* 4—which is to say, the traditional 'body-double' reading. But note this.

It is only *the guilt of Pontius Pilate*, in Cusa's *Sifting the Qur'an*, that can reconcile the *Qur'an* to the historicity of the crucifixion—and, in that way, can begin to reconcile the Christians and Muslims who share so many convictions. The trouble, for Cusa and his late modern adherents, is that Pilate is not named in the *Qur'an*—or in the bulk of Islamic tradition. There is only one premodern Islamic 'passion', to my knowledge, in which Pilate is a player.

The passion according to 'Abd al-Jabbār

'Abd al-Jabbār (died circa 1025) is a Muslim exegete and judge (*qadi*) of the splendid city of Rayy, near modern Tehran.[71] A "gate of commerce" and "bridegroom of the earth" is how one tenth-century geographer, Ibn al-Faqīh, describes medieval Rayy.[72] But in his massive book, *Confirmation of the Proofs of Prophecy* (995 CE), 'Abd al-Jabbār composes (or copies out) a singular 'passion' narrative that is of interest to us.[73]

The *Confirmation* survives in a single manuscript in Istanbul. It first caught the eye of a European scholar in the 1920s[74] and briefly came into vogue (if medieval texts can be in 'vogue') in the 1960s.[75] This text of 'Abd al-Jabbār still has a certain cachet, since it is cited by a Hanbali jurist and radical jihad theorist, Ibn Taymiyya (died 1328)—of twenty-first-century salafist notoriety—and by other radical jurists in Ibn Taymiyya's Syrian milieu.[76]

There can be no doubt that 'Abd al-Jabbār knows of Pilate (Arabic *Filātus*). What is more, 'Abd al-Jabbār knows of Pilate's presence in the Creed of Constantinople (381 CE), which he—like many others— seems to confuse with the earlier Creed of Nicaea (325 CE). For 'Abd al-Jabbār writes in the *Confirmation* that in "a devotion which they call a Creed, which was established in Nicaea within the land of the Romans", the Christians confess that the "Lord Jesus Christ" was "taken, crucified, and killed before Pilate the Roman".[77] 'Abd al-Jabbār even seems to see Pilate as an ancestor of Constantine, whom he calls "the son of Pilate".[78] 'Abd al-Jabbār portrays Constantine as "a wicked, calculating man",[79] but his Pilate is strangely innocent.

The crucifixion of a guiltless man—but not Jesus—in 'Abd al-Jabbār's *Confirmation of the Proofs of Prophecy* is so intriguing, and so chaotic, that it can only be quoted en bloc. It is one eminent Islamic jurist's impression of the canonical passion—and "if the Christians went back over ... what is in their four gospels", he says, "they would know that Christ was *not* the one who was killed and crucified". For this, according to 'Abd al-Jabbār, is what the gospels narrate:

> On the Thursday of Passover, the Jews made out for Herod, the companion of Pilate, King of the Romans, and they said, "There is a man from among us who has corrupted and deluded our youth. According to the stipulation, you are obliged to empower us over someone who [conducts himself] in this way, that we may prosecute him." So [Herod] said to his guards, "Go with these [people] and bring their adversary." Then the guards went out with the Jews ...

> As they walked Judas Iscariot, who was one of the intimate and trusted [friends] and important twelve companions of Christ, met them. He said to them, "Are you looking for Jesus the Nazarene?" They said, "Yes". He said, "What would you give me if I guided you to him?" So one of the Jews let out some of his dirhams, counted thirty and handed them over to him, saying, "This is yours." So Judas said to them, "As you know, he is my friend and I am ashamed to say 'this is he', but stay with me and look at the one to whom I offer my hand and whose head I kiss. Then when I move my hand away from him, take him."

> They went with him, but there were many people from every place in Jerusalem who were meeting there to celebrate the feast. Judas Iscariot offered his hand to someone and kissed his head. He moved his hand away from [the other's head] and dove into the crowd. So the Jews and the guards took [this man].

> The man whom they took said, "What is the matter between us?" He was severely anxious. They said to him, "The ruler wants you." He said, "What is the matter between me and the ruler?" So they took him to [the ruler], bringing him to Herod. He lost his head in fear and anxiety and began to cry. Herod was merciful with him when he saw his fear and commanded them, "Leave him alone." ... [Herod] asked him, "What do you say about what these men claim about you, that you are the Christ, king of the Israelites? Did you say or claim this?" The man denied that he had said or claimed this ... Yet he did not say anything beyond his denial ... Herod said to the Jews: "I do not find that he confirms what you say, nor does he say what you claim ... Bring a basin and water that I may wash my hands from the blood of this man."

> Then Pilate, the great king of the Romans, came to Herod and said to him: "It has come to me that the Jews brought up to you an adversary of

theirs who has wisdom and knowledge. Transfer him to me that I might converse with him and see what he is like." So Herod had the man sent to [Pilate] . . . The king [Pilate] calmed him and asked him about the claim of the Jews that he was the Christ. He denied having said that. [Pilate] continued to question him and soothe him that he might mention something about himself, that [Pilate] might hear from him some wisdom . . . Yet he did not find anything in him. He had nothing [to offer] other than worry, fear, anxiety, crying, and weeping. [Pilate] sent him back to Herod saying: "I did not find in this man what is said about him. There is no good in him." He ascribed to him deficiency and stupidity . . .

On the next day, the Jews came early in the morning, took him, publicly humiliated him . . . and inflicted on him all kinds of torture. Then, towards the end of the day, they whipped him and brought him to a field of melons . . . They crucified him and pierced him with spears that he might die quickly. As he was being crucified he cried out continually in the loudest voice, "My God, why have you forsaken me? My God, why have you abandoned me?" until he died.

When Judas Iscariot met the Jews he said to them, "What did you do with the man whom you took yesterday?" They replied, "We crucified him." [Judas] was amazed at this, finding it unbelievable. So they said to him, "We have done it. If you want to be sure of it, go to the melon field of so and so." When he went there, he saw [the man] and said, "This is innocent blood. This is pure blood." He insulted the Jews and brought out the thirty dirhams that they gave him as a broker, threw it in their faces and went to his house. Then he hanged himself.[80]

In 'Abd al-Jabbār's 'passion', Pilate is given the role of Herod in the canonical passion (namely that of *Luke*), and Herod is made the judge of Jesus (though it is not Jesus, here, who is judged). In formal terms, we could say that—mutatis mutandis—'Abd al-Jabbār fuses the *inculpation of Herod* that can be seen in certain early Christian texts (we will glance at this in the next chapter), and the *body-double theory* seemingly concocted by Basilides (which we have glanced at in this chapter). In 'Abd al-Jabbār's text, as in early Christian texts, both motifs exculpate Pilate.

A critical reading of 'Abd al-Jabba ar's passion

There is a cacophony of influence in 'Abd al-Jabbār's passion, but it is certainly informed by the gospels—most heavily, I suspect, by *Matthew*.

There is much that indicates that 'Abd al-Jabbār read the gospels in Arabic translation.[81] For instance, there is the clear setting of his 'passion' in Jerusalem during the days before Passover.[82] It is Judas Iscariot who agrees to betray Christ, and his blood-price is "thirty". (In *Matthew*, this is thirty pieces of silver,[83] in 'Abd al-Jabbār thirty dirhams.)[84] Christ has a circle of "twelve companions" (where other Islamic traditions count thirteen or seventeen).[85] And the crucified man's final cry is "O my God, why have you forsaken me?"—a clear recollection of Jesus' last cry (*ultima vox*) in the crucifixion scene in *Mark*.[86]

The presence of biblical material accentuates the Islamic character of 'Abd al-Jabbār's passion. For it is not out of ignorance that his text diverges glaringly from the Christian passion—by which I mean, not from the particulars of a given passion narrative (*Matthew*, say, or *John*), but from the common stock of traditions that the canonical gospels share. A monograph could be written on 'Abd al-Jabbār's passion, but we can only notice here a few of his contradictions of the Christian passion.

In the beginning, 'Abd al-Jabbār's Jews are made to initiate Jesus' legal ordeal with *Herod*, who is a "companion of Pilate" (and not, as in *Luke*, on a hostile footing with Pilate until the morning of Jesus' death).[87] Pilate is a "King of the Romans",[88] and not a governor as in the gospels.[89] Jesus' arrest is authorized by *Herod*,[90] and it is with Herod's troops and the Jews—not the Temple elites—that Judas makes a pact to betray Christ.

'Abd al-Jabbār's Judas is ashamed of his betrayal *before* it occurs, and his 'kiss' is a mark of that shame. The arrest is not made at night in a secluded place—as in the four gospels—but in the holy city, and during the day. The man Judas kisses *is not Jesus*, and it is Judas who flees the scene—not Jesus' other disciples, who flee in the gospels. The man who *is not Jesus*, the man who will be crucified, is never named. He is simply, for 'Abd al-Jabbār, 'the man they took'. This pathetic character is confused and terrified—and he is not taken first to a high priest (as in the four gospels), but to Herod.

One of Herod's questions to "the man they took"—namely whether he is "King of Israel"—recollects Pilate's question to Jesus in the gospels, "Are you the King of the Judaeans?"[91] Jesus' reply to Pilate, "You say so",[92] which is not a negation in the gospels, is made a negation by

'Abd al-Jabbār: "It is they who say so *not I.*" It is not Pilate (as in *Matthew*), but Herod who washes his hands to show (what some take to be) his innocence.[93] Pilate's hands are so clean in 'Abd al-Jabbār's passion that they do not even need to be rinsed. Pilate's iconic gesture is therefore left to Herod.

In the gospels, Jesus is flogged by Pilate's legionnaires on the morning of his death.[94] In 'Abd al-Jabbār's passion, "the man they took" is flogged by Jews on the morning of his death. Where Jesus is crucified by Roman troops, most explicitly in *John* 19 ("the soldiers ... crucified Jesus"),[95] "the man they took" is crucified by Jews in this 'passion' of 'Abd al-Jabbār. The man suspended on 'Abd al-Jabbār's cross is not Jesus, and the man who ordered this crucifixion is not Pilate. The "King of the Romans", as 'Abd al-Jabbār calls Pilate, is wholly innocent in this medieval Islamic polemic.

Conclusions

The Islamic 'passion' of 'Abd al-Jabbār mirrors the crucifixion-text in *Qur'an* 4, where it is the Judaeans who declare: "It is we who killed the Christ Jesus son of Mary, the messenger of God."[96] And 'Abd al-Jabbār's 'passion' is in a sense more 'Christian' than the crucifixion narrative in the Babylonian Talmud, which is so intent on claiming the death of Jesus for a Judaean court that it cuts out Judas and the non-Judaean powers (Pilate and Herod), replacing the gentile cross with a stoning (and a posthumous hanging). In both the Judaic and the Islamic 'passions', though, *Pilate is innocent.*

In the Babylonian Talmud, Jesus is a malefactor and a Judaean court punishes him justly. In 'Abd al-Jabbār's *Confirmation*, Jesus is a prophet and a Judaean court punishes *some other man unjustly.* But in neither non-Christian 'passion' is the Roman prefect implicated in Jesus' death. The question now is whether this is a senseless concatenation of late antique and medieval arcana, or whether a political-theological meaning can be discerned here.

I think we must formalize two characteristics of the Christian passion in order to discern the deeper meaning—or the possibility of a deeper meaning—in the pagan, Judaic, and Islamic exculpations of Pilate. To my mind, what the non-Christian passions leave untouched is the archaic temple-state. The pagan and Judaic 'passions' do this by insisting on Jesus' guilt (which renders Pilate innocent); and the Islamic 'passion' does this by removing Jesus from the cross (which renders Pilate innocent).

By way of contrast, in the Christian passion, Jesus is arraigned by the Temple elites because he is a *legal critic* of the first-century 'Mosaic' regime. Jesus' claim to be the Christ during his interrogation by the high priest of Judaea is not blasphemous *in se*, but because of what he represents—namely *a moment of legal critique within the archaic temple-state*.

In the Christian passion, Jesus is not only a legal critic but *an innocent man*—and "Christ, the Son of the Blessed One".[97] Yet Jesus' *innocence* as a 'legal critic' is tied to his claim to be a herald, and a legislator, of a *new type of kingdom*—namely a kingdom of heaven (in *Matthew*), or a kingdom that is not of this world (in *John*).

It is only in the Christian passion that Jesus is both a legal critic *and* an innocent man. And it is only in the Christian passion that Pilate is both a law-observing judge *and* a guilty man. Because the non-Christian passions deny the innocence of the legal critic (pagan and Judaic), or the guilt of the judge (Islamic), they miss, I think, a *splitting of the archaic temple-state* that the Roman trial of Jesus dramatizes.

The pagan and Judaic 'passions' eliminate the moment of legal critique by *punishing* Jesus. The legal critic, they insist, is justly punished by his judges. The Islamic 'passion' eliminates the moment of legal critique by removing Jesus from the cross and *postulating that he is not a legal critic*. It is fascinating that 'Abd al-Jabbār, like many modern New Testament exegetes, insists that the text of the gospels has been corrupted wherever Jesus' sayings conflict with the 'Mosaic' legal regime of first-century Palestine.[98]

The pagan and Judaic 'passions' celebrate Jesus' suffering (a historical fact) and deny his innocence; the Islamic 'passion' celebrates his innocence and denies his suffering (a historical fact).[99] For the Islamic tradition, Jesus is only innocent because he is *not* a legal critic (a theological postulate); but for the pagan and Judaic traditions, Jesus is guilty because he *is* a legal critic (a historical fact). It is only in the Christian passion that a legal critic is revered as *innocent*, and a king—a *mystical* king—is permitted to suffer outrageous violence at the hands of the powers of this 'age' (Greek *aiōn*, Latin *saeculum*).

It could perhaps be expected that this theologico-political drama—a drama that is intolerable (if not inconceivable) for the pagan, Judaic, and Islamic traditions—could produce a novel strain of theologico-political culture. Especially once that drama is linked to the trial and death of Socrates—as it is not only in early Christian texts and the pagan Mara's letter but in 'Abd al-Jabbār's *Confirmation*, where "the man whom they took" (who is *not* Jesus) is charged with Socrates' crime, and where 'Abd al-Jabbār criticizes the Roman ecumene—read, the Byzantine zone—for being infested by "many philosophers".[100]

But curiously, much of 'Abd al-Jabbār's 'passion' is derived not only from the gospels but from other Christian traditions. And in much of the Christian archive, Pilate is not a wicked or corrupt judge but a supernumerary in the passion, or a victim, or a divine functionary—and thus, an innocent man. As this suggests, Jesus' theologico-political drama, as just formalized, may be illegible to much of the Christian tradition. To which we now return.

10

"O ROMAN, SPARE THIS GOD!"

PILATE'S INNOCENCE IN CHRISTIAN TRADITION

For Christians, Jesus' death is a judicial murder and Pilate is a judge on the scene. It might seem that Pilate's guilt would be, for them, inexpungible. Yet Nietzsche complains in the late nineteenth century of a Christian tendency to "set up Pilate ... as an advocate of Christ".[1] And I have already sketched some of the Christian tactics for exonerating Pilate.

The most 'orthodox' tactic for rendering Pilate innocent is just to render him otiose. If the Roman trial of Jesus is a drama without juridical effects, the trial can be theologically edifying—so the reasoning goes—without Pilate being tainted. How could a trial have no juridical effects? The most 'orthodox' reply is formulated by Lactantius in the fourth century: Pilate "did not himself utter a sentence". Jesus' Roman judge gave no judgement, but irregularly "handed him over" to be crucified by Judaeans.[2]

But Christians have exonerated Pilate in other ways that we can sketch in this chapter. The first is to claim that the task of judging Jesus fell not to Pilate—as in the canonical gospels—but to Herod. On whom, a few words.

Jesus and "the jackal"

Not to be confused with his father, Herod I, Herod Antipas held the "tetrarchy" of Galilee for the whole of Jesus' prophetic life. This Herod is a "tetrarch" for complicated reasons, and nothing about the Herodian dynasty is not complicated.[3] According to *Luke* (but only *Luke*), he questioned Jesus on the day of his death. There are conflicting reports, but Herod Antipas seems to have died a half-decade later in a Gallic city (now Lyon, France), after Caligula stripped him of his Palestinian tetrarchy.[4]

It is only *Luke* that tells us that this Herod was in Jerusalem in the days before Jesus' death.[5] And it is only *Luke* that says that Pilate, "when he learned that Jesus was under Herod's jurisdiction, sent him off to Herod".[6] Gabba suggests that this is "a gesture of courtesy" by Pilate.[7] And it may have been perceived this way, since we read in *Luke* that "that same day Herod and Pilate became friends; before this they had been enemies".[8] This friendship of Herod and Pilate, sealed by an urbane gesture on a morning of grisly business, is not hard to believe in.

In *Luke*'s passion, Jesus is taciturn because—he says—his judges will not believe him when he testifies, and will not reply to his questions.[9] Nevertheless, Jesus responds in *Luke* to the Judaean high priest and the Roman prefect.[10] He is laconic, but not mute. With Herod, by way of contrast, *Luke*'s Jesus is stonily silent—because, it seems, his contempt for the tetrarch of Galilee is total. Herod is "very glad" to see Jesus, we read in *Luke*, and "question[s] him at some length". A deputation of Judaean priests and scribes are on the scene, "vehemently accusing" the Galilean prophet to the Galilean tetrarch. But throughout his time before Herod—and this is a unique thing in the gospels' trial scenes— we read that "Jesus gave him no answer."[11]

Jesus' contempt for Herod Antipas in *Luke* seems to have been visceral. "That jackal", Jesus calls him.[12] It is surprising that this has not received more comment in the literature. For Jesus is a Galilean. As such, he legally falls under Herod's jurisdiction or authority (*exousia*, in the gospels' Greek). Of the three 'courts' in which Jesus appears in *Luke*—Judaean, Roman, and Galilean—his clearest *legal* obligation would be to testify before Herod. But it is only before Herod that Jesus refuses to utter a word. Why is this? Because Herod beheaded John the Baptist?[13] *Luke* doesn't speculate. But John the Baptist's killer is not fated to kill Jesus.

We read in *Luke* that "Herod with his soldiers treated Jesus with contempt",[14] and the tetrarch is a master of the arts of degradation. For in *Luke* 7, Jesus contrasts the prophets of God with those who "put on fine clothing" and live "in royal palaces"—referring, here, to the Herodian palaces in Galilee.[15] Much later in *Luke*, we read that Herod draped the Galilean prophet "in an elegant robe" before returning him, sans conviction, to Pilate.[16] With unerring instinct, *Luke* has Herod mock Jesus by turning him into one who "put on fine clothing" in a Herodian palace. In this scene, Jesus is symbolically negated as a prophet *and* a king.

But to restate. In the only canonical trial before Herod, which occurs in *Luke*, Jesus is clearly sent to Pilate *sans conviction*. Herod Antipas is not exactly 'innocent' of Jesus' death in *Luke–Acts*, but he is not a judge who condemns Jesus.[17] This changes in the non-canonical *Gospel of Peter*.

"Then Herod the king commanded"

The *locus classicus* of the idea of Herod's judgement is the fragmentary *Gospel of Peter*, which is probably a second-century concoction. Here, the anti-Judaic bias of the judgement-scene seems to be palpable. We read this:

> Of the Judaeans, none washed their hands—neither Herod, nor any of his judges. And as they would not wash Pilate stood up.
>
> Then Herod the king commanded that the Lord should be taken off saying to them, "What I have commanded you to do to him, do" ... And [Herod] delivered [the Lord Jesus] to the people before the first day of unleavened bread, their feast.
>
> So [the Judaeans] took the Lord and pushed him as they ran and said, "Let us drag the Son of God along now that we have got power over him." ... And they brought two malefactors and crucified the Lord between them. But he held his peace as he felt no pain.[18]

Note the weird resemblances that connect this early Christian apocryphon and 'Abd al-Jabbār's tenth-century Islamic passion. In the *Gospel of Peter*—as in 'Abd al-Jabbār's *Confirmation of the Proofs of Prophecy*—it is Herod, not Pilate, who delivers the one-who-will-be-crucified into the hands of his accusers. And in the *Gospel of Peter*—as in 'Abd al-Jabbār's text—it is not Romans but Judaeans who crucify the one-who-is-crucified. Of course, in the *Gospel of Peter* that is Jesus; for 'Abd al-Jabbār it is not. But the motif of Jesus' non-suffering in the *Gospel of Peter*—"he held his peace as he felt no pain"—is secured, by 'Abd al-Jabbār and much of the Islamic tradition, by other means.[19] Jesus' body is not inhuman or irreal—rather, a body-double is crucified in his place (Simon, Judas, et alia).

The myth of Herod's judgement remains marginal in the Christian tradition because it conflicts too glaringly with the canonical gospels. But Christian poets devised a subtler method of securing Pilate's innocence.

"My song will be Christ's life-giving feats"

Christian poets like to portray Pilate as a Hamlet-like victim. This poetic depiction of Pilate is artfully elaborated no later than the fourth century, when Christians begin to write in a style that modern scholars have called "contrast-imitation" (*Kontrastimitation*). This is a style that survives into the Renaissance (and beyond), and in which Vergil—the epicist of imperial Rome—is both vied with and imitated. Vied with because imitated.

It was a fourth-century Christian poet, Juvencus, who forged the brave new contrast-imitative genre of biblical epic. The first of its kind is Juvencus' *Four Books of the Evangelists* (circa 330), but it would be wrong to think that the influence of Juvencus and his genre is confined to late antiquity. Biblical epic only crests in the late seventeenth century with John Milton's poetic diptych, *Paradise Lost* and *Paradise Regained*. It reasserts itself in the twentieth century with Thomas Mann's massive novel-set, *Joseph and His Brothers*—not to forget the consummate Pilate-trial novels by Mikhail Bulgakov and Roger Caillois. Nor is there reason to doubt that biblical or para-biblical epic has a future.[20]

But returning to Juvencus, he boasts in the preface to his poetic life of Christ that his lines will outlast not only Vergil's epic (they have not) but *the world itself* (that remains to be seen). This is Juvencus, in a bold mood:

> Nothing contained in the structure of the world is immortal—not the globe, not human kingdoms, not golden Rome, not the sea, not the land, not the fire-stars of heaven. For the [divine] Father of all things has set an irrevocable time at which the ultimate scorching conflagration will engulf the whole world. But ... if songs [such as Vergil's *Aeneid*] which attach falsehood to the deeds of men of old have earned such lasting fame, my immovable faith will bestow on me the immortal glory of eternal praise ... For my song will be Christ's life-giving feats (*vitalia gesta*) ... Nor do I fear that the conflagration of the world will engulf this work with it. Indeed, my song will perhaps rescue *me* from the flames at the time when Christ, the resplendent judge ... descends in flame-belching cloud (*flammivoma ... nube*).[21]

In the *Divine Comedy*, Dante is taken higher than his pagan escort, Vergil. And that reverential agon, with its irreverent conclusion, begins here with Juvencus' boast.[22]

More relevant to us, though, is Juvencus' depiction of Pilate in his stanzas on the Roman trial of Jesus. In his monograph *Latin Epics of the New Testament*, R. P. H. Green notes that Juvencus, a high-born Christian priest, "is very lenient on Pontius Pilate".[23] Juvencus whitewashes Pilate in the scenes preceding Jesus' death in much the same way that we have seen in one of Juvencus' contemporaries, Lactantius (in chapter 6).

Green perceptively contrasts Juvencus' Pilate with a harsher image that comes out in a fifth-century Christ-epic by Sedulius, and a sixth-century epic by Arator.[24] Jesus is depicted by Sedulius as a "lamb" (*agnus*) standing before Pilate's dais.[25] (A curious legal note: Sedulius criticizes Pilate for sentencing a king—Jesus—when he was only a prefect.)[26] Green points out that these later poets' handling of Pilate can be traced to the influence of Augustine, who was born roughly twenty-five years after Juvencus wrote *Four Books of the Evangelists*.[27] And the diverging influence of Lactantius and Augustine—the former contriving Pilate's innocence, the latter asserting his guilt—will be a theme in later chapters.

What matters here is just that Juvencus, the inventor of the Christ-epic genre, absolves Pilate of the death of Jesus. In Juvencus' rendition of the Roman phase of Jesus' trial (or what German specialists call the

Pilatus-Prozess), Pilate is intentionally made a figure who is overcome by the vehemence of Jesus' Judaean accusers. More than once, Juvencus calls Pilate a "defeated man" (*victus*). As such, Pilate's judicial decisions are not his own. They are dictated to him by Jesus' non-Roman accusers (or perhaps, as the poet seems to suggest at one point, by Roman law). Finally, Juvencus is at pains to clear Pilate of his reputation for cruelty. *Four Books of the Evangelists* fails to narrate the moment when Pilate commands his legionnaires to scourge Jesus; this omission is almost certainly motivated.[28] And Juvencus' whitewash of Pilate becomes a lasting motif in the epic poetry of Europe.

The relevance of a Medici Christ-epic

The most successful Christ-epic to date is a Renaissance poem by Marco Girolamo Vida, *Christiad* (1535). This is a virtuosic epic of Jesus' last week of natural life—his betrayal, trial, and death—in six books and 6,000 neo-Latin lines. The first scenes of Jesus' post-natural life— his descent into hell, resurrection, and ascension into heaven—are sketched in the last book.

The *Christiad*'s immense, Europe-wide popularity is indicated by it having gone through forty print editions in the sixteenth century— including a Hispano-Flemish version, *Los Cristiados*, which sold in Flanders in the 1550s, and a series of Latin printings at the iconic Antwerp press of Christophe Plantin. The Clarendon Press at Oxford ran a Latin edition of Vida's epic as late as 1725.[29] The *Christiad* was a decisive influence on Torquato Tasso's crusade-epic *Jerusalem Liberated*, and on Milton's *Paradise* diptych.[30] If there is still a European canon, Vida's *Christiad* deserves to be in it.

But what is the relevance here of this Renaissance epic? The *Christiad* is by no means politically (or church-politically) innocent. Without impugning Vida's motives, his poem was commissioned by one Medici pope, Leo X, and completed with the lavish support of another, Clement VII. After it was printed, Vida was handed a bishopric—the see of the city of Cremona—for his labours. Inasmuch as the Medici papacy has a lasting piece of literary propaganda, Vida's *Christiad* may be it. And it is fascinating to find that the deuteragonist of the *Christiad*, after Christ himself, is not, as we might expect, the Virgin Mary or one of Jesus' disciples—Peter, say. It is Pilate. Book V of the *Christiad*, in which Vida dramatizes (or redramatizes) Jesus' Roman trial, is in fact more of a *Pilatiad*. In this book of Vida's epic, to a far greater degree than in the gospels, the foreground of Jesus' Roman trial is occupied by his judge.

The last reason that the *Christiad* is relevant, here, is that Vida's Pilate—like Juvencus' Pilate—is *not* Jesus' judge. Not really—not culpably. For if book V of Vida's epic can be read as a minor epic, an epic-in-brief, of Pilate—a *Pilatiad*—it is an epic treatment of the theme of Pilate's innocence. Let me restate that: Pilate is the deuteragonist in a defining piece of Medici papacy (and Counter-Reformation) propaganda, and Pilate's innocence is the theme in this composition. The poetry of Pilate's innocence originates in the first centuries CE with Juvencus, but it is still salient in Vida's Medici-commissioned epic. A glance at the *Christiad* will have to suffice.

"It is well known your hands were guiltless"

Book I of Vida's poem narrates scenes from the final week of Jesus' natural life. Book II is set in Jerusalem, where Jesus hosts a last supper, is betrayed by Judas, is arrested in Gethsemane, and is tried by the Judaean high priest, Caiaphas.[31] Vida has Caiaphas introduce Pilate, without naming him, towards the end of book II. "It is by the will (*arbitrio*) of the Roman governor that a man lives or dies", says Caiaphas. He is confident that once Pilate has heard the Sanhedrin's accusations, he "will send our enemy, who has no legal defense (*indefensum*), to his death".[32]

The rest of the *Christiad* elaborately suggests that the high priest is half right. Pilate will, as Caiaphas predicts, send Jesus to his death. Vida even gives us Pilate's sentence of death (it is given by none of the gospel-writers). "Let him die", Pilate says in book V, "condemned on a trumped-up charge" (*moriatur crimine falso damnatus*).[33] What Caiaphas is denied, in Vida's poem, is not a sentence of death by a Roman prefect—but, very precisely, Pilate's *will* (*arbitrium*).[34] Pilate is innocent in the *Christiad* because he sends Jesus to his death against his will.

Pilate is not a minor character in the *Christiad*, and his innocence is not a minor theme. Shortly after the high priest introduces "the Roman governor" towards the end of book II, he commands the Temple cohort: "Take [Jesus] ... to the house of the Roman governor and seek the penalty he deserves"—namely death.[35] As if to spare him an indignity, Vida never lets Pilate be named by Caiaphas during the nocturnal trial of Jesus. And when Pilate is finally introduced as "a Roman of distinguished family" (we have no such historical information), it is by the poet himself.

Pilate is struck by Jesus' beauty, which compels him to believe that "the captive must have descended from the gods".[36] The prefect's fateful question to Jesus in the gospels—"Are you the King of the Judaeans?"—is not the echo of a criminal charge against Jesus. It is, for Vida, a sign of Pilate's awe. "Tell me where you come from and who your parents are", his Pilate says to Jesus. "To what scepters do you aspire, what kingdom is your due?"[37]

Pilate's wife senses that Christ is "of the race of gods" (*genus ... deorum*), and she pleads with Pilate—as a voice from heaven has pled with her—"O Roman, spare this god!"[38] The contrast is harsh, between their gentility and the remorseless bloodthirst of the "victorious men of Jerusalem" (*Solymi victores*).[39] To the poet, Jesus' accusers are the "miserable race of Judaea" (*infelix Iudaea propago*).[40] They conquer with unnatural hate the natural piety of the Roman judge and his wife, and Pilate is revealed as a true 'victim' in the first lines of the *Christiad*'s last book.

When Joseph of Arimathea comes to the prefect to request the body of Christ (which is still "unburied and unmourned atop the white hill"), he says to Pilate: "Noblest of the sons of Romulus, it is well known that your hands were guiltless in the death of our dear master, whom our race unjustly and odiously executed, and that you tried with all your might, though in vain, to oppose their blind rage."[41] Pilate—or, as Vida calls him, 'Pontius'—replies to Joseph: "I call the gods to witness, for they know the truth, that I tried everything I could to save this innocent man and to set him free. ... But because the citizens would not allow it, I could do nothing. Their cruel fury carried the day (*vicit*)."[42]

We could contrast Vida's prefect with the 'Pilate' in one of the forgeries we read in chapter 6, who says: "I *did not* strive to the utmost of my power to prevent the loss and suffering of righteous blood."[43] Unlike him, Vida's Pilate "could do nothing". The impotence of Vida's

Pilate is the unenviable proof of his innocence. Rather than Pilate being one of Jesus' tormenters, as in the gospels,[44] Vida's Pilate is himself a tormented man—a sufferer, or, in Latin, a *patiens*, during Jesus' passion.

Conclusions

In the Christian epic tradition that Juvencus and Vida represent, Pilate's judgement is not elucidated—as in the gospels—by reference to his brute political calculations. To be sure, the poets' Pilate is still, in a formal sense, Jesus' judge. They do not relegate his judgement of Jesus to Herod Antipas, as we see in the apocryphal *Gospel of Peter*. Yet their Pilate is literally *conquered* by Caiaphas and the Jerusalemites.

In this sophisticated Christian tradition, the Roman trial of Jesus has not one but two judicial victims—Pilate and Jesus. Vida's interiorization of the Roman trial of Jesus in the *Christiad*, his dramatization of the Roman prefect's inner life, permits the legal reality of Pilate's judgement to be recognized in this Christ-epic, and its moral reality to be annulled. For the poets Juvencus and Vida—as for the courtier Lactantius—the Roman magistrate who interrogates Jesus is guiltless.

It is not only in pagan, Judaic, and Islamic traditions but in early and august Christian traditions that Pilate has enjoyed—in many circles—twenty centuries of innocence. But in the coming chapters, we will begin to retrace the tradition of Pilate's guilt in Latin Christian thought—and the political legacy of this tradition in late medieval and early modern Europe.

PART 4

THE UNLIKELY ORIGINS OF SECULARITY

11

"BEDS INLAID WITH SILVER"

THE *SAECULUM* IN JESUS, PAUL, AND JULIUS PAULUS

The words 'secularity' and 'secularization' are not secular in origin.[1] Ultimately, they stem from pre-Christian Latin words that refer to a space of time. *Saeculum* refers to "a human generation", "a century", or "all the future ages of the world"; and *saecularis* means "belonging to a century" or "to the Roman games celebrating the turn of a century".[2] It is striking, though, that no pre-Christian poet innovates on the Latin word 'secular' to give us a hint of ancient 'secularity' (*saecularitas*). And no pre-Christian orator spins 'secular' out into 'secularization' (*saecularizatio*) in a bid to impress the courts with a flashy new term.[3]

Most striking, perhaps, is that none of pre-Christian Rome's jurists—judging from those who can still be read, if only in sixth-century fragments, in Justinian's massive code of Roman law—feels that the term 'secularization' or 'secularity' might be necessary to describe a mode of Roman life or a sphere of legal reality.[4] The word 'religion' (*religio*) is not rare in the surviving sources of pre-Christian Roman law,[5] but in the vast bulk of Justinian's *Body of Roman Law* there is only one pre-Christian occurrence of the word that we now instinctively contrast with what the Romans call 'religion' (*religio*)—namely what we now call the 'secular' (*saecularis*).[6] And as if to highlight the word's unimportance in pre-Christian Roman legal culture, this solitary use of the word *saecularis* is in a chapter of Justinian's collection that covers "The Legacy of Furniture".[7]

"The following are contained in a legacy"

Justinian's chapter "The Legacy of Furniture" opens with a line from a minor Roman jurist, Florentinus, who defines furniture as "inanimate movable objects".[8] We are then treated to a long paragraph by a highly revered legal commentator, Paul. This is not the apostle, Paul of Tarsus, but Julius Paulus, a third-century pagan jurist who moved in the orbit of the Severan dynasty's most distinguished jurist, Ulpian.[9] Paul begins: "The following are contained in a legacy of furniture—tables, table-legs, three-legged tables, benches, stools, beds *including one inlaid with silver*, mattresses, coverlets, slippers, water jugs, basins, washbasins ..."

Paul's vaguely Borgesian catalogue runs on a bit further like this, but the mention of silver, which I have italicized, is critical. For at the end of this extract, Paul points out that older law-books fail to list silver items among heritable furniture. This is because, he says, the earlier Romans were inclined, "in keeping with the severity of the age (*saeculi severitatem*)", to categorize silver furnishings as pieces of *silver*, and not as household *furniture*.[10] For Paul, as this passage shows, the *saeculum* is simply a space of time. The 'secular' is a temporal concept for him, not a legal one.

In terms of pre-Christian Roman law, the 'secular' begins and ends here—with Paul's paragraph in Justinian's *Digest* on slippers and silver-accented beds. And the interest of this point is not only historical; it has contemporary relevance. For the *Digest* is one of the defining law-books of European history.[11] And it is hardly controversial to claim that the modern history of Europe (and thus, of the Americas) is defined, in large part, by a centuries-long elaboration—and a running contestation—of legal regimes marked by 'secularization' and structured by 'secularity'. There is no one—that I have seen—who wants to trace these epoch-defining European concepts to Paul's scattered lines on heritable furniture in the *Digest*.

If we want to understand ourselves, then, and the inner logic of our own political moment, we have reason to pose the following questions: Who first sharpened the Roman word 'secular' by giving it the forms that we now find indispensable—namely 'secularization' and 'secularity'? When did the word 'secular' cease to refer to a bloc of time—as it did for the pagan lawyer, Paul—and begin to signify a legal and political concept of fundamental importance? And, crucially, *why* did the word 'secular' begin to signify a legal and political concept that has come, by circuitous routes, to define—however much this definition may be, legitimately and illegitimately, challenged—what it means for a form of politics to be modern?[12]

The unlikely origins of secularity

This brings us to the unlikely origins of secularity. For we do not owe the word 'secularity' to a priest-baiting eighteenth-century *philosophe*. It is a coinage of medieval Christian writers.[13] When 'secularity' (*saecularitas*) occurs in a history written by a twelfth-century Shropshire-born monk, Orderic Vitalis,[14] it is sharply contrasted with the monastic form of life (*conversatio monachorum*).[15] And we do not owe the word 'secularization' to a bright-eyed nineteenth-century progressive. It is a creation of late medieval canon law.[16] 'Secularization' originally signified the protocols for laicizing a monastic in the Latin Church (though the medieval term *laicus* is itself highly complex).[17] It often meant no more than permitting a monk to become a secular cleric.

A 'secular cleric'? To us, this looks like a contradiction in terms—and it may have been jarring, too, to twelfth-century Europeans. So a remark by John of Salisbury (died 1180) suggests. But many priests would have been called 'seculars' in the high medieval period. This meant only that secular clerics—unlike monastics—were not committed to a comprehensive rule of life (*regula vitae*) like those that governed the religious houses, hour by hour and minute by minute.[18] A secular priest would not be subject to the forms of "continuous control"—in Foucault's phrase—that high-medieval monastic institutions came to express in a host of new ways.[19]

The crucial thing is this. It is not 'pagan' but Christian law, not civil but canon law, not modern but medieval law that first innovates on the Latin word *saecularis* to give us *saecularizatio*.[20] Originally, 'secularization' designates a judicial process that returns a Latin cleric or monastic to the *saeculum*, to 'the world' (which means different things in different contexts).[21] This is why we can read, for instance, in a medieval English text of a former deacon who "lived *secularly*"—as a Christian, but not as a deacon—"off church revenues".[22]

But the medieval term 'secularization' has one concrete sense that is highly suggestive in a political moment that some call 'post-secular'. For *saecularizatio* is distinguished in medieval texts from *exclaustratio*, the latter term signifying a 'temporary' release from the cloister. Having recourse to *exclaustratio*, a monk, say, could live *extra claustra*— "beyond the walls" of a monastic house—for a time. By way of contrast, *saecularizatio* signifies a perpetual release from the walls, and rules of life, of the monastic estate.[23] It is irrevocable.

This medieval canonistic distinction illuminates one of the looming questions in secularity theory. Are the European civilizations 'secularized' or are they only 'exclaustratized'? Of course, the question is never put this way—but that is, still, the question. Have we *irrevocably* exited a form of life in which our ritual-metaphysical institutions and our legal-political institutions are harmonized ('secularization'), or have we only *temporarily* exited such a form of life ('exclaustration')? In other words, is a restoration of the 'temple-state'—Christian, Islamic, or other—in our future?

That is not our question here. But the possibility of an answer—if there is such a possibility—rests in part on settling the question of the origins of 'secularity'. As just mentioned, the term itself—*saecularitas*—is medieval. But there is another European Ur-text in which *saecularitas* is never used, but in which the concept of an 'age', or *saeculum*, is salient. I am referring to the Latin New Testament.

An echo of Jesus in the letters of Paul

It is often remarked in the critical New Testament literature that Paul rarely cites the words of Jesus. Now, there are thirteen Pauline letters in the New Testament. According to a modern consensus, seven of those letters—*Romans*, *I Corinthians* and *II Corinthians*, *Galatians*, *Philippians*, *I Thessalonians*, and *Philemon*—are certainly from Paul's hand. The rest are contested and may conceivably be pseudonymous.

According to a second-century Christian tradition (not the canonical texts), the author of the *Luke–Acts* diptych is a man named Luke who moved in Paul's orbit and is mentioned by Paul (or pseudo-Paul) as the "beloved physician" in the letter of *Colossians*.[24] This early tradition suggests that the Pauline corpus and *Luke–Acts* are uniquely related. Raymond Brown concludes that this second-century picture is "not impossible"; but it is not, in historical-critical terms, more certain than that.[25]

Whatever bond (or lack of) we conjecture for the author of *Luke–Acts* and Paul, I am intrigued to see that, beyond the close parallels in their eucharistic formulae,[26] one of Jesus' characteristic phrases in *Luke*, "this age",[27] occurs with some frequency in the seven uncontested letters of Paul.[28] In Greek, the phrase is *ho aiōn houtos*, and in Latin, *hoc saeculum*. I should note in passing that for critical exegetes, the Latin New Testament (in its various iterations) is only of marginal interest, since the New Testament is a collection of Greek texts. But concerned as we are with European intellectual history in the *longue durée*, it is the Latin translation that comes to the fore.[29]

This is not the place for a philological demonstration, but I want to briefly suggest that the 'secular' may begin here—with the word *saeculum* in the earliest Latin translations of Jesus' sayings and Paul's letters. The most suggestive occurrence of that word may be in *I Corinthians*, where Paul refers to "the rulers of this age"—in Latin, *principum huius saeculi*—who "crucified the Lord of glory".[30] This line by Paul will reintroduce us to the figure of Pilate—and, conveniently, to the question of his innocence.

The task of parts 4 and 5 of this book is to retrace both questions—of the roots of 'secularity', and the innocence of Pontius Pilate—in conjunction. My suspicion is that they are, in strange and unnoticed ways, connected. Here, we can't give the *saeculum* in Jesus and Paul more than a sidelong glance, but that should suffice to establish that 'this age' is a common motif for both—which is to say, for both of Christianity's most influential figures.

The saeculum *in Jesus*

In what many scholars take to be "the oldest layer of tradition" in the gospels,[31] Jesus speaks in a narrative form called "parable" or "dark saying" (Greek *parabolē*).[32] The parables of Jesus vary in tone and form, but a number of them are—as Joachim Jeremias writes—"so vividly told that it is natural to assume that they arise out of some actual occurrence".[33] And many of them deal with crimes such as theft, embezzlement, assault, and murder. On Jeremias's reading, then, the synoptic gospels become—among other things—a collection of Jesus' true-crime allegories.

We have, for instance, the incident of the Thief in the Night ("an actual happening", Jeremias believes, "about which the whole village is talking"),[34] and the incident of the Cunning Manager ("Jesus is apparently dealing with an actual case which had been indignantly related to him").[35] This parable of the Cunning Manager is unique to *Luke*.[36] And what matters here is only that Jesus concludes this parable, in *Luke* 16, by stating that "the children of this age (Latin *saeculum*) are more shrewd in dealing with their generation than are the children of light".[37] Jesus' Cunning Manager is a figure of 'secular' shrewdness.

To my mind, this logion in *Luke* seems to intimate a novel and a mystical division of humankind. Note that this is not a proto-racist division. For Jesus' circle is marked by a critique of proto-racist thought. In one of the first scenes of *Matthew* and *Luke*—which is the first scene of a conjectural sayings-gospel, Q—John the Baptist tells his hearers that "God is able *from these stones* to raise up children of Abraham."[38] As this suggests, the Baptist's prophetic ministry seems to have been hostile to a fetishization of ancestry. And later in *Matthew* and *Luke* (and Q), a critique of proto-racist thought seems to me to be intrinsic to some of Jesus' sayings.[39] Nietzsche's senses are attuned when he writes that early Christ-belief is "not 'national', not a function of race" (*nicht 'national', nicht rassebedingt*).[40]

Yet Jesus seems to recognize, in his parable of the Cunning Manager, two human 'types'—not totally unlike Hellenes and barbarians, or Judaeans and gentiles. For Jesus, there are those who belong to "this age", and those who belong to an "age to come".[41] The latter are those he calls "children of light". And intriguingly, it is here that Jesus begins to assign the whole realm of commerce—he calls it Mammon (Greek *mamōnas*)—to "this age".[42] Because of this, there can be no doubt that *Luke* 16 is a locus in the history of economic 'secularization'.[43]

Another saying of Jesus' in *Luke* 18 stresses what we can hold on to—or, more critically, relinquish—"in this time". Jesus contrasts here the one thing that can be obtained "in the age to come" to all the things we can acquire in this age. Jesus calls it "eternal life" and suggests that it is more desirable than property or family. Yet it can *only* be obtained—Jesus seems to imply here—in "the age to come".[44]

Most of us have forgotten this, but the premodern theorization of the 'secular' and 'sacred' is mostly elaborated in terms of the 'temporal' and 'eternal'. The 'secular' is a temporal term, and in much premodern theory (and law), it designates what is *essentially* temporal. The church is a 'society' or sphere of concern whose legitimations and horizons are essentially *not* temporal—which is to say, eternal. (Most post-Christians, of course, no longer believe in eternal legitimations and horizons.) That theoretical contrast—which is legally realized in a thousand subtle ways in Byzantine and European canon law (touching property rights, inheritance, etcetera)—may conceivably begin here in *Luke* 18 (and its original, in *Mark* 10).[45]

On the readings I have sketched here, in a necessarily cursory way, Jesus begins in *Luke* 16 to 'secularize' commerce in his logion on the Cunning Manager; and in *Luke* 18, he seems, perhaps less severely, to 'secularize' inheritance and domestic bonds in a logion on "the age to come". In *Luke* 20—which is the last occurrence of *saeculum* in *Luke–Acts*, and the last we will glance at—Jesus seems in some way to 'secularize' the bond of marriage (which, it must be said, he radicalizes in his sayings on divorce).[46] Here, he says that marriage is proper for "the children of this age (Latin *saeculum*)", but that "in the resurrection from the dead", marriage will be a thing of the past.[47] It should not be necessary to stress how this saying, with its parallels in *Mark* and *Matthew*,[48] comes to influence one of the most distinctive traits of the Christian 'sacred', the valorization of virginity—and thereby, the whole monastic edifice of Byzantium and Europe. The history of European 'religion' would be unrecognizable, surely, without Jesus' 'secularization' of marriage in *Luke* 20.

Without concerning ourselves with the prophetic meaning of the *saeculum* in these sayings, it should be clear to us—as it was to countless generations of European theologians and legal theorists—that the 'age' is a motif in *Luke* that touches on the realm of commerce (and of God), on the ordering of families and legacies (and the 'sacred' abandonment of family ties and legacies), and on the marriage bond itself (and the 'apocalyptic' or 'angelic' renunciation of it). For Jesus, I mean to say, the *saeculum* is a concept that introduces a novel set of contrasts and moral imperatives in the life-world of first-century Judaea. I believe that this is a set of contrasts that is still recognizable—in wildly differing forms, of course—in thirteenth-century Paris, fourteenth-century Rome, and fifteenth-century London.

The saeculum *in Paul*

It cannot be unimportant, then, that the *saeculum* is one of the rare motifs in Jesus' sayings that is echoed, in unaltered language, in Paul's letters—meaning, here, only his uncontested letters.[49] It is striking that Paul, in the first lines of *Galatians*—one of his earliest surviving letters (circa 55 CE)—says that Jesus died "to set us free from the present evil age".[50] One of Paul's first claims seems to have been that Jesus died to emancipate us from the *saeculum*. But why is this age "evil"? And why should we hope to be delivered from it?

We can answer that, in part, by glancing at *II Corinthians* 4 (circa 57 CE), where Paul says that there is a "god of this age (Latin *saeculum*)", and that this god conceals and denies the "glory of Christ".[51] As we will see in a moment, Paul seems to think of the *saeculum*, by definition, as a world-order within which the "glory" of Jesus—and particularly, the "glory" of his crucifixion—cannot be recognized. And if the *saeculum* is controlled by hidden powers (by its "god"), it is also governed by a form of time-bound consciousness or a hyper-temporal mentality.

In his letter to the *Romans* (circa 57 CE), Paul urges the Christ-believers in that city—the first century's world-city par excellence—not to be "conformed to this age (Latin *saeculum*)", but to be "transformed by the renovation of your minds".[52] This renovation of the mind must be part of what Paul means by an emancipation from the *saeculum*. According to Paul, "renovation" consists in being lifted out of the mentality of "this age" and living in light of what Jesus calls an "age to come". A highly Platonized vision of this is Ambrose of Milan's *Flight from the World-Age* (*De fuga saeculi*), which ends with him urging fourth-century Christians of the imperial court-city—not Rome, at the time, but Milan—to fly from the *saeculum* "in such a way that it may be said of you, 'Who are these that fly like clouds, and like doves?'"[53]

To my mind, this thought in *Romans* chimes with Paul's proem to *I Corinthians* (circa 50 CE), where he asks—the questions are obviously rhetorical—"Where is the one who is wise? ... Where is the debater of *this age*? Has not God made foolish the wisdom of *the world*?"[54] The logic of the age, Paul claims, is revealed by Jesus' cross to be sophistry. This is his material claim—but note, more formally, how Paul correlates the world and the age (Latin *mundum, saeculum*). This correlation can be traced through many centuries of Christian thought. In the line of thought that originates in the Pauline letters and the gospels, the 'secular' is the 'worldly' and vice versa. And to my awareness, this is not a correlation that can be read off the other defining corpora of the pre-Christian Roman Empire.

Moving on, though, it is in *I Corinthians* 2—our last Pauline text on the *saeculum*—that Paul integrates his theory of the mentality of this age, the governance of this age, and the crucifixion of Jesus. This is Paul:

> Among the mature we do speak wisdom, though it is not a wisdom of this age (*saeculum*) or of the rulers of this age (*saeculum*), who are doomed to perish. But we speak the wisdom of God, mystical and hidden, which God decreed before the ages (*saecula*) for our glory. None of the rulers of this age (*saeculum*) understood this—for if they had, they would not have crucified the Lord of glory.[55]

The Christian 'sacred' seems to be constituted, in its Pauline conception, by an event—or rather, by a sequence of events: the crucifixion and resurrection of Jesus—that is illegible within the form of reasoning, and the form of governance, of the *saeculum*. Or rather, as these lines from *I Corinthians* 2 show, the Christian 'secular' is constituted by an *inevitable failure* of "this age" to recognize the sequence of events that gives human history its mystical and eschatological significance.

The archaic city is or seeks to be—like Plato's definition of time in the *Timaeus*—a moving image of eternity. But Paul believes that Jesus' death on a cross—a fleeting moment on a gibbet-hill in Judaea—is the true revelation of eternity. The archaic 'temple-state'—Judaean and Roman—is reduced, by its failure to recognize that mystery, to a 'secular' status. The rulers of this world, for Paul, are captives of the *saeculum*. It is the ministers of the church—or what Paul calls *ekklēsia*, a "convocation" of Christ—who *truly* participate in eternity.[56] The temple-state, in Paul's thought, becomes a fragile and *essentially* temporal—which is to say, again, a 'secular'—configuration of powers.[57]

Governance in the *saeculum* has its own logic and rationality—Paul calls it the "wisdom of this age". And governance in the church has a different logic and rationality—Paul calls it the "wisdom of God". To recollect a term used by Fustel de Coulanges in his iconic book *The Ancient City*, we might say that, in Paul, the *code* regulating "the relations between humans and their duties towards the gods of the city" is no longer unitary. In Paul, as Fustel formulates it in the mid-nineteenth century, religion ceases to *be* the city, or the empire.[58] In Paul, religion becomes a cultus that elevates a man—"Christ Jesus", as he calls him, and "the Lord Jesus Christ"[59]—who expired on a stake as an enemy of his holy city (Jerusalem) and his god-governed empire (Rome).

For Paul—to put it crudely—the political machine belongs to the *saeculum* (and vice versa), and the church belongs to the *mysterium* (and vice versa). The mystical head of the church died as a criminal reject of the state. How could this be? Note what Paul writes in *I Corinthians*: "None of the rulers of this age (*saeculum*) understood this—for if they had, they would not have crucified the Lord of glory."[60]

This returns us to Pilate—who is now changed, however. Already in the year 50 (or so), Pilate is conceived by Paul—one of the first generation of Christ-believers—as one of "the rulers of this age". Paul's governmental concept of the 'age'—*ho aiōn* in Greek, *saeculum* in Latin—is novel. It has clear antecedents in some of Jesus' sayings (particularly in *Luke*), but not in the ancient corpora of Roman or Judaic law.

Lucian of Samosata may be the first pagan to limn the political contours of Christian religion—a 'religion' that, because it belonged to an age to come, constituted the non-Christian city as 'secular'. Lucian writes this of Christians in second-century Syria:

> Their first lawgiver [Jesus] persuaded them that they are all brothers of one another after they have transgressed once for all by denying the Greek gods and by worshipping that crucified sophist himself and living under his laws. Therefore they despise all things indiscriminately and hold them to be common property.[61]

Jesus is not named here, but Lucian refers to "the Christians" in the preceding sentences.[62] There is no doubt that his "crucified sophist"—not a crucified *philosopher*—is Jesus.[63] And the keeping of common property by Christians (as noted in *Acts of the Apostles*) is registered, by Lucian, as a mark of what a less caustic Syrian writer, Mara bar Serapion, called the "new laws" that Jesus gave.[64] Lucian fails to connect the voluntary communism of early Christians to the hypothetical communism of Plato's ideal city in the *Republic*,[65] but that is a connection Christian legal theorists will make in medieval Europe.[66]

Conclusions

This is how secularity, properly speaking, begins. Within roughly twenty years of Jesus' death, a new term-concept seems to have crystallized, as Nietzsche intuited, in the earliest Christian writings.[67] It is tied in Paul's letters to the fact that he and other early Christ-believers revered a crucified man—as neither pagans nor Judaeans let them forget.[68] That new term-concept is *saeculum*.

12

"YOU ACTED IN IGNORANCE"

WHY THERE ARE NO CHRIST-KILLERS

A novel conception of the 'age' (*saeculum*) seems to be traceable to New Testament texts. But we have not taken note of all that Paul implies in the crucial line that I have quoted from *I Corinthians* 2. "None of the rulers of this age understood this"—by which Paul means, the mystery of the ages and the wisdom of God—"for if they had, they would not have crucified the Lord of glory".[1]

According to Paul, when we read him closely, the crucifixion is not the act of one 'ruler' in the *saeculum*—but of "rulers". This is of course oblique, but it suggests that Paul knew that both Caiaphas and Pilate—the Judaeans and the Romans—had a hand in Jesus' death.[2] Paul's reasoning here suggests, too, that the rulers of the *saeculum* acted in ignorance. The enormity of the act—the destruction of "the Lord of glory"—is a sign, for him, of the blindness of the *saeculum*. Not per se of its evil.

"The inhabitants of Jerusalem and their rulers"

Both aspects of this sentence in *I Corinthians* 2 harmonize nicely with a short statement that is put in Paul's mouth in *Acts of the Apostles* 13, where he says in the synagogue at Antioch: "Because the inhabitants of

Jerusalem and their rulers did not recognize Jesus or understand the words of the prophets that are read every sabbath, they fulfilled those words by condemning him. Even though they found no cause for a sentence of death, they asked Pilate to have him killed."³ The care taken here, in a Syrian synagogue, to restrict the meaning of 'the Judaeans' to "the inhabitants of Jerusalem and their rulers" is notable. There is no consciousness here—as there is, lamentably, in many later Christian texts—of a broader 'Judaean' culpability for Jesus' death.

It is moreover striking that the hand of 'the Judaeans' (*sensu stricto*) in Jesus' death is mitigated in this passage of *Luke–Acts*. Paul is made to say, here, that the Jerusalemites and Temple elites "did not recognize Jesus".⁴ This Lucan claim echoes not only Paul's own reasoning in *I Corinthians* 2⁵ but a uniquely Lucan saying of Jesus on the cross (which is suppressed in many manuscripts).⁶ I am thinking of Jesus' regal line in *Luke* 23: "Father, forgive them—for they do not know what they are doing."⁷ The French theorist René Girard has commented on the luminosity of this utterance: "*They do not know what they are doing* ... In this passage we are given the first definition of the unconscious in human history."⁸

Returning to the sacred page, there is some slight and oblique—but, to my mind, real—confirmation in *Acts of the Apostles* 13 that Paul might have had Pilate in mind, as one of "the rulers of this age", when he wrote *I Corinthians* 2. (I am discounting the clear reference to Jesus' interrogation by Pilate in *I Timothy*, since that seems to be a pseudo-Pauline letter.)⁹ Paul's discourse in Antioch, in *Acts*, is thoroughly Lucan;¹⁰ but it is nevertheless meant to harmonize with—and can be seen to harmonize with—the themes and contents of Paul's teaching in his undisputed letters.¹¹ With that caveat in mind—namely that the Antioch sermon is Lucan—we may still have reason to hear a Pauline recollection of Pilate in *I Corinthians* 2. When Paul insists that "the rulers of this age" would not have crucified Jesus if they had known what they were doing,¹² we can perhaps infer that—for Paul—*Pilate would not have crucified Jesus if he had known what he was doing.*

But if there is some reason to believe that Paul has Pilate (and the Temple elites) in mind in *I Corinthians* 2 (circa 50 CE), then there is some reason to believe, too, that the first Christian to thematize the *saeculum* thought of Pilate (and the Temple elites)—whose judgement of Jesus helps to precipitate the concept of the *saeculum*—as 'innocent'. If our (conjectural) reading of *I Corinthians* 2 is not mistaken, then *before the gospels are written there is some sense of Pilate's innocence.* How could this be? And what could this mean? Before we pursue these questions, our reading of *I Corinthians* 2 can be used to silence an ancient Christian myth that is intimately linked to the question of Pilate's innocence. This is the tenacious Christian myth of 'Christ-killers'.

"The Jews crucified"

There is no need to stress the criminality and hate evoked by the term 'Christ-killers'. The roots of this term in Christian literature are diffuse, but the taproot of Christian anti-Semitism is often taken (with no great accuracy) to be a collection of sermons that John Chrysostom (died 407) preached in Antioch in the autumn months of 386 and 387 CE.[13] This collection has been printed since the seventeenth century under the title *Against the Jews* (*Adversus Iudaeos*), and in the first pages of the first sermon, Chrysostom invokes "Christ, whom *the Jews crucified.*"[14] In Chrysostom's sermons, the idea that "the Jews crucified" Jesus is tied to a myth of undying Jewish blood-guilt. Chrysostom believes that Syrian Jews of the late fourth century CE are marked by, and will be judged for, Jesus' death in Judaea in the early first century CE.[15]

The 'Christ-killer' idea is a tenacious one in the churches—and in Christian and post-Christian nations. It is a source of recurring Christian violence—and thus, of a deep and recurring Christian guilt. However, I believe that it is starkly contradicted in *Luke–Acts* and the Pauline letters (if not in other New Testament texts that "were written in rather diverse milieus" and may, perhaps, differ in their conceptions of the death of Jesus).[16] We should note this in passing—since it bears not only on the question of Pilate's innocence but on Byzantine and European history in the *longue durée*.

"None of the rulers understood"

Paul's logic in *I Corinthians* 2 is illuminating. For him, the idea of crucifying "the Lord of glory" is so repugnant that *the fact* of Jesus' crucifixion *demonstrates* that "none of the rulers of this age understood".[17]The next question to ask, of course, is—understood *what*? Paul is, I believe, the first-century writer who most forcefully argues that there can be no sin (or crime) where there is no law. This is one of Paul's main theses in his letter to the *Romans*—which is, without doubt, one of the most radical pieces of legal critique in ancient literature (and one of the most influential in later centuries).[18] What this means, for Paul, is that there can be no guilt without knowledge.

Paul insists on this in *Romans* 3, where he pre-delineates the nineteenth-century legal formula, *nullum crimen, nulla poena sine lege.*[19] There is no crime, and thus there can be no punishment, where there is no law.[20] But what law brings, according to Paul, is precisely knowledge of crime (or sin). "Through the law", he writes, "comes the knowledge of sin."[21] So when Paul writes that "none of the rulers of this age understood" what they were doing, it is senseless to ask whether they were *guilty*.[22] Paul is a consummate theorist of what Augustine of Hippo later calls—and jurists still call—the "guilty mind" (*mens rea*).[23] And if Paul denies that the "rulers of this age"—Roman *and* Judaean—had a 'guilty mind' when they crucified Jesus, then he denies their guilt. This is beyond doubt.

In *I Corinthians* 2, therefore, Paul asserts the innocence of Caiaphas and Pilate—but *of what* are they innocent? Paul's reasoning here is precise. Jesus *has* been crucified, he writes, but the rulers would not have knowingly crucified *the Lord of glory*. Therefore, the crime (sin) of which Paul absolves both Caiaphas and Pilate is not the murder of Jesus—but, precisely, *the murder of the Lord of glory*. They *are* guilty for having crucified Jesus—a prophet, and an innocent man. But they are *not* guilty as 'Christ-killers', for it is *this*—that Jesus is Christ (so Paul fervently believes)—that "none of the rulers of this age understood".[24] Where there is no 'guilty mind', for Paul, there is no crime—and *he believes that the killers of Jesus did not intend to kill the Christ.*

This is exactly what we find in *Luke–Acts*. There can be no doubt that Jesus' innocence is recognized in Jerusalem in *Luke*. It is recognized by Joseph (a dissenting voice on Caiaphas' Sanhedrin); it is recognized by Herod and Pilate (who nevertheless have Jesus tortured and killed); it is recognized (only in *Luke*) by a malefactor who is crucified with Jesus; it is recognized by a Roman officer who hears

Jesus' last words (and says "Certainly this man was innocent!"); and it is recognized (only in *Luke*) by "the crowds who had gathered ... for this spectacle", but who left the gibbet-hill "beating their breasts" for shame.[25] Despite this thematization of Jesus' innocence in the Lucan passion, it is only in *Luke* that Jesus prays for his killers, saying: "Father, forgive them—for they do not know what they are doing."[26] Given *Luke*'s singular stress on Jesus' innocence, it is logical to ask: What could this prayer by Jesus, unique to *Luke*, mean? How could Jesus' killers *not* know what they are doing?

It is also necessary to ask: Why is Jesus' prayer subtly—yet crucially—different from the prayer of the protomartyr Stephen in *Acts* 7? When he is being lynched, Stephen prays: "Lord, do not hold this sin against them."[27] The resemblance to Jesus' prayer is close—which is precisely why it is so interesting that Stephen's prayer *does not* contain a claim that his killers are acting in ignorance.[28] Jesus says that his killers, for whom he prays, "do not know"; Stephen does not say this. *What* is it, then, that Jesus' killers do not know? It is clear in *Luke–Acts*, as in *I Corinthians*,[29] that the killers of Jesus do not know that he is—per the apostolic faith—the Christ.

"In the presence of Pilate"

Precisely this, on my reading, is the theme of the first Christian homily on record. For, in *Acts* 2, Peter says to "the Israelites" in Jerusalem that "you yourselves know" certain things about Jesus—namely that he is "a man attested to you by God with deeds of power, wonders, and signs".[30] (Peter's assertion in the first chapters of *Acts*, "you yourselves know", may be meant to clarify Jesus' assertion in the last chapters of *Luke*, "they do not know".)[31] That Jesus is "a man attested" is not the theme of Peter's sermon, precisely because—as he says—it is something his hearers know. What, then, is Peter's theme?

"This man", Peter goes on—and note the banality of "this man": Jesus is not yet called 'the Christ'—"you crucified and killed by the hands of those outside the law".[32] The Christian myth that Judaeans— and not Romans—crucified Jesus comes from a slovenly (or malevolent) reading of this verse (and a couple of others in the New Testament). Of course, it is clear from *Acts* 2 that Peter holds the

inhabitants of Jerusalem and their rulers responsible for having crucified and killed "this man", Jesus.[33] But it is no less clear that the crucifying and killing were done "by the hands of" gentiles (Greek *dia
cheiros*, Latin *per manus*).[34] Pilate is not named, here, because his hand
in Jesus' death is one of the things of which Peter can say to his hearers, "you yourselves know".

What is it, then, that Peter's hearers—and Jesus' killers—do *not*
know? It is this—which is the final line of the first Christian homily on
record: "Let the entire house of Israel *know with certainty* that God has
made him both Lord and Christ, this Jesus whom you crucified."[35]
Peter's hearers know that Jerusalem's Temple elite killed "this Jesus";
and they know that the killing was done "by the hands of" gentiles.
What they do *not* know—and what Peter claims—is that "this man" is
the Christ.

If my reading is correct,[36] then the first Christian homily (by which
I mean only the first homily in *Acts*) sharply distinguishes between the
killing of *Jesus*, and the killing of *the Christ*. This distinction structures
Peter's homily, which begins with what the Jerusalemites *know*—that a
man named Jesus, legitimated to them by "marvellous deeds" (in what
may be Josephus' words),[37] had been crucified by Pilate on the insistence of Caiaphas. And it ends with what they *do not know*—that a
crucified man named Jesus had been legitimated to them *by the resurrection as the Christ*.

Of course, the logic of Peter's homily is precisely that Jesus' killers
had killed the Christ. But it is no less precisely that Jesus' killers had
unknowingly killed the Christ. Peter brusquely charges the Jerusalemites
and the Temple elites with killing "this man", "this Jesus", "by the hands
of" gentiles—but *not with killing the Christ*. In *Acts* 2, as in *I Corinthians*
2, therefore—as in *Luke* 23 ("Father, forgive them")—the same conviction is discernible: *Jesus' killers are not guilty as 'Christ-killers'*. The
Judaeans and gentiles who killed Jesus *are not innocent*, since they killed
a prophet and an innocent man—*but they are not guilty of killing 'the
Christ'*.[38] A crucial argument of the first homily in the Christian archive,
then—which was preached in a rather literal sense to *Jesus' killers*—is
that *there are no 'Christ-killers'*.

It is hard to believe this could be a misreading of Peter's first homily
(in *Acts* 2), since it is reiterated in his second homily (in *Acts* 3).

Consider what Peter says one afternoon shortly after Jesus' resurrection, preaching in the portico of Solomon:[39]

> You Israelites, why do you marvel at this? ... The God of our ancestors has glorified his servant Jesus, whom you handed over and rejected in the presence of Pilate, though he had decided to release him. ..., And now, friends, I know that *you acted in ignorance, as did also your rulers.* In this way God fulfilled what he had foretold through all the prophets, that his Christ would suffer.[40]

The most illuminating comment on this Petrine thought (from the writer of *Luke–Acts*) is the extract from Paul's Syrian discourse (in *Acts* 13) that we have already seen: "Because *the inhabitants of Jerusalem and their rulers did not recognize Jesus* or understand the words of the prophets that are read every sabbath, they fulfilled those words by condemning him. Even though they found no cause for a sentence of death, they asked Pilate to have him killed."[41] In both texts, the dramatis personae are Jesus and Pilate, a crowd of Judaeans and their rulers. (Note that Judas is recollected in *Acts* 1, Barabbas in *Acts* 3, and Herod in *Acts* 4.)[42] In both texts, Jesus is innocent; Pilate is reluctant; *the Judaeans and their rulers are ignorant (namely that Jesus is, per the apostolic faith, the Christ).* There are therefore no 'Christ-killers', Roman or Judaean, in the trial of Jesus. This is not just a claim in *Luke–Acts*; it is a theme.

"An unheard-of murder"

The abyssal, homicidal charge of 'deicide' (God-murder) is perhaps first articulated in a Christian homily, *On the Pascha*, attributed to Melito of Sardis,[43] a bishop of the late second century who may himself, conceivably, have been Judaean by birth.[44] Whatever his parentage, it is held that Melito made a pilgrimage to Jerusalem (thought by some to have been the first Christian pilgrimage to Jerusalem),[45] and that his homily *On the Pascha* reveals his knowledge of the Passover Haggadah.[46] Yet no one doubts the anti-Judaic fervour of Melito's lines in *On the Pascha*. "God has been murdered", he thrums, and the murder has been committed "by an Israelite right hand."[47] This is a dark, recurring charge in the history of Christian anti-Semitism. "You killed your Lord", Melito accuses the second-century Judaeans of Anatolia, calling Jesus' death "an unheard-of murder" (Greek *kainos phonos*).[48]

Of course, Melito (or whoever composed this homily) cannot be charged with crimes that postdate him by many centuries. The bishop of Sardis is a poet-theologian of the second century, not a Christian pogromist of the twelfth century or a neo-pagan genocidaire of the twentieth century. Yet he and numerous other Christian exegetes are guilty of effacing a hard, bright line that both Paul and *Luke–Acts* strike between the *conscious* killing of Jesus and the *unconscious* killing of Christ. What is more, Melito's claim that Jesus' death-blow is dealt "by an Israelite right hand" (*hupo dexias Israēlitidos*)[49] is in flagrant conflict with Peter's claim in *Acts* that Jesus is killed "by the hands of those outside the law" (*dia cheiros anomōn*).[50] Both cannot be true; Melito's is false.[51]

Conclusions

The whole anti-Semitic tradition that is engendered by Melito, Chrysostom, and others, reveals not only a deep (and complex) vein of Christian malice and bitterness but a gross failure to comprehend the Christians' canonical texts. Like Jesus' killers, all the Christian exegetes and pogromists who spoke of 'Christ-killers' did not know what they were doing (which is not to say that they were innocent).

It is significant for the arc of this book, though, that the African bishop Augustine of Hippo held that the Judaeans who handed Jesus over to Pilate *did not know* he was the Christ, and that Pilate not only interrogated but *sentenced Jesus*.[52] The anti-Semitic vein of passion-interpretation blurs or denies both of Augustine's conclusions.

The African bishop's reading of the Roman trial of Jesus is not only notable for the way in which it forcefully contradicts the Christian myth of Pilate's innocence (as articulated by the African courtier Lactantius, for instance) but for the way in which it splits the Latin concept of 'dominion' (Latin *regnum*). The divine *regnum*, says Augustine, is radically different from "all human dominions" (*omnia regna terrena*).[53] And Augustine believes that this difference—from which, I suggest, the modern concept of secularity circuitously stems—is stated with world-historical clarity and force during the Roman trial of Jesus.

13

"I OBSTRUCT NOT YOUR DOMINION"

AN AFRICAN SERMON THAT SHAPED HISTORY

We rarely hear it, but one of Europe's defining oeuvres is African. I am referring to the gigantic literary corpus of a man Jean-François Lyotard fondly calls "the old prelate of Hippo"—namely Augustine.[1] Born in Thagaste, an "obscure provincial city" of Roman Numidia,[2] Augustine died in Hippo Regius, a flourishing port city on the Numidian coast.[3] An African by birth, Augustine died in Africa, which had been known for centuries as one of Rome's "most opulent provinces".[4] Though modern Europeans have tended to forget Augustine's African provenance, premodern Christians did not.[5]

For instance, when we flick through Honorius of Autun's twelfth-century book *On the Luminaries of the Church*, we note this description: "Augustine, *an African*, bishop of the city of Hippo ... who wrote so much that it is impossible to read it all."[6] Or when we dip into Prosper of Aquitaine's fifth-century *Epitome of Chronicles*, we read this: "Augustine, disciple of the blessed Ambrose, highly eloquent and excelling in doctrine, ordained bishop of Hippo Regius *in Africa*."[7] As this suggests, to Prosper in fifth-century Marseille and Honorius in twelfth-century Regensburg, Augustine was an African.

"The bread of Africa"

It is clear, too, that Augustine was an African to his contemporaries. One of the bishop's correspondents, Quodvultdeus of Carthage, reverently calls him "the bread of Africa".[8] Since Quodvultdeus is an African priest, Augustine's *africanitas* (or 'being-African') marks a common bond.[9]

It is the same for Augustine's friend, Possidius of Calama (now Guelma, Algeria), who wrote a memoir of Augustine. Possidius retraces Augustine's youth, from his birth "in the African province" to his rhetorical chair at "the head of Africa", namely Carthage.[10] Having crossed the sea to Rome and Milan, where he "received the grace of God" in baptism at the hands of Ambrose, Augustine "determined … to return to Africa (*ad Africam*) to his own home and lands".[11] Later, once the Christians of Hippo Regius had forced him to become a priest—while Augustine wept—he is said to have "preached the word of salvation with all confidence against the African heresies *(Africanas haereses)*".[12]

It was due to Augustine's labours in Hippo, according to Possidius, that "the catholic church in Africa began to lift its head".[13] He writes in a panegyric mood that, beginning in Augustine's basilica and rippling "through the whole body of Africa *(per totum Africae corpus)*, the luminous doctrine and sweet savour of Christ was diffused and made manifest, while the church of God across the sea"—meaning, in the first instance, the churches of Rome and Milan—"heard of it and rejoiced with us".[14] This is not the last we will hear of Augustine's influence in Europe. But not all who were "across the sea" rejoiced.

"Do not scorn this Punic man"

One of Augustine's last and fiercest interlocutors is Julian of Eclanum—a young, high-born Italian bishop who held a radical theory of human freedom. For Julian, Augustine's *africanitas* is a sign that he is uncouth and unreliable.[15] And however much one may sympathize with Julian's theories, his anti-African invective is ugly.[16] Julian jeers, in one place, that Augustine is a "Numidian with a small shield" (*Numida cetratus*).[17] But it is Augustine's Punic ancestry that Julian most savagely mocks. He derides Augustine as a "Punic rhetorician", a "Punic philoso-pher", and "Aristotle of the Punics".[18] It is likely the "faithlessness of the Punics" (*Punica perfidia*), a trope that stems from Rome's ancient hostil-ity to Carthage, which inspires Julian's choice of epithet.[19]

It may be a proto-racist slur when Julian asks in one of his texts: "What is so monstrous as what the Punic fellow says?"[20] In his reply, Augustine is terribly calm:

> Do not in your pride over your earthly origin scorn this Punic man (*istum Poenum*) who warns and admonishes you. Do not, after all, suppose that, because you are a son of Apulia, you must conquer the Punic tribe by your tribe (*gente*), though you cannot conquer them by your mind (*mente*) … You cannot escape the Punic opponents so long as you delight in trusting your own virtue. For blessed Cyprian was also a Punic man, and he said: "We must glory in nothing when noth-ing is ours."[21]

No one doubts that something like Augustine's *africanitas* is deni-grated by Julian, who embodies a late antique strain of aristocratic Christian *romanitas* ('being-Roman'). But it is not the urbane Italian bishop, Julian, who shapes the European idea of what it is to be human. On the contrary, it is Augustine the African who is—regrettably or not—one of the most enduring influences on the European idea of human being, desire, and consciousness.

What Prosper, writing in Marseille, says of Christian Africa—for him, as for Julian, the "church beyond the sea" (*ecclesia transmarina*)[22]—could perhaps be said in the *longue durée* of Augustine himself. This is Prosper: "Africa, it is you who pursues the cause of our faith with the greatest zeal … What you decided has been approved by Rome and followed by the empire."[23] That, basically, is the thesis of this book—and of this chapter. What the bishop of an ancient African port city thought and wrote about the Roman trial of Jesus shaped the history of European law and empire.

"We Africans"

But it is first necessary to establish that Augustine, too, felt himself to be African. One of the strongest signs of this is the name given to his natural son by a lover of many years. This boy died young in Augustine's birthplace, Thagaste, and figures in a couple of his early dialogues, *On the Blissful Life* and *On the Teacher*. The boy's name was Adeodatus, which means "given by God" in Latin. It was a common African name, and derives from the Punic Mutunba'al or Iatanbaal—meaning, "gift of Baal" or "Baal has given".[24]

The sense of belonging that Adeodatus' name reflects is one that is still felt by Augustine during his time as a rhetor in the imperial city of Milan. In the climactic book VIII of the *Confessions*, for instance, Augustine recalls that a man he met there was "a fellow citizen, in that he was an African (*in quantum Afer*)".[25] Even in Rome and Milan, as this shows, Augustine—and his son—were Africans.

In one of Augustine's first surviving letters, after his return to Numidia from Italy, he is replying to a cultured pagan named Maximus who sneers at the African names of many of the Christians martyred in the Numidian city of Madauros, circa 180: Miggin, Sanamo, Lucitas, and Namphamo.[26] Maximus calls these names "hateful" (*odiosa*), and Augustine finds this incredible.[27] "Surely you haven't forgotten", he says to Maximus, "to the point of objecting to Punic names, that you are an African writing to Africans (*homo afer scribens Afris*)—since we both find ourselves in Africa."[28] It is reprehensible, Augustine says in another text, for an African to demean other Africans (*inquinat Afer Afros*),[29] though Augustine is of course willing to sharply criticize other Africans.[30]

In one of his late letters, the bishop of Hippo firmly places himself with those he calls "we Africans" (*nobis Afris*).[31] And Augustine—unlike Julian—senses no inborn conflict between *africanitas* and *romanitas*. Augustine is, in his own mind, a *Roman* African. And this sense of cultural and intellectual *romanitas* is so robust that he argues in a sermon he preached after the sack of Rome in 410: "Perhaps Rome isn't perishing, if Romans aren't perishing ... *What is Rome, after all, but Romans?* I mean, we are not concerned with bricks and mortar, with high apartment blocks and extensive city walls."[32]

Of course, it is unlikely that the Romans *of Rome* would have settled for such an 'African' idea of *romanitas*, when the imperial city lay in ruins. All that matters here is that Augustine held himself to be a bearer of *romanitas* in Africa, and a bearer of *africanitas* in the Roman ecumene. As we will see in a moment, the bishop's idea of *christianitas*—on which his reading of the Roman trial of Jesus turns—is formally very close to the idea of *romanitas* that he articulates in this sermon.

"In a wide world"

We now begin to turn to Augustine's world-historical reflection on the Roman trial of Jesus. And the first thing to note is where this reflection is not situated in Augustine's corpus. There is no mention of Jesus' Roman judge, Pilate—or, for that matter, of his Judaean judge, Caiaphas—in Augustine's thousand-page opus, *The City of God against the Pagans*.[33] Late modern historians tend to see *The City of God* as Augustine's core text of political theory, and there is no denying that *The City of God* is a vast effort in what Foucault might have called counter-memory.

In *The City of God*, Augustine reconceives the cultic and political histories of the Roman ecumene in terms of two invisible cities, which, he claims, drive and traverse the histories of all visible cities (Hippo, Rome, Babylon, etcetera). He writes:

> In a wide world, which has always been inhabited by many differing peoples, that have had, in their time, so many different customs, religions, languages, forms of military organization, and clothing, there have, however, only arisen two groups of human beings—groups we call 'cities', according to the special usage of the scriptures.[34]

And what are these 'cities'? Behind the visible screen of global history, Augustine posits (or intuits) the dim presence and cryptic influence of a divine city that is headed by Christ and constituted by a love of eternity, and a human city that is seduced by "Christ's adversary, the devil" and constituted by a love of the *saeculum* or present age.[35]

If the indexes of *The City of God* are any measure, then Jesus' legal ordeals—and the names of Pilate and Caiaphas—have no bearing on the history of Augustine's divine and human cities. That is highly improbable on the face of it. And the reception-history of Augustine's corpus proves, to my mind, that it is incorrect. For beginning in the late medieval period (as we will see in part 5), the central Augustinian text for European political theorists such as Marsilius of Padua is not Augustine's *City of God*, but his *Homilies on the Gospel of John*. Why might this be? The answer is not hard to come by.

"The government of the whole age"

Augustine's interpretation of one of Jesus' sayings in the passion narrative in *John*—"My kingdom is not of this world"[36]—subverts the high-medieval ideology of a universal papal monarchy.[37] That ideology is crystallized in a line written by Pope Innocent III (reigned 1198–1216), who held that Christ "left to Peter"—meaning, to the first occupant of the Roman see—"the government, not only of the universal church, but of the whole world".[38] This is an audacious conception of papal jurisdiction that intellectual historians call—and that Innocent III himself calls, in the letter from which that line comes[39]—the "fullness of power" (*plenitudo potestatis*).[40]

It is fascinating that when Innocent III claims that his jurisdiction covers "the whole world", what he literally writes is that Christ "left to Peter the government … of the whole *age* (*saeculum*)".[41] This high-medieval 'papal monarch' has recourse to the early Christian term-concept of the *saeculum* in the very act of denying the right of any 'secular'—or indeed, of any 'sacred'—jurisdiction to refuse papal interference in a host of matters. And it is the early Christian concept of the *saeculum*—echoed (and nullified) many centuries on by Innocent III—that Augustine asserts, with astonishing force and colour, in his *Homilies on the Gospel of John*. It is for this reason that the critics of 'papal monarchy' cited the *Homilies*—if only indirectly, through commentaries and florilegia—in the late medieval period.

The papacy à la Innocent III was unimaginable when Augustine composed his *Homilies*, and there is no real indication that the late antique bishop had political concerns in mind. The *Homilies* have an ineluctably political dimension, as we will see, since Jesus' death—which they treat—was court-ordered. But Augustine is operating as an exegete in the *Homilies*, not as a polemicist or theorist of 'cities'. That it is not a political intervention, but the interpretation of New Testament texts that makes Augustine politically useful—many centuries on—for the first theorists of European secularity, helps to set the narrative arc of this book.

But it bears repeating that Augustine is an African exegete. A recognizably African contrast between Christ and Caesar—between the mysteries of the church (*ecclesia*) and the rulers of the age (*saeculum*)—

is sharply felt in Augustine's *Homilies*. We can recall, for instance, Tertullian of Carthage's third-century concession that Caesars are "necessary for the world-age (*saeculum*)", but that it may not be possible for Christians to be Caesars.[42] That is not Augustine's belief. Tertullian was a pre-Constantinian hard-liner. Still, the contrastive tone of African writers such as Tertullian (not to mention Donatist writers such as Tyconius) can be heard throughout Augustine's exegesis of the passion in *John*, when compared with commentaries by fourth-century non-African exegetes—John Chrysostom, to name one.

It is in contrast to non-African exegetes—and to the African courtier at Constantine's court, Lactantius—that Augustine insists in a world-historical way on *the guilt of Pontius Pilate*.

"Pilate judged and condemned Jesus"

Augustine thematizes Pilate's guilt in Jesus' death—or, more precisely, the imputability of Jesus' legal ordeal to Rome—even before Pilate meets Jesus on the day of his death. For in *Homily* 112, on Jesus' arrest in a "garden" (uniquely in *John*),[43] Augustine is convinced that the mention of a "cohort" coming out to seize Jesus (uniquely in *John*)[44] means that he must have been taken by Roman troops on the night before his death. (The reference to the cohort in *John*—is it necessarily Roman?—is still a vexed question.)[45] This is Augustine:

> The cohort was not of Judaeans (*non Iudaeorum*), but of [Roman] troops. Therefore, let the cohort be understood to have been received [by the Judaeans] from the governor [Pilate], as though for arresting a criminal, so that, since the order of legitimate jurisdiction was observed ... no one might dare to resist those making the arrest.[46]

On Augustine's reading, the passion of Jesus is—in a formal, juridical sense—a Roman affair. It ends on a Roman cross, and it begins with a Roman arrest. This is crucial for us. And it is crucial, too, to note the care with which Augustine states that "the order of legitimate jurisdiction was observed" (*servato ordine legitimae potestatis*) on the night before Jesus' death.[47] This stress on the legal validity of the proceedings is distinctive and will become crucial in later, legally attuned reconstructions of Jesus' passion—the exemplary case is Dante Alighieri's treatise *Monarchy*, which we will read in chapter 15.

For Augustine, the formal 'legitimacy' of the proceedings is a legal fact—but what matters most, for him, is that it heightens the mystical drama of Jesus' trial and death. "They bound him", says Augustine, "by whom they ought to have wanted to be unbound!"[48] He marvels that Jesus' "power was so hidden" in the garden, and that his "weakness so concealed it", that the juridical operations of Pilate and the Temple courts "*seemed necessary*" to them.

Nevertheless, the bishop reasons, the man they took by force—and then tortured and killed—was one "to whom nothing could have been done unless he himself willed it". It must be said, here, that Augustine's prose-poetic Latin—throughout his *Homilies*—simply cannot be matched in translation. The original of the last phrase I've quoted is *in quem nihil valuisset nisi quod ipse voluisset*.[49] It was not for nothing that Augustine was made an imperial rhetor in Milan, prior to his conversion.

Returning to the passion, though, Augustine transitions at the close of *Homily* 113 from Jesus' high-priestly interrogations in *John* to "the things done concerning the Lord before the governor, Pontius Pilate".[50] Augustine notes—a rare thing, in the patristic corpus—that Pilate is, for Jesus and his Judaean accusers, "a foreign judge" (*alienigenae iudicis*).[51] And his stress, here, falls—in a striking way—on the brotherhood of Jesus and his accusers. The refusal of the Temple elites to cross the threshold of Pilate's court (unique to *John*) invites this gloss from Augustine:

> They were afraid to be contaminated by the praetorium of a foreign judge, and were not afraid to be contaminated by the blood of an inno-cent brother (*fratris innocentis*)—to say only this, for the time being, in which the conscience of evil men was held guilty (*ubi rea malorum conscientia tenebatur*). For that he was also the Lord who was being led to death by their impiety, and that the Giver of Life was being killed, should not be imputed to their conscience, but to ignorance (*non eorum conscientiae, sed ignorantiae deputetur*).[52]

Augustine, in these lines, rejects the Christian myth of 'Christ-killers', and his echoes of *Acts of the Apostles* in this gloss are unmistak-able.[53] Of course, the figures of 'Judaeans' and 'Judaism' are fraught in Augustine's corpus.[54] But Augustine here subverts the Christian myth of undying Judaean blood-guilt. It is not coincidental, then, that Augustine—unlike the high-born Italian bishop who baptized him,

Ambrose—sees Christian laws as protecting late antique Judaeans.[55] Nor is it coincidental that the myth of Judaean blood-guilt is rejected in the medieval European church precisely where Augustine's influence is the strongest.[56]

Jesus' accusers are guilty, in *Homily* 114, of "the death of a just man (*iustum*)"—but not the death of Christ.[57] On Augustine's reading of the passion, the Temple elites and Pilate are innocent of Christ's death—since they act out of ignorance—and guilty of Jesus' death. Yet Jesus is not only an innocent man; he is the "innocent brother" (*fratris innocentis*) of his Judaean accusers.[58] We are certainly meant to think of Cain and Abel. Because of this, Augustine insists that "the gentiles ... put Jesus to death ... by a lesser crime (*minore scelere*) than the Judaeans".[59]

To tabulate Augustine's judicial findings, as it were, in his reading of *John*'s passion:

1. the Judaeans and Romans are *innocent* of the death of Christ, since they act out of ignorance;
2. the Judaeans and Romans are *guilty* of the death of Jesus, since he is known to be a "just man";
3. the Judaeans are *more* guilty than the Romans in the death of Jesus, since he is their "innocent *brother*"—note that Jesus himself says as much, uniquely in *John*'s passion.[60]

But nevertheless, for Augustine—unlike for much of the Christian tradition, from Aristides in the second century to Agamben in the twenty-first:

4. it is Pontius Pilate who *sentences* Jesus to death.

Who is Pilate? "Pilate was a Roman", says Augustine, "and the Romans had sent him to Judaea as governor."[61] This means that, for Augustine—and he is correct—the sentence under which Jesus dies is a Roman sentence.

The passion is *legally*, for Augustine—unlike for many patristic (and post-patristic) commentators—*a thoroughly Roman affair*. On Augustine's reading: Jesus is arrested by the Romans;[62] the Judaeans formally deny before Pilate their legal right "to put anyone to death";[63] and it is Pilate, a "Roman judge" (*iudex Romanus*), who ultimately sentences Jesus to death.[64] Winter is right to conclude, in his "Marginal

Notes on the Trial of Jesus", that Augustine reads the Johannine trial narrative "more carefully" than other early Christian writers.[65]

The moment in *John*'s trial narrative when Jesus' Judaean accusers renounce their legal right to kill him is not, for Augustine, morally convincing—but it is legally significant. In contrast to much of the Christian tradition, Augustine accepts that it is the Roman *imperium* that most brutally tortures, condemns, and kills Jesus. In his *Harmony of the Gospels*, for instance, Augustine recounts the ugly things that were "done to the Lord"—in his words—"by Pilate".[66] And in his *Harmony*, Augustine assigns the crucifixion to *"John*'s narrative of what was done by Pilate."[67] This is how he concludes his reading of the Roman trial in the *Homilies on the Gospel of John*: "Pilate, seated on his dais, judged and condemned Jesus" (*iudicante atque damnante Pilato pro tribunali*).[68]

Augustine holds, contra Lactantius, that Jesus is killed "by the judgement and power of the governor" (*judicio ac potestate praesidis*).[69] And though he notes the vagueness of some of the language, Augustine denies that there is any juridical uncertainty in the canonical passion narratives. Only Roman troops could have crucified Jesus.[70] This of course means that the Christian myth of a Judaean crucifixion could only be—for the bishop of Hippo—a myth. "It is clear", he concludes in *Homily* 118, that Roman troops "obeyed the governor in crucifying Jesus".[71]

"What more do you want?"

It is Augustine's recognition that Jesus' death is ordered by Pilate and inflicted by Roman legionnaires that permits an African, contrastive logic of church and empire to come to the fore in *Homilies* 115 and 116, which will become stock texts (*loci classici*) in certain late medieval circles—and, in that way, will come to figure decisively in the history of secularity.[72]

Augustine is more keenly aware than most exegetes—ancient or modern—that Jesus is killed as an enemy of his *city*, Jerusalem, and of his *empire*, Rome. The charge of Jesus' enmity to Jerusalem is voiced by his Judaean accusers; and the charge of his enmity to Rome is stated on his *titulus* (composed by Pilate) and brutally symbolized by the cross itself. Because Augustine sees this with singular clarity, and is a passionate believer in Jesus' innocence, he is led—beginning in *Homily* 115—to theorize the reign of God and the kingship of Jesus in a way that radically contrasts them with the 'reign' of any human empire and the 'kingship' of any human sovereign. It is striking that Augustine demarcates Jesus' kingship not only from Rome but from Jerusalem. In this way, he is led to separate the jurisdiction of Jesus' mystical body, the church, from that of any human polity in antiquity—which is to say, from any *coercive* polity, any "domination" (*dominatio*).[73]

For what does Jesus say to Pilate, in *John* 18? "My kingdom is not of this world."[74] In the African bishop's Latin, this is *Regnum meum non est de hoc mundo*.[75] Augustine hears, in this, Jesus' legal defence. But he also hears a delineation, by Jesus, of *a novel form of jurisdiction* that renders all other forms of jurisdiction, *eo ipso*, worldly—which is to say, secular. This is how Augustine opens *Homily* 115:

> "My kingdom is not of this world." ... This is what the good teacher (*bonus magister*) wanted us to know. But first, the vain human opinion about his kingdom had to be pointed out, whether that of the gentiles or the Judaeans (from whom Pilate had heard it). As if Jesus had to be punished with death because he had laid claim to an illicit kingdom (*illicitum ... regnum*). For those who are ruling are usually jealous of those who rule and, of course, care had to be taken that his kingdom should not be opposed (*adversum*) either to the Romans or the Judaeans.[76]

Whatever else this reading may be, it is not politically naïve. Augustine suggests that there is only one "human opinion" (*opinio hominum*) concerning Jesus' kingdom, regardless of whether we turn to "the gentiles or the Judaeans". New kings are a threat to human kingdoms, and Jesus is held to be a threat, because—per Augustine—the Romans and Judaeans share the *one human opinion regarding kings and kingdoms*. It is because this opinion is shared by Jesus' Judaean accusers and his Roman judge that they eye each other—and not only him—with 'jealousy' (*invidentia*). To my mind, this is a commendably hard-headed reading of the text—and of the politics of law.

But if Augustine is right, what Jesus "wanted us to know" (*scire nos voluit*) is that his Roman judge and his Judaean accusers are unenlightened.[77] The "human opinion" about kingdoms that the Roman and Jerusalem elites share is—on Augustine's reading—"vain" (*vana*). But it is only "vain" because Jesus—the accused—is a king. Augustine is so convinced of this that he impersonates Jesus—a taciturn witness in the canonical gospels—in a striking passage that, in strange and circuitous ways, comes to influence the history of European legal thought. This, per the bishop of Hippo, is Jesus' reply to Pilate: "Hear, Judaeans and gentiles! ... Hear, all human dominions! I obstruct not your dominion in this world. 'My kingdom is not of this world.' ... What more do you want? Come to the kingdom which is not of this world; come by believing ..."[78] The question this 'Jesus' poses to the rulers of the age is as peremptory in Latin as it is in English: "What more do you want?" (*quid vultis amplius?*).[79] The medieval opponents of papal monarchy are right to sense that this patristic question—which is ascribed, rhetorically, to Jesus—is one that the high-medieval popes could never pose to the non-clerical rulers of Europe. It is precisely *secular rule* that the first theorists of European secularity, quoting this sermon by Augustine, will later assert.

Returning to Augustine, though, we see that he quickly reverts to his own voice, now glossing what Jesus—through him—has said to all the rulers of this world-age. "'Come to the kingdom which is not of this world; come by believing ...'", says his Jesus. To clarify which, the bishop asks: "For what is Christ's kingdom but *those believing in him*?"[80] There is an arresting echo, here, of Augustine's question after the sack of Rome in the early fifth century. "What is Rome", he asks in *Sermon* 81, "but *Romans?*"[81] And here in *Homily* 115—to read it one more time—he asks: "What is Christ's kingdom but *those believing in him?*"[82]

Neither question is exhaustive—of the idea of Rome or the reign of God—but the formal resemblance is still, I think, suggestive. Augustine's first question is put to a people, or a collection of peoples—'the Romans'—who are *suddenly bereft of an imperial city*. And the second question is meant to limn the contours of a people, or a collection of peoples—'the Christians'—who are *permanently bereft of a terrestrial city*. The situation in which Romans find themselves *after the collapse of their 'eternal city'*, I mean to say, is the situation in which Christians find themselves *in the inaugural scenes of their 'eternal city'*. What is a reign without a city? Perhaps we could say: a *church*. (We see this in the first line of *I Clement*: "The church of God which *sojourns in* Rome to the church of God which *sojourns in* Corinth ...")[83] But

Augustine's church is not the impossible, ideal city of Plato's *Republic*—though some of Augustine's contemporaries read him in that way.[84]

"A foreigner in the world"

There are intimations of a novel concept of jurisdiction in Augustine's lines on the Roman trial of Jesus, and the medieval and early modern philosophers who first theorize 'secularization' will note them (as we will see in part 5). But titanic conflicts and centuries-long processes lie hidden in the fact that Augustine stresses, in his *Homilies on the Gospel of John*, that Jesus does *not* say (à la Plato): "My kingdom is not *in* this world." What Jesus says, rather, is that his kingdom "is not *of* this world". The African bishop clarifies:

> Jesus did not say, "But now my kingdom" is not *here*, but "is not *from here*." For his kingdom *is here* to the very end of the world-age (*saeculi*) ... For the harvest is the end of the world-age (*saeculi*), when the harvesters—that is, the angels—will come and remove out of his kingdom all scandals. And this certainly would not happen if his kingdom were not here—but nevertheless, it is not *from here*, for it is a foreigner in the world.[85]

What could it mean, to testify to a kingdom in the world that is "a foreigner in the world"? There is a beautiful passage in one of Augustine's sermons on the *Psalms* where he recognizes that many of us ask, in life: "What good is my innocence?"[86] This is a real question. Innocence is often worthless—or worse—if we want to "flourish in the world-age (*in saeculo*)", Augustine says in this sermon. (In Geoffrey Hill's line: "Innocence is no earthly weapon.")[87] But Augustine then asks, rhetorically: If 'flourishing in this world-age' were the highest and most desirable thing, "would not your Lord himself have flourished in this world-age (*in hoc saeculo*)?" For believers, of course, the answer is yes. Jesus could have flourished here—and he did not.

Augustine traces out the logic of this—a form of reasoning that only holds within the horizons of Christian faith. Christians can only conclude, says Augustine, that Jesus *chose* not to reveal his power "in this world-age". (Note well—this piece of late antique theological reasoning will become a forceful *political* argument in early modern texts by Hobbes and Pufendorf.) Augustine means by this that Jesus chose "to hide" (*latere*) in his time on earth, and to say to Pontius Pilate ... "My kingdom is not of this world." Therefore, here, your Lord was hidden. And all good persons are hidden here (*omnes boni latent hic*), because their good is *within* them. It is *hidden*. It is in the heart, where faith, love, and hope are—where the "treasure" of good persons is. Are these good things apparent in the world-age (*in saeculo*)? No, they are hidden—and their *reward* is hidden.[88]

It seems to belong to the destiny of the church, in Augustine's thought, to testify to how much good is hidden in this world, and will only be revealed—if it is to be revealed—in a world-age to come.

"Judgements humans pronounce upon humans"

Of course, it is not only "good things" (*bona*) that are hidden in the church. No twenty-first-century reader will miss the aptness of Augustine's choice of words when he says that there will be "scandals" (*scandala*) in the church to "the very end of the world-age (*saeculum*)". Some might ask whether there will be anything *but* scandals in the churches till whatever end comes that we await or dread or posit.

What matters most for us here is the idea of 'secular' justice that is intimated by this picture. Human justice is 'secular', for Augustine, because it is practised *in the absence of true, divine judgement*. 'Secular' justice is, by definition, *imperfect justice*. And the church is a symbol—a presence—in the world of a reign in which *a higher mode of justice is promised*, one that is not of this world-age.

Augustine does not thematize 'secular' justice in the *Homilies*, but he writes powerfully on what he calls "the ignorance of the judge" (*ignorantia iudicis*) in *The City of God*. This is a form of ignorance that, Augustine says, "frequently involves an innocent person in suffering". He is likely referring to the practice of judicial torture in late antiquity.[89] This is a part of Roman legal culture that Augustine notes in passing in *Homily* 115, when he refers to the "injuries that Pilate and his cohort inflicted on Christ"—not after Pilate's judgement, but during Jesus' trial.[90] This judicial torture of Jesus is salient, too, in a couple of early modern legal treatises we will unearth in chapter 19. But the deeper point is that Augustine holds that human, 'secular' judgements—the grim system of courts, and sentences, and punishments—are "necessary in cities". And who could deny this now? They are necessary. But the hard-headed bishop, whose *divine city* is first revealed in the judicial murder of an innocent man (whom Augustine holds to be God), is under no illusion. 'Secular' verdicts are the "judgements humans pronounce upon humans" (*iudicia hominum de hominibus*).[91] As such, they are fallible—and often cruel.

What is 'secular' justice? Most human judgements remain—in Augustine's words—"melancholy and lamentable". They derive not only from human laws and insights but from human ignorance and prejudice. Divine or perfect judgements, they are not—and it is not only in the church that scandals are ineliminable to "the very end of the world-age (*saeculum*)". Secular order is scandalous, too. It is with his eye on human empires—on the machinery of 'secular' governance—that Augustine says in *City of God* XIX that the half-blind imposition of human 'justice' is "a thing to be mourned and, if it were possible, washed away with fountains of tears".[92] He is not referring, here, to the death of Jesus in *John*—but to the deaths of numberless others who never had, or have, any hope of 'secular' justice.

"A great mockery, a great mystery"

Augustine is not only a theorist of the tragic deeps of 'secular' justice. He realizes, too, that much of what passes for human justice is dark comedy. There is a terrific moment in *Homily* 117 in which Augustine shows how Jesus' Roman trial—and even his death—can be seen as gruesomely funny, as a wicked joke staged by Roman justice.[93]

Crucifixion jokes were common in Jesus' day.[94] And Augustine seems to be conscious of the low theatricality of the trial when Pilate and his legionnaires get Jesus up like a slave-convict with a king complex. Pilate offers Jesus to the mob in *John* like a sadistic compere, saying: "Look, the man!" (*Ecce homo*).[95] (See fig. 10.)

Augustine sees how Jesus' disgrace "seethes and cooks" in this scene.[96] The Nazarene is a legal non-entity in Jerusalem, and he is satirized as a deluded claimant to "royal power" (*regiae potestatis*).[97] That phrase—"royal power"—will be crucial for us in the next chapter.

But Augustine is not finished. "Jesus went to the place where he was to be crucified", he says in *Homily* 117, "bearing his own cross." This is a "great spectacle" (*grande spectaculum*), he confesses—but a duplicitous one. As in most trials and executions, it is not entirely clear *who the convict is*. Where some see "a great mockery" (*grande ludibrium*), says Augustine, others will perceive "a great mystery" (*grande mysterium*). "When impiety sees this", he goes on, "it laughs that the 'king' carries a piece of wood on which he will be punished, instead of a rod symbolizing kingly power."[98] The *via dolorosa* has always been, for many, a *via jocosa*.

The Christian idea that the Son of God "is worsted by the devil and punished by him" during the passion is just "ludicrous", Celsus concludes.[99] For this second-century philosopher, the incarnation and passion have the same feel as Old Comedy.[100] Celsus notes that in the gospels, unlike a tragedy by Euripides, "the one who condemned" Jesus to death—Pilate—"did not even suffer any such fate as that of Pentheus by going mad or being torn in pieces". On the contrary, he says, Jesus permitted his tormenters to "put a purple robe round him and the crown of thorns and the reed in his hand"—like the butt of a joke by Aristophanes.[101] A scene from Plautus, if I may, scripted by Pilatus. And it may be in light of such critiques in the first centuries CE that, at the centre of Augustine's reading of the Roman trial in *John*, we find the questions: With *whom* is one to laugh? And *when* is one to laugh?

As Augustine senses, a host of conflicting ironies seems to be inscribed in the text of *John*. The gospel-writer seems (or his editors seem) to have calculated—and Augustine to have intuited—that the comedy or mystery of Jesus' torment and death will be determined by what the reader believes. And what do the Christians of Hippo Regius see, in late antiquity, as Jesus staggers up his gibbet hill? "The king bearing the wood for himself to be fastened on, *which he was going to fasten on the foreheads of kings*."[102] What is the reference here? As Joseph Vogt reminds us, a cross-shaped "monogram with the name of Christ" appears on the helmet of Constantine in the early fourth century and is a common motif on coins and statues of later Christian emperors.[103]

I wonder whether Augustine's line elicited laughter—or a shout—from his congregants in Hippo.[104] And I wonder, too, who is laughing now. In any event, Augustine alludes in this brilliantly constructed line to the mystery of the church—and the history of empire.[105] Which brings us to the letters of an African pope.

14

"THERE ARE TWO"

AN AFRICAN LETTER THAT SHAPED HISTORY

Sometime in the early sixth century, a cleric in the papal archives at
Rome, or *scrinium*, wrote the following in a document called, simply,
The Book of Popes:

> Gelasius, of African nationality, son of Valerius, held the See for four
> years, eight months and eighteen days. He was bishop in the times of
> King Theodoric and Emperor [Anastasius].[1] ... He was one who loved
> the poor, and he increased the numbers of clergy. He freed the Roman
> populace from danger of famine. He made a constitution concerning
> the entire church.[2]

This entry is a catalogue of differences. When we read that Pope
Gelasius I, who reigned from 492 to 496, is "one who loved the poor"
(literally "a lover of the poor", *amator pauperum*),[3] we can infer—though
whoever wrote this may not have meant to convey—that not every
pope exhibits this love.[4] Gelasius "shone with such mercy", we read in
a letter written after his death, that he not only concerned himself with
the poor but chose to "die poor himself".[5] And when we read that
Gelasius "made a constitution concerning the entire church" (*fecit constitutum de omni ecclesia*),[6] we can conclude that not every pope issues
such a constitution. Here, the reference seems to be to one of Gelasius'
letters known as the *General Decree*.

157

The *General Decree* has been a notable source of premodern European law since it circulated, with many of Gelasius' hundred-odd papal letters—or as he called them, "decretal letters"—in an influential legal corpus called the *Dionysian Collection*.[7] This collection of papal rulings was made by a learned monk from the Black Sea region, Dionysius Exiguus, who died in Rome—where he had come at Gelasius' behest.[8] Despite the self-effacing sobriquet (*Exiguus* means "the Little"), Dionysius is not a negligible figure in intellectual history.

One indication of this is the fact that the number of the year in which this book is printed is taken, in convoluted ways, from Dionysius' computation of Jesus' birth- and death-years.[9] The dates we keep in this twenty-first century after the—variously calculated— "year of our Lord's incarnation" (*anno incarnationis Domini*) were not devised in Jacobin Paris or Bolshevik Moscow. The computation of twenty-first-century time, including the designation of this century as 'twenty-first', begins in a sixth-century cloister. The index of European modernity is indelibly premodern and Christian. This is why Nietzsche ends *The Anti-Christ* by designating 30 September 1888 "according to the false calculation of time"—read, according to Dionysius Exiguus' calculation of time—the "first day of year one", by which he means, the first day *after* the end of the Christian Era.[10]

The literally epochal debt that we owe to Dionysius is not a distraction. For my argument in this chapter is that certain lines written in the late fifth century by Gelasius, the pope who called Dionysius to Rome, shape the legal cultures of Europe and many of its former colonies in the early twenty-first century. Like Dionysius' computation of the date of Jesus' birth and death, the lines written by Gelasius are utterly forgotten; but this is no reason to believe that they are irrelevant. Cultural memory is not a sovereign measure of history.

"He made a constitution"

My claim in this chapter is that Gelasius not only "made a constitution concerning the entire church"[11] but that he helped—through the vagaries of a history I will sketch in rough strokes in part 5—to make a *sort of* constitution for the whole of Europe (which, as of this writing, notoriously lacks a ratified constitution). Of course, I have worded this provocatively, but the claim is not contentious.

In his *European Legal History*, Randall Lesaffer foregrounds one of Gelasius' letters (which we will glance at presently) in his sketch of late medieval "secularization".[12] And Lesaffer is merely reflecting a scholarly consensus. Writing in the mid-twentieth century, Francis Dvornik—who rejects the idea that Gelasius is a disruptive figure—concedes that Gelasius' formulations of imperial and papal jurisdiction set the arc of late medieval political theory.[13] One medievalist is tempted to see political theory in Europe, from the eighth to the thirteenth centuries, as nothing but a system of "glosses on, and reactions to, Gelasius".[14] That is hyperbolic, but not meaningless: Gelasius is a critical figure in the history of European politics and law.

But what historians have failed to interrogate is the first element in the sentences on Gelasius in *The Book of Popes*. For how does that entry begin? Gelasius is remembered there as a pope "of African nationality" (*natione Afer*).[15] Like Augustine, Gelasius is an African. And Augustine's influence on Gelasius is a stock observation in the literature.[16] "Gelasius", per Peter Brown, "was an Augustinian."[17] Yet there is no mention of Gelasius in, say, R. A. Markus's *Saeculum*—a path-breaking treatment of the African influence on Augustine's concepts of church and empire.[18] And though it is common for Gelasius to figure in histories of late medieval 'secularization', it is by no means common for Gelasius' role in that history to be *linked* to the fact that he, like Augustine, is an African. Remarkably, this is a link that seems not to have been made.

"Of African nationality"

Since I stress Gelasius' *africanitas*, it is necessary to ask how certain we can be that Gelasius *is* an African, and how much we can *infer* from that claim in Gelasius' entry in *The Book of Popes*. According to the most recent editors of Gelasius' letters, Bronwen Neil and Pauline Allen, there is no reason to doubt his *africanitas*. To be sure, *The Book of Popes* is a much-copied composite text that was augmented (and altered) by countless hands in numerous scriptoria (and printing houses) over many centuries. It is impermissible to assume that any given line in the *Book* is historically reliable; critical reconstruction is a necessity. That caveat being made, *The Book of Popes* seems to be a formal chronicle that emanates from the papal archives,[19] and the "earliest redaction" of the *Book*—per Neil and Allen—seems to date back to the early sixth century. The oldest lines on the late-fifth-century pope Gelasius—including the words, "of African nationality"— were "thus written within living memory of Gelasius' pontificate".[20] The note on Gelasius' *africanitas* seems to be original and credible. But what can we take it to mean?

The sense of Gelasius' *africanitas* is debated in the literature, not least because the pope describes himself in a letter as "Roman born" (*Romanus natus*).[21] How can a 'Roman-born' pope be of 'African nationality'? Opinions differ. Gelasius may have been born in Africa as a Roman citizen; or he may have been born in Rome as a son of Africans. (Whether he may have been a person of colour is a question that seems not to have interested the papal archivists in late antiquity; it thus cannot interest us.) What is not in doubt is that Gelasius, the first pope to have been called the "vicar of Christ",[22] is securely attested as a Roman *and* an African. As with Augustine, there is no discernible conflict between Gelasius' *romanitas* and his *africanitas*.

"I love and respect the Roman emperor"

The letter we will glance at in a moment is one that Gelasius sent from his papal court in Rome to Anastasius I at his imperial court in Constantinople.[23] We may recall from the chapter's opening that Gelasius was bishop of Rome—meaning pope—"in the times of King Theodoric and Emperor [Anastasius]".[24] The difference in titulature, in this line of *The Book of Popes*, is world-historical. For the Balkan-born ruler of Constantinople, Anastasius,[25] is called emperor (or literally, "majestic one", *augustus*).[26] But the Ostrogothic ruler of the Italian peninsula, Theodoric, who held court in the northern city of Ravenna (where his decagonal tomb can still be seen),[27] is called king (*rex*). This is a title for non-Roman rulers in Roman chronicles, such as the "kings of the Franks" (*Francorum regibus*) in Ammianus Marcellinus' *History*.[28]

The letter that concerns us in this chapter is penned in the year 494 by Gelasius, a pope whose bishopric falls within *a post-imperial kingdom* of the Italian peninsula. Yet this post-imperial kingdom is not exactly post-Roman (or 'barbarian'), since its regent, Theodoric, came of age at the court in Constantinople (or in the words of one of his bishop-panegyrists, "in the lap of civilization");[29] and since Theodoric's laws—like Gelasius' decrees—were promulgated in Latin.[30]

During Gelasius' papacy, the imperial power of Constantinople (New Rome)[31] is only fitfully and obliquely felt in Gelasius' episcopal city (Rome). In other words, Gelasius is one of the first bishops of Rome to live with a Romanized *monarch*, but not a Roman *emperor*, in the Latin-speaking core of the Christianized empire.[32] (The imperial court had left Rome for Milan and Ravenna—and other cities—long before Gelasius' time.) The collapse of the Latin empire is commonly dated to the dethronement of Romulus Augustus—or Augustulus, meaning "boy Augustus"—by a Hun warlord, Odoacer, in the year 476. That is less than twenty years before our African pope pens his letter to the emperor in Constantinople.[33] It is imperative to reckon, then, with the fact that Gelasius is one of the first post-imperial bishops of Rome (*sensu lato*).[34]

But Gelasius is not only intricated in the collapse—or rupture—of the Latin imperium.[35] His papacy is epochal because Gelasius, first as secretary to Pope Felix III, and then as pope,[36] deepens a fissure between the bishoprics of the old Rome and the new Rome.[37] What I call a 'fissure' is a thirty-five-year schism that began with Felix III's excommunication of the patriarch of Constantinople, Acacius, in the year 484. Throughout his brief but energetic pontificate, Gelasius steelily refuses to revoke the condemnation of Acacius. And though the Acacian Schism (as it is called) will be brought to a close in the early sixth century[38]—after Gelasius' death—it belongs to a depressing history of incomprehension, intransigence, and brutality that leads to an irreparable breach between the churches of Rome and Constantinople in the mid-eleventh century.[39] By 1203 and 1204, European "crusaders" who had been disavowed by Pope Innocent III in 1202 felt free to burn and raze Constantinople, the city of the first Christianizing emperor.[40]

Of course, Gelasius is nothing like a war criminal or a fomenter of war. He is not remotely culpable for crimes that postdate him by many centuries. "I love, cherish, and respect the Roman emperor", is how he writes to the imperial court at Constantinople in the late fifth century.[41] But Gelasius is a salient figure in the early history of a post-imperial fissure that is still, sadly, observable today in the wary, half-fraternal gestures of twenty-first-century Catholic and Orthodox hierarchs,[42] and in the weird, half-political hostility that hums between London and Moscow, Belgrade and Rome. The conflict between Rome and the New Rome is by no means dead—though the New Rome is.

Power and authority

What is it that Gelasius writes from his papal court in the lands of a non-Roman *rex*, to a Roman *augustus* at his imperial court in the New Rome? What is the world-historical idea—or, if the idea itself is not the African pope's, then *the world-historical form of words*—that he conveys from Rome to Constantinople? Words without which the political history of Rome—and thus, of Europe (and many of its former colonies)—cannot be reconstructed, though this is perhaps not true of Constantinople (and many of its former territories)?

This form of words could not be simpler. Gelasius writes in Latin *duo sunt*. This means in English, "there are two". If roughly a century of historiography can be trusted—most recently, Gilbert Dagron's consummate monograph *Emperor and Priest*—the history of empire is altered by Gelasius' cool insistence that "there are two".[43]

How could such a formal, minimal claim ignite centuries of legal reflection and political contestation in Europe (but not in what modern historians call Byzantium)? Gelasius' intent in this letter is to remind Anastasius that the condemnation of Constantinople's former patriarch, Acacius, concerns a matter of church doctrine—and thus, is a matter of church jurisdiction. The Roman *augustus* has no jurisdiction in matters of doctrine, Gelasius insists. No Caesar is competent to clarify the "venerable mysteries" that are celebrated, and promulgated, by the church.[44] It is nothing but "human presumption" for a Caesar, whose supremacy in imperial matters is secure, to assert himself in matters that touch "the ordinances established by divine judgement" within the church.[45] Only officers of the church, Gelasius warns, can heal the schism—or fissure—in the church. The "august emperor", as he calls Anastasius, is utterly powerless when it comes to the order or symbols of "the worship of the divinity".[46]

The condemnation of Acacius, according to Gelasius, is a matter for "the overseers of religion" (*religionis antistites*).[47] It cannot be lifted by one "who rules in this world-age" (*qui imperas saeculo*).[48] Naturally, one "who rules in this world-age" is contrasted, by Gelasius, with the one who rules "in perpetuity" and "in the future"—namely Christ, whose vicar Gelasius is.[49]

This is what Gelasius means when he writes to Anastasius, *duo sunt*—"there are two". A thirty-five-year conflict between the pontiffs of Rome and Constantinople—which is now a dim memory for the pontiffs of Rome and Constantinople (currently Francis I and Bartholomew I)—could not be adjudicated by the ruler of a centuries-dead empire. At first glance, there is nothing here that is not otiose. But that is a misimpression.

Recall the observation with which I opened chapter 11. 'Religion' (*religio*) is not structurally or symbolically related, in pre-Christian Roman law, to the 'secular' (*saecularis*)—as it is in modern European law. Yet in Gelasius' letter to Anastasius, which circulated for hundreds of years as a crucial legal document, we note a formal and institutional bifurcation of 'religion' and the 'secular'. Gelasius holds that the church is a divinely circumscribed jurisdiction of "religion" (*religio*),[50] and that the empire is a divinely circumscribed jurisdiction of one who only rules in this "world-age" (*saeculum*).[51]

When Gelasius writes calmly, in the fifth century, that "there are two"—*duo sunt*—he is formulating a legal claim that Rousseau is still resisting in the eighteenth century, when, in the last pages of the *Social Contract*, he castigates the church because it "led to the state's ceasing to be one (*cessa d'être un*)".[52] Gelasius is a salient figure in the European history of "the state's ceasing to be one". And though the words post-date him by 1,250 years, Gelasius certainly holds that Christians are subject to—in Rousseau's words—"*two* legislations" (human and divine), "*two* sovereigns" (imperial and ecclesiastical), "*two* fatherlands" (temporal and eternal).[53]

Which finally brings us to the fulgurous lines that give this chapter its title. This is Gelasius: "There are two ways, august emperor, in which this world (*mundus hic*) is chiefly ruled: the sacred authority of the priests (*auctoritas sacra pontificum*), and the royal power (*regalis potestas*)."[54] Gelasius' assignation of 'authority' (*auctoritas*) to ecclesiastical rulers and 'power' (*potestas*) to imperial (and post-imperial) rulers may echo a pre-Christian lexicon of Roman governance. There are already hints in Augustan texts that *auctoritas* is a numinous power that inheres in certain persons (or offices) and is actualized by the 'faith' (*fides*) of those who recognize it; and that *potestas* is a concrete power that can actualize the 'force of law' (*vis legis*).[55] But whatever the sources of Gelasius' terminology, late medieval and early modern theorists of 'secularity' theorize—in his wake—sacred *authority* as a mode of persuasion, and secular *power* as a right to coercion.

And whatever Gelasius' idea of sacred authority, he stresses that it is no threat to the emperor's secular power. In much the same way that Jesus says to Pilate in Augustine's *Homilies on the Gospel of John*, "I obstruct not your dominion in this world",[56] Gelasius says to Anastasius:

> It is certain, emperor, that in your laws you suffer nothing to vanish from the name of Rome, nor do you permit damage to be inflicted ... Indeed, august emperor, if someone were to attempt something against the laws of the government (*leges publicas*)—may it never be!—you would be incapable of allowing it for any reason.[57]

Of course, this is a reasoned move. If Anastasius will not let the name of Rome be diminished, queries Gelasius, then how could he "permit someone"—meaning Acacius—"to inflict loss on religion, on truth, on the integrity of the catholic communion and faith"?[58] If the name of Rome must be honoured, *how much more* must the name of God be honoured? This is a reasoned move. And in much of the early medieval tradition, Gelasius is read as a theorist of papal supremacy—and ultimately, of the papal monarchy. But that is a misinterpretation of Gelasius' letter, which is corrected, to my mind, in some of the late medieval texts we will read in part 5. Gelasius believes that his insistence on "the sacred authority of priests" in Rome *is not a threat* to "the laws of the government" in the New Rome.

This can only be formally coherent if, as Gelasius asserts—and as Hobbes, in chapter 17, will deny—there are "*two ways* ... in which this world is chiefly ruled".[59] The concept of 'secularity' is tied, in immensely complicated ways, to Gelasius' insistence—which derives, I believe, from the African church of the first Christian centuries—that the authority of *religio* differs from, but is not a threat to, the power of the *saeculum*.[60]

Gelasius inherits his conviction that "there are two" from Augustine, who can write in a letter of 401 CE that ecclesiastical verdicts made by a "council of Africa" (*Africae concilio*) cannot be annulled "by the secular powers (*saeculares potestates*) or by any use of violence (*violentias*)".[61] This African terminology of 'secular powers' is cited in some of Gelasius' earliest writings, when he was still secretary of the papal chancery of Felix III.[62] And in one of the letters he composed for Felix, it is eye-catching that Gelasius pleads with a "Christian Emperor", Zeno (died 491), not to violate the integrity of the universal church "which endured much among *those who crucified the Saviour*".[63] Who, for Gelasius, are "those who crucified the Saviour"?

In most Christian texts—Greek and Latin, ancient and medieval— "those who crucified the Saviour" would refer to the Judaeans. But in this fifth-century papal letter, it unmistakably refers to *the pagans*. The church has survived the depredations of a pre-Christian empire, Gelasius reasons in this letter to Zeno. It should hope for more respect from the head of a Christian empire. I take this to mean that Gelasius not only inherits Augustine's terminology of 'secular powers' (unheard of in the pre-Christian empire) but his interpretation of the Roman trial of Jesus.

It is the African prelates Augustine and Gelasius, I believe, who transmit to medieval clerics and legal theorists in Europe a lexicon of 'secular power', and an interpretation of the Roman trial of Jesus that will be cited and reconceived, between the fourteenth and the eighteenth centuries, in continent-shaping ways.[64] Letters written in the chancery of the late antique Roman church, during Gelasius' secretaryship and papacy, are *legal texts* of great importance in medieval and late medieval Europe. It has gone unnoticed that the Augustinian concepts in those letters may reflect the fact that Gelasius, like Augustine, is a prelate "of African nationality".[65]

Conclusions

Beginning with Gratian (reigned 367–83), Christian emperors had renounced the pagan imperial title of "supreme pontiff" (*pontifex maximus*); and as bishop of Rome, Gelasius I would have been styled "highest pontiff" (*summus pontifex*).[66] This is why Gelasius in Rome can write to Anastasius in the New Rome, "there are two".[67] And this is why Justinian I, in his sixth-century incipit to the *Body of Roman Law*, can call himself devout, fortunate, victorious, and majestic—but not supreme pontiff.[68]

It is Gelasius who theorizes this change in titulature as one of the sharpest breaks in Roman history—and the history of empire *tout court*. "Before the coming of Christ", Gelasius writes in his text *On the Bond of an Anathema*, pagan monarchs

> were called emperors (*imperatores*) and supreme pontiffs (*maximi pontifices*). But when the true King and Pontiff came, the emperor no longer took the name of pontiff for himself, nor did the pontiff claim the royal dignity ... For Christ, mindful of human frailty and of what would lead to human salvation, ordered things by a marvellous dispensation. Desiring his own to be saved by a curative humility and not corrupted again by human pride, he divided the offices of the two powers (*officia potestatis utriusque discrevit*) in keeping with their own functions and different dignities, so that Christian emperors would need pontiffs for eternal life (*aeterna vita*), and pontiffs would use imperial policies in the course of temporal things (*temporalium cursu rerum*).[69]

The logic of the new Christian dispensation, says Gelasius, is this. Officers of the Roman church will not entangle themselves in "secular affairs" (*negotiis saecularibus*), and officers of the Roman Empire will not "govern the divine things (*rebus divinis*)". It is by the Christians' division of sacred and secular—or rather, by *Christ's* division of sacred and secular—that a "decency of both orders" (*modestia utriusque ordinis*) can be cultivated.[70] The "decency of both orders" is a rare or non-existent thing in European history, but this African pope's lines pre-delineate a late medieval theory that we can meaningfully call 'secularity'.

Fig. 11: *Image of Lucifer in Dante's* Inferno, by Cornelis Galle the Younger
(after Cigoli, after Jan van der Straet), circa 1595.

Fig. 12: Detail of Galle's *Image of Lucifer in Dante's* Inferno. Note Vergil ("V") carrying Dante ("D") on his back, in two locations, in the foreground. They are just beginning to make their descent into hell. I hazard no conjectures but cannot resist observing that Galle's 1595 engraving bears an eerie resemblance to Abraham Bosse's 1651 etching in the front of Thomas Hobbes's *Leviathan* (see fig. 13).

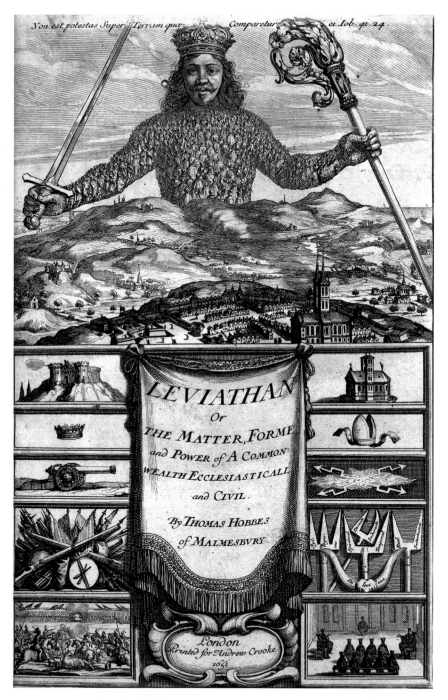

Fig. 13: *Title page of* Leviathan, or the Matter, Form, and Power of a Commonwealth, Ecclesiastical and Civil, *by Thomas Hobbes*, by Abraham Bosse (in consultation with Hobbes), 1651.

Fig. 14: Detail of *Leviathan*'s title page. The motto reads, in the Douay-Rheims translation of *Job* 41:24, from the Latin Vulgate: "There is no power upon earth that can be compared with him." The bishop's crozier is held, here, by the monarch of a modern Protestant state.

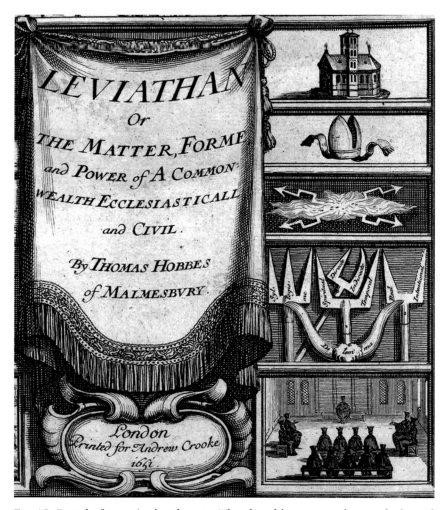

Fig. 15: Detail of *Leviathan*'s title page. The church's courts and councils, logical instruments (and thus, doctrines), powers of condemnation, sacred offices, and properties and assets—reading the images, here, from bottom to top—fall under the control and jurisdiction of a modern Protestant monarch.

Fig. 16: *Portrait of Samuel von Pufendorf*, by Johann Ulrich Kraus, before 1719.

Fig. 17: *Two images of Constantine I with a two-headed eagle*, by Antonio Tempesta, before 1630. The Christianizing emperor, Constantine, is doubled to keep symmetry with a majestic, bicephalous creature. This regal emblem of a two-headed eagle antedates Constantine by many centuries and signifies many things, but Jean-Jacques Rousseau sees it as a symbol of the splitting of European sovereignty—the uncoupling of state power and church authority—which is first dramatized in the Roman trial of Jesus.

Fig. 18: *Christ III*, by Lodewijk Schelfhout, 1919.

PART 5

THE GREAT REFUSAL

15

"I BEHELD THE SHADE"

A REAL TRIAL AND A FAKE DONATION

It is strange that Pontius Pilate is not one of the moody, all-too-human dead that we meet in Dante's *Inferno*. Or is he? In canto III, a swooning Dante and a cold-blooded Vergil are at the gates of hell. They have not yet descended in. (See figs. 11 and 12.)

This is the undecided ground where the newly dead idle before they come to the place of torment. Here, the lost are past all hope, but they have not yet been driven down the coils of the damned. And it is here that Dante sees one of the most mysterious figures in the *Divine Comedy*.

This figure is not unknown to Dante, and that is part of the mystery. Dante knows who it is that he catches sight of, and he tells us that he knows. But he does not tell us who it is. This is what we read:

> I would not have thought
> death had undone so many. When more than one
>
> I recognized had passed, I beheld the shade
> of him who made the great refusal, impelled
> by cowardice.[1]

Who is the coward? He is disowned by the powers of heaven and hell, but he is not unpunished. He is "galled by wasps and flies"—sunk in a cloud of stinging insects—and confined to a dead zone where the

169

lost await their dooms.[2] This must in some coded way symbolize his life (though Dante says, weirdly, that this man belonged to a "dreary guild" of those who were "never alive").[3] And what is "the great refusal" (*il gran rifiuto*)?[4] If we knew that, we would know who made it. But Dante tells us nothing more.

Early theories of the great refusal

The commentary tradition on this scene is intricate and conflicted. One of Dante's sons, Jacopo Alighieri, was the first to comment on *Inferno* III. According to Jacopo, the one who made the great refusal must be Celestine V—a pope who abdicated in the year 1294 (with Dante composing most of the *Inferno* between 1306 and 1308).[5] Papal abdication is an apocalyptically rare thing. The shock of Benedict XVI's abdication in the winter of 2013 is still a source of brooding and melancholy in parts of the Church of Rome—and even in some political circles. Celestine V's renunciation of Peter's see struck most of his contemporaries—and, it seems, Dante—as a monstrosity.

But one of Dante's other sons, Pietro Alighieri, rejects the Celestine theory in his *Comment on Dante's Poem the Comedy*. For Pietro, the one who made the great refusal must be Diocletian—a Roman emperor who abdicated in the year 305.[6] (It is Diocletian's successor, Galerius, who made Maximin Daia—promulgator of the *Memoirs of Pilate*—a Caesar in 305.)[7] The symmetry is clear: Celestine renounced the highest office in the Roman church, and Diocletian renounced the highest office in the Roman Empire. For Dante's sons, and for most fourteenth-century Europeans, no greater renunciations could be imagined.

Other early commentators on the *Inferno* such as Guglielmo Maramauro,[8] Benvenuto da Imola,[9] and novelist Giovanni Boccaccio (whose *Decameron* is still ravishing readers)[10] thought Dante must have had in mind the biblical patriarch Isaac's son, Esau, who sold his birthright for a cup of "red pottage" in the book of *Genesis*.[11] None of these conjectures is thoroughly convincing, to my mind. But the renunciations of Isaac's blessing (Esau), and Caesar's power (Diocletian), and Peter's authority (Celestine) are the early and recurring ones. They have a sort of canonical status in Dante commentaries until the late nineteenth century.[12]

A Renaissance Platonist reads the great refusal

The most sophisticated reading of *Inferno* III 60, where Dante sees the one "who made the great refusal", may have been written circa 1480 by a Renaissance Platonist, Cristoforo Landino, in his *Comment on the Comedy*. It is "not without reason", Landino begins, that the poet decides to give no name here.[13] The lack of a name is not a lack of meaning. On the contrary, it contributes to the meaning of this stanza. Landino's question then becomes: If Dante is silent for a reason, what is his reason?

Landino reads Dante like a philosopher—and indeed, like a Platonist. (As Augustine puts it in *City of God*: "It is hard to perceive Plato's convictions on crucial matters.")[14] Landino notes that Dante not only refuses to tell us *who* he sees but *why* he is silent. The mystery of *il gran rifiuto* is not a sign that Dante's interpreters have failed, but that Dante has succeeded. The poet has constructed a mystery at *Inferno* III 60; it is a sign of his artistry that a mystery remains.

The new question, of course, is: Why the mystery? And Landino is non-dogmatic. He gives three reasons why *Inferno* III 60 might lack a name:

1. Perhaps Dante doesn't want to name a man who held high office and lived a holy life—read Pope Celestine—but who Dante felt had been degraded by his time in government.
2. Perhaps Dante gives no name here *not* because he is thinking of a Celestine (or a Diocletian), but because he is referring to someone "forgettable" or "inglorious" (*sanza fama*): a Florentine non-entity.[15]
3. Or perhaps Dante wants to leave the question open—by which Landino means, to put it in perpetuity "before the judgement of his hearers".[16]

Landino concludes that the vagueness of the one Dante sees at *Inferno* III 60 "creates doubt".[17] And perhaps that is Dante's intention.

It is definitely T. S. Eliot's intention when he restages Dante's scene in the "The Burial of the Dead" stanzas of *The Waste Land*. "So many", is Eliot's strict citation of *Inferno* III 56–7, "I had not thought death had undone so many." He signals with this line that the depressed core of London—"Unreal City"—is the foyer to Dante's hell circa

1920. And Eliot, like Dante, is no stranger to the damned. "I saw one I knew", he then tells us, improvising on *Inferno* III 58–9, "and stopped him, crying 'Stetson! You who were with me in the ships at Mylae!'"[18] Though Eliot names the shade he meets at the brink of hell, he too constructs a mystery—and there is no consensus about who 'Stetson' could be.[19]

A nineteenth-century theory

Returning to Dante, a book printed in New York in the late nineteenth century is eye-wateringly worse than Landino's *Comment*, which was printed in Florence in the late fifteenth century. Like Dante with the coward in *Inferno* III 60, I will not name this book—but only because it is inglorious (*sanza fama*). In it, there is only one idea that matters here—that the blurred-out rogue who is glimpsed at *Inferno* III 60 is none other than Jesus' Roman judge, Pontius Pilate.[20]

This is a neat conjecture, since it places Pilate—who is never named in the *Inferno*—in Dante's hell-cantos. But on a moment's reflection, the placement is confusing. For the shade Dante sees in *Inferno* III—the one "who made the great refusal"—is not in hell itself,[21] but only in hell's vestibule.[22] This may be why, for more than 500 years after Dante wrote the *Inferno*, no one thought Pilate might be the one Dante "beheld" under a cloud of wasps in the *terra nullius* at the outskirts of hell.[23]

A twentieth-century reception

By the turn of the twentieth century, the Pilate-conjecture had crossed the Atlantic. It soon became—and still seems to be—*de rigueur* in certain Italian circles.[24] In 1902, a symbolist poet, Giovanni Pascoli, wrote an essay for the avant-garde magazine *Il Marzocco* titled "Who Is 'the One Who Made the Great Refusal'". For Pascoli, it is Pilate.[25] And more than a century later, Agamben—whom we met in chapter 6— still calls this "Pascoli's hypothesis".[26] It may not be a coincidence that many of Italy's twentieth-century *literati* concluded that Pilate is the coward—or rather, the shade of a coward—that Dante recognizes in *Inferno* III.[27] For I suspect that this stylish Dante-interpretation is linked to a new—or rather, to a *renewed*—interpretation of the Roman trial of Jesus in twentieth-century Italy.

Now, Roman law has a special pride of place in Italian intellectual culture. And Jesus' ordeal in Jerusalem culminates in the most momentous Roman punishment in history. Because of this, there is a rich Italian literature on the topic—the most recent contribution may be Aldo Schiavone's impressive book *Pontius Pilate* (in which Pilate is not 'innocent').[28]

The impetus for much of the modern Italian literature on Pilate and Jesus can be traced to a seminar convened in Turin in 1879, resulting in a volume entitled *The Trial of Jesus Christ*. The Turin seminar's conveners insisted on a modern juridical reading of the gospels' trial narratives. In the wake of this seminar, and a couple of years after Pascoli wrote his essay for *Il Marzocco*, a prominent Italian jurist, Giovanni Rosadi, published a book-length juridical interpretation of the trial—*Il processo di Gesú* in Florence, *The Trial of Jesus* in New York[29]—which he followed with a novel titled *After Jesus*.[30] After Rosadi, a number of articles on Jesus' trials appeared in the Italian journal *Archivio giuridico*, though the topic seems to have cooled by the mid-twentieth century when Aristide Manassero reprised the debate in a historiographical essay, *Ecce Homo: History of the Trial of Jesus*.[31]

The relevance for us of this twentieth-century Italian reception history is real, but complex. To my mind, it is the Italian reception of an early-twentieth-century poet's interpretation of *Inferno* III 60—I mean "Pascoli's hypothesis"—that primes the twentieth-century revival in Italy of an ancient misinterpretation of the Roman trial of Jesus.[32] And it is the same hypothesis—the hypothesis that makes Pilate the coward "who made the great refusal"—that is responsible for a twentieth-century failure to see the significance of Pilate in Dante's political theory. Said differently, a poet's misinterpretation of Dante's lines (at *Inferno* III 60) seems to me to inspire a misinterpretation of the Roman trial of Jesus; and this, in turn, seems to me to foster a misrecognition of Pilate's place in the structure of Dante's political theology.

It is one of the tasks of part 5 to show that a "great refusal" is critical to the history of European secularity in ways that seem to have gone unnoticed—not only in Dante's oeuvre but in other canonical texts. But this *gran rifiuto* is not Pilate's. Quite the contrary.

THE INNOCENCE OF PONTIUS PILATE

Giovanni Rosadi on Pilate's refusal

What is the modern misinterpretation of *Inferno* III 60 that inspires a modern misinterpretation of Pilate's role in Jesus' trial? It can be simply stated: Pilate refuses to judge Jesus. Of course, there is nothing new in this idea. It is not remotely modern. We will recall from chapter 6 how Lactantius insists in the early fourth century that Pilate "did not himself utter a sentence" after he interrogated Jesus. Instead, per Lactantius, the Roman prefect "handed Jesus over to the Judaeans" to be crucified.[33] And we will recall that Agamben's twenty-first-century reprise of Lactantius' reading—which is certainly a misreading—could hardly be more precise.[34] In *Pilate and Jesus*, Agamben writes that Pilate "did not pronounce his sentence", but "simply 'handed over' the accused to the Sanhedrin".[35]

But is the Italian juridical theory of Pilate's non-judgement linked to the Italian theory that Pilate is the coward in *Inferno* III 60? The link is conspicuous in Pascoli's 1902 essay on *il gran rifiuto*,[36] and it enters the 'critical' literature on Jesus' trial a couple of years later in Rosadi's book, *The Trial of Jesus*. Rosadi is certainly thinking of Dante when he writes of "the cowardice" of Pilate's "refusal to act" during Jesus' Roman trial.[37] What is this "refusal to act"? "Pilate refused to choose", Rosadi writes in 1904, "and his refusal was great."[38] No cultured Italian could fail to hear Dante's words, *il gran rifiuto*, in Rosadi's words, "his refusal was great". Rosadi's Pilate is, like Pascoli's, Dante's coward.[39]

Rosadi contradicts Augustine when he insists of the Roman trial of Jesus: "There was in fact no sentence; the prisoner was merely handed over." And his recollection of Lactantius, like Agamben's, could hardly be more exact. For Rosadi then adds, as a corollary: "Jesus ... was not condemned, but He was slain."[40] What could this mean? Rosadi seems to have held that Pilate only uttered an "inarticulate command which was to have the fatal power of a condemnation".[41] And he is not the only modern commentator for whom Jesus' trial is concluded by Pilate's "inarticulate command", whatever that might be. A nod? A glance? A gesture?

"I see the new Pilate"

Is "Pascoli's hypothesis"—by which I mean, the twentieth-century Italian revival of Lactantius' Pilate-interpretation—one possible interpretation of Dante's lines in *Inferno* III?[42] It is not.

The falsity of "Pascoli's hypothesis" is first signalled by the fact that, though Pilate is never named in the *Inferno*, he is named in Dante's *Purgatorio* (most cantos of which appear to have been written between 1309 and 1315).[43] There, Dante portrays a "new Pilate" (*novo Pilato*) who has nothing like the physiognomy of a coward, and nothing like the bearing of a man who, per *Inferno* III 64, never lived.[44] This is Dante, in the only lines of the *Comedy* where Pilate is named:

> I see ...
>
> Christ imprisoned in His vicar.
>
> I see him being mocked a second time;
> I see the vinegar and the gall renewed,
> and between living thieves I see them kill Him.
>
> I see the new Pilate, so cruel
> that this is not enough, without consent sail
> his greedy sails into the Temple.[45]

Commentators have determined that this scene is a late medieval 'passion' play in which the 'new Pilate' is King Philip IV of France, alias Philip the Fair, and 'Christ' is Pope Boniface VIII, who issued the ultra-papalist bull *Unam sanctam* in 1302 and died shortly after being brutalized and imprisoned by Philip's troops in 1303.[46]

Now, much could be said about Boniface VIII in Dante's political imaginary—the poet dubs him "Prince of new Pharisees" in *Inferno* XXVII.[47] Or about the reception of Boniface VIII's novel canonistic definition of "secular persons" (*saecularium personarum*).[48] Or, with an eye to a later chapter, about Boniface VIII's "insufferable usurpation" of secular power in the pages of Pufendorf's *History of the Principal Kingdoms and States of Europe*.[49] But the only thing that matters here is how Dante imagines Pilate in this symbol-rich sketch of the 'passion' of Boniface VIII.

Is the *Purgatorio*'s Pilate a figure of cowardice and indecision? Is he a gutless, contourless figure? On the contrary. The one Dante calls a "new Pilate" is "so cruel" (*sì crudele*) that he can't rest until he—like Pompey in 63 BCE or Titus in 70 CE—profanes the sanctum sanctorum of the Temple.[50] Pilate's ravenousness in this scene, the fact "that this is not enough (*nol sazia*)",[51] plainly refers to the tercet in which Christ—in the person of his vicar, Boniface VIII—is "mocked", given "the vinegar and the gall" to drink, and left to die "between living thieves".

In short: Christ is tortured, here, and crucified "a second time" (*un'altra volta*).[52] And who is responsible for this terrible scene? The one whose cruelty is not sated by it. The one who drives Dante's lines into the innermost chamber of the Temple—a space constructed to be, in Josephus' words, "inaccessible and inviolable".[53] And who is that? Obviously, it is Pilate. And allegorically, it is a new Pilate.

There is no need to press this further. Despite what some modern commentators have said, Dante's lines on Pilate in *Purgatorio* XX terminate the modern hypothesis that Jesus' judge is the one who made "the great refusal" in *Inferno* III.[54] The Pilate of Pascoli and Rosadi in the early twentieth century, and Agamben in this century—which is to say, the Pilate who "did not himself utter a sentence" during Jesus' Roman trial—is not Dante's Pilate.[55]

In *Purgatorio* XX, Pilate seizes Christ, tortures him, and kills him. This suggests that Dante's image of Pilate is not influenced by Lactantius, but Augustine. And the bishop of Hippo seems not only to have informed Dante's image of Pilate in the *Comedy* but in his treatise on political theology, *Monarchy*, which he wrote before completing the *Purgatorio*.[56]

"That unique census of the human race"

The modern hypothesis that Pilate is the one who made "the great refusal" in *Inferno* III reflects a catastrophic misinterpretation of Dante's corpus.[57] I mean two things by this.

First, in Dante's *Monarchy*—as I will show in the coming pages—it is of world-redeeming significance that Pilate judged Jesus. To interpret *Inferno* III 60 in the modern Italian way is to mistake Dante's political theology *in toto*.[58] Second, and perhaps more interesting: Dante believes that a great refusal is made during Jesus' Roman trial; but it is not made by Pilate. For Dante, it is Jesus who makes the great refusal. And this refusal is, of course, not cowardly. We can begin by turning to *Monarchy* II.

Dante's question in *Monarchy* II is "whether the Roman people took on empire by right".[59] Having argued the legitimacy of Roman empire—and of its displaced successor, the Holy Roman Empire—on what he calls "rational principles" for much of book II, Dante formulates a couple of arguments "from the principles of the Christian faith" in the book's final chapters.[60] In chapter 10, he reasons from the circumstances of Jesus' birth—and this is where we will begin to read.

The gospel of *Luke* narrates, Dante writes, that "Christ chose to be born of his Virgin Mother under an edict emanating from Roman authority", by which he means the census that structures the birth-narrative in *Luke* (but not in *Matthew*). This means, Dante reasons, that "Christ chose" to be "enrolled as a man in that unique census of the human race". And that means, he goes on, that "the Son of God ... acknowledged the *validity* of that edict". A citation from Aristotle's *Nicomachean Ethics* proves, for Dante, that the recognition of a law by compliance in act is "more effective" than a mere verbal recognition.[61] The circumstances of Jesus' birth therefore prove, for Dante, that "the jurisdiction of the authority which promulgated" the Roman census— namely, that of the Roman Empire—"is legitimate".[62]

The timing of Christ's birth demonstrates, concretely, that Christ assented to the Roman edict. But it is unjust to assent to an unjust law. And since it is absurd to think—or rather, since it is absurd for a believer to think[63]—that Christ assented unjustly, the Roman edict must be just.[64] This is how Dante reasons from the circumstances of Jesus' birth to the legitimacy of the Roman Empire—and its European successor, the Holy Roman Empire.[65]

"To Pilate to be judged"

Far more intriguing in this context is Dante's reasoning in the next chapter of *Monarchy* II from the circumstances of Jesus' *death* to the legitimacy of the Roman Empire.[66] The strangeness of this argument could call to mind the 'supreme irony' I evoked in chapter 1. How could Dante legitimate Rome's imperium on the grounds that it killed the Son of God? We will see.

Just as the Roman edict in *Luke* is a hinge on which Dante's earlier argument turns, so here he fixes on a single dominical saying in *John*. Dante writes here that "Christ himself, suffering punishment in his own person, says in *John*: 'It is finished.'"[67] These are Jesus' last words in the crucifixion scene in *John*, and they naturally force us to ask: What is finished?

Quoting the Pauline (or pseudo-Pauline) letter of *Ephesians*, Dante infers that what is finished must be our "redemption by [Christ's] blood", and the "remission of [our] sins in accordance with the riches of his glory".[68] Dante is sure that this redemption could not have been secured unless our sins had been "punished in Christ" (a theological claim);[69] and that "'punishment' is not simply 'a penalty imposed on one who does wrong', but 'a penalty imposed on the wrongdoer *by one who has the legal authority* to punish him'" (a legal claim, perhaps taken from Justinian's *Institutes*).[70] This is crucial. For what this means is that, in Dante's mind, the redemption of humankind is legally and theologically unthinkable unless Jesus was *punished*, which is to say, made to suffer—though innocent—*by a legitimate judge*.

Who is Jesus' judge, per Dante? Pontius Pilate. And of necessity, Dante has no use for a Roman judge who refuses to judge Christ. Nothing less than the redemption of the world hangs on the fact that—Dante writes—the sufferings of Christ were inflicted "by an authorized judge" (*sub ordinario iudice*).[71] To deny this is, for Dante, to deny the Christian faith. "This is why Herod", he suggests (referring to a scene that is unique to the gospel of *Luke*), "sent Christ back to Pilate to be judged (*ad iudicandum*)".[72] Why? Because Herod Antipas was a mere client-king of Galilee. But Tiberius Caesar, "whose representative Pilate was, [had] jurisdiction over the whole of mankind (*supra totum humanum genus*)".[73] Only a verdict by Pilate could inflict on Christ a punishment by "the legitimate empire of the world" (*de iure orbis imperium*);[74] and only a punishment by that world-empire, Dante reasons, could exact the redemption of humankind by Christ's blood. When Jesus says, in the death-scene of the gospel of *John*, "It is finished", what Dante believes is finished is *the exaction of a suffering imposed by Jesus' Roman judge, Pilate*.

The judgement of Pilate is no slight question in Dante's political theology. Pilate's judgement is a moment without which—it is not hyperbolic to say—Dante's world-picture becomes incomprehensible. For he believes that first-century Rome held the right to avenge the first humans' sin in paradise, as Beatrice reveals to Dante in the *Paradiso*. It is given to the Roman Empire, she says, through Pilate's sentence of death, to exact the divinely ordained "vengeance of the ancient sin" (*la vendetta del peccato antico*): the crucifixion of Jesus.[75]

Because of this, it is not possible to read Pilate into *Inferno* III, with the Italian modernists. When Dante sees "the shade of him who made the great refusal", he cannot be referring to Pilate.[76] This is certain because of what Dante writes not only in *Purgatorio* XX but in *Monarchy* II. Dante believes that Christ is led before Pilate "to be judged" (*ad Iudicandum*).[77] And Dante believes, in an acutely theorized way, that Pilate did judge Jesus. It is only because Pilate did *not* refuse to judge Jesus that Christ has "freed us from the power of darkness with his blood", as Dante writes in *Monarchy* III.[78] To which we now turn.

"Christ renounced the kingdom"

There is, for Dante, a "great refusal" during the Roman trial of Jesus. He articulates it in *Monarchy* III, where his new question is whether the Roman church—by which he means the papal monarchy of late medieval Europe—holds "the power to confer authority on the Roman prince"—by which he means the Germano-Roman emperor of late medieval Europe.[79]

Given our interest in the presence of Africa and Africans in European legal history, it is arresting that Dante says in *Monarchy* III that "not only all … Africans, but also the greater part of those who live in Europe find the idea abhorrent"—namely the idea of a universal papal monarchy.[80] If it is the Roman church that legitimizes the Roman Empire, Dante reasons here, it is certainly not by "the consent of all men" in the post-Roman territories of late medieval Africa and Europe.[81]

But Dante has a stronger argument in *Monarchy* III that "the authority of the empire does not derive from the authority of the supreme pontiff"—in other words, that the Holy Roman Empire is not legitimated by the Roman church.[82] Further, this is an argument that harmonizes nicely with Dante's reading of the Roman trial of Jesus in *Monarchy* II. In book II, Dante's reading is centred on Pilate; but in book III, it is centred on Jesus. What Pilate accomplishes in *Monarchy* II is the punishment of Christ by his utterance of a formally valid Roman condemnation. What Jesus accomplishes in *Monarchy* III is the renunciation of what Dante calls "the power to confer authority on the kingdom of our mortality".[83] And what Dante calls "the kingdom of our mortality" is roughly what late moderns will call 'secularity'.

179

Dante's reasoning about Christ's renunciation of secular power is clear. It seems to me to recollect Augustine's reading of the Roman trial of Jesus, and it, too, is centred on the trial narrative in *John*. Dante cogently states that "the 'form' of the church is simply the life of Christ". The *vita Christi* is the "exemplar for the church militant, especially for the pastors, and above all for the supreme pastor"—meaning the pope.[84] The question then becomes, what is the testimony of the *vita Christi* with regard to "the kingdom of our mortality" (*regnum nostre mortalitas*)?[85] Dante writes this in *Monarchy* III:

> Christ renounced (*abnegavit*) the kingdom of this world (*huius mundi regnum*) in the presence of Pilate, saying [in *John*]: "My kingdom is not of this world; if my kingdom were of this world, then my servants would fight, that I should not be delivered to the Jews; but now my kingdom is not from hence." Which is not to be understood to mean that Christ, who is God, is not Lord of this kingdom … but that, as exemplar for the church (*exemplar ecclesie*), he had no concern for this kingdom. … From this we deduce that the power to confer authority on the kingdom of this world is against the nature of the church (*contra naturam ecclesie*).[86]

In Dante's *Monarchy*, it is not a coward, but God, who makes the great refusal. It is not Pilate who refuses to judge, but Christ who refuses—in this world (*huius mundi*) and for the present time—*to judge his judge*. Because Pilate judges Jesus, in *Monarchy* II, humankind is redeemed. And because Jesus, in *Monarchy* III, refuses to judge Pilate— in this world (*huius mundi*) and for the present time—the church is born. For Dante, it is because "Christ renounced the kingdom of this world" that there is a kingdom *in* this world that is *not* of this world— namely the church.[87]

Dante believes that he has "sufficiently proved", by means of this Augustinian—or African—reading of the Roman trial in *John*, that "the authority of the empire (*auctoritatem imperii*) in no way derives from the church (*ab ecclesia … dependere*)".[88] Dante states very clearly that the Roman church and its head (the pope) are to be concerned with "happiness in the *eternal* life".[89] By way of contrast, the Roman Empire and its head ("who is called the Roman prince")[90] are to be concerned with "happiness in *this* life".[91] Recollecting the African pope Gelasius for a moment, we could say that, for Dante, the pope is the highest instance of "the sacred authority of the priests" (*auctoritas sacra pontifi-cum*), and the emperor is the highest instance of "the royal power" (*regalis potestas*).[92]

It is a real trial—the Roman trial of Jesus—that legitimizes, for Dante, a formal demarcation between the power of emperors and the authority of prelates. And it is a great refusal, by Jesus, of "the kingdom of this world in the presence of Pilate" that legitimizes the power of emperors to realize a political order that is conducive to "happiness in *this* life".[93]

"That man who weakened your empire"

There is an acute difficulty with this configuration, however, and Dante is keenly aware of it in the early fourteenth century.[94] For most of Dante's contemporaries (though not for Dante), the drama of Jesus' renunciation of secular power in the first century is cancelled out by a counter-drama set in the fourth century. The source of this counter-drama is a portmanteau of fifth- and eighth-century forgeries that came to be called, in the eleventh and twelfth centuries, the *Donation of Constantine*.[95] In this concocted 'donation', Constantine I gives to Pope Sylvester I (reigned 314–35), in thanks for a divine act of healing, the Lateran palace, the city of Rome, and many of his territories, powers, and insignias. In short, in the pages of this *Donation*, the pope is made the *de jure* head of Rome and the western empire, though he is not given Constantinople or the eastern empire.[96]

Thus, when Dante writes to fourteenth-century 'Romans' in the last sentences of *Monarchy* II that it would have been better if "that man who weakened your empire had never been born", he is cursing— from our distance, improbably—the man who Christianized the Roman Empire.[97] Dante seems to fleetingly concede in *Monarchy* that Constantine had "legitimately", in the *Donation*, "handed over into the church's guardianship those things of the empire's which he did hand over".[98] Yet there are many indications that Dante regarded the *Donation*, in Unn Falkeid's words, as "a weak, suspect document" that most convincingly demonstrated "the greed of the church".[99] In *Inferno* XIX, for instance, Dante calls the *Donation of Constantine* the mother of immense wickedness (... *di quanto mal fu matre*).[100] Of how much wickedness, we could ask? In *Paradiso* XX, Dante laments that Constantine's gift had led *the world* to ruination (... *che sia 'l mondo indi distrutto*).[101] Of course, this is hyperbolic. But what could the *Donation*'s ruinous influence on history mean, more concretely, for us in the twenty-first century?

One of the globe-ordering legal fictions derived from the *Donation* may be what a Mexican diplomat-historian, Luis Weckmann, styled the "all-islands doctrine" (*doctrina omni-insular*) in his 1949 doctoral thesis, "Constantine the Great and Christopher Columbus".[102] Weckmann's task in his thesis, which is introduced by Ernst Kantorowicz, is to clarify the legal doctrines behind a number of papal bulls written in the horizon-dissolving year 1493. And this is how Weckmann restates his thesis in a still-illuminating 1951 article, "The Middle Ages in the Conquest of America":

> Columbus, the first link between the Old World and the New, stands in a clearer light, perhaps, if we envisage him not so much as the first of the modern explorers but as the last of the great mediaeval travelers ... In all his travels, when navigating through the Antilles ... he thought (as his diary shows) that he was visiting the many islands which, as he said, were depicted in mediaeval maps at the end of the Orient ... If such were the geographical convictions of the discoverer, what then is strange in the fact that the papacy, barely a few months after the discovery, divided these newly-found lands, *mainly islands* ... on the basis of *the then uncontested doctrine that all islands belong to the Holy See*, a curious mediaeval theory whose ultimate basis lay, as I have tried to prove [in the 1949 thesis], in the *Donation of Constantine*?[103]

Because of this "curious medieval theory", namely "that all islands belong to the Holy See", it seems that legal efforts were made in the early modern period to define the Americas, *in toto*, as an archipelago.[104] Naturally, this calls to mind the fact that Columbus's celebrated letter to King Ferdinand of Spain, printed in Basel in 1493, is titled *Epistle on the Islands Recently Discovered*.[105] What Columbus calls "the islands", we call the Americas.

It is not certain that Weckmann proved his theory that the "all-islands doctrine" is rooted in the *Donation of Constantine*, and I am not competent to judge the dossier of papal communications that he, and later researchers, seek to interpret.[106] One of his early critics writes that, "for all its massive documentation and often brilliant reasoning",

Weckmann's thesis "fails to carry conviction".[107] Yet the question seems not to be whether there is a medieval "all-islands doctrine",[108] for a medieval papal claim to "island sovereignty" is already noted in the 1890s by the eminent Belgian jurist and justice at The Hague Ernest Nys.[109] The question seems to be whether this papal 'doctrine' stems from late medieval readings of the *Donation of Constantine*, and thus whether the *Donation* informs the 1493 papal bulls on 'the islands recently discovered'.

Johannes Fried, an authority on the *Donation*, seems to affirm both ideas—which is to say, Weckmann's thesis—in a study published in 2015. Fried writes this: "Direct consequences from the *Donation* were first drawn under the rule of Pope Urban II, who in 1098 laid claim to all the islands of the Earth, thereby establishing an idiosyncratic theory of islands, which was still operative in 1493 when Pope Alexander VI divided the world up."[110] It is not without interest that the man who "divided the world up" in 1493 is Pope Alexander VI (reigned 1492–1503), the notorious Borgia paterfamilias that many called a Supreme Pest (*Pestis Maxima*), not a Supreme Pontiff (*Pontifex Maximus*).[111] Alexander held the degree of doctor of "both laws" (*utrumque ius*) from the University of Bologna. He had certainly read the *Donation*, and could draw on its interpretive traditions.

All this digression on Weckmann and the "all-islands doctrine" is meant to suggest is that the *Donation of Constantine* is one of premodern Europe's world-altering documents, though it may not have destroyed the world (à la Dante in *Paradiso* XX).[112] Its exposure as a fake is world-altering, too. Roughly 130 years after Dante wrote *Monarchy*, Valla demonstrates the spuriousness of the *Donation*.[113] And in the pages of Valla's exposé, as in Dante's *Monarchy*, the Roman trial of Jesus is decisive.[114]

"A secular kingdom had nothing to do with him"

Medieval political theology is shaped by a 'great refusal' that Constantine was thought to have made in his *Donation* to a fourth-century pope, Sylvester. And early modern political theology is marked—perhaps inaugurated—by Valla's demonstration that the *Donation* is a fake.[115] It is immensely symbolic that Valla's exposé, written in 1440, went to press for the first time in the epochal year 1517—the year to which Martin Luther's continent-shaping protest is dated.[116]

Luther himself read Valla's critique not much later, in February 1520, and it is Valla who seems to have convinced the Saxon monk-militant that the Roman pontiff was the Antichrist warned of in *II Thessalonians*.[117] "I have here at my disposal [Ulrich von Hutten's] edition of Lorenzo Valla's *Confutation of the Donation of Constantine*", Luther writes in a 1520 letter to a confidant, the Bavarian humanist Georg Spalatin. "I am greatly tormented", Luther tells Spalatin, "[and] I do not even doubt that the pope is properly the Antichrist."[118] Within months, in his polemic *On the Papacy at Rome*, Luther can ask: "Why then does the Roman see so furiously desire the whole world ... as if it were the Antichrist?" By the summer of 1520 in Luther's new, billowing circles, this question is rhetorical.[119]

A chasm separates Valla's reading of the *Donation* from Luther's feverish end-times reading of Valla. The point here is this. It is only because the *Donation of Constantine* is spurious—as revealed by Valla in the fifteenth century—that Christ's "great refusal" ceases to be cancelled out, in sixteenth-century political theology and ultimately in Protestant politics, by Constantine's 'great refusal'.

Returning to Valla, late modern historians tend to see the force and significance of his text *On the Forged and Mendacious Donation of Constantine* in his epoch-inaugurating philological reasoning—which also led him to conclude that the Apostles' Creed is not the apostles' work (as the medieval church held); and that the apostle Paul's correspondence with the philosopher Seneca (much loved by medieval Christians) is a later concoction.[120] Without diminishing the rigour and ingenuity of Valla's text-critical tour de force, it is worth remembering that much of his reasoning on the spurious *Donation* is theological (if pitched in a highly rhetorical register).

Valla once wrote to a friend, Giovanni Tortelli, that his critique of the *Donation* is "concerned with canon law and theology but opposed to all canon lawyers and theologians".[121] Valla's text could not have survived or influenced early modern political theory and literary culture if it had truly been "opposed to *all* theologians". And on closer inspection, it proves not to be. Indeed, on the crucial question of Jesus' renunciation of secular power Valla echoes not only Dante, and the

Augustinian tradition that structures our narrative, but Marsilius of Padua—on whom, more in the coming chapter.[122]

The part of Valla's text that concerns us is a fictional reply by Sylvester I to a fictional donation by Constantine I, which would have conferred on the Roman pontiff the secular powers, fiscs, and holdings of the western Roman Empire. Valla is certain on historical grounds that the *Donation* is fake. He reasons, for instance, that Constantine would have been assassinated if he had tried to alienate the powers and territories of imperial Rome. (A convincing historical objection.)[123] But Valla is certain, too, on theological grounds that the *Donation* must be a fake.

For it is not only absurd that a fourth-century emperor would have 'donated' the empire to a pope. It is absurd that a fourth-century pope would have *accepted* the empire, because—Valla argues—temporal dominion conflicts with the early Christian idea of the pontificate. It is this second argument of Valla's that interests us here, since it suggests that Dante had refuted the *Donation of Constantine* on *a priori* theological grounds in *Monarchy* before Valla demolished it on *a posteriori* philological grounds. The real trial of Jesus—Valla concurs with Dante—exposes the fake donation of Constantine.[124]

To begin with, Valla's pope states his concern that "secular affairs" (*secularium negotiorum*) will corrupt the priesthood.[125] Note the terminology. We saw the same in Gelasius' text *On the Bond of an Anathema*, where Christ divides the offices of pontiff and emperor so as to shelter his ministers from the cares and temptations of "secular affairs" (*negotiis saecularibus*).[126] It is after this seeming echo of Gelasius that Valla's papal speech crescendos.

"Tell me", the humanist's half-imagined pope says to his half-imagined emperor, "do you want to make me a king or rather a Caesar—a ruler of kings?" Valla's pope presses on:

> When the Lord Jesus Christ, God and man, king and priest, acknowledged that he was a king (*se regem affirmaret*), listen to what he said: "My kingdom", he said, "is not of this world. For if my kingdom were of this world, my ministers would assuredly fight back." ... When he said these things, did he not declare that a secular kingdom (*regnum seculare*) had nothing to do with him? ... Therefore I have no need of your donation, by which I would assume a task that it would be as wrong for me to bear as it is impossible.[127]

Valla then lets his half-fictional fourth-century pope reformulate Jesus' *gran rifiuto*. This is Valla's Sylvester, admonishing his Constantine:

> Caesar—allow me to say this without offence—do not play the devil for me, you who tell Christ, namely me, to accept kingdoms of the world (*regna mundi*) that are given by you. I prefer to despise (*spernere*) them than to possess them. ... Even if you should offer it a thousand times, I would never accept.[128]

The genre of this scene could perhaps be called historical romance. But Valla is playing, here—like Dante and his "new Pilate"—with a historical drama that controlled the European imaginary for at least a thousand years. Valla's late antique pope is staying true to the passion—meaning, here, to Christ's renunciation of temporal power—and in that way he reveals the corruption (to Valla's mind) of the papal monarchy and its defenders. This is a far cry, however, from Luther's abhorrence of the pope as "Antichrist". It is only necessary to recall that Valla is writing as a future secretary at the court of Pope Nicholas V (reigned 1447–55).[129] When Valla insists that it is impossible for a pope to imitate Christ if he does not "despise" secular rule, he is not per se hostile to the Renaissance papacy.

Conclusions

We will not hear of *il gran rifiuto* "a thousand times" in the rest of part 5, but Jesus' renunciation of "kingdoms of the world" in Pilate's tribunal is a drama that recurs in a succession of canonical philosophical texts, at structurally critical moments, in late medieval and early modern Europe. If Jesus had not made his "great refusal", that is to say—as formulated by Augustine and received in a certain vein of Augustinian tradition—there is reason to believe that the secular could not have been theorized, or progressively actualized, in late medieval and early modern Europe.[130]

16

"CHRIST WILLED HIMSELF TO LACK AUTHORITY"

A *SUCCÈS DE SCANDALE* AND A CHAIN OF GOLD

One of the first rectors of the University of Paris, Marsilius of Padua, is commonly seen as the first architectonic theorist of secularity.[1] Like most premodern political theorists, Marsilius' theory is dramatic. A sacred drama structures his theory of human and divine law, coercion and jurisdiction, in his incendiary *Defender of the Peace* and "slanderous little book", the *Lesser Defender*.[2] In light of the last chapter, it is intriguing that Dante and Marsilius may have met in the decade in which the poet wrote *Monarchy*. For as Falkeid reminds us, they "were both at Verona ... during the second decade of the fourteenth century, both under the patronage of Cangrande della Scala"—then Lord of Verona— "and both were staunch defenders of the Holy Roman Empire".[3] Both, too, were reprobated by popes and condemned by cities.[4]

Marsilius is a salient actor in a brash, scarring conflict between the Roman church and empire in the early fourteenth century. His life is dramatic. A son of the church but a fierce partisan of the empire, Marsilius belongs—like Dante—to the Ghibelline (imperial) faction of certain north Italian cities.[5] Because of this, a papal bull of 1327 thunders that Marsilius—then sheltering in the Tyrolean city of Trent—is a "son of perdition".[6] And it should not be forgotten that Marsilius' books were banned in the vast Tridentine blocs of early modern Europe, as were Dante's (as Boccaccio tells us), Valla's, and Hobbes's (taken up in the next chapter). Most of the writers who figure in part 5 were listed for centuries on the Roman Curia's *Index of Prohibited Books*.[7]

The turbulent drama of Marsilius' life as a court philosopher of Ludwig of Bavaria, a restive emperor excommunicated by the second Avignon pope, John XXII, is informed by his reading of Europe's Ur-drama in ways that I will sketch in this chapter. It is Marsilius' interpretation of the Roman trial of Jesus, in defence of which he cites Augustine's *Homilies on the Gospel of John*, that permits him to condemn, in 'orthodox' terms, the political and juridical order of late medieval Europe—and more concretely, the political theology of the Avignon papacy.

It is because Marsilius reads the Pilate trial in an Augustinian vein, not only like Dante but like the English Franciscan and radical nominalist William of Ockham (on whom there will be more in chapter 17),[8] that he can theorize the late medieval popes' holding of "supreme coercive jurisdiction" as a shocking drama of *usurpation*.[9] Marsilius is sure that the papal monarchy's "fullness of power" (*plenitudo potestatis*), as it is called in the late medieval European lexicon, is not full of grace.

"Outrageous and dangerous"

For Marsilius, as for other theorists in part 5, the continental tremors and ruptures of European history—the tectonic shifts and abrasions of church and empire that ultimately break out in the Protestant revolutions and wars of religion—force us to revisit the Roman trial of Jesus. Marsilius cites the Pilate trial once in his *Lesser Defender* and scrutinizes it closely in a decisive chapter of discourse II in *Defender of the Peace*, which is "by far the longest" of the treatise's three discourses.[10] For him, papal usurpation is only 'usurpation'—rather than a legitimate rule or domination of Europe—because of its place in sacred history.

Before we come to the political theories of real Protestants, the *homines novi* of early modern philosophy—such as Hobbes, Pufendorf, and Thomasius—we can ask what significance the Pilate trial had for a medieval 'Protestant'. This crude descriptor is not only inspired by Marsilius' excommunication by the pope in April 1327 (a couple of years before a papal legate burned copies of Dante's *Monarchy*),[11] and by Marsilius' condemnation for heresy in October 1327 (in a bull that damns *Defender of the Peace* as "outrageous and dangerous"),[12] but by his early modern reception. For centuries, Marsilius is cited—like Dante—by partisans of both Reformation and Counter-Reformation, as a Protestant *avant la lettre*.[13] One sign of Marsilius' radical chic is that Henry VIII's vice-regent, Thomas Cromwell, who dissolved hundreds of English monasteries, commissioned a translation of Marsilius' *Defender of the Peace* (as *The Defence of Peace*) in 1535.[14] And it is striking that the translator of Marsilius' *Defender of the Peace*, William Marshall, also put Valla's demolition of the *Donation of Constantine* into English, as *A Treatise of the Donation Given unto Sylvester Pope of Rome*, in 1534.[15]

I am convinced that Jesus' trial is of fundamental importance for Marsilius, as for Dante and Valla (in chapter 15). I would even hazard the claim that neither the structure nor the conceptual architecture of his *Defender of the Peace* or *Lesser Defender* can be reconstructed without close attention to the Roman trial of Jesus. It is strange, then, that the Pilate trial has never been thematized in the literature on Marsilius.[16]

"Authority in this age"

The Pilate trial is not salient in Marsilius' *Lesser Defender*. Jesus' words to Pilate are only quoted once in this text, in a chapter in which Marsilius asserts the supremacy of divine law over human decrees. It is in this setting that Marsilius writes that "Christ *willed himself to lack* authority in this world-age in so far as he was human, in as much as he said [to Pilate]: 'My kingdom is not of this world.'"[17]

At first glance, the drama that Marsilius evokes here is the same one that we reconstructed in Dante's and Valla's texts. Jesus is standing before Pilate, confessing that his "kingdom is not of this world". The dramatis personae are Jesus and Pilate, and the kingdom in question is Jesus' kingdom—the kingdom that is *not* of this world. But this rushed interpretation of Marsilius' words is flawed. The drama that Marsilius conjures up, here, is a *metaphysical* one—and it is this *metaphysical drama* that underlies Marsilius' political theory in a far more elaborate form than we find in Dante or Valla. For notice that Pilate is a supernumerary in Marsilius' narration of the scene. It is only Christ

189

who acts. And notice that, on Marsilius' telling, the kingdom in question is the kingdom *of* this world—and only obliquely a kingdom that is *not* of this world. We can read Marsilius' sentence again, more analytically. "Christ willed himself to lack authority in this world-age in so far as he was human", he writes, "in as much as he said: 'My kingdom is not of this world.'"[18]

To repeat, it is only Christ who acts in this sentence—by *willing*, and only incidentally by testifying before Pilate. And Christ's act of willing concerns "*this* world-age"—and only indirectly, the kingdom that is "*not* of this world". Note, especially, Marsilius' terminology. Rendered literally, what Marsilius writes is that "Christ willed himself to lack authority in *this age (hoc saeculo)*", because he said, "My kingdom is not of *this world (hoc mundo)*."[19] Marsilius' term *hoc saeculum* is, here, a precise counterpart to Jesus' phrase *hoc mundum* in *John* 18. No one denies that it is impossible to reconstruct Marsilius' thought without clarifying his notion of the *saeculum*—the mundane, human order. What, then, is the sublime drama hidden in this epitomic sentence by Marsilius?

"Christ *willed himself to lack* authority in this world-age", we read. And this willing, I believe, this divine renunciation of coercive power, by Christ, "in so far as he was human" (*inquantum homo*), is the dramatic act that shapes the structure of Marsilius' *Lesser Defender*—and more clearly, of his *Defender of the Peace*. This is a vast argument, of course, which I can only begin to justify in the coming pages.

"Transgressors in this world-age"

To begin, the section of the *Lesser Defender* in which this sentence appears becomes much clearer once we have noticed exactly what Marsilius says in the line I have just quoted. In the paragraph that comes before, for instance, we then notice that Marsilius asserts that the author of divine law—the Christians' God—"has decided to be a judge of transgressors on the basis of this law"—divine law—"only, and to restrain them by means of punishment in the future world-age *only*, and not in the present one (*in futuro saeculo ... non in isto*)".[20] Here, the jurisdiction of human law—and the punishment of transgressors of human law—is constituted by *a divine limitation of the divine jurisdiction*. The dramatic logic of this sentence is identical to the one we just analysed.

And this dramatic logic is clarified by a formulation one paragraph before, where Marsilius states: "According to divine law, there is a coercive judge (*iudex ... coactivus*), about whom Saint James said in his letter: 'There is one lawgiver and one judge (*Unus est legislator et iudex*), he who can condemn and deliver', namely Christ."[21] This last clarification—"namely Christ" (*Christus videlicet*)—is Marsilius' gloss on the verse from *James* 4 that he cites here.[22] The One lawgiver, the One judge, is Christ. And it is this assertion that lies behind Marsilius' claim that "Christ *willed himself to lack* authority in this world-age."[23] For a kingdom in which the One lawgiver is *not* the sole lawgiver, and a jurisdiction in which the One judge is *not* the sole judge, could only be constituted by a decision of that lawgiver and judge to *cede jurisdiction*. And this—precisely this, for Marsilius—is what occurs in Jesus' appearance before Pilate.

Before we move from the *Lesser Defender* to *Defender of the Peace*, note that Marsilius cites the same line from *James* 4, "There is one lawgiver and one judge", in the first paragraphs of the *Lesser Defender*.[24] There, Marsilius asserts that divine laws are "coercive precepts" for "transgressors in this world-age (*hoc saeculo*)", but that divine laws carry punishments "to be carried out in the future rather than the present world-age (*in futuro saeculo, non in isto*)".[25] His terminology, from the first paragraphs of the *Lesser Defender*, is that of the *saeculum* (this *saeculum*, a future *saeculum*). And from the first paragraphs of the *Lesser Defender*, Marsilius is clearing a space for human coercive power—which is to say, for human jurisdiction—by insisting upon a divine limitation of divine coercive power to a future world-age (*saeculum futurum*).

The *saeculum* is written into Marsilius' definition of human law. Marsilius formulates "human law" as a "coercive precept ... on account of the pursuit of immediate ends *in the present world-age* and under threat of punishment to be inflicted upon transgressors *in that realm alone*".[26] This definition depends, for its logical articulation—and indeed, for its political force in late medieval Europe—on the dictum concerning "this world" in Jesus' reply to Pilate. Thus, though it is only cited once in Marsilius' *Lesser Defender*, the Pilate trial is of fundamental importance from the first sentences of the work, where we read that human "coercive precepts"—which is to say, human laws—only impinge on "transgressors *in this world-age*".[27]

Christ's dramatic renunciation of secular jurisdiction in the Pilate trial is structurally decisive before it is cited in the *Lesser Defender*, precisely because Christ is the "one lawgiver and one judge" in that epitomic text.

"Caesar's viceregent Pontius Pilate"

The Roman trial's structural significance is far more visible in Marsilius' *Defender of the Peace*. In the first paragraphs of *Defender of the Peace*, he quotes from the Pilate trial in *John* 18, where Jesus says: "'For this reason I have come into the world, that I should bear witness unto the truth.'"[28] That is Jesus' gloss, in *John* 18:37, on his statement in *John* 18:36 that his "kingdom is not of this world" (a gloss that is decisive for Pufendorf's reading of the Pilate trial, as we will see in a later chapter). There is an echo, then, of the Pilate trial in the first pages of *Defender of the Peace* I—an echo that late modern readers are likely to miss, but that Marsilius' first readers were not.

I do not take it to be a coincidence that Pilate is named in the last pages of *Defender of the Peace* I, where Marsilius states that Christ is "one individual who [is] simultaneously God and man", and who "suffered and died ... under Caesar's viceregent Pontius Pilate".[29] It is between his echo of *John* 18 in *Defender of the Peace* I, chapter 1, and his mention of Pilate in *Defender of the Peace* I, chapter 19, that discourse I of Marsilius' iconic text could, perhaps, be fruitfully reread. But these textual data are too negligible to suggest a new reading of *Defender of the Peace* I.

Or they would be, if they were not structurally integrated—in *Defender of the Peace*, as in the *Lesser Defender*—with Marsilius' claim that Christ is the "one lawgiver and one judge" (*James* 4:12). That, we recall, is an assertion that necessitates—and, within Marsilius' system, derives from—the sacred drama of Christ's renunciation of coercive power in secular affairs in the *Lesser Defender*. And at the end of *Defender of the Peace* I, the assertion of Christ's lordship takes a rather shocking form. Marsilius veers perilously close to the justificatory logic of papal 'fullness of power' in the last paragraphs of book I.[30]

Marsilius' opponents, the defenders of universal papal monarchy, hold that Christ—"and this is true", Marsilius concedes—is "king of kings and lord of lords, of all persons and things universally (*universo-rum omnium personarum et rerum*)". Marsilius' only objection is that the inference that his opponents want to make "does not follow from this at all, as will become clear ... in what follows".[31] As Marsilius states here, the task of *Defender of the Peace* II is to demonstrate that the real *plenitudo potestatis* of Christ, far from justifying the *plenitudo potestatis* of the bishop of Rome, invalidates the papal claim as a sign of what Marsilius calls, several pages on, "perverse desire for government".[32]

The political jurisdiction—meaning, the coercive power in secular affairs—claimed by theorists of papal supremacy is, for Marsilius, a usurpation. This is the continental drama in which Marsilius inter-venes—he seeks to demonstrate that the Roman pontiff is a usurper of the Roman emperor's office. Yet Marsilius believes—or, what comes to the same in this context, he insists that he believes—that the One the Roman pontiff serves *is* possessed of *plenitudo potestatis*. The only way, then, in which the pretenders to that power—namely popes—can be shown to be usurpers, is if the rightful claimant to that power—namely Christ—had renounced it for himself (*in persona propria inquantum homo* is the salient caveat that we will recall from the *Lesser Defender*),[33] and forbade it to his successors.

Precisely this is what occurs in Marsilius' reading of the Roman trial of Jesus in *Defender of the Peace* II, chapter 4. It is Jesus' renunciation of coercive power in *John*—and less dramatically, in the other gospels—that delegitimizes the papal claims to temporal jurisdiction. And Marsilius indicates, as early as *Defender of the Peace* I, chapter 1, that in this—Marsilius' most urgent task—Aristotle is no help at all. This is because, as he writes there, "Aristotle could not perceive" late medieval Europe's "singular cause of strife"—meaning, the Avignon popes' claims, which compel Marsilius to write his treatise.[34]

It is inexact to say that Aristotle is 'no help at all'. For in the last sentences of *Defender of the Peace* I, Marsilius mines Aristotle's *Politics* for a claim that the office of priest "is to be kept apart from political governments".[35] But that technocratic line of Aristotle's, commented on by many generations of European scholastics, would be inert against the soaring claims of the papal monarchy if it were not for the sacred drama of *John* 18. This is why Marsilius writes *Defender of the Peace* II.

"Jurisdiction in this world-age"

Marsilius' difficulty—and the centrality, for him, of the Pilate trial—is most sharply stated in *Defender of the Peace* II, chapter 4:

> All Christian faithful are certain that Christ, who was true God and true man, was able to confer, not just upon the apostles but upon anyone else, coercive authority or jurisdiction in this world-age (*in hoc saeculo*) over all princes or principates of this world-age and over all individual persons; and perhaps even greater authority than this (*et hac ampliorem fortasse*), for example of creating beings, of destroying and restoring heaven and earth and all that are therein.[36]

There is some satirical bite in this suggestion, however doctrinally rooted, that the papacy's claims to universal jurisdiction are, set in a certain light, incredibly modest. A bold pope might hope for the right, not merely to rule this world-age, but to *make* worlds …

No matter. This is a sharp statement of the situation—the *dramatic situation*—that we observed in Marsilius' *Lesser Defender*. There is One judge and One lawgiver—the creator. Because God is the creator, his divine jurisdiction is—by rights—the world. The only conceivable limitation on the divine jurisdiction would be a *self-limitation*. Such a self-limitation, such a *renunciation* of coercive power in this world-age, would—in an instant—cede legitimacy to a 'secular' human jurisdiction (the concern of *Defender of the Peace* I), and decide the illegitimacy of the papal claims to human jurisdiction (the concern of *Defender of the Peace* II).

"Subject to the powers of this world-age"

Christ's renunciation of coercive power in this world-age is what Marsilius sees in the action of *John* 18—or, more accurately, this renunciation is *half* of what Marsilius sees in that action. For *Defender of the Peace* II, chapter 4—where Marsilius interprets the Pilate trial—has two parts (and a proem),[37] in both of which Marsilius reflects on the scene in *John*'s gospel where Jesus converses with Pilate.

As Marsilius tells us, he reads in the Roman trial of Jesus a demonstration that Christ "excluded himself and wanted to exclude himself" from all "government, judgement, or worldly coercive power (*coactiva potestate mundana*)".[38] The sphere of human jurisdiction that Marsilius delineates in *Defender of the Peace* I is the sphere of jurisdiction from which Christ, here in *Defender of the Peace* II, "excluded himself". And what is more, it is this act of divine self-exclusion that reveals the papal claims to be those of a usurper.

Late in the chapter,[39] Marsilius reads in the Roman trial of Jesus a demonstration that it was Christ's "will that he should be subject to the princes and the powers of this world-age (*seculi potestatibus*) in coercive jurisdiction".[40] Christ's subjection to human jurisdiction, which reveals and confirms the self-limitation of divine jurisdiction, is most decisively proved, for Marsilius, by the fact that "a sentence of death was passed upon Christ". By whom? The sentence under which Jesus dies is not uttered by a Judaean high priest, but by "Pilate sitting in his tribunal". And who crucified Christ? Not the Judaeans. "By his authority", Marsilius writes—that is, by the Roman prefect's—"the sentence was executed."[41]

It is Pilate's sentence of death—denied by Lactantius, asserted by Augustine—that Marsilius anticipates when he writes in the last pages of *Defender of the Peace* I that Christ "suffered and died … under Caesar's viceregent".[42] The judicial sentence that ends the *political* drama of Christ's life on earth (but not the mystical or theological drama) is no less critical for Marsilius in *Defender of the Peace* II than for Dante in *Monarchy* II. For both iconic Ghibellines, who were read and cited in early modern Europe as Protestants *avant la lettre*, it is Jesus' great refusal during the Pilate trial that constitutes the secular.[43]

"Christ willed himself to lack authority in this world-age (*in hoc saeculo*)", is Marsilius' epochal line.[44] This is the renunciation drama that invites Europe's first master-thinker of the secular to delineate a space of pure, though not absolute, human jurisdiction. Pilate's death sentence is a sign, for Marsilius—or less dogmatically, in Marsilius' texts—of a divine will that is revealed in *John*'s narrative of the Roman trial of Jesus. The legitimacy of secularity (*Defender of the Peace* I), and the illegitimacy of papal monarchy (*Defender of the Peace* II), can both be traced to Marsilius' reading of the Roman trial of Jesus. The critical chapter of *Defender of the Peace*, on this reconstruction, would be the one in which Marsilius' "one lawgiver and one judge" (*unus legislator et iudex*)—the mystic head of the Roman church—wills to let an officer of the Roman Empire take his natural life.[45]

Conclusions

Marsilius frequently cites Augustine's *Homilies on the Gospel of John*, but it is not certain he had read them. One probable line of transmission for Augustine's interpretation of the Pilate trial seems to be a patristic (and Byzantine) commentary on *John* edited by Thomas Aquinas, called *The Chain of Gold*. Augustine's commentary on the Pilate trial is salient in this text of Aquinas'.[46] A critical examination of Marsilius' citations of Augustine in *Defender of the Peace* and Aquinas' in *Chain of Gold* has not yet been made. But regardless of Aquinas' own legal theories, he may have had a hand in the creation of one of the fourteenth century's most radical texts—by putting the African bishop's exegesis into the hands of Marsilius. Aquinas may have a significant place in the history of secularity, not for anything that he wrote, but for something he copied.[47]

17

"A POWER WHICH HE REFUSED"

THE MOMENTARY ORTHODOXY OF THOMAS HOBBES

Hobbes is a thinker of immense force and originality, and no one denies his tectonic influence on early modern—and for that matter, late modern—political theory. Hobbes is, to lift one of his own images, a behemoth.[1] His thought is a huge, untameable presence in European modernity. "His bones are as strong pieces of brass", as the book of *Job* says of behemoth.[2] But Hobbes is fascinating not because he is brazenly modern—a hard-core nominalist, a de facto materialist, and so on—but because he is so *strangely* modern.

A bishop of the then-nascent Church of England had already noted this in a letter he wrote in July 1651—the year in which *Leviathan* appeared. "As in the man, so there are strange mixtures in the book", Bishop Duppa wrote of Hobbes and his *Leviathan*, adding, "and many things so wildly and unchristianly [said], that I can scarce have so much charity ... as to think he was ever Christian."[3] Christian or not, Hobbes was demonstrably—like the bishop—Anglican, and it was reported by a cleric who knew him that, in his final weeks, Hobbes had "received the Sacrament ... with seeming devotion, and in humble, and reverent posture".[4] It is impossible not to notice the word "seeming", but irresponsible—and perhaps, uncharitable—to forget Hobbes's "reverent posture".

"Strange mixtures in the book"

Hobbes is a strange thinker—which is to say, an original one—in a host of ways. Hobbes locks his commitments into a novel system of thought that evokes—or should evoke—surprise. For instance, Hobbes revives many theses of the ancient Epicureans—a materialist, hedonist sect that certain friends of his in Paris, such as philosopher-priest Pierre Gassendi, sought to blend with Christian faith.[5] But the Epicureans were notorious for their renunciation of both politics and religion—neither of which, they reasonably held, brought more pleasure than pain. Being hedonists, they decided to let the gods of earth and heaven—or more precisely, of the "interworlds"—be.[6] Epicureans retreated from both temple and city into the lush, semi-monastic seclusion of a sect that came to be known as the Garden (on the model of the Platonists' Academy, the Aristotelians' Lyceum, and the Stoics' Porch).[7]

Hobbes is a neo-Epicurean, but he is by no means a philosopher of the Garden. In radical contrast to a pagan Epicurean like Lucretius (the epic poet) or a Christian Epicurean like Gassendi (an erudite priest), neither of whom concern themselves with political theory, Hobbes takes his neo-Epicurean notions and convictions and forges them into an ultra-political philosophy in which religion, as we will see, is a salient concern. This is a bold and unexpected thing.

Strange, too, is Hobbes's 'modernity'. For his hostility to the harmonization of Christian and Aristotelian philosophy in the late medieval universities cannot be doubted.[8] Hobbes is a programmatic 'modernist'. And yet, it is uniquely Hobbes who insists on interpreting the political present—*any* political present, and not only that of his brutal and volatile seventeenth century—in light of a primaeval drama that he calls the "War of Every One against Every One".[9] Hobbes is a modernist who believes that the chaos and savagery of human prehistory lurk in the heart of every modern European polity. The messianic hope of 'perpetual peace' that eighteenth-century philosophers will nurture—I of course have in mind the Abbé Charles-Irénée de Saint-Pierre, Rousseau, and Kant—is not only deeply unrealistic for Hobbes. For the seventeenth-century 'modernist', the idea of perpetual peace is formally incoherent. The only 'peace' that political order generates is, by Hobbes's definition, that of a *truce*.

One of the most intriguing aspects of Hobbes's 'war of every one against every one' is that this primaeval drama is a constant threat to peace precisely because nature has made us, so Hobbes writes, "so equal".[10] Where modern leftists reason from natural equality to doctrines of political equality, and modern rightists reason from doctrines of natural inequality to political inequality, Hobbes boldly opens his iconic book, *Leviathan*, by asserting that the necessity of iron-bound *political inequalities* can logically be derived from humans' radical *natural equality*.[11] This is a strange, but weighty, move.

Why is it weighty? Because Hobbes notes in the first (and most famous) pages of *Leviathan* that it is easiest for humans to *hurt* others. Our radical equality lies, for Hobbes, just in that—a natural power to inflict harm. It is most clearly in this that we are made by nature, in Hobbes's words, "so equal".[12] Human equality lies in a capacity for fear and conflict and harm. Trust and peace and security—that is to say, the city, and thus, 'civility'—are generated by a form of inequality that Hobbes, with other early modern theorists (emblematically, Jean Bodin), calls sovereignty. The sovereign state or commonwealth—what Hobbes styles a Mortal God[13]—is generated in the moment when humans renounce their natural equality. The form of this renunciation is what Hobbes calls a "contract". And the renunciation of our natural right to harm—and thus, of our natural equality—is the only conceivable drama by which, according to Hobbes, we leave a condition of natural war and enter a condition of artificial peace. This is the great refusal—recalling Dante's lines—without which modern politics, conceived as a Hobbesian contract, is unthinkable. But this is not, predictably, the only *gran rifiuto* in Hobbes.

"Of power ecclesiastical"

As we have seen in Dante's *Monarchy*, Marsilius' *Defender of the Peace*, and Valla's refutation of the *Donation of Constantine*, so we can see in Hobbes's political theory in the *Leviathan*.[14] In the *Leviathan*, as in other early modern treatises, a philosophical defence of secular jurisdiction is coupled with a theological defence of the secular. In the case of Hobbes, his philosophical argument is made in parts I and II of *Leviathan* ("Of Man" and "Of Common-Wealth"), and his theological argument is made in parts III and IV ("Of a Christian Common-Wealth" and "Of the Kingdom of Darkness"). Parts III and IV of *Leviathan* are of no interest to most late modern readers, but to early modern readers—and censors—the opposite was the case. Many iconic texts in European history—from Dante to Hobbes—may owe most of their influence to forms of reasoning, and to blocs of text, that interest late modern readers the least.

The naturalistic 'great refusal' that underlies Hobbes's contract theory is common knowledge. But who remembers the sacred drama of a 'great refusal' in Hobbes? Without this sacred drama, Hobbes's singular idea "of a Christian common-wealth" in the *Leviathan* would have been differently elaborated; and what Hobbes calls "a Christian common-wealth" is one potent conception of what we still call a modern or 'Westphalian' state. (European states may now be 'post-Westphalian', but the spectre of Westphalia lives in that term.) What is this other 'great refusal'? I am of course referring to Jesus' renunciation of temporal power—or what Hobbes calls "jurisdiction"—during his interrogation by Pilate.

Now, Hobbes is a critical figure in the book's narrative. This is the case for more than one reason. In the first place, Hobbes diverges from the late medieval juridical reading of Jesus' Roman trial, in which—as in Augustine (and his excerpter, Aquinas)—a Roman crucifixion is thematized. For reasons that invite further reflection, Hobbes—like other seventeenth-century English writers, such as poet George Herbert—seems to pin Jesus' crucifixion on 'the Jews'. In much of the Christian tradition, the myth of a Judaean crucifixion is linked to the myth of Pilate's innocence. But in the same breath that Hobbes affirms the first myth, he denies the second. Hobbes seems to countenance a Judaean crucifixion, I mean to say, but he sharply denies Pilate's innocence. This is what Hobbes writes in *Leviathan*, chapter 42: "Pilate ... unjustly, without finding fault in him, delivered [our Saviour] to the Jews to be crucified."[15]

For Hobbes, Pilate's guilt lies in his recognition of Jesus' innocence. Though the Roman judge is not convinced of Jesus' guilt, in the *Leviathan* he "delivered him ... to be crucified" (which reads *crucifigendum tradidit* in the Latin version of the *Leviathan*).[16] It is not stated, but Hobbes's construction seems to imply that the pitiless work of nailing

Jesus up is left, by the Romans, to 'the Jews'. This contradicts the Augustinian tradition upheld by Dante and Marsilius, and marks a con-cession—conscious or unconscious—to anti-Judaic readings of the gospels' crucifixion narratives. Yet this is not a concession that renders Pilate innocent. On the contrary, for Hobbes Pilate is a symbol of the unjust or hated judge. And this injustice, or hatefulness, is useful in the argument of the *Leviathan*.

We may recall how Augustine notes in his *Homilies on the Gospel of John* that Pilate is "a foreign judge" in first-century Judaea.[17] It is not Pilate's foreignness that catches Hobbes's eye, but his paganness. Hobbes stresses Pilate's paganness in his refutation of one of the hottest theories of the seventeenth century—namely the idea "that Christians are not to tolerate Infidel,'or Heretical Kings".[18] This refutation comes at the end of *Leviathan* chapter 42, "Of Power Ecclesiastical", which is one of Hobbes's structuring questions. One indication of this is this chapter's length: "Of Power Ecclesiastical" is by far the longest chapter of *Leviathan*.

Much of this chapter consists of Hobbes's rebuttal of a text, *On the Highest Pontiff*, written by a cardinal of the century-old Jesuit order, Robert Bellarmine (died 1621).[19] A curious biographical note is that in 1614 Hobbes, then a man in his twenties, had seen Pope Paul V, Cardinal Bellarmine, and other princes of the church celebrate the eucharist in the papal chapel in Rome.[20] But there is no nostalgia for Rome in *Leviathan*. On Hobbes's irate and *engagé* reading of *On the Highest Pontiff*, Bellarmine annuls the authority of 'heretical kings' (Protestant monarchs), who may therefore be deposed by 'the supreme pontiff' (the pope). In this and other respects, Hobbes sees Bellarmine as defending a fading late medieval order in Europe—one that may anticipate, in certain ways, a fading late modern world order in which regime change can be imposed or orchestrated by global hegemons, or continental bureaucracies, or ad hoc tribunals.

In the Europe of Hobbes's and Bellarmine's day, the highest court in Europe, the only European bureaucracy, and the *de facto* European hege-mon were all centred—in a contested, byzantine fashion—on the papal court in Rome. Could Rome use its "indirect power" (*potestas indirecta*) to topple 'heretical'—meaning, in the first instance, Protestant—regimes in Europe?[21]

"Christ had no kingdom"

Where Cardinal Bellarmine is sanguine about regime change, the statist Hobbes is choleric. Hobbes is sure, as the frontispiece of *Leviathan* blares, that—in the words of the biblical verse-drama *Job*—the modern sovereign is one of whom it must be said: "There is no power upon earth that can be compared with him."[22] (See figs. 13, 14 and 15.)

Because of this, per Hobbes, it is formally incoherent to hold—in Bellarmine's fashion—that a sovereign can be deposed.

Having defined the sovereign—or, in his monstrous 'modern' imaginary, the *leviathan* (a figure of depravity in the medieval canon law tradition)[23]—as a "power upon earth" to which none "can be compared", Hobbes has theoretically precluded the trial or deposition of any sovereign. But Bellarmine, of course, is making theological arguments—and the theological arguments for regime change were being made, in Hobbes's day, on every side.[24] It is the Roman trial of Jesus that permits Hobbes—in his own mind, and the minds of many of his early readers—to *theologically* refute the high-churchman Bellarmine and to offer what Hobbes himself calls, in the final sentences of *Leviathan*, his "New Wine".[25]

What is Hobbes's 'new wine'? The first thing to note is that this is no slight boast.[26] It is an echo of Jesus himself—as Hobbes and his first readers knew—who in *Matthew*, *Mark*, and *Luke* seems to compare his prophetic doctrine to a "new wine" that must be poured into "fresh wine-skins".[27] However suspect it may be for Hobbes to ventriloquize Jesus in this way, it is not 'blasphemous' for him to do so—I say this in the sense of his seventeenth-century milieu—because Hobbes believes, or claims to believe—in any event, he *insists*—that his 'new wine' in *Leviathan* is none other than the 'new wine' of the gospels. And what is that?

First, Hobbes writes in *Leviathan* chapter 41 that "Christ while he was on Earth"—past tense—"had no Kingdom in this World."[28] And second, Hobbes writes in chapter 42 that "the Kingdom of Christ is not"—present tense—"of this World".[29] In both statements—and there are many more in *Leviathan*, as we will see—Hobbes is of course citing Jesus' reply to Pilate in *John* 18: "My kingdom is not of this world."[30] This returns us to Pilate's guilt, and paganness—both of which are important for Hobbes.

"Our Saviour might have had twelve legions of angels"

Pilate's guilt is stated in the line that we have already seen, where Hobbes writes that "Pilate ... *unjustly*, without finding fault in him, delivered [our Saviour] to the Jews to be crucified."³¹ Though Hobbes echoes, here, a centuries-old anti-Judaic trope, he is uninterested in 'the Jews'. This is because the Judaean rulers have a certain Mosaic legitimacy in the gospels, as Hobbes points out in *Leviathan* chapter 41.³² It is only the Romans who interest Hobbes, because their blank disinterest in Israel's deity demonstrates, for him, the inviolability of 'heathen' sovereignty. This is Hobbes:

> To depose [a sovereign], when he is chosen, is in no case Just. For it is always a violation of faith, and consequently against the Law of Nature, which is the eternal Law of God. Nor do we read, that any such Doctrine was accounted Christian in the time of the Apostles; nor in the time of the Roman Emperors ...

> But to this [Bellarmine] hath replied, that the Christians of old, deposed not Nero, nor Diocletian, nor Julian ... for this cause only, that they wanted Temporal forces. Perhaps so. But did our Saviour, who for calling for, might have had twelve Legions of immortal, invulnerable Angels to assist him, want forces to depose Caesar, or at least Pilate, that unjustly, without finding fault in him, delivered him to the Jews to be crucified? Or if the Apostles wanted Temporal forces to depose Nero, was it therefore necessary for them in their Epistles to the new made Christians, to teach them (as they did) to obey the Powers constituted over them, (whereof Nero in that time was one,) and that they ought to obey them, not for fear of their wrath, but for conscience sake? ...

> It is not therefore for want of strength, but for conscience sake, that Christians are to tolerate their Heathen Princes, or Princes (for I cannot call any one whose Doctrine is the Public Doctrine, an Heretic) that authorize the teaching of an Error.³³

While Hobbes argues from the Roman trial of Jesus that "Christians are to tolerate their Heathen Princes", Pufendorf will argue in the next chapter, from the Roman trial of Jesus, that Christian princes are to tolerate dissenting citizens. The logic of religious intolerance is therefore broken, not once but twice, by Hobbes and Pufendorf, in light of their readings of Jesus' interrogation by Pilate. This suggests that the modern logic of tolerance is linked to early modern readings of the Roman trial of Jesus. But the main thing for us to notice here is Hobbes's allusion to Jesus' claim, in his arrest scene in *Matthew*, that he could summon "twelve legions of angels" to thwart his enemies.[34] It is precisely Christians' belief that Jesus *could* have judged his Judaean, Galilean, and Roman judges—contrary to all appearances—that gives meaning to his ordeal. "I lay down my life", as Jesus says in *John* 10. "No one takes it from me", he underscores, "but I lay it down of my own accord."[35]

The question for Christians then becomes, why would Jesus relinquish his life before a pagan judge? And why would Jesus' disciples—as Hobbes notes—not only lay down their lives as martyrs[36] but instruct the earliest Christians not to resist pagan monarchs like Nero, and not to fight unjust judges like Pilate? For Hobbes, there can be no doubt. It is because the kingdom that Jesus prefigures is "not of this world".[37] This line that Jesus utters before Pilate is no less crucial for Hobbes in *Leviathan* than for Dante in *Monarchy* and Marsilius in *Defender of the Peace*. This is what I call the 'momentary orthodoxy' of Hobbes, which can be traced back, through Aquinas' *Chain of Gold*, to Augustine's *Homilies* on the Roman trial in *John*.

"Our Saviour was not king"

Jesus' words to Pilate are taken in *Leviathan* chapter 41, "Of the Office of Our Blessed Saviour", as the title of a section: "Christ's Kingdom not of this world".[38] In that section, Hobbes cites them again, writing:

> It is manifest, that our Saviour (as man) was not King of those that he Redeemed, before he suffered death; that is, during that time he conversed bodily on the Earth. I say, he was not then King in present … According whereunto, our Saviour himself expressly saith, (*John* 18.36.) "My Kingdom is not of this world."[39]

Now, something radical is being alleged here that we will clarify in a moment. But Hobbes's stress on the Johannine line on Jesus' kingdom being "not of this world" is in keeping with the Augustinian line that we have been retracing in part 5. Before we come back to Hobbes's bold new reading of the Roman trial of Jesus, it is reasonable to ask whether his citation of the trial is a conscious one. And it is.

Jesus' words to Pilate function like an ostinato in the latter chapters of *Leviathan*. As Mogens Lærke indicates, this is in keeping with Hobbes's earlier treatise *On the Citizen*.[40] There is more in *Leviathan* about the kingdom of Christ being 'not of this world' than there is about the 'war of every one against every one', though there is nothing like parity in the literature on Hobbes. I have already commented that Pilate's guilt, for Hobbes, is determined by his sense of Jesus' innocence. This is restated by Hobbes in *Leviathan* chapter 41: "For though Pilate himself (to gratify the Jews) delivered [Christ] to be crucified; yet before he did so, he pronounced openly, that he found no fault in him."[41] It is his enunciation of Jesus' innocence that renders Pilate guilty in Hobbes's eyes, since he finally delivers an innocent man "to be crucified". But if this is why Hobbes's Pilate is guilty—why, we could ask, is his Jesus innocent? And Hobbes tells us:

> *The Kingdom he claimed was to be in another world*; He taught all men to obey in the mean time ... [and] to give Caesar his tribute, and refused to take upon himself to be a judge. How then could his words, or actions be seditious, or tend to the overthrow of their then Civil Government?[42]

The guilt of Hobbes's Pilate is constituted by his recognition of Jesus' innocence, and Jesus' innocence is constituted by his utterance to Pilate in *John* 18.[43] It is this utterance, too, that proves to Hobbes the guilt of Bellarmine and other theologians, of the Counter-Reformation *and the Reformation*, who hold that "the Church now on Earth, is the Kingdom of Christ".[44] To hold that, according to Hobbes, is to hold that the church *is* a "Kingdom ... of this World". And to hold *that*, Hobbes insists, is to betray Christ.[45]

Hobbes believes that there can be no 'kingdom' without sovereignty, no sovereignty without coercion, and that "there is no Coercive Power left them"—meaning ecclesiastics—"by our Saviour".[46] Ecclesiastics "have not ... Regal Power *in this world*", Hobbes writes, for the simple reason that "the Kingdom of Christ is not *of this world*".[47] It is only because of this—which is to say, because of the Roman trial of Jesus—that Hobbes can definitively state that "Faith hath no relation to, nor dependence at all upon Compulsion."[48]

It is because of Jesus' utterance before Pilate that Hobbes can argue that "the Ministers of Christ *in this world*, have no Power ... to Punish

any man for not Believing, or for Contradicting what they say".[49]
Hobbes himself restates this many times. "The ministers of Christ *in
this present world*", he stresses, "have no right of Commanding." And this
lack of a 'right of commanding' in the church, Hobbes states, is precisely mirrored by what he calls "the lawful Authority which Christ
hath left to all Princes".[50] The structure is identical in form—though
not in content—to what we found in Marsilius. And the logic of papal
usurpation in the *Leviathan* is identical, too, to that in *Defender of the
Peace*. Hobbes writes: "The Pope in taking upon him to give Laws to all
Christian Kings, and Nations, *usurpeth a Kingdom in this world, which
Christ took not on him.*"[51] No seventeenth-century reader could fail to
hear, in this sentence, echoes of the world-historical meeting of Pilate
and Jesus. But the seventeenth-century popes, in Hobbes's mind, had
positioned themselves—in Jesus' name—on Pilate's dais.

"Spiritual commonwealth there is none"

What is the first move in this world-historical usurpation drama,
which, Hobbes is not alone in believing, shapes the history of Europe?
The first move is the church's claim that "there is *now in this world* a
Spiritual Commonwealth, distinct from a Civil Commonwealth".[52]
Hobbes calls this "the greatest, and main abuse of Scripture ... to
which almost all the rest are either consequent, or subservient".[53] This
is the source of what Hobbes calls the "Night amongst us", or "at least
a Mist"—a night, or a mist, in which European wars and civil wars of
religion are not only inevitable but in principle irresolvable.[54]

Hobbes's solution to this European difficulty is perhaps more pagan
or Islamic, as Rousseau will later imply, than Christian. Hobbes himself
writes that "the Religion of the Gentiles"—that is, of the pagans—"was
a Part of their Policy".[55] This is the unitary or 'integral' model that
modern European Christians must, Hobbes urges, return to. Where
there has been a distinction in Christian texts, from the earliest days—
and arguably, as we have seen, from the pages of the New Testament—
between the powers of this age (state) and the age to come (church),
Hobbes abolishes the distinction. "This distinction of Temporal, and
Spiritual Power", he concludes, "is but words"—by which he means,
specious and unreal.[56]

Hobbes is not—in his words—"charmed with the word *Power Spiritual*".[57] Because there can be no 'commonwealth' without sovereignty, no 'sovereignty' without power, and no 'power' without coercion—for Hobbes, all this is definitional—there can therefore be no 'spiritual commonwealth' and no 'spiritual power'. The church, therefore, is not—for Hobbes—a 'kingdom'. He sharply denies "that there is *now in this world* a Spiritual Commonwealth, distinct from a Civil Commonwealth".[58] Is there an echo, here, of the Roman trial of Jesus? Hobbes himself tells us that there is. "Spiritual Commonwealth there is *none in this world*", he reiterates, "for it is the same thing with the Kingdom of Christ; which he himself saith, is *not of this world*."[59]

From the much-commented-upon title page of the *Leviathan*,[60] in which the bishop's crozier is held by a monarch—a ruler 'of this world'—Hobbes's grand claim is this: "Spiritual Commonwealth there is none in this world." That is the signal innovation of *Leviathan*. That is what Hobbes calls his 'new wine'. After the *Leviathan*, the European 'secular' can be theorized without a counter-power in the 'religious'. Incidentally, this may be why Hobbes—unlike Bellarmine, and other traditionalists—never uses the word 'secular'. After Hobbes, as *Leviathan*'s Vulgate-lifted motto blasts, the state is to have no conceivable judge on earth. And where is Hobbes's theological rationale for this located? In the Roman trial of Jesus. His parallel construction, which we have just seen, could not make this clearer. "Spiritual Commonwealth there is *none in this world*", is Hobbes's institution-negating claim, "for it is the same thing with the Kingdom of Christ; which he himself saith, is *not of this world*."[61]

"Constantine was that bishop"

Hobbes is not, strictly speaking, a theorist of 'secularization'. His preferred term is 'dissolution', as when he calls for "the *dissolution* of the preter-political Church Government".[62] What this "dissolution of the preter-political" means, precisely, is that there is to be no *'government' within the state that is not statal*. Hobbes rejects "the distinction between the Civil and the Canon Laws"—a distinction we may recall from chapter 1.[63] Hobbes is nostalgic—as Rousseau, citing Hobbes, will later be nostalgic—for the imperial office of *pontifex maximus* in the 'pagan' empire. Precisely this, again, is the meaning of the 'monstrous' frontis-piece of Hobbes's *Leviathan*. His monarch is a neo-pagan emperor—not only *caesar augustus* (signified by the sword) but *pontifex maximus* of the modern European state (signified by the crozier).

Hobbes could not be more explicit in his desire—which, a century later, is Rousseau's desire, too—of reversing the Gelasian vision (which Gelasius, of course, believed to be Christ's vision). *Pontifex maximus*, Hobbes writes in a section of *Leviathan* titled "The name of Pontifex", was "the name of him that in the ancient Commonwealth of Rome, had the Supreme Authority under the Senate and People, of regulating all Ceremonies, and Doctrines concerning their Religion".[64]

Modern sovereigns are to be, on Hobbes's conception, the supreme pontiffs of Europe—or, in his own words, "Supreme Pastors ... in their own Dominions".[65]

Naturally, Hobbes cannot plead for a neo-pagan (or quasi-Islamic) settlement. He therefore suggests that the 'dissolution' of church law and government that he calls for would return the modern state to a Constantinian order. In no more than a sentence, by arguing that Constantine was rightly the "Supreme Pastor" of the Roman Empire (because Christ's kingdom is "not of this world"), Hobbes parodies Valla's theological refutation of the *Donation of Constantine*.[66]

In Valla's text, we will recall, Pope Sylvester refuses Constantine's gift because it would corrupt the bishop of Rome to hold the impe-rial fisc and territories. And in Valla's text, Sylvester cites Jesus' words to Pilate in *John* 18. Hobbes parodies this in a way that is only possible once he has—notionally—returned the office of *pontifex maximus* to the emperor. For Hobbes, Sylvester cannot receive Constantine's gift to the bishop of Rome because *Sylvester is not the true bishop of Rome*. Who is? Why, Constantine, of course. This is Hobbes: "If by Bishop of Rome, be understood either the Monarch of the Church, or the Supreme Pastor of it; not Silvester, but Constantine (who was the first Christian Emperor) was that Bishop; and as Constantine, so all other Christian Emperors were of Right Supreme Bishops of the Roman Empire."[67]

Constantine is rumoured to have called himself "the bishop of those who are outside".[68] The meaning of that comment is still debated: Is he referring to those outside the church (the empire's pagans, say, and

Judaeans)? Or is he referring to Christians outside the empire (the Christians of Persia, say, on whose behalf Constantine may have threatened invasions)?[69] Hobbes, by historical dictat—as required by his novel theory of a post-Catholic European state—makes Constantine the bishop of those who are *inside*. In this regard, he breaks with the entire Augustinian line of thought that we have been tracing in part 5. Nevertheless, the 'momentary orthodoxy' of Hobbes lies in his entire political theology—and his iconic text of political theory, *Leviathan*—turning upon the Roman trial of Jesus in the gospel of *John*.

Conclusions

Hobbes is momentarily orthodox when he insists in the *Leviathan* that coercive jurisdiction is "a Power which [our Saviour] refused to take upon himself, saying, 'Who made me a Judge, or a Divider, amongst you?' and in another place, 'My Kingdom is not of this world.'"[70] The first citation here, by Hobbes, evokes a scene in *Luke* 12 that is cited by other early theorists of secularity, perhaps beginning with the fourteenth-century radical Franciscan William of Ockham, who lived much of his life—like Marsilius of Padua—attached to the imperial court of Ludwig of Bavaria.

In this scene in *Luke* 12, Jesus refuses to settle an inheritance because he is not a 'judge'. This is Ockham's comment, in his text *On the Jurisdiction of Emperors and Popes*, on the Lucan pericope that is later cited by Hobbes:

> Christ was not made a judge—by God or by humankind—of secular things (*temporalibus*) or a divider of inheritances. For when, as we read in *Luke* 12, a certain man said to him: "Master, speak to my brother, so that he divides the inheritance with me", Christ replied, "Man, who made me a judge or a divider over you?"—as if to say, "No one" (*Nullus*). Therefore, he was not a king in secular things, since it belongs to a secular king (*regem temporalem*) to judge concerning secular things.[71]

Hobbes's second citation—"and in another place, 'My Kingdom is not of this world'"[72]—is of course the line in *John* 18, uttered by Jesus before Pilate, which runs like a gold thread through this book, and through much of the *Leviathan*. Like Hobbes, Ockham cites this Johannine line of Jesus' after his citation of *Luke* 12. Again, this is Ockham:

> Christ refused the secular kingdom (*regnum temporale*) offered to him [in the wilderness by the devil] ... And as he says of himself ... "My kingdom is not of this world" ... that is to say, "I have no secular kingdom (*regnum ... temporale*) against the will of Caesar, but a spiritual one." And Pilate, who understood this though he was an unbeliever, afterwards stated that he could find no cause in Christ why he should be put to death—which he would not have done if Christ had testified that he was a secular king (*regem temporalem*), since he was not made a king by Caesar.[73]

It is not in Hobbes's theorization of the "Power which Christ refused to take upon himself" that he differs from Ockham or Marsilius—or, indeed, from Augustine or Gelasius. It is only in his theorization of the power that Christ *did* take upon himself—that is to say, it is not in Hobbes's theory of the secular, but of the *sacred*— that he breaks with the tradition we have been retracing in parts 4 and 5. His contemporaries noticed the rupture, and one of them— Pufendorf—tried to correct it.

18

"TRUTH IS NOT SUBJECT TO HUMAN EMPIRE"

SAMUEL PUFENDORF AND THE LOGIC OF TOLERANCE

Thomas Hobbes is "the very worst framer of theological opinions".[1] Or
that is what we read in a text by one of Hobbes's younger contemporaries, Samuel Pufendorf. (See fig. 16.)

Now a niche figure in intellectual history, Pufendorf was one of the
great lights of what some call the early Enlightenment (*Frühaufklärung*),[2]
with Kant being the Copernican sun of the late Enlightenment
(*Spätaufklärung*).[3] Pufendorf was read for many decades throughout
Europe, not only by scholars but by the members of a rising, continent-
wide bourgeoisie. His treatise *On the Law of Nature and Nations* was one
of the most cited texts of legal and political theory in the long eighteenth century,[4] though a German historian could already say in 1875
that Pufendorf's name was "gone and forgotten".[5]

Anglophone historiography is illiberally fixated on the Ur-liberal,
John Locke, who first made his name as a gentleman's physician and
trade secretary.[6] But Locke himself rates Pufendorf highly. Locke
writes in a 1697 letter: "Pufendorf *On the Duty of Man and Citizen* and
On the Law of Nature and Nations and Aristotle and above all the New
Testament"—a canonical list, clearly—are the books from which a
European "may learn how to live".[7] Yet Pufendorf is not only an ethi-
cist. A professor of the law of nature and nations in Lund, and later, a
privy councillor in Stockholm and a diplomat-historian in Berlin,

Pufendorf is Locke's rival in forging the modern logic of toleration.[8] And though Locke has pages on the Roman trial of Jesus, Pufendorf's handling of it is far more interesting.[9]

What is odd about Pufendorf's harsh verdict on the "theological opinions" of *Leviathan* is that Pufendorf is, in Fiammetta Palladini's phrase, a "disciple of Hobbes".[10] Or, as Noel Malcolm writes, he is a legal theorist who is marked by "the depth of his engagement with— and indebtedness to—Hobbes's ideas".[11] Pufendorf notes this in the first pages of his first treatise, *Elements of Universal Jurisprudence*, saying that he "does not owe a little to Thomas Hobbes". Hobbes's theory, writes Pufendorf—less than a decade after *Leviathan* appeared—has "a certain savour of impiety", but is "nevertheless for the most part quite penetrating and sound".[12]

In a later text on the political history of Europe, Pufendorf stresses that "mankind in general, politically considered, is like wild unruly creatures".[13] Civil war—a war of "wild unruly creatures"—is an ineliminable threat for Pufendorf, no less than for Hobbes. And Pufendorf's intent, here, is not to denigrate 'wild creatures' that are *not human*. On the contrary, as he writes in the first book of his treatise *On the Duty of Man and Citizen*, humans are

> seen to have a greater tendency to do harm than any of the beasts ... [for many] passions and desires are found in the human race unknown to the beasts, as, greed for unnecessary possessions, avarice, desire of glory and of surpassing others, envy, rivalry and intellectual strife. It is indicative that many of the wars by which the human race is broken and bruised are waged for reasons unknown to the beasts. And all these things can and do incite humans to inflict harm on each other.[14]

Pufendorf certainly wants us to think of the confessional wars 'unknown to beasts' that ravaged early modern Europe, without forgetting the wars lit by avarice and other secular passions (and without forgetting that confessional wars may be lit by secular passions).[15] Like Hobbes, Pufendorf holds to a "quasi-Epicurean anthropology", as Ian Hunter calls it, in which passion and not reason is dominant. The contrast Hunter makes is to a "Christian Platonic anthropology" held by the Protestant scholastic Valentin Alberti (died 1697) and the incomparable savant G. W. Leibniz (died 1716), both of whom wrote demolitionary critiques of Pufendorf.[16]

But it is precisely because Pufendorf is a sort of 'Hobbist' who denounces Hobbes as the "worst framer of theological opinions" that it is necessary—and will be interesting—to try to identify where and how Pufendorf rejects Hobbes's political theology in *Leviathan*.

"The dissolution of the preter-political church"

From what I can tell, Pufendorf's core objection seems to be to Hobbes's 'dissolution' of the church—namely Hobbes's insistence that the doctrine and liturgy of the church can be decided, and can *only* be decided, by the temporal rulers of the state. This is what Pufendorf calls the *Leviathan*'s doctrine of "unlimited power"—of which he calls Hobbes "the first inventer".[17] We will of course remember the frontispiece of *Leviathan*, where it is the "Mortal God" of this age who holds the pontiff's crozier, governing the courts and controlling the doctrinal rulings of the church.[18] Pufendorf seems to have found this repugnant. And he is by no means alone.

It is the total dissolution of church authority that a hard-core 'Hobbist' of the early eighteenth century, Nicolaus Gundling—a rector of the University of Halle and friend of Thomasius (whom we will meet in chapter 19)—criticized in his 1707 treatise, *Hobbes Freed from Atheism*. And it is instructive that, on the question of the church in post-Reformation Europe, Gundling cites a 1687 text by Pufendorf, *On the Bearing of Christian Religion on Civil Life*.[19] For reasons that will become clear in a moment, that text by Pufendorf not only helps the rector of Halle to extricate Hobbes from the charge of 'atheism' but will help us to retrace the influence of Pilate and Jesus on the theory of tolerance in the early Enlightenment.

Hobbes, we will remember, calls for "the dissolution of the preter-political Church Government".[20] He means, by this, that a modern political settlement should resemble pre-Christian Rome, a legal order in which—as Hobbes writes—"the Religion of the Gentiles was a part of their Policy".[21] For Hobbes, the 'civil sovereign' is by right (*de jure*) the highest arbiter of religious questions. And what he calls the 'dissolution' of church government is mirrored by what he calls a "*consolidation* of the Right Politique, and Ecclesiastique in Christian Sovereigns". What is the effect of this 'consolidation' of secular power, which entails a 'dissolution' of sacred authority? Early modern sovereigns, writes Hobbes, have by right "all manner of Power over their Subjects, that can be given to man, for the government of men's external actions, both in Policy, and Religion".[22] How are we to interpret this? "Christian Civil Sovereigns in their own Dominions", for Hobbes, are "Supreme Pastors". It is not the pope, but the early modern prince, who is "Monarch of the Church".[23] It is not the pope, but the early modern sovereign, who is high priest in his, or supreme pontiff in her, "own dominions".

What is happening here? Hobbes defines real power as "sovereign, and coercive",[24] and observes—with Augustine, Aquinas, and Marsilius—that this is "a Power which [our Saviour] refused to take upon himself".[25] Hobbes concludes, from his reading of the Roman trial of Jesus, that a "Power to proclaim the Kingdom of Christ"— which he also calls a "power to teach"—is the only power held by the churches and their ministers.[26] So far, so 'orthodox'. However, Hobbes then insists that "the Right of Teaching is inseparably annexed" to what he calls "the Sovereignty".[27] There is therefore no true difference, in *Leviathan*, between the power of coercion (secular) and the power of proclamation (sacred). The latter is held by the former, which is to say, the power to teach 'dissolves' into the power to coerce. The church is not only stripped of its doctrinal authority and internal jurisdiction, but it is denied an intrinsic "Right of Teaching".

The question of truth, for Hobbes, is reduced (in a complicated fashion) to a question of jurisdiction, and the *Leviathan* recognizes only one type of jurisdiction—that of the 'civil sovereign'. There is no non-statal locus of truth, or of the question concerning truth, in *Leviathan*. The question concerning truth is to be controlled, by right (*de jure*), by the one who has the right to coerce. The church's right to confess truth or codify doctrine or judge ecclesiastical matters is specious. For Hobbes, that right belongs to the state.

This is what Pufendorf cannot accept. And it is Pufendorf's reading of the Roman trial of Jesus, in his book *On the Bearing of Christian Religion on Civil Life*, which permits him to break with Hobbes—and to recover a motif in the Johannine trial of Jesus that is strangely absent from much of the commentary tradition that we have covered in the preceding chapters. That motif is truth.

"A king of truth"

Hobbes uses the Johannine Pilate trial in a glaringly novel, that is, untraditional (or 'heretical') way, to argue that Jesus *is in no sense* a king in this world-age, and that the church *is in no sense* a kingdom in this world age. The dubiousness of this reading is brought out when we recall that the arch-humanist and jurist Grotius—writing a couple of decades before Hobbes—says that Jesus, in his reply to Pilate, claims to be "a king *in a certain sense*".[28] Where Grotius holds that Jesus is a king, but not "in the vulgar sense",[29] Hobbes shoots back that 'the vulgar sense' is the only sense.

Pufendorf's contribution to the tradition is exegetically and legally brilliant and deepens the modern logic of tolerance. According to Pufendorf, the sense in which Jesus is a king in this world-age is that he is "a King of Truth", and the sense in which the church is a kingdom in this world-age is that it is "a Kingdom of Truth".[30] Contra Hobbes, Pufendorf believes that the rights of the churches to formulate or celebrate the Truth of Christ are not 'dissolved' into the secular order, because, in Pufendorf's unforgettable phrase: "Truth is not subject to human empire."[31]

Situating truth and the question of truth outside the early modern state's jurisdiction suggests—and Pufendorf sees this—that much error will fall outside the state's jurisdiction. And that is how Pufendorf's theory of the church informs his theory of tolerance. Like philosophy, he says, Christianity can thrive in numerous jurisdictions—even hostile ones.[32] This bare fact indicates, to Pufendorf, the limits of "human empire". Note the formulation: Pufendorf says that "truth *is not subject* to human empire". It is of the essence of truth, he suggests, to be undecidable by means of human courts or edicts.

Pufendorf seems to voice a proto-romantic or a progressive conviction—for him, it is merely Protestant and Christian—that it is of the essence of truth "to be convincing in itself".[33] It is a divine right of truth, Pufendorf thinks, to convince and convict—even bureaucrats, judges, and monarchs. Pilate's jibe might be relevant, here: "What is truth?"[34] But Pufendorf, unlike the seventeenth-century philosopher-Lord Chancellor Francis Bacon, does not read that as a joke.[35] Which returns us to the Roman trial of Jesus.

Pufendorf offers his interpretation of the Pilate trial in a treatise he wrote at a time when, as he states in the first paragraphs of *On the Bearing of Christian Religion on Civil Life*, "some of the greatest princes in Christendom (setting aside the ancient way of converting people by reason and force of arguments) have now recourse to open violence", seeking to "force their miserable subjects to a religion" they cannot honestly confess.[36] Confessional repression and coercion are not national problems in the late seventeenth century. They are European problems.

In this treatise, Pufendorf wants to "trace the very original of religion in general, and of the Christian religion in particular", in the hopes of determining whether it is licit for any government—sacred or secular—to "compel their subjects to obedience by force of arms, in matters of religion".[37] It is inevitable that, in tracing the "very original" of Christianity, Pufendorf—like Dante and Marsilius, Grotius and Hobbes—would have to articulate the meaning, for him, of Jesus' Roman trial.

"God alone is the judge"

Pufendorf agrees with Hobbes that, in Pufendorf's words, "Christ and his Apostles, during the time of Grace, here upon Earth, did not intend to set up a judicial Court, but to preach."[38] Jesus calls his contemporaries to repent—that is, to confess their sins and crimes. But Pufendorf notes that the mode of confession that Jesus' circle practised—and he cites Plato's *Laws*, here, to good effect—is not "like to those Confessions, which in Judicial Courts are required to be made by Offenders", but rather "has a resemblance to those Confessions, that are made to Physicians, by such of their Patients as labour under a secret Distemper, hoping thereby for Relief in their Diseases".[39]

Like a judge, Jesus wants the guilty to confess. But the confession he seeks is not juridical in a human sense, because the judgement it anticipates is not a human judgement. This is Pufendorf:

> God alone is the Judge of our Faith, and even our Thoughts; but Men can only give their Judgment according to such Circumstances, or outward Signs, as effect our Senses, which often prove deceitful, and far different from what we keep concealed within us. And, though in Civil

Courts of Judicature it is sufficient, if Judgment be given in a case, according to what is proved by Evidence, notwithstanding the same may be contrary to Truth; it is quite otherwise with God Almighty, who, searching into the very bottom of our Hearts, cannot be deceived by Hypocrisie.[40]

Pufendorf's conviction that "truth is not subject to human empire" is discernible in this gloss on repentance and the motif of forgiveness of sins in the gospels. "What is proved by *Evidence*", Pufendorf writes here, "may be contrary to *Truth*."[41] The court that Jesus convenes during his prophetic life is not a court of evidence, then—a *forum externum*, in canon law terminology—but a court of conscience, a *forum internum*. This is a court in which even 'secular' judges are judged, and in which no human can judge another. Only God and conscience, here, are the judges.[42] This *forum internum* is vividly conjured in a letter written by Ambrose of Milan in the winter of 379. Though we may be "enclosed in the house, surrounded by darkness, without a witness", says Ambrose, we are held in the double-gaze of our inner experience, and of a divine judge "whom nothing deceives".[43] Though the phrase is not Pufendorf's (or Ambrose's), we could perhaps say that Jesus convenes a 'Court of Truth' during his prophetic life. And Pufendorf's contrast between the judgements of truth and evidence is, indeed, rooted in the gospels. For it is Jesus who says in *John*: "Do not judge by appearances, but judge with right judgement."[44]

"The great mystery of this kingdom"

If the court that Jesus convened was not like the "Civil Courts of Judicature", on Pufendorf's reading,[45] so too the kingdom that Jesus inaugurated "had not the least relation to the Establishment of a Sovereign State".[46] It is fascinating to see how Pufendorf limns what he calls "the great Mystery of this Kingdom",[47] for he seems to contradict, point by point, the logic of human kingdoms that concerns him in much of his oeuvre. Consider the following:

1. "Gold and Silver", says Pufendorf, are "the Sinews of a State"—a nice mercantilist (or cameralist) formula. But what is Jesus' counsel to his disciples? "As you have received [the Gift] for nothing, so

you shall give it for nothing."[48] The logic of Jesus' kingdom is anti-mercantilist.

2. It is "a sure Maxim of State" that enemies must be resisted. But Jesus tells his disciples that they must overcome "Persecutions and Dangers ... not by Force, but by Patience, by showing their Innocence, or flying to another Place". This is the contrary of what is "practiced in Temporal Governments", Pufendorf notes—and this is not Jesus' counsel *for* 'temporal governments'. Yet non-resistance and flight are the anti-realpolitik maxims of Jesus' disciples, qua disciples of Jesus.[49]

3. "It is allowable by the Civil Constitutions", says Pufendorf, "for everyone to pursue his Right." It is perhaps definitional of a 'crime' that its victim cannot be commanded to forgive it. Redress is the *raison d'être* of a law court. But "in the kingdom of Christ", Pufendorf—a celebrated jurist—reminds us, anyone "who will not remit a Trespass to his brother" is seen as a bad citizen. The law-code of Jesus' kingdom is anti-litigious.[50]

4. "Those that pretend to lay the Foundation of a new State", Pufendorf writes, "must have Territories belonging to them, where their new subjects may settle themselves." But the church has been, from the very beginning, non-territorial. "Neither Christ, nor his Apostles", he observes—noting the contrast with Moses and Romulus—"did ever remove Christians from their Habitations to other Places." It is in the century when the modern territorial state is crystallizing in Europe that Pufendorf stresses that the 'kingdom of truth' is not territorial.[51]

Other interesting contrasts are made—the church, for instance, is not constituted by a Hobbesian contract but by a divine covenant.[52] The crux, though, is that Pufendorf's church is a "Mystical Body".[53] For Pufendorf, the non-statal logic of the gospels and the early church demonstrate that "the Church, according to the intention of Christ and his Apostles, neither was, *nor could be* a State".[54] The church eludes human jurisdiction in the same way that truth eludes human empire.

What, then, is *The Bearing of Christian Religion on Civil Life*? Pufendorf concludes, against Hobbes, that:

> It is without question, that the Union of Believers under Christ, their King, ought to be considered a Kingdom or Empire, but such a one as

is *not of this World*, and consequently of a quite different nature from
that Sovereign Power, which is exercised in a Civil Government. ...
That Civil Power does not reach this Kingdom; true Piety being not to
be implanted by Human Force ... For, the Kingdom of Christ being a
Kingdom of Truth, it requires no Civil Power or Force.[55]

The linkage between early modern Christianity and violence, which
occasions Pufendorf's book, is broken—not by a 'dissolution' of the
church, as in the *Leviathan*, but by a re-elaboration of the Augustinian
tradition we have been retracing in part 5. Jesus *is* a king, says
Pufendorf, but his kingdom is *not of this world*. A correct reading of the
Roman trial of Jesus is thus, according to Pufendorf, a *sine qua non* of a
European political culture in which ritual and confessional differences
are tolerated. Pufendorf therefore gives us what is, to his mind, a correct reading of the trial.

"A kingdom of truth"

Jesus "did not deny" the charge of being a king in his interrogation by
Pilate. This marks Pufendorf's critical break with Hobbes, for whom
Jesus is not a king during his trial and death. Rather, Pufendorf goes
on, Jesus "witnessed a good confession"—an echo of *I Timothy* 6, and of
Grotius' gloss on *John* 18 (see chapter 2). And what, for Pufendorf, is
the 'good confession' that Jesus made on the morning of his death?
"That his Kingdom was *not of this World*, which is as much as to say: His
kingdom was not like those of Temporal Princes, who exercise Acts of
Sovereignty over their Subjects."

The right to coerce and punish the body is definitional of 'temporal'—which is to say, 'secular'—jurisdiction. Note that Pufendorf still
uses this patristic and medieval lexicon, which Hobbes, who rejects the
distinction between 'temporal' and 'spiritual' power, had abandoned.
It is precisely this right to coerce that Jesus' utterance before Pilate, on
Pufendorf's interpretation, renounces. A "Kingdom of Truth" is a kingdom that only has recourse to "the force of Truth". It is because of
this—that "the Kingdom of Christ ... is a Kingdom of Truth"—that
"the Kingdom of Christ needs not to be maintained by the same forc-
ible means and Rules, by which Subjects must be kept in Obedience to
the Civil Powers". Just like philosophy—a love of truth—needs no

"particular State" with militias and war machines, so the church needs no "separate Commonwealth" with criminal courts and prisons.[56]

What then is Pufendorf's church? In a word, a 'college'. More precisely, he theorizes the church as a "private college" (*privatum collegium*).[57] We cannot enter into the legal ontology of corporations, societies, and colleges. But it is striking that Pufendorf quotes two authorities for his theory: Jesus and Tertullian. "Does not our Saviour himself say?" asks Pufendorf, "'Where two or three are gathered in my name, there am I in the midst of them.'" He then observes that it is Jesus' words that "moved Tertullian to say, 'Three make up a church, as well as a college' (*Tres faciunt ecclesiam, sicut collegium*)".[58] Though synagogues could be called 'colleges' in the first centuries CE,[59] it is worth remembering that a number of third-century legal decisions reflect the pre-Christian empire's recognition of the church as a sort of 'college'—and that Tertullian, like Augustine, was an African.[60]

"Pilate understood this did not fall under his cognizance"

Pufendorf's kingdom of truth is not a state because "Truth is not subject to human empire."[61] It is curious, though, that Pufendorf places this ultra-tolerant line on the lips of Jesus' Roman judge. It is Pilate who says this, not Jesus—for reasons that will become clear in a moment. First, the passage is worth reading in full. It marks a high point of the *gran rifiuto* tradition we have been retracing, from the early fourteenth to the late seventeenth century, in part 5. This is Pufendorf:

> Jesus therefore being examined by Pilate concerning this Accusation [that he made himself out to be a King], did not deny it, but witnessed a good Confession (*I Timothy* 6:13), namely, "That his Kingdom was not of this World", which is as much as to say; "His Kingdom was not like those of Temporal Princes, who exercise Acts of Sovereignty over their Subjects."
>
> For, if Jesus had pretended to the same Prerogatives, he might have commanded his Servants—not his timorous Disciples, but those strong Legions of Angels, who always stand ready to his Command (*Matthew* 4:11)—to protect their Lord from falling into the Hands of Pilate. And when Pilate replied, "That he then professed himself to be a King", Jesus answered, "That he was King, but a King of Truth, and that for this

cause he came into the World, that he should bear witness unto Truth (*John* 1:17)."

Pilate, by what Christ had professed, soon understood that this matter did not fall under his Cognizance, and therefore answered, "What is Truth?" As if he would have said, "If nothing else can be objected against you, but that you make profession of Truth, I have no further business with you; for Truth is not subject to any Human empire (*veritas imperio humano non subsit*)."

Neither did the Laws of the Roman Empire, wherein so many Nations were comprehended, take any Cognizance at that time, of the various Opinions of their Subjects in matters of Religion, as it plainly appears out of *Acts of the Apostles* 18:14–15, 24:29, 26:31–32 … It was for this reason that Pilate would have discharged him, if he had not at last thought it more convenient, to appease the rage of the Jews by Sacrificing him, though Innocent, to their Fury.

But after Christ had once made this open Confession, he refused to make any further answer to Pilate, being sensible that Pilate was not desirous to be instructed in this Truth. The Kingdom of Christ therefore, is a Kingdom of Truth (*regnum veritatis*), where he, by the force of Truth, brings over our Souls to his Obedience.[62]

The first thing to note is that this is the first place in Pufendorf's *On the Bearing of Christian Religion on Civil Life* where the formulation 'kingdom of truth' is used. This is a structuring moment in the book, and a memorable one in the intellectual history of tolerance in early modern Europe. For the 'kingdom of truth' idea is what leads Pufendorf to conclude, in the last sentences of his book, that "a prince sins (*peccat*) who harasses his citizens due only to a difference of religion".[63] And it is because the church is a 'kingdom of truth' that it renounces—or rather, that it must renounce—the logic and tactics of "human dominion and coercion" (*imperio humano et coactione*).[64] Christianity's break with the realpolitik of human 'empire' (*imperium*) is irreplaceably dramatized, on Pufendorf's reading, in the Roman trial of Jesus.

What is more, Pufendorf is clearly cognizant of part of the tradition that we have been retracing in this book. We have already noticed the echo of Grotius' *Annotations on the New Testament*, when Pufendorf cites *I Timothy* 6:13 on the 'good confession'. But there is likely an echo, too, of Hobbes in this passage. We may recall Hobbes's rhetorical question in *Leviathan* III: "But did our Saviour, who for calling for, might have had

221

twelve Legions of immortal, invulnerable Angels to assist him, want forces to depose Caesar, or at least Pilate?"[65] I see no reason to doubt that this inspires Pufendorf's line about "strong Legions of Angels, who always stand ready", and who could have prevented "their Lord from falling into the Hands of Pilate".[66] Later in the book, Pufendorf returns to the angels; and here, like Hobbes, he stresses their revolutionary potential: "Never did anybody shew a greater Love to Mankind than our Saviour, who sacrificed himself for our Salvation; Yet he made use of no other ways to propagate his Doctrine, than Teaching, when he might have commanded Twelve Legions of Angels to force Mankind to Obedience."[67] This is not a common line of reasoning in the commentaries. It is likely a sign of Hobbes's influence.

"A public act of terror"

Hobbes's influence is cancelled out, though, when Pufendorf comes to Pilate's brusque question to Jesus: "What is truth?" For with this question, on Pufendorf's reading, Pilate denies that questions of truth—and thus, questions of religion—come within his civil jurisdiction. "If nothing else can be objected against you", this Pilate says to Jesus, "but that you make profession of Truth, I have no further business with you."[68] What is happening here? Pufendorf is depicting Pilate as more humane—and, in a sense, more 'Christian'—than many of the Christian judges of seventeenth-century Europe. Is Pufendorf whitewashing Pilate?

He is not. And we know this because Pufendorf returns to the Roman trial of Jesus, and turns to the question of Pilate's innocence, in an appendix in which he fiercely criticizes a text by a Dutch 'Hobbist', Adrian Houtuyn (died 1733).[69] Pufendorf is shocked that Houtuyn, "who passes himself off as a jurisconsult", is impressed by Pilate's handling of Jesus. (Houtuyn's reading of the Roman trial is determined by his 'Hobbist' commitments. For him, a 'secular' tribunal can do no wrong in religious matters.) Pufendorf fumes that there is "not one iota of legitimate process" in the Roman trial of Jesus, which is nothing but "a public act of terror" (*latrocinium publicum*).[70]

Pufendorf's Pilate is a terrible judge—a murderous judge. Why is it, then, that Pilate and not Jesus utters Pufendorf's luminous line about 'truth not being subject to human empire'? The reason for this lies not in Pufendorf's idea of Pilate, but in his idea of Rome. According to Hobbes, we may recall, the religion of the Romans "was a Part of their Policy".[71] This historical claim is crucial to Hobbes's political philosophy—as it will be, in the eighteenth century, to Rousseau's. But Pufendorf is not convinced. For him—and this will become the doctrinaire Enlightenment line—pre-Christian Rome was a basically humane, religiously tolerant legal culture.[72]

In the long passage on Jesus and Pilate we just read, Pufendorf denies that "the laws of the Roman Empire" were concerned "at that time" with "the various opinions of their subjects in matters of religion". "It was for this reason", Pufendorf continues, "that Pilate would have discharged Christ ..."[73] Pilate's reluctance to kill Jesus has nothing to do with Pilate's innocence, for Pufendorf; it merely reflects his interpretation of Roman legal culture in the first century. Because of his early Enlightenment theory of pre-Christian law, Pufendorf could hold both that Pilate's handling of Jesus was "a public act of terror", and that Pilate had no desire to crucify Jesus.[74] This is interesting.

Conclusions

The question of Pilate's innocence is debated with greater legal sophistication at the end of the seventeenth century than ever before. And it is one of Pufendorf's disciples, Thomasius, who insists—in the Augustinian vein that has held us throughout part 5—that Pilate is not a humane judge, but a judicial murderer. But what provokes Thomasius to write on the question is a notorious legal text by the title of *Pilate Defended*, which will draw our narrative towards a conclusion.

19

"PILATE DEFENDED"

THE NATURE OF JESUS' TRIAL AND THE RISE
OF SECULARIZATION

Though 'secularization' (*saecularizatio*) is a creation of medieval canon
law, it only becomes a regime-defining term in seventeenth-century
Europe. It is not hard to identify the reason for this. In early modern
Europe, 'secularization' is a term on hand to describe the expropriation of monastic estates (and other church holdings), and the
Protestant revolutions led to a mass expropriation of monastic estates
(and other church holdings) in the north of Europe.[1] It is because of
the Protestant revolutions that a minor process of medieval canon
law—'secularization'—became a revolutionary, continent-shaping
technique of early modern civil law.

Pufendorf cites a northern European rhyme that already felt cli-
chéd by the end of the seventeenth century: "Whoever governs the
region decides the religion." In Pufendorf's Latin: *cuius est regio, illius
est religio*.[2] The idea is that any 'state-holder' may decide whether
their state—and, crucially, whether their *citizens*—will cut ties to
the old Roman church and become allied with one of the new
Protestant communions. Wherever a 'state-holder' went with the
Lutherans or Calvinists, 'secularization' occurred—meaning that
vast, centuries-old church complexes were seized and incorporated

225

into the secular economies of government or the burgeoning early capitalist market.

Emblematic of this was Henry VIII, who "destroyed" the great monastic houses of England, as Simon Grimm puts it in a 1687 dissertation, *On the Profanation of Sacred Things, which Is Called in the Vernacular, 'Secularization'*.[3] Henry's policy, incidentally, seems to have been inspired by his need for ready cash.[4] The walled-in wealth of the monasteries was liquefied by fiat and poured into Henry's many, early nationalist wars—and the Henrician settlement was then theorized, by Hobbes (in chapter 17), in light of the Roman trial of Jesus.

Profanation, secularization, incorporation

Note Grimm's title: *On the Profanation of Sacred Things*. He leads with 'profanation' (*profanatio*), a pre-Christian term for the seizure of temples, altars, and consecrated vessels.[5] And it is common for seventeenth-century jurists to signal that *saecularizatio* is a dubious term.[6] It is a "barbarism", says jurist Johann Rhetz—meaning, a post-classical term—and "according to those who write in a more elegant Latin, it should not be used".[7] In a 1683 dissertation, *On Secularization*, Johann Baumgart notes that *saecularizatio* is "not really a Latin" concept at all, since it never occurs in Justinian's *Body of Roman Law*. But Baumgart then concedes that *saecularizatio* seems to have "usurped" a place in modern European politics and law—one that, mutatis mutandis, it holds to this day.

And what, for Baumgart, is the meaning of the pseudo-Latin term, *saecularizatio*? It is "to make something that belongs to the church into something that belongs to the age" (*ex ecclesiastico facere aliquid seculare*).[8] In the first instance, modern 'secularization' is a form of expropriation. And it is worth remembering that it is a form of expropriation—as one young jurist notes—that cancels out "the last will and intention" of numberless Christians who left their lands to the church, wishing them to be "perpetual holdings of the church".[9]

It is worth remembering that 'incorporation' (*incorporatio*) is a seventeenth-century term for 'secularization'. We see this in Erich Mauritius's 1666 book *On the Secularization of Church Holdings*, one of the first modern legal treatments of the topic. "Incorporation of church

holdings", Mauritius writes, is "a different way of saying secularization".[10] In Hobbes's *Leviathan*, we may recall, a 'dissolution' of church
authority is mirrored in what Hobbes calls a 'consolidation' of the
power of the early modern state. And what Mauritius's comment
reveals—to my mind—is that 'secularization' denotes the loss sustained by the church (Hobbes's 'dissolution'), and 'incorporation'
denotes the gain made by the state or secular economy that expropri-
ates the church's holdings (Hobbes's 'consolidation').

In other words, 'incorporation' reminds us that there is inevitably a
cui-bono question to be asked wherever modern 'secularization' is
occurring. One blood-curdling *exemplum* in a seventeenth-century treatise, *On Justice and Right*, by an illustrious Flemish theologian-jurist,
Leonard Lessius (died 1623), illustrates the high stakes of an ultra-
sectarian moment in which a single adverse judgement might lead to a
religious house being seized and asset-stripped. "Calumniators [might]
succeed in falsely accusing an entire monastery", as Wim Decock
recounts Lessius' *exemplum*, "with a capital crime, such as treason [or]
idolatry."[11] *Incorporatio* is a forgotten term that signals the benefits that
can accrue, justly or not, to a secular order as the result of *saecularizatio*. However that may be, 'secularization' is the term that has lasted—
not 'profanation', and not 'incorporation'.

"The power of magistrates to secularize"

The novelty of early modern 'secularization' is not only terminologi-
cal. Antecedents for the mass seizure of basilicas, bishops' palaces, and
consecrated houses—by Christians—were hard to come by. Mauritius
comments that Julian the Apostate, a "bitter persecutor of the
Christian name", had seized all the "ecclesiastical holdings that
Constantine had granted".[12]

For Mauritius, of course, Julian's 'profanation' of Christian properties is not a legitimating history. And the histories that Mauritius and
other seventeenth-century Protestants could not foresee are not, perhaps, legitimating either. In the wake of the Protestant revolution, the
real breakers of secularization that razed Europe's thousand-year
monastic estates came with the Jacobins in the eighteenth century,
Bonapartists in the nineteenth century, Nazis and Bolsheviks in the

twentieth century—and now, late capitalism (or neoliberalism) in the twenty-first century. But what is the relevance of this?

To clarify, we can glance at a 1707 doctoral dissertation *On the Nature of Secularized Holdings*, defended at the then-new University of Halle, which stages a "defence of the justice of secularization against infinite objections" in a striking way.[13] "None of this controversy over the power of political magistrates to secularize church holdings", writes Bernhard Heinrich Pagendarm in this dissertation, "can be defined by Justinian's civil law, or by canon law".[14]

The two continent-shaping legal traditions I introduced in chapter 1 are declared inert, here, by a young doctor of laws in the first decade of the eighteenth century. But if neither of the premodern European law-codes can justify 'secularization', what form of law possibly can? The right to 'secularize' can only be defined, says Pagendarm, "by the law of nature".[15]

This manoeuvre is interesting for two reasons. First, because it is typical of a post-Reformation legal tradition that rises continuously in the seventeenth century and dominates the eighteenth century. And second, because it is identical to the reasoning of a professor of law in Halle, Thomasius—the professor, incidentally, to whom Pagendarm submitted his dissertation—in a 1675 text, *On the Unjust Judgement of Pontius Pilate*.[16] Thomasius is one of the master-thinkers of 'secularization' in the early Westphalian era in Europe.[17]

Writing in the front pages of a 1709 German translation of Thomasius' *Institutes of Divine Jurisprudence*—first published in Latin, in 1688—a young economic theorist, Ephraim Gerhard (died 1718), concluded that those with an "enlightened understanding (*aufgeklährtern Verstand*) could only take pleasure in the lights" that stream from the books of "Grotius, Pufendorf, Thomasius".[18] Grotius, Pufendorf, and Thomasius. They form a sort of Orion's belt of early Enlightenment legal theory—one that seems, strangely, to be invisible to most post-Kantian intellectual historians.[19] But as Ian Hunter documents in *Rival Enlightenments*, Grotius, Pufendorf, and Thomasius are the luminaries of a distinctive culture of "civil enlightenment" in the long eighteenth century.[20] It is significant that they are all Protestants, and that they all publish legally astute, philosophically motivated interpretations of the Roman trial of Jesus.

Grotius comments on the Pilate trial, word by word and line by line, in his *Annotations on the New Testament* (touched on in chapter 2); and Pufendorf offers his reading of the Pilate trial in his text *On the Bearing of Christian Religion on Civil Life* (considered in chapter 18). Thomasius, too, has a text on Pilate—a high point, if not the high point, of legal reasoning on the innocence (or not) of Jesus' judge. But Thomasius' interpretation of the Pilate trial is written in reply to two other texts. We will turn to them, before returning to Thomasius.

"Notorious for defending Pilate"

From what I can determine, the 'secularization' genre is born in the second half of the seventeenth century in the states that now comprise the German Republic. And it is eye-catching, in light of this book's narrative arc—which connects the Pilate trial and the history of secularity—that in 1674 a legal text went to press in Dresden with the shocking title *A Defence of Pontius Pilate*.[21] It was reprinted a couple of years later in Leipzig—with a pair of rebuttals we will glance at in a moment—under the briefer title *Pilate Defended*.[22]

One of the critics of *Pilate Defended* calls it, coolly, a "singular treatise".[23] And it is. In just forty-nine pages, a doctoral candidate in "both laws" at the University of Jena—it is hard to believe he is not yet a doctor[24]—insists that Pilate is not, as he is vulgarly conceived, "the exemplar of the most-unjust judge".[25] On the contrary, what subtler readers of the gospels will perceive is "the justice of the just judge, Pilate" (*justitiam judicis justi, Pilati*).[26] German theologians reprobated this idea, and Protestant censors banned *Pilate Defended*, but that only heightened its allure.[27]

The name on this slim book's title page is Johann Steller, signed *Leisnicensis*—meaning, "from Leisnig" (an obscure town in Saxony).[28] Unless I am mistaken, not much more is known about this Steller, though one Catholic historian, Joseph Zola, is keen to convey decades later that Steller is a Protestant.[29] We can take that as read. What the young Protestant jurist wants to prove, Steller writes in *Pilate Defended*, is "the innocence of Pontius Pilate" (*innocentia Pontii Pilati*).[30] That idea had been extant, as we have seen, since the first centuries CE. But "the innocence of Pontius Pilate" seems to have been formulated for the first time, with such force and clarity, by Steller—a provincial *doctorandus* in the late seventeenth century. This may be why the eminent dramatist and cultural philosopher Gottfried Ephraim Lessing remembers Steller in the mid-eighteenth century, saying that he had become "notorious for defending Pilate".[31]

Lessing will himself become "notorious for defending Pilate" during the so-called 'fragment-controversy' (*Fragmentenstreit*) that raged in the German states after he unearthed, as head of the ducal library at Wolfenbüttel, a set of secret notebooks by a learned Hebraist, Hermann Samuel Reimarus (died 1768). Lessing's edition of Reimarus' fragments on the gospels, *The Goal of Jesus and His Disciples* (Braunschweig, 1778), is hugely important.[32] For Reimarus is the first European intellectual to revive the ancient theory that Jesus was a prophet-militant, a 'secular' aspirant king—and thus, destined for a Roman cross.

In a fourth-century 'pagan' fragment I cited in chapter 4, seemingly traceable to Sossianus Hierocles, Jesus is alleged to have led "a force of 900 men".[33] That is not Reimarus' theory in the eighteenth century, or Eisler's in the twentieth, but there is a filament-thin tradition that ties Hierocles to Reimarus and his heirs. There is a history yet to be written of *the inculpation of Jesus* in Europe in the late seventeenth and eighteenth centuries, as a rebel or an impostor, for the first time since late antiquity.[34]

Like the 'innocence' of Pontius Pilate, the 'guilt' of Jesus is not only an intellectual but a legal and political history. But this is not the place to ask how Lessing's edition of Reimarus might have influenced nineteenth- and twentieth-century philosophy and politics—helping to give rise, for instance, to a voluminous Marxist archive on the life of Jesus and the rise of Christianity.[35] Our question here is, rather: What are young Steller's arguments in *Pilate Defended*?

"The innocence of Pontius Pilate"

Pilate Defended has three chapters, and three arguments. In the first, Steller claims that the Temple court of Caiaphas—the Sanhedrin—held the right to kill (*ius gladii*) in Jerusalem and passed a binding sentence on Jesus. Steller therefore believes that the sentence of death under which Jesus died—by Roman hands—was that of the Temple court, and not Pilate's tribunal. This could perhaps be harmonized with the 'passion' narratives in the early modern *Toledot Yeshu* tradition, though it differs at crucial points.

In the second chapter, Steller suggests that the custom (*consuetudo*) that Pilate invoked in the scene with Barabbas—the *privilegium pas-chale*—legally obligated him to free Barabbas and crucify Jesus. To my knowledge, this is a totally original argument. It is highly interesting, and it seems to anticipate a line of reasoning about the Barabbas refer-endum that twentieth-century Europe's most revered legal theorist, Hans Kelsen, will make. (Note that Kelsen wrote his doctoral thesis on a text that is much concerned with Jesus' Roman trial: Dante's *Monarchy*.)[36] For those who hold that Jesus is the "witness of the abso-lute truth", writes Kelsen—a Christian convert of Jewish descent—the scene with Barabbas "is certainly a strong argument against demo-cracy". A strong argument—but not, for Kelsen, conclusive.[37] Steller has no interest in democracy, but he is convinced that the Barabbas referendum is binding on Pilate—which is to say, conclusive.

Neither Steller nor his critics (nor Kelsen) seem to note this, but the clearest objection to his argument from the Barabbas incident may be exegetical. (It is not till the nineteenth century that the historicity of this incident begins to be questioned.) Steller infers that once the 'crowds' massed at Pilate's tribunal, who are controlled by the Temple elites,[38] call for Barabbas to be freed, Pilate is legally obligated to crucify Jesus. But our texts only tell us that the prefect had this cus-tom in Jerusalem: to release a prisoner at Passover.[39] A close reading of the texts implies that Pilate *is* legally obligated (by force of *consue-tudo*) to liberate Barabbas on the insistence of the 'crowds'. But it cannot be inferred from the canonical texts that the paschal referen-dum—Jesus or Barabbas?—decided Jesus' fate. The *privilegium pas-chale* is pictured in the gospels as an emancipatory custom, not a puni-tive (or sacrificial) one.

In the third chapter, Steller tries to definitively cancel out the scan-dalous "injustice of Pilate" (*injustitia Pilati*). To do this, he must disprove the vulgar Christian notion that Pilate "condemned to death" the only human—Jesus—who "could truly be charged with no fault what-ever".[40] Having argued in his first chapter that Caiaphas *did* condemn

Jesus (in a legally binding manner); and in the second chapter that the Barabbas referendum obligated Pilate to *crucify* Jesus (through the binding force of custom); Steller now denies that Pilate condemned Jesus. This is the crux of Steller's defence in *Pilate Defended*. The Roman prefect gives his nod to the "mere execution" (*nudam executionem*) of Jesus, but he utters no sentence of death.[41]

According to Steller, it is Caiaphas' sentence of death, which is 'democratically' ratified by the Barabbas plebiscite, that destines Jesus to the cross. (The term 'democratic' is Kelsen's, not Steller's.) Pilate did not, himself, condemn "that righteous man" (as Pilate's wife calls Jesus in *Matthew*).[42] Thus, although Steller believes that a judge is *strictly* obligated "to judge according to what is *alleged* and *proven*" (unlike certain other early modern jurists);[43] and although Steller believes that the gravest political crime alleged in Jesus' Roman trial—sedition—is *not* proven (unlike certain modern New Testament scholars, who follow Reimarus): Steller's Pilate is innocent. This is because, according to Steller, Pilate never uttered "the most-unjust sentence" he is wrongly thought, by most Christians, to have uttered.[44] The only "sentence of death" under which Jesus died was uttered by Caiaphas and ratified by the 'crowd'.[45]

Steller's argument in the second chapter of *Pilate Defended*—from the Barabbas incident—is highly original. Not so with the idea in his third chapter that Pilate never sentences Jesus. Nor does Steller want us to think that his idea of a "mere execution" is original. Steller reminds us where we have heard it—and its opposite—before. He cites the *Divine Institutes* of Lactantius, where Constantine's courtier insists that Pilate "did not himself pronounce a sentence", but merely "handed Jesus over" to be crucified.[46] That is a crystalline early Christian formulation, Steller tells us, of the "innocence of Pontius Pilate".[47] Other patristic formulations of Pilate's innocence are made by Eusebius of Emesa (died 359/60),[48] by Chrysostom,[49] and by a forged letter from Pilate to Tiberius (at which we glanced in chapter 6).[50]

Contra Pilate's innocence are the Africans—though Steller does not call them that. He cites Cyprian more than once,[51] and Tertullian (as hard to make out).[52] Steller avoids the African father par excellence, Augustine (though Steller's critics will not). And the one 'Greek' that

Steller cites in opposition to Pilate's innocence is the medieval Byzantine commentator Theophylact of Ohrid (died 1107).[53] This is interesting, since Theophylact enters the Latin commentary tradition—and late medieval political theory—through Aquinas' *Chain of Gold* (mentioned in chapter 16).

Steller is young and bold, and signals a new mood of 'protest' in northern Europe, but his use of Theophylact shows that he is not cut off from the commentary traditions that informed Dante and Marsilius, say, in the fourteenth century.

"The iniquity of Pilate"

The first critique of Steller is dully titled *A Refutation of the Defence of Pontius Pilate*.[54] It is signed "Daniel Maphanasus", which is the nom de guerre of Daniel Hartnaccius, *Pomerani* ("from Pomerania"). This is not the place to delve into Hartnaccius' biography, but we can note that he edited and supplemented a bulky (700-page) book of *Natural Wonders* in which neat answers are given to hundreds of questions,[55] such as: "Whether nymphs and women-of-the-waves are monsters?" This is denied. They are "spectral" creatures, not natural ones; they are not therefore monsters.[56]

More relevant for us is a massive (1,300-page) *System of All the Histories of the Church*, which Hartnaccius re-edited, and to which he contributed.[57] It is curious to see a list of the most daring lines in Thomas Browne's *Religio Medici* (*Religion of a Doctor*),[58] barbed comments on the free-thinking of a Johann Spinoza (*sic*), and a rapid-fire critique of "the sect of the Cartesians" in the final pages of this *System*.[59] But who could write a *System of All the Histories of the Church* without referring to Jesus' judge?

The "cruelty of Pilate" (*immanitas Pilati*) is entered into Hartnaccius' *System*,[60] and we note one place where Pilate's sin is compared to Lucifer's rebellion.[61] Pilate's world-historical sin can only be what the *System* calls his "tyrannical" crucifixion of Jesus.[62] And it is crucial that the reconstruction of the passion in this huge tome concludes that Jesus was "condemned to death by Pilate".[63] In several pages on the empire-wide persecution of Christians by the Tetrarchy in the early fourth century, the *System* notes that Maximin Daia stoked the masses' hatred by promulgating his "*Acts of Pilate and of the Saviour*, full of blasphemies, confected by priests".[64] Not only this, but the *System* sketches the (half-historical or fictional) scene from Hegesippus in which Jesus' cousins instruct the emperor Domitian in Palestine, telling him that "the kingdom of Christ spurns all worldly kingdoms".[65]

No one would expect a co-labourer on this *System* to be convinced by young Steller's *Defence of Pontius Pilate*. But for us, two things are striking about Hartnaccius' *Refutation of the Defence of Pontius Pilate*. First, the titles of no fewer than seven of Hartnaccius' chapters (of thirty-two) begin with the words: "On the Iniquity of Pilate ..." (*De iniquitate Pilati ...*). Just as the idea of Pilate's innocence had never been so sharply formulated before Steller, so the idea of his guilt had never been so intently catalogued before Hartnaccius. His *Refutation of the Defence of Pontius Pilate* faults Pilate for

1. hearing hostile witnesses (chapter 13),
2. perverting the custom of the *privilegium paschale*—a sharp rebuke to Steller (chapter 14),
3. judicially torturing an innocent man (chapter 15),
4. abusing his power throughout the interrogation of Jesus (chapter 16),
5. feigning his fear of a Judaean riot—and of Caesar's wrath (chapter 17),
6. caving to Jesus' accusers by condemning him to death (chapter 19), and
7. rushing his interrogation of Jesus—and the crucifixion (chapter 24).

Hartnaccius is an able humanist, and he sources every point in this catalogue from the archives. What is innovative is the catalogue itself. Hartnaccius' reading of the trial is no less legalistic than Steller's, but with the *Refutation* it becomes possible to read the Pilate trial, scene by scene—with a humanistic apparatus—as a mistrial.

The second striking thing in *A Refutation of the Defence of Pontius Pilate* is the cool-headedness with which Hartnaccius columnizes the diverging strains of Christian tradition concerning Pilate. This is the topic of chapter 20 of Hartnaccius' *Refutation*,[66] in which—as in the narrative of this book—the lines of thought that hold to Pilate's innocence and guilt could be placed under the rubrics of 'Lactantius' and 'Augustine'.

Now, Hartnaccius criticizes Steller's interpretation of Lactantius—and mine. He opens chapter 20 of his *Refutation* by denying that Lactantius or any early Christian writer "expressly defended" Pilate. This comment is, perhaps, deceptively weak. For Lactantius *did* defend Pilate, if he did not *expressly* defend him. And Hartnaccius concedes this, introducing Lactantius with the words, "Yet I confess ..." (*fateor tamen*), and then copying out the lines from *Divine Institutes* IV that we have read more than once: Pilate "did not himself utter a sentence, but handed Jesus over to the Judaeans".[67] Hartnaccius cites Chrysostom, too, 'in defence of Pontius Pilate'. He is unsure about Eusebius of Emesa. But even on Hartnaccius' telling, there is a Christian tradition within which Steller's little book, *Pilate Defended*, can be placed. And who, on Hartnaccius' telling, most forcefully rejects that tradition? Augustine in the *Homilies on the Gospel of John*, which we read from in chapter 13.[68]

Steller is a crude biblical exegete, and Hartnaccius is not a stellar jurist. But it seems fair to say that they mark high points in the early modern reception of the conflicting Latin traditions—seeded by Lactantius and Augustine—of reading the Roman trial of Jesus in a juridical vein.[69] It is with Steller and Hartnaccius that early Christian theories of Pilate's innocence and guilt are most comprehensively stated, and that modern refinements are most clearly made.

But the most impressive critique of Steller's *Pilate Defended* is not Hartnaccius' *Refutation*. And though this other critique of Steller is 'Augustinian' in its contours, it is notable for a total lack of patristic and medieval citations. In this second critique of Steller—to which we now turn—the old-school 'humanistic' method shared by Steller and Hartnaccius is replaced by a sleeker, more 'critical' style. Only newly edited original texts and modern scholarship—meaning, here, the gospels and seventeenth-century writers such as Grotius—are cited. It is therefore possible to read this second critique of Steller without knowing, or while forgetting, that it is 'Augustinian'.

"Measured against the law of nature"

Shortly after Hartnaccius' *Refutation* appeared, a second critique of Steller went to press. There is no false name on the title page of this text, *On the Unjust Judgement of Pontius Pilate* (Leipzig, 1675). Its author is Thomasius, who signs as a Leipzig man (*Lipsiensis*) and a Master of Philosophy (*Phil. M.*).[70] Thomasius is no minor figure in European intellectual history. Heavily influenced by Grotius, Hobbes, and Pufendorf,[71] he is a potent early theorist of the secularized state.[72]

We will recall that it was Thomasius, as a professor of law at the University of Halle (or 'Fridericiana'), who judged Pagendarm's 1707 dissertation *On the Nature of Secularized Holdings*. And we will recall Pagendarm's certainty, in that dissertation, that the Protestant magistrate's power to "secularize church holdings" cannot be validated "by Justinian's civil law or by canon law", but only by "by the law of nature".[73] This is a sure sign of Thomasius' influence.

There is much of interest in Thomasius' salvo *On the Unjust Judgement of Pontius Pilate*. For instance, he undermines Steller's narrative before the Pilate trial even begins, by claiming—with Augustine, but without citing him—that the 'cohort' mentioned in *John* signals the presence of Roman troops on the night of Jesus' arrest.[74] Later, Thomasius underscores a line from the gospels that Steller omits from his *Defence of Pontius Pilate*—the line, of course, in which Jesus says to Pilate (in my free translation of Thomasius' free rendering) that "his kingdom is not secular but spiritual" (*regnum suum non mundanum sed spirituale*). This line is crucial in Thomasius' reading of the Pilate trial, since—he tells us—it rebuts the charge that Jesus is guilty of sedition (*laesae majestatis*).[75] But what is more, this line is crucial to Thomasius' theory of a humane early modern state. For what I now quote is paragraph 45, *in toto*, of Thomasius' text "The Right of a Christian Prince in Religious Matters": "Christ's kingdom is *not of this world* and has nothing in common with civil or human power."[76] Like Pufendorf, Grotius, and those before, Thomasius cites *John*—as interpreted by the African bishop, Augustine—when he is demarcating the 'secular' as a sphere of legal reality.

But for us, here, Thomasius' text *On the Unjust Judgement of Pontius Pilate* is only significant for one reason. Thirty years before young Pagendarm insists that neither Roman civil law nor Roman church law—but only 'natural law'—can clarify the epoch-making question of secularization, young Thomasius insists that neither Roman civil law nor Roman church law—but only 'natural law'—can clarify the epoch-making trial of Jesus, in which the judge is guilty and the convict is supremely innocent. This is Thomasius:

> It is to be denied that Pilate, in judging Christ, acted justly and fulfilled the offices of a good judge ... [But both that] in which Pilate erred, and the office of the judge, are to be measured against the law of nature, and not against the civil law of Justinian, *such as it then was*, or even canon law, *which at that time did not even exist*.[77]

What is the novelty here? Why is this curt, introductory comment in the second, juridical part of Thomasius' text so telling?

There is not much new, in Thomasius' text, on the question of Pilate's guilt. Where Hartnaccius enumerates seven heinous sins of Jesus' Roman judge, Thomasius calculates five:

1. after declaring Jesus innocent, Pilate assures the Temple elites that he will have him flogged (paragraph 34),
2. Pilate injuriously associates Jesus with "a hardened thug", namely Barabbas (paragraphs 35–6),
3. having wronged Jesus by *promising* to have him flogged, Pilate commits a much graver injury (*injuria*) by having him flogged (paragraphs 37–8),
4. Pilate scales "the very heights of injustice" (*summum injustitiae gradum*), when, "against his own conscience, he condemned Christ to death" (paragraphs 39–40).[78]

Pilate's fifth sin seems to come to Thomasius as an afterthought. It is this:

5. Pilate speaks "arrogantly" (*arroganter*) to Jesus during the trial, threatening him in ways that suggest "tyrannical cruelty, and not legitimate authority" (paragraph 46).[79]

And there is not much new in Thomasius' idea that a 'law of nature' is older and deeper than the civil laws of Rome or the canon laws of the Church of Rome. Not only the writings of Augustine but the letters of Paul—and, conceivably, the sayings of Jesus—reflect that idea. And a sophisticated concept of 'natural law' is written into the corpora of both Roman civil and canon law. There are practised gestures towards a 'law of nature' in the opening pages of both Justinian's *Institutes* and Gratian's *Decretum*.[80]

But we may recall one of Hartnaccius' objections to *Pilate Defended*. No early Christian writers, Hartnaccius wants to say, *expressly* defended Pilate. Hartnaccius argues, in other words, that Steller has predecessors but that his *tone* is new. I think something similar could be said here of Thomasius and his protégé, Pagendarm. If there is not much new in their insistence on a 'law of nature', there is something new in the *tone* in which they assure us that this 'law' will make inconceivably intricate, regime-defining legal questions vanish.[81] For Pagendarm in *On the Nature of Secularized Holdings*, this is the question of secularization. Church law, says Pagendarm, cannot determine the nature of church holdings—but natural law can. For Thomasius in *On the Unjust Judgement of Pontius Pilate*, this is the question of Pilate's innocence. Civil law cannot determine the office of Jesus' judge, says Thomasius—but natural law can.

The depths and conflicts hidden in such questions had barred premodern legal thinkers, it seems, from reducing the mass 'profanation' of consecrated structures, or the sentencing and death of one held to be the Son of God, to a question of 'nature' or the 'law of nature' (Latin *jus naturae*, German *Naturrecht*).[82] What we sense in this manoeuvre of Thomasius, then, is that, though his text *On the Unjust Judgement of Pontius Pilate* is informed by a tradition that stems from patristic literature (and the gospels), 'nature' is invoked in a novel way. It is a just and radiant 'nature' that can flood with light—so Thomasius asserts—the most mysterious trial in human history. That is new.

Conclusions

Thomasius is an *Aufklärer* and a pietist Christian with a liberal's instincts. But roughly a century after his little book *On the Unjust Judgement of Pontius Pilate*, his gesture towards a 'law of nature' will be torqued by post-Christians and neo-pagans—I have in mind the Jacobins—in ways that make the biblical-juridical controversies and Christian 'secularizations' of the late seventeenth century look medieval.[83]

EPILOGUE

THE UNFINISHED HISTORY OF PILATE AND JESUS

It is hardly a cliché in the literature on Rousseau—and it should be—
that this philosopher-novelist and "citizen of Geneva", as he signs his
books, rejects the Christian political legacy on the strength of his interpretation of the Roman trial of Jesus.[1] For, on Rousseau's telling in the
last pages of *On the Social Contract, or Principles of Political Right*
(Amsterdam, 1762), that trial is the origin of Christian Europe's deca-
dent, fissile politics.

Though the drama of Pilate and Jesus had been a *topos* in European
political texts since the fourteenth century—as we will recall from our
readings in Dante's *Monarchy* and Marsilius' *Defender of the Peace*—
Rousseau is the first European master-thinker after Porphyry, a devastating third-century critic of Christianity, *to inculpate Jesus*. Because of
his shift from a neo-Augustinian interpretation of the Pilate trial (à la
Dante) to a neo-pagan critique of Jesus' political legacy (à la Porphyry),
Rousseau is a coda for this book—though it must be said that his relations to Christianity are formidably complex. Our only interest in the
coming pages is with Rousseau's critique of Christian *politics* in
European history.

Rousseau's critique of Christian politics belongs to the history of
European *Realpolitik*. For Rousseau's "little treatise", as he calls *Social
Contract*, is canonized in revolutionary Paris.[2] Of course, the real influ-
ence of this "little treatise" is disputed, but it is indicative that *Social
Contract* went through seven editions in the febrile years 1790 and

239

1791.[3] And that Rousseau's treatise is revered by the Jacobin Club links his reading, in it, of a sacred king-killing drama—Pilate's judicial murder of a 'King of the Judaeans'—to the most iconic secular king-killing of modern history—the judicial murder of Louis Capet, as the revolutionary court styled the doomed Bourbon king, Louis XVI (died 1793).[4]

It is unnecessary to labour the interest, for us, of the presence of the Pilate trial, and the rejection of the Christian political legacy, *in one of the Jacobins' core texts*. And the presence of an 'innocent' Pilate in Rousseau's most 'Jacobin' text begins to crystallize into some sort of obscure sign when we recall that, in his last will and testament, Louis Capet recollects Jesus' words from the cross in *Luke* 23. Where a convict-king of first-century Judaea says, "Father, forgive them", a convict-king of eighteenth-century Europe says, "I, with all my heart, forgive those who are become my enemies."[5] It seems to me that Louis' recitation of Jesus' words invites us to set Louis' death within a new symbolic sequence.

Reflect, for a moment, on the fact that king-killing is not only the nasty *auto-da-fé* of the Pilate trial, and an inaugural moment of the Christian revolution of the first centuries CE. King-killing is an inaugural moment, too, of the Puritan, Jacobin, and Bolshevik revolutions—an axe for Charles I, a guillotine for Louis XVI (and his wife), and a hail of bullets for Nicholas II (and his wife and children). And validating this symbolic sequence are the last words of Charles Stuart (died 1649), who says, like the Galilean convict-king before him and the Bourbon convict-king after him: "I have forgiven all the World, and even those in particular, that have been the chief Causers of my Death."[6]

Unless I am mistaken, there is no history of Jesus' trials and crucifixion as they figure in the regicide literatures, and scenes, of modern Europe.[7]

This book has sought to demonstrate that theories of Jesus' Roman trial and theories of modern 'secularity' share a genealogy. And there is nothing contentious, as such, in the modern line of influence that I have sketched in this book—from a jurist-exegete, Grotius, to a counter-revolutionary theorist, Hobbes; from Hobbes to a diplomat-historian, Pufendorf; and from Pufendorf to a professor-*Aufklärer*, Thomasius.

Of course, that they are all Protestants—and that Dante, Marsilius, and Valla are long regarded as Protestants *avant la lettre*—is

not a coincidence. Europe's early modern revolutions, which reconceived medieval canon-law 'secularization' (*saecularizatio*) as a radical
civil-law technique with a novel natural-law rationale, were
Protestant. And it is no secret that the writings of Grotius and
Hobbes, Pufendorf and Thomasius influence the political thought of
the post-Protestant Rousseau.[8]

But before we come to Rousseau's interpretation of Pilate and
Jesus in the penultimate chapter of *Social Contract*, it is interesting to
note that in the same chapter, "Of Civil Religion", he forcefully contradicts an anti-Christian bias that is articulated in his day by
François-Marie d'Arouet, alias Voltaire (died 1778).[9] This bias—the
Voltaire bias, I will call it—holds that Christianity is a singularly cruel
and destructive faith.

First coming into vogue in the eighteenth century, the Voltaire bias
is now *de rigueur* in much of Europe and the Americas. For a trenchant
formulation of this bias we can glance at a letter Voltaire sent to the
brilliant Hohenzollern sceptic-king, Frederick II of Prussia, in January
1767. Christianity is the bloodiest faith in human history—*la plus san-
guinaire*—Voltaire says to this post-Christian sovereign.[10] A contemporary reconception of the Voltaire bias is Gil Anidjar's *Blood: A Critique of
Christianity*, which I have criticized in print.[11]

A bare litany of historic European conflicts serves Voltaire and
Anidjar—and many others—as a sort of anti-Christian *credo*. To nullify
the Christian political legacy, it is only necessary to refer to the crusades and inquisitions, to the old-world wars of religion and new-world
wars of conquest. The Voltaire bias voices a double suspicion: (1) that
the integration of human political machinery and divine authority is
uniquely strong, and intolerant, in Christianity; and (2) that
Christianity, as a result, is—Voltaire says it best—the bloodiest faith in
human history.

In the penultimate chapter of *Social Contract*, Rousseau brusquely
contradicts this notion. Like Voltaire, he expresses nothing but contempt for the Christian legacy in European politics. Nevertheless,
Rousseau argues in this chapter (1) that the integration of secular
power and sacred authority is singularly weak in Christianity; and (2)
that Christianity, as a result, is a perilously irenic faith. Since Rousseau's
reasoning concerning Christianity so flagrantly negates a late modern
cliché (or *communis opinio*), there is reason to sketch it out here.[12]

Rousseau's grounds for (1) are that "Jesus came to establish a spiritual kingdom (*un royaume spirituel*)", and that Christianity, in its primitive form, is "a totally spiritual religion (*une religion toute spirituelle*), solely concerned with the things of heaven". Because of this, Christianity as such "has no particular relation to the body politic", and, "far from attaching the hearts of citizens to the state, it detaches them from it as from all the things of earth".[13]

Rousseau's grounds for (2) are what he calls "the mildness of the Christian" (*la douceur du chrétien*). Even the most rudimentary acts of political resistance, says Rousseau—"resorting to violence, spilling blood", and so on—are hard for Christians to justify. The "essential thing" for a Christian, Rousseau observes, is not to govern in this life but to "get to paradise"—and "resignation (*la résignation*) is but one more means to that end". The natural fate of a Christian people is therefore not to conquer and enslave. On the contrary, it is to be "beaten, crushed, destroyed before they have time to realize what is happening to them".[14] It cannot be forgotten—and it was never forgotten by 'pagans' in the first centuries CE—that Christians venerate a man (or, as they believe, a God-Man) who was "beaten, crushed" by a foreign power in his own holy city.

The eighteenth-century objection to Rousseau's line of reasoning is still in circulation. "I will be referred to the crusades", he says dully. Rousseau is bored, but this is where things become interesting. "Strictly speaking", he tells us, "this belongs under the heading of paganism (*le paganisme*)." What could Rousseau mean by this? In what sense could the crusades be regarded as a 'pagan' affair? The idea will strike most of us as crazy.

Before we clarify Rousseau's bid to 'paganize' the crusades, it is useful to note that he claims that "holy war" (*guerre sacrée*) is not a Christian phenomenon. More emphatically, he says that it is "impossible among Christians". His reason for this claim? "The gospel does not establish a national religion (*une religion nationale*)."[15] (Though a partisan of Voltaire, Nietzsche echoes this—consciously or not—when he writes, more than a century on, that early Christ-belief is "not 'national', not a function of race".)[16] Rousseau's reasoning is less circular than it appears. He is not merely saying that, because holy war is not a Christian phenomenon, *manifestly Christian* holy wars are not *truly*

Christian. Rousseau is rather asserting that holy war is an *archaic human phenomenon*—and in that capacious sense, a 'pagan' phenomenon—that is rooted in a *total integration of a political body and a ritual cultus*.

By establishing a religion that is *not* constitutive of a territorial *locus* or an ancestral *corpus*—in other words, of a political body— Christianity is a strangely non-political faith (though Rousseau, like Georges Bataille in the twentieth century, compares it to Tibetan Buddhism).[17] When Christian polities wage what are ritually and legally 'holy wars', they are therefore not introducing a novel, Christian practice. On the contrary, says Rousseau, they are behaving *just like any archaic polity*. "Under paganism", Rousseau asserts, a temple-city or temple-state "drew no distinction between its gods and its laws. Political war was also theological".[18] There is much to confirm this in Alan Watson's slim volume *International Law in Archaic Rome: War and Religion*.[19]

What is striking about the European "wars of religion" (*guerres de religion*), says Rousseau, is not at all that they occurred. For when have wars not occurred? No, he insists, what is striking is that Europeans call them wars *of religion*. That is the mark of Christian influence—not that wars raged, but that only *certain* wars were *religious*. In 'pagan' antiquity, war was, by law and by ritual, *an intrinsically religious matter*. "The Romans extended their cult and their gods along with their empire", he reminds us. And according to Rousseau, the early Islamic caliphs resemble the 'pagans' of Rome, rather than the Christians of Rome in the centuries before Constantine. "Under the caliphs", he says, "government was totally unitary (*exactement un*), and in this respect good."[20]

If Rousseau can be trusted, the integration of secular power and sacred authority is strong in pagan Rome and Islamic Baghdad, and bizarrely weak in Europe, where Christians are subjected to "*two* legislations, *two* sovereigns, *two* fatherlands"—human and divine, imperial and ecclesiastical, temporal and eternal.[21] Of course, we will recall the late antique African pope Gelasius I, who theorized this division in one of his decretal letters to the Roman emperor at Constantinople. "There are two ways", writes Gelasius, "in which this world is chiefly ruled: the sacred authority (*auctoritas*) of the priests, and the royal power (*potestas*)."[22]

Gelasius' thousand-year-old division of the Christian pontificate and the Roman Empire, which is informed by his readings in Augustine's corpus, is Rousseau's *bête noire*. And if Rousseau can be trusted, it is Hobbes's *bête noire*, too.

"Of all Christian writers", Rousseau holds, "the philosopher *Hobbes* is the only one who clearly saw the evil and the remedy, who dared to propose the reunion of the two heads of the eagle"—see, for this emblem, fig. 17—"and the restoration throughout [Christian Europe] of political unity".[23]

We will recall the logic of Hobbes's "restoration" of a pre-Christian "political unity" and the salience, in it, of Jesus' Roman trial. Further, Rousseau can write in one breath of his interlocutors "Hobbes and Grotius", and we will recall Grotius' dramatic and hermeneutical texts on the Pilate trial.[24] But where is the drama of Pilate and Jesus in Rousseau's post-Grotian, post-Hobbesian chapter, "Of Civil Religion"?

Like Hobbes in *Leviathan*, Rousseau cites the Pilate trial at a critical moment of his treatise. This is Rousseau:

> Jesus came to set up on earth a spiritual kingdom (*un royaume spiri-tuel*), which, by separating the theological system from the political system, led to the state's ceasing to be one (*cessa d'être un*), and caused the internal divisions which have never ceased to convulse Christian peoples. As this new idea of a kingdom of the other world could never have entered the heads of pagans (*cette idée nouvelle d'un royaume de l'autre monde n'ayant pu jamais entrer dans la tête des païens*), they always looked on the Christians as true rebels ... This was the cause of the persecutions.[25]

One critical moment in Rousseau's theory of the history of empire—and perhaps, mutatis mutandis, of some of the Jacobins'—is the moment when Jesus testifies to what Rousseau calls, in one place, his "so-called kingdom of the other world" (*prétendu royaume de l'autre monde*).[26] And when is that? None of Rousseau's eighteenth- or nine-teenth-century readers could have failed to hear, in this, Jesus' utter-ance before Pilate's dais: "My kingdom is not of this world" (*John* 18:36). That, for Rousseau, is the world-historical idea of Jesus that "could never have entered the head of pagans".

And like Hobbes in *Leviathan*, Rousseau cites Jesus' world-historical testimony more than once. "The Christian's fatherland (*patrie*)", Rousseau insists, "is not of this world (*n'est pas de ce monde*)."[27] If this is not proof that the Pilate trial inspires his political critique of Christian

Europe in "Of Civil Religion", I would ask with Augustine—what more do you want?[28]

William Blake is right in his mocking line: "Mock on Mock on Voltaire Rousseau."[29] Rousseau, like Voltaire, denigrates the Christian legacy in politics. In that respect, both he and Voltaire represent the caustic mood of the *philosophes*. Yet Rousseau deconstructs what I have called the Voltaire bias. Though Blake would not have cared, "Voltaire Rousseau" spurn the Christian legacy in radically different ways.

This is interesting for us, since late modern critics of Christianity would tend to assume that Rousseau's argument—"Jesus came to set up on earth a spiritual kingdom ... by separating the theological system from the political system"—is partisan, by which I mean slyly or subconsciously pro-Christian.[30] But that is only because most of us would assume that the theologico-political disintegration we call 'secularity'—a culture of religio-political governance that has ceased to be, in Rousseau's phrase, "totally unitary"—is a *good thing*. And that is precisely what Rousseau, like Hobbes, denies. For what does Rousseau call 'good'? "Under the caliphs", he opines, "government was totally unitary, and in this respect good."[31]

To my mind, Rousseau's demolition of the Voltaire bias is not partisan. Indeed, it is Rousseau—not Voltaire—who provincializes Europe, and European Christianity. Voltaire's notion that Christianity is humankind's bloodiest faith is suited to a letter between eighteenth-century *philosophes*, but it has no correlate in global history.[32] It is a salon-ready *bon mot*, not a serious hypothesis. Rousseau's critique of Christian political history, however, has theoretical force.

A dark commingling of temple and state, and of the temple-state and violence, is unremarkable in global history. It is lamentable, but it is certainly not remarkable. What Voltaire treats as most *uncommon* in Christianity—its cult-implicated, cult-sanctioned violence—is what Rousseau treats as most *common* in global history. Voltaire is obsessed, in a thoroughly provincial way, with the infamies of Christian Europe. Rousseau, levelling his eye on further horizons, realizes that it is Christianity's *critique* of cultic violence, and its *unease* with the archaic temple-state, that must be entered into what Paul Veyne called the "inventory of differences" of global history.[33]

Something that Voltaire is blind to in global history, namely the split-ting of the archaic temple-state, is precisely what holds Rousseau's eye. And I have come to believe that the significance of Christianity, in terms of political history in the *longue durée*, is not at all that it erects a temple-state (à la Voltaire), but rather that it critiques the temple-state (à la Rousseau). The institutional effect of that critique, originally rooted in New Testament texts and Augustine's African corpus, is what comes to be called 'secularity'—a Latin Christian term, as we have seen.

Jesus is the first figure in history to prophetically decouple the temple-state, and to radically alter the concept of a temple, by claiming to be the head of "a spiritual kingdom".[34] Before the life and death of Jesus, no such concept is on record—though we should note Plato's evocation of an ideal city in the heavens in *Republic* IX.[35]

The Voltaire bias is a late modern orthodoxy. But if Rousseau is in the minority, he is not alone. In fact, Rousseau's theory is taken up by one of the nineteenth century's most imposing historians of antiquity, Numa Denis Fustel de Coulanges (died 1889). In the last chapter of his book *The Ancient City*, Fustel seems to recollect Rousseau without, however, citing him.[36]

Like Rousseau, Fustel asserts that a pre-Christian state is by defini-tion a temple-state. And like Rousseau, Fustel traces the influence of early Christianity on what he calls "the conditions of government" in the first centuries CE.[37] This is Fustel de Coulanges:

> In the pre-Christian ages, religion and the state formed nothing but a unity; every people adored its own god, and every god governed his own people; the same code regulated the relations between humans and their duties towards the gods of the city ... In place of this, Jesus Christ teaches that his empire is not of this world ... It is the first time that God and the state are so clearly distinguished. For Caesar in that period was still the *pontifex maximus*, the chief and the principal organ of the Roman religion ... [Caesar] held the cult and the dogmas in his hands ... But now Jesus Christ breaks the alliance which paganism and the empire wished to renew; he proclaims that religion is no longer the state, and that to obey Caesar is no longer the same as to obey God.[38]

It is "in place" (*au lieu*) of the archaic temple-state that Jesus says to Pilate, *within* an archaic temple-city (Jerusalem) and temple-state (the

Roman Empire), that "his empire is not of this world" (*son empire n'est pas de ce monde*).

For Rousseau in the eighteenth century, and for Fustel de Coulanges in the nineteenth, Jesus' utterance before Pilate marks a point of divergence—and a new thing (*novum*)—in the history of empire.

I have come to believe that Rousseau and Fustel de Coulanges were right. What we call the 'secular' can first be glimpsed in the gospels—and, most clearly, in the Roman trial of Jesus in *John*. For that is where, though only "in speech" (as Socrates says in the *Republic*), Jesus splits the archaic temple-state and ascribes different logics or codes to all the polities of *this* world-age, and to the divine polity of a world-age *to come*.

In *John*'s dramatization of Jesus' Roman trial, and in Augustine's interpretation of that drama, Pilate is a legate of the Roman temple-state in the Judaean temple-city. For Pilate, as for the Judaean Temple elites who charge Jesus with blasphemy and treason, the codes of *religio* and the *saeculum* had not been decoupled. It is in part because Jesus decouples them that he is sent to the cross. (See fig. 18.)

And it is in part through his convict's death, signified by the cross, that he still shapes history.

LIST OF PREMODERN TITLES

ABB. *Taf.* Pseudo-Ibn 'Abbas, *Commentary on the Qur'an*

Acta Pil. *The Acts of Pilate*

AGO. *Jud. Sup.* Agobard of Lyon, *On the Superstitions of Jews*

Alc. Lat. Renaissance Latin edition of *The Qur'an*

AMBR. *Epist.* Ambrose of Milan, *Letters*

AMBR. *Fug. Saec.* Ambrose of Milan, *Flight from the World-Age*

AMM. *Rer. Gest.* Ammianus Marcellinus, *History*

AQUIN. *Cat. Aur.* Thomas Aquinas, *The Chain of Gold*

AQUIN. *Summ. Theol.* Thomas Aquinas, *Summa Theologiae*

ARIST. *Apol. Gr.* Aristides, *Greek Apology*

ARIST. *Apol. Syr.* Aristides, *Syriac Apology*

ARN. *Adv. Nat.* Arnobius of Sicca, *Against the Pagans*

ATH. *Leg.* Athenagoras of Athens, *Plea for Christians*

AUG. *Civ. Dei* Augustine of Hippo, *City of God against the Pagans*

AUG. *Conf.* Augustine of Hippo, *Confessions*

AUG. *Cons. Ev.* Augustine of Hippo, *Harmony of the Gospels*

AUG. *Enar. Ps.* Augustine of Hippo, *Expositions on the Psalms*

AUG. *Epist.* Augustine of Hippo, *Letters*

AUG. *Retract.* Augustine of Hippo, *Two Books of Recensions*

AUG. *Serm.* Augustine of Hippo, *Sermons*

AUG. *Tract.* Augustine of Hippo, *Homilies on the Gospel of John*

BEN. IMOLA *Com.* Benvenuto da Imola, *Comment on the Comedy of Dante Alighieri*

BOCC. *Exp.*	Giovanni Boccaccio, *Expositions on the Comedy of Dante*
CAES. AREL. *Serm.*	Caesarius of Arles, *Sermons*
CHRY. *Adv. Iud.*	John Chrysostom, *Discourses against Jews*
CIC. *Nat. Deor.*	Cicero, *On the Nature of the Gods*
Clem.	*First Letter of Clement to the Corinthians*
CUS. *Crib. Alk.*	Nicholas of Cusa, *Sifting the Qur'an*
CUS. *Pac. Fid.*	Nicholas of Cusa, *On the Peace of Faith*
DAM. *Adv. Haer.*	John of Damascus, *Against the Heresies*
DAM. *Bar. Ioas.*	John of Damascus, *The Lives of Barlaam and Ioasaph*
DAN. *Inf.*	Dante Alighieri, *Inferno*
DAN. *Mon.*	Dante Alighieri, *Monarchy*
DAN. *Para.*	Dante Alighieri, *Paradiso*
DAN. *Purg.*	Dante Alighieri, *Purgatorio*
Did. Apost.	*Doctrine of the Apostles*
DIM. *Jaw.*	al-Dimashqi, *Response to the Letter from the People of Cyprus*
DIO CASS. *Hist. Rom.*	Dio Cassius, *The Roman History*
DIO. LAER. *Vit. Phil.*	Diogenes Laertius, *Lives of the Philosophers*
EPIC. *Enchir.*	Epictetus, *Handbook*
Epic. Christ.	Christian paraphrase of Epictetus' *Handbook*
EPIPH. *Panar.*	Epiphanius of Salamis, *Medicine Chest*
Epist. Mar.	*Letter of Mara bar Sarapion*
EUS. *C. Hier.*	Eusebius of Caesarea, *Against Hierocles*
EUS. *Dem. Ev.*	Eusebius of Caesarea, *Demonstration of the Gospel*
EUS. *Hist. Eccl.*	Eusebius of Caesarea, *Ecclesiastical History*
Ev. Petr.	*The Gospel of Peter*
GEL. I *Epist.*	Gelasius I, *Letters*
GEL. I *Tom.*	Gelasius I, *On the Bond of an Anathema*
GRAT. *Dec.*	Gratian, *Decretum, or Harmony of Inharmonious Canons*
HER. *Frag.*	Heraclitus of Ephesus, *Fragments*
Hist. Aug.	*Augustan History*
HON. *Lum. Eccl.*	Honorius of Autun, *Luminaries of the Church*
IGN. *Ep. Mag.*	Ignatius of Antioch, *Letter to the Church in Magnesia*

IGN. *Ep. Smyr.*	Ignatius of Antioch, *Letter to the Church in Smyrna*
INN. III *Reg.*	Innocent III, *Responses, or Letters*
IREN. *Adv. Haer.*	Irenaeus of Lyon, *Against the Heresies*
IREN. *Dem. Apost.*	Irenaeus of Lyon, *Demonstration of the Apostolic Preaching*
ISID. *Etym.*	Isidore of Seville, *Etymologies*
JABB. *Tathb.*	'Abd al-Jabbār, *Critique of Christian Origins* (within *Confirmation of the Proofs of Prophecy*)
JAC. AL. *Comm.*	Jacopo Alighieri, *Comment*
JAL. *Taf.*	Jalāl al Mahalli and Jalāl al Suyūtī, *Commentary on the Qur'an*
JOS. *Ant. Jud.*	Flavius Josephus, *Judaic Antiquities*
JOS. *Bell. Jud.*	Flavius Josephus, *The Judaean War*
JOS. *Vita*	Flavius Josephus, *Life of Josephus*
JOS. SLAV. *Bell. Jud.*	Old Russian Version of Flavius Josephus, *The Judaean War*
JUST. *Apol. I*	Justin the Philosopher, *First Apology*
JUSTIN. *Dig.*	Justinian I, *Digest*
JUSTIN. *Inst.*	Justinian I, *Institutes*
JUV. *Evang.*	Juvencus, *The Four Books of the Evangelists*
LACT. *Div. Inst.*	Firmianus Lactantius, *Divine Institutes*
LACT. *Mort. Pers.*	Firmianus Lactantius, *Deaths of the Persecutors*
LAND. *Com.*	Cristoforo Landino, *Comment on the Comedy*
Leg. Aur.	Jacobus de Voragine, *The Golden Legend*
Lib. Pont.	*The Book of Popes*
LUC. *Mort. Per.*	Lucian of Samosata, *The Passing of Peregrinus*
MAC. *Apoc.*	Macarius of Magnesia, *Response*
MAIM. *Mish. Tor.*	Maimonides, *Repetition of the Torah*
MARA. *Exp.*	Guglielmo Maramauro, *Exposition on the Inferno of Dante Alighieri*
MARS. PAD. *Def. Min.*	Marsilius of Padua, *Lesser Defender*
MARS. PAD. *Def. Pac.*	Marsilius of Padua, *Defender of the Peace*
MEL. *P. Pas.*	Melito of Sardis, *On Pascha*
MIN. FEL. *Oct.*	Minutius Felix, *Octavius*
Mors Pil.	*The Death of Pilate*
NAG. HAMM. *Seth II*	Nag Hammadi Codex, *Second Treatise of the Great Seth*

OCK. *Imp. Pont.*	William of Ockham, *On the Jurisdiction of Emperors and Popes*
ORIG. *C. Cels.*	Origen of Caesarea, *Against Celsus*
PHIL. *Leg.*	Philo of Alexandria, *Embassy to Gaius*
PIET. AL. *Com.*	Pietro Alighieri, *Comment on Dante's Poem the Comedy*
PL. *Apol.*	Plato, *Apology*
PL. *Resp.*	Plato, *Republic*
PLIN. *Epist.*	Pliny the Younger, *Letters*
PLIN. *Hist. Nat.*	Pliny the Elder, *Natural History*
PLUT. *Mor.*	Plutarch, *Morals*
POSS. *Vita Aug.*	Possidius of Calama, *Life of Augustine*
PROC. *Anec.*	Procopius of Caesarea, *The Secret History*
PROSP. *Chron.*	Prosper of Aquitaine, *Chronicle*
PS.-LACT. *Pass. Dom.*	Pseudo-Lactantius, *Poem on the Lord's Passion*
QUOD. *Epist.*	Quodvultdeus of Carthage, *Letters*
Qur.	*The Qur'an*
SUET. *Vit. XII*	Suetonius, *Lives of the Twelve Caesars*
TAB. *Jam.*	al-Ṭabarī, *Commentary on the Qur'an*
TAC. *Ann.*	Tacitus, *Annals*
TAL. BAB. *San.*	Babylonian Talmud, *Sanhedrin*
TERT. *Anim.*	Tertullian of Carthage, *On the Soul*
TERT. *Apol.*	Tertullian of Carthage, *Apology*
THEO. *Autol.*	Theophilus of Antioch, *To Autolycus*
Tol. Yesh. Byz.	Byzantine Version of *Toledot Yeshu* or *The Life of Jesus*
Tol. Yesh. Eur.	European Version of *Toledot Yeshu* or *The Life of Jesus*
Tol. Yesh. Or.	Eastern Versions of *Toledot Yeshu* or *The Life of Jesus*
TREB. *Aut. Dox.*	George of Trebizond, *On the Eternal Glory of the Autocrat*
VALL. *Don. Const.*	Lorenzo Valla, *On the Donation of Constantine*
VIDA *Christ.*	Marco Girolamo Vida, *The Christ Epic*
WYC. *Nov. Test.*	John Wycliffe (and others), *The New Testament*

NOTES

AUTHOR'S NOTE

1. E. H. Kantorowicz, *The King's Two Bodies: A Study in Medieval Political Theology* (Princeton, 1957), vii. Kantorowicz is referring to American legal historian Max Radin. And it is worth remembering that Radin, the son of a German rabbi, wrote a book entitled *The Trial of Jesus of Nazareth* (Chicago, 1931). In it, Radin concludes that it is likely that "Jesus was tried and condemned by what purported to be the Jerusalem Sanhedrin", that "his execution was ordered by the Roman governor"—Pilate—and that "Herod, the tetrarch of Galilee, waived any claim he might have" to condemn Jesus (176–7).
2. M. Houellebecq, *Serotonin*, trans. S. Whiteside (New York, 2019).

PROLOGUE

1. P. R. Blum, "Europa: Ein Appellbegriff", *Archiv für Begriffsgeschichte* 43 (2001), 149–71; J. Patočka, *Plato and Europe*, trans. P. Lom (Stanford, 2002); M. Foucault, *Security, Territory, Population: Lectures at the Collège de France, 1977–1978*, ed. M. Senellart, trans. G. Burchell (New York, 2007), 294–306; J. Kristeva, *This Incredible Need to Believe*, trans. B. B. Brahic (New York, 2011); U. Eco, "European Roots", *Chronicles of a Liquid Society*, trans. R. Dixon (New York, 2017); and O. Roy, *Is Europe Christian?* (London, 2020). This book's narrative is centred on the west (after many caveats, Catholic and Protestant Europe), rather than the east (after many caveats, Orthodox Europe). This is because the reception of Augustine of Hippo's corpus—written in Latin, received in the west—is decisive for us. I am not forgetting the august old synagogues and mosques of Europe—but to my mind they cast in relief, rather than blurring, a continent-wide prevalence of the cross. The 'history' in my title is thus what Michel Foucault calls "the form of Western political life and the form of Western history": Foucault, *Security, Territory, Population*, 294.

pp. [xvii–xviii]   NOTES

2. F. Braudel, *A History of Civilizations*, trans. R. Mayne (London, 1993), 301–573.
3. For Baltimore: J. Lacan, "Of Structure as an Inmixing of an Otherness Prerequisite to Any Subject Whatever", *The Structuralist Controversy: The Languages of Criticism and the Sciences of Man*, ed. R. Macksey and E. Donato (Baltimore, 1972), 189. And for Lacan's intense, if eccentric, Catholicism: J. Lacan, *The Triumph of Religion, Preceded by Discourse to Catholics*, trans. B. Fink (Cambridge, 2013).
4. I take "Galilean prophet" from *Matthew* 21:11, where we read: "This is the prophet Jesus from Nazareth of Galilee." There will be more in chapter 14 on the dating of Jesus' birth. Writing in the early third century CE, Hippolytus of Rome calculates that Jesus was *conceived* on 2 April in 2 BCE and died on 25 March in 29 CE. Hippolytus' statements seem to imply that Jesus was *born* on 25 December in 2 BCE (or perhaps, on 2 January in 1 BCE). A fascinating reconstruction is made in T. C. Schmidt, "Calculating December 25 as the Birth of Jesus in Hippolytus' Canon and Chronicon", *Vigiliae Christianae* 69, 5 (2015), 542–63. Modern calculations of Jesus' dates do not differ greatly from those run by Hippolytus.
5. P. McKechnie, "Judaean Embassies and Cases before Roman Emperors, AD 44–66", *Journal of Theological Studies* (NS) 56, 2 (2005), 339–61, here 356. Emilio Gabba gives Festus' dates in Judaea as circa 60–2 CE, and, remarkably, he concludes from this passage in *Acts of the Apostles* that "the taking of Paul to Felix at Caesarea, and the rest of the account in the Acts—all this offers a realistic illustration both of conditions in Judaea during the governorship of Antonius Felix, and of the procurator himself": E. Gabba, "The Social, Economic, and Political History of Palestine 63 BCE–CE 70", *The Cambridge History of Judaism, Volume Three: The Early Roman Period*, ed. W. Horbury, W. Davies, and J. Sturdy (Cambridge, 1999), 145–6.
6. *Acts of the Apostles* 25:19. The translation of this verse is taken from McKechnie, "Judaean Embassies and Cases before Roman Emperors", 359.
7. For the dating of Jesus' death: H. K. Bond, "Dating the Death of Jesus: Memory and the Religious Imagination", *New Testament Studies* 59, 4 (2013), 461–75.
8. J. Taylor, "Why Were the Disciples First Called 'Christians' at Antioch? (Acts 11, 26)", *Revue Biblique* 101, 1 (1994), 75–94.
9. It is a Roman who says of Jesus, in *Luke* 23:47, "Certainly this man was innocent!"
10. E. J. Bickerman, "The Name of Christians", *Studies in Jewish and Christian History: A New Edition in English Including The God of the Maccabees*, ed. A. Tropper (Leiden, 2007—reprint of a 1949 article), 119; G. S. Reynolds, "On the Qur'anic Accusation of Scriptural Falsification (*tahrīf*) and Christian Anti-Jewish Polemic", *Journal of the American Oriental Society* 130, 2 (2010), 189–202, here 200.

11. *John* 19:7.
12. *Mark* 12:29 (Jesus); *John* 1:18 and *I John* 4:12 (John). Compare Jesus' confession to Paul's asseveration: "There is one God" (*I Corinthians* 8:6).
13. It is worth noting that Pilatus' *nomen*, Pontius, is only attested in the New Testament at *I Timothy* 6:13 (a proto-creedal text). In the gospels and *Acts of the Apostles*, the Roman prefect is known by his *cognomen* only Pilatus in Greek, from *Pilatus* in Latin: A. N. Sherwin-White, *Roman Society and Roman Law in the New Testament: The Sarum Lectures, 1960–1961* (Oxford, 1963), 159–60, 162. Though some have held that Pilate governed Judaea from 17/18 CE, the accepted dates are still 26 to 36/37 CE: D. W. Chapman and E. J. Schnabel, *The Trial and Crucifixion of Jesus: Texts and Commentary* (Tübingen, 2015), 158–63.
14. TAC. *Ann.* XV 44: *Auctor nominis eius Christus Tiberio imperitante per procuratorem Pontium Pilatum supplicio adfectus erat.*
15. IGN. *Ep. Mag.* 11.1.
16. G. Agamben, *Pilate and Jesus*, trans. A. Kotsko (Stanford, 2015), 55; idem, *Pilato e Gesù* (Rome, 2014), 76.
17. Foucault, *Security, Territory, Population*, 294. (Typography lightly modified.)
18. *Matthew* 27:19. And Kierkegaard writes here, too: "Pilate's wife had been much troubled by her dream that day and therefore advised against the conviction of Christ. But Pilate did not dream by day; he understood that if he did not convict Christ, he would be no friend of the emperor—and he condemned him." S. Kierkegaard, *Søren Kierkegaard's Journals and Papers, Volume 1*, ed. and trans. H. V. Hong and E. H. Hong (Bloomington, 1967), 139.
19. For "rabbi": *Matthew* 26:49 and *Mark* 14:45.
20. Charcoal fire: *John* 18:18. Open gate: *John* 18:16. Melancholy glance: *Luke* 22:61. Relentless girl: *Mark* 14:66–70. Naked boy: *Mark* 14:51–2. Blindfold: *Mark* 14:65, *Luke* 22:64. Bird's call: *Matthew* 26:74, *Mark* 14:72, *Luke* 22:60, *John* 18:27.
21. R. Bultmann, *The History of the Synoptic Tradition, Revised Edition*, trans. J. Marsh (Oxford, 1972), 261, 273.
22. "In general", as Elias Bickerman put it in 1935, "it is the Gospel accounts [of Jesus' trial] that hold water, and the critics who are wrong": E. J. Bickerman, "Utilitas Crucis: Observations on the Accounts of the Trial of Jesus in the Canonical Gospels", *Studies in Jewish and Christian History*, 2: 779. Compare Sherwin-White, *Roman Society and Roman Law in the New Testament*, 186–93, here 191: "The impression of a historical tradition [in the gospels] is nowhere more strongly felt than in the various accounts of the trial of Christ."
23. The provincial status of Roman Judaea is not entirely clear. I rely here on E. Schürer, *The History of the Jewish People in the Age of Jesus Christ (175 B.C.–A.D. 135)*, rev. and ed. G. Vermes and F. Millar, with P. Vermes and M. Black (Edinburgh, 1973), 1:357, where he writes that the prefect of Judaea remained,

in our period, "to some extent subordinate to the imperial legate, *legatus Augusti pro praetore*, in Syria". Judaea thus belongs to what Schürer calls a "third class of imperial provinces". This is confirmed, and Strabo is cited, in H. K. Bond, *Pontius Pilate in History and Interpretation* (Cambridge, 1998), 4.

24. Compare *Matthew* 26:65–6 and *Mark* 14:63.

25. *Luke* 22:66–71. It is worth noting that only *John*—the most 'anti-Judaean' of the gospels, per much of the modern criticism—reports no Judaean verdict.

26. Gabba, "History of Palestine 63 BCE–CE 70", 158–9.

27. For the entirety of Millar's gloss on this pericope, with the conclusion that "its inauthenticity certainly cannot be demonstrated": F. Millar, "Reflections on the Trials of Jesus", *A Tribute to Geza Vermes: Essays on Jewish and Christian Literature and History*, ed. P. R. Davies and R. T. White (Sheffield, 1990), 368–9.

28. *Luke* 23:4, 14–15, 22.

29. *Luke* 23:14–15.

30. The figure of Herod Antipas in *Luke* is "wholly evil": J. A. Darr, *Herod the Fox: Audience Criticism and Lukan Characterization* (Sheffield, 1998), 167.

31. Compare JOS. *Ant. Jud.* XVIII 136; *Matthew* 14:3–4; *Mark* 6:17–18; and Schürer, *History of the Jewish People*, 1:344.

32. *Luke* 13:32. Translating from a conjectural Aramaic substrate: J. Jeremias, *The Parables of Jesus*, trans. S. H. Hooke (London, 1954), 123, 123 note 90. The Greek is "fox".

33. *Luke* 23:12.

34. Gabba sees no reason to doubt the historicity of this: Gabba, "History of Palestine 63 BCE–CE 70", 131.

35. *Luke* 23:6–11 (introducing the name, Jesus, at "treated *him* with contempt").

36. *Luke* 23:22, 24.

37. W. von Ammon, "Das Strafverfahren gegen Jesus von Nazareth", *Nachrichten der Evangelisch-Lutherischen Kirche in Bayern* 8 (1953), 69–72, here 71; cit. J. Blinzler, "Der Entscheid des Pilatus—Exekutionsbefehl oder Todesurteil?", *Münchener theologische Zeitschrift* 5, 3 (1954), 171–84, here 172. Eerily, the topic of von Ammon's doctoral thesis is "the binding unlawful command": W. von Ammon, *Der bindende rechtswidrige Befehl* (Breslau, 1926—reprinted 1977). After the Second World War, von Ammon was convicted of crimes against humanity by the Nuremberg Tribunal. The prosecution cited his enforcement of the notorious *Nacht und Nebel* decree of 7 December 1941—which is to say, his enforcement of a 'binding unlawful command'.

38. J. Blinzler, *Der Prozess Jesu: Das jüdische und das römische Gerichtsverfahren gegen Jesus Christus auf Grund der ältesten Zeugnisse dargestellt und beurteilt* (Regensburg, 1955), 171–2. I wish to thank A. S. Dusenbury for advice on the translation of Blinzler's statement.

39. Millar, "Reflections on the Trials of Jesus", 378 (my stress). *Nota bene*—Millar

highlights differences between the synoptic and Johannine trial narratives. However, he writes here: "As with the other Gospels, in John the decision by Pilate to have Jesus executed ..."

40. Compare Luke 23:40 ("under the same sentence of condemnation"), 24:20 ("sentenced to death"); and D. L. Dusenbury, "The Judgment of Pontius Pilate: A Critique of Giorgio Agamben", *Journal of Law and Religion* 32, 2 (2017), 340–65, here 355–6.

41. Bickerman, "Utilitas Crucis", 2:778.

42. Compare *Matthew* 27:26 (here) and *Mark* 15:15. For the Roman-legal import of the gospels' wording: Sherwin-White, *Roman Society and Roman Law in the New Testament*, 26–7.

43. *Luke* 23:24; Dusenbury, "Judgment of Pontius Pilate", 352–8. There is a clear reference in *Luke* 23:24b, "that their demand should be granted", back to *Luke* 23:23a: "they were ... demanding with loud cries that he should be crucified". Despite twenty centuries of misinterpretation, then, a simple transposition from verse 23a to verse 24b elucidates *Luke*'s claim. When *Luke* writes (without transposition): "Pilate gave sentence *that their demand should be granted*" (*Luke* 23:24); what he means is that (with transposition): "Pilate gave sentence *that he should be crucified.*" That is, unmistakably, a report of Pilate's sentence of death—which is then referred to once during the crucifixion (*Luke* 23:40), once after the resurrection (*Luke* 24:20), and more than once in *Acts of the Apostles* (2:23, 3:13, 4:27–8).

44. Compare *Luke* 23:24, 23:40, and 24:20; *Acts of the Apostles* 2:23, 3:13, and 4:27–8.

45. *John* 19:13 (judgement seat), 19:16 (handing over).

46. *John* 19:23.

47. *Matthew* 27:26–38, here 27: *hoi stratiōtai tou hēgemonos*. Compare *Mark* 15:15–27; *Luke* 23:24–34.

48. The troops who seized and crucified Jesus would not have been legionnaires (Roman citizens), but auxiliaries conscripted by Rome from the non-Judaean populations in Roman Judaea, for, Judaeans were exempt. The troops under Pilate's command would therefore have been *neither* Roman *nor* Judaean— gentiles, but not citizens of the empire: Schürer, *History of the Jewish People*, 1:362–3.

49. *Acts of the Apostles* 2:23: *dia cheiros anomōn.*

50. *Luke* 13:1.

51. *Acts of the Apostles* 4:26–8 (note the Nestle-Aland reading *laois Israēl*, "peoples of Israel", rather than the singular *laos*, "people", which is attested in some manuscripts).

52. *I Timothy* 6:13.

53. Sherwin-White, *Roman Society and Roman Law in the New Testament*, 1–47.

54. For Hamann as "meta-critic" of Kantian philosophy: J. G. Hamann,

"Metacritique on the Purism of Reason (Written in 1784)", *Writings on Philosophy and Language*, ed. K. Haynes (Cambridge, 2007); G. Griffith Dixon, *Johann Georg Hamann's Relational Metacriticism* (Berlin, 1995). For the citation of Hamann: S. Kierkegaard, *Philosophical Fragments: Johannes Climacus*, ed. and trans. H. V. Hong and E. H. Hong (Princeton, 1985), 109–10 (Kierkegaard), 320 note 51 (Hamann in a letter to Johann Kaspar Lavater).

55. F. Nietzsche, *Human, All Too Human: A Book for Free Spirits*, ed. R. J. Hollingdale, trans. R. Schacht (Cambridge, 1996), 216; idem, *Menschliches, Allzumenschliches: Zweiter Band; Nachgelassene Fragmente; Frühling 1878 bis November 1879*, ed. G. Colli and M. Montinari (Berlin, 1967), 19–20.

56. There is more on Celsus and Porphyry in the coming chapters. The pages of Bloch that I have in mind are E. Bloch, *Atheism in Christianity: The Religion of the Exodus and the Kingdom*, trans. J. T. Swann (London, 2009), 110–23.

57. For more on this: D. L. Dusenbury, "'A World like a Russian Novel': The Trials of Socrates and Jesus", *TLS: The Times Literary Supplement* (10 April 2020), 21.

58. F. Nietzsche, *The Anti-Christ, Ecce Homo, Twilight of the Idols, and Other Writings*, ed. A. Ridley and J. Norman, trans. J. Norman (Cambridge, 2005), 45 (Nietzsche's stresses).

59. One notable contribution is Y. Yovel, *Les juifs selon Hegel et Nietzsche: La clef d'une énigme* (Paris, 2001).

60. John 18:38; Nietzsche, *Anti-Christ, Ecce Homo, Twilight of the Idols*, 45 (Nietzsche's stresses).

61. John 19:5.

62. Letter of 20 November 1888 to Georg Brandes: F. Nietzsche, *Friedrich Nietzsche Briefe: Januar 1887–Januar 1889*, ed. G. Colli and M. Montinari with H. Anania-Hess (Berlin, 1984), 482 (my translation): "Ich habe jetzt mit einem Cynismus, der welthistorisch warden wird, mich selbst erzählt: das Buch heißt 'Ecce homo' und ist ein Attentat ohne die geringste Rücksicht auf den Gekreuzigten: es endet in Donnern und Wetterschlägen gegen Alles, was christlich oder christlich-infekt ist, bei denen Einem Sehn und Hören vergeht."

63. Letter of 4 January 1889 to Cardinal Mariano Rampolla (whom Nietzsche calls "*Kardinal Mariani*") in Nietzsche, *Briefe: Januar 1887–Januar 1889*, 577. He signs: "*Der Gekreuzigte*". And letter of 4 January 1889 to Umberto I, king of Italy, in Nietzsche, *Briefe: Januar 1887–Januar 1889*, 577. He signs: "*Der Gekreuzigte*".

64. Nietzsche, *Anti-Christ, Ecce Homo, Twilight of the Idols*, 147 (Nietzsche's stress).

65. Augustine only begins to be rendered into Greek and read in the Byzantine zone in the late thirteenth and fourteenth centuries: J. Herrin, *The Formation of Christendom* (Princeton, 1987), 11–12.

66. T. Hobbes, *Leviathan: Volume 1*, ed. G. A. J. Rogers and K. Schuhmann (London–New York, 2005), 382–3 (III, 41). (Typography lightly modernized.)

pp. [3–5]

1. "IN THE NAME OF OUR LORD": THE MOST SUBLIME IRONY IN THE HISTORY OF EMPIRE

1. R. H. Helmholz, *The Ius Commune in England: Four Studies* (Oxford, 2001).
2. An exemplary study of the delayed but marked influence of canon law on early modern Protestant, specifically Lutheran, jurisdictions is J. Witte, *Law and Protestantism: The Legal Teachings of the Lutheran Reformation* (Cambridge, 2002).
3. This is still salient in Denis Diderot and Jean d'Alembert's unsigned article "Testament", *Encyclopédie ou dictionnaire raisonné des sciences, des arts et des métiers* (Paris, 1765).
4. Compare *I Corinthians* 11:25 (in a quasi-legal setting: *I Corinthians* 11:17–34); and *II Corinthians* 3:14 (in a quasi-legal setting: *II Corinthians* 3:4–17). Note that in *II Corinthians* 3:6, Paul calls himself one of the "ministers of a new covenant" (*diakonous kainēs diathēkēs*); and that it is the *reading* of the law that concerns him in *II Corinthians* 3:14.
5. LACT. *Mort. Pers.* 2.
6. LACT. *Mort. Pers.* 10: *legem aut religionem dei*.
7. P. Courcelle, "Anti-Christian Arguments and Christian Platonism: From Arnobius to St. Ambrose", *The Conflict between Paganism and Christianity in the Fourth Century*, ed. A. Momigliano (Oxford, 1963), 159–60.
8. ORIG. *C. Cels.* VII 18. For an ingenious reconstruction of Celsus' logic, here: J. G. Cook, *The Interpretation of the New Testament in Greco-Roman Paganism* (Tübingen, 2000), 41–3.
9. Thus Ptolemy, a disciple of Valentinus (flourished 130s CE): EPIPH. *Panar.* 33.3.1–6. "Enormous body of legislation": P. Fredriksen, *Paul: The Pagans' Apostle* (New Haven, 2017), 15.
10. Cit. J. Moorhead, "The Word *Modernus*", *Latomus* 65, 2 (2006), 425–33, here 427. On Ennodius' letters: S. A. H. Kennell, *Magnus Felix Ennodius: A Gentleman of the Church* (Ann Arbor, 2000).
11. Cit. Moorhead, "Word *Modernus*", 425–6. Note, too, that one of Ennodius' other contemporaries, Cassiodorus, writes non-condemningly of "modern times" (*modernis saeculis*) (427). For more on "modern times" in Cassiodorus: R. A. Markus, *The End of Ancient Christianity* (Cambridge, 1998), 219–20. And Paul Veyne notes that the rise of 'modern' institutions in the wake of Constantine was signalled by a wave of new terms. A house for non-citizens (Greek *xenodochium*), a house for unprotected children (*orphanotrophium*), and a house for the poor (*ptochotrophium*) "appear only with the Christian epoch", he writes, "the very names for them being neologisms": P. Veyne, *Bread and Circuses: Historical Sociology and Political Pluralism*, trans. B. Pearce, ed. O. Murray (London, 1990), 63 note 45.
12. H. R. Jauss, "Modernity and Literary Tradition", *Critical Inquiry* 31, 2 (2005),

329–64, here 333. The definitive study, which Markus and Jauss both cite, is: W. Freund, *Modernus und andere Zeitbegriffe des Mittelalters* (Cologne, 1957). And for a pre-Christian (late-third-century) legal invocation of "the spirit of our times" (*disciplina nostrorum temporum*): J. M. Schott, *Christianity, Empire, and the Making of Religion in Late Antiquity* (Philadelphia, 2008).

13. A sophisticated medieval treatment of this is AQUIN. *Summ. Theol.* part I–II (Prima Secundae) questions 97–108. For the origins of a pre-Christian, Platonic tradition of legal critique and legal innovation: D. L. Dusenbury, *Platonic Legislations: An Essay on Legal Critique in Ancient Greece* (Cham, 2017).

14. Earlier (in biblical chronology), and fewer in number than the laws of Moses (tabulated in *Exodus, Leviticus, Numbers,* and *Deuteronomy*), are the laws of Noah (promulgated in *Genesis* 9:1–7). A brilliant study of the re-theorizations of the 'Noachide laws' in early modern Europe is E. Nelson, *The Hebrew Republic: Jewish Sources and the Transformation of European Political Thought* (Cambridge, Mass., 2010). For the early American context, see N. Goodman, *The Puritan Cosmopolis: The Law of Nations and the Early American Imagination* (Oxford, 2018), 25–82.

15. *Did. Apost.* 26. Compare R. H. Connolly, ed., *Didascalia Apostolorum: The Syriac Version Translated and Accompanied by the Verona Latin Fragments* (Oxford, 1929), 216–19, 224–5, 238–41.

16. This convolution of old and new laws may be traceable to certain of Jesus' sayings—by which I only mean, in this context, *logia* in the canonical gospels: H. J. Schoeps, "*Restitutio principii* as the Basis for the *Nova Lex Jesu*", *Journal of Biblical Literature* 66, 4 (1947), 453–64, here 454–7.

17. One fine study of the origins of canon law is H. Hess, *The Early Development of Canon Law and the Council of Serdica* (Oxford, 2002).

18. This is of course not to diminish the vast, unceasing work of harmonization and hybridization that intricates Roman and non-Roman legal cultures—signally, for us, in the Roman trial of Jesus. To mention one relevant study out of hundreds: R. M. Frakes, *Compiling the* Collatio legum Mosaicarum et Romanarum *in Late Antiquity* (Oxford, 2011).

19. A. Z. Bryen, "Judging Empire: Courts and Culture in Rome's Eastern Provinces", *Law and History Review* 30, 3 (2012), 771–811, here 777.

20. I. Shahîd, *Rome and the Arabs: A Prolegomenon to the Study of Byzantium and the Arabs* (Washington, D.C., 1984), 33–5, 150–1. Domna and her nieces, Julia Sohaemia and Julia Mammaea, bore three half-Arab emperors in the early third century CE: Caracalla (son of Domna), Elagabalus (son of Sohaemia), and Severus Alexander (son of Mammaea). And for the seemingly Arabic origins of the *cognomina* of the Severan dynasty's four Julias (Domna, Maesa, Sohaemia, and Mammaea): Shahîd, *Rome and the Arabs*, 41–2.

21. F. Millar, *The Roman Near East, 31 BC–AD 337* (Cambridge, Mass., 1993), 305–9.

22. In fact, canon 3 of the Council of Constantinople (381) asserts that Constantinople is the New Rome (*Nova Roma*). See A. D. Lee, *From Rome to Byzantium, AD 363 to 565: The Transformation of Ancient Rome* (Edinburgh, 2013), 57–78, here 70–3.

23. PLIN. *Hist. Nat.* XXXIV 11.21. For more on this: F. Gary, *A Critical History of Early Rome: From Prehistory to the First Punic War* (Berkeley, 2005), 66–8, 209–11; C. F. Amunátegui Perelló, "The Twelve Tables and the *Leges regiae*: A Problem of Validity", *Roman Law before the Twelve Tables: An Interdisciplinary Approach*, ed. S. W. Bell and P. J. du Plessis (Edinburgh, 2020), 61–6.

24. HER. *Frag.* 114 (Diels–Kranz).

25. Gary, *Critical History of Early Rome*, 201. For modern doubts about the historicity of the Twelve Tables—first voiced by Giambattista Vico in his iconoclastic *New Science*: M. Steinberg, "The Twelve Tables and Their Origins: An Eighteenth-Century Debate", *Journal of the History of Ideas* 43, 3 (1982), 379–96.

26. JUSTIN. *Inst.* "Imperial Majesty". (Translation of Birks and McLeod modified.)

27. L. Capogrossi Colognesi, "Niebuhr and Bachofen: New Forms of Evidence on Roman History", *Roman Law before the Twelve Tables*, 155.

28. J. Bloemendal, "Introduction: Bilingualism, Multilingualism, and the Formation of Europe", in *Bilingual Europe: Latin and Vernacular Cultures, Examples of Bilingualism and Multilingualism c. 1300–1800*, ed. J. Bloemendal (Leiden, 2015), 1.

29. A. Grafton with A. Shelford and N. Siraisi, *New Worlds, Ancient Texts: The Power of Tradition and the Shock of Discovery* (Cambridge, Mass., 1992), 75.

30. M. Prinz, "Christian Thomasius' frühe akademische Programmschriften im Kontext zeitgenössischer Praktiken der Vorlesungsankündigung", *Vernakuläre Wissenschaftskommunikation: Beiträge zur Entstehung und Frühgeschichte der modernen deutschen Wissenschaftssprachen*, ed. M. Prinz and J. Schiewe (Berlin, 2018), here 301–9, 313–17. Compare I. Hunter, *Rival Enlightenments: Civil and Metaphysical Philosophy in Early Modern Europe* (Cambridge, 2001), 198–9.

31. Consult S. Naragon, "Reading Kant in Herder's Notes", and R. Pozzo, "Kant's Latin in Class", both in *Reading Kant's Lectures*, ed. R. R. Clewis (Berlin, 2015).

32. However, the Latin tradition is not 'innocent': A. Patten, "The Humanist Roots of Linguistic Nationalism", *History of Political Thought* 27, 2 (2006), 223–62.

33. For Italian as the Mediterranean *lingua franca* of the sixteenth and seventeenth centuries (and in parts of the Ottoman Empire, into the nineteenth century): E. R. Dursteler, "Speaking in Tongues: Language and Communication in the Early Modern Mediterranean", *Past & Present* 217 (2012), 47–77, here 68–73.

34. H. Kahane and R. Kahane, "'Lingua Franca': The Story of a Term", *Romance Philology* 30, 1 (1976), 25–41, here 34–6.

35. JUSTIN. *Inst.* "Imperial Majesty". (Translation of Birks and McLeod modified.)

36. P. Sarris, *Empires of Faith: The Fall of Rome to the Rise of Islam, 500–700* (Oxford, 2011), 171–7.

37. In contrast, say, to the use of *Britannicus* and *Britannicus maximus* during the Severan dynasty: P. Bureth, *Les titulatures impériales dans les papyrus, les ostraca et les inscriptions d'Égypte (30 a.c.–284 p.c.)* (Brussels, 1964), 127. On which: M. Heil, "On the Date of the Title *Britannicus Maximus* of Septimius Severus and His Sons", *Britannia* 34 (2003), 268–71. For the question of Britain's *romanitas* in Justinian's reign: J. O. Ward, "Procopius, 'Bellum Gothicum' II.6.28: The Problem of Contacts between Justinian I and Britain", *Byzantion* 38, 2 (1968), 460–71. And for Justinian's Britannic policy: Sarris, *Empires of Faith*, 195–204.

38. A brilliant study of this is J. Conant, *Staying Roman: Conquest and Identity in Africa and the Mediterranean, 439–700* (Cambridge, 2012).

39. JUSTIN. *Inst.* I 2.2. (Translation of Birks and McLeod modified.)

40. The epochal first sentence of book I, chapter 1, is not, technically, the first of the treatise. See J.-J. Rousseau, *Du contrat social*, ed. with intro. and annot. R. Grimsley (Oxford, 1972), 103: "L'homme est né libre, et partout il est dans les fers."

41. Compare the question of war and the origins of slavery in the first pages of Rousseau, *Contrat social*, 103–13, and JUSTIN. *Inst.* I 2.2 and I 3.1–5.

42. That there is much variation in the 'traditional imperial titulature' is borne out by the material collected in Bureth, *Les titulatures impériales dans les papyrus*, and more recently in Z. M. Packman, "Epithets with the Title Despotes in Regnal Formulas in Document Dates and in the Imperial Oath", *Zeitschrift für Papyrologie und Epigraphik* 90 (1992), 251–7; idem, "Regnal Formulas in Document Date and in the Imperial Oath", *Zeitschrift für Papyrologie und Epigraphik* 91 (1992), 61–76.

43. Or rather, in Eusebius' Greek, *anikētos Sebastos, archiereus megistos*: EUS. *Hist. Eccl.* VIII 17.3–4.

44. T. Whitmarsh, *Battling the Gods: Atheism in the Ancient World* (New York, 2015), 235.

45. For the imperial titulature evinced here, and the question of its echoes in the New Testament: T. H. Kim, "The Anarthrous υἱός θεοῦ in Mark 15,39 and the Roman Imperial Cult", *Biblica* 79, 2 (1998), 221–41, here 225–37; R. L. Mowery, "Son of God in Roman Imperial Titles and Matthew", *Biblica* 83, 1 (2002), 100–10, here 101–5; M. D. Litwa, *Iesus Deus: The Early Christian Depiction of Jesus as a Mediterranean God* (Minneapolis, 2014), 181–214.

46. A. Cameron, "The Imperial Pontifex", *Harvard Studies in Classical Philology* 103 (2007), 341–84, here 355. Consult, too: A. Cameron, "Pontifex Maximus: From Augustus to Gratian—and Beyond", *Emperors and the Divine: Rome and Its Influence*, ed. M. Kahlos (Helsinki, 2016); R. Dijkstra and D. van Espelo, "Anchoring Pontifical Authority: A Reconsideration of the Papal Employment of the Title *Pontifex Maximus*", *Journal of Religious History* 41, 3 (2017), 312–25.

47. Cameron, "Imperial Pontifex", 355–6.
48. Cameron, "Imperial Pontifex", 361; I. Kajanto, "Pontifex Maximus as the Title of the Pope", *Arctos* 15 (1981), 37–51.
49. Cameron, "Imperial Pontifex", 362.
50. Cameron, "Imperial Pontifex", 364, 371.
51. A. Watson, *The State, Law, and Religion: Pagan Rome* (Athens, Ga., 1992).
52. However biased, the *locus classicus* on Justinian's religious intolerance is PROC. *Anec.* XIII 7: "It did not seem to him to be murder (*phonos*) if the victims happened not to be of his own creed." For more on Justinian's religious policies: J. Meyendorff, "Justinian, the Empire, and the Church", *Dumbarton Oaks Papers* 22 (1968), 43–60, here 45–52; Sarris, *Empires of Faith*, 160–8; Lee, *From Rome to Byzantium*, 264–85; S. J. Shoemaker, *The Apocalypse of Empire: Imperial Eschatology in Late Antiquity and Early Islam* (Philadelphia, 2018), 64–74. And for the question of Procopius' own religious commitments (or lack of them): A. M. Cameron, "The 'Scepticism' of Procopius", *Historia: Zeitschrift für Alte Geschichte* 15, 4 (1966), 466–82.
53. For more on Justinian's sanctification and legitimation of Roman law: M. Maas, "Roman History and Christian Ideology in Justinianic Reform Legislation", *Dumbarton Oaks Papers* 40 (1986), 17–31. A different but related irony is articulated in a second-century anti-Christian text (as transmitted by a Christian text): ORIG. *C. Cels.* II 44. "Why may we not think", counters Celsus, "that everyone else … who has been condemned and come to an unfortunate end is an angel greater and more divine than Jesus?" And he presses on: "Anyone with similar shamelessness could say even of a robber and murderer who had been punished that he … was not a robber but a god."
54. That the longest discourse in *The Divine Comedy* is made by Justinian I in *Paradiso* VI, and is linked in manifold ways to the political theology of Dante's *Monarchy*, which is centred, as we will see, on the cross, is a single instance of how the legal irony—or ironies—of the cross can lead to new, global readings of canonical texts: U. Falkeid, *The Avignon Papacy Contested: An Intellectual History from Dante to Catherine of Siena* (Cambridge, Mass., 2017), 25–51.
55. Notable contributions to a rich literature on the laws and customs reflected in the Judaean and Roman trials of Jesus are: Bickerman, "Utilitas Crucis"; Blinzler, *Der Prozess Jesu*; Sherwin-White, *Roman Society and Roman Law in the New Testament*, 1–47; Millar, "Reflections on the Trials of Jesus"; R. E. Brown, *The Death of the Messiah: From Gethsemane to the Grave* (New York, 1994), 1:661–877; and A. Schiavone, *Pontius Pilate: Deciphering a Memory* (New York, 2017).
56. For brief reflections on their twinned deaths: Nietzsche, *Human, All Too Human*, 233; Dusenbury, "'A World like a Russian Novel'", 21.
57. MEL. *P. Pas.* 96.

2. "YOU SAY I AM A KING": THE MOMENT WHEN JESUS CONFESSES TO PILATE

1. *I Timothy* 6:13 in the WYC. *N. Test.* (translation lightly modified), and in R. Lattimore, *Acts and Letters of the Apostles: Newly Translated from the Greek* (New York, 1982), 207.

2. "It was not called this ['Vulgate'] until the sixteenth century, nor was it generally accepted as the official version [of the Latin church] until well into the eighth": Herrin, *Formation of Christendom*, 91.

3. It is fascinating that a Byzantine funerary inscription in North Galatia echoes *I Timothy* 6:13. "This is the grave of a most distinguished man", the inscription reads, "whom the Lord Jesus Christ, *bearing witness before Pontius Pilate to a fair confession*, and salvation, shall help. Amen." Text given in Chapman and Schnabel, *Trial and Crucifixion of Jesus*, 164–5. (My italics.)

4. This appellation is used in *Acts* 3:14 (by Peter), 7:52 (by Stephen), and 22:14 (by Paul); and in *James* 5:6 (by the letter's author). See A. Watson, *The Trial of Stephen: The First Christian Martyr* (Athens, Ga., 2012), 89, 141.

5. PHIL. *Leg.* 299–305; JOS. *Bell. Jud.* II 169–77; JOS. *Ant. Jud.* XVIII 55–64, 85–7. It is a cliché in the modern critical literature that the gospels' Pilate differs radically from Philo's and Josephus' Pilate. Thus, Paul Winter writes that "there *could not be a greater discrepancy* between the Pilate known from history and the feeble figure ... in the Passion Drama": P. Winter, "Marginal Notes on the Trial of Jesus, II", *Zeitschrift für die neutestamentliche Wissenschaft und die Kunde der älteren Kirche* 50 (1959), 221–51, here 237 (my italics). I cannot go into this question, but I am convinced that this reflects a poor reading of the canonical and non-canonical texts on Pilate.

6. I am grateful to Jos Verheyden for reminding me of this distinction, and for many other learned comments, in a letter of 18 June 2020.

7. M. Foucault, *On the Government of the Living: Lectures at the Collège de France, 1979–1980*, ed. M. Senellart, trans. G. Burchell (New York, 2012), 84. (My italics.) For more on this theme in the late Foucault: P. Chevallier, "Michel Foucault et le 'soi' chrétien", *Astérion* 11 (2013), archived online at https://journals.openedition.org/asterion/2403; accessed 13 August 2019.

8. *John* 18:38; R. Lattimore, *The Four Gospels and the Revelation* (New York, 1979), 241.

9. *I Timothy* 6:13 in the WYC. *N. Test.* (translation lightly modified), and in Lattimore, *Acts and Letters of the Apostles*, 207.

10. B. Dehandschutter, "Martyr—Martyrium: Quelques observation à propos d'un christianisme sémantique", *Eulogia: Mélanges offerts à Antoon R. Bastiaensen à l'occasion de son soixante-cinquième anniversaire*, ed. G. J. M. Bartelink, A. Hilhorst, and C. H. J. M. Kneepkens (Turnhout, 1991).

11. P. Keresztes, "Law and Arbitrariness in the Persecution of the Christians and

Justin's *First Apology*", *Vigiliae Christianae* 18 (1964), 204–14; J. N. Bremmer, "'Christianus sum': The Early Christian Martyrs and Christ", *Eulogia: Mélanges offerts à Antoon R. Bastiaensen*. And for Vestia's *Christiana sum*: H. A. Gärtner, "Die Acta Scillitanorum in literarischer Interpretation", *Wiener Studien* 102 (1989), 149–67, here 154–5; Schott, *Christianity, Empire, and the Making of Religion*, 2.

12. P. Wintour, "Persecution of Christians 'Coming Close to Genocide' in Middle East", *The Guardian* (2 May 2019), archived online at https://www.theguardian.com/world/2019/may/02/persecution-driving-christians-out-of-middle-east-report; accessed 27 October 2020.

13. For "unnamed other Christ-believers", see *Acts* 8:1–3. For the death of James that may, or may not, have been preceded by a Herodian trial, see *Acts* 12:1–5. For the other trials referred to here: A. A. Trites, "The Importance of Legal Scenes and Language in the Book of Acts", *Novum Testamentum* 16, 4 (1974), 278–84; D. P. Moessner, "'The Christ Must Suffer': New Light on the Jesus–Peter, Stephen, Paul Parallels in Luke–Acts", *Novum Testamentum* 28, 3 (1986), 220–56. And it is imperative to note that *Acts* is not only structured by legal actions *against* Christians but by the first scene of a (sort of) trial *among* Christians, culminating in two preternatural deaths: J. A. Harrill, "Divine Judgment against Ananias and Sapphira (Acts 5:1–11): A Stock Scene of Perjury and Death", *Journal of Biblical Literature* 130, 2 (2011), 351–69.

14. Nietzsche, *Anti-Christ, Ecce Homo, Twilight of the Idols*, 35.

15. *Acts* 11:26. On which, see E. Haenchen, *The Acts of the Apostles: A Commentary*, trans. B. Noble and G. Shinn with H. Anderson, rev. R. McL. Wilson (Philadelphia, 1971), 371–2.

16. A different interpretation from the one offered here, which notably suggests that *I Timothy* 6:13 contains echoes of the Johannine scene of Jesus' interrogation by Pilate, is M. Gourgues, "Jesus's Testimony before Pilate in 1 Timothy 6:13", *Journal of Biblical Literature* 135, 3 (2016), 639–48, here 646–8.

17. Note, though, that the letter's recipient is urged to "take hold of the eternal life … for which *you confessed the good confession* (*hōmologēsas tēn kalēn homologian*) in the presence of many witnesses (*marturōn*)" (*I Tim.* 6:12). This is not the place for careful exegesis or even a brief excursion in the commentary traditions, but one can glance at the hymn-like or creed-like lines of *I Tim.* 2:5–6 and 3:16.

18. *I Tim.* 6:12–17; Lattimore, *Acts and Letters of the Apostles*, 207. (Translation modified.)

19. *I Tim.* 6:16; Lattimore, *Acts and Letters of the Apostles*, 207 ("power everlasting"); and WYC. *N. Test.* ("empire without end").

20. *I Tim.* 2:1–4; Lattimore, *Acts and Letters of the Apostles*, 201. (Translation modified.)

21. *I Tim.* 6:16 in the WYC. *N. Test.*

22. Even Paul, whose anthropology is exultantly unitary (*Acts* 17:26), writes to the church in Rome that his gospel is going out to "barbarians" (*barbarois*), and not only to "Hellenes" (*Romans* 1:14). See C. D. Stanley, "The Ethnic Context of Paul's Letters", *Christian Origins and Greco-Roman Culture, Social Literary Contexts for the New Testament: Early Christianity in Its Hellenistic Context*, ed. S. E. Porter and A. W. Pitts (Leiden, 2013).

23. Consult the brief interpretation of this passage by a second-century Syrian bishop, Theophilus of Antioch, at THEO. *Autol.* III 14.

24. TERT. *Apol.* 39.2. "We pray", he says here, "for the emperors, for their ministers and those in power, for a stable world, for universal peace, and"—*nota bene*—"for the delay of the coming end of the world."

25. "What St. Paul says, *I Tim.* 2:2, is very well worth taking notice of", suggests Samuel Pufendorf in the 1670s. For his gloss on this passage: S. Pufendorf, *Of the Nature and Qualification of Religion in Reference to Civil Society*, trans. J. Crull, ed. S. Zurbuchen (Indianapolis, 2002), 129.

26. K. Smith, *Constantine and the Captive Christians of Persia: Martyrdom and Religious Identity in Late Antiquity* (Oakland, Calif., 2016).

27. *I Tim.* 3:16; Lattimore, *Acts and Letters of the Apostles*, 203. (Translation modified.)

28. EUS. *Hist. Eccl.* III 39.12.

29. *I Tim.* 2:4; Lattimore, *Acts and Letters of the Apostles*, 201.

30. For a modern gloss on this text in *I Timothy* 6: M. Dibelius and H. Conzelmann, *The Pastoral Epistles: A Commentary on the Pastoral Epistles*, ed. H. Koester, trans. P. Buttolph and A. Yarbro (Philadelphia, 1972), 88–9.

31. H. Grotius, *The Free Sea, with William Welwod's Critique and Grotius's Reply*, trans. R. Hakluyt, ed. D. Armitage (Indianapolis, 2004); W. E. Butler, "Grotius and the Law of the Sea", *Hugo Grotius and International Relations*, ed. H. Bull, B. Kingsbury, and A. Roberts (Oxford, 1990).

32. H. Grotius, *The Rights of War and Peace*, trans. J. Barbeyrac, ed. R. Tuck (Indianapolis, 2005); R. Tuck, *The Rights of War and Peace: Political Thought and the International Order from Grotius to Kant* (Oxford, 1999), 109–225.

33. M. Koskenniemi, "Imagining the Rule of Law: Rereading the Grotian 'Tradition'", *The European Journal of International Law* 30, 1 (2019), 17–52, here 21. In the conclusion of the article (51–2), Koskenniemi seems, in a nuanced way, to echo this claim.

34. Grotius is also a formidable reader of patristic literature—which, needless to say, he turns to his own ends: S.-P. Bergjan, "The Patristic Context in Early Grotius", *Grotiana* 26, 1 (2007), 127–46, here 127–8: "Grotius draws on Augustine, Ambrose, Cyprian, Lactantius, somewhat less often on Athanasius, Justin, and the historians Eusebius, Socrates and Theodoret, and occasionally on Chrysostom." Bergjan notes, however, that Grotius' patristic citations do not necessarily reflect his own readings in the early Christian archive. They are often lifted from "the writings of his contemporaries" (129).

35. Exceptional contributions are M. Somos, "Secularization in *De iure praedae*: From Bible Criticism to International Law", *Grotiana* 26, 1 (2007), 147–91; D. van Miert, *The Emancipation of Biblical Philology in the Dutch Republic, 1590–1670* (Oxford, 2018), 133–69. Of the various editions of Grotius' commentaries, consult H. Grotius, *Annotationes ad Vetus Testamentum* (Paris, 1644); idem, *Annotationes in Novum Testamentum: Denuo emendatius editae* (Groningen, 1826–34); and a reprint of the 1679 Amsterdam edition in H. Grotius, *Opera omnia theologica* (Stuttgart, 1972).

36. J. H. Bentley, *Humanists and Holy Writ: New Testament Scholarship in the Renaissance* (Princeton, 1983), 32–69 (Valla), 112–93 (Erasmus).

37. John 18:37; Lattimore, *Four Gospels and the Revelation*, 241. (Translation modified.)

38. Grotius, *Annotationes in Novum Testamentum*, 4:259. (All translations from Grotius' *Annotationes* are mine.)

39. A. Watson, *The Trial of Jesus* (Athens, Ga., 1995), 41.

40. S. E. Fassberg, "Which Semitic Language Did Jesus and Other Contemporary Jews Speak?", *The Catholic Biblical Quarterly* 74, 2 (2012), 263–80, here 280: "There is no denying that Jesus spoke Aramaic: the transliterated words attributed to him in the [New Testament] are Aramaic. As a Jew from the Galilee, he must have spoken some form of Galilean Aramaic … But as a Jew living in Palestine, he must also have spoken Hebrew."

41. S. Krauss, *The Jewish–Christian Controversy from the Earliest Times to 1789: Volume I; History*, ed. and rev. W. Horbury (Tübingen, 1995), 136.

42. Grotius, *Annotationes in Novum Testamentum*, 4:259.

43. Eus. *Hist. Eccl.* III 20.3–6. (Translation modified.)

44. Grotius, *Annotationes in Novum Testamentum*, 4:258.

45. Grotius, *Annotationes in Novum Testamentum*, 4:259.

46. C. Thomasius, *De injusto Pontii Pilati judicio* … (Leipzig, 1675).

47. For Grotius' critical relation to the Senecan model: J. A. Parente, *Religious Drama and the Humanist Tradition: Christian Theater in Germany and in the Netherlands, 1500–1681* (Leiden, 1987), 54–8.

48. H. J. M. Nellen, *Hugo Grotius: A Lifelong Struggle for Peace in Church and State, 1583–1645*, trans. J. C. Grayson (Leiden, 2015), 102–12.

49. H. Grotius, *Christ's Passion: A Tragedie, with Annotations*, trans. G. Sandys (London, 1640), 31 (act III, line 106).

50. For Sandys' connections to Thomas Hobbes, and, with Hobbes, to the legal cultures and commercial ventures that shaped the early English colonies: N. Malcolm, *Aspects of Hobbes* (Oxford, 2002), 74–5; C. Warren, "Hobbes's *Thucydides* and the Colonial Law of Nations", *The Seventeenth Century* 24, 2 (2013), 260–86, here 275–7.

51. Grotius, *Christ's Passion*, 31 (act III, lines 107–10). (Here and below, I have lightly modernized Sandys' typography.)

52. *Matthew* 27:24–6.

53. One irony (of many) is that the scene of Pilate's handwashing reflects the gospel's Judaean setting and origins: Winter, "Marginal Notes on the Trial of Jesus", 241.

54. Grotius, *Annotationes in Novum Testamentum*, 2:352–4.

55. *King Richard the Second* IV 1,237–42, in W. *Shakespeare, King Richard II*, ed. and annot. A. Gurr (Cambridge, 1990), 147 (typography.) Compare this to what I believe is the only other Shakespearean mention of Pilate, at *King Richard the Third* I 4,259–61: "A bloody deed, and desperately dispatched! How fain, like Pilate, would I wash my hands Of this most grievous murder." (W. Shakespeare, *Richard III*, ed. and annot. B. Raffel (New Haven, 2008), 59–60.) And I am grateful to Dante Fedele for reminding me of Macbeth's desperate question, at *Macbeth* II 2,63–4: "Will all great Neptune's ocean wash this blood clean from my hand?" (W. Shakespeare, *Macbeth*, ed. and annot. A. R. Braunmuller (Cambridge, 1997), 146.)

56. For Pilate's sentence in Grotius' *Annotationes*, see Dusenbury, "Judgment of Pontius Pilate", 358–64.

57. Grotius, *Christ's Passion*, 35–36 (act III, lines 209–24).

58. G. Herbert, "The Sacrifice", *The Temple: Sacred Poems, and Private Ejaculations: By the Rev. George Herbert; Late Orator of the University of Cambridge ...* (Bristol, 1799), 37. (Typography lightly modernized.)

59. H. S. Reimarus, *The Goal of Jesus and His Disciples*, trans. G. W. Buchanan (Leiden, 1970).

3. "THESE THINGS WERE REPORTED TO TIBERIUS": THE MYSTERY OF WHAT PILATE WROTE

1. G. Scholem, *Walter Benjamin: The Story of a Friendship*, trans. H. Zohn (Philadelphia, 1981), 130–1.

2. R. Eisler, *Iesous Basileus ou Basileusas: Die Messianische Unabhängigkeitsbwegung vom auftreten Johannes des Täufers bis zum Untergang Jakobs des Gerechten nach der neuerschlossenen Eroberung von Jerusalem des Flavius Josephus und den christlichen Quellen*, 2 vols. (Heidelberg, 1929–30).

3. R. Eisler, *The Messiah Jesus and John the Baptist according to Flavius Josephus' Recently Rediscovered 'Capture of Jerusalem' and the Other Jewish and Christian Sources*, trans. A. H. Krappe (New York, 1931).

4. Eisler, *Messiah Jesus and John the Baptist*, 480.

5. Eisler, *Messiah Jesus and John the Baptist*, 483–7.

6. G. Vidal, "Live from Golgotha: An Excerpt from the Novel", *New England Review* 14, 3 (1992), 127–33, here 127: "At the head of an army of rebellion, Jesus occupied the Temple."

7. Eisler, *Messiah Jesus and John the Baptist*, 501.

8. Eisler, *Messiah Jesus and John the Baptist*, 485.

9. Eisler, *Messiah Jesus and John the Baptist*, 513.

10. Controverted texts by Josephus (late first century) and Tacitus (early second century) reference the Pilate trial, but no one doubts that our only surviving first-century 'narratives' are in the canonical gospels. Compare JOS. *Ant. Jud.* XVIII 63–4; TAC. *Ann.* XV 44.

11. Scholem, *Walter Benjamin*, 131; B. Collins, "By Post or by Ghost: Ruminations on Visions and Epistolary Archives", *Jewish Quarterly Review* 107, 3 (2017), 397–408, here 402.

12. R. Eisler, "The Frontispiece to Sigismondo Fanti's *Triompho di Fortuna*", *Journal of the Warburg and Courtauld Institutes* 10 (1947), 155–9.

13. Eisler states that he was "Wykeham Professor of Philosophy in 1941": R. Eisler, *Man into Wolf: An Anthropological Interpretation of Sadism, Masochism, and Lycanthropy* (London, 1951), 253. To date, I have not been able to confirm this.

14. Collins, "By Post or by Ghost", 403.

15. Eisler, *Man into Wolf*, 16.

16. "Robert Eisler", *Wiener Kunst Geschichte Gesichtet*, archived online at univie. ac.at/geschichtegesichtet/r_eisler.html; accessed 5 August 2019.

17. R. Eisler, *Stable Money: The Remedy for the Economic World Crisis; A Programme of Financial Reconstruction for the International Conference, 1933* (London, 1932); K. Rogoff, "Dealing with Monetary Paralysis at the Zero Bound", *Journal of Economic Perspectives* 31, 3 (2017), 47–66, here 58–9; W. H. Buiter, "Is Numerairology the Future of Monetary Economics? Unbundling Numeraire and Medium of Exchange through a Virtual Currency and a Shadow Exchange Rate", Working Paper 12839, National Bureau of Economic Research (2007), 1–41, archived online at http://www.nber.org/papers/w12839; accessed 5 August 2019.

18. Buiter, "Is Numerairology the Future?", 34–5.

19. R. Eisler, *Studien zur Werttheorie* (Leipzig, 1902).

20. R. Eisler, *Orpheus—The Fisher: Comparative Studies in Orphic and Early Christian Symbolism* (London, 1921).

21. R. Eisler, *The Enigma of the Fourth Gospel: Its Author and Its Writer* (London, 1938).

22. R. Eisler, *Man into Wolf*, 264–70.

23. Scholem, *Walter Benjamin*, 131.

24. Classic treatments of this immensely complex, diffuse, and protracted process are found in Ramsay MacMullen, *Constantine* (New York, 1971); idem, *Christianizing the Roman Empire (A.D. 100–400)* (New Haven, 1984); and idem, *Christianity and Paganism in the Fourth to Eighth Centuries* (New Haven, 1997). A concise, more recent contribution is E. Watts, "Christianization", *Late Ancient Knowing: Explorations in Intellectual History*, ed. C. M. Chin and M. Vidas (Oakland, 2015).

25. E. Bammel, "The Revolution Theory from Reimarus to Brandon", *Jesus and the Politics of His Day*, ed. E. Bammel and C. F. D. Moule (Cambridge, 1984), 32.

26. Cit. Grotius, *Annotationes in Novum Testamentum*, 2:360: *literas causam mortis indicantes*. And consult P. L. Maier, "The Inscription on the Cross of Jesus of Nazareth", *Hermes* 124, 1 (1996), 58–75.

27. Winter, "Marginal Notes on the Trial of Jesus", 250: "There are cogent reasons which forbid the reader to consider the ἐπιγραφὴ τῆς αἰτίας αὐτοῦ (Mc 15 26) to be anything else than bare historical fact." For a defence of the historicity of Pilate's inscription in *Mark* as a warning "against any sympathy for messianic kings": N. Förster, "Der *titulus crucis*: Demütigung der Judäer und Proklamation des Messias", *Novum Testamentum* 56, 2 (2014), 113–33, here 122 (my translation).

28. Compare SUET. *Vit. XII* Gaius Caligula 32.2: "preceded by a notice (*titulo*) giving the reason for his punishment"; and Domitianus 10.1: "with this notice (*hoc titulo*): 'A favourer of the Thracians who spoke impiously.'"

29. Maier, "Inscription on the Cross", 60–1.

30. Winter, "Marginal Notes on the Trial of Jesus", 250–1 (citing Cyril of Alexandria's *Commentary on Matthew*).

31. J. Joyce, *Ulysses* (London, 2000), 100.

32. For Aramaic, rather than Hebrew: Maier, "Inscription on the Cross", 68–9.

33. John 19:19–22; Lattimore, *Four Gospels and the Revelation*, 243. (Translation modified.)

34. Eisler, *Messiah Jesus and John the Baptist*, 514.

35. J. K. Elliott, *The Apocryphal New Testament: A Collection of Apocryphal Christian Literature in an English Translation* (Oxford, 1993), 164.

36. Elliott, *Apocryphal New Testament*, 210.

37. The Slavonic Josephus manuscripts (not only those known to Popov), and their dates (between the fifteenth and eighteenth centuries), are catalogued by N. A. Meščerskij, "Introduction: A Literary and Historical Study", *Josephus' Jewish War and Its Slavonic Version: A Synoptic Comparison of the English Translation by H. St. J. Thackeray with the Critical Edition by N. A. Meščerskij of the Slavonic Version in the Vilna Manuscript*, ed. and trans. H. Leeming and K. Leeming (Leiden, 2003), 7–11.

38. Eisler, *Messiah Jesus and John the Baptist*, 79–80. For Berendts's historical reasonings on the Slavonic Josephus: A. Berendts, *Die Zeugnisse vom Christentum im slavischen "De Bello Judaico" des Josephus* (Leipzig, 1906). The question of the origins of the Slavonic Josephus texts are cautiously probed in A. Rubinstein, "Observations on the Old Russian Version of Josephus' Wars", *Journal of Semitic Studies* 2, 4 (1957), 329–48. A fuller history of the modern reception is sketched in Meščerskij, "Introduction", 1–6.

39. Cit. Eisler, *Messiah Jesus and John the Baptist*, 394. Note that 'horse-faced' is

my idiomatic rendering of *makroprosōpos* in a text by John of Damascus that is adduced by Eisler.

40. Meščerskij, "Introduction", 4: "Within a few pages of putting forward a hypothesis, [Eisler] often took it as proved beyond question, and then built further conclusions on its basis."

41. Eisler, *Messiah Jesus and John the Baptist*, 218–29.

42. Consult JOS. SLAV. *Bell. Jud.* II 174–5, V 195, V 214, and VI 313.

43. P. Bilde, *Flavius Josephus between Jerusalem and Rome: His Life, His Works, and Their Importance* (Sheffield, 1988), 64.

44. Though it is, of course, conceivable that they might yet be unearthed: D. R. Schwartz, "Composition and Sources in *Antiquities* 18: The Case of Pontius Pilate", *Flavius Josephus: Interpretation and History*, ed. Z. Rodgers (Leiden, 2007), 143.

45. Meščerskij, "Introduction", 4–6, here 5.

46. J. N. Carleton Paget, "Some Observations on Josephus and Christianity", *The Journal of Theological Studies* (NS) 52, 2 (2001), 539–624, here 545 note 25.

47. Scholem, *Walter Benjamin*, 132.

48. Eisler, *Messiah Jesus and John the Baptist*, 13.

49. JUST. *Apol. I* 35.

50. JUST. *Apol. I* 48.

51. TERT. *Apol.* 21.1, 18.

52. A limestone block was uncovered at Caesarea in Israel, in 1961, which bears a lacunar inscription in which Pilate is named as the "prefect of Judaea". For a reconstructed text, translation, and level-headed interpretation of this find: Chapman and Schnabel, *Trial and Crucifixion of Jesus*, 165–7. Pilate's presence in Judaea, though not his office, may have found new material confirmation in the course of a dig at Herodium: S. Amorai-Stark et al., "An Inscribed Copper-Alloy Finger Ring from Herodium Depicting a Krater", *Israel Exploration Journal* 68, 2 (2018), 208–20. I wish to thank Talila Michaeli for obtaining a copy of this article for me.

53. TERT. *Apol.* 21.24.

54. M. Foucault, "The Confession of the Flesh", *Power/Knowledge: Selected Interviews and Other Writings, 1972–1977*, ed. C. Gordon (New York, 1980), 211.

55. TERT. *Apol.* 21.24.

56. With a stress, here, on the words 'declares himself to be'. Philip I "the Arab" (*Philippus Arabus*) may have been the first Christian emperor—but, if so, Philip never declared his commitments. Consult Shahîd, *Rome and the Arabs*, 36–7, 46–7, 65–93, 97, 103–4; M. Sordi, *The Christians and the Roman Empire*, trans. A. Bedini (London, 1994), 91, 96–107. Arguments from silence are rarely convincing, but one of Shahîd's seems to me to have weight: "It is noticeable that in the [*Ecclesiastical History*] Eusebius does not refer to ... Constantine as the first Christian emperor, which would have been expected from a pane-

gyrist and a historian of the Church who had based his chronological system on the reigns of Roman emperors, most of whom had been non-Christian or anti-Christian. This is indirect evidence that Constantine was not the first; Eusebius could not very well have presented him as such in a work that had referred to one of his predecessors, namely, Philip, if not as *primus*, at least as Christian": Shahîd, *Rome and the Arabs*, 79–82, here 82. Other arguments pro and contra Philip's Christian identity are J. M. York, "The Image of Philip the Arab", *Historia: Zeitschrift für Alte Geschichte* 21, 2 (1972), 320–32; H. Crouzel, "Le christianisme de l'empereur Philippe l'Arabe", *Gregorianum* 56, 3 (1975), 545–50; and H. A. Pohlsander, "Philip the Arab and Christianity", *Historia: Zeitschrift für Alte Geschichte* 29, 4 (1980), 463–73. York's article (pro) is well constructed; Crouzel's note (pro) argues for an Antiochene tradition that is distinct from Eusebius' report; and though Pohlsander's tone is strong (contra), his reasoning is weak. By way of contrast, Shahîd's evidence (pro) is stronger than he realizes—according to David Graf in his "Review of *Rome and the Arabs: A Prolegomenon to the Study of Byzantium and the Arabs* by Irfan Shahîd and *Byzantium and the Arabs in the Fourth Century* by Irfan Shahîd", *Bulletin of the American Schools of Oriental Research* 275 (1989), 71–3, here 71.

57. JOS. SLAV. *Bell. Jud.* V 195.

58. See the reasonings sketched lightly in D. L. Dusenbury, "Unfortunate Galilean: The Passion as Seen by Two Poetic Herberts", *TLS: The Times Literary Supplement* (19 April 2019), 13–14.

59. N. A. Pedersen, "Aristides", *In Defence of Christianity: Early Christian Apologists*, ed. J. Engberg, A.-C. Jacobsen, and J. Ulrich (Frankfurt am Main, 2014), 35–6.

60. ARIST. *Apol. Syr.* 2.4; ed. Pouderon et al., 190–1.

61. LACT. *Div. Inst.* IV 10,18.

4. "CHRIST HIMSELF COMMITTED ROBBERIES": THE *MEMOIRS OF PILATE* AND THE LAST PAGAN EMPEROR

1. P. Springborg, "Hobbes, Heresy, and the *Historia ecclesiastica*", *Journal of the History of Ideas* 55, 4 (1994), 553–71; idem, "The Politics of Hobbes's *Historia ecclesiastica*", *Hobbes on Politics and Religion*, ed. L. van Apeldoorn and R. Douglass (Oxford, 2018), here 150.

2. I simplify. As Patricia Springborg notes, Eusebius is only the first to use this title. The early genre is represented "by Eusebius, Rufinus, Socrates of Constantinople, by Sozomen and Evagrius, by the Arian Philostorgius and the Nestorian Theodoret". For more on Hobbes's sources: Springborg, "Politics of Hobbes's *Historia ecclesiastica*", 150, 158–9.

3. For a concise account: R. Rees, *Diocletian and the Tetrarchy* (Edinburgh, 2004), 59–71.

4. Compare W. H. C. Frend, "Prelude to the Great Persecution: The Propaganda War", *Journal of Ecclesiastical History* 38 (1987), 1–18, here 10; E. DePalma Digeser, "Lactantius, Porphyry, and the Debate over Religious Toleration", *The Journal of Roman Studies* 88 (1998), 129–46, here 145–6.

5. LACT. *Mort. Pers.* 11. Note, too, that pagan oracles sustained the persecution: S. Mitchell, "Maximinus and the Christians in A.D. 312: A New Latin Inscription", *The Journal of Roman Studies* 78 (1988), 105–24, here 120.

6. Rees, *Diocletian and the Tetrarchy*, 62.

7. LACT. *Mort. Pers.* 12. Perhaps the intention "was not to exterminate the Christians root and branch, but to provide the most explicit possible symbol of imperial hostility to them, and the greatest encouragement to loyal pagans": Mitchell, "Maximinus and the Christians in A.D. 312", 121.

8. Consult B. Ward-Perkins, "Old and New Rome Compared: The Rise of Constantinople", and A. Kaldellis, "From Rome to New Rome, from Empire to Nation-State: Reopening the Question of Byzantium's Roman Identity", both collected in *Two Romes: Rome and Constantinople in Late Antiquity*, ed. L. Grig and G. Kelly (Oxford, 2012).

9. EUS. *Hist. Eccl.* X 1.4.

10. E. DePalma Digeser, *A Threat to Public Piety: Christians, Platonists, and the Great Persecution* (Ithaca, N.Y., 2012); J. Harries, *Imperial Rome AD 284 to 363: The New Empire* (Edinburgh, 2012), 80–101.

11. Harries, *Imperial Rome*, 95.

12. EUS. *Hist. Eccl.* X 3.3.

13. EUS. *Hist. Eccl.* X 3.4.

14. As in the unforgettable scene in LACT. *Mort. Pers.* 10, where Diocletian's augurs are unable to read the signs because "some attendants of his, who were Christians, stood by, and ... put the immortal sign on their foreheads (*imposuerunt frontibus suis inmortale signum*)". It is fascinating what the augurs then say to Diocletian: "There are profane persons (*profani homines*) here, who obstruct the divine rites."

15. LACT. *Mort. Pers.* 44.

16. T. D. Barnes, *Constantine and Eusebius* (Cambridge, Mass., 1981), 48.

17. LACT. *Mort. Pers.* 44. After Constantine and his armies saw a cross blazing in the heavens: O. Nicholson, "Constantine's Vision of the Cross", *Vigiliae Christianae* 54, 3 (2000), 309–23, here 311: "There is no need to doubt that a cross in the sky could have appeared. The physical phenomenon is a well-known one ... What is important is not what the emperor saw but what he *thought* he saw ... Constantine himself, according to Eusebius, was at first perplexed; he had the experience but missed the meaning." (My italics.)

18. Barnes, *Constantine and Eusebius*, 161–2.

19. It is worth noting that in his dialogue *Octavius* (circa 200), the African Christian legist, Marcus Minucius Felix, not only denies the 'pagan' charge of

"worship of a malefactor and his cross" in Christianity but alleges that the Roman state-cult—*nota bene*: roughly a century before Constantine—unconsciously features "the sign of the cross". Referring to certain Roman military flags, he asks what they are if not "gilded and decorated crosses"; and gesturing to certain Roman cultic symbols, he says to 'pagans' that "the objects of your cult" include the cross: MIN. FEL. *Oct.* 29.2, 6–8. For the seeming *africanitas* of the *Octavius* author: M. von Albrecht, "M. Minucius Felix as a Christian Humanist", *Illinois Classical Studies* 12, 1 (1987), 157–68, here 157–8, 161, 164, 167.

20. EUS. *Hist. Eccl.* X 3.3.

21. According to *Acts of the Apostles* 9:11, Saul—later Paul—is "a man of Tarsus". Compare *Acts* 9:30, 11:25, 21:39, 22:3; and Sherwin-White, *Roman Society and Roman Law in the New Testament*, 151, 151 note 5. Paula Fredriksen, who dates *Luke–Acts* to the second century, seems to believe that Paul may have been a Damascene: Fredriksen, *Paul: The Pagans' Apostle*, 92. But for other early attestations of Paul's connection to Tarsus: R. L. Mullen, *The Expansion of Christianity: A Gazeteer of Its First Three Centuries* (Leiden, 2004), 82 (under "Tarsus").

22. Compare LACT. *Mort. Pers.* 49. For the Christian rumours surrounding Daia's death: R. M. Grant, "The Religion of Maximin Daia", *Christianity, Judaism, and other Greco-Roman Cults ... Part Four*, ed. J. Neusner (Leiden, 1975), 165–6.

23. Barnes, *Constantine and Eusebius*, 148. 'Daza' may be the correct form of Maximin's patronymic, but in imperial texts he is neither 'Daia' nor 'Daza', but Galerius Valerius Maximinus. I have preferred 'Daia' since it is the form attested in one of our crucial authors, Lactantius (though the manuscript tradition of LACT. *Mort. Pers.* may, conceivably, have been corrupted, with a copyist mis-rendering Lactantius' accusative *Dazam* to *Daiam*): C. S. Mackay, "Lactantius and the Succession to Diocletian", *Classical Philology* 94, 2 (1999), 198–209, here 207–9.

24. Barnes, *Constantine and Eusebius*, 26. For more precise datings, and a chronology of Maximin's control of the dioceses of Asia (*Diocesis Asiana*) and Pontus (*Diocesis Pontica*): J. van Heesch, "The Last Civic Coinages and the Religious Policy of Maximinus Daza (AD 312)", *The Numismatic Chronicle* 153 (1993), 65–75, here 72–3.

25. Grant, "Religion of Maximin Daia", 143; Mackay, "Lactantius and the Succession to Diocletian", 209.

26. Harries, *Imperial Rome*, 25, 31.

27. EUS. *Hist. Eccl.* IX 1.1.

28. Mitchell, "Maximinus and the Christians in A.D. 312", 111–16.

29. EUS. *Hist. Eccl.* IX 11,1. Compare LACT. *Mort. Pers.* 43: "Of the adversaries of God, there still remained one"—namely Daia.

30. One admirable study is C. P. Jones, *Between Pagan and Christian* (Cambridge, Mass., 2014).

31. Barnes, *Constantine and Eusebius*, 62–72.

32. Harries, *Imperial Rome*, 113, 115.

33. Harries, *Imperial Rome*, 111–12.

34. LACT. *Mort. Pers.* 48.

35. H. C. Teitler, *The Last Pagan Emperor: Julian the Apostate and the War against Christianity* (Oxford, 2017)

36. Harries, *Imperial Rome*, 294–318.

37. There is a huge, complicated literature on the question of whether Constantine 'converted'. Sometimes the simplest argument is the best. Joseph Vogt of Tübingen says in the 1960s: "We prefer to trust the emperor Julian's bitter reproach to his uncle of having deserted [the sun god] Helios." That is one line worth 1,000 pages: J. Vogt, "Pagans and Christians in the Family of Constantine the Great", *Conflict between Paganism and Christianity in the Fourth Century*, 40.

38. I. Shahîd, *Byzantium and the Arabs in the Fourth Century* (Washington, D.C., 1984), 124–32. Only rumours survive concerning the death of Julian: N. H. Baynes, "The Death of Julian the Apostate in a Christian Legend", *The Journal of Roman Studies* 27, 1 (1937), 22–9; D. Woods, "Gregory of Nazianzus on the Death of Julian the Apostate (*Or.* 5.13)", *Mnemosyne* 68, 2 (2015), 297–303.

39. EUS. *Hist. Eccl.* IX 11.1.

40. S. Elm, *Sons of Hellenism, Fathers of the Church: Emperor Julian, Gregory of Nazianzus, and the Vision of Rome* (Berkeley, 2012).

41. D. N. Greenwood, "Five Latin Inscriptions from Julian's Pagan Restoration", *Bulletin of the Institute of Classical Studies* 57, 2 (2014), 101–19, here 108–11.

42. Sordi, *Christians and the Roman Empire*, 141–2: "*In extremis* … Maximinus himself, forger of the Acts of Pilate, tried to gain Constantine's support by issuing an edict—at Nicomedia or Cappadocia in May 313—giving total freedom to Christians and restoring church property … Although it added nothing to the edict of Milan, we can say that the publication of Maximinus' edict finally marked the end of the conflict between Christianity and the Roman Empire."

43. EUS. *Hist. Eccl.* X 3.3.

44. Note the brief mentions in van Heesch, "Last Civic Coinages and the Religious Policy of Maximinus Daza", 74; A. Kofsky, *Eusebius of Caesarea against Paganism* (Leiden, 2000), 16; and A. J. Carriker, *The Library of Eusebius of Caesarea* (Leiden, 2003), 281–2.

45. W. Horbury, "Christ as Brigand in Ancient Anti-Christian Polemic", *Jesus and the Politics of His Day*, 184–5.

46. EUS. *Hist. Eccl.* I 10.1.

47. A numismatic defence of Eusebius' critique of Pilate's dates in Daia's *Memoirs of Pilate*—and a critique of Robert Eisler—is P. L. Hedley, "Pilate's Arrival in

Judaea", *The Journal of Theological Studies* 35, 137 (1934), 56–8. I have not traced up Hedley's evidence in the subsequent literature.

48. Note, however, that "Josephus was important to Eusebius because he was *not* a Christian": S. Inowlocki, *Eusebius and the Jewish Authors: His Citation Technique in an Apologetic Context* (Leiden, 2006), 209 (my italics).

49. Eus. *Hist. Eccl.* I 9.2–4.

50. The origin of the *Testimonium Flavianum* in Eusebius is a question that "may be insolvable": Carriker, *Library of Eusebius of Caesarea*, 160–1. But for a meticulous analysis of Eusebius' use of Josephus' lines on Jesus (and John the Baptist): Inowlocki, *Eusebius and the Jewish Authors*, 171–2, 187–8, 206–11, 278–81. Inowlocki firmly rejects the idea that the *Testimonium Flavianum* is a whole-cloth fabrication by Eusebius, writing (on 207) that "the creation of a whole passage seems too remote from Eusebius' common practice. One can hardly deny that he occasionally felt free to modify some texts … or that he warped the meaning of events reported by some Jewish authors. However, it would be unfair to attribute to him the composition of a forgery."

51. Eus. *Hist. Eccl.* I 11.8–9.

52. Eus. *Hist. Eccl.* II 3.4–6.

53. B. D. Ehrmann, *Forgery and Counter-forgery: The Use of Literary Deceit in Early Christian Polemics* (Oxford, 2013), 351.

54. Eus. *Hist. Eccl.* II 2.1–3.

55. Among other passages: Mac. *Apoc.* 2.14, 2.19, 3.1. On which: Cook, *Interpretation of the New Testament*, 172–3 (Porphyry? Julian?), 195–6, 198–200 (Pilate). For more on the identity of the 'pagan': E. DePalma Digeser, "Porphyry, Julian, or Hierokles? The Anonymous Hellene in Makarios Magnēs *Apokritikos*", *The Journal of Theological Studies* (NS) 53, 2 (2002), 466–502.

56. Eus. *Hist. Eccl.* II 2.1–3.

57. Eus. *Hist. Eccl.* IX 4.1–3. Compare Lact. *Mort. Pers.* 36, where we read that Daia instructed his priests "to compel the Christians to sacrifice to idols, and, on their refusal, to bring them before the civil magistrate". For more on this 'reactionary' priesthood: Grant, "Religion of Maximin Daia", 157–60, who reminds us (on 160) that Maximin was—and later, Julian the Apostate was—"naturally … *pontifex maximus*" of the imperial cultus.

58. Eus. *Hist. Eccl.* IX 5.1.

59. This possibility seems to be hinted at by P. Lémonon, *Pilate et le gouvernement de la Judée: Textes et monuments* (Paris, 1981), 256.

60. The pagan *Memoirs* may not have been forged for the occasion. See R. M. Grant, "The Occasion of Luke III: 1–2", *The Harvard Theological Review* 33, 2 (1940), 151–4, here 152–3: "it seems unlikely that Eusebius himself thought such memoirs new".

61. Eus. *Hist. Eccl.* IX 6.4–7.1.

62. Eus. *Hist. Eccl.* IX 7.1.

63. Eus. *Hist. Eccl.* IX 5.1.

64. Eus. *Hist. Eccl.* IX 7.1.

65. In her introduction to Eusebius' *Against Hierocles*, Marguerite Forrat cites the same fragment of Hierocles in connection to Daia's lost *Memoirs of Pilate*: M. Forrat, "Introduction", *Eusèbe de Césarée, Contre Hiéroclès*, ed. E. des Places, trans. and annot. M. Forrat (Paris, 1986), 24–5.

66. Eusebius is thought to have written a polemic *Against Hierocles*, on which T. D. Barnes, "Sossianus Hierocles and the Antecedents of the 'Great Persecution'", *Harvard Studies in Classical Philology* 80 (1976), 239–52, here 240–3. Eusebius' authorship is contested, most recently by A. P. Johnson, "The Author of the *Against Hierocles*: A Response to Borzì and Jones", *The Journal of Theological Studies* (NS) 64, 2 (2013), 574–94. But the Eusebian attribution is now upheld by F. Montinaro and L. Neumann, "Eusebius Was the Author of the *Contra Hieroclem*", *Zeitschrift für Antikes Christentum* 22, 2 (2018), 322–6.

67. On the question of Lactantius' name: T. D. Barnes, "Lactantius and Constantine", *The Journal of Roman Studies* 63 (1973), 29–46, here 39.

68. LACT. *Inst. Div.* V 3. On this piece of *antichristiana* (as Horbury calls it): Horbury, "Christ as Brigand", 188–95.

69. LACT. *Inst. Div.* V 3.

70. A genealogy of this concept is D. Heller-Roazen, *The Enemy of All: Piracy and the Law of Nations* (New York, 2009).

71. Consult the definitions of 'enemies' (*hostes*) and 'brigands', 'gangsters', or 'terrorists' (*latrones*) at JUSTIN. *Dig.* 50.16.118 (from Pomponius, *Quintus Mucius*, book 2).

72. Frend, "Prelude to the Great Persecution", 13–14; Barnes, "Sossianus Hierocles", 243–6.

73. LACT. *Inst. Div.* V 3. Compare EUS. *C. Hier.* 1.

74. LACT. *Inst. Div.* V 2.

75. LACT. *Inst. Div.* V 2: "[Hierocles] tried to reveal falsity in sacred scripture … for certain chapters … seemed to contradict themselves, he exposed, *enumerating so many and such internal points of detail that, at times, he seems to have been of the same training.*"

76. Cook, *Interpretation of the New Testament*, 269–70.

77. *Acts* 21:27–39; B. D. Shaw, "The Myth of the Neronian Persecution", *The Journal of Roman Studies* 105 (2015), 73–100, here 76.

5. "DOMITIAN DID NOT CONDEMN THEM": ECHOES OF JESUS IN THE TRIAL OF HIS COUSINS

1. Schott, *Christianity, Empire, and the Making of Religion*, 136–65.

2. Eus. *Hist. Eccl.* I 3.7–11.

3. Eisler, *Messiah Jesus and John the Baptist*, 589–60.
4. EUS. *Hist. Eccl.* I 7.11. A rare study is R. Bauckham, *Jude and the Relatives of Jesus in the Early Church* (Edinburgh, 1990).
5. EUS. *Hist. Eccl.* I 7.14; Bauckham, *Jude and the Relatives of Jesus*, 361.
6. I Cor. 9:5: *hoi adelphoi tou kuriou*; Bauckham, *Jude and the Relatives of Jesus*, 61–2.
7. EUS. *Hist. Eccl.* III 11.1; Bauckham, *Jude and the Relatives of Jesus*, 82–3.
8. "Julius the African": EUS. *Hist. Eccl.* I 7.1, 17. "Library at the Pantheon": F. Granger, "Julius Africanus and the Library of the Pantheon", *The Journal of Theological Studies* (OS) 34 (1933), 157–61; L. D. Bruce, "The *Procurator Bibliothecarum* at Rome", *The Journal of Library History* 18, 2 (1983), 143–62, here 148, 153–4. For Julius' importance in early Christian historiography: M. Wallraff, "The Beginnings of Christian Universal History: From Tatian to Julius Africanus", *Zeitschrift für Antikes Christentum* 14, 3 (2011), 540–55.
9. Bauckham, *Jude and the Relatives of Jesus*, 354–67.
10. EUS. *Hist. Eccl.* I 7.14. Compare Bauckham, *Jude and the Relatives of Jesus*, 60–7; Mullen, *Expansion of Christianity*, 25–6 (Cochaba), 29 (Nazareth).
11. EUS. *Hist. Eccl.* III 19.1.
12. On Domitian's relevance for *Revelation*: P. Keresztes, "The Jews, the Christians, and Emperor Domitian", *Vigiliae Christianae* 27, 1 (1973), 1–28, here 23–7; G. Biguzzi, "Ephesus, Its Artemision, Its Temple to the Flavian Emperors, and Idolatry in Revelation", *Novum Testamentum* 40, 3 (1998), 276–90.
13. EUS. *Hist. Eccl.* III 19.1. In Eusebius, they are 'grandsons' (*huiōnoi*), but Epiphanius Monachus calls them 'sons' (*huioi*). 'Grandsons' seems to be the better reading: Bauckham, *Jude and the Relatives of Jesus*, 98–9.
14. But it is by no means irrelevant for many other conjectures regarding Christian origins. This "ancient story" should have been analysed, for instance, in E. Laupot, "Tacitus' Fragment 2: The Anti-Roman Movement of the *Christiani* and the Nazoreans", *Vigiliae Christianae* 54, 3 (2000), 233–47.
15. G. W. Bowersock, *Fiction as History: Nero to Julian* (Berkeley, 1994).
16. Citing *Romans* 1:3 at Bauckham, *Jude and the Relatives of Jesus*, 355. Compare Fredriksen, *Paul: The Pagans' Apostle*, 136: "[Paul] designates [Jesus] explicitly as the *Davidic* messiah only twice, both times in his letter to the Romans (1.3 and 15.12)." (Fredriksen's italics.)
17. EUS. *Hist. Eccl.* IV 22.8; Bauckham, *Jude and the Relatives of Jesus*, 80; T. C. G. Thornton, "High-Priestly Succession in Jewish Apologetics and Episcopal Succession in Hegesippus", *The Journal of Theological Studies* (NS) 54, 1 (2003), 160–3, here 162.
18. EUS. *Hist. Eccl.* III 12; Winter, "Marginal Notes on the Trial of Jesus", 247–8; and M. Bockmuehl, "The Son of David and His Mother", *The Journal of Theological Studies* (NS) 62, 2 (2011), 476–93, here 488. For material evidence of Jerusalemites claiming descent from "the house of David" in the second or third century CE: Bauckham, *Jude and the Relatives of Jesus*, 360–1.

19. I have read the hostile Anglophone reviews of Sordi, *Christians and the Roman Empire*, and found them less impressive than her book. This is of course not to say that I find her book to be, throughout, convincing.

20. Alessandro Galimberti suggests that "Vespasian's search for descendants of the family of David after the Jewish war" was later "resumed under Trajan": A. Galimberti, "Hadrian, Eleusis, and the Beginning of Christian Apologetics", *Hadrian and the Christians*, ed. M. Rizzi (Berlin, 2010), 73.

21. Sordi, *Christians and the Roman Empire*, 38–43. Compare Bauckham, *Jude and the Relatives of Jesus*, 99–106, here 104: "Allowing for the apologetic and hagiographical concerns of the tradition, we may accept as reliable that the two grandsons of Jude were prominent leaders in the Jewish Christian churches and that they came under suspicion by the Roman authorities because they were known to be ... relatives of Jesus whom they claimed to be the Messiah, the son of David. Their appearance before Domitian and the connection of their arrest with a Domitianic persecution of Christians must be considered rather doubtful."

22. Pilate's first words to Jesus, in all four canonical gospels, take the form of this question: "Are you the King of the Judaeans?" Compare *Matthew* 27:11; *Mark* 15:2; *Luke* 23:3; *John* 18:33.

23. EUS. *Hist. Eccl.* III 20.1–2.

24. *I Timothy* 6:13.

25. Bauckham, *Jude and the Relatives of Jesus*, 104: "the size of their smallholding (39 plethra, valued at 9000 denarii) is so precisely stated that perhaps this ... is accurate tradition".

26. EUS. *Hist. Eccl.* III 20.3–6. Compare *Hist. Eccl.* III 32.5–6; Bauckham, *Jude and the Relatives of Jesus*, 94–7.

27. EUS. *Hist. Eccl.* III 20.7 (quoting from TERT. *Apol.* 5.3–4).

28. Compare P. Fredriksen, *When Christians Were Jews: The First Generation* (New Haven, 2019), 125–6: "The prefect ... had known for years that this group around Jesus presented no serious political or military threat. He had never acted against them before that Passover when he struck Jesus down."

29. *John* 18:35–6.

30. Bauckham, *Jude and the Relatives of Jesus*, 102–4. Bauckham writes that, of all the canonical echoes in this passage ('come in glory', etc.), the "relation between Hegesippus' text and John 18:36 is of special interest", precisely because John is *not likely* to be Hegesippus' source: Bauckham, *Jude and the Relatives of Jesus*, 103.

31. Compare JUST. *Apol. I* 11.1–2.

32. EUS. *Hist. Eccl.* III 20.4.

33. According to Sordi, this scene may illuminate the Flavians' toleration of Christians (until the harsh final years of Domitian's reign): Sordi, *Christians and the Roman Empire*, 42–3. It receives a bare mention in T. D. Barnes,

"Legislation against the Christians", *The Journal of Roman Studies* 58 (1968), 32–50, here 35.

6. "PILATE DID NOT UTTER A SENTENCE": THE FORGERIES OF 'PILATE' AND THE COURT OF CONSTANTINE

1. P.-D. Huet in a letter to Gilles Ménage dated 23 January 1662 (manuscript held at the Bibliothèque nationale de France); as translated and cited by A. Shelford, "The Quest for Certainty in Fact and Faith: Pierre-Daniel Huet and Josephus' *Testimonium Flavianum*", *Essays in Renaissance Thought and Letters*, ed. A. Frazier and P. Nold (Leiden, 2015), 228.
2. Elliott, *Apocryphal New Testament*, 164–5: "It is not impossible that the apocryphal Acts of Pilate originated as a Christian reaction to [the spurious Acts of Pilate circulated by Maximin Daia] ... The genesis of the stories behind the Acts of Pilate may be much earlier than the fifth century: indeed Epiphanius ... writing c.375, refers to details known to us now from the Acts."
3. *Matthew* 21:11.
4. Elliott, *Apocryphal New Testament*, 205.
5. Bizarrely—but not, of course, without reason. The text is IREN. *Dem. Apost.* 74: "Herod ... and Pontius Pilate, procurator of Claudius Caesar (*Claudii Caesaris procurator*), came together and condemned him to be crucified." Paul Maier concludes that patristic literature is highly variable on the date of Jesus' death: P. L. Maier, "Sejanus, Pilate, and the Date of the Crucifixion", *Church History* 37, 1 (1968), 3–13, here 13. A critical rereading of SUET. *Vit. XII Claudius* 25.3.4 by Henri Janne in the 1930s briefly revived the chronological question of Jesus and Claudius. For a concise elucidation of the whole question: Grant, "Occasion of Luke III: 1–2", 151–4.
6. Elliott, *Apocryphal New Testament*, 205–6. (Translation modified.)
7. *Acts* 5:28. For 'newly reconstituted': *Acts* 1:12–26.
8. Elliott, *Apocryphal New Testament*, 209.
9. Elliott, *Apocryphal New Testament*, 210–11. (Translation modified.)
10. Elliott, *Apocryphal New Testament*, 211.
11. Elliott, *Apocryphal New Testament*, 206.
12. JOS. *Ant. Jud.* XVIII 89. Compare H. W. Hoehner, *Herod Antipas* (Cambridge, 1972), 313–16; Chapman and Schnabel, *Trial and Crucifixion of Jesus*, 189–92.
13. Elliott, *Apocryphal New Testament*, 207–8.
14. Elliott, *Apocryphal New Testament*, 208.
15. For the early Christianization of Ethiopia: Mullen, *Expansion of Christianity*, 330–2. In a fifth- or sixth-century Ethiopic (Ge'ez) text derived from an Arabic apocryphon, not only Pilate's wife but his daughters, Makara and Dorta, and sons, Adorokonadi and Awlogis, offer to die in Jesus' place. Though

Pilate is forced to give his nod to the crucifixion, Jesus exonerates him before going to the cross: P. Piovanelli, "Exploring the Ethiopic *Book of the Cock*: An Apocryphal Passion Gospel from Late Antiquity", *The Harvard Theological Review* 96, 4 (2003), 427–54, here 428–30.

16. The most credible report of Pilate's suicide is EUS. *Hist. Eccl.* II 7. For other sources of the tradition of his suicide: P. I. Maier, "The Fate of Pontius Pilate", *Hermes* 99, 3 (1971), 362–71, here 369–70. And for the vicissitudes of Pilate's corpse: Elliott, *Apocryphal New Testament*, 216–17.

17. Maier, "Fate of Pontius Pilate", 362.

18. Elliott, *Apocryphal New Testament*, 217. (Translation modified.)

19. Schürer, *History of the Jewish People*, 1:351–3.

20. S. G. F. Brandon, *The Trial of Jesus of Nazareth* (New York, 1968), 154.

21. TERT. *Apol.* 21.

22. C. Hourihane, *Pontius Pilate, Anti-Semitism, and the Passion in Medieval Art* (Princeton, 2009). For a different—and, to my mind, ungenerous—characterization of Hourihane's book: J. Elsner, Untitled review of *Pontius Pilate, Anti-Semitism, and the Passion in Medieval Art* by Colum Hourihane, *Church History* 80, 4 (2011), 876–7.

23. Hourihane, *Pontius Pilate, Anti-Semitism, and the Passion*, 92.

24. Hourihane, *Pontius Pilate, Anti-Semitism, and the Passion*, 146.

25. Or, perhaps, 'Christian Romans' against 'Jewish Romans' in 'the post-Roman West': P. Fredriksen, "Jewish Romans, Christian Romans, and the Post-Roman West: The Social Correlates of the *Contra Iudaeos* Tradition", *Conflict and Religious Conversation in Latin Christendom*, ed. I. J. Yuval and R. Ben-Shalom (Turnhout, 2014).

26. PS.-LACT. *Pass. Dom.*

27. It is highly improbable that the *Acts of Pilate* cited at JUST. *Apol. I* 35 is the extant *Acts of Pilate*, which has been given a fourth-century date falling somewhere between 320 and 380: R. Gounelle, "Un nouvel évangile Judéo-Chrétien?", *The Apocryphal Gospels within the Context of Early Christian Theology*, ed. J. Schröter (Leuven, 2013), 371. Even if we date the extant *Acts of Pilate* to the fifth or sixth century, it likely has roots in the late third or early fourth century: Elliott, *Apocryphal New Testament*, 164–5.

28. Elliott, *Apocryphal New Testament*, 166.

29. *Acta Pil.* A 3.2; Elliott, *Apocryphal New Testament*, 173. (Translation modified.)

30. *Acta Pil.* A 3.2.

31. *Acta Pil.* A 9.5.

32. *Luke* 23:32: *kakourgoi duo*; *Acta Pil.* A 9.5: *duo kakourgoi*. A fascinating study of whom is J. D. M. Derrett, "The Two Malefactors (Luke xxiii 33, 39–43)", *Studies in the New Testament, Volume Three: Midrash, Haggadah, and the Character of the Community* (Leiden, 1982), 200–14.

33. *Matthew* 27:33; *Mark* 15:22; *Luke* 23:33; *John* 19:17.

34. *John* 18:35.
35. *Luke* 23:24. For the importance of which: Dusenbury, "Judgment of Pontius Pilate", 353–8.
36. *Acta Pil.* A 9.5; Elliott, Apocryphal New Testament, 176.
37. *Acta Pil.* A 3.2; Elliott, Apocryphal New Testament, 173.
38. P. Winter, *On the Trial of Jesus* (Berlin, 1961), 56.
39. The troops who crucified Jesus would not have been legionnaires (Roman citizens), but auxiliaries conscripted by Rome from the *non-Judaean populations* within the provinces of Syria and Judaea—for Judaeans were exempt. The troops under Pilate's command would therefore have been gentiles, but not Roman citizens: Schürer, *History of the Jewish People*, 1:362–3.
40. Dusenbury, "Judgment of Pontius Pilate", 344–8; idem, "Pilate Schemes", *TLS: The Times Literary Supplement* (25 March 2016), 15.
41. *Luke* 23:24; Dusenbury, "Judgment of Pontius Pilate", 353–8.
42. *John* 19:23. Compare *Matthew* 27:27, 31, 35–6; and *Mark* 15:16, 20, 24. And my reasoning, here, is hardly original. One of many juridical–hermeneutical texts that could be cited is W. Goesius, *Pilatus Judex, ad virum illustrem Constantinum Hugenium, equitem, Zulichemi Toparcham, &c.* ... (The Hague, 1681).
43. Winter, *Trial of Jesus*, 58.
44. N. A. Pedersen, "Aristides", *In Defence of Christianity: Early Christian Apologists*, ed. J. Engberg, A.-C. Jacobsen, and J. Ulrich (Frankfurt am Main, 2014), 35–6.
45. Pedersen, "Aristides", 36–7, 47–8.
46. DAM. *Bar. Ioas.* 7.53–5 (where "the gentiles" are implicated, too); *Leg. Aur.* Barlaam and Josaphat. A charming introduction is R. Manselli, "The Legend of Barlaam and Joasaph: In Byzantium and in the Romance Europe", *East and West* 7, 4 (1957), 331–40.
47. Consult the essays in *Barlaam und Josaphat: Neue Perspektiven auf ein europäisches Phänomen*, ed. C. Cordoni and M. Meyer with N. Hable (Berlin, 2015).
48. ARIST. *Apol. Gr.* 14.2; ed. Pouderon et al., 284–5, here 285 note 2: "Ce passage ... très sévère envers les juifs, a été suspecté d'interpolation, dans la mesure où il ne figure pas dans le texte syriaque correspondant ..."
49. ARIST. *Apol. Syr.* 2.4; ed. Pouderon et al., 190–1.
50. *John* 19:31–7; ARIST. *Apol. Syr.* 2.4; ed. Pouderon et al., 190 note 1.
51. DIM. *Jaw.* 77(v)–78(v).
52. Note, though, that much of LACT. *Div. Inst.* seems to have been composed during the Great Persecution: N. L. Thomas, *Defending Christ: The Latin Apologists before Augustine* (Turnhout, 2011), 165.
53. LACT. *Div. Inst.* V 2–3; Thomas, *Defending Christ*, 166.
54. Frend, "Prelude to the Great Persecution", 13–14; Barnes, "Sossianus Hierocles", 243–6.
55. LACT. *Div. Inst.* IV 1,1. The inscriptions to Constantine were made in "a new

edition of the *Divine Institutes*" that Lactantius circulated after the Great Persecution: O. Nicholson, "Constantine's Vision of the Cross", *Vigiliae Christianae* 54, 3 (2000), 309–23, here 317.

56. LACT. *Div. Inst.* IV 10,18.

57. LACT. *Mort. Pers.* 2.

58. Bloch, *Atheism in Christianity*, 119

59. *Pace* Winter, "Marginal Notes on the Trial of Jesus", 249: "The Edict of Milan (312) made it unnecessary for the Church to have in Pilate a witness that 'he found no guilt in [Jesus]'"; and 249 note 119: "the depiction of Pilate as a friend of Jesus comes to a stop under Constantine".

60. LACT. *Div. Inst.* IV 18,6–9.

61. LACT. *Div. Inst.* IV 18,4.

62. LACT. *Div. Inst.* IV 18,6.

63. Agamben, *Pilato e Gesú*; Agamben, *Pilate and Jesus*.

64. Agamben, *Pilate and Jesus*, 47; Agamben, *Pilato e Gesú*, 65: "ma il giudice alla fine non ha pronunciato la sua sentenza, ha semplicemente 'consegnato' l'accusato ai sinedriti e ai carnefici".

65. LACT. *Div. Inst.* IV 18,6.

66. LACT. *Div. Inst.* IV 18,6–9.

67. In his second gloss, Agamben contrasts *Matthew*'s account of the crucifixion— in which it is clearly "the soldiers of the governor" (27:27) who "led Jesus away to crucify him" (27:31)—with *Luke*'s account. "Significantly," writes Agamben, "in Luke there is not a word (*non si fa parola*) about the soldiers": Agamben, *Pilate and Jesus*, 50–1; Agamben, *Pilato e Gesú*, 69–70. Agamben does not detail the precise significance that this supposed omission has for him—but in any case, there is no such omission. We find a reference to Pilate's troops at *Luke* 23:36 ("and the soldiers also mocked him"), and again at *Luke* 23:47 ("Now the centurion ... said, 'Certainly this man was inno-cent!'"). The indistinctness of Luke's crucifixion narrative—he says only that "*they* crucified him" (*Luke* 23:33)—has nothing to do with the later myth of a Judaic crucifixion. Rather, it is accounted for by *Luke*'s reprise of Jesus' death in *Acts* 4:24–8, where the parties culpable for the crucifixion are enu-merated as "both Herod and Pontius Pilate, with the gentiles and the peoples of Israel". According to the writer of *Luke–Acts*, the whole of Roman Judaea killed Jesus.

7. "THE MAN WHO WAS CRUCIFIED IN PALESTINE": PILATE'S INNOCENCE IN PAGAN TRADITION

1. LUC. *Mort. Per.* 11. Two relevant contributions are M. J. Edwards, "Lucian of Samosata in the Christian Memory", *Byzantion* 80 (2010), 142–56; J. N. Bremmer, "Lucian on Peregrinus and Alexander of Abonuteichos: A Sceptical View of Two

Religious Entrepreneurs", *Beyond Priesthood: Religious Entrepreneurs and Innovators in the Roman Empire*, ed. R. L. Gordon, G. Petridou, and J. Rüpke (Berlin, 2017), 49–78.

2. The persecution of Christians in pre-Christian Rome, dating back to the first century CE, reflects "a strong feeling that only ancestral Gods ought to be worshipped, and in the traditional way": Barnes, "Legislation against the Christians", 48–50.

3. EPIC. *Enchir.* 31. Compare the definition of piety as "love of humankind" (*philanthrōpia*) at *Epic. Christ.* 10.6; *Commentaire sur la* Paraphrase Chrétienne *du Manuel d'Épictète*, Greek with French trans., ed. and comm. M. Spanneut (Paris, 2007), 236–7.

4. ORIG. *C. Cels.* V 34. For Celsus' identity, about which "Origen himself seems unsure": Cook, *Interpretation of the New Testament*, 17–18. And for more on Celsus' conservativism: R. L. Wilken, *The Christians as the Romans Saw Them* (New Haven, 1984), 117–25; Schott, *Christianity, Empire, and the Making of Religion*, 45–50.

5. LACT. *Mort. Pers.* 34.

6. SUET. *Vit. XII* Nero 16.2: *afflicti suppliciis Christiani, genus hominum superstitionis novae ac maleficae.* Note that "Suetonius records (among Nero's *good deeds*) merely the fact that Christians were done to death": Barnes, "Legislation against the Christians", 34 (my italics).

7. ORIG. *C. Cels.* VIII 12.

8. DIO CASS. *Hist.* LII 36.1–2; cit. Sordi, *Christians and the Roman Empire*, 90.

9. See, for instance, a sophisticated late-second-century defence against the charge of 'atheism' at ATH. *Leg.* 4–22. For the argument concerning "the gods of the cities" (*tais polesin theous*): ATH. *Leg.* 14.

10. Rome has acquired a veneer of 'secularity' in modern historiography. This is deceptive. For *even in Judaea*, sacrifice lay at the centre of the Roman polity. To be sure, the emperor-cult was not enforced in Judaea (as in certain other Roman provinces), but every morning and evening, sacrifices were offered by Judaean priests in the Jerusalem Temple "for Caesar and the Roman nation". The daily immolation seems to have consisted of an ox and two lambs. And according to Josephus, Judaea's world-historical conflict with Rome began when a zealot-priest halted the Romans' sacrifice in Jerusalem. This interruption of the imperial sacrifice constituted an act of rebellion. Compare JOS. *Bell. Jud.* II 408–21; Schürer, *History of the Jewish People*, 1:381–2. Relevant, too, is a comment by Guy Stroumsa: "In the ancient world, religion was above all a matter of state ... The heart of religious cult was public, from Egypt and Babylonia to Rome. The Jerusalem Temple reflected the Israelite version of ancient civic religion (as best expressed in Varro's conception of *religio civilis*)." See G. G. Stroumsa, *The Making of the Abrahamic Religions in Late Antiquity* (Oxford, 2015), 108.

11. CIC. *Nat. Deor.* III 2.5; Watson, *State, Law, and Religion*; C. Ando, *The Matter of the Gods: Religion and the Roman Empire* (Berkeley, 2008); J. Scheid, *The Gods, the State, and the Individual: Reflections on Civic Religion in Rome*, trans. C. Ando (Philadelphia, 2015). And as Clifford Ando reminds us, "Roman lawyers and theologians ... described [the city's] gods *as citizens*": C. Ando, "The Ontology of Religious Institutions", *History of Religions* 50, 1 (2010), 54–79, here 60. (My italics.)

12. ORIG. *C. Cels.* VIII 2. Compare *C. Cels.* III 5, V 33; and Cook, *Interpretation of the New Testament*, 89–90, 94–7.

13. Consult the argument of J. J. O'Donnell, *Pagans: The End of Traditional Religion and the Rise of Christianity* (New York, 2015).

14. ORIG. *C. Cels.* VIII 63.

15. ORIG. *C. Cels.* VIII 55.

16. *I Corinthians* 8:4–6. This is not to imply that Paul, like later Christian writers, is a full-blown euhemerist, but consult: Schott, *Christianity, Empire, and the Making of Religion*, 28–39.

17. *I Peter* 1:18; here in the translation of P. J. Achtemeier, *1 Peter: A Commentary on First Peter*, ed. E. J. Epp (Minneapolis, 1996), 123. My notice was drawn to this text by W. C. van Unnik, "The Critique of Paganism in I Peter 1:18", *Neotestamentica et Semitica: Studies in Honour of Matthew Black*, ed. E. E. Ellis and M. Wilcox (Edinburgh, 1969), 129–42. And for a succinct comment on the letter's provenance: Achtemeier, *1 Peter*, 38–50.

18. For the Roman suppression of the cult of Bacchus, and the 'Bacchic' character—in Greco-Roman imagination—of early Christianity: Wilken, *Christians as the Romans Saw Them*, 16–20, 96. For the 'Bacchic' extremes of certain marginal Christian communities: S. Benko, "The Libertine Gnostic Sect of the Phibionites according to Epiphanius", *Vigiliae Christianae* 21, 2 (1967), 103–19; I. Jurasz, "Carpocrate et Epiphane: Chrétiens et platoniciens radicaux", *Vigiliae Christianae* 71, 2 (2017), 134–67. And for the idea that Euripides' *Bacchae* may have influenced the composition of the gospel of *John*: D. R. MacDonald, *The Dionysian Gospel: The Fourth Gospel and Euripides* (Minneapolis, 2017).

19. DIO. LAER. *Vit. Phil.* II 5.40: *hetera de kaina daimonia eisēgoumenos*.

20. For more on this: Courcelle, "Anti-Christian Arguments and Christian Platonism".

21. TERT. *Anim.* 28.3: *Neque veritas desiderat vetustatem neque mendacium devitat novellitatem.*

22. It postdates Tertullian, however, by roughly two centuries: Moorhead, "Word *Modernus*", 425–33.

23. G. G. Stroumsa, *The Scriptural Universe of Ancient Christianity* (Cambridge, Mass., 2016), 35, 123. (My italics.)

24. Stroumsa, *Making of the Abrahamic Religions*, 37, 39.

25. TAC. *Ann.* XV 44.

26. L. T. Johnson, *Among the Gentiles: Greco-Roman Religion and Christianity* (New Haven, 2009), 55–63.

27. ARN. *Adv. Nat.* II 66; cit. Courcelle, "Anti-Christian Arguments and Christian Platonism", 155, 172 note 61.

28. TAC. *Ann.* XV 44.

29. Shaw, "Myth of the Neronian Persecution", 74 ("never happened"), 94–6 ("mirage").

30. C. P. Jones, "The Historicity of the Neronian Persecution: A Response to Brent Shaw", *New Testament Studies* 63, 1 (2017), 146–52. For the structural integrity of the scenes, and the mention of Pilate, compare R. Syme, *Tacitus* (Oxford, 1958), 2:468–9.

31. The original reading is likely *Chrestians*: Shaw, "Myth of the Neronian Persecution", 80–1; Jones, "Historicity of the Neronian Persecution", 148–51. But Tertullian notes that second-century bureaucrats tended to soften the Greek-derived 'Christian' into a Latin-sounding 'Chrestian' (*Chrestianus*): TERT. *Apol.* 3.5. Tacitus may be punning on this confusion, if we accept the ingenious reading of TAC. *Ann.* XV 44 offered by Haenchen, *Acts of the Apostles*, 65; and a *Chrestus–Christus* pun may even be present in the New Testament manuscript tradition: T. S. Caulley, "The *Chrestos/Christos* Pun (1 Pet 2:3) in P⁷² and P¹²⁵", *Novum Testamentum* 53, 4 (2011), 376–87.

32. TAC. *Ann.* XV 44.

33. ORIG. *C. Cels.* VII 40. Compare *C. Cels.* VIII 39, for the crucifixion of Christians. And to clarify what Celsus means by "gods who are made manifest": Cook, *Interpretation of the New Testament*, 58–9.

34. ORIG. *C. Cels.* V 64.

35. ORIG. *C. Cels.* I 3.

36. Cit. Frend, "Prelude to the Great Persecution", 13 note 89.

37. LACT. *Mort. Pers.* 2.

38. Fredriksen, *Paul: The Pagans' Apostle*, 90. (Fredriksen's italics.)

39. IGN. *Ep. Mag.* 11.1.

40. IGN. *Ep. Smyr.* 1.2.

41. JUST. *Apol. I* 13. Note that *Apol. I* was arguably written as early as 139 CE: P. L. Buck, "Justin Martyr's *Apologies*: Their Number, Destination, and Form," *Journal of Theological Studies* (NS) 54, 1 (2003), 45–59, here 55; and that Justin does not foreground Pilate's hand in the crucifixion in his anti-Judaic *Dialogue with Trypho*: M. Mach, "Justin Martyr's *Dialogus cum Tryphone Iudaeo* and the Development of Christian Anti-Judaism", *Contra Iudaeos*, 32.

42. Justin seems to have been a 'pagan' convert from Neapolis (present-day Nablus): Mach, "Justin Martyr's *Dialogus cum Tryphone Iudaeo*", 32 note 21.

43. MacMullen, *Christianizing the Roman Empire*, 104.

44. Compare A. R. Birley, "Pliny's Family, Pliny's Career", *The Epistles of Pliny*,

ed. R. Gibson and C. Whitton (Oxford, 2016), 65–6; and J. Corke-Webster, "Trouble in Pontus: The Pliny–Trajan Correspondence on the Christians Reconsidered", *Transactions of the American Philological Association* 147, 2 (2017), 371–411, here 371: "The precise date of Pliny's tenure is unclear; 109–111, 110–112 and 111–113 C.E. are all possible."

45. *1 Peter* 1·1. I owe both fascinating observations to Mullen, *Expansion of Christianity*, 117 (under "Bithynia").

46. PLIN. *Epist.* X 96.3. (Translation modified.) For a vigorous defence of the letter's authenticity: A. N. Sherwin-White, *The Letters of Pliny: A Historical and Social Commentary* (Oxford, 1966), 691–3.

47. Corke-Webster, "Trouble in Pontus", 382. Compare Sherwin-White, *Letters of Pliny*, 697–8; Wilken, *Christians as the Romans Saw Them*, 22–5.

48. PLIN. *Epist.* X 96.4; Sherwin-White, *Letters of Pliny*, 699–700.

49. *Acts of the Apostles* 25:6–12, here 25:10. Inevitably, Paul's citizenship has been doubted: E. R. Goodenough, *Goodenough on the Beginnings of Christianity*, ed. A. T. Kraabel (Leiden, 2020), 119–21, 138–9. For the lawcourt setting of much of the drama in *Acts*: Sherwin-White, *Roman Society and Roman Law in the New Testament*, 48–119, esp. 144–71 (on Paul's citizenship); A. A. Trites, "The Importance of Legal Scenes and Language in the Book of Acts", *Novum Testamentum* 16, 4 (1974), 278–84, here 282. And for a juridical reading of the first trial in *Acts*—a Judaean, not a Roman process: Watson, *Trial of Stephen*, 12.

50. Meaning, only, that Paul could have invoked a right to be heard 'in Caesar's tribunal' in any city of the empire. For the narratives of Paul's troubles in Corinth: *Acts of the Apostles* 18:1–17; in Lystra: *Acts* 14:8–20; and in Caesarea Maritima: *Acts* 23:11–25:4. For the tradition of Paul's death in Rome: LACT. *Mort. Pers.* 2.

51. PLIN. *Epist.* X 96.8; Sherwin-White, *Letters of Pliny*, 702–10. If the *index locorum* can be trusted, there is no mention of these ill-treated *ancillae* in J. M. Carlon, *Pliny's Women: Constructing Virtue and Creating Identity in the Roman World* (Cambridge, 2009).

52. Lee, *From Rome to Byzantium*, 141–2.

53. PLIN. *Epist.* X 97.1. (Translation modified.) Consult Sherwin-White, *Letters of Pliny*, 710–12.

54. PLIN. *Epist.* X 96.7. (Translation modified.)

55. Sherwin-White, *Letters of Pliny*, 699–700, 708; Wilken, *Christians as the Romans Saw Them*, 8–25, 33–5.

56. *Matthew* 27:57–66; *Mark* 15:42–7; *Luke* 23:50–5; *John* 19:38–42.

57. A. Kalthoff, *Das Christus-Problem: Grundlinien zu einer Sozial-theologie* (Leipzig, 1903), 43; cit. Bammel, "Revolution Theory from Reimarus to Brandon", 19: "[A. Kalthoff, who revives Bruno Bauer's myth-theory, sees the canonical] accounts of the passion as reflections of what happened in the time of the persecution under Trajan, [and] he sees Pliny under the mask of Pilate ..."

58. *Acts* 18:12–17 (Gallio), 23:23–4:27 (Felix). For more on Paul's vicissitudes: Sherwin-White, *Roman Society and Roman Law in the New Testament*, 48–119. And for the earliest Christian traditions on Paul's martyrdom: D. L. Eastman, *Paul the Martyr: The Cult of the Apostle in the Latin West* (Atlanta, 2011), 15–114.

59. Keresztes, "Jews, the Christians, and Emperor Domitian", 22–5.

60. Compare Lactantius' witness to a similar oracle of Apollo: LACT. *Div. Inst.* IV 13,11; though they are judged by some to be "completely different": S. Freund, "Christian Use and Valuation of Theological Oracles: The Case of Lactantius' *Divine Institutes*", *Vigiliae Christianae* 60, 3 (2006), 269–84, here 276–9.

61. Compare PLUT. *Mor.* 140d. "It is becoming for a wife to worship", in Plutarch of Chaeronea's opinion, "only those gods that her husband believes in."

62. AUG. *Civ. Dei* XIX 23. That Augustine is transmitting Porphyrian material is deemed credible: A. Busine, *Paroles d'Apollon: Pratiques et traditions oraculaires dans l'Antiquité tardive (IIe–VIe siècles)* (Leiden, 2005), 279–80.

63. See the contemptuous portrayal of Mary Magdalene (by Porphyry? Julian?) as "a coarse woman ... from a wretched little village", at MAC. *Apoc.* II 14; here in the translation of Cook, *Interpretation of the New Testament*, 198.

64. *Matthew* 28:1–8; *Mark* 16:1–8; *Luke* 24:1–9; *John* 20:1–10. For the salience of women in Jesus' prophetic life, culminating in the passion and resurrection narratives: B. Witherington, *Women and the Genesis of Christianity*, ed. A. Witherington (Cambridge, 1990), 88–120.

65. ORIG. *C. Cels.* II 55. For a reading of this passage: Cook, *Interpretation of the New Testament*, 55–6. And for more on the 'hysterical female' trope: M. Y. MacDonald, *Early Christian Women and Pagan Opinion: The Power of the Hysterical Woman* (Cambridge, 1996), 104–6.

66. The second-century philosopher Celsus denies that Jesus can even be called a 'dead god' or a 'phantom'. What the Christians worship, according to Celsus, is "a man who is more wretched even than what *really are* phantoms, and who is *not even* any longer a phantom, but is in fact *dead*": ORIG. *C. Cels.* VII 40.

67. AUG. *Civ. Dei* XIX 23. For other places in *Philosophy from Oracles* where Porphyry commends Judaeans (and faults Christians): Wilken, *Christians as the Romans Saw Them*, 151–2.

68. J. J. O'Meara, *Porphyry's Philosophy from Oracles in Augustine* (Paris, 1959), 50–1.

69. To echo a memorable title: P. Schäfer, *Judeophobia: Attitudes toward the Jews in the Ancient World* (Cambridge, Mass., 1997).

70. Markus, *End of Ancient Christianity*, 210.

71. For Mara, it seems, Jesus is condemned by Judaeans only, not by Pilate. Much later dates have been suggested for the neglected *Letter of Mara bar Sarapion*, but I concur with Millar, *Roman Near East*, 461: "If there is an appropriate context [for Mara's *Letter*], it is the early 70s." On Mara's allusion to Jesus, I

concur with P. Pokorný, "Jesus as the Ever-Living Lawgiver in the *Letter* of Mara bar Sarapion", *The Letter of Mara bar Sarapion in Context: Proceedings of the Symposium Held at Utrecht University, 10–12 December 2009*, ed. A. Merz and T. Tieleman (Leiden, 2012), 131: "The reference to Jesus appears in ch. 18. It is rather short and, from the point of view of the general intention of the letter, only illustrative. The intention of the letter is a Stoic one"; 134: "The suggestion that the Wise King may have been some other person [than Jesus] cannot be substantiated. ... The Wise King was obviously a title given by the author or some of his contemporaries to Jesus of Nazareth"; and 135: "It is unthinkable that somebody would have composed the whole *Letter* in order that the sentences about Jesus might be noticed by the readers. It follows that the reference to Jesus has a certain historical value. ... [Mara's *Letter*] does reproduce rumours circulating about him about a hundred years after Easter and the Christian creed as reflected in [Syrian] society at large." Finally, a sensitive new reading of Mara on Jesus—the "wise king"—is I. Jurasz, "Lettre de Mara bar Sérapion et la *paideia* hellénistique", *Babelao* 7 (2018), 81–135, here 103–9.

72. *Hist. Aug.* "Severus Alexander", 29.1–2; S. Swain, *Hellenism and Empire: Language, Classicism, and Power in the Greek World, AD 50–250* (Oxford, 1996), 382. For more on Severus Alexander: Shahîd, *Rome and the Arabs*, 36–7, 71; Sordi, *Christians and the Roman Empire*, 88–91.

73. "Synagogue-going pagans": Fredriksen, *When Christians Were Jews*, 188.

74. AUG. *Cons. Ev.* I 7.11.

75. EUS. *Dem. Ev.* III 7. Compare the Latin parallel in AUG. *Civ. Dei* XIX 23.

76. ORIG. *C. Cels.* I 9.

77. To those who enquire about Christ's death, Hecate says only: "The body ... is always exposed to torments, but the souls of the righteous dwell in heaven." Though Christ is a righteous soul, says Hecate, the Christians are "hated by the gods"—because they worship Christ as God: AUG. *Civ. Dei* XIX 23.2. For the most recent comment on this oracle: Busine, *Paroles d'Apollon*, 281.

78. AUG. *Civ. Dei* XIX 23. And compare AUG. *Cons. Ev.* I 7.12; PL. *Apol.* 20d–23b. It is not without interest that Porphyry's verdict comes from the same god—Apollo—who judged that there was "no one wiser" than Socrates in the fifth century before Jesus' death. For Socrates, too, died as a convict.

8. "JESUS IS GOING TO BE STONED": PILATE'S INNOCENCE IN JUDAIC TRADITION

1. Nor for that matter is Paula Fredriksen, who defends the historicity of "aristocratic priestly involvement in Jesus' arrest and execution": Fredriksen, *When Christians Were Jews*, 70. Of numerous other texts that could be cited, here: M. Goodman, *The Ruling Class of Judaea: The Origins of the Jewish Revolt against Rome A.D. 66–70* (Cambridge, 1987), 113, 115.

2. For a similar line of reasoning: D. Catchpole, *The Trial of Jesus: A Study in the Gospels and Jewish Historiography from 1770 to the Present Day* (Leiden, 1971), 5–7.

3. Fredriksen, *When Christians Were Jews*, 186: "All of these New Testament texts are often read as antagonistic to Jews and to Judaism. I think that this is due ... to the long shadow of later Christian anti-Judaism"—and, as I suggest here, to non-Christian (or post-Christian) anti-Semitism of the nineteenth and twentieth centuries (shared, lamentably, by many practising Christians).

4. B.-S. Albert, "*Adversus Iudaeos* in the Carolingian Empire", *Contra Iudaeos*, 132.

5. Similarly, there are cogent reasons to believe that Jesus' clashes with Pharisees and Sadducees "belong to a distinct stratum in the Gospel tradition", and "did not really determine" the Christians' mid-second-century (and subsequent) *Adversus Judaeos* genre: Mach, "Justin Martyr's *Dialogus cum Tryphone Iudaeo*", 27–9.

6. *Jos. Ant.* XX 199. He is referring, here, to the Sadducees—on whom: G. Stemberger, "The Sadducees: Their History and Doctrines", *The Cambridge History of Judaism, Volume Three: The Early Roman Period*, ed. W. Horbury, W. Davies, and J. Sturdy (Cambridge, 1999).

7. JOS. *Vita* 1–7.

8. Vespasian made him a Roman citizen: JOS. *Vita* 423. Compare W. den Hollander, *Josephus, the Emperors, and the City of Rome: From Hostage to Historian* (Leiden, 2014), 67 note 194.

9. For Caiaphas' likely connection to Josephus' father: Fredriksen, *When Christians Were Jews*, 4. To be sure, *Matthew* is the only gospel that names Caiaphas in a scene of Jesus' interrogation by a high priest. But Caiaphas' high-priesthood is confirmed by *John*, and obliquely by *Luke–Acts*. What is more, *John* implies that Jesus may have been interrogated by Caiaphas (whom he names) on the night before his death.

10. I have consulted the texts and translations in JOS. *Ant. Jud.* XVIII 63–4; Schürer, *History of the Jewish People*, 1:437; and J. P. Meier, *A Marginal Jew: Rethinking the Historical Jesus, Volume One: The Roots of the Problem and the Person* (New York, 1991), 61.

11. H. J. De Jonge, "Joseph Scaliger's Historical Criticism of the New Testament", *Novum Testamentum* 38, 2 (1996), 176–93, here 189–91; A. Whealey, *Josephus on Jesus: The Testimonium Flavianum Controversy from Late Antiquity to Modern Times* (New York, 2003). For a defence by a seventeenth-century humanist bishop (and Christian sceptic), Pierre-Daniel Huet—"no novice in matters of textual criticism"—see Shelford, "Quest for Certainty in Fact and Faith", 228.

12. Schürer, *History of the Jewish People*, 1:428–41; Fredriksen, *When Christians Were Jews*, 70–2, 80–1.

13. Carleton Paget, "Some Observations on Josephus and Christianity", 565.

14. JOS. *Ant. Jud.* XX 199–203; S. Schwartz, *Josephus and Judaean Politics* (Leiden, 1990), 65–7.

15. For more on the context of this killing: B. Reicke, "Judaeo-Christianity and the Jewish Establishment, A.D. 33–66", *Jesus and the Politics of His Day*, 198. And for a fragment of 'Josephus' that ties the fall of Jerusalem in 70 CE to the killing of James—this fragment is cited by Origen and Eusebius, and may belong to Hegesippus: G. W. H. Lampe, "A.D. 70 in Christian Reflection", *Jesus and the Politics of His Day*, 167–8

16. To limit myself to a single attack, which occurred during my first week living in Jerusalem in the autumn of 2019: P. Oltermann, "Germany: Mass Shooting Attempt that Killed Two Was Antisemitic Attack, Minister Says", *The Guardian* (9 October 2019), archived online at https://www.theguardian.com/world/2019/oct/09/two-people-killed-in-shooting-in-german-city-of-halle; accessed 28 October 2020.

17. For a subtle introduction to a formidable set of vexed questions: G. G. Stroumsa, "From Anti-Judaism to Antisemitism in Early Christianity?", *Contra Iudaeos*.

18. This is subtly argued for Celsus (via Origen) in J. N. Carleton Paget, "The Jew of Celsus and *Adversus Judaeos* Literature", *Zeitschrift für Antikes Christentum* 21, 2 (2017), 201–42. Note that Carleton Paget's argument resembles an earlier one concerning the 'Judaean' reports in Justin: W. Horbury, *Jews and Christians in Contact and Controversy* (Edinburgh, 1998), 103–7. For further references: Cook, *Interpretation of the New Testament*, 27–8; and for an important new argument: M. R. Niehoff, "A Jewish Critique of Christianity from Second-Century Alexandria: Revisiting the Jew Mentioned in *Contra Celsum*", *Journal of Early Christian Studies* 21, 2 (2013), 151–75.

19. ORIG. *C. Cels.* II 10.

20. When Celsus' Judaean figure alludes to Pilate, it is in reference to both Euripides and the gospels. "But the one who condemned him"—read Pilate—"did not even suffer any such fate as that of Pentheus by going mad or being torn in pieces." Rather, Jesus permitted "those who mocked him" to "put a purple robe round him and the crown of thorns and the reed in his hand": ORIG. *C. Cels.* II 34.

21. ORIG. *C. Cels.* II 5. John Granger Cook underlines that "Celsus does not mention any role for the Romans in Jesus' destiny": Cook, *Interpretation of the New Testament*, 49.

22. AUG. *Civ. Dei* XIX 23.

23. ORIG. *C. Cels.* VI 10.

24. A composite of ORIG. *C. Cels.* II 31, 44. For a precis of Celsus' critique of the passion: Cook, *Interpretation of the New Testament*, 48–54.

25. What Guy Stroumsa says of the Midrash could be said of Talmud, too—and, mutatis mutandis, of the canonical gospels and the Qur'an. "The fact that it was composed and redacted orally, and only later committed to writing, makes the exact dating of the texts quite difficult": Stroumsa, *Making of the Abrahamic Religions*, 113.

26. Some have even treated the name 'Jesus' as a post-Talmudic insertion—though Gunther Mark and others have presented incisive arguments in favour of the name's authenticity: G. Mark, "Jesus 'Was Close to the Authorities': The Historical Background of a Talmudic Pericope", *Journal of Theological Studies* (NS) 60, 2 (2009), 437–66, here 441, 446–50.

27. J. Maier, *Jesus von Nazareth in der talmudischen Überlieferung* (Darmstadt, 1978). Compare the respectful, yet fundamental criticisms of Maier's study in: Horbury, *Jews and Christians*, 19–20; P. Schäfer, *Jesus in the Talmud* (Princeton, 2007), 5–8.

28. Schäfer, *Jesus in the Talmud*, 7: "I start with the deliberately naive assumption that the relevant sources do refer to the figure of Jesus unless proven otherwise."

29. P. Frankopan, *The Silk Roads: A New History of the World* (New York, 2017), 57–8.

30. M. Bar-Asher Siegal, *Early Christian Monastic Literature and the Babylonian Talmud* (Cambridge, 2013), 9–10, 60–1, here 10.

31. Murcia situates himself between the minimalism of Johann Maier and the maximalism of I. J. Yuval, *Two Nations in Your Womb: Perceptions of Jews and Christians in Late Antiquity and the Middle Ages* (Berkeley, 2006), at T. Murcia, *Jésus dans le Talmud et la littérature rabbinique ancienne* (Turnhout, 2014), 32. For his unease with some of Schäfer's formulations: Murcia, *Jésus dans le Talmud*, 41–4, 432–3, 438–9, 472–3.

32. W. Horbury, "The Trial of Jesus in Jewish Tradition", *The Trial of Jesus: Cambridge Studies in Honour of C. F. D. Moule*, ed. E. Bammel (Naperville, Ill., 1970), 111–12.

33. Krauss, *Jewish–Christian Controversy*, 9–13, here 11–12.

34. Murcia, *Jésus dans le Talmud*, 335: "il ne fait aucun doute que les rédacteurs des *Toledot Yeshu* ont utilisé et amplifié les traditions rabbiniques ... pour façonner leur personnage composite censé représenter Jésus. Mais l'échange a parfaitement pu fonctionner à divers niveaux en croisant plusieurs sources: Celse, Tosefta, Yerushalmi, *Toledot*, Babli."

35. On Talmudic indications of "the deep attraction the figure of the Virgin Mary exercised on many Jews"—noting that "the Virgin Mary was not only attractive, but also repulsive": M. Himmelfarb, "The Mother of the Messiah in the Talmud Yerushalmi and Sefer Zerubbabel", *The Talmud Yerushalmi and Graeco-Roman Culture*, ed. P. Schäfer (Tübingen, 2002), 389.

36. TAL. BAB. *San.* 106b.

37. This is noted in Horbury, *Jews and Christians*, 17–20, 103–7, 177–8; W. Horbury, "The Depiction of Judaeo-Christians in the Toledot Yeshu", *The Image of the Judaeo-Christians in Ancient Jewish and Christian Literature*, ed. P. J. Tomson and D. Lambers-Petry (Tübingen, 2003), 283, 286: "There is ... much to suggest that the Toledot Yeshu preserve early Jewish polemical tra-

dition on Christianity, often post-Constantinian but developing material already known in connected forms in the second century." The same lineage is sketched in Meerson and Schäfer, "Introduction", *Toledot Yeshu*, 4–9.

38. The critical Talmudic text on Jesus' death—TAL. BAB. *San.* 43a—is "incorporated into the Toledot Yeshu narrative (without any express reference to the Talmud)": Horbury, "Depiction of Judaeo-Christians in the Toledot Yeshu", 282–3.

39. I am thinking of R. M. Meelführer, *Jesus in Talmude* (Altdorf, 1699). Cit. Krauss, *Jewish–Christian Controversy*, 142.

40. Here and below, I take 'Jesus the Nazarene' from Schäfer, *Jesus in the Talmud*, 64–5. Note that TAL. BAB. *San.* 43a prints 'Yeshu', here, stating in a note that 'Nazarean' is attested in the manuscript tradition. 'Nazarene' is a contested rendering of the fuller text: Mark, "Jesus 'Was Close to the Authorities'", 438 note 2. Thierry Murcia prefers to transcribe the Hebrew, 'Yeshu ha-Notsri', of the fuller text: Murcia, *Jésus dans le Talmud*, 332, 423–4. Note, finally, that one text-critical interpreter of this *baraita* suggests that the lines, "On the eve of the Passover Jesus the Nazarene was hanged" and "Jesus the Nazarene … practiced sorcery and seduced Israel to idolatry", might be "older than their immediate context": Horbury, *Jews and Christians*, 105.

41. Compare the translations in TAL. BAB. *San.* 43a; and Schäfer, *Jesus in the Talmud*, 64–5.

42. L. Jacobs, *The Talmudic Argument: A Study in Talmudic Reasoning and Methodology* (Cambridge, 1984), 1–7.

43. *John* 18:28, 19:14, 19:31. There is a still more precise recollection of *John* 19:31 in a Florentine manuscript of the Babylonian Talmud. In this Florentine variant, the hanging of Jesus occurs on "the eve of the Sabbath and the eve of the Passover": Murcia, *Jésus dans le Talmud*, 332 note 109, 423 note 3, 430–5.

44. Murcia, *Jésus dans le Talmud*, 333: "En réalité, *B. Sanhedrin* 43a … présenté *sa version* de la mort de Jésus—condamné, pendu, lapidé, la veille de Pâque (et du sabbat) en un lieu *non précisé* (Jérusalem)." (Murcia's italics.)

45. Murcia, *Jésus dans le Talmud*, 423: "le Talmud de Babylone possède lui aussi sa propre version de l'exécution de Jésus" (my translation).

46. Murcia, *Jésus dans le Talmud*, 425–30, here 428: "Ce sont ces deux traditions—juives et chrétiennes—réinterprétées, qui convergent en *B. Sanhédrin* 43a: Yeshu est condamné a être lapidé et il finit 'pendu'." (My translation.)

47. ORIG. *C. Cels.* II 10.

48. *Qur.* 4:157–8. For the relevance of Quranic doctrine to Judaic narratives of Jesus' life and death (and vice versa): P. Alexander, "The *Toledot Yeshu* in the Context of Jewish–Muslim Debate", *Toledot Yeshu ("The Life Story of Jesus")* *Revisited: A Princeton Conference*, ed. P. Schäfer, M. Meerson, and Y. Deutsch (Tübingen, 2011), 149–57.

49. The rabbinic 'hanging' referred to is certainly not crucifixion: TAL. BAB. *San.* 46a.

50. On the vexed question of Judaean crucifixions in antiquity (to which there is no allusion in this *baraita*): D. W. Chapman, *Ancient Jewish and Christian Perceptions of Crucifixion* (Tübingen, 2008), 2–177.

51. TAL. BAB. *San.* 43a; Schäfer, *Jesus in the Talmud*, 64–5. For a subtle suggestion that 'the government', in this Babylonian *baraita*, is a late antique Christian Rome retrojected into the first century CE: Murcia, *Jésus dans le Talmud*, 441–2. For broader Judaic perceptions of 'the government' in late antiquity: A. M. Sivertsev, *Judaism and Imperial Ideology in Late Antiquity* (Cambridge, 2011). And for a fourth-century Palestinian rabbi who is 'close to the Romans'—indeed, Rabbi Abahu is rumoured to be one of "the House of Caesar": L. I. Levine, "R. Abbahu of Caesarea", *Christianity, Judaism, and Other Greco-Roman Cults ... Part Four: Judaism after 70, Other Greco-Roman Cults ...*, ed. J. Neusner (Leiden, 1975), 66–75.

52. Schäfer, *Jesus in the Talmud*, 73.

53. TAL. BAB. *San.* 43a; Schäfer, *Jesus in the Talmud*, 64–5.

54. Cit. W. Bacher, "Joseph Perles: 1835–1894", *The Jewish Quarterly Review* 7, 1 (1894), 1–23, here 17.

55. Perles noted, too, that a Roman crucifixion of Jesus is recollected in the Targum—meaning, here, in Aramaic versions of the Hebrew book of Esther: J. Perles, "Bileam-Jesus und Pontius Pilatus", *Monatsschrift für Geschichte und Wissenschaft des Judentums* 21 (1872), 266–7. Cit. Murcia, *Jésus dans le Talmud*, 622.

56. TAL. BAB. *San.* 106b. (Note that TAL. BAB. *San.* 106b prints "thirty years old". I take "thirty-three or thirty-four years old" from Murcia, *Jésus dans le Talmud*, 621, 633–5, 651–2.)

57. Murcia, *Jésus dans le Talmud*, 438.

58. The critical history is reprised by Murcia, *Jésus dans le Talmud*, 621–6.

59. *Numbers* 22–4; N. Cave, *And the Ass Saw the Angel* (London, 2013).

60. It is interesting to recall, in this context, the scathing references to Balaam in three New Testament texts: *II Peter* 2:15 ("the way of Balaam ... who loved gain from wrongdoing"); *Jude* 11 ("Balaam's error"); and *Revelation* 2:14 ("the teaching of Balaam, who ... put a stumbling block before the sons of Israel").

61. There are other recurring typologies. In both Judaean and Christian texts, for instance, Haman's impalement in *Esther* is made to resemble Jesus' crucifixion. For the Haman–Jesus typology: Yuval, *Two Nations in Your Womb*, 229–31; S. Kattan Gribetz, "Hanged and Crucified: The Book of Esther and the *Toledot Yeshu*", *Toledot Yeshu ("The Life Story of Jesus") Revisited*, 159–61. And for the sanguinary history of the Haman–Jesus typology in medieval Europe: Yuval, *Two Nations in Your Womb*, 165–7.

62. *Luke* 3:23; Murcia, *Jésus dans le Talmud*, 633.

63. Murcia, *Jésus dans le Talmud*, 638–41, here 638: "Judas lui-même ... le défenseur le plus zélé de la religion mosaïque menacée."

64. Murcia, *Jésus dans le Talmud*, 652.

65. TAL. BAB. *San.* 82a; Murcia, *Jésus dans le Talmud*, 622–3.

66. For Balaam's age, compare TAL. BAB. *San.* 106b; Murcia, *Jésus dans le Talmud*, 621, 633–5, 651–2.

67. D. W. Halivni, *The Formation of the Babylonian Talmud* (Oxford, 2013), 65.

68. Krauss, *Jewish–Christian Controversy*, 12: "Based on the Talmud, especially as regards the birth and death of Jesus, is the Jewish history of Jesus called *Toldoth Jeshu*."

69. For a path-breaking study of the birth-narratives, to balance my concentration here on the death-narratives: M. Goldstein, "Early Judeo-Arabic Birth Narratives in the Polemical Story 'Life of Jesus' (Toledot Yeshu)", *Harvard Theological Review* 113, 3 (2020), 354–77.

70. Alexander, "*Toledot Yeshu* in the Context of Jewish–Muslim Debate", 149–57. For indications that the *The Life of Jesus* came to fill a "semi-liturgical" function in the Jewish communities of Christian Europe, while remaining a "humorous semi-fictional" text in the Islamicate lands in which it originates: M. Goldstein, "A Polemical Tale and Its Function in the Jewish Communities of the Mediterranean and the Near East: Toledot Yeshu in Judeo-Arabic", *Intellectual History of the Islamicate World* 7 (2019), 192–227, here 195–7, 215–16.

71. Albert, "*Adversus Iudaeos* in the Carolingian Empire", 120–1, 135–8, 141–2.

72. Albert, "*Adversus Iudaeos* in the Carolingian Empire", 142: "Although the Jews were not yet generally regarded as hated and outcasts [in the 820s], the more hostile attitude introduced by Agobard ... was ultimately to prevail, both in exegesis and in Canon Law." For Agobard's defence of the rights of slaves in Jewish households: J. A. Cabaniss, "Agobard of Lyons", *Speculum* 26, 1 (1951), 50–76, here 59–60. For the role of Jewish merchants in medieval slave trades, and its relevance for Agobard: M. McCormick, "New Light on the 'Dark Ages': How the Slave Trade Fuelled the Carolingian Economy", *Past & Present* 177 (2002), 17–54; J. Elukin, *Living Together, Living Apart: Rethinking Jewish–Christian Relations in the Middle Ages* (Princeton, 2007), 48–50; Frankopan, *Silk Roads*, 118. For the intrication of Agobard's theology and politics: J. Cohen, *Living Letters of the Law: Ideas of the Jew in Medieval Christianity* (Berkeley, 1999), 123–45.

73. For the idea that Agobard signals "a significant shift in attitudes to the supernatural" in Carolingian legal culture: P. R. L. Brown, *The Rise of Western Christendom: Triumph and Diversity, AD 200–1000* (Oxford, 1996), 291–3.

74. Cabaniss, "Agobard of Lyons", 51–3.

75. Albert, "*Adversus Iudaeos* in the Carolingian Empire", 122–3.

76. AGO. *Jud. Sup.* 10; Meerson and Schäfer, "Introduction", 3–5. (Translation lightly modified.) And compare: Cabaniss, "Agobard of Lyons", 62.

77. Meerson and Schäfer, "Introduction", 4, 92–3.

78. Y. Deutsch, "The Second Life of the Life of Jesus: Christian Reception of *Toledot Yeshu*", *Toledot Yeshu ("The Life Story of Jesus") Revisited.*
79. Krauss, *Jewish–Christian Controversy*, 12–13; Meerson and Schäfer, "Introduction", 4–6.
80. Meerson and Schäfer, "Introduction", 29.
81. *Tol. Yesh. Or.* in *Toledot Yeshu: The Life Story of Jesus*, ed. and trans. M. Meerson and P. Schäfer (Tübingen, 2014), 1:128–9.
82. *Tol. Yesh. Or.*, ed. and trans. Meerson and Schäfer, 1:131.
83. *Tol. Yesh. Or.*, ed. and trans. Meerson and Schäfer, 1:132–3.
84. *Tol. Yesh. Or.*, ed. and trans. Meerson and Schäfer, 1:131. See, however, a later list of names in the same manuscript where "Tiberius Caesar ... and Pilate the governor, and Rabbi Yehoshuah ben Perahiah, and Marinus the Great Elder of the Jews" are credited with having "brought and hanged" Jesus: *Tol. Yesh. Or.*, ed. and trans. Meerson and Schäfer, 1:134.
85. Meerson and Schäfer, "Introduction", 29.
86. See Lémonon, *Pilate et le gouvernement de la Judée*, 256.
87. *Tol. Yesh. Byz.*, ed. and trans. Meerson and Schäfer, 1:155. (Translation modified: Meerson and Schäfer print "Yeshu ha-Notsri".)
88. *Tol. Yesh. Byz.*, ed. and trans. Meerson and Schäfer, 1:159.
89. *Tol. Yesh. Byz.*, ed. and trans. Meerson and Schäfer, 1:159, 163.
90. *Tol. Yesh. Byz.*, ed. and trans. Meerson and Schäfer, 1:163.
91. Compare MEL. *P. Pas.* 96; *Tol. Yesh. Byz.*, ed. and trans. Meerson and Schäfer, 1:164 (translation lightly modified).
92. Meerson and Schäfer, "Introduction", 32.
93. *Tol. Yesh. Eur.*, ed. and trans. Meerson and Schäfer, 1:198.
94. Grotius, *Annotationes in Novum Testamentum*, 4:259.
95. *Tol. Yesh. Eur.*, ed. and trans. Meerson and Schäfer, 1:198.
96. *John* 19:13–16.
97. *Tol. Yesh. Eur.*, ed. and trans. Meerson and Schäfer, 1:199. (Translation lightly modified.)
98. *Tol. Yesh. Eur.*, ed. and trans. Meerson and Schäfer, 1:199. (Translation lightly modified.)
99. *Tol. Yesh. Or.*, ed. and trans. Meerson and Schäfer, 1:140.
100. Meerson and Schäfer, "Introduction", 32.
101. Schäfer, *Jesus in the Talmud*, 73. (My italics.)
102. Murcia, *Jésus dans le Talmud*, 41–4, 432–3, 438–9, 472–3.
103. Compare the translations in TAL. BAB. *San.* 43a; Schäfer, *Jesus in the Talmud*, 64–5.
104. For Voltaire: Meerson and Schäfer, "Introduction", 17–18. His interest in the *Toledot Yeshu* is purely tactical. Voltaire notoriously refers to eighteenth-century European Jewry as "this vile people, superstitious, ignorant ...": A. Sutcliffe, *Judaism and Enlightenment* (Cambridge, 2003), 231–46, here 231.

105. For a more appreciative premodern Judaic narrative about Jesus: R. Ben-Shalom, "The Foundation of Christianity in the Historical Perceptions of Medieval Jewry as Expressed in the Anonymous *Various Elements on the Topic of Christian Faith* (London, BL, MS Addit. 27129, pp. 88b–92a)", *Conflict and Religious Conversation in Latin Christendom: Studies in Honour of Ora Limor*, ed. I, J, Yuval and R, Ben-Shalom (Turnhout, 2014),

106. A subtle reflection on the *Mishneh Torah*'s legal and formal innovativeness, and on its Almohad *Sitz im Leben*, is S. Stroumsa, *Maimonides in His World: Portrait of a Mediterranean Thinker* (Princeton, 2009), 59–70.

107. MAIM. *Mish. Tor.* Book of Judges (*Sefer Shoftim*), Laws of Kings and Their Wars (*Hilchot Melachim*) 11.4; here in the translation of Krauss, *Jewish–Christian Controversy*, 226. However, *caveat lector*. This Jesus-text is not printed in the Yale edition of Maimonides' revered commentary, nor is the lacuna noted: Maimonides, *The Code of Maimonides, Book Fourteen: The Book of Judges*, trans. A. M. Hershman (New Haven, 1977), 239–40. It is only present in parts of the Hebrew tradition of *Mishneh Torah*, having been censored in the late medieval period. (I am grateful to Oded Irshai and Sarah Stroumsa for helping to elucidate the transmission-history, and suppression-history, of this Jesus-text.) I am therefore relying on Krauss, though the interpretation offered here is my own.

108. J. Cohen, *The Friars and the Jews: The Evolution of Medieval Anti-Semitism* (Ithaca, N.Y., 1982), 51–76. For a survey of church-ordered Talmud burning (and banning) from the thirteenth to the sixteenth century: K. R. Stow, "The Burning of the Talmud in 1553, in Light of Sixteenth Century Catholic Attitudes toward the Talmud", *Bibliothèque d'humanisme et Renaissance* 34, 3 (1972), 435–59, here 435–43.

109. H. Bloom, *Jesus and Yahweh: The Names Divine* (New York, 2005), 112.

9. "CHRIST WAS NOT THE ONE CRUCIFIED": PILATE'S INNOCENCE IN ISLAMIC TRADITION

1. T. Nöldeke et al., *The History of the Qur'ān*, ed. and trans. W. H. Behn (Leiden, 2013), 592. For a gorgeous display of the mechanics of sura division in one of the earliest sets of *Qur'an* copies, the invaluable 'Sanaa palimpsest': A. Hilali, *The Sanaa Palimpsest: The Transmission of the Qur'an in the First Centuries AH* (Oxford, 2017), 75–9. Hilali notes that some suras in the Sanaa palimpsest are titled, and some are not (40–3).

2. Nöldeke et al., *History of the Qur'ān*, 244.

3. Nöldeke et al., *History of the Qur'ān*, 48–50. For the renaming of Yathrib from the Arabic *madinat al-nabi*, "city of the prophet": F. M. Donner, *Muhammad and the Believers: At the Origins of Islam* (Cambridge, Mass., 2010), 42–3.

4. Nöldeke et al., *History of the Qur'ān*, 158–66.

5. Reynolds, "On the Qur'anic Accusation of Scriptural Falsification", 200.

6. *Qur'an* 4:152–68 (Judaeans), 4:169–74 (Christians): Nöldeke et al., *History of the Qur'ān*, 165.

7. Alexander, "*Toledot Yeshu* in the Context of Jewish–Muslim Debate", 153.

8. *Qur.* 4:153 (People of the Book), 160 (Judaeans).

9. For the origins of this charge: G. S. Reynolds, "On the Qur'ān and the Theme of Jews as 'Killers of the Prophets'", *Al-Bayān: Journal of Qur'an and Hadith Studies* 10, 2 (2012), 9–32.

10. Note that aspersions of Mary are common in the *Toledot Yeshu* genre. For instance, before giving the names of Jesus' brothers and sisters a 'Byzantine' version tells us that "Miriam became pregnant ... by harlotry, more than once": *Tol. Yesh. Byz.*, in *Toledot Yeshu*, ed. and trans. Meerson and Schäfer, 1:156.

11. G. S. Reynolds, "The Muslim Jesus: Dead or Alive?", *Bulletin of the School of Oriental and African Studies* 72, 2 (2009), 237–58, here 257.

12. This is not the view of G. S. Reynolds, *The Qur'an and Its Biblical Subtext* (London, 2010), 153–4: "with the killing of Jesus the Qur'ān turns a Biblical accusation (cf. Acts 3.14; 4.10; 7.52) into a proclamation of the Jews (Q. 4.157)".

13. As intimated very early in ARIST. *Apol. Syr.* 2.4; ed. Pouderon et al., 190–1.

14. *Qur.* 4:157–58; Reynolds, "Muslim Jesus", 238 and 238 note 6.

15. *Qur.* 4:157–9.

16. The only clear, premodern references to Pilate are made by the eleventh-century jurist 'Abd al-Jabbār, whom we will meet later in the chapter. Other confused references are cited here: T. Lawson, *The Crucifixion and the Qur'an: A Study in the History of Muslim Thought* (Oxford, 2009), 134–5 (*Ikhwan al-Safa*), 163–4 (ibn Kathīr).

17. Jesus was certainly not killed by Judaeans in the *Qur'an*, but whether he died is a vexed question: Reynolds, "Muslim Jesus", 238–40.

18. TAL. BAB. *San.* 106b; Murcia, *Jésus dans le Talmud*, 499–664.

19. S. M. Stern, "Quotations from Apocryphal Gospels in 'Abd al-Jabbār", *The Journal of Theological Studies* (NS) 18, 1 (1967), 34–57, here 45–6; Lawson, *Crucifixion and the Qur'an*, 63–169; Reynolds, "Muslim Jesus", 240–5.

20. Voltaire calls Sale, in a 1738 letter, "a devil of an Englishman who has done a very beautiful translation of the holy Alcoran". Cit. A. Bevilacqua, "The Qur'an Translations of Marracci and Sale", *Journal of the Warburg and Courtauld Institutes* 76 (2013), 93–130, here 93.

21. G. Sale, *The Koran, Commonly Called The Alcoran of Mohammed, Translated into English Immediately from the Original Arabic* ... (London, 1734), 42 (of chapter 3). (Typography lightly modernized.) For more on Sale, about whom "remarkably little is known", and his impressive translation of the *Qur'an*: Bevilacqua, "Qur'an Translations of Marracci and Sale", 100–2, 112–20.

22. For a change of tone in twentieth-century commentaries: Lawson, *Crucifixion and the Qur'an*, 171–215.

23. In a contribution entitled "Jesus in the Islamic Tradition", for instance, Asma Afsaruddin unhesitatingly refers to the "Qur'anic denial of the killing of Jesus" (citing sura 4). She presents as Islamic doctrine that "it only appeared as if Jesus was crucified". Yet Afsaruddin is silent on the question of *what* appeared during the crucifixion: A. Afsaruddin, "The Messiah 'Isa, Son of Mary: Jesus in the Islamic Tradition", *Nicholas of Cusa and Islam: Polemic and Dialogue in the Late Middle Ages*, ed. I. C. Levy, R. George-Tvrtković, and D. Duclow (Leiden, 2014), 189–90.

24. The name 'Cyrene bar Mansur' is from a text by the thirteenth-century Syrian polyhistor Gregory bar Ahron, aka Bar Hebraeus (died 1286), who cites "a certain Damascene author"—the context indicates that this is our John—"who was named Cyrene bar Mansūr": S. W. Anthony, "Fixing John Damascene's Biography: Historical Notes and His Family Background", *Journal of Early Christian Studies* 23, 4 (2015), 607–27, here 625–6. John's pre-monastic name is uncertain; according to a modern *communis opinio*, it is 'Mansur ibn Sarjun'. But I have deferred to a convincing new reconstruction of John's life that shows that Mansur ibn Sarjun seems to be John's father; that Mansur is not "John's pre-monastic name" but "simply John's *ancestral* name"; and that John's given name is, more probably, Cyrene bar Mansur: Anthony, "Fixing John Damascene's Biography", 618–27 (Anthony's stress). I am grateful to Samuel Noble for alerting me to this debate, and for referring me to Anthony's contribution.

25. R. Le Coz, "Jean Damascène: Vie et œuvre", *Jean Damascène: Écrits sur l'Islam*, Greek with French trans. and comm. R. Le Coz (Paris, 1992), 54. Compare D. J. Sahas, *John of Damascus on Islam: The "Heresy of the Ishmaelites"* (Leiden, 1972), 43–5.

26. A. Louth, *St John Damascene: Tradition and Originality in Byzantine Theology* (Oxford, 2002), 3–8. Compare Sahas, *John of Damascus on Islam*, 47–8. Inevitably, the historicity of John's connection to Saint Sabbas has been doubted: Anthony, "Fixing John Damascene's Biography", 624 note 57. And though I give a conventional date for John's death, here, it is conceivable that he "may have remained active well into the 760s": Anthony, "Fixing John Damascene's Biography", 626–7.

27. Brown, *Rise of Western Christendom*, 189–90; A. Louth, "St John Damascene: Preacher and Poet", *Preacher and Audience: Studies in Early Christian and Byzantine Homiletics*, ed. M. B. Cunningham and P. Allen (Leiden, 1998), 247–9. As Daniel Sahas notes, John's writings "bear mostly the name 'John of Damascus' and sometimes simply 'John presbyter and monachus'": Sahas, *John of Damascus on Islam*, 7. However, when he is anathematized by the Iconoclastic Synod of 754, the name used is 'Mansur' (or rather, in the synod's Greek records, *Mansour*): Sahas, *John of Damascus on Islam*, 3–9.

28. P. Schadler, *John of Damascus and Islam: Christian Heresiology and the Intellectual Background to Earliest Christian-Muslim Relations* (Leiden, 2018), 110. Compare Sahas, *John of Damascus on Islam*, 45–7. Given the Syrian milieu, it is worth noting that the *Qur'an* contains "a large number of loan words, mostly Syriac", and that the orthography of the *Qur'an* is "strongly imprinted by Syriac models": A. Neuwirth, "Qur'an and History: A Disputed Relationship; Some Reflections on Qur'anic History and History in the Qur'an", *Journal of Qur'anic Studies* 5 (2003), 1–18, here 7. For the more than 300 non-Arabic words in the *Qur'an*—a collection the *Qur'an* itself says is composed in "Arabic" (*'arabī*): H. Motzki, "Alternative Accounts of the Qur'ān's Formation", *The Cambridge Companion to the Qur'ān*, ed. J. McAuliffe (Cambridge, 2006), 67–8.

29. Here in the translation of Anthony, "Fixing John Damascene's Biography", 618–19. Compare Sahas, *John of Damascus on Islam*, 4 note 2: "Anathema to Mansūr, who has ... Saracen opinions."

30. Schadler, *John of Damascus and Islam*, 110–19, here 111–13.

31. DAM. *Adv. Haer.* 100 6.2–3: *hē graphē "tēs gunaikos"*. For John as a witness to the names of the suras: Sahas, *John of Damascus on Islam*, 89–90, 93.

32. For "Hagarism": Sahas, *John of Damascus on Islam*, 120 note 3, 156–7. And for the originality of "the number 100", though in some editions—notably, in Migne's Patrologia Graeca—this is chapter 101: Sahas, *John of Damascus on Islam*, 57–8. For more on John's ordering of the heresies, culminating in Islam—or, in his words, "the superstition of the Ishmaelites": Stroumsa, *Making of the Abrahamic Religions*, 69–70, 185–6.

33. DAM. *Adv. Haer.* 100 2.7–11. Here in the translation of Schadler, *John of Damascus and Islam*, 115–16 (lightly modified). I have transposed 'Jesus' from DAM. *Adv. Haer.* 100 2.6–7: "Jesus, who was a prophet and servant of God."

34. Schadler, *John of Damascus and Islam*, 118. Compare Sahas, *John of Damascus on Islam*, 78–9 and 84–6, here 79: "This passage is one of the most convincing evidences of the accuracy of John of Damascus' knowledge of ... the wording of the Qur'ān."

35. DAM. *Adv. Haer.* 100 2.9–10: *ho Christos ouk estaurōthē ... oute apethanen.*

36. *Qur.* 4:157–8.

37. Reynolds, *Qur'an and Its Biblical Subtext*, 219, 221.

38. J. D. McAuliffe, "Quranic Hermeneutics: The Views of al-Tabarī and Ibn Kathīr", *Approaches to the History of the Interpretation of the Qur'ān* (Oxford, 1988), 47–8.

39. Compare Stern, "Apocryphal Gospels", 46, 46 notes 3–4; Reynolds, "Muslim Jesus", 241.

40. W. A. Saleh, *The Formation of the Classical Tafsīr Tradition: The Qur'ān Commentary of al-Tha'labī (d. 427/1035)* (Leiden, 2004), 28–52, here 41.

41. Stern, "Apocryphal Gospels", 47.

42. ABB. *Taf.* 4:156–8 *ad loc.* (Note that I have lightly modified the typography

and inserted Khalidi's *Qur'an* translation—the one relied on in this chapter—
for clarity of exposition.)

43. In the *Tafsīr al-Jalālayn*, a revered Egyptian commentary by Jalāl al-Dīn al
Mahalli (died 1459) and Jalāl al-Dīn al Suyūtī (died 1505), Jesus' body double is not given a name. But "the one slain and crucified" is called "a companion of theirs": JAL. *Taf.* 4:157 *ad loc.* (Translation modified.)

44. Nöldeke et al., *History of the Qur'ān*, 6: "There can be no doubt that
Muhammad's prime source of information was ... uncanonical liturgical and
dogmatic literature. For this reason ... [his] New Testament stories ... display some common features with the reports of the apocryphal Gospels."

45. Stroumsa, "From Anti-Judaism to Antisemitism", 16.

46. W. Schneemelcher, *New Testament Apocrypha*, trans. R. McL. Wilson (Louisville,
2003), 1:397–9.

47. J. L. Borges, "Three Versions of Judas", *Ficciones*, trans. A. Kerrigan (New York,
1962); idem, "A Defense of Basilides the False", *Selected Non-fictions*, ed.
E. Weinberger, trans. E. Allen, S. J. Levine, and E. Weinberger (London,
2000).

48. IREN. *Adv. Haer.* I 24.4.

49. G. G. Stroumsa, "Christ's Laughter: Docetic Origins Reconsidered", *Journal
of Early Christian Studies* 12, 3 (2004), 267–88, here 271.

50. *Mark* 15:21. For 'Pilate's troops': *Mark* 15:15–20. (Revised Standard Version.)
For the political-cultural resonance of the names of Simon's sons: R. Westall,
"Simon of Cyrene, a Roman Citizen?", *Historia: Zeitschrift für Alte Geschichte*
59, 4 (2010), 489–500.

51. M. Dibelius, *From Tradition to Gospel*, trans. B. L. Woolf (Cambridge, 1982),
182–3, 192.

52. Eisler, *Messiah Jesus and John the Baptist*, 513.

53. For the symbolism: Stroumsa, "Christ's Laughter", 280–8.

54. Stroumsa, "Christ's Laughter", 270 note 14.

55. NAG. HAMM. *Seth II* 55–6. Cit. Stroumsa, "Christ's Laughter", 270–1.

56. ABB. *Taf.* 4:156–58 *ad loc.*

57. This title, assumed by Mehmed II, "became an integral part of his and his
descendants' *intitulatio*": D. Kolodziejczyk, "Khan, Caliph, Tsar, and Imperator:
The Multiple Identities of the Ottoman Sultan", *Universal Empire: A Comparative
Approach to Imperial Culture and Representation in Eurasian History*, ed. P. Fibiger
Bang and D. Kolodziejczyk (Cambridge, 2012), 183.

58. TREB. *Aut. Dox.* 15.4.

59. TREB. *Aut. Dox.* 15.5. This can be contrasted with a passage in Cusa that
reveals no memory—or represses a memory?—of Basilides. See CUS. *Crib.
Alk.* II 14.122: "The chronicles of that period speak harmoniously [about
Christ's crucifixion]; and all Christians, Jews, and pagans held this belief for
some six hundred years before the time of Mohammed."

60. TREB. *Aut. Dox.* 15.9.

61. TREB. *Aut. Dox.* 15.4. The definitive work on Trebizond's fascinating and tumul-
tuous life is J. Monfasani, *George of Trebizond: A Biography and a Study of His
Rhetoric and Logic* (Leiden, 1976).

62. *Alc. Lat.* 1, which begins, in the sixteenth-century edition of Theodore
Bibliander—which reprints a twelfth-century translation by Robert of Ketton
(and a Muslim convert known only as Muhammad): *In nomine Dei misericor-
dis, miseratoris.* How must that Quranic invocation have sounded in the
Christian stronghold of Pamplona in the 1150s? Or for that matter, in
Reformation-era Basel in the 1540s? For more on the Bibliander edition:
T. E. Burman, *Reading the Qur'an in Latin Christendom, 1140–1560* (Philadelphia,
2007), 110–21.

63. For a contrast of these texts by Cusa, and an analysis of his sources in *Sifting
the Qur'an*, see M. Costigliolo, "Qur'anic Sources of Nicholas of Cusa",
Mediaevistik 24 (2011), 219–38.

64. CUS. *Pac. Fid.* 47.

65. TREB. *Aut. Dox.* 22.5.

66. CUS. *Pac. Fid.* 47.

67. Though he alludes to this common misperception at CUS. *Crib. Alk.* II 14.122:
"Christians … believe that Christ … was crucified on the cross by altogether
unbelieving Jews."

68. CUS. *Crib. Alk.* II 14.126. Cusa now seems to think that Muhammad "states",
in sura 4, that the Jews "hung up someone else who resembled Christ". That
is inexact. The body-double theory—on which, more presently—is a 'theory'
precisely because it is not stated in the *Qur'an.*

69. See the brief comments on medieval Islamic theories of Jesus' death (or non-
death) in J. Kritzeck, *Peter the Venerable and Islam* (Princeton, 1964), 120–1.
These are confirmed by the only book, to date, on Jesus' crucifixion in the
Quranic commentary tradition—which notes, though, that there are rare
Islamic affirmations of the crucifixion, mainly in the Isma'ili vein of Shi'ism:
Lawson, *Crucifixion and the Qur'an*, 144–5. For more on the Isma'ilis, see
F. Daftary, *The Ismā'īlis: Their History and Doctrines* (Cambridge, 1990).

70. CUS. *Crib. Alk.* II 14.129.

71. For his dates and biography: M. T. Heemskerk, *Suffering in the Mu'tazilite
Theology: 'Abd al'Jabbār's Teaching on Pain and Divine Justice* (Leiden, 2000),
36–53; G. S. Reynolds, "The Rise and Fall of Qadi 'Abd al-Jabbar", *International
Journal of Middle East Studies* 37, 1 (2005), 3–18.

72. Cit. Frankopan, *Silk Roads*, 104.

73. I am grateful to Gabriel Said Reynolds for confirming in a letter of 13 June
2020 that 'Abd al-Jabbar's account of the crucifixion is, to his knowledge,
unique.

74. G. S. Reynolds, *A Muslim Theologian in the Sectarian Milieu: 'Abd al-Jabbār and
the Critique of Christian Origins* (Leiden, 2004), 75–7.

75. E. Bammel, "Excerpts from a New Gospel?", *Novum Testamentum* 10, 1 (1968), 1–9; Reynolds, *Muslim Theologian in the Sectarian Milieu*, 1–2.

76. For Ibn Taymiyya's Syrian milieu: Reynolds, *Muslim Theologian in the Sectarian Milieu*, 79. For a sidelong glance at Ibn Taymiyya's radical chic: N. Feldman, *The Fall and Rise of the Islamic State* (Princeton, 2008), 32–3, 112. For more on jihad circles in twenty-first-century Syria: G. Wood, *The Way of the Strangers: Encounters with the Islamic State* (New York, 2019).

77. Cit. Reynolds, *Muslim Theologian in the Sectarian Milieu*, 114. (Translation modified.)

78. Reynolds, *Muslim Theologian in the Sectarian Milieu*, 114–15.

79. Reynolds, *Muslim Theologian in the Sectarian Milieu*, 111.

80. I have compared the translations in Stern, "Apocryphal Gospels", 42–4; Reynolds, *Muslim Theologian in the Sectarian Milieu*, 128–9; and JABB. *Tathb*. 396–477 in 'Abd al-Jabbār, *Critique of Christian Origins*, ed. and trans. G. S. Reynolds and S. K. Samir (Provo, Utah, 2010), 71–80.

81. Reynolds, *Muslim Theologian in the Sectarian Milieu*, 95–107. Nor is he alone. See the introductory chapters to a fifteenth-century Islamic treatise on the New Testament, which is centred on the gospels (and regrettably, not yet translated): W. A. Saleh, "The Qur'ān Commentary, the Bible Controversy, and the Treatise", *In Defense of the Bible: A Critical Edition and an Introduction to al-Biqā'īs Bible Treatise* (Leiden, 2008).

82. For the crucifixion occurring on a Friday (or a Thursday): Brown, *Death of the Messiah*, 2:1350–1.

83. *Matthew* 27:3.

84. The tradition of 'thirty dirhams' is early and can be found in the *Qur'an* commentary of Muhammad Ibn Ishaq (died 767/8): Lawson, *Crucifixion and the Qur'an*, 95–6.

85. Reynolds, "Muslim Jesus", 243.

86. *Mark* 15:34.

87. *Luke* 23:12.

88. As at DIM. *Jaw.* 89(v)–90(r): "you [Christians] claim that Christ was crucified and died in the presence of the people of … Jerusalem, who at that time were numerous, including *King Pilate*, the populace, citizens, nobles and ordinary people".

89. *Matthew* 27:2; *Luke* 20:20; etc.

90. Compare the reasoning of "the Jews" before Herod to *John* 18:30, 19:7.

91. *Matthew* 27:11; *Mark* 15:2; *Luke* 23:3; *John* 18:33.

92. *Matthew* 27:11; *Mark* 15:2; *Luke* 23:3; *John* 18:37.

93. *Matthew* 27:24.

94. In *Luke* 23:11, it is done by Herod and his troops.

95. *Matthew* 27:27, 31, 35; *Mark* 15:16, 20, 24; *Luke* 23:25, 32–3, 36; *John* 19:23.

96. *Qur.* 4:157–8.

97. Mark 14:61.
98. Reynolds, *Muslim Theologian in the Sectarian Milieu*, 96–105.
99. It is worth noting that 'Abd al-Jabbār has an elaborate theory of penal suffering: Heemskerk, *Suffering in the Mu'tazilite Theology*, 72–191.
100. Cit. Reynolds, *Muslim Theologian in the Sectarian Milieu*, 111. And for context: I. Alon, *Socrates in Medieval Arabic Literature* (Leiden, 1991).

10. "O ROMAN, SPARE THIS GOD!": PILATE'S INNOCENCE IN CHRISTIAN TRADITION

1. Nietzsche, *Human, All Too Human*, 216; idem, *Menschliches, Allzumenschliches*, 19–20.
2. LACT. *Div. Inst.* IV 18,6.
3. Schürer, *History of the Jewish People*, 1:341–2.
4. Schürer, *History of the Jewish People*, 1:351–3.
5. *Luke* 23:7.
6. *Luke* 23:6.
7. Gabba, "Social, Economic, and Political History of Palestine", 158–9.
8. *Luke* 23:12.
9. *Luke* 22:67–8.
10. *Luke* 22:70, 23:3.
11. *Luke* 23:8–10.
12. *Luke* 13:32. Translating from a (conjectural) Aramaic substrate: J. Jeremias, *The Parables of Jesus*, trans. S. H. Hooke (London, 1954), 123, 123 note 90.
13. *Luke* 9:7–9, compare *Matthew* 14:1–12 and *Mark* 6:14–29.
14. *Luke* 23:11.
15. *Luke* 7:24–6, compare *Matthew* 11:7–9.
16. *Luke* 23:11.
17. *Acts* 4:26–8.
18. *Ev. Petr.* 1.1–4.11.
19. *Ev. Petr.* 4.10.
20. J. Milton, *"Paradise Lost: A Poem Written in Ten Books"; An Authoritative Text of the 1667 First Edition*, ed. with comm. J. T. Shawcross and M. Lieb (Pittsburgh, 2007); idem, *The 1671 Poems: Paradise Regain'd and Samson Agonistes*, ed. and annot. with comm. L. L. Knoppers (Oxford, 2008); T. Mann, *Joseph and His Brothers*, trans. H. T. Lowe-Porter (London, 1956); M. Bulgakov, *The Master and Margarita*, trans. M. Ginsburg (New York, 1995); R. Caillois, *Pontius Pilate: A Novel*, trans. C. L. Markmann (Charlottesville, Va., 2006); G. Spiró, *Captivity*, trans. T. Wilkinson (Brooklyn, N.Y., 2015); K. O. Knausgaard, *A Time for Everything*, trans. J. Anderson (Brooklyn, N.Y., 2008).
21. JUV. *Evang.* 1–27. I have thoroughly revised, here, the translation of this stanza in R. P. H. Green, *Latin Epics of the New Testament: Juvencus, Sedulius, Arator* (Oxford, 2006), 15–16.

22. C. Kallendorf, "From Virgil to Vida: The *Poeta Theologus* in Italian Renaissance Commentary", *Journal of the History of Ideas* 56, 1 (1995), 41–62, esp. 58–62 (on Vida).

23. Green, *Latin Epics of the New Testament*, xiii.

24. Green, *Latin Epics of the New Testament*, xii–xiii.

25. C. P. E. Springer, *The Gospel as Epic in Late Antiquity· The Paschala Carmen of Sedulius* (Leiden, 1988), 98.

26. Green, *Latin Epics of the New Testament*, 205.

27. Green, *Latin Epics of the New Testament*, 205, 239.

28. I am here following the summary in Green, *Latin Epics of the New Testament*, 110–11.

29. My source here is James Gardner's bibliography in the I Tatti edition of VIDA *Christ*.

30. On the last, see E. Haan, "Milton's Latin Poetry and Vida", *Humanistica Lovaniensia* 44 (1995), 282–304, here 282–3: "It is evident that an intimate awareness of Vida's Latin writings underlies the Miltonic corpus ... from his earliest juvenilia ... right through to his most mature vernacular *magnum opus*."

31. Jesus' night-trial before the Judaean council is narrated at VIDA *Christ*. II 875–917.

32. VIDA *Christ*. II 887–91.

33. VIDA *Christ*. V 358–9.

34. This is one justifiable reading, within the dramatic horizons of Vida's epic. However, *caveat lector*. I am grateful to Dante Fedele for stressing, in a letter of June 2020, that—in his words—"in the late medieval and early modern legal language, *arbitrium* could rather be translated with 'judgement'". For more on this: M. Meccarelli, *Arbitrium: Un aspetto sistematico degli ordinamenti giuridici in età di diritto comune* (Milan, 1998), 3–158.

35. VIDA *Christ*. II 916–17.

36. VIDA *Christ*. II 969–1001.

37. VIDA *Christ*. II 989–90.

38. VIDA *Christ*. V 295–6.

39. VIDA *Christ*. V 401.

40. VIDA *Christ*. V 721.

41. VIDA *Christ*. VI 1–16.

42. VIDA *Christ*. VI 23–9.

43. Elliott, *Apocryphal New Testament*, 208.

44. *Matthew* 27:26–31; *Mark* 15:15–20; *Luke* 23:16, 24–5; *John* 19:1–5, 13–16.

11. "BEDS INLAID WITH SILVER": THE *SAECULUM* IN JESUS, PAUL, AND JULIUS PAULUS

1. G. Marramao, "Säkularisierung", *Historisches Wörterbuch der Philosophie*, ed. J. Ritter and K. Gründer (Basel, 1992), 8:1133–61, here 1133: "ursprünglich

ein Terminus technicus im Bereich des kanonischen und des Staatskirchenrechts ('saecularisatio' von 'saecularis', 'saeculum')".

2. *Oxford Latin Dictionary*, ed. P. G. W. Glare (Oxford, 1996), 1676 (under *saecularis* and *saeculum*). Compare G. Goetz, *Thesaurus glossarum emendatarum* ... *Pars posterior, accedit index Graecus Guilelmi Heraei* (Leipzig, 1901), 222 (under *saecularis* and *saeculum*). For a subtle treatment of Rome's "secular festivals" and the Christianization of time: Markus, *End of Ancient Christianity*, 107–35. And since the "generation" is a recurring theme in Jesus' sayings, it is interesting to note that *saeculum* seems to have originally denoted a generation. The etymological tie is already noted by Isidore of Seville at ISID. *Etym.* V 38.1, and, most recently, by M. A. C. de Vaan, *Etymological Dictionary of Latin and the Other Italic Languages* (Leiden, 2008), 533 (under *saeculum*): "'generation, breed, lifetime'".

3. Æ. Forcellini, *Lexicon totius Latinitatis*, comp. J. Facciolati and Æ. Forcellini (Padua, 1771), 4:9–10 (under *sæcularis* and *sæculum*).

4. Unlike most late modern texts on secularization, early modern treatises often begin by noting this fact. Consult E. Mauritius, *De secularisatione bonorum ecclesiasticorum ex jure divino et humano praestertim...* (Sine loco, 1666), chapter II, section I (no page); J. F. Rhetius, "De secularisatione", *Disputationes juris publici undecim* ... (Frankfurt an der Oder, 1678), 97–8; J. B. Baumgart, *Dissertatio academica, de secularisatione* ... (Helmstedt, 1683), 75(r). I will return to this in chapter 19.

5. *Vocabularium iurisprudentiae Romanae, ex auctoritate Academiae Borussicae compositum, tomus V*, ed. B. Kübler (Berlin, 1931), 63 (under *religio* and *religiosus*).

6. *Vocabularium iurisprudentiae Romanae*, 234 (under *saeculum*).

7. The only substantive occurrences of *saecularis* in the whole of Justinian's *Body of Roman Law* are clustered at *Cod. Just.* I 3.54.2–7: R. Mayr, ed., *Vocabularium codicis Iustiniani, I: Pars Latina* (Hildesheim, 1965), 2176 (under *saecularis*). Note that the lines are *Justinianic*—meaning, they are not pre-Christian. Note, too, that they pertain to marriage and monasticism: H.-W. Strätz, "Säkularisation, Säkularisierung, II: Der kanonistische und staatskirchenrechtliche Begriff", *Geschichtliche Grundbegriffe: Historisches Lexikon zur politisch-sozialen Sprache in Deutschland*, ed. O. Brunner, W. Conze, and R. Koselleck (Stuttgart, 1984), 796. Strätz seems to miss the lines by Paul that I glance at in this chapter, but he confirms that *Cod. Just.* I 3.54.2–7 contain the first black-letter legal instance of the Christian Latin term, *saecularis*.

8. JUSTIN. *Dig.* 33.10.2 (from Florentinus, *Institutes*, book 11).

9. *Hist. Aug.* "Severus Alexander" 68.1; E. Daalder, "The *Decreta* and *Imperiales sententiae* of Julius Paulus: Law and Justice in the Judicial Decisions of Septimius Severus", *The Impact of Justice on the Roman Empire*, ed. O. Hekster and K. Verboven (Leiden, 2019), 50–1. For a clarification of the apostle's *cognomen*, Paulus: Sherwin-White, *Roman Society and Roman Law*, 152–4.

10. JUSTIN. *Dig.* 33.10.3 (from Paulus, *Sabinus*, book 4). This, at least, is how I

read him: "Neither a silver bowl nor any silver vessel was included in furniture [in older texts] in accordance with the severity of an age which did not yet admit (*admittentis*) silver furniture ..." Compare JUSTIN. *Dig*. 33.10.1 (from Pomponius, *Sabinus*, book 6): "Furniture ... is not reckoned with silver or gold articles or clothing."

11. For aspects of the twentieth-century influence, see the essays in K. Tuori and H. Björklund, eds, *Roman Law and the Idea of Europe* (London, 2019).

12. For critical reflections on the secularity–modernity configuration: T. Asad, *Formations of the Secular: Christianity, Islam, Modernity* (Stanford, 2003); É. Balibar, *Saeculum: Culture, religion, idéologie* (Paris, 2012).

13. For the nineteenth-century origins of what we now mean by 'secularity' and 'secularization': I. Hunter, "Secularization: The Birth of a Modern Combat Concept", *Modern Intellectual History* 12, 1 (2015), 1–32.

14. M. Chibnall, *The World of Orderic Vitalis: Norman Monks and Norman Knights* (Woodbridge, Suffolk, 1984); C. C. Rozier et al., eds, *Orderic Vitalis: Life, Works and Interpretations* (Woodbridge, Suffolk, 2016).

15. D. Du Cange et al., *Glossarium mediae et infimae Latinitatis ... Tomus sextus* (Graz, 1954), 264 (under *saecularis, saeculum*, and *saecularitas*).

16. Giacomo Marramao's article on "Säkularisierung" in the *Historisches Wörterbuch der Philosophie* is frequently misread. When Marramao writes that the first occurrence of the term *séculariser* can be dated to May 1646 ("der Ausdruck 'séculariser' (säkularisieren) erstmals am 8. Mai 1646 in Münster benutzt worden sei"), he is only referring to the first *vernacular* use of the Latin term, *saecularizatio*. The original legal sense of *saecularizatio*—what Marramao calls its "institutionally unmistakable core of meaning" ("institutionell unmißverständlichen Bedeutungskern")—is forged in late medieval, and not early modern, Europe. Compare Marramao, "Säkularisierung", *Historisches Wörterbuch der Philosophie*, 8:1133; and J. N. Bremmer, "Secularization: Notes toward a Genealogy", *Religion: Beyond a Concept*, ed. Hent de Vries (New York, 2008), 433–4.

17. A. Blaise, *Lexicon Latinitatis Medii Aevi* (Turnhout, 1975), 812 (under *saecularizatio*): "action de séculariser un religieux"; R. E. Latham, *Revised Medieval Latin Word-List from British and Irish Sources* (London, 1965), 429 (under *seculum*, not *saeculum*): "[*secul]arior*, more secular 1378; [*secul]aritas*, worldliness, worldly life c 1130, c 1610; [*secul]ariter*, in a worldly fashion c 1115, 15c.; [*secul]arizo*, to live a worldly life 1378". For the unclarity of *laicus* and *laici* in medieval England: H. M. Thomas, *The Secular Clergy in England, 1066–1216* (Oxford, 2014), 14.

18. Thomas, *Secular Clergy in England*, 12.

19. Foucault, *On the Government of the Living*, 195. A fascinating reflection on the 'rule', informed by Foucault, is G. Agamben, *The Highest Poverty: Monastic Rules and Form-of-Life*, trans. A. Kotsko (Stanford, 2013).

20. This, too, is noted in Rhetius, "De secularisatione", *Disputationes* (1678), 98–101; and Baumgart, *De secularisatione* ... (1683), 75(r–v).

21. Blaise, *Lexicon Latinitatis Medii Aevi*, 812 (under *saeculum*): "le monde"; J. F. Niemeyer, *Mediae Latinitatis lexicon minus: Lexique Latin médiéval* (Leiden, 1967), 2:951 (under *saeculum*): "le monde qui prend fin ... la vie présente, les choses temporelles ... le monde terrestre, le siècle, les hommes".

22. Cit. Thomas, *Secular Clergy in England*, 13. (Translation lightly modified.)

23. Blaise, *Lexicon Latinitatis Medii Aevi*, 354 (under *exclaustratio*): "permission de demeurer pour un temps hors du cloître ... différent de *saecularizatio*, permission d'y demeurer définitivement".

24. *Colossians* 4:14.

25. R. Brown, *An Introduction to the New Testament* (New York, 1997), 326–7.

26. *Luke* 22:19–20; *I Corinthians* 11:24–5; Brown, *Introduction to the New Testament*, 324.

27. *Luke* 16:8, 18:30, and 20:34. For an interpretation of the *saeculum* in *Luke–Acts* that differs markedly from the one offered in the coming pages: A. Brent, "Luke–Acts and the Imperial Cult in Asia Minor", *The Journal of Theological Studies* (NS) 48, 2 (1997), 411–38.

28. *Romans* 12:2; *I Corinthians* 1:20, 2:6, 2:8, 3:18; *II Corinthians* 4:4; *Galatians* 1:4.

29. An important study, but with only scattered allusions to *saeculum*, is P. Burton, *The Old Latin Gospels: A Study of Their Texts and Language* (Oxford, 2000).

30. *I Corinthians* 2:8.

31. This is, of course, not uncontested: J. Jeremias, *The Parables of Jesus*, trans. S. H. Hooke (London, 1954), 11.

32. For *parabolē* as "dark saying": Jeremias, *Parables of Jesus*, 14 note 21.

33. Jeremias, *Parables of Jesus*, 20.

34. Jeremias, *Parables of Jesus*, 38–9.

35. Jeremias, *Parables of Jesus*, 127–8.

36. For a 'haggadic' reading of this parable: J. A. Fitzmyer, *The Semitic Background of the New Testament* (Grand Rapids, Mich., 1997), 161–84.

37. *Luke* 16:8–9 (Greek *aiōnos toutou*; Latin *huius saeculi*). Compare the expressions in what may be Paul's first letter, *I Thessalonians* 5:1–11, here 5 and 8: "For you are all sons of light (*huioi phōtos*) and sons of the day (*huioi hēmeras*) ... [and] we belong to the day."

38. Compare *Matthew* 3:9; *Luke* 3:8; and "Q 3:1a–8" in J. M. Robinson, P. Hoffmann, and J. S. Kloppenborg, eds, *The Critical Edition of Q: Synopsis Including the Gospels of Matthew and Luke, Mark and Thomas* ... (Leuven, 2000), 4–13, here 10–11. The medical philosopher Galen of Pergamum seems to have heard of this saying—and to have objected to it, for reasons having nothing to do with race: Wilken, *Christians as the Romans Saw Them*, 84–8.

39. Compare *Matthew* 8:11–12; *Luke* 13:28–30; and "Q 13:28–30" in Robinson, Hoffmann, and Kloppenborg, *Critical Edition of Q*, 414–19.

40. Nietzsche, *Anti-Christ, Ecce Homo, Twilight of the Idols*, 50; idem, *Der Fall Wagner, Götzen-Dämmerung* ... *Der Antichrist, Ecce homo, Dionyso-Dithyramben, Nietzsche contra Wagner*, ed. G. Colli and M. Montinari (Berlin, 1969), 230.

41. Compare *Luke* 18:30 with the uniquely Matthaean contrast, in *Matthew* 12:32, between forgiveness in "this age" and "the age to come".

42. Compare *Luke* 16:8 ("dirty currency") and 16:13 ("God and Currency")

43. On this theme: G. Agamben, *The Kingdom and the Glory: For a Theological Genealogy of Economy and Government*, trans. L. Chiesa with M. Mandarini (Stanford, 2011); and less convincingly, D. Leshem, *The Origins of Neoliberalism: Modeling the Economy from Jesus to Foucault* (New York, 2016).

44. *Luke* 18:28–30 (Greek *en kairōi toutōi*; Latin *in hoc tempore*).

45. *Mark* 10:29–31.

46. Compare *Matthew* 19:3–12 and *Mark* 10:2–12.

47. *Luke* 20:34–35 (Greek *aiōnos toutou* ... *aiōnos ekeinou*; Latin *saeculi huius* ... *saeculo illo*).

48. Compare *Matthew* 22:23–33; *Mark* 12:18–27; and *Luke* 20:27–38.

49. Other relevant passages in the Pauline corpus are *Ephesians* 1:21, 2:2; *I Timothy* 6:17; *II Timothy* 4:10; and *Titus* 2:12.

50. *Galatians* 1:4 (Greek *ek tou aiōnos*; Latin *de praesenti saeculo*).

51. *II Corinthians* 4:4 (Greek *ho theos tou aiōnos toutou*; Latin *deus huius saeculi*).

52. *Romans* 12:2 (Greek *aiōni toutōi*; Latin *huic saeculo*).

53. AMBR. *Fug. Saec.* 9.58.

54. *I Corinthians* 1:20 (Greek *aiōnos toutou* ... *tou kosmou*; Latin *huius saeculi* ... *huius mundi*).

55. *I Corinthians* 2:6–8 (Greek *aiōnos toutou* ... *aiōnos toutou* ... *pro tōn aiōniōn* ... *aiōnos toutou*; Latin *huius saeculi* ... *huius saeculi* ... *ante saecula* ... *huius saeculi*).

56. Paul's term for 'church', *ekklēsia*, originally denoted a quorum of some 2,000 to 6,000 free Athenian males when they convened to decide matters of state: M. H. Hansen, *The Athenian Ecclesia: A Collection of Articles, 1976–1983* (Copenhagen, 1983). The Christian *ekklēsia*, by way of contrast—and this is a contrast that Paul makes in *Galatians*, one of his first surviving letters—is composed of all Christ-believers, gentile and Judaean, female and male, slave and free (*Galatians* 3:28).

57. This is of course not to deny Paul's divine legitimation of the state in *Romans* 13:1–7.

58. N. D. F. de Coulanges, *The Ancient City: A Study on the Religion, Laws, and Institutions of Greece and Rome* (Baltimore, 1980), 385. (Translation modified.) I owe this Fustel reference to F. Oakley, *Kingship: The Politics of Enchantment* (Oxford, 2006), 60–1.

59. *I Corinthians* 1:3–4.

60. *I Corinthians* 2:8 (Greek *aiōnos toutou*; Latin *huius saeculi*).

61. LUC. *Mort. Per.* 13.

62. LUC. *Mort. Per.* 11–13.

63. *Pace* Lucian is a compelling new study: R. M. Thorsteinsson, *Jesus as Philosopher: The Moral Sage in the Synoptic Gospels* (Oxford, 2018).

64. *Epist. Mar.*—or, simply, "the laws which he promulgated"; *Spicilegium Syriacum: Containing Remains of Bardesan, Meliton, Ambrose, and Mara bar Serapion*, ed. with English trans. and notes W. Cureton (London, 1855), 70–6, here 73,28–74,7. The date of this neglected letter is contested, but I am relying, here, on the judgement of Millar, *Roman Near East*, 461.

65. A fascinating text on the influence of Platonic communism in radical Christian circles of the first centuries CE is I. Jurasz, "Carpocrate et epiphane: Chrétiens et platoniciens radicaux", *Vigiliae Christianae* 71, 2 (2017), 134–67.

66. GRAT. *Dec.* 8.1.1; Gratian, *The Treatise on Laws (Decretum DD. 1–20), with the Ordinary Gloss*, trans. A. Thompson and J. Gordley (Washington, D.C., 1993), 24.

67. I have in mind, here, his comments on believers and the *biōtika*—the "things of this life"—in *I Corinthians* 6:2–3: Nietzsche, *Anti-Christ, Ecce Homo, Twilight of the Idols*, 43. "Unfortunately", Nietzsche says, "these are not just the words of a madman." The passage in question has to do with the formation of Christian 'courts' in the mid-first century. It is an Ur-text of the canon law tradition.

68. Of a hundred texts that could be cited, beginning with Paul's exultant lines on the 'scandal' of the cross: LACT. *Div. Inst.* IV 16,1.

12. "YOU ACTED IN IGNORANCE": WHY THERE ARE NO CHRIST-KILLERS

1. *I Corinthians* 2:8. I reject the twentieth-century (and Origenist) tendency to construe these 'rulers' as "demonic beings". For a conclusive defence of the ancient interpretation—which is mine here—namely that "the archons [are] the rulers who connived at the crucifixion of Jesus, i.e. Pilate, Herod and Caiaphas": W. Carr, "The Rulers of This Age: I Corinthians ii.6–8", *New Testament Studies* 23 (1977), 20–35, here 20–1. Paul's reasoning here, Carr writes (32–3), conforms to "the primitive kerygma" of early Christ-believers "concerning the rulers of the world". And this means? "The men who had crucified Jesus are only temporarily powerful. Their rule is declining."

2. If we conjecture that Paul and the writer of *Luke–Acts* knew each other, Paul might have known of Herod's interrogation of Jesus—a scene that is unique to *Luke–Acts*. No aspect of that scene is neglected—or uncontested—in the colossal literature: J. M. Harrington, *The Lukan Passion Narrative: The Markan Material in Luke 22,54–23,25; A Historical Survey; 1891–1997* (Leiden, 2000), 691–804.

3. *Acts* 13:27–9. One notable comment on the meaning of the phrase "they found no cause for a sentence of death" in *Luke–Acts* is made by Winter, "Marginal

Notes on the Trial of Jesus," 232: "The absence of a report [in Luke 22] of a death sentence passed by the Sanhedrin must have been deliberately intended ... [and we] have in Acts 13 27. 28 the explanation why the Third Gospel nowhere mentions that the Sanhedrin sentenced Jesus to death."

4. In contrast to the bitter anti-Judaic invective in *I Thessalonians* 2:13–16. The tone of the latter text is so hostile—and so unlike, say, Romans 9 to 11—that commentators have suspected an interpolation. For a reasoned defence of a post-70 CE, probably second-century interpolation, and for further references: Fredriksen, *When Christians Were Jews*, 216 note 27.

5. Not to mention Peter's concession in *Acts* 3:17, in one of his discourses in Jerusalem: "And now, friends, I know that you acted in ignorance, as did also your rulers."

6. N. Eubank, "A Disconcerting Prayer: On the Originality of Luke 23:34a", *Journal of Biblical Literature* 129, 3 (2010), 521–36.

7. *Luke* 23:34. Wesley Carr concludes that the "theme of ignorance is identical" in *I Corinthians* 2:6–8 and the crucifixion scene in *Luke* 23: Carr, "Rulers of This Age", 27.

8. R. Girard, *The Scapegoat*, trans. Y. Freccero (Baltimore, 1989), 111.

9. *I Timothy* 6:13.

10. Haenchen, *Acts of the Apostles*, 405–18.

11. Goodenough, *Goodenough on the Beginnings of Christianity*, 139: "much can be found in Paul's letters that resembles his speeches in Acts".

12. *I Corinthians* 2:8.

13. An orienting study is R. L. Wilken, *John Chrysostom and the Jews: Rhetoric and Reality in the Later Fourth Century* (Berkeley, 1983). "No great accuracy": Stroumsa, "From Anti-Judaism to Antisemitism", 8–9, 12; and idem, *Making of the Abrahamic Religions*, 104–5; "autumn months": W. Pradels, R. Brändle, and M. Heimgartner, "The Sequence and Dating of the Series of John Chrysostom's Eight Discourses *Adversus Iudaeos*", *Zeitschrift für Antikes Christentum* 6 (2002), 90–116.

14. CHRY. *Adv. Iud.* I 5. In Chrysostom's Greek: *ton hup' autōn staurōthenta Christon*; and in Latin translation: *Christum ab ipsis crucifixum*.

15. For a sketch of the idea that "Chrysostom's discourses *kata tōn ioudaiōn* reveal a new trend" in Christian polemics of the late fourth century CE: Stroumsa, "From Anti-Judaism to Antisemitism", 23–5.

16. Stroumsa, "From Anti-Judaism to Antisemitism", 5.

17. *I Corinthians* 2:8.

18. I am thinking, here, in the last decades of J. Taubes, *The Political Theology of Paul*, ed. A. Assmann and J. Assmann with H. Folker, D.-W. Hartwich, and C. Schulte, trans. D. Hollander (Stanford, 2004); A. Badiou, *Saint Paul: The Foundation of Universalism*, trans. R. Brassier (Stanford, 2003); G. Agamben, *The Time That Remains: A Commentary on the Letter to the Romans*, trans. P. Dailey

(Stanford, 2005); and W. Blanton and H. de Vries, eds, *Paul and the Philosophers* (New York, 2013).

19. V. Krey, *Keine Strafe ohne Gesetz: Einführung in die Dogmengeschichte des Satzes 'nullum crimen, nulla poena sine lege'* (Berlin, 1983), 18–19.

20. In the absence of law and a legal judgement, the infliction of harm is regarded as 'injury' (*iniuria*), not 'punishment' (*punitio*): JUSTIN. *Inst.* 4.1.

21. *Romans* 3:20. See the patristic glosses collected in G. Bray, ed., *Ancient Christian Commentary on Scripture: New Testament VI; Romans* (Chicago, 1998), 95–7.

22. *I Corinthians* 2:8.

23. AUG. *Serm.* 180 2.2. The current term for a 'criminal intent', *mens rea*, seems to first be attested in Augustine's sermon: M. E. Badar, *The Concept of Mens Rea in International Criminal Law: The Case for a Unified Approach* (Oxford, 2013), 25 note 78.

24. *I Corinthians* 2:8.

25. *Luke* 23:13–15 (Herod and Pilate), 40–2 (malefactor), 46–7 (officer), 48 (crowds), 50–1 (Joseph).

26. *Luke* 23:34.

27. *Acts* 7:60.

28. Surprisingly, the difference is not noted in Haenchen, *Acts of the Apostles*, 293 note 9, 296.

29. *Pace* Haenchen, *Acts of the Apostles*, 207 note 4: "The stressing of the fact [in *Acts* 3:17] that even the Jewish ἄρχοντες shared the ἄγνοια has nothing in common with I Cor. 2. 8."

30. *Acts* 2:22; Haenchen, *Acts of the Apostles*, 180 note 8.

31. *Luke* 23:34 (*ou gar oidasin*); *Acts* 2:22 (*kathōs autoi oidate*).

32. *Acts* 2:23.

33. Note the similarity between Peter's phrase in Jerusalem, "men of Judaea and all who live in Jerusalem" (*Acts* 2:14), and Paul's in Antioch, "the residents of Jerusalem and their rulers" (*Acts* 13:27). Jesus' death is tied to the *temple-city*, and not the 'race', of Judaeans.

34. This is commonly blurred (or denied) in the literature; perhaps most recently in Fredriksen, *When Christians Were Jews*, 124, 126. And for the 'lawless' as gentiles: Haenchen, *Acts of the Apostles*, 180 note 11.

35. *Acts* 2:36.

36. *Pace* Haenchen, *Acts of the Apostles*, 183, 183 note 5.

37. JOS. *Ant. Jud.* XVIII 63 (translation modified). Compare *Luke* 5:26, which I believe is the only place in the New Testament where *paradoxos* is used to describe Jesus' doings.

38. This seems to be the claim made by Caesarius of Arles in the sixth century, at CAES. AREL. *Serm.* 142.6: "You heard Jesus now telling them: What have I done to you? If you have found sin in me, prove it. But they answered:

'Crucify him! Crucify him!' *They thought he was a man, even though an innocent one.*"

39. *Acts* 3:1 (afternoon), 3:11 (portico).

40. *Acts* 3:12–18.

41. *Acts* 13:27–9.

42. *Acts* 1:16–19 (Judas), 3:14 (Barabbas), 4:27 (Herod)

43. D. Satran, "Anti-Jewish Polemic in the *Peri Pascha* of Melito of Sardis: The Problem of Social Context", *Contra Iudaeos*, 52–3.

44. For the conjecture that Melito is himself a Judaean: A. S. Sykes, "Melito's Anti-Judaism", *Journal of Early Christian Studies* 5, 2 (1997), 271–83, here 273–5, 277–9. This conjecture is rejected—not as false, but unproven—by L. H. Cohick, *The* Peri Pascha *Attributed to Melito of Sardis: Setting, Purpose, and Sources* (Providence, R.I., 2000), 13–15.

45. Satran, "Anti-Jewish Polemic in the *Peri Pascha*", 51.

46. Yuval, *Two Nations in Your Womb*, 68–77.

47. MEL. *P. Pas.* 96.

48. MEL. *P. Pas.* 93–4. (Translation modified.)

49. MEL. *P. Pas.* 96.

50. *Acts* 2:23.

51. For more on anti-Judaic motifs in this homily: Cohick, Peri Pascha *Attributed to Melito of Sardis*, 52–87.

52. J. Cohen, "The Jews as the Killers of Christ in the Latin Tradition, from Augustine to the Friars", *Traditio* 39 (1983), 1–37, here 8–10.

53. AUG. *Tract.* 115 2.

13. "I OBSTRUCT NOT YOUR DOMINION": AN AFRICAN SERMON THAT SHAPED HISTORY

1. J.-F. Lyotard, *The Confession of Augustine*, trans. R. Beardsworth (Stanford, 2000), 95. For more on Lyotard's reading of Augustine: D. L. Dusenbury, *The Space of Time: A Sensualist Interpretation of Time in Augustine, Confessions X to XII* (Leiden, 2014), 11–16, 96–9.

2. Now Souk Ahras, Algeria: C. Lepelley, *Aspects de l'Afrique Romaine: Les cités, la vie rurale, le christianisme* (Bari, 2001), 329; Mullen, *Expansion of Christianity*, 318.

3. Now Annaba/Bône, Algeria: Mullen, *Expansion of Christianity*, 315. In Augustine's lifetime, Hippo was "overshadowed only by Carthage": J. E. Merdinger, *Rome and the African Church in the Time of Augustine* (New Haven, 1997), 68.

4. LACT. *Mort. Pers.* 8: *opulentissimae provinciae*.

5. Note that 'Africa' denotes a Roman province, here, not a continent. "In Roman parlance", as Judith Herrin writes, "'Africa' is always [the] western half of the north African coastline, while the eastern half is 'Egypt'": Herrin, *Formation of Christendom*, 22–3.

6. HON. *Lum. Eccl.* II 38. Cit. Dusenbury, *Space of Time*, 2 note 8.

7. PROSP. *Chron.* 737. (Migne col. 588). (Migne col. 588.) Cit. Dusenbury, *Space of Time*, 2 note 8.

8. QUOD. *Epist.* = AUG. *Epist.* 223.3.

9. R. A. Markus, *Saeculum: History and Society in the Theology of St Augustine* (Cambridge, 1970), 115: "Africanity".

10. POSS. *Vita Aug.* 1.

11. POSS. *Vita Aug.* 3.

12. POSS. *Vita Aug.* 7.

13. POSS. *Vita Aug.* 7.

14. POSS. *Vita* 6.

15. Here and below, I draw on the materials collected in M. J. G. P. Lamberigts, "The Italian Julian of Æclanum about the African Augustine of Hippo"; D. Weber, "'For What Is so Monstrous as What the Punic Fellow Says?' Reflections on the Literary Background of Julian's Polemical Attacks on Augustine's Homeland"; and J. K. Coyle, "The Self-identity of North African Christians in Augustine's Time"—all of which are printed in *Augustinus Afer*.

16. Note that 'anti-African' is imprecise. According to Weber, "'What Is so Monstrous as What the Punic Fellow Says?'", 79: "Julian does not use words as 'man from Africa' (*Afer* or *Africanus*), which have a mere geographical meaning, to disparage Augustine ... but he does use 'Punic' (*Poenus*) and 'Numidian' (*Numida*) to do this. Both have a strong negative connotation [in a late antique Roman context]."

17. Cit. Weber, "'What Is so Monstrous as What the Punic Fellow Says?'", 79, 79 note 33.

18. Cit. Weber, "'What Is so Monstrous as What the Punic Fellow Says?'", 79–80; and Lamberigts, "Italian Julian of Æclanum about the African Augustine", 85–7.

19. Weber, "'What Is so Monstrous as What the Punic Fellow Says?'", 81.

20. Cit. Weber, "'What Is so Monstrous as What the Punic Fellow Says?'", 75, 81.

21. Cit. Weber, "'What Is so Monstrous as What the Punic Fellow Says?'", 81. (Translation modified.)

22. F. Decret, *Le Christianisme en Afrique du Nord ancienne* (Paris, 1996), 239; idem, *Early Christianity in North Africa*, trans. E. Smither (Eugene, Oreg., 2009), 181.

23. Cit. Decret, *Christianisme en Afrique du Nord ancienne*, 232; idem, *Early Christianity in North Africa*, 176.

24. J. N. Adams, *Bilingualism and the Latin Language* (Cambridge, 2003), 238.

25. AUG. *Conf.* VIII 6.14; cit. Coyle, "Self-identity of North African Christians", 63.

26. Mullen, *Expansion of Christianity*, 316 (under "Madauros"). Augustine will later write that Africa is "full of the bodies of the blessed martyrs": AUG. *Epist.* 78.3; cit. Markus, *End of Ancient Christianity*, 93. And it is again today. Of hun-

dreds of reports that could be cited: Agence France-Presse in Ouagadougou, "Burkina Faso Church Attack Leaves 24 Dead", *The Guardian* (17 February 2020), archived online at https://www.theguardian.com/world/2020/feb/17/burkina-faso-church-attack-dead-wounded; accessed 29 October 2020.

27. Cit. Decret, *Early Christianity in North Africa*, 147.

28. AUG. *Epist*. 17.4; cit. Coyle, "Self-identity of North African Christians", 63, Decret, *Early Christianity in North Africa*, 159.

29. Cit. Coyle, "Self-identity of North African Christians", 63.

30. M. A. Gaumer, *Augustine's Cyprian: Authority in Roman Africa* (Leiden, 2016), 33–8.

31. AUG. *Epist*. 138 4.19; cit. Coyle, "Self-identity of North African Christians", 63.

32. AUG. *Serm*. 81.9; cit. Decret, *Early Christianity in North Africa*, 190.

33. I owe this thought to Gert-Jan Van de Voorde, "'What More do You Want?': The Use of the Roman Trial of Jesus by St. Augustine and Marsilius of Padua", paper read at the conference "Marsilius of Padua between History, Philosophy, and Politics", held at the University of Leuven, 6–7 September 2018.

34. AUG. *Civ. Dei* XIV 1; here in the translation of Brown, *Rise of Western Christendom*, 53.

35. AUG. *Civ. Dei* XIV 13.

36. *John* 18:35–6.

37. C. Morris, *The Papal Monarchy: The Western Church from 1050 to 1250* (Oxford, 1989).

38. INN. III, *Reg*. II 209; cit. Morris, *Papal Monarchy*, 431 (translation modified).

39. INN. III, *Reg*. II 209. Innocent is writing to the archbishop of Constantinople, who calls himself—in his fraternal letter to Innocent—"the Patriarch of New Rome" (*Novae Romae patriarcha*): INN. III, *Reg*. II 208.

40. INN. III, *Reg*. II 209: *ut nihil eis de potestatis plenitudine deperiret*.

41. INN. III, *Reg*. II 209; cit. Morris, *Papal Monarchy*, 431 (translation modified).

42. TERT. *Apol*. 21.24.

43. Augustine knows that the "garden" is a Johannine touch: AUG. *Cons. Ev*. III 4.10.

44. Augustine knows that the "cohort" is unique to *John*: AUG. *Cons. Ev*. III 6.19.

45. Winter, "Marginal Notes on the Trial of Jesus", 233–4: "It was more likely a *decurio* than a *tribunus militaris* who arrested Jesus ... [but there] is nothing incredible in the account of Jn 18 ... which states that a Roman military commander, having arrested Jesus, conducted him to a local Jewish official with the order to prepare the judicial proceedings for the procurator's court and, this done, to hand him back to the imperial authority."

46. AUG. *Tract*. 112.2.

47. AUG. *Tract*. 112.2.

48. AUG. *Tract*. 112.6.

49. AUG. *Tract.* 112.2.
50. AUG. *Tract.* 113.6.
51. AUG. *Tract.* 114.2.
52. AUG. *Tract.* 114.2.
53. *Acts of the Apostles* 2:22–3, 3:13–15, etc.
54. P. Fredriksen, *Augustine and the Jews: A Christian Defense of Jews and Judaism* (New York, 2008); J. Cohen, "Revisiting Augustine's Doctrine of Jewish Witness", *The Journal of Religion* 89, 4 (2009), 564–78; G. W. Lee, "Israel between the Two Cities: Augustine's Theology of the Jews and Judaism", *Journal of Early Christian Studies* 24, 4 (2016), 523–51.
55. Stroumsa, "From Anti-Judaism to Antisemitism", 22; idem, *Making of the Abrahamic Religions*, 111–12.
56. Cohen, *Friars and the Jews*, 14–15, 19–22; Cohen, "Jews as the Killers of Christ".
57. AUG. *Tract.* 114.4.
58. AUG. *Tract.* 114.2.
59. AUG. *Tract.* 114.5.
60. *John* 19:11.
61. AUG. *Tract.* 114.5.
62. AUG. *Tract.* 112.2.
63. AUG. *Tract.* 114.4.
64. AUG. *Tract.* 114.5.
65. Winter, "Marginal Notes on the Trial of Jesus", 242 note 98.
66. AUG. *Cons. Ev.* III 8.32: *per Pilatum gesta de Domino.*
67. AUG. *Cons. Ev.* III 8.35: *Haec narravit Ioannes per Pilatum gesta.*
68. AUG. *Tract.* 117.1.
69. AUG. *Tract.* 116.9.
70. AUG. *Tract.* 116.9.
71. AUG. *Tract.* 118.2: *unde apparet quatuor fuisse* milites *qui in eo crucifigendo praesidi paruerunt.*
72. The troops who seized and crucified Jesus would not technically have been legionnaires, but they would have been gentiles: Schürer, *History of the Jewish People*, 1:362–3.
73. AUG. *Tract.* 115.2.
74. *John* 18:36.
75. AUG. *Tract.* 115.1.
76. AUG. *Tract.* 115.1.
77. AUG. *Tract.* 115.1.
78. AUG. *Tract.* 115.2.
79. AUG. *Tract.* 115.2.
80. AUG. *Tract.* 115.2.
81. AUG. *Serm.* 81.9; cit. Decret, *Early Christianity in North Africa*, 190.
82. AUG. *Tract.* 115.2.

83. *Clem.* 1:1: *paroikousa ... paroikousē.*
84. PL. *Resp.* IX 592b. For the late Augustine's contrast of Christian and Platonic theories of "two worlds" (*duos mundos*)—of the intelligible world of Plato, and the otherworldly kingdom of Jesus (formulated in the Roman trial in *John*): AUG. *Retract.* I 3.2.
85. AUG. *Tract.* 115.2.
86. AUG. *Enar. Ps.* 54.3 (53.3 in the Latin numbering): *Quid mihi prodest innocentia?*
87. G. Hill, "Ovid in the Third Reich", *These Hard and Shining Things: Rowan Evans, Geoffrey Hill, Toby Martinez de las Rivas* (London, 2018), 40.
88. AUG. *Enar. Ps.* 54.3 (53.3 in the Latin numbering).
89. AUG. *Civ. Dei* XIX 6.
90. AUG. *Tract.* 115.2.
91. AUG. *Civ. Dei* XIX 6.
92. AUG. *Civ. Dei* XIX 6.
93. Consider Alfred Jarry's piece for *Le canard sauvage* in 1903, "La Passion considérée comme course du côte", which has been put into English as "The Passion Considered as an Uphill Bicycle Race", *Selected Works of Alfred Jarry*, ed. R. Shattuck and S. W. Taylor (London, 1965).
94. For the prevalence in Hellenistic literature of "vulgar witticism[s] tied to the cross": Chapman and Schnabel, *Trial and Crucifixion of Jesus*, 748–54.
95. *John* 19:1–5.
96. AUG. *Tract.* 116.2.
97. AUG. *Tract.* 116.3.
98. AUG. *Tract.* 117.3.
99. ORIG. *C. Cels.* VI 42.
100. ORIG. *C. Cels.* VI 78.
101. ORIG. *C. Cels.* II 34 (Origen states that Pilate is meant here). John Granger Cook clarifies, writing that "[w]hat Celsus would like to see is the courage and power shown by Bacchus in Euripides' *Bacchae* 498 ... [Celsus] wants Jesus to at least show some of Dionysius' threatening power": Cook, *Interpretation of the New Testament*, 52–3.
102. AUG. *Tract.* 117.3.
103. Vogt, "Pagans and Christians in the Family of Constantine the Great", 40. Note that this not only occurred in images of Christian emperors—but of pre-Christian ones, too. As Peter Brown writes: "With the sign of the Cross engraved neatly on their foreheads, the statues of Augustus and Livia, that had stood for centuries in ... Ephesus, now gazed down serenely on the Christian bishops assembled by Theodosius II—the most orthodox, direct successor of Augustus—to the momentous council of 431." See Brown, *Rise of Western Christendom*, 98.
104. On shouts and acclamations during Augustine's sermons, see P. R. L. Brown, *Through the Eye of a Needle: Wealth, the Fall of Rome, and the Making of*

Christianity in the West, 350–550 AD (Princeton, 2012), 339–44, here 344: "The Christian *populus* ... remained a *populus* in the old Roman sense—a citizen body with a right to shout and riot. Augustine faced this *populus* in his basilica."

105. AUG. *Tract.* 116.1: "So the kingdom that was not of this world conquered this proud world not by the ferocity of fighting, but by the humility of suffering."

14. "THERE ARE TWO": AN AFRICAN LETTER THAT SHAPED HISTORY

1. Confusingly, the text states that Gelasius held the Roman See "in the time of King Theodoric and Emperor *Zeno*"; but Zeno died in 491, a year before Gelasius became pope. For Zeno's reign: Lee, *From Rome to Byzantium*, 100–1.

2. *Lib. Pont.* I "Gelasius"; cit. B. Neil and P. Allen, *The Letters of Gelasius I (492–496): Pastor and Micro-manager of the Church of Rome* (Turnhout, 2014), 71. (Translation modified.)

3. For the bishop as a "lover of the poor" (Greek *philoptōchos*, Latin *amator pauperum*), consult P. R. L. Brown, "'Lover of the Poor': The Creation of a Public Virtue", *Poverty and Leadership in the Later Roman Empire: The Menahem Stern Jerusalem Lectures* (London, 2002), 1–44.

4. This likely refers to Gelasius' decree that a quarter of the church's income must be distributed to the poor: A. K. Ziegler, "Pope Gelasius I and His Teaching on the Relation of Church and State", *The Catholic Historical Review* 27, 4 (1942), 412–37, here 417.

5. Letter from Dionysius Exiguus to a priest ordained by Gelasius. Here in the translation of Ziegler, "Pope Gelasius I and His Teaching", 416–17.

6. *Lib. Pont.* I "Gelasius"; cit. Neil and Allen, *Letters of Gelasius I*, 71. (Translation modified.)

7. B. Neil, "Papal Letters and Letter Collections", *Late Antique Letter Collections: A Critical Introduction and Reference Guide*, ed. C. Sogno, B. K. Storin, and E. J. Watts (Oakland, Calif., 2017), 452, 457–8.

8. Neil and Allen, *Letters of Gelasius I*, 57–8.

9. C. P. E. Nothaft, *Dating the Passion: The Life of Jesus and the Emergence of Scientific Chronology (200–1600)* (Leiden, 2012), 69–80.

10. Nietzsche, *Anti-Christ, Ecce Homo, Twilight of the Idols*, 66.

11. *Lib. Pont.* I "Gelasius"; cit. Neil and Allen, *Letters of Gelasius I*, 71. (Translation modified.)

12. R. Lesaffer, *European Legal History: A Cultural and Political Perspective*, trans. J. Arriens (Cambridge, 2009), 143–4, 212–27, here 225.

13. F. Dvornik, "Emperors, Popes, and General Councils", *Dumbarton Oaks Papers* 6 (1951), 3–23, here 19–21.

14. R. L. Benson, "The Gelasian Doctrine: Uses and Transformations", *La notion d'autorité au Moyen Age: Islam, Byzance, Occident*, ed. G. Makdisi and D. Sourdel (Paris, 1982), 13.

15. *Lib. Pont.* I "Gelasius"; cit. Neil and Allen, *Letters of Gelasius I*, 71.

16. G. Dagron, *Emperor and Priest: The Imperial Office in Byzantium*, trans. J. Birrell (Cambridge, 2003), 295–306.

17. In the context of the Pelagian controversy: Brown, *Through the Eye of a Needle*, 474.

18. Markus, *Saeculum*, 105–32.

19. T. F. X. Noble, "A New Look at the *Liber pontificalis*", *Archivum historiae pontificiae* 23 (1985), 347–58, here 354; B. Neil, "Crisis and Wealth in Byzantine Italy: The *Libri pontificales* of Rome and Ravenna", *Byzantion* 82 (2012), 279–303, here 283.

20. Neil and Allen, *Letters of Gelasius I*, 70.

21. *Lib. Pont.* I "Gelasius"; cit. Neil and Allen, *Letters of Gelasius I*, 73.

22. GEL. I *Epist.* 30.15; cit. Neil and Allen, *Letters of Gelasius I*, 50.

23. For Anastasius' reign: Lee, *From Rome to Byzantium*, 159–77.

24. *Lib. Pont.* I "Gelasius"; cit. Neil and Allen, *Letters of Gelasius I*, 71. (Translation modified.) Once again, note that the text claims that Gelasius held the Roman See "in the time of King Theodoric and Emperor *Zeno*". I have emended for clarity.

25. Anastasius seems to have been born in "Latin-speaking Dyrrachium" (now Durrës, Albania): Lee, *From Rome to Byzantium*, 160.

26. *Lib. Pont.* I "Gelasius"; cit. Neil and Allen, *Letters of Gelasius I*, 73.

27. The definitive new study is J. Herrin, *Ravenna: Capital of Empire, Crucible of Europe* (Princeton, 2019).

28. AMM. *Rer. Gest.* XVI 3,2.

29. Cit. Lee, *From Rome to Byzantium*, 123–4.

30. H. Wolfram, "The Shaping of the Early Medieval Kingdom", *Viator* 1 (1971), 11–20, here 19; S. Corcoran, "Roman Law in Ravenna", *Ravenna: Its Role in Earlier Medieval Change and Exchange*, ed. J. Herrin and J. Nelson (London, 2016), 166–8; C. Scholl, "Imitatio Imperii? Elements of Imperial Rule in the Barbarian Successor States of the Roman West", *Transcultural Approaches to the Concept of Imperial Rule in the Middle Ages*, ed. C. Scholl, T. R. Gebhardt, and J. Clauss (Berlin, 2017), 25–6.

31. One of the canons of the First Council of Constantinople (381 CE) states that "Constantinople is the New Rome"; cit. Lee, *From Rome to Byzantium*, 73.

32. This is the basic configuration that will hold until Charlemagne 'restores' the Latin Roman Empire in Europe, beginning with his coronation—in Rome, by the pope—in 800. Significantly, Charlemagne's pre-800 titulature calls him a "king by the grace of God" (*gratia dei rex*) and "patrician of the Romans" (*patricius Romanorum*): Herrin, *Formation of Christendom*, 400.

33. Lee, *From Rome to Byzantium*, 96.

34. Though it is worth remembering that, in the year 536, "the troops of the east Roman emperor Justinian entered Rome, making it once again an 'imperial' city. By that time, however, the Roman empire had become little more than a memory along the [western] frontiers … that lay at many weeks' journey to the north of Marseilles and Rome." Brown, *Rise of Western Christendom*, 75.

35. Within a colossal literature on the question of 'collapse', one orienting text—precisely because it remains controversial—is B. Ward-Perkins, *The Fall of Rome and the End of Civilization* (Oxford, 2005).

36. Dagron, *Emperor and Priest*, 300–1.

37. Rome as "eternal city" is a late antique cliché: AMM. *Rer. Gest.* XIV 6,1.

38. For the Roman political culture that generated the schism, see M. R. Salzman, "Lay Aristocrats and Ecclesiastical Politics: A New View of the Papacy of Felix III (483–492 C.E.) and the Acacian Schism", *Journal of Early Christian Studies* 27, 3 (2019), 465–89.

39. For the ravaging of Constantinople in 1203 and 1204: J. J. Norwich, *A Short History of Byzantium* (New York, 1999), 291–306.

40. Norwich, *Short History of Byzantium*, 300.

41. GEL. I *Epist.* 12.1; Neil and Allen, *Letters of Gelasius I*, 73. As Peter Brown notes: "Up to AD 800, every papal document sent to western bishops and to western rulers was dated by the regnal year of the emperor in Constantinople." See Brown, *Rise of Western Christendom*, 124.

42. Dagron, *Emperor and Priest*, 302–3, 317–18.

43. Dagron, *Emperor and Priest*, 295–306.

44. GEL. I *Epist.* 12.2; Neil and Allen, *Letters of Gelasius I*, 74.

45. GEL. I *Epist.* 12.3; Neil and Allen, *Letters of Gelasius I*, 75.

46. GEL. I *Epist.* 12.2; Neil and Allen, *Letters of Gelasius I*, 74.

47. GEL. I *Epist.* 12.2; Neil and Allen, *Letters of Gelasius I*, 74.

48. GEL. I *Epist.* 12.4; Neil and Allen, *Letters of Gelasius I*, 75. (Translation modified.)

49. GEL. I *Epist.* 12.4; Neil and Allen, *Letters of Gelasius I*, 75.

50. GEL. I *Epist.* 12.2; Neil and Allen, *Letters of Gelasius I*, 74.

51. GEL. I *Epist.* 12.4; Neil and Allen, *Letters of Gelasius I*, 75. (Translation modified.)

52. J.-J. Rousseau, *The Social Contract and Other Later Political Writings*, ed. and trans. V. Gourevitch (Cambridge, 1997), 144; idem, *Du contrat social*, ed. with intro. and annot. R. Grimsley (Oxford, 1972), 223. (Translation modified.)

53. Rousseau, *Social Contract*, 146; idem, *Contrat social*, 226. (Translation modified.)

54. GEL. I *Epist.* 12.2; Neil and Allen, *Letters of Gelasius I*, 74. (Translation modified.)

55. A comprehensive study of the origins of such influence is A. Brent, *The*

Imperial Cult and the Development of Church Order: Concepts and Images of Authority in Paganism and Early Christianity before the Age of Cyprian (Leiden, 1999).

56. AUG. *Tract.* 115.2.

57. GEL. I *Epist.* 12.4, 12.10; Neil and Allen, *Letters of Gelasius I*, 75, 79. (Translation modified.)

58. GEL. I *Epist.* 12.4; Neil and Allen, *Letters of Gelasius I*, 75. (Translation modified.)

59. GEL. I *Epist.* 12.2; Neil and Allen, *Letters of Gelasius I*, 74. (Translation modified.)

60. I am not the first to suggest this: G. Essen, "Autonomer Geltungssinn und religiöser Begründungszusammenhang: Papst Gelasius I. († 496) als Fallstudie zur religionspolitischen Differenzsemantik", *Archiv für Rechts- und Sozialphilosophie* 99, 1 (2013), 1–10.

61. AUG. *Epist.* 64.4.

62. Benson, "Gelasian Doctrine", 19.

63. Letter from Felix III (written by Gelasius) to Zeno. Here in the translation of Ziegler, "Pope Gelasius I and His Teaching", 426–7.

64. There is a notable lag in Gelasius' influence, as "the papal chancery apparently forgot about 'Duo sunt' for almost 250 years": Benson, "Gelasian Doctrine", 20.

65. *Lib. Pont.* I "Gelasius"; cit. Neil and Allen, *Letters of Gelasius I*, 73.

66. Ziegler, "Pope Gelasius I and His Teaching", 421.

67. GEL. I *Epist.* 12.2; Neil and Allen, *Letters of Gelasius I*, 74. (Translation modified.)

68. JUSTIN. *Inst.* "Imperial Majesty".

69. GEL. I *Tom.* (no textual divisions). Here and below, I am translating from *Patrologia Latina* 59, columns 102–10, in consultation of Benson, "Gelasian Doctrine", 16; Ziegler, "Pope Gelasius I and His Teaching", 434–5.

70. GEL. I *Tom.* (no textual divisions).

15. "I BEHELD THE SHADE": A REAL TRIAL AND A FAKE DONATION

1. DAN. *Inf.* III 56–60; *The Inferno of Dante: A New Verse Translation*, Italian with trans. R. Pinsky, annot. N. Pinsky (New York, 1994), 20–1 (typography lightly modified). Consult C. S. Singleton, *The Divine Comedy: Inferno, vol. 2: Commentary* (Princeton, 1977), 47–52.

2. DAN. *Inf.* III 66.

3. DAN. *Inf.* III 61–9. For more on this: M. Colish, "*Sanza 'nfama e sanza lodo*: Moral Neutrality from Alan of Lille to Dante", *Alain de Lille, le Docteur Universel*, ed. J.-L. Solère, A. Vasiliu, and A. Galonnier (Turnhout, 2015).

4. DAN. *Inf.* III 60.

5. JAC. AL. *Comm. ad loc.* (DAN. *Inf.* III 58–60). The Celestine reading is upheld

by Natalino Sapegno in the apparatus of N. Sapegno, *La Divina Commedia: Vol. I; Inferno* (Florence, 1980), 39–40. For the *Inferno*'s dates of composition: M. Santagata, *Dante: The Story of His Life*, trans. R. Dixon (Cambridge, Mass., 2016), 219.

6. PIET. AL. *Com.* ad loc. (DAN. *Inf.* III 34–60). Note that I am citing, here, the third edition of Pietro's *Comment*.

7. For some of the questions touching this succession: C. S. Mackay, "Lactantius and the Succession to Diocletian", *Classical Philology* 94, 2 (1999), 198–209.

8. MARA. *Exp.* ad loc. (DAN. *Inf.* III 58–60).

9. BEN. IMOLA *Com.* ad loc. (DAN. *Inf.* III 58–60).

10. BOCC. *Exp.* ad loc. (DAN. *Inf.* III 58–60). Note that Boccaccio is not only one of the first commentators on the *Divine Comedy* but Dante's first biographer: Falkeid, *Avignon Papacy Contested*, 52–4.

11. *Genesis* 25:29–34 (Authorized Version).

12. See the commentary of Baldassarre Lombardi, in which the only possibility other than Celestine, Diocletian, and Esau is a Florentine known to Dante, such as Torrigiano de' Cerchi: B. Lombardi, *La Divina Commedia, novamente corretta, spiegata e difesa* ... (Rome, 1791–2) ad loc. (DAN. *Inf.* III 59–60).

13. LAND. *Com.* ad loc. (DAN. *Inf.* III 58–60).

14. AUG. *Civ. Dei* VIII 4.

15. Vieri de' Cerchi and Giano della Bella have been proposed: Singleton, *Inferno, vol. 2: Commentary*, 59.

16. LAND. *Com.* ad loc. (DAN. *Inf.* III 58–60).

17. I say "concludes", not because this line about doubt is placed at the end of Landino's comment; but rather, because it seems to me to capture his point: LAND. *Com.* ad loc. (DAN. *Inf.* III 58–60).

18. T. S. Eliot, *Collected Poems, 1909–1962* (New York, 1963), 55 (lines 60–70).

19. There is a small 'Stetson' literature. One charming (not convincing) possibility is that 'Stetson' is an anagram taken from 'Stearns Eliot': V. Thorpe, "Who Is the Mysterious 'Stetson' in T. S. Eliot's Waste Land?", *The Observer* (8 November 2015). Archived online at https://www.theguardian.com/books/2015/nov/08/ts-eliot-waste-land-stetson-anagram-riddle; accessed 29 October 2020.

20. P. Schaff, *Literature and Poetry* (New York, 1890), 380. This is not meant to impugn the oeuvre of Philip Schaff (died 1893), who wrote an irenic *History of the Christian Church* (eight volumes) and edited a collection of *Early Church Fathers* (thirty-eight volumes) that I have consulted hundreds of times.

21. DAN. *Inf.* III 58–60.

22. For "vestibule of Hell" and a concise reception-history of *Inferno* III 60 (in which the Pilate-conjecture gets no more than a mention): Singleton, *Inferno, vol. 2: Commentary*, 47–52.

23. DAN. *Inf.* III 59.

24. It is perplexing to me that the Pilate-conjecture is called "the most credible" (*il piú attendibile*), after Celestine V, in the commentary of U. Bosco and G. Reggio, eds, *La Divina Commedia: Inferno* (Florence, 1979), 34–5. Like Landino, Bosco and Reggio are non-dogmatic; and they say that the Pilate-conjecture is not convincing. But to my mind, it is *far less* credible than all the others (Celestine, Diocletian, Esau), for reasons that will be stated in a moment.

25. G. Pascoli, "Chi sia 'colui che fece il gran rifiuto'", *Il Marzocco* 6 (27 July 1902), reprinted in *Prose, II* (Milan, 1952), 1469–87. Before this: E. Barbarani, *Due chiose dantesche* (Verona, 1897); cit. A. Penna, "Pilato, Ponzio", *Enciclopedia Dantesca*, ed. U. Bosco (Rome, 1973).

26. Agamben, *Pilato e Gesú*, 68; idem, *Pilate and Jesus*, 50.

27. Though it is rejected by Natalino Sapegno in his apparatus: Sapegno, *La Divina Commedia: Vol. I*, 39–40.

28. Schiavone, *Pontius Pilate*. For an Italian collection: F. Amarelli and F. Lucrezi, eds, *Il processo contro Gesù* (Naples, 1999).

29. G. Rosadi, *Il processo di Gesú* (Florence, 1904); idem, *The Trial of Jesus*, trans. E. Reich (New York, 1905).

30. G. Rosadi, *Dopo Gesù* (Florence, 1919).

31. A. Manassero, *Ecce Homo: Storia del processo di Gesú* (Milan, 1952), 7–11.

32. Agamben, *Pilato e Gesú*, 68; idem, *Pilate and Jesus*, 50.

33. LACT. *Div. Inst.* IV 18,6.

34. Dusenbury, "Judgment of Pontius Pilate".

35. Agamben, *Pilate and Jesus*, 47.

36. G. Pascoli, "Chi sia 'colui che fece il gran rifiuto'", *Il Marzocco* 6 (27 July 1902), reprinted in *Prose, II* (Milan, 1952), 1469–87.

37. Rosadi, *Trial of Jesus*, 260.

38. Rosadi, *Trial of Jesus*, 222–4.

39. It must be said that Rosadi denies Pilate's *moral* innocence. Rosadi, *Trial of Jesus*, 260: "We have no intention of shielding the *moral* guilt of Lucius Pontius …" (My italics.)

40. Rosadi, *Trial of Jesus*, 294. (Translation modified. My italics.)

41. Rosadi, *Trial of Jesus*, 300.

42. Agamben, *Pilato e Gesú*, 68; idem, *Pilate and Jesus*, 50.

43. Santagata, *Dante*, 219, 225.

44. DAN. *Purg.* XX 91 (new Pilate); *Inf.* III 64 (never lived).

45. DAN. *Purg.* XX 86–93. Consult C. S. Singleton, *The Divine Comedy: Purgatorio, vol. 2: Commentary* (Princeton, 1973), 486–9.

46. Falkeid, *Avignon Papacy Contested*, 26–7, 73. For the influence of this conflict on political theory: G. Briguglia, *La questione del potere: Teologi e teoria politica nella disputa tra Bonifacio VIII e Filippo il Bello* (Milan, 2010).

47. DAN. *Inf.* XXVII 85; R. Artinian, "Dante's Parody of Boniface VIII", *Dante Studies* 85 (1967), 71–4.

48. Cit. H.-W. Strätz, "Säkularisation, Säkularisierung, II: Der kanonistische und staatskirchenrechtliche Begriff", *Geschichtliche Grundbegriffe: Historisches Lexikon zur politisch-sozialen Sprache in Deutschland*, ed. O. Brunner, W. Conze, and R. Koselleck (Stuttgart, 1984), 799 note 58: "Liber sextus decretalium D. Bonifacii Papae VIII ... *i. Saeculares, i. saecularium personarum* ..."

49. S. Pufendorf, *An Introduction to the History of the Principal Kingdoms and States of Europe*, trans. J. Crull, ed. M. J. Seidler (Indianapolis, 2013), 460–5.

50. DAN. *Purg.* XX 91–3.

51. DAN. *Purg.* XX 92.

52. DAN. *Purg.* XX 88–90.

53. JOS. *Bell. Jud.* V 219.

54. DAN. *Inf.* III 60.

55. LACT. *Div. Inst.* IV 18,6.

56. Santagata, *Dante*, 261–75, 284–95.

57. DAN. *Inf.* III 60.

58. Italian correctives are C. Di Fonzo, "La legittimazione dell'Impero e del popolo romano presso Dante", *Dante* 6 (2009), 39–64; and S. Cecotti, "La legittima validità dell'impero: Analisi degli argomenti sviluppati secondo la semantica della validità nel secondo libro della *Monarchia* di Dante condotta a partire dalla confutazione fattane da fra' Guido Vernani da Rimini nel suo *De Reprobatione monarchiae*", *Divus Thomas* 115, 1 (2012), 390–412. It is necessary to register a "volte-face" in Dante's politics between his composition of *Inferno* and *Purgatorio*: Santagata, *Dante*, 284.

59. DAN. *Mon.* III 16.16.

60. DAN. *Mon.* II 10.1.

61. DAN. *Mon.* II 10.6.

62. DAN. *Mon.* II 10.8.

63. DAN. *Mon.* II 10.5; trans. Shaw (1996), 59: "If someone is a believer, he allows that this is false; if he does not allow it, he is not a believer, and if he is not a believer, this argument is not for him."

64. DAN. *Mon.* II 10.9–10.

65. For the influence of Peter of Spain on Dante's reasoning here: Falkeid, *Avignon Papacy Contested*, 35–6.

66. For the sources of Dante's arguments: Cecotti, "La legittima validità dell'impero", 401–7.

67. DAN. *Mon.* II 11.3.

68. DAN. *Mon.* II 11.3.

69. DAN. *Mon.* II 11.1.

70. DAN. *Mon.* II 11.4.

71. DAN. *Mon.* II 11.4.

72. DAN. *Mon.* II 11.6.

73. DAN. *Mon.* II 11.5.

74. DAN. *Mon.* II 11.7.
75. DAN. *Para.* VI 82–93, here 93. I owe this to Falkeid, *Avignon Papacy Contested*, 33–4. The divine vengeance taken by Rome, in Jerusalem, at the crucifixion, is then divinely avenged by Rome, in Jerusalem, with the destruction of the Temple by Titus in 70 CE. For Dante's derivation of the last idea from the writings of Paulus Orosius (one of Augustine's protégés): C. S. Singleton, *The Divine Comedy. Paradiso, vol. 2: Commentary* (Princeton, 1975), 123–4.
76. DAN. *Inf.* III 58–60.
77. DAN. *Mon.* II 11.6.
78. DAN. *Mon.* III 1.3.
79. DAN. *Mon.* III 14.1.
80. DAN. *Mon.* III 14.7.
81. DAN. *Mon.* III 14.1.
82. DAN. *Mon.* III 16.1.
83. DAN. *Mon.* III 15.1.
84. DAN. *Mon.* III 15.3.
85. DAN. *Mon.* III 15.1.
86. DAN. *Mon.* III 15.5–9.
87. DAN. *Mon.* III 15.5.
88. DAN. *Mon.* III 15.10.
89. DAN. *Mon.* III 16.7.
90. DAN. *Mon.* III 16.11.
91. DAN. *Mon.* III 16.7.
92. GEL. I, *Epist.* 12.2; Neil and Allen, *Letters of Gelasius I*, 74. (Translation modified.)
93. DAN. *Mon.* III 15.5–9 and III 16.7.
94. D. G. Park, "Dante and the Donation of Constantine", *Dante Studies* 130 (2012), 67–161.
95. Park, "Dante and the Donation of Constantine", 68–70; J. Fried, *The "Donation of Constantine" and "Constitutum Constantini": The Misinterpretation of a Fiction and Its Original Meaning* (Berlin, 2007).
96. Park, "Dante and the Donation of Constantine", 67; B. E. Whalen, *Dominion of God: Christendom and Apocalypse in the Middle Ages* (Cambridge, Mass., 2009), 18–26.
97. DAN. *Mon.* II 11.8. Dante's tercets on the *Donation of Constantine* were written in the same period: DAN. *Para.* VI 1–9; Falkeid, *Avignon Papacy Contested*, 33–4.
98. DAN. *Mon.* III 13.7.
99. Falkeid, *Avignon Papacy Contested*, 42–3. Compare V. S. Benfell, *The Biblical Dante* (Toronto, 2011), 101, 181–8.
100. DAN. *Inf.* XIX 115–17; Park, "Dante and the Donation of Constantine", 72.
101. DAN. *Para.* XX 55–60; Park, "Dante and the Donation of Constantine", 73–4.

102. Citing here the bolder and more informative title of the book's reprint in 1992, shortly before Weckmann's death in 1995: L. Weckmann, *Las Bulas Alejandrinas de 1493 y la Teoría política del papado medieval: Estudio de la supremacía papal sobre islas (1091–1493)*, intro. E. H. Kantorowicz (Mexico City, 1949); idem, *Constantino el Grande y Cristóbal Colón: Estudio de la supremacía papal sobre islas (1091–1493)*, intro. E. H. Kantorowicz (Mexico City, 1992).

103. L. Weckmann, "The Middle Ages in the Conquest of America", *Speculum* 26, 1 (1951), 130–41, here 130–1 (my italics in the text, and at *Donation of Constantine*). For more on Columbus as a medieval traveller: V. I. J. Flint, *The Imaginative Landscape of Christopher Columbus* (Princeton, 1992). Compare, too, the pages on "Columbus as a great reader": A. Grafton, with A. Shelford and N. Siraisi, *New Worlds, Ancient Texts: The Power of Tradition and the Shock of Discovery* (Cambridge, Mass., 1992), 63–5, 75–82.

104. J. McClure, *The Franciscan Invention of the New World* (Cham, 2017), 118–20. A new study in which Dante's *Monarchy* features, and that I have not managed to consult, is A. W. Devereux, *The Other Side of Empire: Just War in the Mediterranean and the Rise of Early Modern Spain* (Ithaca, N.Y., 2020).

105. There are many editions, and many titles, but I am relying here on Grafton, with Shelford and Siraisi, *New Worlds, Ancient Texts*, 80 (with frontispiece): *Epistula de Insulis nuper inventis*.

106. Compare C. J. Bishko, untitled review of *Las Bulas Alejandrinas de 1493 y la Teoría política del papado medieval* by Luis Weckmann, *Speculum* 25, 2 (1950), 306–11; H. de la Costa, untitled review of *Las Bulas Alejandrinas de 1493 y la Teoría política del papado medieval* by Luis Weckmann, *Traditio* 7 (1951), 516–18; and J. Muldoon, "Papal Responsibility for the Infidel: Another Look at Alexander VI's *Inter caetera*", *The Catholic Historical Review* 64, 2 (1978), 168–84, here 169 note 2: "Weckmann's argument that papal claims to control of unclaimed regions was rooted in the Donation of Constantine cannot be accepted, [but] he was correct in seeking the legal tradition that influenced Alexander VI in drawing up the bull [*Inter caetera*]."

107. Bishko, untitled review of *Las Bulas Alejandrinas de 1493*, 307. I am grateful to Dante Fedele for referring me to this review.

108. De la Costa, untitled review of *Las Bulas Alejandrinas de 1493*, 518: "With regard to the 'omni-insular doctrine' itself, there seems to be no question that it was invoked by Urban II and Adrian IV, and it is reasonable to suppose that these are not isolated instances."

109. De la Costa, untitled review of *Las Bulas Alejandrinas de 1493*, 517.

110. J. Fried, *The Middle Ages* (Cambridge, Mass., 2015), 147–8 (my italics at *Donation*).

111. J. N. Hillgarth, "The Image of Alexander VI and Cesare Borgia in the Sixteenth and Seventeenth Centuries", *Journal of the Warburg and Courtauld*

Institutes 59 (1996), 119–29, here 121. False rumours that Alexander was a Marrano, or "secret Jew"—he was a Catalan who gave refuge, in Rome, to Jews expelled by Ferdinand and Isabella—seem to have enraged many of his detractors (121–2, 129).

112. The political history of the *Donation*'s reception is not limited to Europe: J. L. Wieczynski, "The Donation of Constantine in Medieval Russia", *The Catholic Historical Review* 55, 2 (1969), 159–72.

113. The novelty of Valla's text is debated: J. C. Linde, "Lorenzo Valla and the Authenticity of Sacred Texts", *Humanistica Lovaniensia* 60 (2011), 35–63, here 38–9.

114. I am grateful to Paul Richard Blum for insisting that I read Valla during an August 2019 conversation at Loyola University Maryland, and for providing me with the relevant texts. Among his many pages on Valla are P. R. Blum, *Philosophy of Religion in the Renaissance* (New York, 2010), 77–94.

115. For 'modern' traits in the thought of Reginald Pecock, who concurrently— and differently—exposed the *Donation*: J. M. Levine, "Reginald Pecock and Lorenzo Valla on the *Donation of Constantine*", *Studies in the Renaissance* 20 (1973), 118–43.

116. For the date of composition (and Nicholas of Cusa's influence on Valla's text): R. Fubini, "Humanism and Truth: Valla Writes against the Donation of Constantine", *Journal of the History of Ideas* 57, 1 (1996), 79–86, here 82–3; and Linde, "Lorenzo Valla", 36–8. For the 1517 first edition: D. M. Whitford, "The Papal Antichrist: Martin Luther and the Underappreciated Influence of Lorenzo Valla", *Renaissance Quarterly* 61, 1 (2008), 26–52, here 28 note 5, 40.

117. Whitford, "Papal Antichrist", 28, 36–7, 40.

118. Cit. Whitford, "Papal Antichrist", 40. (Whitford's translation.)

119. Cit. Whitford, "Papal Antichrist", 41. (Whitford's translation.)

120. J. H. Bentley, *Humanists and Holy Writ: New Testament Scholarship in the Renaissance* (Princeton, 1983), 46–7.

121. Cit. L. Valla, *On the Donation of Constantine*, trans. G. W. Bowersock (Cambridge, Mass., 2007), viii. (Translation modified.)

122. For Dante's and Marsilius' critiques of the *Donation of Constantine*, with Marsilius—like Valla—citing the Roman trial of Jesus: Falkeid, *Avignon Papacy Contested*, 42–4 (Dante), 62 (Marsilius).

123. VALLA *Don. Const.* 20.

124. The same could be said of Marsilius of Padua's *Defender of the Peace*—a point I owe to the descriptions in Falkeid, *Avignon Papacy Contested*, 62–4.

125. VALLA *Don. Const.* 22.

126. GEL. I *Tom.* (no textual divisions).

127. VALLA *Don. Const.* 24–5.

128. VALLA *Don. Const.* 26.

129. Bentley, *Humanists and Holy Writ*, 57; Linde, "Lorenzo Valla", 59–60.

130. This is not to deny that Valla could be a harsh critic of Augustine, who often confined his exegesis to the *Vetus Latina* renderings he had on hand in North Africa: Bentley, *Humanists and Holy Writ*, 41, 60.

16. "CHRIST WILLED HIMSELF TO LACK AUTHORITY": A *SUCCÈS DE SCAN-DALE* AND A CHAIN OF GOLD

1. One of Unn Falkeid's clarifications is germane here: "This does not mean, however, that [Marsilius] reckoned on a society of nonbelievers. He accepted that the citizens of his perfect state would be Christians. Nonetheless, he presented a political structure where God was placed in the background as a remote rather than a direct cause." Falkeid, *Avignon Papacy Contested*, 57–8.
2. From a condemnation issued in June 1331 by the city of Milan of the "erroneous beliefs" held by Marsilius and of the "slanderous" little books (*libelli*) that he circulated: F. Godthardt, "The Life of Marsilius of Padua", *A Companion to Marsilius of Padua*, ed. G. Moreno-Riano and C. J. Nederman (Leiden, 2012), 30–1, here 31: "The *libelli* referred to in the bull were probably 'pamphlets,' i.e., short propaganda texts. Perhaps Marsilius' tract *De translatio Imperii* was one of these shorter texts composed in Milan." Marsilius wrote the *Lesser Defender* much later than the Milan condemnation: Godthardt, "Life of Marsilius", 55; C. J. Nederman, "From *Defensor pacis* to *Defensor minor*: The Problem of Empire in Marsiglio of Padua", *History of Political Thought* 16, 3 (1995), 313–29, here 313.
3. Falkeid, *Avignon Papacy Contested*, 53.
4. Godthardt, "Life of Marsilius of Padua", 16–19; Falkeid, *Avignon Papacy Contested*, 53–4.
5. A Guelf (papal) partisan by birth and long by conviction, Dante's ties to the Ghibellines are immensely complex: Falkeid, *Avignon Papacy Contested*, 28–32; Santagata, *Dante: The Story of His Life*, 43–88, 187–301.
6. Pope John XXII's bull *Quia iuxta doctrinam* in fact calls out "two worthless men, sons of perdition ... one of whom lets himself be called Marsilius of Padua and the other John of Jandun". Cit. Godthardt, "Life of Marsilius", 25–8.
7. Falkeid, *Avignon Papacy Contested*, 52–4; T. M. Izbicki, "The Reception of Marsilius", *Companion to Marsilius of Padua*, 309.
8. OCK. *Imp. Pont.* 27.565–701.
9. MARS. PAD. *Def. Pac.* II 1.3: *suprema ... coactiva jurisdictio.*
10. Falkeid, *Avignon Papacy Contested*, 62.
11. G. Corbett, *Dante's Christian Ethics: Purgatory and Its Moral Contexts* (Cambridge, 2020), 48–9. A study of *Monarchy*'s notoriety is A. K. Cassell, *The Monarchia Controversy: An Historical Study with Accompanying Translations of Dante Alighieri's Monarchia, Guido Vernani's Refutation of the "Monarchia" Composed by Dante, and Pope John XXII's Bull Si fratrum* (Washington, D.C., 2004). And for 'Protestant'

fore-echoes in Dante, as in the breathtaking lines at DAN. *Para.* IX 133–8: Falkeid, *Avignon Papacy Contested*, 48.

12. Godthardt, "Life of Marsilius of Padua", 32–4.

13. For several illuminating proofs of the Dante–Marsilius reception (or more precisely, citation) by sixteenth-century English Protestants: J. C. Boswell, "Dante's Fame in England: 1536–1586", *Dante Studies* 111 (1993), 235–43, here 237–9, 242.

14. Izbicki, "Reception of Marsilius", 309–10. For Henry's world-historical dissolution of monasteries: D. Knowles, *The Religious Orders in England, Volume III: The Tudor Age* (Cambridge, 1957–60); idem, *Bare Ruined Choirs: The Dissolution of the English Monasteries* (Cambridge, 1976); and for a micro-history: G. Moorhouse, *The Last Office: 1539 and the Dissolution of a Monastery* (London, 2008). I am grateful to Arnold Hunt for these references, and for a state-of-the-art letter on the "long process" of dissolution in April 2020.

15. S. Lockwood, "Marsilius of Padua and the Case for the Royal Ecclesiastical Supremacy", *Transactions of the Royal Historical Society* 1 (1991), 89–119, here 90.

16. I wish to thank two Marsilius scholars, Jürgen Miethke and Gianluca Briguglia, for confirming this in conversations at the University of Leuven in September 2018. It is indicative that a fine essay on Marsilius' political theology contains no mention of the Pilate trial: B. Koch, "Marsilius of Padua on Church and State", *Companion to Marsilius of Padua*.

17. MARS. PAD. *Def. Min.* 13.9.

18. MARS. PAD. *Def. Min.* 13.9: *tali auctoritate Christus in hoc saeculo carere voluit, in persona propria inquantum homo, dum dixit: 'Regnum meum non est de hoc mundo'*.

19. MARS. PAD. *Def. Min.* 13.9.

20. MARS. PAD. *Def. Min.* 13.8.

21. MARS. PAD. *Def. Min.* 13.7.

22. *James* 4:12.

23. MARS. PAD. *Def. Min.* 13.9.

24. MARS. PAD. *Def. Min.* 1.2.

25. Marsilius of Padua, *Œuvres mineures. Defensor Minor. De Translatione Imperii*, ed., trans. and annot. C. Jeudy and J. Quillet (Paris, 1979), 172.

26. MARS. PAD. *Def. Min.* 13.6.

27. MARS. PAD. *Def. Min.* 1.2.

28. MARS. PAD. *Def. Pac.* I 1.5.

29. MARS. PAD. *Def. Pac.* I 19.4.

30. MARS. PAD. *Def. Pac.* I 19.9.

31. MARS. PAD. *Def. Pac.* I 19.9.

32. MARS. PAD. *Def. Pac.* I 19.12: *perversa ... affeccio principatus*.

33. MARS. PAD. *Def. Min.* 13.9.

34. MARS. PAD. *Def. Pac.* I 1.7.

35. MARS. PAD. *Def. Pac.* I 19.12.
36. MARS. PAD. *Def. Pac.* II 4.2.
37. MARS. PAD. *Def. Pac.* II 4.1–3.
38. MARS. PAD. *Def. Pac.* II 4.13.
39. MARS. PAD. *Def. Pac.* II 4.8–13.
40. MARS. PAD. *Def. Pac.* II 4.13.
41. MARS. PAD. *Def. Pac.* II 4.12.
42. MARS. PAD. *Def. Pac.* I 19.4.
43. Izbicki, "Reception of Marsilius", 314–32; F. Cheneval, "La réception de la 'Monarchie' de Dante ou Les métamorphoses d'une œuvre philosophique", *Vivarium* 34, 2 (1996), 254–67, here 261–4.
44. MARS. PAD. *Def. Min.* 13.9.
45. MARS. PAD. *Def. Pac.* II 4.
46. AQUIN. *Cat. Aur.* In Ioannem 18–19.
47. I nevertheless agree with Unn Falkeid that Dante's *Monarchy* and Marsilius' *Defender of the Peace* must be read in light of "the Gelasian theory of the two swords, later echoed in the Thomistic idea of the twofold goal and the twofold happiness of man": Falkeid, *Avignon Papacy Contested*, 52.

17. "A POWER WHICH HE REFUSED": THE MOMENTARY ORTHODOXY OF THOMAS HOBBES

1. T. Hobbes, *Behemoth or The Long Parliament*, ed. P. Seaward (Oxford, 2010).
2. *Job* 40:15–24 (Authorized Version).
3. Cit. N. Malcolm, *Aspects of Hobbes* (Oxford, 2002), 21, 21 note 88.
4. Cit. Malcolm, *Aspects of Hobbes*, 25. (Typography modified.)
5. Noting the stark limitations that Gassendi set on this 'blend': M. R. Johnson, "Was Gassendi an Epicurean?", *History of Philosophy Quarterly* 20, 4 (2003), 339–60, here 340–4.
6. Though Epicurus' theology is hard to reconstruct, he is hostile to radical atheism, calling it "total madness" (according to Philodemus of Gadara): J. Mansfeld, "Aspects of Epicurean Theology", *Mnemosyne* 46, 2 (1993), 172–210, here 183–8. Epicurus and Lucretius seem to differ on the question of worship, but for Lucretius' "forceful renunciation" of the first-century BCE Roman cultus: K. Summers, "Lucretius and the Epicurean Tradition of Piety", *Classical Philology* 90, 1 (1995), 32–57, here 41–4. Peter Green notes that "the void between the worlds" of Epicurean theory—in Latin, *intermundia*—are "described (though, oddly, never named as such) by Lucretius": P. Green, *Alexander to Actium: The Historical Evolution of the Hellenistic Age* (Berkeley, 1990), 622.
7. Green, *Alexander to Actium*, 618–30.
8. Malcolm, *Aspects of Hobbes*, 22: "[Hobbes's] attack on [the universities] in *Leviathan* became suddenly topical when a proposal was made in the Barebones Parliament in 1653 to abolish them altogether."

9. T. Hobbes, *Leviathan: Volume 1*, ed. G. A. J. Rogers and K. Schuhmann (London—New York, 2005), 101 (I, 13, variant reading; compare "War, as if of every man, against every man"). (Here and throughout, typography lightly modernized.)

10. Hobbes, *Leviathan*, 99 (I, 13).

11 Hobbes therefore opens his *Leviathan* with a rejection of the disastrous notion of "natural slavery" with which Aristotle opens his *Politics*: G. M. Vaughan, "The Audience of Leviathan and the Audience of Hobbes's Political Philosophy", *History of Political Thought* 22, 3 (2001), 448–71, here 452. For the recrudescence of Aristotle's slave-theory—alien to much medieval Christian thought—during the Renaissance: A. Pagden, *The Fall of Natural Man: The American Indian and the Origins of Comparative Ethnology* (Cambridge, 1999), 27–56.

12. Hobbes, *Leviathan*, 99 (I, 13).

13. Hobbes, *Leviathan*, 137 (II, 17).

14. It is not clear why Hobbes never cites Marsilius: Izbicki, "Reception of Marsilius", 332–3.

15. T. Hobbes, *Leviathan, Volume 3: The English and Latin Texts (ii)*, ed. N. Malcolm (Oxford, 2012), 922. (Typography lightly modified.)

16. Hobbes, *Leviathan, Volume 3*, 922–3.

17. AUG. *Tract.* 114.2.

18. Hobbes, *Leviathan*, 461 (III, 42).

19. Hobbes, *Leviathan*, 436 (III, 42).

20. M. Rose, "Hobbes contra Bellarmine", *Journal of Moral Theology* 4, 2 (2015), 43–62, here 43.

21. Hobbes is in no mood, nor is he the kind of man, to register the subtleties of Bellarmine's arguments. For the context of this intervention by a Jesuit master-thinker: E. de Bom, "Political Thought", *Jesuit Philosophy on the Eve of Modernity*, ed. C. Casalini (Leiden, 2019).

22. *Job* 41:24 (Douay–Rheims Version). It strikes me that the text-history of *Leviathan*'s motto contradicts the argument of *Leviathan*. For Hobbes prefers the Vulgate rendering of this verse to a 'modern' version of *Job* that was translated from the Hebrew. I of course have in mind the rendering commissioned by James I of England in 1604 and published in 1611. The Authorized Version of this line, "Upon earth there is not his like, who is made without fear" (*Job* 41:33), is not nearly as useful for Hobbes. That Hobbes abandoned the text that was *commissioned by an English sovereign* is vertigo-inducing—and droll—since *Leviathan* is a revolutionary defence of 'secular' sovereigns as the highest arbiters of 'religious' truth.

23. GRAT. *Dec.* 13.2.1. See, too: G. Agamben, *Stasis: Civil War as a Political Paradigm*, trans. N. Heron (Stanford, 2015), 43–8. Already in the second century CE, philosopher Celsus claims to have seen a Christian cosmogram—likely gnostic—composed of ten circles that were "held together by a single

circle, which was said to be the soul of the universe and was called Leviathan (*Leuiathan*)": ORIG. *C. Cels.* VI 25.

24. H. Höpfl, "Tyrannicide and the Oath of Allegiance", *Jesuit Political Thought: The Society of Jesus and the State, c.1540–1630* (Cambridge, 2004); P.-A. Mellet, *Les traités monarchomaques: Confusion des temps, résistance armée et monarchie parfaite, 1560–1600* (Geneva, 2007).

25. Hobbes, *Leviathan*, 527 (IV, 45), 565 (A Review, and Conclusion).

26. It is this image of Hobbes's that gives a title to a brilliant counter-history of medieval Europe: F. Oakley, *Empty Bottles of Gentilism: Kingship and the Divine in Late Antiquity and the Early Middle Ages (to 1050)* (New Haven, 2010). Note that there is an incisive passage on the Pilate trial (57–60).

27. *Mark* 2:18–22, compare *Matthew* 9:14–17 and *Luke* 5:33–9. The meaning of this 'new wine' image is immensely complicated by a unique statement in *Luke*, where Jesus says that "no one after drinking old wine desires new wine, but says, 'The old is good'" (*Luke* 5:39).

28. Hobbes, *Leviathan*, 384 (III, 41).

29. Hobbes, *Leviathan*, 392 (III, 42).

30. *John* 18:36.

31. Hobbes, *Leviathan, Volume 3*, 922. (Typography lightly modified.)

32. Compare *Matthew* 23:2 and Hobbes, *Leviathan*, 384–5 (III, 41).

33. Hobbes, *Leviathan*, 461–2 (III, 42).

34. *Matthew* 26:53. Note—as Hobbes does not—that the Greek for "legions" (*legiōnas*) in this saying is a loan-word from the Latin. *Matthew*'s Jesus is echoing, here, the military lexicon of Rome.

35. *John* 10:17–18.

36. Hobbes has a highly restrictive definition of Christian martyrdom, which the earliest Christians, on his interpretation, met: Hobbes, *Leviathan*, 396–7 (III, 42).

37. *John* 18:36.

38. Hobbes, *Leviathan*, 382 (III, 41).

39. Hobbes, *Leviathan*, 382–3 (III, 41).

40. M. Lærke, "Leibniz on Church and State: Presumptive Logic and Perplexing Cases", *Journal of the History of Philosophy* 56, 4 (2018), 629–57, here 637–8.

41. Hobbes, *Leviathan*, 385 (III, 41).

42. Hobbes, *Leviathan*, 385 (III, 41).

43. Note the occurrence in Hobbes, *Leviathan*, 384 (III, 41): "Christ while he was on Earth, had no Kingdom in this world."

44. Hobbes, *Leviathan*, 548 (IV, 47).

45. Hobbes, *Leviathan*, 548–51 (IV, 47).

46. Hobbes, *Leviathan*, 392 (III, 42).

47. Hobbes, *Leviathan*, 392 (III, 42).

48. Hobbes, *Leviathan*, 393 (III, 42).

49. Hobbes, *Leviathan*, 393 (III, 42).
50. Hobbes, *Leviathan*, 393 (III, 42).
51. Hobbes, *Leviathan*, 441 (III, 42).
52. Hobbes, *Leviathan*, 460 (III, 42).
53. Hobbes, *Leviathan*, 483 (IV, 44).
54. Hobbes, *Leviathan*, 483 (IV, 44).
55. Hobbes, *Leviathan*, 95 (I, 12).
56. Hobbes, *Leviathan*, 457 (III, 42).
57. Hobbes, *Leviathan*, 547 (IV, 47).
58. Hobbes, *Leviathan*, 460 (III, 42).
59. Hobbes, *Leviathan*, 460 (III, 42).
60. Malcolm, *Aspects of Hobbes*, 200–33; and Agamben, *Stasis*, 19–54.
61. Hobbes, *Leviathan*, 460 (III, 42).
62. Hobbes, *Leviathan*, 553 (IV, 47). For a brilliant reconstruction of how this moment of 'dissolution' is, in Hobbes's mind, a moment of constitution— namely the constitution of a post-Catholic church and state *as a single entity*: J. Olsthoorn, "The Theocratic *Leviathan*: Hobbes's Arguments for the Identity of Church and State", *Hobbes on Politics and Religion*, ed. L. van Apeldoorn and R. Douglass (Oxford, 2018).
63. Hobbes, *Leviathan*, 485 (IV, 44).
64. Hobbes, *Leviathan*, 525 (IV, 45).
65. Hobbes, *Leviathan*, 439 (III, 42).
66. Hobbes, *Leviathan*, 439 (III, 42).
67. Hobbes, *Leviathan*, 439 (III, 42).
68. W. Seston, "Constantine as a 'Bishop'", *The Journal of Roman Studies* 37 (1947), 127–31; C. Rapp, "Imperial Ideology in the Making: Eusebius of Caesarea on Constantine as 'Bishop'", *The Journal of Theological Studies* (NS) 49, 2 (1998), 685–95; K. Smith, *Constantine and the Captive Christians of Persia: Martyrdom and Religious Identity in Late Antiquity* (Oakland, Calif., 2016), 34–7.
69. The persecution of minority cults in Persia, including Christianity, is a Sasanian practice that antedates Constantine, and that claimed the life of the third-century prophet Mani, whose adherents—the Manichaeans—were persecuted by non-Christian Persia and by Christian Rome: Frankopan, *Silk Roads*, 32–5, 39–40. Concise treatments of Constantine's concern for Persia's Christians are T. D. Barnes, "Constantine and the Christians of Persia", *The Journal of Roman Studies* 75 (1985), 126–36, here 130–3; and Frankopan, *Silk Roads*, 42–4. A more comprehensive study is Smith, *Constantine and the Captive Christians of Persia*. Note, too, that "Christian 'refugees' from Iran" remain a factor in fifth-century geopolitics: G. Fisher, *Between Empires: Arabs, Romans, and Sasanians in Late Antiquity* (Oxford, 2011), 32.
70. Hobbes, *Leviathan, Volume 3*, 900. (Typography lightly modified.)
71. OCK. *Imp. Pont.* 27.665–71.

72. Hobbes, *Leviathan, Volume 3*, 900. (Typography lightly modified.)
73. OCK. *Imp. Pont.* 27.672–81.

18. "TRUTH IS NOT SUBJECT TO HUMAN EMPIRE": SAMUEL PUFENDORF AND THE LOGIC OF TOLERANCE

1. S. Pufendorf, *Of the Nature and Qualification of Religion in Reference to Civil Society*, trans. J. Crull, ed. S. Zurbuchen (Indianapolis, 2002), 139: "Mr. Thomas Hobbes, the worst interpreter that ever was in divinity." Here in the translation of Pufendorf's Latin—*Thomas Hobbes, pessimus sententiarum Theologicarum autor*—given in N. Malcolm, *Aspects of Hobbes* (Oxford, 2002), 524.
2. The term is not innocent, and Ian Hunter critiques it. Hunter's concept of a rival "civil enlightenment" led by Pufendorf and Thomasius is convincing: Hunter, *Rival Enlightenments*, 18–19.
3. For a tripartition of the German Enlightenment under the rubrics of (Pufendorf's heir) Christian Thomasius/*Frühaufklärung*, Christian Wolff/*Hochaufklärung*, and Immanuel Kant/*Spätaufklärung*: N. Hinske, "Eklektik, Selbstdenken, Mündigkeit: Drei verschiedene Formulierungen einer und derselben Programmidee", *Aufklärung* 1, 1 (1986), 5–7. But note, again, the critique of this historiographic tradition in Hunter, *Rival Enlightenments*, 15–21.
4. Malcolm, *Aspects of Hobbes*, 524.
5. Comment by Heinrich von Treitschke (died 1896), a voluminous writer and a hard-line member of the Reichstag; cit. F. Palladini, *Samuel Pufendorf Disciple of Hobbes: For a Re-interpretation of Modern Natural Law*, intro. I. Hunter, trans. D. Saunders (Leiden, 2020), 245.
6. M. Cranston, *John Locke: A Biography* (London, 1957), 88–115 (gentleman's physician), 153–9 (trade secretary).
7. J. Locke, *Selected Correspondence*, ed. M. Goldie (Oxford, 2002), 253. (Pufendorf's titles have been translated from Locke's Latin, and the typography lightly modernized.)
8. F. Lezius, *Der Toleranzbegriff Lockes und Pufendorfs: Ein Beitrag zur Geschichte der Gewissensfreiheit* (Leipzig, 1900); and S. Zurbuchen, *Naturrecht und natürliche Religion: Zur Geschichte des Toleranzproblems von Samuel Pufendorf bis Jean-Jacques Rousseau* (Würzburg, 1991).
9. J. Locke, "The Reasonableness of Christianity, as Delivered in the Scriptures", *Writings on Religion*, ed. V. Nuovo (Oxford, 2002), 114–22, 146–52.
10. F. Palladini, *Samuel Pufendorf discepolo di Hobbes: Per una reinterpretazione del giusnaturalismo modern* (Bologna, 1990).
11. Malcolm, *Aspects of Hobbes*, 521.
12. Malcolm, *Aspects of Hobbes*, 521.
13. S. Pufendorf, *An Introduction to the History of the Principal Kingdoms and States*

of Europe, trans. J. Crull, ed. M. J. Seidler (Indianapolis, 2013), 31–2. (Typography lightly modified.)

14. S. Pufendorf, *On the Duty of Man and Citizen according to Natural Law*, ed. J. Tully, trans. M. Silverthorne (Cambridge, 1991), 34. (Translation lightly modified.)

15. Hunter, *Rival Enlightenments*, 148, 171

16. Hunter, *Rival Enlightenments*, 133–6 (on Alberti), 95–8 (on Leibniz), 152–3 (on Pufendorf). And for more on this: I. Hunter, "The Invention of Human Nature: The Intention and Reception of Pufendorf's *Entia moralia* Doctrine", *History of European Ideas* 45, 7 (2019), 933–52. A neglected master-thinker of Platonic–Christian anthropology, who is likely a demonstrable (but, as yet, undemonstrated) influence on figures like Alberti and Leibniz, via pre-Reformation scholasticism and seventeenth-century Protestant scholasticism, is Nemesius of Emesa (died circa 400). His treatise *On Human Nature* (*De natura hominis*) circulated in two Latin versions in the late medieval period, significantly influencing scholastic masters such as William of Conches, Alexander of Hales, Albert the Great, and Thomas Aquinas. During the early modern period, Nemesius' text saw a flurry of Greek, Latin, and vernacular editions. For more on this: D. L. Dusenbury, *Nemesius of Emesa on Human Nature: A Cosmopolitan Anthropology from Roman Syria* (Oxford, 2021).

17. Pufendorf, *Religion in Reference to Civil Society*, 139: "The first inventer of this unlimited power ... was Mr. Thomas Hobbes, the worst interpreter that ever was in divinity."

18. Hobbes, *Leviathan*, 137 (II, 17).

19. Malcolm, *Aspects of Hobbes*, 533–4. (The translation of Pufendorf's title is mine.)

20. Hobbes, *Leviathan*, 553 (IV, 47).

21. Hobbes, *Leviathan*, 95 (I, 12).

22. Hobbes, *Leviathan*, 435 (III, 42).

23. Hobbes, *Leviathan*, 439 (III, 42).

24. Hobbes, *Leviathan*, 392 (III, 42).

25. Hobbes, *Leviathan, Volume 3*, 900. (Typography lightly modified.)

26. Hobbes, *Leviathan*, 391–2 (III, 42).

27. Hobbes, *Leviathan*, 439 (III, 42).

28. Grotius, *Annotationes in Novum Testamentum*, 4:259. (All translations from Grotius' *Annotationes* are mine.)

29. Grotius, *Annotationes in Novum Testamentum*, 4:258.

30. Pufendorf, *Religion in Reference to Civil Society*, 35.

31. Pufendorf, *Religion in Reference to Civil Society*, 35.

32. Pufendorf, *Religion in Reference to Civil Society*, 35–6.

33. Pufendorf, *Religion in Reference to Civil Society*, 36.

34. *John* 18:38.

35. F. Bacon, "Of Truth", *The Essayes or Counsels, Civill and Morall*, ed. with comm. M. Kiernan (Cambridge, Mass., 1985), 7: "*What is Truth*; said jesting *Pilate*; And would not stay for an Answer." Whence the title of A. Huxley, *Jesting Pilate* (London, 1926).

36. Pufendorf, *Religion in Reference to Civil Society*, 12.

37. Pufendorf, *Religion in Reference to Civil Society*, 12.

38. Pufendorf, *Religion in Reference to Civil Society*, 48.

39. Pufendorf, *Religion in Reference to Civil Society*, 47.

40. Pufendorf, *Religion in Reference to Civil Society*, 48.

41. Pufendorf, *Religion in Reference to Civil Society*, 48.

42. For an 'interiorization' of the *forum internum*, so to speak, in early Protestant culture and legal theory—a shift that is reflected in my formulations here: W. Decock, "The Judge's Conscience and the Protection of the Criminal Defendant: Moral Safeguards against Judicial Arbitrariness", *From the Judge's Arbitrium to the Legality Principle: Legislation as a Source of Law in Criminal Trials*, ed. G. Martyn, A. Musson, and H. Pihlajamäki (Berlin, 2013), 79–80.

43. AMBR. *Epist.* 2 (in the Benedictine numbering: to Constantius).

44. *John* 7:24.

45. Pufendorf, *Religion in Reference to Civil Society*, 48.

46. Pufendorf, *Religion in Reference to Civil Society*, 54.

47. Pufendorf, *Religion in Reference to Civil Society*, 58.

48. Pufendorf, *Religion in Reference to Civil Society*, 54.

49. Pufendorf, *Religion in Reference to Civil Society*, 55. Note, in this connection, an ancient tradition that Christians fled to Pella before Jerusalem fell in 70 CE. The tradition is attested by Hegesippus in EUS. *Hist. Eccl.* III 5.3 and EPIPH. *Panar.* 29.7.1–8, 30.2.1–9. It is defended by Bammel, "Revolution Theory from Reimarus to Brandon", 40–1.

50. Pufendorf, *Religion in Reference to Civil Society*, 58.

51. Pufendorf, *Religion in Reference to Civil Society*, 65–6.

52. Pufendorf, *Religion in Reference to Civil Society*, 67–8.

53. Pufendorf, *Religion in Reference to Civil Society*, 59: "that Mystical Body, whose Head is Christ"; 63: "this Mystical Body".

54. Pufendorf, *Religion in Reference to Civil Society*, 59.

55. Pufendorf, *Religion in Reference to Civil Society*, 56–7.

56. Pufendorf, *Religion in Reference to Civil Society*, 34–6.

57. Pufendorf, *De Habitu Religionis Christianae*, 88. (My translation.)

58. Pufendorf, *Religion in Reference to Civil Society*, 65; Pufendorf, *De habitu religionis Christianae*, 95.

59. Fredriksen, *Paul: The Pagans' Apostle*, 55: "Jews referred to their communities by various names: *hieron, proseuchē, politeuma,* collegium, *synodos, koinon, thiasos, ekklēsia, synagōgē.*" (My stress.)

60. Frend, "Prelude to the Great Persecution", 1–2. For the church as a Greco-Roman 'college': Wilken, *Christians as the Romans Saw Them*, 45–7.

61. Pufendorf, *Religion in Reference to Civil Society*, 35.
62. Pufendorf, *Religion in Reference to Civil Society*, 34–5. The Latin and biblical citations are taken from S. Pufendorf, *De habitu religionis Christianae ad vitam civilem, liber singularis: Accedunt animadversiones ad aliqua loca è Politica Adriani Houtuyn* ... (Bremen, 1687), 45–7.
63. Pufendorf, *De habitu religionis Christianae*, 193–4 (My translation.)
64. Pufendorf, *De habitu religionis Christianae*, 82. (My translation.)
65. Hobbes, *Leviathan*, 461 (III, 42).
66. Pufendorf, *Religion in Reference to Civil Society*, 35.
67. Pufendorf, *Religion in Reference to Civil Society*, 105.
68. Pufendorf, *Religion in Reference to Civil Society*, 35.
69. A. Houtuyn, *Politica contracta generalis, notis illustrata* ... *Ad calcem errores Hobbesiani indicantur* (The Hague, 1681). Also of interest in this context is Houtuyn, *Monarchia Hebraeorum, quae est imperio monarchico in populum Hebraeum probatio ab Abrahamo ad dispersam gentem* (Leiden, 1685).
70. Pufendorf, *De habitu religionis Christianae*, 214–15. (My translation.)
71. Hobbes, *Leviathan*, 95 (I, 12).
72. Early Christians made the same argument, even in times of persecution. See, for instance, the opening of Athenagoras' plea (177 CE) to Marcus Aurelius and his son Commodus: ATH. *Leg.* 1.1.
73. Pufendorf, *Religion in Reference to Civil Society*, 35.
74. Pufendorf, *De habitu religionis Christianae*, 214–15. (My translation.)

19. "PILATE DEFENDED": THE NATURE OF JESUS' TRIAL AND THE RISE OF SECULARIZATION

1. The literature is immense, but compare Bremmer, "Secularization: Notes toward a Genealogy", 434. For a different reconstruction: Hunter, *Rival Enlightenments*, 13–14; citing M. Heckel, "Das Säkularisierungsproblem in der Entwicklung des deutschen Staatskirchenrechts", *Christentums und modernes Recht: Beiträge zum Problem der Säkularisation*, ed. G. Dilcher and I. Staff (Frankfurt am Main, 1984); idem, "Religionsbann und landesherrliches Kirchenregiment", *Die lutherische Konfessionalisierung in Deutschland*, ed. H.-C. Rublack (Gütersloh, 1992).
2. S. Pufendorf, *De habitu religionis Christianae ad vitam civilem, liber singularis* (Bremen, 1687), 193; idem, *Of the Nature and Qualification of Religion*, 120.
3. S. Grimm, *De profanatione rei sacrae, Vulgo Secularisirung Geistlicher Güter* (Giessen, 1687), 5.
4. For a more political read of Henry's motives: G. W. Bernard, "The Making of Religious Policy, 1533–1546: Henry VIII and the Search for the Middle Way", *The Historical Journal* 41, 2 (1998), 321–49, here 327–31; idem, "The Dissolution of the Monasteries", *History* 96, 4 (2011), 390–409; and for a more theological read: R. Rex, "The Religion of Henry VIII", *The Historical Journal* 57, 1 (2014), 1–32, here 20–32.

5. This is common in the late-seventeenth-century literature. Consider J. B. Baumgart, *Dissertatio academica, de secularisatione* ... (Helmstedt, 1683), 75(r): "Quod enim Romani dixerunt *profanum* ... et sacro, vel religioso opposuerunt, hoc postmodum à scriptoribus dici coepit *res seculi*, item *seculare*, unde *miles seculi, seculare negotium, res secularis*, et *persona secularis*."

6. J. F. Rhetius, "De secularisatione", *Disputationes juris publici undecim* ... (Frankfurt an der Oder, 1678), 97–8.

7. E. Mauritius, *De secularisatione bonorum ecclesiasticorum ex jure divino et humano praestertim* ... (*Sine loco*: Joachim Reumann, 1666), chapter II, section 1 (no page number): "Alio nomine secularisatio enim vocatur *incorporatio bonorum Ecclesiasticorum*. Verum ambo vocabula, & secularisatio & incorporatio, barbara sunt, & apud elegantioris Latinitatis Scriptores non reperiuntur ..." (My translation.) Compare Grimm, *De profanatione rei sacrae*, 3: "Alias vocatur Alienatio, et crasse Secularisatio sive Incorporatio bonorum ecclesiasticorum."

8. Baumgart, *De secularisatione*, 75(r): "Thesis I. *Secularisationis* vocabulum, quamvis minus latinum, & in jure Romano, ubi de hac materia agitur, non occurrat, id tamen passim usurpari tantum non omnes norunt. Et videtur descendere ex verbo itidem non Romano *Secularisare*, quod idem est ac ex spirituali facere temporale, seu ex Ecclesiastico facere aliquid seculare ..." (My translation.)

9. B. H. Pagendarm, *De bonorum secularisatorum natura* (Halle, 1748), 21–2. That Pagendarm deflects this objection does not lessen its historical—and legal—interest.

10. Mauritius, *De secularisatione bonorum ecclesiasticorum*, chapter II, section 1 (no page number). (My translation.)

11. I stress that this is a legal-theoretical *exemplum*, not a historical scene, which illustrates for us the stakes involved in early modern 'secularization'. This is not Lessius' direct concern in the passage, where he is rather insisting that no one (in Decock's words) "would dare to say ... that those monks must suffer punishment by burning at the stake or quartering, if the judge knew that those monks were innocent": Decock, "Judge's Conscience and the Protection of the Criminal Defendant", 90–1.

12. Mauritius, *De secularisatione bonorum ecclesiasticorum*, chapter II, section 4 (no page number). (My translation.)

13. Pagendarm, *De bonorum secularisatorum natura*, 1. (My translation.)

14. Pagendarm, *De bonorum secularisatorum natura*, 14: "Totam hanc controversiam de potestate magistratus politici circa secularisationem bonorum ecclesiasticorum, non definiendam esse ex Jure Justinianeo vel Canonico." (My free translation.)

15. Pagendarm, *De bonorum secularisatorum natura*, 14: "Totam hanc controversiam de potestate magistratus politici circa secularisationem bonorum ecclesiasticorum, non definiendam esse ex Jure Justinianeo vel Canonico, sed ex solo

jure Naturae et Gentium." (My free translation. I omit "law of peoples" for clarity of exposition—though it is interesting, since Pilate and Jesus do not belong to the same 'peoples'.)

16. C. Thomasius, *De injusto Pontii Pilati judicio* ... (Leipzig, 1675).

17. I. Hunter, "Christian Thomasius and the Desacralization of Philosophy", *Journal of the History of Ideas* 61, 4 (2000), 595–616; idem, *The Secularisation of the Confessional State: The Political Thought of Christian Thomasius* (Cambridge, 2007). Compare K. R. Eskildsen, "How Germany Left the Republic of Letters", *Journal of the History of Ideas* 65, 3 (2004), 421–32, here 422–9.

18. Cit. Hunter, *Rival Enlightenments*, 4. Note that Hunter himself recognizes the historical importance of this legal-theoretical trinity—Grotius, Pufendorf, and Thomasius: Hunter, *Rival Enlightenments*, 14.

19. To cite only one contribution, which, however, belies this: J. Olsthoorn, "Grotius and Pufendorf", *The Cambridge Companion to Natural Law Ethics*, ed. T. Angier (Cambridge, 2019).

20. For "civil enlightenment", and for the curious invisibility of the Grotius–Pufendorf–Thomasius triad in modern historiography: Hunter, *Rival Enlightenments*, 15–21.

21. J. Steller, *Defensum Pontium Pilatum ... Amicorum eruditorum examini exponit Ad 23. Aprilis 1674* (Dresden, 1674).

22. J. Steller, *Pilatus defensus*, in *Johannis Stelleri, J. U. Doctoris Jenensis Pilatus defensus unà cum Danielis Maphanasi Mulchentinensis confutatione scripti illius et disputatione academica Christiani: Thomasii Ph M adversus idem paradoxon* (Leipzig, 1676).

23. C. Thomasius, *Injustum judicium Pontii Pilati*, in *Johannis Stelleri, J. U. Doctoris Jenensis Pilatus defensus unà cum Danielis Maphanasi Mulchentinensis confutatione scripti illius et disputatione academica Christiani: Thomasii Ph M adversus idem paradoxon* (Leipzig, 1676), preface (no page).

24. For 'doctorandus': Steller, *Defensum Pontium Pilatum*, title page; and Thomasius, *Injustum judicium Pontii Pilati*, preface (no page).

25. Steller, *Pilatus defensus*, preliminaria 1 (no page): "exemplar judicis injustissimi". (My free translation.)

26. Steller, *Pilatus defensus*, chapter 2, paragraph 1 (no page).

27. Thomasius, *Injustum judicium Pontii Pilati*, preface (no page).

28. Steller, *Defensum Pontium Pilatum*, title page. Confirmed by Thomasius, *Injustum judicium Pontii Pilati*, preface (no page).

29. Zola also mentions the critiques of *Pilate Defended* by Hartnaccius (aka Maphanasus) and Thomasius ("men of the same sect", namely Lutherans). See J. Zola, *Commentariorum de rebus Christianis ante Const. Magnum: Liber I* (Pavia, 1793), 236–9, here 236: "erat enim Stellerus Lutheranus".

30. Steller, *Pilatus defensus*, chapter 1, paragraphs 72–3 (no page): "innocentiam et defensionem Pontii Pilati". (My translation. Elided for clarity. Note that Steller is citing Lactantius—with whom he concurs.)

31. G. E. Lessing, *Rettung des* Inepti Religiosi, *und seines ungenanten Berfassers*, in *Vermischte Schriften: Dritte Theil* (Berlin, 1784), 185: "gingen meine Gedanken auf den Johann Steller, welcher sich durch die Vertheidigung des Pilatus berüchtigt hat".

32. Reimarus, *Goal of Jesus and His Disciples*; U. Groetsch, *Hermann Samuel Reimarus (1694–1768): Classicist, Hebraist, Enlightenment Radical in Disguise* (Leiden, 2015).

33. LACT. *Inst. Div.* V 3. On this piece of *antichristiana* (as Horbury calls it): Horbury, "Christ as Brigand", 188–95.

34. For more on the rise of Jesus as "impostor": M. Benitez, "La diffusion du *Traité des trois imposteurs* au XVIIIe siècle", *Revue d'histoire moderne et contemporaine* 40, 1 (1993), 137–51.

35. I have in mind, here: Kalthoff, *Das Christus-Problem*; K. Kautsky, *Foundations of Christianity*, trans. H. F. Mins (New York, 1908); Bloch, *Atheism in Christianity*.

36. H. Kelsen, *Die Staatslehre des Dante Alighieri* (Vienna, 1905); M. Cau, "To the Roots of the Universal Juridical Order: Hans Kelsen and the *Staatslehre* of Dante Alighieri", *Hans Kelsen and the Natural Law Tradition*, ed. P. Langford, I. Bryan, and J. McGarry (Leiden, 2019); O. Lepsius, "Hans Kelsen on Dante Alighieri's Political Philosophy", *The European Journal of International Law* 27, 4 (2016), 1153–67.

37. Note, though, that Kelsen calls the Barabbas incident a 'plebiscite'—which might imply that Pilate (*pace* Steller) is not legally bound to enforce it: H. Kelsen, "Absolutism and Relativism in Philosophy and Politics", *The American Political Science Review* 42, 5 (1948), 906–14, here 915; Kelsen, "Foundations of Democracy", *Ethics: An International Journal of Social, Legal, and Political Philosophy* 66, 1 (1955), 1–101, here 39. And more recently, in Kelsen's wake, there is a learned essay by an Italian high-court justice, Gustavo Zagrebelsky, in which the 'democratic' choice to free Barabbas and crucify Jesus is thematized: G. Zagrebelsky, *Il "Crucifige!" e la democrazia* (Turin, 2007). I wish to thank Dante Fedele for bringing this essay to my notice.

38. Elite control of this lynch mob is explicit in *Mark* 15:11 and *Matthew* 27:20, and subtly observed in *John* 19:6. It is somewhat blurred in *Luke* 23:13–18.

39. *Matthew* 27:15; *Mark* 15:6; *Luke* 23:17 (a poorly attested verse); *John* 18:39.

40. Steller, *Pilatus defensus*, chapter 3, paragraph 1 (no page): "Et quidem quod Jesum, qui omnino de peccato nullo vere accusari poterat, ad mortem condemnaverit."

41. Steller, *Pilatus defensus*, chapter 3, paragraph 14 (no page).

42. *Matthew* 27:19.

43. Steller, *Pilatus defensus*, chapter 3, paragraph 14 (no page): "Nos adfirmamus judicem adstrictum esse ad judicandum secundum allegata et probata." For notes on the history of the hard question of whether a court's evidence or a judge's conscience must determine the verdict—a question that, as Wim

Decock writes, is "already present in the *Noctes Atticae* of the second century Roman polymath Aulus Gellius": Decock, "Judge's Conscience and the Protection of the Criminal", 80–6.

44. Steller, *Pilatus defensus*, chapter 1, paragraph 84 (no page).

45. Steller, *Pilatus defensus*, chapter 1, paragraphs 66–8, 82–3 (no pages).

46. LACT. *Div. Inst.* IV 18.6. Note that Steller, unlike Lactantius, concedes that Romans crucified Jesus: Steller, *Pilatus defensus*, chapter 3, paragraphs 72–3, 91 (no pages).

47. Steller, *Pilatus defensus*, chapter 1, paragraphs 72–3 (no page): "innocentiam et defensionem Pontii Pilati". (My translation. Elided for clarity.) A further citation of Lactantius is *Pilatus defensus*, chapter 3, paragraph 54 (no page).

48. Steller, *Pilatus defensus*, chapter 1, paragraph 74 (no page). For context: R. Hennings, "Eusebius von Emesa und die Juden", *Zeitschrift für Antikes Christentum* 5 (2001), 240–60.

49. Steller, *Pilatus defensus*, chapter 3, paragraph 54 (no page).

50. Steller, *Pilatus defensus*, chapter 1, paragraph 75 (no page).

51. Steller, *Pilatus defensus*, chapter 3, paragraph 3 (no page). Steller's contents make it clear that there is a later reference to Cyprian (*sine nomine*) at *Pilatus defensus*, chapter 3, paragraph 58 (no page).

52. Steller, *Pilatus defensus*, chapter 3, paragraph 53 (no page).

53. Steller, *Pilatus defensus*, chapter 3, paragraph 57 (no page).

54. D. Hartnaccius (pseudonym: "Daniel Maphanasus"), *Confutationis Pontii Pilati defensi*, in *Johannis Stelleri, J. U. Doctoris Jenensis Pilatus defensus unà cum Danielis Maphanasi Mulchentinensis confutatione scripti illius et disputatione academica Christiani. Thomasii Ph M adversus idem paradoxon* (Leipzig, 1676).

55. D. Hartnaccius, *Admiranda physica, sive observationes singulares ... quas curiossi-simi in universa penè Europa naturae scrutatores, summa non minus diligentia, quàm judicio singulari annotarunt: Ita digestae, ut ad Celeberrimi Joh. Sperlingii synopsisi quasi commentarii sint perpetui ...* (Leipzig, 1683).

56. Hartnaccius, *Admiranda physica, sive observationes singulares*, 81.

57. D. Hartnaccius, *Johannis Micraelii syntagma historiarum ecclesiae omnium ... ut beneficio Indicis locupletissimi, tabularumque chronologicarum instar lexici historiae ecclesiasticae esse possit* (Leipzig, 1679).

58. Hartnaccius, *Syntagma historiarum ecclesiae omnium*, 1030–2.

59. Hartnaccius, *Syntagma historiarum ecclesiae omnium*, 1254–6, here 1254.

60. Interestingly, this is not a reference to the passion, but to Pilate's slaughter of Galileans in *Luke* 13:1: Hartnaccius, *Syntagma historiarum ecclesiae omnium*, 130.

61. Hartnaccius, *Syntagma historiarum ecclesiae omnium*, 594.

62. Hartnaccius, *Syntagma historiarum ecclesiae omnium*, 266: "*tyrranide* sub Pilato Dominus pro salute generis humani crucifixus est". (Original italics.)

63. Hartnaccius, *Syntagma historiarum ecclesiae omnium*, 215: "et ad mortem à Pilato condemnatus".

64. Hartnaccius, *Syntagma historiarum ecclesiae omnium*, 274–5: "plebem in odium Christiani nominis animavit: acta Pilati et Servatoris, blasphemiae plena, per sacrificulos confingi, et juventuti inculcari curavit".

65. Hartnaccius, *Syntagma historiarum ecclesiae omnium*, 226: "cum eum de regno Christi, omnia mundana respuente, erudiissent, tyrannum à persecutione Christianorum avocasse animum".

66. Though this is not the 'duplicity' (*duplici via*) in the title of chapter 20, which refers to Pilate's failings by virtue of decisions he should have made (*ferenda*), or has made (*lata*).

67. LACT. *Div. Inst.* IV 18,6.

68. Hartnaccius, *Confutationis Pontii Pilati defensi*, chapter 20 (no pages).

69. It should be noted that Christoph Paulus is seeking to revive Steller's hypothesis: C. G. Paulus, *Der Prozess Jesu: Aus römisch-rechtlicher Perspektive* (Berlin, 2016), 35–6.

70. C. Thomasius, *De injusto Pontii Pilati judicio* ... (Leipzig, 1675).

71. P. Schröder, "Thomas Hobbes, Christian Thomasius, and the Seventeenth Century Debate on the Church and State", *History of European Ideas* 23 (1997), 59–79.

72. Hunter, *Secularisation of the Confessional State*; Hunter, "Thomasius and the Desacralization of Philosophy".

73. Pagendarm, *De bonorum secularisatorum natura*, 14. (My free translation.)

74. Compare AUG. *Tract.* 112.2; Thomasius, *Injustum judicium Pontii Pilati*, part 1, paragraph 7 (no pages).

75. Thomasius, *Injustum judicium Pontii Pilati*, part 1, paragraph 14 (no pages).

76. C. Thomasius, "The Right of a Christian Prince in Religious Matters", *Essays on Church, State, and Politics*, ed. and trans. I. Hunter, T. Ahnert, and F. Grunert (Indianapolis, 2007). (My italics.)

77. Thomasius, *Injustum judicium Pontii Pilati*, part 2, paragraph 23 (no pages): "An Pilatus in judicando Christo justè egerit, officiumque boni judicis impleverit? Negatur ... in quo peccaverit Pilatus & officium judicis (quod tamen non juxta Jus Civile Justinianeum, quatenus tale, vel etiam Canonicum, utpote quae tunc non fuerunt, sed juxta Legem naturae metiendum) ..." (My free translation; my italics.)

78. Thomasius, *Injustum judicium Pontii Pilati*, part 2, paragraphs 34–40 (no pages).

79. Thomasius, *Injustum judicium Pontii Pilati*, part 2, paragraph 46 (no page).

80. GRAT. *Dec.* 1.1.1–7; JUSTIN. *Inst.* 2.1–11. Early modern receptions and re-conceptions of Roman civil and canon-legal theories of natural law are, of course, various and immensely complex.

81. For more on Thomasius' interpretation of nature: T. Ahnert, *Religion and the Origins of the German Enlightenment: Faith and the Reform of Learning in the Thought of Christian Thomasius* (Rochester, N.Y., 2006), 107–20.

82. It would be fascinating to compare the Pilate trial in two seventeenth- and

eighteenth-century legal-theoretical corpora—namely "the 'civil' natural law [corpus] of Grotius, Hobbes, Pufendorf, and Thomasius; and the 'Christian' natural law [corpus] of Althusius, Alberti, Prasch, Veltheim, Placcius, Rachel, and, most famously (retrospectively), Leibniz, who attacked the civil philosophers from the high ground of Protestant scholasticism": Hunter, *Rival Enlightenments*, 27–8. It is only writers of the first corpus who are touched on in this book.

83. For the revolutionary 'cult of nature' in late-eighteenth-century France: D. Edelstein, *The Terror of Natural Right: Republicanism, the Cult of Nature, and the French Revolution* (Chicago, 2009). 'Neo-pagan' is suggested, here, by the Jacobins' reception of Rousseau's *Social Contract*—which valorizes the 'pagan' (or quasi-Islamic) political theology of Hobbes's *Leviathan*. There is inevitably an echo, too, of P. Gay, *The Enlightenment: An Interpretation; The Rise of Modern Paganism* (New York, 1966), 9–10.

EPILOGUE: THE UNFINISHED HISTORY OF PILATE AND JESUS

1. J.-J. Rousseau, *Du contrat social*, ed. with intro. and annot. R. Grimsley (Oxford, 1972), 97: "J. J. Rousseau Citoyen de Genève."

2. Rousseau, *Contrat social*, 102 (*ce petit traité*), and 102 note 2 (*un petit ouvrage*).

3. I take the number of editions from G. H. McNeil, "The Cult of Rousseau and the French Revolution", *Journal of the History of Ideas* 6, 2 (1945), 197–212, here 202; and from G. Garrard, *Rousseau's Counter-Enlightenment: A Republican Critique of the Philosophes* (Albany, 2003), 36. Compare J. Swenson, *On Jean-Jacques Rousseau: Considered as One of the First Authors of the Revolution* (Stanford, 2000), 159–226, here 170.

4. I only graze questions in this epilogue, and gesture towards histories, that have vast and rich literatures. One text that comes to mind, here, is M. Gauchet, *La révolution des droits de l'homme* (Paris, 1989).

5. *Luke* 23:34; Louis Capet, "The Last Will of Louis XVI", *Judgment and Execution of Louis XVI: King of France*, ed. and trans. H. Goudemetz (Sine loco, sine anno), 236, 238. Compare J. Hardman, *Louis XVI* (New Haven, 1993), 230–2.

6. *England's Black Tribunal Containing, I. The Complete Tryal of King Charles the First, by the Pretended High Court of Justice in Westminster-Hall ... Together with His Majesty's Speech on the Scaffold...* (London, 1747), 53 (Charles Stuart), 65 (last words).

7. One masterful contribution, however, is S. Dunn, *The Deaths of Louis XVI: Regicide and the French Political Imagination* (Princeton, 1994).

8. Rousseau knew Thomasius' ideas, though perhaps only by way of the oeuvre of a Genevan jurist, Jean-Jacques Burlamaqui (died 1748). By intent, "post-Protestant" means many things, here—many of them vague—beginning, and only beginning, with Rousseau's youthful conversion to Catholicism.

9. Some of Voltaire's livid marginal notes on this chapter are included in Ronald Grimsley's edition: Rousseau, *Contrat social*, 221–32.

10. Letter to Frederick II dated 3 January 1767: F.-M. d'Arouet, *Œuvres complètes de Voltaire avec des notes ... tome dixième* (Paris, 1869), 281.

11. D. L. Dusenbury, "Red Cells and Grey", *TLS: The Times Literary Supplement* (3 October 2014), 32.

12. I stress that this is a *sketch*. A close reading of Rousseau's "Of Civil Religion" will bear out how many nuances, and shifts in argumentation, cannot be dealt with here.

13. Rousseau, *Social Contract*, 144, 147–8; idem, *Contrat social*, 223, 227–8. (Here and hereafter, translation modified.)

14. Rousseau, *Social Contract*, 148–9; idem, *Contrat social*, 228–9.

15. Rousseau, *Social Contract*, 149; idem, *Contrat social*, 229.

16. Nietzsche, *Anti-Christ, Ecce Homo, Twilight of the Idols*, 50; idem, *Der Fall Wagner*, 230: *nicht 'national', nicht rassebedingt.*

17. G. Bataille, *The Accursed Share: Volume I*, trans. R. Hurley (New York, 1991), 93.

18. Rousseau, *Social Contract*, 143; idem, *Contrat social*, 222.

19. A. Watson, *International Law in Archaic Rome: War and Religion* (Baltimore, 1993).

20. Rousseau, *Social Contract*, 143–5; idem, *Contrat social*, 222–4.

21. Rousseau, *Social Contract*, 146–7; idem, *Contrat social*, 226.

22. GEL. I *Epist.* 12.2; Neil and Allen, *Letters of Gelasius I*, 74. (Translation modified.)

23. Rousseau, *Social Contract*, 146; idem, *Contrat social*, 225.

24. Rousseau, *Social Contract*, 43; idem, *Contrat social*, 106.

25. Rousseau, *Social Contract*, 144; idem, *Contrat social*, 223.

26. Rousseau, *Social Contract*, 145; idem, *Contrat social*, 224.

27. Rousseau, *Social Contract*, 148; idem, *Contrat social*, 228.

28. AUG. *Tract.* 115.2: *quid vultis amplius?*

29. W. Blake, *Blake's Poetry and Designs*, ed. M. L. Johnson and J. E. Grant (New York, 1979), 184. For the theologico-political dimension of Blake's contempt for both men, see his Christian-Jacobin lines, here cited by Bloch, *Atheism in Christianity*, 110: "The spirit of turmoil shot down from the Saviour, And in the vineyards of red France appear'd the light of his fury."

30. Rousseau, *Social Contract*, 144; idem, *Contrat social*, 223.

31. Rousseau, *Social Contract*, 145; idem, *Contrat social*, 224.

32. Arouet, *Œuvres complètes de Voltaire*, 281.

33. P. Veyne, "The Inventory of Differences", *Economy and Society* 11, no. 2 (1982), 173–98.

34. Rousseau, *Social Contract*, 144; idem, *Contrat social*, 223.

35. PL. *Resp.* IX 592b.

36. I owe this reference to F. Oakley, *Kingship: The Politics of Enchantment* (Oxford, 2006), 60–1.

37. N. D. Fustel de Coulanges, *The Ancient City: A Study on the Religion, Laws, and Institutions of Greece and Rome* (Baltimore, 1980), 381. His last chapter is titled, "Christianity Changes the Conditions of Government".

38. Fustel de Coulanges, *Ancient City*, 385. (Translation modified.)

SELECT BIBLIOGRAPHY

Premodern works (before 1600)

ABB. *Taf.*   Pseudo-Ibn 'Abbas. *Tafsīr Ibn 'Abbas.* Trans. M. Guezzou. Amman, 2008.

Acta Pil.   (I)   *Evangelia apocrypha, adhibitis plurimis codicibus Graecis et Latinis maximam partem nunc primum consultis* ... Ed. C. de Tischendorf. Leipzig: Hermann Mendelssohn, 1876.

                         (II) *The Apocryphal New Testament: A Collection of Apocryphal Christian Literature in an English Translation.* Ed. and trans. J. K. Elliott. Oxford, 1993.

AGO. *Jud. Sup.*   Agobard of Lyon. *De Judaicis Superstitionibus.* (Patrologia Latina 104.) Ed. J.-P. Migne. Paris, 1865.

Alc. Lat.   *Machumetis Saracenorum principis* ... *Alcoran, quo velut authentico legum divinarum codice Agareni et Turcae* ... Ed. T. Bibliander. Basel (Basilea): Johannes Oporinus, 1543.

AMBR. *Epist.*   Ambrose of Milan. *Letters.* Trans. M. M. Beyenka. Washington, D.C., 1954.

AMBR. *Fug. Saec.*   Ambrose of Milan. *Seven Exegetical Works.* Trans. M. P. McHugh. Washington, D.C., 1971.

AMM. *Rer. Gest.*   Ammianus Marcellinus. *Ammianus Marcellinus, Volume I.* Latin with trans. J. C. Rolfe. London, 1950.

AQUIN. *Summ. Theol.* (I)   Thomas Aquinas. *Summa Theologiae*, Volume 28 (1a2ae. 90–97). Latin with trans. and annot. T. Gilby. Cambridge, 2006.

347

(II) *Summa Theologiae*, Volume 29 (1a2ae. 98–105). Latin with trans. and annot. D. Bourke. Cambridge, 2006.

(III) *Summa Theologiae*, Volume 30 (1a2ae. 106–114). Latin with trans. and annot. E. Cornelius. Cambridge, 2006.

ARIST. *Apol. Gr.* Aristides. *Apologie.* Ed., trans., and comm. B. Pouderon and M.-J. Pierre, with B. Outtier, and M. Guiorgadzé. Paris, 2003.

ARIST. *Apol. Syr.* Ibid.

ATH. *Leg.* (I) Athenagoras of Athens. *Legatio and De resurrectione.* Greek with trans. W. R. Schroedel. Oxford, 1972.

(II) *Legatio pro Christianis.* Ed. M. Marcovich. Berlin, 1990.

AUG. *Conf.* (I) Augustine of Hippo. *Confessions, I: Introduction and Text.* Ed. J. J. O'Donnell. Oxford, 1992.

(II) *Confessions.* Trans. and annot. H. Chadwick. Oxford, 1991.

AUG. *Civ. Dei* (I) Augustine of Hippo. *La cité de Dieu.* Ed. B. Dombart and A. Kalb. Trans. G. Combès. Annot. G. Bardy. Paris, 1959–1960. 5 vols.

(II) *The City of God against the Pagans.* Ed. and trans. R. W. Dyson. Cambridge, 1998.

AUG. *Cons. Ev.* (I) Augustine of Hippo. *De Consensu Evangelistarum.* Ed. and comm. F. Weihrich. Leipzig, 1904.

(II) *Harmony Of The Gospels.* Ed. P. Schaff. New York, 1887 (reprinted 1974).

AUG. *Enar. Ps.* (I) Augustine of Hippo. *Enarrationes in Psalmos.* (Patrologia Latina 36.) Ed. J.-P. Migne. Paris, 1861.

(II) Augustine. *Expositions on the Book of Psalms.* Ed. A. C. Coxe. Edinburgh, 1888 (reprinted 1974).

AUG. *Epist.* (I) *Epistulae LVI–C.* Ed. Kl. D. Daur. Turnhout, 2005.

(II) *The Confessions and Letters of St. Augustin.* Ed. P. Schaff. New York, 1888.

AUG. *Retract.* Augustine of Hippo. *Retractationum libri II.* Ed. A. Mutzenbecher. Turnhout, 1984.

SELECT BIBLIOGRAPHY

AUG. *Serm.*   Augustine of Hippo. *Sermones in Epistolas Apostolicas II.* Ed. S. Boodts, F. Dolbeau, G. Partoens, et al. Turnhout, 2016.

AUG. *Tract.*   (I)   *In Iohannis Evangelium tractatus CXXIV.* Ed. R. Willems. Turnhout, 1954.
(II)   *In Joannis Evangelium tractatus LXXIV.* (Patrologia Latina 35.) Ed. J.-P. Migne. Paris, 1902.
(III)   *Homilies on the Gospel of John.* Trans. J. Gibb and J. Innes. Ed. P. Schaff. New York, 1888.

BEN. IMOLA *Com.*   Benvenuto da Imola. *Comentum super Dantis Aldigherij Comoediam* ... Ed. W. W. Vernon and J. P. Lacaita. Florence, 1887. Archived online by Dartmouth College.

BOCC. *Exp.*   Giovanni Boccaccio. *Esposizioni sopra la Comedia di Dante.* Ed. G. Padoan. Milan, 1965. Archived online by Dartmouth College.

CAES. AREL. *Serm.*   Caesarius of Arles. *Sermons, Volume II (81–186).* Trans. M. M. Mueller. Washington, D.C., 1964.

CHRY. *Adv. Iud.*   (I)   John Chrysostom. *Adversus Judaeos orationes.* (Patrologia Graeca 48.) Ed. J.-P. Migne. Paris, 1862.
(II)   *Discourses against Judaizing Christians.* Trans. P. W. Harkins. Washington, D.C., 1979.

CIC. *Nat. Deor.*   Cicero. *De natura deorum; Academica.* Latin with trans. H. Rackham. London, 1933.

Clem.   *I Clement.* In: *The Apostolic Fathers.* Greek with trans. K. Lake. 2 vols. London, 1912.

CUS. *Crib. Alk.*   Nicholas of Cusa. *De pace fidei and Cribratio Alkorani: Translation and Analysis.* Trans. and annot. J. Hopkins. Minneapolis, 1994.

CUS. *Pac. Fid.*   Ibid.

DAM. *Adv. Haer.*   John of Damascus. *Écrits sur l'Islam.* Greek with French trans. and comm. R. Le Coz. Paris, 1992.

DAM. *Bar. Ioas.*   John of Damascus. *Barlaam and Ioasaph.* Greek with trans. G. R. Woodward and H. Mattingly. Cambridge, Mass., 1914.

DAN. *Inf.*   (I)   Dante Alighieri. *La Divina Commedia: Vol. I; Inferno.* Ed. N. Sapegno. Florence, 1980.

349

SELECT BIBLIOGRAPHY

	(II) *The Inferno of Dante: A New Verse Translation*. Italian with trans. R. Pinsky. Annot. N. Pinsky. New York, 1994.
DAN. *Mon.*	(I) Dante Alighieri. *Monarchia*. Ed. P. Chiesa and A. Tabarroni with D. Ellero. Rome, 2013.
	(II) *Monarchy*. Ed. and trans. P. Shaw. Cambridge, 1996.
	(III) *Dante's Monarchia*. Trans. and comm. R. Kay. Toronto, 1998.
DAN. *Para.*	Dante Alighieri. *The Divine Comedy: Paradiso, vol. 1; Italian Text and Translation*. Trans. and comm. C. S. Singleton. Princeton, 1975.
DAN. *Purg.*	Dante Alighieri. *Purgatorio: A New Verse Translation*. Italian with trans. W. S. Merwin. New York, 2000.
Did. Apost.	*Didascalia Apostolorum: The Syriac Version Translated and Accompanied by the Verona Latin Fragments*. Ed. and trans. R. H. Connolly. Oxford, 1929.
DIM. *Jaw.*	*Muslim–Christian Polemic during the Crusades: The Letter from the People of Cyprus and Ibn Abī Tālib al-Dimashqī's Response*. Arabic with trans. R. Ebied and D. Thomas. Leiden, 2005.
DIO CASS. *Hist. Rom.*	Dio Cassius. *Roman History*. Greek with trans. E. Cary. 9 vols. London, 1917.
DIO. LAER. *Vit. Phil.*	Diogenes Laertius. *Lives of Eminent Philosophers*. Greek with trans. R. D. Hicks. 2 vols. London, 1925.
EPIC. *Enchir.*	Epictetus. *The Discourses as Reported by Arrian, the Manual, and Fragments*. Greek with trans. W. A. Oldfather. 2 vols. London, 1925.
Epic. *Christ.*	*Commentaire sur la Paraphrase Chrétienne du Manuel d'Épictète*. Greek with French trans., ed. and comm. M. Spanneut. Paris, 2007.
EPIPH. *Panar.*	Epiphanius of Salamis. *Ancoratus und Panarion, Erster Band: Ancoratus und Panarion Haer. 1–33*. Ed. K. Holl. Leipzig, 1915.
Epist. *Mar.*	"The Epistle of Mara, Son of Serapion" (*sic*). *Spicilegium Syriacum: Containing Remains of Bardesan, Meliton, Ambrose, and Mara bar Serapion*. Ed. Syriac with English trans. and notes W. Cureton. London, 1855.

SELECT BIBLIOGRAPHY

EUS. *C. Hier.*   Eusebius of Caesarea. *Reply to Hierocles.* In: Philostratus, *The Life of Apollonius of Tyana.* Greek with trans. C. P. Jones. Vol. 3. Cambridge, Mass., 2006.

EUS. *Dem. Ev.*   Eusebius of Caesarea. *The Proof of the Gospel.* Ed. and trans. W. J. Ferrar. London, 1920 (reprinted 2001).

EUS. *Hist. Eccl.*   (I) Eusebius of Caesarea. *The Ecclesiastical History.* Greek with trans. K. Lake. 2 vols. Cambridge, Mass., 1926.
(II) *The Ecclesiastical History, Volume II.* Ed. J. E. L. Oulton and H. J. Lawlor. Greek with trans. J. E. L. Oulton. Cambridge, Mass., 1932.

Ev. Petr.   "The Gospel of Peter." *The Apocryphal New Testament: A Collection of Apocryphal Christian Literature in an English Translation.* Ed. and trans. J. K. Elliott. Oxford, 1993.

GEL. I *Epist.*   (I) Gelasius I. *Epistolae et Decreta.* (Patrologia Latina 59.) Ed. J.-P. Migne. Paris, 1862.
(II) *The Letters of Gelasius I (492–496): Pastor and Micro-Manager of the Church of Rome.* Ed., trans., and annot. B. Neil and P. Allen. Turnhout, 2014.

GEL. I *Tom.*   Gelasius I. *Tomus de Anathematis vinculo.* (Patrologia Latina 59.) Ed. J.-P. Migne. Paris, 1862.

GRAT. *Dec.*   (I) Gratian. *Decretum Gratiani ... post Justi Henningii Boehmeri.* (Patrologia Latina 187.) Ed. J.-P. Migne. Paris, 1861.
(II) *The Treatise on Laws (Decretum DD. 1–20), with the Ordinary Gloss.* Trans. A. Thompson and J. Gordley. Washington, D.C., 1993.

HER. *Frag.*   *The Art and Thought of Heraclitus: An Edition of the Fragments with Translation and Commentary.* Greek with trans. and comm. C. H. Kahn. Cambridge, 1979.

Hist. Aug.   *The Scriptores historiae Augustae.* Latin with English trans. D. Magie. Cambridge, Mass., 1960

HON. *Lum. Eccl.*   Honorius of Autun. *De luminaribus ecclesiae sive de scriptoribus ecclesiasticis libelli quatuor.* (Patrologia Latina 172.) Ed. J.-P. Migne. Paris, 1895.

IGN. *Ep. Mag.*   "Ignatius to the Magnesians." In: *The Apostolic Fathers.* Greek with trans. K. Lake. 2 vols. London, 1912.

IGN. *Ep. Smyr.*   "Ignatius to the Smyrnaeans." In: *The Apostolic Fathers.* Greek with trans. K. Lake. 2 vols. London, 1912.

INN. III, *Reg.* Innocent III. *Regesta sive Epistolae.* (Patrologia Latina 214.) Ed. J.-P. Migne. Paris, 1855.

IREN. *Adv. Haer.* (I) Irenaeus of Lyon. *Contre les hérésies: Livre I.* Latin with French trans. A. Rousseau and L. Doutreleau. Paris, 1979.

(II) *Irenaeus against Heresies.* In: *The Apostolic Fathers with Justin Martyr and Irenaeus.* Ed. A. C. Coxe. Edinburgh, 1884 (reprinted 1996).

IREN. *Dem. Apost.* (I) Irenaeus of Lyon. *Démonstration de la prédication apostolique.* Latin with French trans. A. Rousseau. Paris, 1995.

(II) *Proof of the Apostolic Preaching.* Trans. and annot. J. N. D. Kelly. London, 1955.

ISID. *Etym.* *The Etymologies of Isidore of Seville.* Trans. S. A. Barney, W. J. Lewis, J. A. Beach, and O. Berghof, with M. Hall. Cambridge, 2006.

JABB. *Tathb.* 'Abd Al-Jabbār. *Critique of Christian Origins.* Ed. and trans. G. S. Reynolds and S. K. Samir. Provo, Utah, 2010.

JAC. AL. *Comm.* Jacopo Alighieri. *Chiose alla Cantica dell'Inferno di Dante Alighieri scritte da Jacopo Alighieri* ... Ed. G. Piccini. Florence, 1915. Archived online by Dartmouth College.

JAL. *Taf.* Jalāl al Mahalli and Jalāl al Suyūtī. *Tafsīr al-Jalālayn.* Trans. F. Hamza. Amman, 2008.

JOS. *Ant. Jud.* Flavius Josephus. *Jewish Antiquities.* Greek with trans. H. St. J. Thackeray, R. Marcus, A. Wikgren, and L. Feldman. 6 vols. Cambridge, Mass., 1957–65.

JOS. *Bell. Jud.* Flavius Josephus. *The Jewish War.* Greek with trans. H. St. J. Thackeray. 2 vols. Cambridge, Mass., 1927–8.

JOS. *Vita* Flavius Josephus. *Life of Josephus.* Trans. with comm. S. Mason. Boston–Leiden, 2003.

JOS. SLAV. *Bell. Jud.* *Josephus' Jewish War and Its Slavonic Version: A Synoptic Comparison of the English Translation by H. St. J. Thackeray with the Critical Edition by N. A. Meščerskij of the Slavonic Version in the Vilna Manuscript* ... Ed. and trans. H. Leeming and K. Leeming. Leiden, 2003.

JUST. *Apol. I* (I) Justin the Philosopher. *Apologie pour les chrétiens.*

Greek with trans. and annot. C. Munier. Paris, 2006.

(II) *The First Apology*. In: *Saint Justin Martyr*. Trans. T. Falls. Washington, D.C., 1948 (reprinted 1977).

JUSTIN, *Dig.* *The Digest of Justinian*. Ed. T. Mommsen with P. Krueger. Trans. A. Watson. 4 vols. Philadelphia, 1985.

JUSTIN. *Inst.* (I) Justinian I. *Imperatoris Iustiniani Institutionum libri quattuor*. Latin with intro. and annot. J. B. Moyle. Oxford, 1883 (reprinted 1964).

(II) *The Institutes of Justinian*. Latin with trans. and annot. T. C. Sandars. London, 1922 (reprinted 1970).

(III) *Justinian's* Institutes *with the Latin Text of Paul Krueger*. Trans. P. Birks and G. McLeod. London, 2001.

LACT. *Div. Inst.* (I) Firmianus Lactantius. *Institutions Divines. Livre 4.* Ed. and annot. Pierre Monat. Paris, 1992.

(II) *Divine Institutes*. Trans. A. Bowen and P. Garnsey. Liverpool, 2003.

(III) *The Divine Institutes, Books I–VII*. Trans. M. F. McDonald. Washington, D.C., 1964.

LACT. *Mort. Pers.* (I) Firmianus Lactantius. *Liber de Mortibus persecuto-rum*. (Patrologia Latina 7.) Ed. J.-P. Migne. Paris, 1844.

(II) *The Deaths of the Persecutors*. In: *The Minor Works*. Trans. M. F. McDonald. Washington, D.C., 1965.

LAND. *Com.* Cristoforo Landino. *Comento sopra la Comedia*. Florence, 1481. Archived online by Dartmouth College.

Leg. Aur. Jacobus de Voragine. *The Golden Legend: Readings on the Saints*. Trans. W. G. Ryan. Princeton, 2012.

LUC. *Mort. Per.* *Lucian V*. Greek with trans. A. M. Harmon. London, 1936.

MAC. *Apoc.* Macarius of Magnesia. *Apocriticus*. Trans. J. M. Schott and M. J. Edwards. Liverpool, 2015.

MAIM. *Mish. Tor.* Maimonides. *The Code of Maimonides, Book Fourteen: The Book of Judges*. Trans. A. M. Hershman. New Haven, 1977.

SELECT BIBLIOGRAPHY

MARA. *Exp.*

Guglielmo Maramauro. *Expositione sopra l'"Inferno" di Dante Alighieri.* Ed. G. Pisoni and S. Bellomo. Padua, 1998. Archived online by Dartmouth College.

MARS. PAD. *Def. Min.*

(I) Marsilius of Padua. *Œuvres mineures. Defensor Minor. De Translatione Imperii.* Ed., trans. and annot. C. Jeudy and J. Quillet. Paris, 1979.

(II) *Writings on the Empire: Defensor minor and De translatione imperii.* Ed. C. J. Nederman. Cambridge, 1993.

MARS. PAD. *Def. Pac.*

(I) Marsilius of Padua. *Defensor pacis.* Ed. R. Scholz. Hannover, 1932.

(II) *Le défenseur de la paix.* French trans. and annot. J. Quillet. Paris, 1968.

(III) *The Defender of the Peace.* Ed. and trans. A. S. Brett. Cambridge, 2005.

MEL. *P. Pas.*

Melito of Sardis. *On Pascha and Fragments.* Greek with trans. S. G. Hall. Oxford, 1979.

MIN. FEL. *Oct.*

(I) Minucius Felix. *Octavius.* Ed. B. Kytzler. Leipzig, 1992.

(II) *Octavius.* In: *Tertullian, Apologetical Works, and Minucius Felix, Octavius.* Trans. R. Arbesmann, E. J. Daly, and E. A. Quain. Washington, D.C., 1950.

Mors Pil.

"The Death of Pilate." In: *The Apocryphal New Testament: A Collection of Apocryphal Christian Literature in an English Translation.* Ed. and trans. J. K. Elliott. Oxford, 1993.

NAG. HAMM. *Seth II*

Second Treatise of the Great Seth. Coptic with trans. and annot. G. Riley. In: *Nag Hammadi Codex VII.* Ed. B. A. Pearson. Leiden, 1996.

OCK. *Imp. Pont.*

(I) William of Ockham. *Opera politica IV.* Ed. H. S. Offler. Oxford, 1997.

(II) *On the Power of Emperors and Popes.* Ed. and trans. A. S. Brett. Bristol, 1998.

ORIG. *C. Cels.*

(I) Origen of Caesarea. *Contra Celsum libri VIII.* Ed. M. Marcovich. Leiden, 2001.

(II) *Contre Celse.* Greek with French trans. M. Borret. 5 vols. Paris, 1967–76.

(III) *Contra Celsum.* Trans. and annot. H. Chadwick. Cambridge, 1965 (reprinted 2003).

PHIL. *Leg.* Philo of Alexandria. *The Embassy to Gaius.* Greek with trans. F. H. Colson. Cambridge, Mass., 1971.

PIET. AL. *Com.* Pietro Alighieri. *Comentum super poema Comedie Dantis: A Critical Edition of the Third and Final Draft of Pietro Alighieri's "Commentary on Dante's 'Divine Comedy'".* Ed. M. Chiamenti. Tempe, Ariz., 2002. Archived online by Dartmouth College.

PL. *Apol.* Plato. *Euthyphro, Apology, Crito, Phaedo, Phaedrus.* Greek with trans. H. N. Fowler. London, 1971.

PL. *Resp.* Plato. *The Republic.* Greek with trans. P. Shorey. 2 vols. Cambridge, Mass., 1935–7.

PLIN. *Epist.* Pliny the Younger. *Letters and Panegyricus.* Latin with trans. B. Radice. 2 vols. London, 1969.

PLIN. *Hist. Nat.* Pliny the Elder. *Natural History, Volume IX: Libri XXXIII– XXXV.* Latin with trans. H. Rackham. London, 1952.

PLUT. *Mor.* Plutarch. *Plutarch's Moralia, II: 86B–171F.* Greek with trans. F. C. Babbitt. London, 1928.

POSS. *Vita Aug.* Possidius of Calama. *Sancti Augustini Vita scripta a Possidio Episcopo.* Ed. with trans. H. T. Weiskotten. Princeton, 1919.

PROC. *Anec.* Procopius of Caesarea. *The Anecdota or Secret History.* Greek with trans. H. B. Dewing. 7 vols. London, 1953–4.

PROSP. *Chron.* Prosper of Aquitaine. *Chronicon.* (Patrologia Latina 51.) Ed. J.-P. Migne. Paris, 1861.

PS.-LACT. *Pass. Dom.* (I) Pseudo-Lactantius. "Incerti Auctoris Carmen de Passione Domini." (Patrologia Latina 7.) Ed. J.-P. Migne. Paris, 1844.
(II) "Poem—at Times Attributed to Lactantius, *On the Passion of the Lord.*" In: *The Minor Works.* Trans. M. F. McDonald. Washington, D.C., 1965.

QUOD. *Epist.* (I) Quodvultdeus of Carthage. Letters 221 and 223 in Augustine of Hippo. *Letters 211–270, 1*–29*.* Ed. B. Ramsey. Trans. R. Teske. Hyde Park, N.Y., 2005.
(II) "Les deux lettres de Quodvultdeus à Augustin." *Opera Quodvultdeo Carthaginiensi episcopo tributa.* Ed. R. Braun. Turnhout, 1976.

Qur.	*The Qur'an. A New Translation.* Trans. T. Khalidi. London, 2008.
SUET. *Vit. XII*	*Suetonius.* Latin with trans. J. C. Rolfe. 2 vols. London, 1913–14.
TAB. *Jam.*	A. J. M. b. Jarīr Al-Tabarī. *The Commentary on the Qur'an ... Volume I.* Ed. W. F. Madelung and A. Jones. Annot. J. Cooper. Oxford, 1987.
TAC. *Ann.*	Tacitus. *The Annals: Books XIII–XVI.* Latin with trans. J. Jackson. London, 1981.
TAL. BAB. *San.*	*The Babylonian Talmud: Sanhedrin.* Trans. J. Schachter and H. Freedman. Ed. I. Epstein. 2 vols. London, 1935.
TERT. *Anim.*	(I) Tertullian of Carthage. *De Anima.* Ed. and comm. J. H. Waszink. Leiden—Boston, 2010. (II) *A Treatise on the Soul.* In: *The Writings of Tertullian.* Ed. A. C. Coxe. Edinburgh, 1870 (reprinted 1978).
TERT. *Apol.*	(I) Tertullian of Carthage. *Apologeticus pro Christianis.* (Patrologia Latina 1.) Ed. J.-P. Migne. Paris, 1844. (II) Tertullian of Carthage. *Apology.* In: *Tertullian, Apologetical Works, and Minucius Felix, Octavius.* Trans. R. Arbesmann, E. J. Daly, and E. A. Quain. Washington, D.C., 1950. (III) *Christian and Pagan in the Roman Empire: The Witness of Tertullian.* Ed. R. D. Sider. Washington, D.C., 2001.
TH. AQ. *Cat. Aur.*	Thomas Aquinas. *Catena aurea: Commentary on the Four Gospels Collected out of the Works of the Fathers by St. Thomas Aquinas.* Ed. J. H. Newman. Intro. A. Nichols. 4 vols. London, 1999.
THEO. *Autol.*	Theophilus of Antioch. *Ad Autolycum.* Greek with trans. R. M. Grant. Oxford, 1970.
Tol. Yesh. Byz.	*Toledot Yeshu: The Life Story of Jesus.* Ed. and trans. M. Meerson and P. Schäfer. 2 vols. Tübingen, 2014.
Tol. Yesh. Eur.	Ibid.
Tol. Yesh. Or.	Ibid.
TREB. *Aut. Dox.*	George of Trebizond. *Collectanea Trapezuntiana: Texts,*

SELECT BIBLIOGRAPHY

Documents, and Bibliographies of George of Trebizond. Ed.
J. Monfasani. Binghampton, New York, 1984.

VALLA *Don. Const.* Lorenzo Valla. *On the Donation of Constantine.* Latin
with trans. G. W. Bowersock. Cambridge, Mass.,
2007.

VIDA *Christ.* Marco Girolamo Vida. *Christiad.* Latin with trans.
J. Gardner. Cambridge, Mass., 2009.

WYC. *Nov. Test.* *The Wycliffe New Testament (1388): An Edition in Modern
Spelling.* Ed. W. R. Cooper. London, 2002.

Modern works (after 1600)

Abulafia, A. S. "Twelfth-Century Humanism and the Jews." *Contra Iudaeos:
Ancient and Medieval Polemics between Christians and Jews.* Ed. O. Limor and
G. G. Stroumsa. Tübingen, 1996.

Achtemeier, P. J. *1 Peter: A Commentary on First Peter.* Ed. E. J. Epp. Minneapolis,
1996.

Adams, J. N. *Bilingualism and the Latin Language.* Cambridge, 2003.

———— *The Regional Diversification of Latin 200 BC–AD 600.* Cambridge,
2007.

Afsaruddin, A. "The Messiah 'Isa, Son of Mary: Jesus in the Islamic Tradition."
Nicholas of Cusa and Islam: Polemic and Dialogue in the Late Middle Ages. Ed.
I. C. Levy, R. George-Tvrtković, and D. Duclow. Leiden, 2014.

Agamben, G. *The Highest Poverty: Monastic Rules and Form-of-Life.* Trans.
A. Kotsko. Stanford, 2013.

———— *The Kingdom and the Glory: For a Theological Genealogy of Economy and
Government.* Trans. L. Chiesa with M. Mandarini. Stanford, 2011.

———— *Pilate and Jesus.* Trans. A. Kotsko. Stanford, 2015.

———— *Pilato e Gesù.* Rome, 2014.

———— *Stasis: Civil War as a Political Paradigm.* Trans. N. Heron. Stanford,
2015.

———— *The Time That Remains: A Commentary on the Letter to the Romans.* Trans.
P. Dailey. Stanford, 2005.

Agence France-Presse in Ouagadougou. "Burkina Faso Church Attack Leaves
24 Dead." *The Guardian* (17 February 2020). Archived online at https://
www.theguardian.com/world/2020/feb/17/burkina-faso-church-
attack-dead-wounded.

Ahnert, T. *Religion and the Origins of the German Enlightenment: Faith and the
Reform of Learning in the Thought of Christian Thomasius.* Rochester, N.Y.,
2006.

Albert, B.-S. "*Adversus Iudaeos* in the Carolingian Empire." *Contra Iudaeos:*

SELECT BIBLIOGRAPHY

Ancient and Medieval Polemics between Christians and Jews. Ed. O. Limor and G. G. Stroumsa. Tübingen, 1996.

Alexander, P. "The *Toledot Yeshu* in the Context of Jewish–Muslim Debate." *Toledot Yeshu ("The Life Story of Jesus")* Revisited: A *Princeton Conference*. Ed. P. Schäfer, M. Meerson, and Y. Deutsch. Tübingen, 2011.

Alon, I. *Socrates in Medieval Arabic Literature*. Leiden, 1991.

Amarelli, F., and F. Lucrezi, eds. *Il processo contro Gesù*. Naples, 1999.

Amorai-Stark, S., Y. Kalman, M. Hershkovitz, R. Chachy, G. Forster, and R. Porat. "An Inscribed Copper-Alloy Finger Ring from Herodium Depicting a Krater." *Israel Exploration Journal* 68, 2 (2018), 208–20.

Amunátegui Perelló, C. F. "The Twelve Tables and the *Leges regiae*: A Problem of Validity." *Roman Law before the Twelve Tables: An Interdisciplinary Approach*. Ed. S. W. Bell and P. J. du Plessis. Edinburgh, 2020.

Ando, C. *The Matter of the Gods: Religion and the Roman Empire*. Berkeley, 2008.

——— "The Ontology of Religious Institutions." *History of Religions* 50, 1 (2010), 54–79.

Anidjar, G. *Blood: A Critique of Christianity*. New York, 2014.

Anthony, S. W. "Fixing John Damascene's Biography: Historical Notes and His Family Background." *Journal of Early Christian Studies* 23, 4 (2015), 607–27.

Arnold, G. *Lotionem manuum, disquisitione historica ad factum Pontii Pilati recensitam* ... Wittenberg (Wittenberga): Matthaeus Henckel (Henckelius), 1689.

Arouet, F.-M. d'. *Œuvres complètes de Voltaire avec des notes ... tome dixième*. Paris: Firmin Didot Frères, Fils et Cⁱᵉ., 1869.

Artinian, R. "Dante's Parody of Boniface VIII." *Dante Studies* 85 (1967), 71–4.

Asad, T. *Formations of the Secular: Christianity, Islam, Modernity*. Stanford, 2003.

Auden, W. H. *Selected Poems*. Ed. E. Mendelson. London, 2009.

Bach, O. "Natur als juridisches Argument an der Schwelle zur Aufklärung: Zu den theonomen, rationalistischen und voluntaristischen Systemstellen des Denkens vom Naturzustand bei Samuel Pufendorf und Christian Thomasius." *Aufklärung* 25 (2013), 23–50.

Bacher, W. "Joseph Perles: 1835–1894." *The Jewish Quarterly Review* 7, 1 (1894), 1–23.

Bacon, F. "Of Truth." *The Essayes or Counsels, Civill and Morall*. Ed. with comm. M. Kiernan. Cambridge, Mass., 1985.

Badar, M. E. *The Concept of Mens Rea in International Criminal Law: The Case for a Unified Approach*. Oxford, 2013.

Badiou, A. *Saint Paul: The Foundation of Universalism*. Trans. R. Brassier. Stanford, 2003.

Balibar, É. *Saeculum: Culture, religion, idéologie*. Paris, 2012.

Bammel, E. "Excerpts from a New Gospel?" *Novum Testamentum* 10, 1 (1968), 1–9.

SELECT BIBLIOGRAPHY

———— "The Revolution Theory from Reimarus to Brandon." *Jesus and the Politics of His Day*. Ed. E. Bammel and C. F. D. Moule. Cambridge, 1984.

Bar-Asher Siegal, M. *Early Christian Monastic Literature and the Babylonian Talmud*. Cambridge, 2013.

Barbarani, E. *Due chiose dantesche*. Verona, 1897.

Barnes, T. D. "Constantine and the Christians of Persia." *The Journal of Roman Studies* 75 (1985), 126–36.

———— *Constantine and Eusebius*. Cambridge, Mass., 1981.

———— "Lactantius and Constantine." *The Journal of Roman Studies* 63 (1973), 29–46.

———— "Legislation against the Christians." *The Journal of Roman Studies* 58 (1968), 32–50.

———— "Sossianus Hierocles and the Antecedents of the 'Great Persecution'." *Harvard Studies in Classical Philology* 80 (1976), 239–52.

———— "Was There a Constantinian Revolution?" *Journal of Late Antiquity* 2, 2 (2009), 374–84.

Bataille, G. *The Accursed Share: Volume I*. Trans. R. Hurley. New York, 1991.

Bauckham, R. *Gospel Women: Studies of the Named Women in the Gospels*. Grand Rapids, Mich., 2002.

———— *Jude and the Relatives of Jesus in the Early Church*. Edinburgh, 1990.

Baudoin, A.-C. "La femme de Pilate dans les *Actes des Pilate*, recension grecque A (II, 1)." *Apocrypha* 21 (2010), 133–49.

———— "Truth in the Details: The *Report of Pilate to Tiberius* as an Authentic Forgery." *Splendide Mendax: Rethinking Fakes and Forgeries in Classical, Late Antique, and Early Christian Literature*. Ed. E. P. Cueva and J. Martínez. Groningen, 2016.

Bauman, R. A. *Impietas in Principem: A Study of Treason against the Roman Emperor with Special Reference to the First Century A.D*. Munich, 1974.

Baumgart, J. B. *Dissertatio academica, de secularisatione ...* Helmstedt (Helmestadium): Georg-Wolfgang Hamm (Hammius), 1683.

Baynes, N. H. "The Death of Julian the Apostate in a Christian Legend." *The Journal of Roman Studies* 27, 1 (1937), 22–9.

Behrent, M. "The Genealogy of Genealogy: Foucault's 1970–1971 Course on The Will to Know." *Foucault Studies* 13 (2012), 157–78.

Benfell, V. S. *The Biblical Dante*. Toronto, 2011.

Benitez, M. "La diffusion du *Traité des trois imposteurs* au XVIIIe siècle." *Revue d'histoire moderne et contemporaine* 40, 1 (1993), 137–51.

Benko, S. "The Libertine Gnostic Sect of the Phibionites According to Epiphanius." *Vigiliae Christianae* 21, 2 (1967), 103–19.

Ben-Shalom, R. "The Foundation of Christianity in the Historical Perceptions of Medieval Jewry as Expressed in the Anonymous *Various Elements on the Topic of Christian Faith* (London, BL, MS Addit. 27129, pp. 88b–92a)."

Conflict and Religious Conversation in Latin Christendom: Studies in Honour of Ora Limor. Ed. I. J. Yuval and R. Ben-Shalom. Turnhout, 2014.

Benson, R. L. "The Gelasian Doctrine: Uses and Transformations." *La notion d'autorité au Moyen Age: Islam, Byzance, Occident*. Ed. G. Makdisi and D. Sourdel. Paris, 1982.

Bentley, J. H. "Biblical Philology and Christian Humanism: Lorenzo Valla and Erasmus as Scholars of the Gospels." *The Sixteenth Century Journal* 8, 2 (1977), 8–28.

———— *Humanists and Holy Writ: New Testament Scholarship in the Renaissance*. Princeton, 1983.

Berendts, A. *Die Zeugnisse vom Christentum im slavischen "De Bello Judaico" des Josephus*. Leipzig, 1906.

Bergjan, S.-P. "The Patristic Context in Early Grotius." *Grotiana* 26–8 (2007), 127–46.

Bernard, G. W. "The Dissolution of the Monasteries." *History* 96, 4 (2011), 390–409.

———— "The Making of Religious Policy, 1533–1546: Henry VIII and the Search for the Middle Way." *The Historical Journal* 41, 2 (1998), 321–49.

Bevilacqua, A. "The Qur'an Translations of Marracci and Sale." *Journal of the Warburg and Courtauld Institutes* 76 (2013), 93–130.

Bickerman, E. J. "The Name of Christians." *Studies in Jewish and Christian History: A New Edition in English Including The God of the Maccabees*. Ed. A. Tropper. Leiden, 2007 (reprint of a 1949 article).

———— "Utilitas Crucis: Observations on the Accounts of the Trial of Jesus in the Canonical Gospels." *Studies in Jewish and Christian History: A New Edition in English Including The God of the Maccabees*. Ed. A. Tropper. Leiden, 2007 (reprint of a 1935 article).

Biguzzi, G. "Ephesus, Its Artemision, Its Temple to the Flavian Emperors, and Idolatry in Revelation." *Novum Testamentum* 40, 3 (1998), 276–90.

Bilde, P. *Flavius Josephus between Jerusalem and Rome: His Life, His Works, and Their Importance*. Sheffield, 1988.

Birley, A. R. "Pliny's Family, Pliny's Career." *The Epistles of Pliny*. Ed. R. Gibson and C. Whitton. Oxford, 2016.

Bishko, C. J. Untitled review of *Las Bulas Alejandrinas de 1493 y la Teoría política del papado medieval* by Luis Weckmann. *Speculum* 25, 2 (1950), 306–11.

Blaise, A. *Lexicon Latinitatis Medii Aevi*. Turnhout, 1975.

Blake, W. *Blake's Poetry and Designs*. Ed. M. L. Johnson and J. E. Grant. New York–London, 1979.

Blanton, W., and H. de Vries, eds. *Paul and the Philosophers*. New York, 2013.

Blinzler, J. "Der Entscheid des Pilatus: Exekutionsbefehl oder Todesurteil?" *Münchener theologische Zeitschrift* 5, 3 (1954), 171–84.

———— "Die Niedermetzelung von Galiläern durch Pilatus." *Novum Testamentum* 2, 1 (1957), 24–39.

SELECT BIBLIOGRAPHY

———— *Der Prozess Jesu: Das jüdische und das römische Gerichtsverfahren gegen Jesus Christus auf Grund der ältesten Zeugnisse dargestellt und beurteilt.* Regensburg, 1955.

Bloch, E. *Atheism in Christianity: The Religion of the Exodus and the Kingdom.* Trans. J. T. Swann. London, 2009.

Bloemendal, J. "Bilingualism, Multilingualism, and the Formation of Europe." *Bilingual Europe: Latin and Vernacular Cultures, Examples of Bilingualism and Multilingualism c.1300–1800.* Ed. J. Bloemendal. Leiden, 2015.

———— "Hugo Grotius (1583–1645): Jurist, Philologist, and Theologian; A Christian Humanist, His Works, and His Correspondence." *Nederlands archief voor kerkgeschiedenis* 82, 2 (2002), 342–49.

Bloom, H. *Jesus and Yahweh: The Names Divine.* New York, 2005.

Blum, P. R. "Europa: Ein Appellbegriff." *Archiv für Begriffsgeschichte* 43 (2001), 149–71.

———— *Philosophy of Religion in the Renaissance.* New York, 2010.

Bockmuehl, M. "The Son of David and His Mother." *The Journal of Theological Studies* (NS) 62, 2 (2011), 476–93.

Bond, H. K. "The Coins of Pontius Pilate: Part of an Attempt to Provoke the People or to Integrate Them into the Empire?" *Journal for the Study of Judaism in the Persian, Hellenistic, and Roman Period* 27, 3 (1996), 241–62.

———— "Dating the Death of Jesus: Memory and the Religious Imagination." *New Testament Studies* 59, 4 (2013), 461–75.

———— *Pontius Pilate in History and Interpretation.* Cambridge, 1998.

Borges, J. L. "A Defense of Basilides the False." *Selected Non-fictions.* Ed. E. Weinberger. Trans. E. Allen, S. J. Levine, and E. Weinberger. London, 2000.

———— "Three Versions of Judas." *Ficciones.* Trans. A. Kerrigan. New York, 1962.

Bosco, U., and G. Reggio, eds. *La Divina Commedia: Inferno.* Florence, 1979.

Boswell, J. C. "Dante's Fame in England: 1536–1586." *Dante Studies* 111 (1993), 235–43.

Botterill, S. "Not of This World: Spiritual and Temporal Powers in Dante and Bernard of Clairvaux." *Lectura Dantis* 10 (1992), 8–21.

Bowersock, G. W. *Fiction as History: Nero to Julian.* Berkeley, 1994.

Brague, R. *The Kingdom of Man: Genesis and the Failure of the Modern Project.* Trans. P. Seaton. Notre Dame, 2018.

———— *The Law of God: The Philosophical History of an Idea.* Trans. L. G. Cochrane. Chicago, 2007.

———— *The Wisdom of the World: The Human Experience of the Universe in Western Thought.* Trans. T. L. Fagan. Chicago, 2003.

Brandon, S. G. F. *The Trial of Jesus of Nazareth.* New York, 1968.

Braudel, F. *A History of Civilizations.* Trans. R. Mayne. London, 1993.

SELECT BIBLIOGRAPHY

Bray, G., ed. *Ancient Christian Commentary on Scripture: New Testament VI; Romans.* Chicago–London, 1998.

Bremmer, J. N. "'Christianus sum': The Early Christian Martyrs and Christ." *Eulogia: Mélanges offerts à Antoon R. Bastiaensen à l'occasion de son soixante-cinquième anniversaire.* Ed. G. J. M. Bartelink, A. Hilhorst, and C. H. J. M. Kneepkens. Turnhout, 1991.

———— "Lucian on Peregrinus and Alexander of Abonuteichos: A Sceptical View of Two Religious Entrepreneurs." *Beyond Priesthood: Religious Entrepreneurs and Innovators in the Roman Empire.* Ed. R. L. Gordon, G. Petridou, and J. Rüpke. Berlin, 2017.

———— "Secularization: Notes toward a Genealogy." *Religion: Beyond a Concept.* Ed. H. de Vries. New York, 2008.

Brent, A. *The Imperial Cult and the Development of Church Order: Concepts and Images of Authority in Paganism and Early Christianity before the Age of Cyprian.* Leiden, 1999.

———— "Luke–Acts and the Imperial Cult in Asia Minor." *The Journal of Theological Studies* (NS) 48, 2 (1997), 411–38.

Briguglia, G. *La questione del potere: Teologi e teoria politica nella disputa tra Bonifacio VIII e Filippo il Bello.* Milan, 2010.

Brown, P. R. L. "'Lover of the Poor': The Creation of a Public Virtue." *Poverty and Leadership in the Later Roman Empire: The Menahem Stern Jerusalem Lectures.* London, 2002.

———— *The Rise of Western Christendom: Triumph and Diversity, AD 200–1000.* Oxford, 1996.

———— *Through the Eye of a Needle: Wealth, the Fall of Rome, and the Making of Christianity in the West, 350–550 AD.* Princeton, 2012.

Brown, R. E. *The Death of the Messiah: From Gethsemane to the Grave.* New York, 1994.

———— *An Introduction to the New Testament.* New York, 1997.

Bruce, L. D. "The *Procurator bibliothecarum* at Rome." *The Journal of Library History* 18, 2 (1983), 143–62.

Bryen, A. Z. "Judging Empire: Courts and Culture in Rome's Eastern Provinces." *Law and History Review* 30, 3 (2012), 771–811.

Buck, P. L. "Justin Martyr's *Apologies*: Their Number, Destination, and Form." *Journal of Theological Studies* (NS) 54, 1 (2003), 45–59.

Buiter, W. H. "Is Numerairology the Future of Monetary Economics? Unbundling Numeraire and Medium of Exchange through a Virtual Currency and a Shadow Exchange Rate." Working Paper 12839, National Bureau of Economic Research (2007), 1–41. Archived online at http://www.nber.org/papers/w12839.

Bulgakov, M. *The Master and Margarita.* Trans. M. Ginsburg. New York, 1995.

Bultmann, R. *The History of the Synoptic Tradition, Revised Edition.* Trans. J. Marsh. Oxford, 1972.

SELECT BIBLIOGRAPHY

Bureth, P. *Les titulatures impériales dans les papyrus, les ostraca et les inscriptions d'Égypte (30 a.C.–284 p.C.)*. Brussels, 1964.

Burkett, D. "The Parable of the Unrighteous Steward (Luke 16.1–9): A Prudent Use of Mammon." *New Testament Studies* 64, 3 (2018), 326–42.

Burman, T. E. *Reading the Qur'an in Latin Christendom, 1140–1560*. Philadelphia, 2007.

Burton, P. *The Old Latin Gospels: A Study of Their Texts and Language*. Oxford, 2000.

Busine, A. *Paroles d'Apollon: Pratiques et traditions oraculaires dans l'antiquité tardive (IIᵉ–VIᵉ siècles)*. Leiden, 2005.

Butler, W. E. "Grotius and the Law of the Sea." *Hugo Grotius and International Relations*. Ed. H. Bull, B. Kingsbury, and A. Roberts. Oxford, 1990.

Cabaniss, J. A. "Agobard of Lyons." *Speculum* 26, 1 (1951), 50–76.

Caillois, R. *Pontius Pilate: A Novel*. Trans. C. L. Markmann. Charlottesville, Va., 2006.

Cameron, A. "The Imperial Pontifex." *Harvard Studies in Classical Philology* 103 (2007), 341–84.

——— "*Pontifex Maximus*: From Augustus to Gratian—and Beyond." *Emperors and the Divine: Rome and Its Influence*. Ed. M. Kahlos. Helsinki, 2016.

Cameron, A. M. "The 'Scepticism' of Procopius." *Historia: Zeitschrift für Alte Geschichte* 15, 4 (1966), 466–82.

Canning, J. *Ideas of Power in the Late Middle Ages, 1296–1417*. Cambridge, 2011.

Capet, L. "The Last Will of Louis XVI." *Judgment and Execution of Louis XVI: King of France*. Ed. and trans. H. Goudemetz. Sine loco: Sine nomine, sine anno.

Capogrossi Colognesi, L. "Niebuhr and Bachofen: New Forms of Evidence on Roman History." *Roman Law before the Twelve Tables: An Interdisciplinary Approach*. Ed. S. W. Bell and P. J. du Plessis. Edinburgh, 2020.

Carleton Paget, J. N. "The Jew of Celsus and *Adversus Judaeos* Literature." *Zeitschrift für Antikes Christentum* 21, 2 (2017), 201–42.

——— "Some Observations on Josephus and Christianity." *The Journal of Theological Studies* (NS) 52, 2 (2001), 539–624.

Carlon, J. M. *Pliny's Women: Constructing Virtue and Creating Identity in the Roman World*. Cambridge, 2009.

Carr, W. "The Rulers of This Age: I Corinthians ii.6–8." *New Testament Studies* 23 (1977), 20–35.

Carriker, A. J. *The Library of Eusebius of Caesarea*. Leiden, 2003.

Cassell, A. K. *The Monarchia Controversy: An Historical Study with Accompanying Translations of Dante Alighieri's Monarchia, Guido Vernani's Refutation of the "Monarchia" Composed by Dante, and Pope John XXII's Bull Si fratrum*. Washington, D.C., 2004.

SELECT BIBLIOGRAPHY

Catchpole, D. *The Trial of Jesus: A Study in the Gospels and Jewish Historiography from 1770 to the Present Day*. Leiden, 1971.

Cau, M. "To the Roots of the Universal Juridical Order: Hans Kelsen and the *Staatslehre* of Dante Alighieri." *Hans Kelsen and the Natural Law Tradition*. Ed. P. Langford, I. Bryan, and J. McGarry. Leiden, 2019.

Caulley, T. S. "The *Chrestos/Christos* Pun (1 Pet 2:3) in P[72] and P[125]." *Novum Testamentum* 53, 4 (2011), 376–87.

Cave, N. *And the Ass Saw the Angel*. London, 2013.

Cecotti, S. "La legittima validità dell'impero: Analisi degli argomenti sviluppati secondo la semantica della validità nel secondo libro della *Monarchia* di Dante condotta a partire dalla confutazione fattane da fra' Guido Vernani da Rimini nel suo *De reprobatione monarchiae*." *Divus Thomas* 115, 1 (2012), 390–412.

Celenza, C. *The Lost Italian Renaissance: Humanists, Historians, and Latin's Legacy*. Baltimore, 2004.

Champion, J. "Decoding the *Leviathan*: Doing the History of Ideas through Images, 1651–1714." *Printed Images in Early Modern Britain: Essays in Interpretation*. Ed. M. Hunter. Farnham, Surrey, 2010.

Chapman, D. W. *Ancient Jewish and Christian Perceptions of Crucifixion*. Tübingen, 2008.

Chapman, D. W., and E. J. Schnabel. *The Trial and Crucifixion of Jesus: Texts and Commentary*. Tübingen, 2015.

Cheneval, F. "La réception de la 'Monarchie' de Dante ou Les métamorphoses d'une œuvre philosophique." *Vivarium* 34, 2 (1996), 254–67.

Chevallier, P. "Michel Foucault et le 'soi' chrétien." *Astérion* 11 (2013). Archived online at https://journals.openedition.org/asterion/2403.

Chibnall, M. *The World of Orderic Vitalis: Norman Monks and Norman Knights*. Woodbridge, Suffolk, 1984.

Cohen, J. *The Friars and the Jews: The Evolution of Medieval Anti-Semitism*. Ithaca, N.Y., 1982.

———— "The Jews as the Killers of Christ in the Latin Tradition, from Augustine to the Friars." *Traditio* 39 (1983), 1–37.

———— *Living Letters of the Law: Ideas of the Jew in Medieval Christianity*. Berkeley, 1999.

———— "Revisiting Augustine's Doctrine of Jewish Witness." *The Journal of Religion* 89, 4 (2009), 564–78.

Cohick, L. H. *The Peri Pascha attributed to Melito of Sardis: Setting, Purpose, and Sources*. Providence, R.I., 2000.

Colish, M. "*Sanza 'nfama e sanza lodo*: Moral Neutrality from Alan of Lille to Dante." *Alain de Lille, le Docteur Universel*. Ed. J.-L. Solère, A. Vasiliu, and A. Galonnier. Turnhout, 2015.

Collins, B. "By Post or by Ghost: Ruminations on Visions and Epistolary Archives." *Jewish Quarterly Review* 107, 3 (2017), 397–408.

SELECT BIBLIOGRAPHY

Collins, J. "Christian Ecclesiology and the Composition of *Leviathan*: A Newly Discovered Letter to Thomas Hobbes." *The Historical Journal* 43, 1 (2000), 217–31.

Conant, J. *Staying Roman: Conquest and Identity in Africa and the Mediterranean, 439–700*. Cambridge, 2012.

Connolly, R. H., ed. *Didascalia Apostolorum: The Syriac Version Translated and Accompanied by the Verona Latin Fragments*. Oxford, 1929.

Cook, J. G. *The Interpretation of the New Testament in Greco-Roman Paganism*. Tübingen, 2000.

Corbett, G. *Dante's Christian Ethics: Purgatory and Its Moral Contexts*. Cambridge, 2020.

Corcoran, S. "Roman Law in Ravenna." *Ravenna: Its Role in Earlier Medieval Change and Exchange*. Ed. J. Herrin and J. Nelson. London, 2016.

Cordoni, C., and M. Meyer, with N. Hable, eds. *Barlaam und Josaphat: Neue Perspektiven auf ein europäisches Phänomen*. Berlin, 2015.

Corke-Webster, J. "Trouble in Pontus: The Pliny–Trajan Correspondence on the Christians Reconsidered." *Transactions of the American Philological Association* 147, 2 (2017), 371–411.

Costigliolo, M. "Perspectives on Islam in Italy and Byzantium in the Middle Ages and Renaissance." *Nicholas of Cusa and Islam: Polemic and Dialogue in the Late Middle Ages*. Ed. I. C. Levy, R. George-Tvrtković, and D. Duclow. Leiden, 2014.

———— "Qur'anic Sources of Nicholas of Cusa." *Mediaevistik* 24 (2011), 219–38.

Courcelle, P. "Anti-Christian Arguments and Christian Platonism: From Arnobius to St. Ambrose." *The Conflict between Paganism and Christianity in the Fourth Century*. Ed. A. Momigliano. Oxford, 1963.

Coyle, J. K. "The Self-identity of North African Christians in Augustine's Time." *Augustinus Afer: Saint Augustin; africanité et universalité ...* Ed. P.-Y. Fux, J.-M. Roessli, and O. Wermelinger. Fribourg, 2003.

Cranston, M. *John Locke: A Biography*. London, 1957.

Crouzel, H. "Le christianisme de l'empereur Philippe l'Arabe." *Gregorianum* 56, 3 (1975), 545–50.

Daalder, E. "The *Decreta* and *Imperiales sententiae* of Julius Paulus: Law and Justice in the Judicial Decisions of Septimius Severus." *The Impact of Justice on the Roman Empire*. Ed. O. Hekster and K. Verboven. Leiden, 2019.

Daftary, F. *The Ismāʿīlīs: Their History and Doctrines*. Cambridge, 1990.

Dagron, G. *Emperor and Priest: The Imperial Office in Byzantium*. Trans. J. Birrell. Cambridge, 2003.

Darr, J. A. *Herod the Fox: Audience Criticism and Lukan Characterization*. Sheffield, 1998.

De Bom, E. "Political Thought." *Jesuit Philosophy on the Eve of Modernity*. Ed. C. Casalini. Leiden, 2019.

SELECT BIBLIOGRAPHY

Decock, W. "The Judge's Conscience and the Protection of the Criminal Defendant: Moral Safeguards against Judicial Arbitrariness." *From the Judge's Arbitrium to the Legality Principle: Legislation as a Source of Law in Criminal Trials.* Ed. G. Martyn, A. Musson, and H. Pihlajamäki. Berlin, 2013.

Decret, F. *Early Christianity in North Africa.* Trans. E. Smither. Eugene, Oregon, 2009.

———— *Le Christianisme en Afrique du Nord ancienne.* Paris, 1996.

Dehandschutter, B. "Martyr—Martyrium: Quelques observation, à propos d'un christianisme sémantique." *Eulogia: Mélanges offerts à Antoon R. Bastiaensen à l'occasion de son soixante-cinquième anniversaire.* Ed. G. J. M. Bartelink, A. Hilhorst, and C. H. J. M. Kneepkens. Turnhout, 1991.

De Jonge, H. J. "Joseph Scaliger's Historical Criticism of the New Testament." *Novum Testamentum* 38, 2 (1996), 176–93.

De la Costa, H. Untitled review of *Las Bulas Alejandrinas de 1493 y la Teoría política del papado medieval* by Luis Weckmann. *Traditio* 7 (1951), 516–18.

Den Hollander, W. *Josephus, the Emperors, and the City of Rome: From Hostage to Historian.* Leiden, 2014.

DePalma Digeser, E. "Lactantius, Porphyry, and the Debate over Religious Toleration." *The Journal of Roman Studies* 88 (1998), 129–46.

———— "Porphyry, Julian, or Hierokles? The Anonymous Hellene in Makarios Magnēs *Apokritikos.*" *The Journal of Theological Studies* (NS) 53, 2 (2002), 466–502.

———— *A Threat to Public Piety: Christians, Platonists, and the Great Persecution.* Ithaca, N.Y., 2012.

Derrett, J. D. M. "The Two Malefactors (Luke xxiii 33, 39–43)." *Studies in the New Testament, Volume Three: Midrash, Haggadah, and the Character of the Community.* Leiden, 1982.

Deutsch, Y. "The Second Life of the Life of Jesus: Christian Reception of *Toledot Yeshu.*" *Toledot Yeshu ("The Life Story of Jesus") Revisited: A Princeton Conference.* Ed. P. Schäfer, M. Meerson, and Y. Deutsch. Tübingen, 2011.

De Vaan, M. A. C., *Etymological Dictionary of Latin and the Other Italic Languages.* Leiden, 2008.

Devereux, A. W. *The Other Side of Empire: Just War in the Mediterranean and the Rise of Early Modern Spain.* Ithaca, New York, 2020.

Dibelius, M. *From Tradition to Gospel.* Trans. B. L. Woolf. Cambridge, 1982.

Dibelius, M., and H. Conzelmann. *The Pastoral Epistles: A Commentary on the Pastoral Epistles.* Ed. H. Koester. Trans. P. Buttolph and A. Yarbro. Philadelphia, 1972.

Di Fonzo, C. "La legittimazione dell'Impero e del popolo romano presso Dante." *Dante* 6 (2009), 39–64.

Dijkstra, R., and D. van Espelo. "Anchoring Pontifical Authority: A

SELECT BIBLIOGRAPHY

Reconsideration of the Papal Employment of the Title *Pontifex Maximus*." *Journal of Religious History* 41, 3 (2017), 312–25.

Donner, F. M. *Muhammad and the Believers: At the Origins of Islam*. Cambridge, Mass., 2010.

Döring, D. "Säkularisierung und Moraltheologie bei Samuel von Pufendorf." *Zeitschrift für Theologie und Kirche* 90, 2 (1993), 156–74

Du Cange, D., et al. *Glossarium mediae et infimae Latinitatis ... Tomus sextus*. (Facsimile of the 1883–7 edition.) Graz, 1954.

Dunn, S. *The Deaths of Louis XVI: Regicide and the French Political Imagination*. Princeton, 1994.

Dursteler, E. R. "Speaking in Tongues: Language and Communication in the Early Modern Mediterranean." *Past & Present* 217 (2012), 47–77.

Dusenbury, D. L. "The Judgment of Pontius Pilate: A Critique of Giorgio Agamben." *Journal of Law and Religion* 32, 2 (2017), 340–65.

——— *Nemesius of Emesa on Human Nature: A Cosmopolitan Anthropology from Roman Syria*. Oxford, 2021.

——— "Pilate Schemes." *TLS: The Times Literary Supplement* (25 March 2016), 15.

——— *Platonic Legislations: An Essay on Legal Critique in Ancient Greece*. Cham, 2017.

——— "Red Cells and Grey." *TLS: The Times Literary Supplement* (3 October 2014), 32.

——— "Socrate e Gesù di nuovo a processo." *La lettura: Corriere della Sera* (19 July 2020), 8–9.

——— *The Space of Time: A Sensualist Interpretation of Time in Augustine, Confessions X to XII*. Leiden–Boston, 2014. Note that I signed this book, for obscure reasons, David van Dusen.

——— "Unfortunate Galilean: The Passion as Seen by Two Poetic Herberts." *TLS: The Times Literary Supplement* (19 April 2019), 13–14.

——— "'A World like a Russian Novel': The Trials of Socrates and Jesus." *TLS: The Times Literary Supplement* (10 April 2020), 21.

Dvornik, F. *Early Christian and Byzantine Political Philosophy: Origins and Background*. 2 vols. Washington, D.C., 1966.

——— "Emperors, Popes, and General Councils." *Dumbarton Oaks Papers* 6 (1951), 3–23.

Eastman, D. L. *Paul the Martyr: The Cult of the Apostle in the Latin West*. Atlanta, 2011.

Eco, U. "European Roots." *Chronicles of a Liquid Society*. Trans. R. Dixon. New York, 2017.

Edelstein, D. *The Terror of Natural Right: Republicanism, the Cult of Nature, and the French Revolution*. Chicago, 2009.

Edwards, M. J. "Constantine's Donation to the 'Bishop and Pope of the City of Rome'." *The Journal of Theological Studies* (NS) 56, 1 (2005), 115–21.

SELECT BIBLIOGRAPHY

———— "Lucian of Samosata in the Christian Memory." *Byzantion* 80 (2010), 142–56.

Ehrmann, B. D. *Forgery and Counter-forgery: The Use of Literary Deceit in Early Christian Polemics.* Oxford, 2013.

Eisler, R. *The Enigma of the Fourth Gospel: Its Author and Its Writer.* London, 1938.

———— "The Frontispiece to Sigismondo Fanti's *Triompho di Fortuna.*" *Journal of the Warburg and Courtauld Institutes* 10 (1947), 155–9.

———— *Iesous Basileus ou Basileusas. Die Messianische Unabhängigkeitsbewegung vom auftreten Johannes des Täufers bis zum Untergang Jakobs des Gerechten nach der neuerschlossenen Eroberung von Jerusalem des Flavius Josephus und den christlichen Quellen.* 2 vols. Heidelberg, 1929–30.

———— *Man into Wolf: An Anthropological Interpretation of Sadism, Masochism, and Lycanthropy.* London, 1951.

———— *The Messiah Jesus and John the Baptist according to Flavius Josephus' Recently Rediscovered 'Capture of Jerusalem' and the Other Jewish and Christian Sources.* Trans. A. H. Krappe. New York, 1931.

———— *Orpheus—The Fisher: Comparative Studies in Orphic and Early Christian Symbolism.* London, 1921.

———— *Stable Money: The Remedy for the Economic World Crisis; A Programme of Financial Reconstruction for the International Conference, 1933.* London, 1932.

———— *Studien zur Werttheorie.* Leipzig, 1902.

Eliot, T. S. *Collected Poems, 1909–1962.* New York–London, 1963.

Elliott, J. K. *The Apocryphal New Testament: A Collection of Apocryphal Christian Literature in an English Translation.* Oxford, 1993.

Elm, S. *Sons of Hellenism, Fathers of the Church: Emperor Julian, Gregory of Nazianzus, and the Vision of Rome.* Berkeley, 2012.

Elsner, J. Untitled review of *Pontius Pilate, Anti-Semitism, and the Passion in Medieval Art* by Colum Hourihane. *Church History* 80, 4 (2011), 876–7.

Elukin, J. *Living Together, Living Apart: Rethinking Jewish–Christian Relations in the Middle Ages.* Princeton, 2007.

England's Black Tribunal Containing, I. The Complete Tryal of King Charles the First, by the Pretended High Court of Justice ... Together with His Majesty's Speech on the Scaffold, London: R. Freeman, in Fleet-Street, 1747.

Eskildsen, K. R. "How Germany Left the Republic of Letters." *Journal of the History of Ideas* 65, 3 (2004), 421–32.

Essen, G. "Autonomer Geltungssinn und religiöser Begründungszusammenhang: Papst Gelasius I. († 496) als Fallstudie zur religionspolitischen Differenzsemantik." *Archiv für Rechts- und Sozialphilosophie* 99, 1 (2013), 1–10.

Eubank, N. "A Disconcerting Prayer: On the Originality of Luke 23:34a." *Journal of Biblical Literature* 129, 3 (2010), 521–36.

Euler, W. A. "A Critical Survey of Cusanus's Writings on Islam." *Nicholas of*

SELECT BIBLIOGRAPHY

Cusa and Islam: Polemic and Dialogue in the Late Middle Ages. Ed. I. C. Levy, R. George-Tvrtković, and D. Duclow. Leiden, 2014.

Falkeid, U. *The Avignon Papacy Contested: An Intellectual History from Dante to Catherine of Siena*. Cambridge, Mass., 2017.

Fassberg, S. E. "Which Semitic Language Did Jesus and Other Contemporary Jews Speak?" *The Catholic Biblical Quarterly* 74, 2 (2012), 263–80.

Feldman, L. H. "The Slavonic Version." *Josephus and Modern Scholarship (1937–1980)*. Berlin, 1984.

Feldman, N. *The Fall and Rise of the Islamic State*. Princeton, 2008.

Fisher, G. *Between Empires: Arabs, Romans, and Sasanians in Late Antiquity*. Oxford, 2011.

Fitzmyer, J. A. *The Semitic Background of the New Testament*. Grand Rapids, Mich., 1997.

Flint, V. I. J. *The Imaginative Landscape of Christopher Columbus*. Princeton, 1992.

Forcellini, Æ. *Lexicon Totius Latinitatis*. Comp. J. Facciolati and Æ. Forcellini. Padua (Patavium): Typis Seminarii apud Joannem Manfrè, 1771.

Forrat, M. "Introduction." *Eusèbe de Césarée, Contre Hiéroclès*. Ed. E. des Places. Trans. and annot. M. Forrat. Paris, 1986.

Förster, N. "Der *titulus crucis*: Demütigung der Judäer und Proklamation des Messias." *Novum Testamentum* 56, 2 (2014), 113–33.

Foucault, M. *The Birth of Biopolitics: Lectures at the Collège de France, 1978–1979*. Ed. M. Senellart et al. Trans. G. Burchell. New York, 2004.

———— "The Confession of the Flesh." *Power / Knowledge: Selected Interviews and Other Writings, 1972–1977*. Ed. C. Gordon. New York, 1980.

———— *On the Government of the Living: Lectures at the Collège de France, 1979–1980*. Ed. M. Senellart. Trans. G. Burchell. New York, 2012.

———— *Security, Territory, Population: Lectures at the Collège de France, 1977–1978*. Ed. M. Senellart. Trans. G. Burchell. New York, 2007.

Frakes, R. M. *Compiling the* Collatio legum Mosaicarum et Romanarum *in Late Antiquity*. Oxford, 2011.

Frankopan, P. *The Silk Roads: A New History of the World*. New York, 2017.

Fredriksen, P. *Augustine and the Jews: A Christian Defense of Jews and Judaism*. New York, 2008.

———— "Jewish Romans, Christian Romans, and the Post-Roman West: The Social Correlates of the *Contra Iudaeos* Tradition." *Conflict and Religious Conversation in Latin Christendom: Studies in Honour of Ora Limor*. Ed. I. J. Yuval and R. Ben-Shalom. Turnhout, 2014.

———— *Paul: The Pagans' Apostle*. New Haven, 2017.

————"Roman Christianity and the Post-Roman West: The Social Correlates of the *Contra Iudaeos* Tradition." *Jews, Christians, and the Roman Empire: The Poetics of Power in Late Antiquity*. Ed. N. B. Dohrmann and A. Y. Reed. Philadelphia, 2013.

————— *When Christians Were Jews: The First Generation.* New Haven, 2019.

Frend, W. H. C. "Prelude to the Great Persecution: The Propaganda War." *Journal of Ecclesiastical History* 38 (1987), 1–18.

Freund, S. "Christian Use and Valuation of Theological Oracles: The Case of Lactantius' *Divine Institutes.*" *Vigiliae Christianae* 60, 3 (2006), 269–84.

Freund, W. *Modernus und andere Zeitbegriffe des Mittelalters.* Cologne, 1957.

Fried, J. *The "Donation of Constantine" and "Constitutum Constantini": The Misinterpretation of a Fiction and Its Original Meaning.* Berlin, 2007.

————— *The Middle Ages.* Cambridge, Mass., 2015.

Fritsch, A. "Secularisatio bonorum ecclesiasticorum." *Orbis novus literatorum, praeprimis jurisconsultorum detectus, sive continuatio thesauri practici Besoldiani* ... Ed. C. L. Dietherr with A. Fritsch. Nuremberg (Norimberga): Sons of Johann Andreas Endter (Endteri Filiorum), 1699.

Fubini, R. *Humanism and Secularization: From Petrarch to Valla.* Trans. M. King. Durham, N. Car., 2003.

————— "Humanism and Truth: Valla Writes against the Donation of Constantine." *Journal of the History of Ideas* 57, 1 (1996), 79–86.

Fustel de Coulanges, N. D. *The Ancient City: A Study on the Religion, Laws, and Institutions of Greece and Rome.* Baltimore, 1980.

Gabba, E. "The Social, Economic and Political History of Palestine 63 BCE–CE 70." *The Cambridge History of Judaism, Volume Three: The Early Roman Period.* Ed. W. Horbury, W. Davies, and J. Sturdy. Cambridge, 1999.

Gaddis, M. *There Is No Crime for Those Who Have Christ: Religious Violence in the Christian Roman Empire.* Berkeley, 2005.

Galimberti, A. "Hadrian, Eleusis, and the Beginning of Christian Apologetics." *Hadrian and the Christians.* Ed. M. Rizzi. Berlin, 2010.

Garrard, G. *Rousseau's Counter-Enlightenment: A Republican Critique of the Philosophes.* Albany, 2003.

Gärtner, H. A. "Die Acta Scillitanorum in literarischer Interpretation." *Wiener Studien* 102 (1989), 149–67.

Gary, F. *A Critical History of Early Rome: From Prehistory to the First Punic War.* Berkeley, 2005.

Gauchet, M. *La révolution des droits de l'homme.* Paris, 1989.

Gaumer, M. A. *Augustine's Cyprian: Authority in Roman Africa.* Leiden, 2016.

Gay, P. *The Enlightenment: An Interpretation; The Rise of Modern Paganism.* New York, 1966.

Girard, R. *The Scapegoat.* Trans. Y. Freccero. Baltimore, 1989.

Godthardt, F. "The Life of Marsilius of Padua." *A Companion to Marsilius of Padua.* Ed. G. Moreno-Riano and C. J. Nederman. Leiden, 2012.

Godwin, R. T. *Persian Christians at the Chinese Court: The Xi'an Stele and the Early Medieval Church of the East.* London, 2018.

Goesius, W. *Pilatus Judex, ad virum illustrem Constantinum Hugenium, equitem,*

SELECT BIBLIOGRAPHY

Zulichemi Toparcham, &c. ... The Hague (Haga Comitis): Johan Tongerloo, 1681.

Goetz, G. *Thesaurus glossarum emendatarum* ... *Pars posterior, accedit index Graecus Guilelmi Heraei.* Leipzig (Lipsia), 1901.

Goldstein, M. "Early Judeo-Arabic Birth Narratives in the Polemical Story 'Life of Jesus' (Toledot Yeshu)." *Harvard Theological Review* 113, 3 (2020), 354–77.

———— "A Polemical Tale and Its Function in the Jewish Communities of the Mediterranean and the Near East: *Toledot Yeshu* in Judeo-Arabic." *Intellectual History of the Islamicate World* 7 (2019), 192–227.

Goodenough, E. R. *Goodenough on the Beginnings of Christianity.* Ed. A. T. Kraabel. Leiden, 2020.

Goodman, M. *The Ruling Class of Judaea: The Origins of the Jewish Revolt against Rome A.D. 66–70.* Cambridge, 1987

Goodman, N. *The Puritan Cosmopolis: The Law of Nations and the Early American Imagination.* Oxford, 2018.

Gounelle, R. "Un nouvel évangile judéo-chrétien?" *The Apocryphal Gospels within the Context of Early Christian Theology.* Ed. J. Schröter. Leuven, 2013.

Gourgues, M. "Jesus's Testimony before Pilate in 1 Timothy 6:13." *Journal of Biblical Literature* 135, 3 (2016), 639–48.

Graf, D. F. Untitled review of *Rome and the Arabs: A Prolegomenon to the Study of Byzantium and the Arabs* by Irfan Shahîd and *Byzantium and the Arabs in the Fourth Century* by Irfan Shahîd. *Bulletin of the American Schools of Oriental Research* 275 (1989) 71–3.

Grafton, A., with A. Shelford and N. Siraisi. *New Worlds, Ancient Texts: The Power of Tradition and the Shock of Discovery.* Cambridge, Mass., 1992.

Granger, F. "Julius Africanus and the Library of the Pantheon." *The Journal of Theological Studies* (OS) 34 (1933), 157–61.

Grant, R. M. "The Occasion of Luke III: 1–2." *The Harvard Theological Review* 33, 2 (1940), 151–4.

———— "The Religion of Maximin Daia." *Christianity, Judaism, and other Greco-Roman Cults* ... *Part Four: Judaism after 70, Other Greco-Roman Cults* ... Ed. J. Neusner. Leiden, 1975.

Green, E. "The Impossible Future of Christians in the Middle East: An Ancient Faith Is Disappearing from the Lands in Which It First Took Root." *The Atlantic* (23 May 2019). Archived online at https://www.theatlantic.com/international/archive/2019/05/iraqi-christians-nineveh-plain/589819/.

Green, P. *Alexander to Actium: The Historical Evolution of the Hellenistic Age.* Berkeley, 1990.

Green, R. P. H. *Latin Epics of the New Testament: Juvencus, Sedulius, Arator.* Oxford, 2006.

Greenwood, D. N. "Five Latin Inscriptions from Julian's Pagan Restoration." *Bulletin of the Institute of Classical Studies* 57, 2 (2014), 101–19.

Griffith Dixon, G. *Johann Georg Hamann's Relational Metacriticism.* Berlin, 1995.

Grimm, S. *Dissertatio inauguralis juridica, de profanatione rei sacrae, vulgo Secularisirung Geistlicher Güter.* Giessen (Gissa Hassorum): Christoph Hermann Karger (Kargerus), 1687.

Griswold, E. "Is This the End of Christianity in the Middle East? ISIS and Other Extremist Movements across the Region Are Enslaving, Killing, and Uprooting Christians, with No Aid in Sight." *The New York Times Magazine* (22 July 2015). Archived online at https://www.nytimes.com/2015/07/26/magazine/is-this-the-end-of-christianity-in-the-middle-east.html.

Groetsch, U. *Hermann Samuel Reimarus (1694–1768): Classicist, Hebraist, Enlightenment Radical in Disguise.* Leiden, 2015.

Grotius, H. *Annotationes ad Vetus Testamentum.* 3 vols. Paris: S. Cramoisy, 1644.

———— *Annotationes in Novum Testamentum: Denuo emendatius editae.* 9 vols. Groningen: W. Zuidema, 1826–34.

———— *Christ's Passion: A Tragedie, with Annotations.* Trans. G. Sandys. London: John Legatt, 1640.

———— *The Free Sea, with William Welwod's Critique and Grotius's Reply.* Trans. R. Hakluyt. Ed. D. Armitage. Indianapolis, 2004.

———— *Opera omnia theologica.* 4 vols. Stuttgart, 1972.

———— *The Rights of War and Peace.* Trans. J. Barbeyrac. Ed. R. Tuck. 3 vols. Indianapolis, 2005.

Haan, E. "Milton's Latin Poetry and Vida." *Humanistica Lovaniensia* 44 (1995), 282–304.

Haenchen, E. *The Acts of the Apostles: A Commentary.* Trans. B. Noble and G. Shinn with H. Anderson. Rev. R. McL. Wilson. Philadelphia, 1971.

Halivni, D. W. *The Formation of the Babylonian Talmud.* Oxford, 2013.

Hamann, J. G. "Metacritique on the Purism of Reason (Written in 1784)." *Writings on Philosophy and Language.* Ed. K. Haynes. Cambridge, 2007.

Hankins, J. "Religion and the Modernity of Renaissance Humanism." *Interpretations of Renaissance Humanism.* Ed. A. Mazzocco. Leiden, 2006.

Hansen, M. H. *The Athenian Ecclesia: A Collection of Articles, 1976–1983.* Copenhagen, 1983.

Hardman, J. *Louis XVI.* New Haven, 1993.

Harries, J. *Imperial Rome AD 284 to 363: The New Empire.* Edinburgh, 2012.

Harrill, J. A. "Divine Judgment against Ananias and Sapphira (Acts 5:1–11): A Stock Scene of Perjury and Death." *Journal of Biblical Literature* 130, 2 (2011), 351–69.

Harrington, J. M. *The Lukan Passion Narrative: The Markan Material in Luke 22,54–23,25; A Historical Survey; 1891–1997.* Leiden, 2000.

SELECT BIBLIOGRAPHY

Harrison, E. D. R. "The Nazi Dissolution of the Monasteries: A Case-Study." *The English Historical Review* 109, 431 (1994), 323–55.

Hartnaccius, D. *Admiranda physica, sive observationes singulares ... quas curiossisimi in universa penè Europa naturae scrutatores, summa non minus diligentia, quàm judicio singulari annotarunt ...* Leipzig (Lipsia): Bauerianae, 1683.

———— (Pseudonym: "Daniel Maphanasus".) *Confutationis Pontii Pilati defensi* In: *Johannis Stelleri, J. U. doctoris Jenensis Pilatus defensus unà cum Danielis Maphanasi Mulchentinensis confutatione scripti illius et disputatione academica Christiani: Thomasii Ph M adversus idem paradoxon.* Leipzig (Lipsia): Johann Christoph Mieth (Miethius), 1676.

———— *Johannis Micraelii syntagma historiarum ecclesiae omnium ... ut beneficio Indicis locupletissimi, tabularumque chronologicarum instar lexici historiae ecclesiasticae esse possit.* (Fourth edition.) Leipzig (Lipsia): Johann Lüderwald, 1679.

Heckel, M. "Religionsbann und landesherrliches Kirchenregiment." *Die lutherische Konfessionalisierung in Deutschland.* Ed. H.-C. Rublack. Gütersloh, 1992.

———— "Das Säkularisierungsproblem in der Entwicklung des deutschen Staatskirchensrechts." *Christentums und modernes Recht. Beiträge zum Problem der Säkularisation.* Ed. G. Dilcher and I. Staff. Frankfurt am Main, 1984.

Hedley, P. L. "Pilate's Arrival in Judaea." *The Journal of Theological Studies* 35 (1934), 56–8.

Heemskerk, M. T. *Suffering in the Mu'tazilite Theology: 'Abd al' Jabbār's Teaching on Pain and Divine Justice.* Leiden, 2000.

Heil, M. "On the Date of the Title *Britannicus Maximus* of Septimius Severus and His Sons." *Britannia* 34 (2003), 268–71.

Heller-Roazen, D. *The Enemy of All: Piracy and the Law of Nations.* New York, 2009.

Helmholz, R. H. *The Ius Commune in England: Four Studies.* Oxford, 2001.

Hennings, R. "Eusebius von Emesa und die Juden." *Zeitschrift für Antikes Christentum* 5 (2001), 240–60.

Herbert, G. "The Sacrifice." *The Temple: Sacred Poems, and Private Ejaculations; By the Rev. George Herbert; Late Orator of the University of Cambridge ...* Bristol: R. Edwards (printer), and London: T. Hurst (seller), 1799.

Herrin, J. *The Formation of Christendom.* Princeton, 1987.

———— *Ravenna: Capital of Empire, Crucible of Europe.* Princeton, 2019.

Hess, H. *The Early Development of Canon Law and the Council of Serdica.* Oxford, 2002.

Hilali, A. *The Sanaa Palimpsest: The Transmission of the Qur'an in the First Centuries AH.* Oxford, 2017.

Hill, G. "Ovid in the Third Reich." *These Hard and Shining Things: Rowan Evans, Geoffrey Hill, Toby Martinez de las Rivas.* London, 2018.

SELECT BIBLIOGRAPHY

Hillgarth, J. N. "The Image of Alexander VI and Cesare Borgia in the Sixteenth and Seventeenth Centuries." *Journal of the Warburg and Courtauld Institutes* 59 (1996), 119–29.

Himmelfarb, M. "The Mother of the Messiah in the Talmud Yerushalmi and Sefer Zerubbabel." *The Talmud Yerushalmi and Graeco-Roman Culture*. Ed. P. Schäfer. Tübingen, 2002.

Hinske, N. "Eklektik, Selbstdenken, Mündigkeit: Drei verschiedene Formulierungen einer und derselben Programmidee." *Aufklärung* 1, 1 (1986), 5–7.

Hobbes, T. *Behemoth or The Long Parliament*. Ed. P. Seaward. Oxford, 2010.

———— *Leviathan: Volume 1*. Ed. G. A. J. Rogers and K. Schuhmann. London—New York, 2005.

———— *Leviathan, Volume 3: The English and Latin Texts (ii)*. Ed. N. Malcolm. Oxford, 2012.

Hoehner, H. W. *Herod Antipas*. Cambridge, 1972.

Höpfl, H. "Tyrannicide and the Oath of Allegiance." *Jesuit Political Thought: The Society of Jesus and the State, c.1540–1630*. Cambridge, 2004.

Horbury, W. "Christ as Brigand in Ancient Anti-Christian Polemic." *Jesus and the Politics of His Day*. Ed. E. Bammel and C. F. D. Moule. Cambridge, 1984.

———— "The Depiction of Judaeo-Christians in the Toledot Yeshu." *The Image of the Judaeo-Christians in Ancient Jewish and Christian Literature*. Ed. P. J. Tomson and D. Lambers-Petry. Tübingen, 2003.

———— *Jews and Christians in Contact and Controversy*. Edinburgh, 1998.

———— "The Trial of Jesus in Jewish Tradition." *The Trial of Jesus: Cambridge Studies in Honour of C. F. D. Moule*. Ed. E. Bammel. Naperville, Ill., 1970.

Houellebecq, M. *Serotonin*. Trans. S. Whiteside. New York, 2019.

Hourihane, C. *Pontius Pilate, Anti-Semitism, and the Passion in Medieval Art*. Princeton, 2009.

Houtuyn, A. *Monarchia Hebraeorum, quae est imperio monarchico in populum Hebraeum probatio ab Abrahamo ad dispersam gentem*. Leiden (Lugdunum Batavorum): Felix Lopez de Haro, 1685.

———— *Politica contracta generalis, notis illustrata ... Ad calcem errores Hobbesiani indicantur*. The Hague (Haga-Comitis): Gerard Rammazin, 1681.

Hunter, I. "Christian Thomasius and the Desacralization of Philosophy." *Journal of the History of Ideas* 61, 4 (2000), 595–616.

———— "The Invention of Human Nature: The Intention and Reception of/ Pufendorf's *Entia moralia* Doctrine." *History of European Ideas* 45, 7 (2019), 933–52.

———— *Rival Enlightenments: Civil and Metaphysical Philosophy in Early Modern Europe*. Cambridge, 2001.

———— *The Secularisation of the Confessional State: The Political Thought of Christian Thomasius*. Cambridge, 2007.

SELECT BIBLIOGRAPHY

———— "Secularization: The Birth of a Modern Combat Concept." *Modern Intellectual History* 12, 1 (2015), 1–32.

Huxley, A. *Jesting Pilate*. London, 1926.

Inowlocki, S. *Eusebius and the Jewish Authors: His Citation Technique in an Apologetic Context*. Leiden, 2006.

Izbicki, T. M. "The Reception of Marsilius." *A Companion to Marsilius of Padua*. Ed. G. Moreno-Riano and C. J. Nederman. Leiden, 2012.

Jacobs, L. *The Talmudic Argument: A Study in Talmudic Reasoning and Methodology*. Cambridge, 1984.

Jarry, A. "The Passion Considered as an Uphill Bicycle Race." *Selected Works of Alfred Jarry*. Ed. R. Shattuck and S. W. Taylor. London, 1965.

Jauss, H. R. "Modernity and Literary Tradition." *Critical Inquiry* 31, 2 (2005), 329–64.

Jeremias, J. *The Parables of Jesus*. Trans. S. H. Hooke. London, 1954.

Johnson, A. P. "The Author of the *Against Hierocles*: A Response to Borzì and Jones." *The Journal of Theological Studies* (NS) 64, 2 (2013), 574–94.

Johnson, L. T. *Among the Gentiles: Greco-Roman Religion and Christianity*. New Haven, 2009.

Johnson, M. R. "Was Gassendi an Epicurean?" *History of Philosophy Quarterly* 20, 4 (2003), 339–60.

Jones, C. P. *Between Pagan and Christian*. Cambridge, Mass., 2014.

———— "The Historicity of the Neronian Persecution: A Response to Brent Shaw." *New Testament Studies* 63, 1 (2017), 146–52.

Joyce, J. *Ulysses*. London, 2000.

Jurasz, I. "Carpocrate et Epiphane: Chrétiens et platoniciens radicaux." *Vigiliae Christianae* 71, 2 (2017), 134–67.

———— "Lettre de Mara bar Sérapion et la *paideia* hellénistique." *Babelao* 7 (2018), 81–135.

Kahane, H., and R. Kahane. "'Lingua Franca': The Story of a Term." *Romance Philology* 30, 1 (1976), 25–41.

Kajanto, I. "Pontifex Maximus as the Title of the Pope." *Arctos* 15 (1981), 37–51.

Kaldellis, A. "From Rome to New Rome, from Empire to Nation-State: Reopening the Question of Byzantium's Roman Identity." *Two Romes: Rome and Constantinople in Late Antiquity*. Ed. L. Grig and G. Kelly. Oxford, 2012.

Kallendorf, C. "From Virgil to Vida: The *Poeta Theologus* in Italian Renaissance Commentary." *Journal of the History of Ideas* 56, 1 (1995), 41–62.

Kalthoff, A. *Das Christus-Problem: Grundlinien zu einer Sozial-theologie*. Leipzig, 1903.

Kannengiesser, C. *Handbook of Patristic Exegesis: The Bible in Ancient Christianity*. 2 vols. Leiden, 2004.

Kantorowicz, E. H. *The King's Two Bodies: A Study in Medieval Political Theology*. Princeton, 1957.

SELECT BIBLIOGRAPHY

Kattan Gribetz, S. "Hanged and Crucified: The Book of Esther and the *Toledot Yeshu.*" *Toledot Yeshu ("The Life Story of Jesus") Revisited: A Princeton Conference.* Ed. P. Schäfer, M. Meerson, and Y. Deutsch. Tübingen, 2011.

Kautsky, K. *Der Ursprung des Christentums.* Stuttgart, 1920.

Kelhoffer, J. A. "Basilides's Gospel and *Exegetica* (*Treatises*)." *Vigiliae Christianae* 59, 2 (2005), 115–34.

Kelsen, H. "Absolutism and Relativism in Philosophy and Politics." *The American Political Science Review* 42, 5 (1948), 906–14.

———— *Die Staatslehre des Dante Alighieri.* Vienna, 1905.

———— "Foundations of Democracy." *Ethics: An International Journal of Social, Legal, and Political Philosophy* 66, 1 (1955), 1–101.

Kennell, S. A. H. *Magnus Felix Ennodius: A Gentleman of the Church.* Ann Arbor, 2000.

Keresztes, P. "The Jews, the Christians, and Emperor Domitian." *Vigiliae Christianae* 27, 1 (1973), 1–28.

———— "Law and Arbitrariness in the Persecution of the Christians and Justin's *First Apology.*" *Vigiliae Christianae* 18 (1964), 204–14.

Kierkegaard, S. *Philosophical Fragments: Johannes Climacus.* Ed. and trans. H. V. Hong and E. H. Hong. Princeton, 1985.

———— *Søren Kierkegaard's Journals and Papers, Volume 1.* Ed. and trans. H. V. Hong and E. H. Hong. Bloomington, 1967.

Kim, T. H. "The Anarthrous υἱὸς θεοῦ in Mark 15,39 and the Roman Imperial Cult." *Biblica* 79, 2 (1998), 221–41.

Knausgaard, K. O. *A Time for Everything.* Trans. J. Anderson. Brooklyn, New York, 2008.

Knowles, D. *Bare Ruined Choirs: The Dissolution of the English Monasteries.* Cambridge, 1976.

———— *The Religious Orders in England, Volume III: The Tudor Age.* Cambridge, 1957–60.

Koch, B. "Marsilius of Padua on Church and State." *A Companion to Marsilius of Padua.* Ed. G. Moreno-Riano and C. J. Nederman. Leiden, 2012.

Kofsky, A. *Eusebius of Caesarea against Paganism.* Leiden, 2000.

Kolodziejczyk, D. "Khan, Caliph, Tsar, and Imperator: The Multiple Identities of the Ottoman Sultan." *Universal Empire: A Comparative Approach to Imperial Culture and Representation in Eurasian History.* Ed. P. Fibiger Bang and D. Kolodziejczyk. Cambridge, 2012.

Koskenniemi, M. "Imagining the Rule of Law: Rereading the Grotian 'Tradition'." *The European Journal of International Law* 30, 1 (2019), 17–52.

Krauss, S. *The Jewish–Christian Controversy from the Earliest Times to 1789: Volume I; History.* Ed. and rev. W. Horbury. Tübingen, 1995.

Krey, V. *Keine Strafe ohne Gesetz: Einführung in die Dogmengeschichte des Satzes 'nullum crimen, nulla poena sine lege'.* Berlin, 1983.

SELECT BIBLIOGRAPHY

Kristeva, J. *This Incredible Need to Believe*. Trans. B. B. Brahic. New York, 2011.

Kritzeck, J. *Peter the Venerable and Islam*. Princeton, 1964.

Krop, H. "From Religion in the Singular to Religions in the Plural: 1700, a Faultline in the Conceptual History of Religion." *Enlightened Religion: From Confessional Churches to Polite Piety in the Dutch Republic*. Ed. J. Spaans and J. Touber. Leiden, 2019.

Lacan, J. "Of Structure as an Inmixing of an Otherness Prerequisite to Any Subject Whatever." *The Structuralist Controversy: The Languages of Criticism and the Sciences of Man*. Ed. R. Macksey and E. Donato. Baltimore, 1972.

——— *The Triumph of Religion, Preceded by Discourse to Catholics*. Trans. B. Fink. Cambridge, 2013.

Lærke, M. "*Jus circa sacra*: Elements of Theological Politics in 17th Century Rationalism; From Hobbes and Spinoza to Leibniz." *Distinktion* 10 (2005), 41–64.

——— "Leibniz on Church and State: Presumptive Logic and Perplexing Cases." *Journal of the History of Philosophy* 56, 4 (2018), 629–57.

Lamberigts, M. J. G. P. "The Italian Julian of Æclanum about the African Augustine of Hippo." *Augustinus Afer: Saint Augustin; africanité et universalité ... *Ed. P.-Y. Fux, J.-M. Roessli, and O. Wermelinger. Fribourg, 2003.

Lampe, G. W. H. "A.D. 70 in Christian Reflection." *Jesus and the Politics of His Day*. Ed. E. Bammel and C. F. D. Moule. Cambridge, 1984.

——— "The Trial of Jesus in the *Acta Pilati*." *Jesus and the Politics of His Day*. Ed. E. Bammel and C. F. D. Moule. Cambridge, 1984.

Latham, R. E. *Revised Medieval Latin Word-List from British and Irish Sources*. London, 1965.

Lattimore, R. *Acts and Letters of the Apostles: Newly Translated from the Greek*. New York, 1982.

——— *The Four Gospels and the Revelation*. New York, 1979.

Laupot, E. "Tacitus' Fragment 2: The Anti-Roman Movement of the *Christiani* and the Nazoreans." *Vigiliae Christianae* 54, 3 (2000), 233–47.

Lawson, T. *The Crucifixion and the Qur'an: A Study in the History of Muslim Thought*. Oxford, 2009.

Le Coz, R. "Jean Damascène: Vie et œuvre." *Jean Damascène: Écrits sur l'Islam*. Greek with French trans. and comm. R. Le Coz. Paris, 1992.

Lee, A. D. *From Rome to Byzantium, AD 363 to 565: The Transformation of Ancient Rome*. Edinburgh, 2013.

Lee, G. W. "Israel between the Two Cities: Augustine's Theology of the Jews and Judaism." *Journal of Early Christian Studies* 24, 4 (2016), 523–51.

Lémonon, P. *Pilate et le gouvernement de la Judée: Textes et monuments*. Paris, 1981.

Lenski, N. "Constantine and the Donatists: Exploring the Limits of Religious Toleration." *Religiöse Toleranz: 1700 Jahre nach dem Edikt von Mailand*. Ed. M. Wallraff. Berlin, 2016.

SELECT BIBLIOGRAPHY

Lepelley, C. *Aspects de l'Afrique Romaine: Les cités, la vie rurale, le christianisme.* Bari, 2001.

Lepsius, O. "Hans Kelsen on Dante Alighieri's Political Philosophy." *The European Journal of International Law* 27, 4 (2016), 1153–67.

Lesaffer, R. *European Legal History: A Cultural and Political Perspective.* Trans. J. Arriens. Cambridge, 2009.

Leshem, D. *The Origins of Neoliberalism: Modeling the Economy from Jesus to Foucault.* New York, 2016.

Lessing, G. E. *Rettung des* Inepti Religiosi, *und seines ungenanten Berfassers.* In: *Vermischte Schriften. Dritte Theil.* Berlin: Christian Friedrich Boss und Sohn, 1784.

Levieils, X. "Étude historique du récit d'Hégésippe sur la comparution des petits-fils de Jude devant Domitien." *Revue des études juives* 173, 3–4 (2014), 297–323.

Levine, J. M. "Reginald Pecock and Lorenzo Valla on the *Donation of Constantine.*" *Studies in the Renaissance* 20 (1973), 118–43.

Levine, L. I. "R. Abbahu of Caesarea." *Christianity, Judaism, and other Greco-Roman Cults ... Part Four: Judaism after 70, Other Greco-Roman Cults ...* Ed. J. Neusner. Leiden, 1975.

Levitin, D. "From Sacred History to the History of Religion: Paganism, Judaism, and Christianity in European Historiography from Reformation to the 'Enlightenment'." *The Historical Journal* 55, 4 (2012), 1117–60.

Lezius, F. *Der Toleranzbegriff Lockes und Pufendorfs: Ein Beitrag zur Geschichte der Gewissensfreiheit.* Leipzig, 1900 (reprinted 1987).

Linde, J. C. "Lorenzo Valla and the Authenticity of Sacred Texts." *Humanistica Lovaniensia* 60 (2011), 35–63.

Lipsius, J. *De cruce libri tres, ad sacram profanamque historiam utiles: Unà cum notis, ac figuris.* Leiden (Lugduni Batavorum), 1695.

Litwa, M. D. *Iesus Deus: The Early Christian Depiction of Jesus as a Mediterranean God.* Minneapolis, 2014.

Locke, J. "The Reasonableness of Christianity, as Delivered in the Scriptures." *Writings on Religion.* Ed. V. Nuovo. Oxford, 2002.

———— *Selected Correspondence.* Ed. M. Goldie. Oxford, 2002.

Lockwood, S. "Marsilius of Padua and the Case for the Royal Ecclesiastical Supremacy." *Transactions of the Royal Historical Society* 1 (1991), 89–119.

Lombardi, B., ed. and comm. *La divina commedia, novamente corretta, spiegata e difesa ...* Rome, 1791–2. Archived online by Dartmouth College.

Louth, A. "St John Damascene: Preacher and Poet." *Preacher and Audience: Studies in Early Christian and Byzantine Homiletics.* Ed. M. B. Cunningham and P. Allen. Leiden, 1998.

———— *St John Damascene: Tradition and Originality in Byzantine Theology.* Oxford, 2002.

SELECT BIBLIOGRAPHY

Lübbe, H. *Säkularisierung. Geschichte eines ideenpolitischen Begriffs.* Freiburg, 1965.

Lyotard, J.-F. *The Confession of Augustine.* Trans. R. Beardsworth. Stanford, 2000.

Maas, M. "Roman History and Christian Ideology in Justinianic Reform Legislation." *Dumbarton Oaks Papers* 40 (1986), 17–31.

MacDonald, D. R. *The Dionysian Gospel: The Fourth Gospel and Euripides.* Minneapolis, 2017.

MacDonald, M. Y. *Early Christian Women and Pagan Opinion: The Power of the Hysterical Woman.* Cambridge, 1996.

Mach, M. "Justin Martyr's *Dialogus cum Tryphone Iudaeo* and the Development of Christian Anti-Judaism." *Contra Iudaeos: Ancient and Medieval Polemics between Christians and Jews.* Ed. O. Limor and G. G. Stroumsa. Tübingen, 1996.

Mackay, C. S. "Lactantius and the Succession to Diocletian." *Classical Philology* 94, 2 (1999), 198–209.

MacMullen, R. *Christianity and Paganism in the Fourth to Eighth Centuries.* New Haven, 1997.

———— *Christianizing the Roman Empire (A.D. 100–400).* New Haven, 1984.

———— *Constantine.* New York, 1971.

Maier, J. *Jesus von Nazareth in der talmudischen Überlieferung.* Darmstadt, 1978.

McKechnie, P. "Judaean Embassies and Cases before Roman Emperors, AD 44–66." *Journal of Theological Studies* (NS) 56, 2 (2005), 339–61.

Meier, J. P. *A Marginal Jew: Rethinking the Historical Jesus, Volume One: The Roots of the Problem and the Person.* New York, 1991.

Maier, P. L. "The Fate of Pontius Pilate." *Hermes* 99, 3 (1971), 362–71.

———— "The Inscription on the Cross of Jesus of Nazareth." *Hermes* 124, 1 (1996), 58–75.

———— "Sejanus, Pilate, and the Date of the Crucifixion." *Church History* 37, 1 (1968), 3–13.

Malcolm, N. *Aspects of Hobbes.* Oxford, 2002.

Manassero, A. *Ecce Homo: Storia del processo di Gesù.* Milan, 1952.

Mann, T. *Joseph and His Brothers.* Trans. H. T. Lowe-Porter. London, 1956.

Manselli, R. "The Legend of Barlaam and Joasaph: In Byzantium and in the Romance Europe." *East and West* 7, 4 (1957), 331–40.

Mansfeld, J. "Aspects of Epicurean Theology." *Mnemosyne* 46, 2 (1993), 172–210.

Mark, G. "Jesus 'Was Close to the Authorities': The Historical Background of a Talmudic Pericope." *Journal of Theological Studies* (NS) 60, 2 (2009), 437–66.

Markus, R. A. *The End of Ancient Christianity.* Cambridge, 1998.

———— *Saeculum: History and Society in the Theology of St Augustine.* Cambridge, 1970.

SELECT BIBLIOGRAPHY

Marramao, G. "Säkularisierung." *Historisches Wörterbuch der Philosophie*. Ed. J. Ritter and K. Gründer. Basel, 1992.

———— *Die Säkularisierung der westlichen Welt.* Trans. G. Memmert. Frankfurt am Main, 1996.

Mauritius, E. *De secularisatione bonorum ecclesiasticorum ex jure divino et humano praestertim ...* Sine loco (Kiel): Joachim Reumann (Reumannus), 1666.

Mayr, R., ed. *Vocabularium codicis Iustiniani, I: Pars Latina*. Hildesheim, 1965.

McAuliffe, J. D. "Quranic Hermeneutics: The Views of al-Ṭabarī and Ibn Kathīr." *Approaches to the History of the Interpretation of the Qur'ān*. Oxford, 1988.

McClure, J. *The Franciscan Invention of the New World*. Cham, 2017.

McCormick, M. "New Light on the 'Dark Ages': How the Slave Trade Fuelled the Carolingian Economy." *Past & Present* 177 (2002), 17–54.

McNeil, G. H. "The Cult of Rousseau and the French Revolution." *Journal of the History of Ideas* 6, 2 (1945), 197–212.

McQueen, A. "'A Rhapsody of Heresies': The Scriptural Politics of *On the Citizen*." *Hobbes's On the Citizen: A Critical Guide*. Ed. R. Douglass and J. Olsthoorn. Cambridge, 2019.

Meccarelli, M. *Arbitrium: Un aspetto sistematico degli ordinamenti giuridici in età di diritto comune*. Milan, 1998.

Meerson, M., and P. Schäfer. "Introduction." *Toledot Yeshu: The Life Story of Jesus ... Volume I; Introduction and Translation*. Ed. and trans. M. Meerson and P. Schäfer. Tübingen, 2014.

Mellet, P.-A. *Les traités monarchomaques: Confusion des temps, résistance armée et monarchie parfaite, 1560–1600*. Geneva, 2007.

Merdinger, J. E. *Rome and the African Church in the Time of Augustine*. New Haven, 1997.

Meščerskij, N. A. "Introduction: A Literary and Historical Study." *Josephus' Jewish War and Its Slavonic Version: A Synoptic Comparison of the English Translation by H. St. J. Thackeray with the Critical Edition by N. A. Meščerskij of the Slavonic Version in the Vilna Manuscript ...* Ed. and trans. H. Leeming and K. Leeming. Leiden, 2003.

Meyendorff, J. "Justinian, the Empire, and the Church." *Dumbarton Oaks Papers* 22 (1968), 43–60.

Milbank, J. *Being Reconciled: Ontology and Pardon*. London–New York, 2003.

———— "Christ the Exception." *New Blackfriars* 82 (2001), 541–56.

Millar, F. "Reflections on the Trials of Jesus." *A Tribute to Geza Vermes: Essays on Jewish and Christian Literature and History*. Ed. P. R. Davies and R. T. White. Sheffield, 1990.

———— *The Roman Near East, 31 BC–AD 337*. Cambridge, Mass., 1993.

Milton, J. *The 1671 Poems: Paradise Regain'd and Samson Agonistes*. Ed. and annot. with comm. L. L. Knoppers. Oxford, 2008.

———. *"Paradise Lost: A Poem Written in Ten Books"; An Authoritative Text of the 1667*

SELECT BIBLIOGRAPHY

First Edition. Ed. with comm. J. T. Shawcross and M. Lieb. Pittsburgh, 2007.

Mitchell, S. "Maximinus and the Christians in A.D. 312: A New Latin Inscription." *The Journal of Roman Studies* 78 (1988), 105–24.

Moessner, D. P. "'The Christ Must Suffer': New Light on the Jesus–Peter, Stephen, Paul Parallels in Luke–Acts." *Novum Testamentum* 28, 3 (1986), 220–56.

Moorhouse, G. *The Last Office: 1539 and the Dissolution of a Monastery.* London, 2008.

Moorhead, J. "The Word *Modernus.*" *Latomus* 65, 2 (2006), 425–33.

Monateri, P. G. *Dominus mundi: Political Sublime and the World Order.* Oxford, 2018.

Monfasani, J. *George of Trebizond: A Biography and a Study of His Rhetoric and Logic.* Leiden, 1976.

Montinaro, F., and L. Neumann. "Eusebius Was the Author of the *Contra Hieroclem.*" *Zeitschrift für Antikes Christentum* 22, 2 (2018), 322–6.

Morris, C. *The Papal Monarchy: The Western Church from 1050 to 1250.* Oxford, 1989.

Motzki, H. "Alternative Accounts of the Qur'ān's Formation." *The Cambridge Companion to the Qur'ān.* Ed. J. McAuliffe. Cambridge, 2006.

Mounier, P. J. J. *Specimen academicum, de Pontii Pilati in causa Servatoris Agendi Ratione.* Leiden (Lugduni Batavorum): H. W. Hazenberg, 1825.

Mowery, R. L. "Son of God in Roman Imperial Titles and Matthew." *Biblica* 83, 1 (2002), 100–10.

Muldoon, J. "Papal Responsibility for the Infidel: Another Look at Alexander VI's *Inter caetera.*" *The Catholic Historical Review* 64, 2 (1978), 168–84.

Mullen, R. L. *The Expansion of Christianity: A Gazeteer of Its First Three Centuries.* Leiden, 2004.

Murcia, T. *Jésus dans le Talmud et la littérature rabbinique ancienne.* Turnhout, 2014.

Naragon, S. "Reading Kant in Herder's Notes." *Reading Kant's Lectures.* Ed. R. R. Clewis. Berlin, 2015.

Nederman, C. J. "From *Defensor pacis* to *Defensor minor*: The Problem of Empire in Marsiglio of Padua." *History of Political Thought* 16, 3 (1995), 313–29.

Negro, P. "Intorno alle fonti scolastiche in Hugo Grotius." *Divus Thomas* 103, 3 (2000), 200–51.

Neil, B. "Crisis and Wealth in Byzantine Italy: The *Libri pontificales* of Rome and Ravenna." *Byzantion* 82 (2012), 279–303.

———— "Papal Letters and Letter Collections." *Late Antique Letter Collections: A Critical Introduction and Reference Guide.* Ed. C. Sogno, B. K. Storin, and E. J. Watts. Oakland, Calif., 2017.

SELECT BIBLIOGRAPHY

Neil, B., and P. Allen. *The Letters of Gelasius I (492–496): Pastor and Micro-manager of the Church of Rome.* Turnhout, 2014.

Nellen, H. J. M. *Hugo Grotius: A Lifelong Struggle for Peace in Church and State, 1583–1645.* Trans. J. C. Grayson. Leiden, 2015.

Nelson, E. *The Hebrew Republic: Jewish Sources and the Transformation of European Political Thought.* Cambridge, Mass., 2010.

Neuwirth, A. "Qur'an and History: A Disputed Relationship; Some Reflections on Qur'anic History and History in the Qur'an." *Journal of Qur'anic Studies* 5 (2003), 1–18.

Nicholson, O. "Constantine's Vision of the Cross." *Vigiliae Christianae* 54, 3 (2000), 309–23.

Niehoff, M. R. "A Jewish Critique of Christianity from Second-Century Alexandria: Revisiting the Jew Mentioned in *Contra Celsum.*" *Journal of Early Christian Studies* 21, 2 (2013), 151–75.

Niemeyer, J. F. *Mediae Latinitatis lexicon minus: Lexique Latin médiéval.* Leiden, 1967.

Nietzsche, F. *The Anti-Christ, Ecce Homo, Twilight of the Idols, and Other Writings.* Ed. A. Ridley and J. Norman. Trans. J. Norman. Cambridge, 2005.

——— *Der Fall Wagner, Götzen-Dämmerung … Der Antichrist, Ecce homo, Dionyso-Dithyramben, Nietzsche contra Wagner.* Ed. G. Colli and M. Montinari. Berlin, 1969.

——— *Friedrich Nietzsche Briefe: Januar 1887–Januar 1889.* Ed. G. Colli and M. Montinari with H. Anania-Hess. Berlin, 1984.

——— *Human, All Too Human: A Book for Free Spirits.* Ed. R. J. Hollingdale. Trans. R. Schacht. Cambridge, 1996.

——— *Menschliches, Allzumenschliches: Zweiter Band; Nachgelassene Fragmente; Frühling 1878 bis November 1879.* Ed. G. Colli and M. Montinari. Berlin, 1967.

——— *Nachgelassene Fragmente: Herbst 1887 bis März 1888.* Ed. G. Colli and M. Montinari. Berlin, 1970.

Noble, T. F. X. "A New Look at the *Liber pontificalis.*" *Archivum historiae ponti-ficiae* 23 (1985), 347–58.

Nöldeke, T., F. Schwally, G. Berstrásser, and O. Pretzl. *The History of the Qur'ān.* Ed. and trans. W. H. Behn. Leiden, 2013.

Norwich, J. J. *A Short History of Byzantium.* New York, 1999.

Nothaft, C. P. E. *Dating the Passion: The Life of Jesus and the Emergence of Scientific Chronology (200–1600).* Leiden, 2012.

Oakley, F. *Empty Bottles of Gentilism: Kingship and the Divine in Late Antiquity and the Early Middle Ages (to 1050).* New Haven, 2010.

——— *Kingship: The Politics of Enchantment.* Oxford, 2006.

——— *The Mortgage of the Past: Reshaping the Ancient Political Inheritance (1050–1300).* New Haven, 2012.

———— *The Watershed of Modern Politics: Law, Virtue, Kingship, and Consent (1300–1650)*. New Haven, 2015.

O'Donnell, J. J. *Pagans: The End of Traditional Religion and the Rise of Christianity*. New York, 2015.

Olsthoorn, J. "Grotius and Pufendorf." *The Cambridge Companion to Natural Law Ethics*. Ed. T. Angier. Cambridge, 2019.

———— "The Theocratic *Leviathan*: Hobbes's Arguments for the Identity of Church and State." *Hobbes on Politics and Religion*. Ed. L. van Apeldoorn and R. Douglass. Oxford, 2018.

Oltermann, P. "Germany: Mass Shooting Attempt That Killed Two Was Antisemitic Attack, Minister Says." *The Guardian* (9 October 2019). Archived online at https://www.theguardian.com/world/2019/oct/09/two-people-killed-in-shooting-in-german-city-of-halle.

O'Meara, J. J. *Porphyry's Philosophy from Oracles in Augustine*. Paris, 1959.

Oxford Latin Dictionary. Ed. P. G. W. Glare. Oxford, 1996 (reprinted 2010).

Packman, Z. M. "Epithets with the Title Despotes in Regnal Formulas in Document Dates and in the Imperial Oath." *Zeitschrift für Papyrologie und Epigraphik* 90 (1992), 251–7.

———— "Regnal Formulas in Document Date and in the Imperial Oath." *Zeitschrift für Papyrologie und Epigraphik* 91 (1992), 61–76.

Pagden, A. *The Fall of Natural Man: The American Indian and the Origins of Comparative Ethnology*. Cambridge, 1999.

Pagendarm, B. H. *Dissertatio inauguralis juridica, de bonorum secularisatorum natura*. (Doctoral dissertation submitted to the University of Halle in 1707; Christian Thomasius presided at the defence.) Halle (Hala Magdeburgica): Johann Christian Grunert (Grunertus), 1748.

Palazzini, P. "Sécularisation." *Dictionnaire de droit canonique*. Ed. R. Naz. Vol. VII, Paris, 1965.

Palladini, F. *Samuel Pufendorf discepolo di Hobbes: Per una reinterpretazione del giusnaturalismo moderno*. Bologna, 1990.

———— *Samuel Pufendorf Disciple of Hobbes: For a Re-interpretation of Modern Natural Law*. Intro. I. Hunter. Trans. D. Saunders. Leiden, 2020.

Parente, J. A. *Religious Drama and the Humanist Tradition: Christian Theater in Germany and in the Netherlands, 1500–1681*. Leiden, 1987.

Park, D. G. "Dante and the Donation of Constantine." *Dante Studies* 130 (2012), 67–161.

Pascoli, G. "Chi sia 'colui che fece il gran rifiuto'." *Il Marzocco* 6 (27 July 1902). Reprinted in G. Pascoli, *Prose, II* (Milan, 1952).

Patočka, J. *Plato and Europe*. Trans. P. Lom. Stanford, 2002.

Patten, A. "The Humanist Roots of Linguistic Nationalism." *History of Political Thought* 27, 2 (2006), 223–62.

Paulus, C. G. *Der Prozess Jesu aus römisch-rechtlicher Perspektive*. Berlin, 2016.

SELECT BIBLIOGRAPHY

Pedersen, N. A. "Aristides." In *Defence of Christianity: Early Christian Apologists*. Ed. J. Engberg, A.-C. Jacobsen, and J. Ulrich. Frankfurt am Main, 2014.

Penna, A. "Pilato, Ponzio." *Enciclopedia Dantesca*. Ed. U. Bosco. Rome, 1973.

Perles, J. "Bileam-Jesus und Pontius Pilatus." *Monatsschrift für Geschichte und Wissenschaft des Judentums* 21 (1872), 266–7.

Peterson, E. "Monotheism as a Political Problem: A Contribution to the History of Political Theology in the Roman Empire." *Theological Tractates*. Ed. and trans. M. J. Hollerich. Stanford, 2011.

Piovanelli, P. "Exploring the Ethiopic *Book of the Cock*: An Apocryphal Passion Gospel from Late Antiquity." *The Harvard Theological Review* 96, 4 (2003), 427–54.

————— "The *Toledot Yeshu* and Christian Apocryphal Literature: The Formative Years." *Toledot Yeshu ("The Life Story of Jesus")* Revisited: A Princeton Conference. Ed. P. Schäfer, M. Meerson, and Y. Deutsch. Tübingen, 2011.

Pohlsander, H. A. "Philip the Arab and Christianity." *Historia: Zeitschrift für Alte Geschichte* 29, 4 (1980), 463–73.

Pokorný, P. "Jesus as the Ever-Living Lawgiver in the *Letter* of Mara bar Sarapion." *The Letter of Mara bar Sarapion in Context: Proceedings of the Symposium Held at Utrecht University, 10–12 December 2009*. Ed. A. Merz and T. Tieleman. Leiden, 2012.

Pozzo, R. "Kant's Latin in Class." *Reading Kant's Lectures*. Ed. R. R. Clewis. Berlin, 2015.

Pradels, W., R. Brändle, and M. Heimgartner. "The Sequence and Dating of the Series of John Chrysostom's Eight Discourses *Adversus Iudaeos*." *Zeitschrift für Antikes Christentum* 6 (2002), 90–116.

Prinz, M. "Christian Thomasius' frühe akademische Programmschriften im Kontext zeitgenössischer Praktiken der Vorlesungsankündigung." *Vernakuläre Wissenschaftskommunikation: Beiträge zur Entstehung und Frühgeschichte der modernen deutschen Wissenschaftssprachen*. Ed. M. Prinz and J. Schiewe. Berlin, 2018.

Pufendorf, S. *An Introduction to the History of the Principal Kingdoms and States of Europe*. Trans. J. Crull. Ed. M. J. Seidler. Indianapolis, 2013.

————— *De habitu religionis Christianae ad vitam civilem, liber singularis: Accedunt animadversiones ad aliqua loca è politica Adriani Houtuyn ...* Bremen (Brema): Anthony Gunther Schwerdfeger, 1687.

————— *Of the Nature and Qualification of Religion in Reference to Civil Society*. Trans. J. Crull. Ed. S. Zurbuchen. Indianapolis, 2002.

————— *On the Duty of Man and Citizen according to Natural Law*. Ed. J. Tully. Trans. M. Silverthorne. Cambridge, 1991.

Radin, M. *The Trial of Jesus of Nazareth*. Chicago, 1931.

Rapp, C. "Imperial Ideology in the Making: Eusebius of Caesarea on Constantine as 'Bishop'." *The Journal of Theological Studies* (NS) 49, 2 (1998), 685–95.

SELECT BIBLIOGRAPHY

Rauscher, A., ed. *Säkularisierung und Säkularisation vor 1800*. Munich, 1976.

Rees, R. *Diocletian and the Tetrarchy*. Edinburgh, 2004.

Reicke, B. "Judaeo-Christianity and the Jewish Establishment, A.D. 33–66." *Jesus and the Politics of His Day*. Ed. E. Bammel and C. F. D. Moule. Cambridge, 1984.

Reimarus, H. S. *The Goal of Jesus and His Disciples*. Trans. G. W. Buchanan. Leiden, 1970.

Reisiger, G. *Dissertatio juridica inauguralis, de jurisdictione Pilati, quam adspirante summo numine* ... Harderwijk (Harderovicus): Johan Moojen, 1759.

Rex, R. "The Religion of Henry VIII." *The Historical Journal* 57, 1 (2014), 1–32.

Reynolds, G. S. "The Muslim Jesus: Dead or Alive?" *Bulletin of the School of Oriental and African Studies* 72, 2 (2009), 237–58.

——— *A Muslim Theologian in the Sectarian Milieu: 'Abd al-Jabbār and the Critique of Christian Origins*. Leiden, 2004.

——— "On the Qur'anic Accusation of Scriptural Falsification (*tahrīf*) and Christian Anti-Jewish Polemic." *Journal of the American Oriental Society* 130, 2 (2010), 189–202.

——— "On the Qur'ān and the Theme of Jews as 'Killers of the Prophets'." *Al-Bayān: Journal of Qur'an and Hadith Studies* 10, 2 (2012), 9–32.

——— *The Qur'an and Its Biblical Subtext*. London, 2010.

———*The Qur'an and the Bible: Text and Commentary*. Qur'an trans. A. Q. Qarai. New Haven, 2018.

——— "The Rise and Fall of Qadi 'Abd al-Jabbar." *International Journal of Middle East Studies* 37, 1 (2005), 3–18.

Rhetius, J. F. "De secularisatione." *Disputationes juris publici undecim* ... Frankfurt an der Oder (Francofurti ad Viadrum): Jeremias Schrey, 1678.

"Robert Eisler." *Wiener Kunst Geschichte Gesichtet*. Archived online at univie. ac.at/geschichtegesichtet/r_eisler.html.

Robinson, J. M., P. Hoffmann, and J. S. Kloppenborg, eds. *The Critical Edition of Q: Synopsis, Including the Gospels of Matthew and Luke, Mark and Thomas* ... Leuven, 2000.

Rogoff, K. "Dealing with Monetary Paralysis at the Zero Bound." *Journal of Economic Perspectives* 31, 3 (2017), 47–66.

Rosadi, G. *Dopo Gesù*. Florence, 1919.

——— *Il processo di Gesú*. Florence, 1904.

——— *The Trial of Jesus*. Trans. E. Reich. New York, 1905.

Rose, M. "Hobbes contra Bellarmine." *Journal of Moral Theology* 4, 2 (2015), 43–62.

Rosenberg, A. W., and H. S. Lake. "Hugo Grotius as Hebraist." *Studia Rosenthaliana* 12, 1 (1978), 62–90.

Rousseau, J.-J. *Du contrat social*. Ed. with intro. and annot. R. Grimsley. Oxford, 1972.

———— *The Plan for Perpetual Peace, On the Government of Poland, and Other Writings on History and Politics.* Ed. C. Kelly. Trans. C. Kelly and J. Bush. Hanover, 2005.

———— *The Social Contract and Other Later Political Writings.* Ed. and trans. V. Gourevitch. Cambridge, 1997.

Roy, O. *Is Europe Christian?* London, 2020.

Rozier, C. C., D. Roach, G. E. M. Gasper, and E. van Houts, eds. *Orderic Vitalis: Life, Works, and Interpretations.* Woodbridge, Suffolk, 2016.

Rubinstein, A. "Observations on the Old Russian Version of Josephus' *Wars.*" *Journal of Semitic Studies* 2, 4 (1957), 329–48.

Saastamoinen, K. "Pufendorf on the Law of Sociality and the Law of Nations." *The Law of Nations and Natural Law 1625–1800.* Ed. S. Zurbuchen. Leiden, 2019.

Sahas, D. J. *John of Damascus on Islam: The "Heresy of the Ishmaelites".* Leiden, 1972.

Sale, G. *The Koran, Commonly Called The Alcoran of Mohammed, Translated into English Immediately from the Original Arabic* ... London, 1734.

Saleh, W. A. *The Formation of the Classical Tafsīr Tradition: The Qurʾān Commentary of al-Thaʿlabī (d. 427/1035).* Leiden, 2004.

———— "The Qurʾān Commentary, the Bible Controversy, and the Treatise." *In Defense of the Bible: A Critical Edition and an Introduction to al-Biqāʿīs Bible Treatise.* Leiden, 2008.

Salzman, M. R. "Lay Aristocrats and Ecclesiastical Politics: A New View of the Papacy of Felix III (483–492 C.E.) and the Acacian Schism." *Journal of Early Christian Studies* 27, 3 (2019), 465–89.

Santagata, M. *Dante: The Story of His Life.* Trans. R. Dixon. Cambridge, Mass., 2016.

Sapegno, N., ed. *La divina commedia: Vol. I; Inferno.* Florence, 1980.

Sarris, P. *Empires of Faith: The Fall of Rome to the Rise of Islam, 500–700.* Oxford, 2011.

Satran, D. "Anti-Jewish Polemic in the *Peri Pascha* of Melito of Sardis: The Problem of Social Context." *Contra Iudaeos: Ancient and Medieval Polemics between Christians and Jews.* Ed. O. Limor and G. G. Stroumsa. Tübingen, 1996.

Schadler, P. *John of Damascus and Islam: Christian Heresiology and the Intellectual Background to Earliest Christian–Muslim Relations.* Leiden, 2018.

Schäfer, P. *Jesus in the Talmud.* Princeton, 2007.

———— *Judeophobia: Attitudes toward the Jews in the Ancient World.* Cambridge, Mass., 1997.

Schaff, P. *Literature and Poetry.* New York, 1890.

Scheid, J. *The Gods, the State, and the Individual: Reflections on Civic Religion in Rome.* Trans. C. Ando. Philadelphia, 2015.

SELECT BIBLIOGRAPHY

Schiavone, A. *Pontius Pilate: Deciphering a Memory*. New York–London, 2017.

Schmidt, T. C. "Calculating December 25 as the Birth of Jesus in Hippolytus' *Canon* and *Chronicon*." *Vigiliae Christianae* 69, 5 (2015), 542–63.

Schmitt, C. *Political Theology: Four Chapters on the Concept of Sovereignty*. Trans. G. Schwab. Chicago, 2005.

———— *Political Theology II: The Myth of the Closure of Any Political Theology* Trans. M. Hoelzl and G. Ward. Cambridge, 2008.

Schneemelcher, W. *New Testament Apocrypha*. Trans. R. McL. Wilson. 2 vols. Louisville, 2003.

Schoeps, H. J. "*Restitutio Principii* as the Basis for the *Nova Lex Jesu*." *Journal of Biblical Literature* 66, 4 (1947), 453–64.

Scholem, G. *Walter Benjamin: The Story of a Friendship*. Trans. H. Zohn. Philadelphia, 1981.

Scholl, C. "Imitatio Imperii? Elements of Imperial Rule in the Barbarian Successor States of the Roman West." *Transcultural Approaches to the Concept of Imperial Rule in the Middle Ages*. Ed. C. Scholl, T. R. Gebhardt, and J. Clauss. Berlin, 2017.

Schott, J. M. *Christianity, Empire, and the Making of Religion in Late Antiquity*. Philadelphia, 2008.

Schröder, P. "Thomas Hobbes, Christian Thomasius, and the Seventeenth-Century Debate on the Church and State." *History of European Ideas* 23 (1997), 59–79.

Schürer, E. *The History of the Jewish People in the Age of Jesus Christ (175 B.C.– A.D. 135)*. Rev. and ed. G. Vermes and F. Millar, with P. Vermes and M. Black. 2 vols. Edinburgh, 1973.

Schwartz, D. R. "Composition and Sources in *Antiquities* 18: The Case of Pontius Pilate." *Flavius Josephus: Interpretation and History*. Ed. Z. Rodgers. Leiden, 2007.

Schwartz, S. *Josephus and Judaean Politics*. Leiden, 1990.

Senellart, M. "Course Context." In: M. Foucault. *On the Government of the Living: Lectures at the Collège de France, 1979–1980*. Ed. M. Senellart. Trans. G. Burchell. New York, 2012.

Seston, W. "Constantine as a 'Bishop'." *The Journal of Roman Studies* 37 (1947), 127–31.

Shahîd, I. *Byzantium and the Arabs in the Fourth Century*. Washington, D.C., 1984.

———— *Rome and the Arabs: A Prolegomenon to the Study of Byzantium and the Arabs*. Washington, D.C., 1984.

Shakespeare, W. *King Richard II*. Ed. and annot. A. Gurr. Cambridge, 1990.

———— *Macbeth*. Ed. and annot. A. R. Braunmuller. Cambridge, 1997.

———— *Richard III*. Ed. and annot. B. Raffel. New Haven, 2008.

Shaw, B. D. "The Myth of the Neronian Persecution." *The Journal of Roman Studies* 105 (2015), 73–100.

———— *Sacred Violence: African Christians and Sectarian Hatred in the Age of Augustine*. Cambridge, 2011.

Shelford, A. "The Quest for Certainty in Fact and Faith: Pierre-Daniel Huet and Josephus' *Testimonium Flavianum*." *Essays in Renaissance Thought and Letters*. Ed. A. Frazier and P. Nold. Leiden, 2015.

Sherwin-White, A. N. *The Letters of Pliny: A Historical and Social Commentary*. Oxford, 1966.

———— *Roman Society and Roman Law in the New Testament: The Sarum Lectures, 1960–1961*. Oxford, 1963.

Shoemaker, S. J. *The Apocalypse of Empire: Imperial Eschatology in Late Antiquity and Early Islam*. Philadelphia, 2018.

Singleton, C. S. *The Divine Comedy: Inferno, vol. 2; Commentary*. Princeton, 1977.

———— *The Divine Comedy: Paradiso, vol. 2; Commentary*. Princeton, 1975.

———— *The Divine Comedy: Purgatorio, vol. 2; Commentary*. Princeton, 1973.

Sivertsev, A. M. *Judaism and Imperial Ideology in Late Antiquity*. Cambridge, 2011.

Smith, K. *Constantine and the Captive Christians of Persia: Martyrdom and Religious Identity in Late Antiquity*. Oakland, Calif., 2016.

Somos, M. "Secularization in *De iure praedae*: From Bible Criticism to International Law." *Grotiana* 26, 1 (2007), 147–91.

Sordi, M. *The Christians and the Roman Empire*. Trans. A. Bedini. London, 1994.

Sorkin, D. *The Religious Enlightenment: Protestants, Jews, and Catholics from London to Vienna*. Princeton, 2008.

Spiró, G. *Captivity*. Trans. T. Wilkinson. Brooklyn, N.Y., 2015.

Springborg, P. "Hobbes's Biblical Beasts: *Leviathan* and *Behemoth*." *Political Theory* 23, 2 (1995), 353–75.

———— "Hobbes, Heresy, and the *Historia ecclesiastica*." *Journal of the History of Ideas* 55, 4 (1994), 553–71.

———— "The Politics of Hobbes's *Historia ecclesiastica*." *Hobbes on Politics and Religion*. Ed. L. van Apeldoorn and R. Douglass. Oxford, 2018.

———— "Thomas Hobbes and Cardinal Bellarmine: Leviathan and 'the Ghost of the Roman Empire'." *History of Political Thought* 16, 4 (1995), 503–31.

Springer, C. P. E. *The Gospel as Epic in Late Antiquity: The Paschale Carmen of Sedulius*. Leiden, 1988.

Stanley, C. D. "The Ethnic Context of Paul's Letters." *Christian Origins and Greco-Roman Culture, Social Literary Contexts for the New Testament: Early Christianity in Its Hellenistic Context*. Ed. S. E. Porter and A. W. Pitts. Leiden, 2013.

Steinberg, M. "The Twelve Tables and Their Origins: An Eighteenth-Century Debate." *Journal of the History of Ideas* 43, 3 (1982), 379–96.

Steller, J. *Liberatoris Jesu Subsidio! Defensum Pontium Pilatum ... Amicorum eruditorum examini exponit Ad 23. Aprilis 1674*. Dresden (Dresdae): Melchior Bergen, 1674.

SELECT BIBLIOGRAPHY

————— *Pilatus defensus*. In: *Johannis Stelleri, J. U. doctoris Jenensis Pilatus defensus unà cum Danielis Maphanasi Mulchentinensis confutatione scripti illius et disputatione academica Christiani: Thomasii Ph M Adversus idem paradoxon*. Leipzig (Lipsia): Johann Christoph Mieth (Miethius), 1676.

Stemberger, G. "The Sadducees: Their History and Doctrines." *The Cambridge History of Judaism, Volume Three: The Early Roman Period.* Ed. W. Horbury, W. Davies, and J. Sturdy. Cambridge, 1999.

Stern, S. M. "Quotations from Apocryphal Gospels in 'Abd al-Jabbār." *The Journal of Theological Studies* (NS) 18, 1 (1967), 34–57.

Stinger, C. "Italian Renaissance Learning and the Church Fathers." *The Reception of the Christian Fathers in the West: From the Carolingians to the Maurists*. 2 vols. Ed. I. Backus. Leiden, 1997.

Stow, K. R. "The Burning of the Talmud in 1553, in Light of Sixteenth-Century Catholic Attitudes toward the Talmud." *Bibliothèque d'humanisme et Renaissance* 34, 3 (1972), 435–59.

Strätz, H.-W. "Säkularisation, Säkularisierung, II: Der kanonistische und staatskirchenrechtliche Begriff." *Geschichtliche Grundbegriffe: Historisches Lexikon zur politisch-sozialen Sprache in Deutschland*. Ed. O. Brunner, W. Conze, and R. Koselleck. Stuttgart, 1984.

Straus, J. V. *Dissertatio juridica inauguralis historico-canonico-publica, de possessore Catholico non obligato ad bona secularisata pristinis usibus ecclesiasticis restituenda* … Mainz (Moguntia): Ex Typographejo privilegiato Franckenbergico, 1740.

Stroumsa, G. G. "Christ's Laughter: Docetic Origins Reconsidered." *Journal of Early Christian Studies* 12, 3 (2004), 267–88.

————— *The End of Sacrifice: Religious Transformations in Late Antiquity*. Trans. S. Emanuel. Chicago, 2009.

————— "From Anti-Judaism to Antisemitism in Early Christianity?" *Contra Iudaeos: Ancient and Medieval Polemics between Christians and Jews*. Ed. O. Limor and G. G. Stroumsa. Tübingen, 1996.

————— *The Making of the Abrahamic Religions in Late Antiquity*. Oxford, 2015.

————— *A New Science: The Discovery of Religion in the Age of Reason*. Cambridge, Mass., 2010.

————— *The Scriptural Universe of Ancient Christianity*. Cambridge, Mass., 2016.

Stroumsa, S. *Maimonides in His World: Portrait of a Mediterranean Thinker*. Princeton, 2009.

Summers, K. "Lucretius and the Epicurean Tradition of Piety." *Classical Philology* 90, 1 (1995), 32–57.

Sutcliffe, A. *Judaism and Enlightenment*. Cambridge, 2003.

Swain, S. *Hellenism and Empire: Language, Classicism, and Power in the Greek World, AD 50–250*. Oxford, 1996.

SELECT BIBLIOGRAPHY

Swenson, J. *On Jean-Jacques Rousseau: Considered as One of the First Authors of the Revolution*. Stanford, 2000.

Sykes, A. S. "Melito's Anti-Judaism." *Journal of Early Christian Studies* 5, 2 (1997), 271–83.

Syme, R. *Tacitus*. 2 vols. Oxford, 1958 (reprinted 1989).

Syros, V. *Marsilius of Padua at the Intersection of Ancient and Medieval Traditions of Political Thought*. Toronto, 2012.

Tardieu, M. "Le procès de Jésus vu par les Manichéens." *Apocrypha* 8 (1997), 9–24.

Taubes, J. *The Political Theology of Paul*. Ed. A. Assmann and J. Assmann with H. Folker, D.-W. Hartwich, and C. Schulte. Trans. D. Hollander. Stanford, 2004.

Taylor, J. "Why Were the Disciples First Called 'Christians' at Antioch? (Acts 11, 26)." *Revue Biblique* 101, 1 (1994), 75–94.

Taylor, J. E. "Pontius Pilate and the Imperial Cult in Roman Judaea." *New Testament Studies* 52, 4 (2006), 555–82.

Teitler, H. C. *The Last Pagan Emperor: Julian the Apostate and the War against Christianity*. Oxford, 2017.

"Testament." *Encyclopédie ou dictionnaire raisonné des sciences, des arts et des métiers*. Paris, 1765.

Thomas, G. S. R. "Maximin Daia's Policy and the Edicts of Toleration." *L'antiquité classique* 37, 1 (1968), 172–85.

Thomas, H. M. *The Secular Clergy in England, 1066–1216*. Oxford, 2014.

Thomas, N. L. *Defending Christ: The Latin Apologists before Augustine*. Turnhout, 2011.

Thomasius, C. *De injusto Pontii Pilati Judicio, habita d. 25 Nov. 1675 ... ADDITIO I. Joh. Stelleri Pilatus defensus*. In: *Dissertationes juridicae, varii argumenti, in Academia Lipsiensi ab ipso publice habitae, nunc conjunctim editae* ... Halle (Hala): Christoph. Salfedius—Leipzig (Lipsia): Joh. Grossius, 1695.

——— *Disputatio juridica, de injusto Pontii Pilati Judicio* ... Leipzig (Lipsia): Johann Georg (Georgi), 1675.

——— *Injustum judicium Pontii Pilati*. In: *Johannis Stelleri, J. U. doctoris Jenensis Pilatus defensus unà cum Danielis Maphanasi Mulchentinensis confutatione scripti illius et disputatione academica Christiani: Thomasii Ph M Adversus idem paradoxon*. Leipzig (Lipsia): Johann Christoph Mieth (Miethius), 1676.

——— "The Right of a Christian Prince in Religious Matters." *Essays on Church, State, and Politics*. Ed. and trans. I. Hunter, T. Ahnert, and F. Grunert. Indianapolis, 2007.

Thompson, E. A. "Christianity and the Northern Barbarians." *The Conflict between Paganism and Christianity in the Fourth Century*. Ed. A. Momigliano. Oxford, 1963.

Thornton, T. C. G. "High-Priestly Succession in Jewish Apologetics and

SELECT BIBLIOGRAPHY

Episcopal Succession in Hegesippus." *The Journal of Theological Studies* (NS) 54, 1 (2003), 160–3.

Thorpe, V. "Who Is the Mysterious 'Stetson' in T. S. Eliot's Waste Land?" *The Observer* (8 November 2015). Archived online at https://www.theguardian.com/books/2015/nov/08/ts-eliot-waste-land-stetson-anagram-riddle.

Thorsteinsson, R. M. *Jesus as Philosopher: The Moral Sage in the Synoptic Gospels.* Oxford, 2018.

Trites, A. A. "The Importance of Legal Scenes and Language in the Book of Acts." *Novum Testamentum* 16, 4 (1974), 278–84.

Tuck, R. *The Rights of War and Peace: Political Thought and the International Order from Grotius to Kant.* Oxford, 1999.

Tuori, K., and H. Björklund, eds. *Roman Law and the Idea of Europe.* London, 2019.

Turner, J. *Philology: The Forgotten Origins of the Modern Humanities.* Princeton, 2014.

Van Dam, H.-J. "Italian Friends: Grotius, De Dominis, Sarpi, and the Church." *Nederlands archief voor kerkgeschiedenis* 75, 2 (1995), 198–215.

Van de Voorde, G.-J. "'What More do You Want?' The Use of the Roman Trial of Jesus by St. Augustine and Marsilius of Padua." Paper read at the conference Marsilius of Padua between History, Philosophy and Politics. Katholieke Universiteit Leuven, 6–7 September 2018.

Van Heesch, J. "The Last Civic Coinages and the Religious Policy of Maximinus Daza (AD 312)." *The Numismatic Chronicle* 153 (1993), 65–75.

Van Henten, J. W. "Jewish Martyrdom and Jesus' Death." *Deutungen des Todes Jesu im Neuen Testament.* Ed. J. Frey and J. Schröter. Tübingen, 2005.

Van Miert, D. *The Emancipation of Biblical Philology in the Dutch Republic, 1590–1670.* Oxford, 2018.

Van Oort, J. "Tyconius' Apocalypse Commentary, Its Reconstruction, and Its Significance for Augustine's Doctrine of the Two Cities." *Vigiliae Christianae* 72, 5 (2018), 513–32.

Van Unnik, W. C. "The Critique of Paganism in I Peter 1:18." *Neotestamentica et Semitica: Studies in Honour of Matthew Black.* Ed. E. E. Ellis and M. Wilcox. Edinburgh, 1969.

——— "Hugo Grotius als uitlegger van het Nieuwe Testament." *Nederlands archief voor kerkgeschiedenis* (NS) 25 (1932), 1–48.

Vaughan, G. M. "The Audience of *Leviathan* and the Audience of Hobbes's Political Philosophy." *History of Political Thought* 22, 3 (2001), 448–71.

Vermes, G. *Jesus: Nativity—Passion—Resurrection.* London, 2010.

Versnel, H. S. "Making Sense of Jesus' Death: The Pagan Contribution." *Deutungen des Todes Jesu im Neuen Testament.* Ed. J. Frey and J. Schröter. Tübingen, 2005.

SELECT BIBLIOGRAPHY

Veyne, P. *Bread and Circuses: Historical Sociology and Political Pluralism.* Trans. B. Pearce. Ed. O. Murray. London–New York, 1990.

Vidal, G. "Live from Golgotha: An Excerpt from the Novel." *New England Review* 14, 3 (1992), 127–33.

Vocabularium iurisprudentiae Romanae, ex auctoritate Academiae Borussicae compositum, tomus V. Ed. B. Kübler. Berlin, 1931.

Vogt, J. "Pagans and Christians in the Family of Constantine the Great." *The Conflict between Paganism and Christianity in the Fourth Century.* Ed. A. Momigliano. Oxford, 1963.

Von Albrecht, M. "M. Minucius Felix as a Christian Humanist." *Illinois Classical Studies* 12, 1 (1987), 157–68.

Von Ammon, W. *Der bindende rechtswidrige Befehl.* Breslau, 1926 (reprinted 1977).

———— "Das Strafverfahren gegen Jesus von Nazareth." *Nachrichten der Evangelisch-Lutherischen Kirche in Bayern* 8 (1953), 69–72.

Wallraff, M. "The Beginnings of Christian Universal History: From Tatian to Julius Africanus." *Zeitschrift für Antikes Christentum* 14, 3 (2011), 540–55.

Ward, J. O. "Procopius, 'Bellum Gothicum' II.6.28: The Problem of Contacts between Justinian I and Britain." *Byzantion* 38, 2 (1968), 460–71.

Ward-Perkins, B. *The Fall of Rome and the End of Civilization.* Oxford, 2005.

———— "Old and New Rome Compared: The Rise of Constantinople." *Two Romes: Rome and Constantinople in Late Antiquity.* Ed. L. Grig and G. Kelly. Oxford, 2012.

Warren, C. "Hobbes's *Thucydides* and the Colonial Law of Nations." *The Seventeenth Century* 24, 2 (2013), 260–86.

Watson, A. *International Law in Archaic Rome: War and Religion.* Baltimore, 1993.

———— *The State, Law and Religion: Pagan Rome.* Athens, Ga. 1992.

———— *The Trial of Jesus.* Athens, Ga. 1995.

———— *The Trial of Stephen: The First Christian Martyr.* Athens, Ga., 2012.

Watts, E. "Christianization." *Late Ancient Knowing: Explorations in Intellectual History.* Ed. C. M. Chin and M. Vidas. Oakland, 2015.

Weber, D. "'For What Is so Monstrous as What the Punic Fellow Says?' Reflections on the Literary Background of Julian's Polemical Attacks on Augustine's Homeland." *Augustinus Afer: Saint Augustin; Africanité et universalité ...* Ed. P.-Y. Fux, J.-M. Roessli, and O. Wermelinger. Fribourg, 2003.

Weckmann, L. *Las Bulas Alejandrinas de 1493 y la Teoría política del papado medieval: Estudio de la supremacía papal sobre islas (1091–1493).* Intro. E. H. Kantorowicz. Mexico City, 1949.

———— *Constantino el Grande y Cristóbal Colón: Estudio de la supremacía papal sobre islas (1091–1493).* Intro. E. H. Kantorowicz. Mexico City, 1992 (reprint of 1949 book).

SELECT BIBLIOGRAPHY

———— "The Middle Ages in the Conquest of America." *Speculum* 26, 1 (1951), 130–41.

Weiss, J. *Die Predigt Jesu vom Reiche Gottes.* Göttingen, 1892.

Werckmeister, J. "The Reception of the Church Fathers in Canon Law." *The Reception of the Christian Fathers in the West: From the Carolingians to the Maurists.* Ed. I. Backus. Leiden, 1997. 2 vols.

Westall, R. "Simon of Cyrene, a Roman Citizen?" *Historia: Zeitschrift für Alte Geschichte* 59, 4 (2010), 489–500.

Whalen, B. E. *Dominion of God: Christendom and Apocalypse in the Middle Ages.* Cambridge, Mass., 2009.

Whealey, A. *Josephus on Jesus: The Testimonium Flavianum Controversy from Late Antiquity to Modern Times.* New York, 2003.

Whitford, D. M. "The Papal Antichrist: Martin Luther and the Under-appreciated Influence of Lorenzo Valla." *Renaissance Quarterly* 61, 1 (2008), 26–52.

Whitmarsh, T. *Battling the Gods: Atheism in the Ancient World.* New York, 2015.

Wieczynski, J. L. "The Donation of Constantine in Medieval Russia." *The Catholic Historical Review* 55, 2 (1969), 159–72.

Wilken, R. L. *The Christians as the Romans Saw Them.* New Haven, 1984.

———— *John Chrysostom and the Jews: Rhetoric and Reality in the Later Fourth Century.* Berkeley, 1983.

Winter, P. "Marginal Notes on the Trial of Jesus, II." *Zeitschrift für die neutestamentliche Wissenschaft und die Kunde der älteren Kirche* 50 (1959), 221–51.

———— *On the Trial of Jesus.* Berlin, 1961.

Wintour, P. "Persecution of Christians 'Coming Close to Genocide' in Middle East." *The Guardian* (2 May 2019). Archived online at https://www.theguardian.com/world/2019/may/02/persecution-driving-christians-out-of-middle-east-report.

Witherington, B. *Women and the Genesis of Christianity.* Ed. A. Witherington. Cambridge, 1990.

Witte, J. *Law and Protestantism: The Legal Teachings of the Lutheran Reformation.* Cambridge, 2002.

Wolfram, H. "The Shaping of the Early Medieval Kingdom." *Viator* 1 (1971), 11–20.

Wood, G. *The Way of the Strangers: Encounters with the Islamic State.* New York, 2019.

Woods, D. "Gregory of Nazianzus on the Death of Julian the Apostate (*Or.* 5.13)." *Mnemosyne* 68, 2 (2015), 297–303.

York, J. M. "The Image of Philip the Arab." *Historia: Zeitschrift für Alte Geschichte* 21, 2 (1972), 320–32.

Young, J. *Friedrich Nietzsche: A Philosophical Biography.* Cambridge, 2010.

Yovel, Y. *Les juifs selon Hegel et Nietzsche: La clef d'une énigme.* Paris, 2001.

SELECT BIBLIOGRAPHY

Yuval, I. J. *Two Nations in Your Womb: Perceptions of Jews and Christians in Late Antiquity and the Middle Ages*. Trans. B. Harshav and J. Chipman. Berkeley, 2006.

Zabel, H. "Säkularisation, Säkularisierung, III: Der geschichtsphilosophische Begriff." *Geschichtliche Grundbegriffe: Historisches Lexikon zur politisch-sozialen Sprache in Deutschland*. Ed. O. Brunner, W. Conze, and R. Koselleck. Stuttgart, 1984.

Zagrebelsky, G. *Il "Crucifige!" e la democrazia*. Turin, 2007.

Zallentin, H. M. *Rabbinic Parodies of Jewish and Christian Literature*. Tübingen, 2011.

Zedler, J. H. *Grosses vollständiges Universal Lexicon Aller Wissenschafften und Künste ... Sechs und Dreissigster Band ...* Leipzig–Halle: Johann Heinrich Zedler, 1743.

Ziegler, A. K. "Pope Gelasius I and His Teaching on the Relation of Church and State." *The Catholic Historical Review* 27, 4 (1942), 412–37.

Zola, J. *Commentariorum de Rebus Christianis ante Const. Magnum. Liber I*. Pavia (Ticinum): Balthass. Comini, 1793.

Zurbuchen, S. *Naturrecht und natürliche Religion: Zur Geschichte des Toleranzproblems von Samuel Pufendorf bis Jean-Jacques Rousseau*. Würzburg, 1991.

——— ed. *The Law of Nations and Natural Law 1625–1800*. Leiden, 2019.

INDEX

395

INDEX

INDEX

INDEX

INDEX

409

INDEX

secularity, xxv–xxvi, 246
  concept of, 164
  legitimacy of, 195
  origins of, 123–4
secularization
  creation of medieval canon law, 225
  as judicial process, 123–4
  origin of, 121–3
Sedulius (poet), 113
Seneca (philosopher), 184
Serapion, Mara bar (philosopher), 76, 107, 131, 288–9n71
Severan dynasty (Rome), 6, 76, 122
Shakespeare, William, 22, 268n55
Siegal, Michal Bar-Asher, 82
Sifting the Qur'an (Cusa), 99, 100
Simon of Cyrene, 97–8
Slavonic Josephus, 31, 34
Social Contract (Rousseau), 10, 163, 239–40, 241
Socrates, 12, 69, 107, 289n78
Sordi, Marta, 42, 51
Spalatin, Georg, 184
Spinoza, 233
Steller, Johann, 229–33, 235, 238
  on 'innocence' of Pontius Pilate, 229–33
Stephen (protomartyr), 137
Stroumsa, Guy, 69, 98, 284n10, 291n25
Stuart, Charles (King of England), 240
Studies on Value-Theory (Eisler), 28
Suetonius, 29, 67–8
supreme pontiff (*pontifex maximus*), 10–11, 165–6
Sylvester I (Pope), 181–2, 208
  Constantine I, donation to, 181–2, 183–6
Syria, 40, 45–6, 55, 91

basilicas of, 40
Christians persecuted in, 45
Jews of, 135
Syrian dynasty (Rome), 6, 260n20
System of All the Histories of the Church (Hartnaccius), 233

al-Tabari (Qur'an commentator), 96
  body-double theory, 96–7
Tacitus, xviii, 69–70
  Pliny's letter to, 72
Tafsīr Ibn 'Abbas (Qur'an commentary), 97, 98
Talmud, 82–6, 90, 95, 105
  death of Jesus in, 83–5
  Pilate and Jesus in, 85–6
  question of Jesus' presence in, 82–3
Tarsus (city), 40
Tasso, Torquato, 114
Tatianos, 97
Teitler, Hans, 42
Temple elites (Jerusalem), 134, 138, 148, 247
temple-state, 243, 245–7
  Paul on, 129–30
Tertullian of Carthage, 18, 33–4, 44, 69, 147, 220, 232
Testimony of Josephus (*Testimonium Flavianum*), 44, 80, 276n50
Tetrarchy, 41, 47, 233
al-Tha'labi (Qur'an commentator), 96–7
Thagaste (village), 141, 144
Theodoric (King of the Ostrogoths), 160
Theophylact of Ohrid (bishop), 233
Thomasius, Christian, 8, 18, 20, 62–3, 64, 188, 223, 228, 236, 240, 241